The Modernist Imagination

THE MODERNIST IMAGINATION
*Intellectual History and Critical Theory
Essays in Honor of Martin Jay*

Edited by
Warren Breckman, Peter E. Gordon, A. Dirk Moses,
Samuel Moyn, and Elliot Neaman

Berghahn Books
New York • Oxford

First published in 2009 by
Berghahn Books
www.berghahnbooks.com

©2009, 2011 Warren Breckman, Peter E. Gordon, A. Dirk Moses,
Samuel Moyn, and Elliot Neaman
First paperback edition published in 2011

All rights reserved. Except for the quotation of short passages
for the purposes of criticism and review, no part of this book
may be reproduced in any form or by any means, electronic or
mechanical, including photocopying, recording, or any information
storage and retrieval system now known or to be invented,
without written permission of the publisher.

Library of Congress Cataloging-in-Publication Data
The modernist imagination : intellectual history and critical theory : essays in honor of
Martin Jay / Warren Breckman ... [et al.] eds.
    p. cm.
Includes bibliographical references and index.
ISBN 978-1-84545-428-9 (hbk) -- ISBN 978-0-85745-307-5 (pbk)
  1. History—Philosophy. 2. Intellectual life—History—Historiography. 3. Critical
theory. I. Breckman, Warren, 1963– II. Jay, Martin, 1944–
D16.9.M53 2009
901—dc22

                                                   2008031380

British Library Cataloguing in Publication Data
A catalogue record for this book is available from the British Library

Printed in the United States on acid-free paper.

ISBN: 978-1-84545-428-9 (hardback)
ISBN: 978-0-85745-307-5 (paperback)

Contents

List of Figures	vii
Preface	viii
Martin Jay and the Dialectics of Intellectual History *Lloyd Kramer*	xi

Part I: Intellectual History

"The Kiss of Lamourette": "Possibilism" or "Christian Democracy"? *David Sorkin*	3
Selves without Qualities? Duchamp, Musil, and the History of Selfhood *Jerrold Seigel*	24
Liberty and the "Coming-into-Being" of Natural Law: Hans Kelsen and Ernst Cassirer *Gregory B. Moynahan*	55
The Artwork beyond Itself: Adorno, Beethoven, and Late Style *Peter E. Gordon*	77
Marxism and Alterity: Claude Lefort and the Critique of Totality *Samuel Moyn*	99
The Return of the King: Hegelianism and Post-Marxism in Zizek and Nancy *Warren Breckman*	117
Paradigm Shift: The *Speculation* of *Downcast Eyes* *Rosalind Krauss*	137

Part II: Violence, Memory, Identity

Memory Culture at an Impasse: Memorials in Berlin and New York 151
Andreas Huyssen

Against Grandiloquence: "Victim's Culture" and Jewish Memory 162
Carolyn J. Dean

Paris, Capital of Anti-Fascism 183
Anson Rabinbach

Toward a Critique of Violence 210
Dominick LaCapra

Democratization, Turks, and the Burden of German History 242
Rita Chin

West German Generations and the *Gewaltfrage*: The Conflict of the Sixty-Eighters and the Forty-Fivers 268
A. Dirk Moses and Elliot Neaman

Part III: Critical Theory and Global Politics

From "the Dialectic of Enlightenment" to "the Origins of Totalitarianism" and the Genocide Convention: Adorno and Horkheimer in the Company of Arendt and Lemkin 299
Seyla Benhabib

The Anti-Totalitarian Left between Morality and Politics 331
Dick Howard

Sovereign Equality vs. Imperial Right: The Battle over the "New World Order" 346
Jean L. Cohen

The Myths of Modern Identity as Ersatz Ideologies 368
Detlev Claussen and Michael Werz

Part IV: Coda

Ten Questions for Martin Jay 385
Publications of Martin Jay 393
Doctoral Students Directed by Martin Jay 404
Contributors 405
Index 410

Figures

Figure 1 Marcel Duchamp, "Paradise (Adam and Eve)," 1910–11. The Philadelphia Museum of Art/Art Resource, NY © 2007 Artists Rights Society (ARS), New York/ADAGP, Paris/Succession Marcel Duchamp. 27

Figure 2 Marcel Duchamp, "The Bride Stripped Bare by Her Bachelors, Even," 1915–23. The Philadelphia Museum of Art/Art Resource, NY © 2007 Artists Rights Society (ARS), New York/ADAGP, Paris/Succession Marcel Duchamp. 28

Figure 3 Marcel Duchamp, "Sculpture (50 cc of Paris Air)," 1919. The Philadelphia Museum of Art/Art Resource, NY © 2007 Artists Rights Society (ARS), New York/ADAGP, Paris/Succession Marcel Duchamp. 29

Figure 4 Marcel Duchamp, "Bottlerack," 1961 (replica of 1914 original). The Philadelphia Museum of Art/Art Resource, NY © 2007 Artists Rights Society (ARS), New York/ADAGP, Paris/Succession on Marcel Duchamp. 31

Figure 5 Marcel Duchamp, "Marcel Duchamp as Rrose Sélavy," ca. 1920–21. The Philadelphia Museum of Art/Art Resource, NY © 2007 Artists Rights Society (ARS), New York/ADAGP, Paris/Succession Marcel Duchamp. 32

Figure 6 Marcel Duchamp, "3 Stoppages Étalon," 1913–14. Digital Image © The Museum of Modern Art/Licensed by SCALA/Art Resource, NY © 2007 Artists Rights Society (ARS), New York/ADAGP, Paris/Succession Marcel Duchamp. 33

Figure 7 Cindy Sherman, "Untitled #167," 1985. Courtesy of the artist and Metro Pictures. 144

Figure 8 William Kentridge, "History of the Main Complaint," 1996. Charcoal and pastel on paper. Courtesy of Marian Goodman Gallery, New York. 146

Preface

This volume brings together a remarkably diverse group of scholars, intellectual historians, art historians, political theorists, and literary and cultural critics, all of whom wished to pay homage to the incomparable lifework of our mentor, colleague, and friend, Martin Jay, on the occasion of his sixty-fifth birthday. We could think of no better means to express our admiration and gratitude than the admittedly somewhat traditional and unmistakably Central European format of a *Festschrift*, though we are mindful that the very best homage should be one that not only acknowledges, but also contributes to Jay's ongoing achievements.

In the present case, any such contribution could only be partial. Martin Jay has inspired so many scholars across such a broad range of disciplines that any attempt to include all of those he has touched or to register the totality of his impact was bound to fail. Since he first burst upon the scene in 1973 with his path-breaking study, *The Dialectical Imagination: A History of the Frankfurt School and the Institute of Social Research, 1923–1950*, Jay has remained perhaps the most lucid and self-critical expositor of the Frankfurt School tradition of critical theory, a reputation further solidified by *Marxism and Totality: The Adventures of a Concept from Lukács to Habermas* (1984), his smaller volume, *Adorno* (1984), for the "Modern Masters" series, and by his innumerable essays on affiliated figures of the Central European intellectual left, such as Karl Mannheim, Leo Löwenthal, Siegfried Kraucauer, and many others. In more recent years, Jay has turned toward even more comprehensive themes in intellectual and cultural modernism, highlighted by his study of the anti-ocular prejudice in twentieth-century French thought, *Downcast Eyes: The Denigration of Vision in Twentieth-Century French Thought* (1993), and his breathtakingly synoptic treatment of the very category of experience, *Songs of Experience: Modern American and European Variations on a Universal Theme* (2005). These major works have punctuated a career that has also seen a constant outpouring of scholarly and contemporary interventions too numerous to summarize and too diverse to categorize here. But it seems fair to say that throughout his career, Jay has remained faithful to a certain conception of *intellectual critique*, animated most of all by an undiminished belief in the possibility—one should say the *necessity*—of modernity as both a theoretical and practical ideal.

No doubt throughout the twentieth century and into our own most immediate present, this ideal has confronted an array of important challenges: Nietzschean and post-Nietzschean strains of irrationalism, along with various strands of meta-political existentialism and political theology, postmodernism and identitarian-populism, have all conspired (despite their internecine rivalries) to dismantle or at least to destabilize the intellectual heritage of the Enlightenment and the "unfinished" project of emancipatory critique. The modernist intellectual's ideal of a universal yet unforced consensus has frequently seemed no longer viable. Yet notwithstanding his subtle appreciation of the force of these manifold challenges, Jay has remained committed to the notion that modernity warrants intellectual support and that only a failure of imagination would permit the conclusion that modernism has somehow reached its end. The essays assembled here offer testimony to Jay's continued power to inspire scholars in a great many disciplines. This breadth of influence made it fitting to include essays in intellectual history as well as art history, political theory, and cultural critique. In the diversity of their voices, they all bear witness to both the history and persistence of the modernist imagination.

The editors of this volume—all five of us—were trained in intellectual history under Martin Jay's supervision at the University of California at Berkeley. For those of us who have been fortunate enough to work with him, it would be difficult to convey the depth of our admiration and our gratitude. To be sure, Jay is best known for his breadth of erudition and his always judicious and never intemperate critical perspective. His is a model of learning difficult to emulate, but worthy of emulation. Amongst his graduate students in the 1970s, 1980s, and 1990s, there circulated a rumor—one that seemed to all of us quite plausible—that Marty's erudition was so vast, his knowledge of various spheres of literature in the human sciences so immense, that there were perhaps only five books he had not read. (Why we supposed the number was precisely five is mysterious.) It would of course happen on very rare occasions that one of his students would chance to mention one of those five books, provoking Marty to smile beneath his moustache and raise his eyebrows with a rare expression of surprise. The dismaying fact about this anecdote is that, in the interim since this particular cohort of students left Berkeley and assumed positions across the country and the globe, we are now certain Marty has had more than enough time to read those five books. His erudition seems boundless.

But together with this prodigious learning and his constant engagement in contemporary debates across a great number of disciplines, Marty is still astonishingly generous with his time for both students and colleagues. Discerning yet gentle with his criticism, Marty has taught and continues to teach all of us—students, colleagues, and friends—how to sustain the often-difficult balance between scholarship and pedagogy. In this respect, too, Marty remains a model and we offer him our heartfelt gratitude.

It seemed to us that the best way to express this gratitude was to bring together some of Martin Jay's many colleagues and students—it would naturally be impossible to include them all—to demonstrate the vitality of those modern intellectual traditions and critical potentialities he has mined with such prodigious energy and insight throughout his career. In this way, we hope not merely to mark an occasion but also to signal some directions for future scholarship in several of the overlapping fields that Jay has made his own. With this hopeful purpose, we offer this volume to Martin Jay, colleague, teacher, friend.

The editors would like to thank Catherine Gallagher for her advice and complicity throughout (in particular, for providing the complete bibliography of Martin Jay's published works), Marion Berghahn for her steadfast commitment to this project, Columbia University students James Chappel and Jennifer L. Wilson for assistance with the bibliographies and index, Ann Przyzycki and Melissa Spinelli for guiding the manuscript through the press.

Martin Jay and the Dialectics of Intellectual History

Lloyd Kramer

Intellectual history is the sub-discipline of historical studies that describes and interprets the creative work of past thinkers and artists, but intellectual historians have the widest influence when they also engage in the cultural debates of their own era. Intellectual history therefore provides insights into contemporary historical problems as well as new perspectives on the history of ideas and the cultural contexts in which earlier intellectuals have lived and worked. The best intellectual historians resemble the creative thinkers they write about because they often see unexpected connections among apparently diverse ideas and because they think critically about inherited assumptions or long-developing cultural conflicts. Intellectual historians also analyze the deep structures of thought shaping social life, thereby providing self-conscious accounts of ideas that are not so explicitly defined in everyday life or in the books of other historians. These general patterns of intellectual history all appear in the influential work of Martin Jay, whose contributions to this lively, evolving sub-discipline have made him an intellectual leader in the field.

Jay clearly believes that intellectual historians should be "intellectuals" who connect the ideas of thinkers in different historical contexts and then show how past intellectual debates can still provide theoretical resources for ongoing debates in our own culture. Although his most notable scholarship appears in four major historical books that have been published at roughly ten-year intervals over four decades (1973, 1984, 1993, 2005), Jay has also produced a steady stream of essays, conference papers, and journal articles on the methodological arguments of intellectual historians, the well-publicized conflicts of recent "culture wars," and the perennial arguments about "theory" and "praxis" in modern political movements.[1]

All of Jay's work examines the question of what it means to be an "intellectual" and typically uses a "dialectical" or "dialogic" method to lay out the alternative positions in every theoretical debate. He stresses the fluidity of ideas or cultural traditions and usually comes to a critically informed "middle position" that offers a provocative starting point for future discussion. His historical narratives (as Jay himself notes) provide a "synoptic content analysis" of the ways in which thinkers have developed their ideas on a particular theme, compares these ideas to the theories of other thinkers, notes the criticisms that have been directed against each thinker's theories, and then suggests how earlier debates can continue in other contexts. His analytical method is "dialectical" in that he constantly explores the history of debates, exchanges, and interactions among opposing intellectual movements and theorists; but his work is also "dialogic" in that he seeks to place himself and his readers in an active, present-day dialogue with influential thinkers across the long intellectual history of Western culture.[2]

My goal in this essay is to examine Jay's wide-ranging work through a brief "synoptic content analysis" that notes both his recurring intellectual themes and his method for exploring these themes. I will therefore focus on his conceptions of intellectual labor, his synoptic method of writing about past thinkers, his dialectical exploration of alternative positions, his attempts to sustain critical dialogues by finding a rigorous "middle way" between competing theoretical perspectives, his interest in reaching audiences beyond the academic community of intellectual historians, and his debates with critics. For Jay, the "force fields" that develop around certain intellectual problems must remain open and dynamic cultural "constellations" that illuminate social praxis, even when they evolve on the most abstract levels of cultural life.[3] Rejecting the anti-intellectualism that runs through much of American mass culture, Jay insists that theoretical arguments make a difference in the social world and that intellectual historians should make critical judgments about the competing ideas in both past and present intellectual debates. If such judgments lead to charges of intellectual elitism, Jay is willing to accept the criticism as the cultural cost of a firm commitment to Enlightenment traditions of critical analysis and rational communication.

The Meaning of Intellectual Labor

All of Jay's historical work focuses on the history of intellectuals, so it is important to understand how he describes the meaning of intellectual labor. In general, he views intellectuals as theoretically informed critics who move between the dichotomous cultural poles of "critique and affirmation." Summarizing the nature of intellectual work in one of his essays, for example, Jay notes the "fundamental inclination to problematize the self-evident, complexify the simple and unpack the apparently solid, leaving many questions still unanswered ..." Such inclinations give intellectuals the identity of a "critical gadfly" in cultural life, and they establish what Jay calls the "congenial intellectual stance of negativity."[4] This is the familiar identity of the intellectual critic, and Jay's work usually focuses on such critical-minded figures, including Marxists, critical theorists, and postmodern philosophers.

At the same time, however, Jay also recognizes the value of another kind of intellectual labor—the work of an expert on, say, intellectual history—which conveys knowledge about cultural traditions or provides reliable information about the past. This role (like the role of the critic) derives from an Enlightenment belief in the value of carrying knowledge to a wider public (as in the famous eighteenth-century *Encyclopédie*), and intellectual expertise is an important theme in Jay's account of the intellectual historian: "The stance of faithful preserver and disseminator of the cultural riches of the past and the nurturer of new—but not too new—cultural creation has ... frequently been seen as the pedagogue's main function." Like other "pedagogues," Jay does this kind of intellectual work whenever he sets out to describe the "cultural riches of the past" as a foundation for future critical work. He thus warns that it would "be a mistake to reify the distinction between critical intellectuals and constructive pedagogues,"[5] and Jay himself approaches intellectual history as a dialectical journey between the different but overlapping roles of critic and expert. The critics attract most of his attention, however, and become the analytical object of his historical expertise.

The work of intellectual criticism depends on several related perspectives that Jay brings to each of his projects. In the first place, good intellectual critics examine cultural or political issues with historical perspectives enabling them to challenge dominant cultural assumptions. When cultures lack historical knowledge, intellectual historians become critical thinkers simply by tracing the forgotten historical lineage of certain ideas or cultural assumptions that have become ascendant and largely unquestioned in contemporary societies. As he notes in one of his (sympathetic) commentaries on historical work, the study of past cultures immerses one "in the flow of historical becoming, compensating for the one-sided and partial character of our own personal experience through opening ourselves to that of others."[6] Historical knowledge, in short, challenges or transforms the meaning of personal experience and cultural traditions as well as the assumptions of modern social and political ideologies.

Historical perspective also contributes to a second component of critical intellectual labor, which Jay usually calls "theory." As Jay describes it, theory enters into the intellectual's work at "a moment of reflexive self-distancing, a moment that subverts the self-sufficient immanence of whatever we happen to be thinking about," and this self-conscious theorizing often gives intellectuals their distinctive cultural identities or social roles. Theoretical work is embedded in social life, but it goes beyond a simple reflection of the social world in which it appears because critical theorists seek a perspective that extends or questions the social realities they encounter. This dialectical theorizing process means that "those who yearn for an entirely immanent position [within the social world] are as deluded as those who think they can find one that is entirely transcendent." Here, too, one finds a fluid intellectual movement between dialectical poles that are never reached in final closures, "for absolute proximity is as hard to come by as that unbridgeable spectatorial distance supposedly allowing theoretical contemplation from afar."[7] The quest for self-conscious theoretical perspectives is nevertheless a second key attribute of intellectual work, and Jay affirms the critical value of "grand theories" that postmodern thinkers have generally rejected.

Finally, Jay supports the traditional Enlightenment conception of intellectual labor as a process of rational communication. The intellectual must convince others by arguing for an idea rather than by compelling consent through social power or producing an irrational public spectacle. Rational analysis becomes for Jay the essential and difficult work that intellectuals should pursue. "The neutral culture of critical discourse in which persuasive ideas come before personal authority and disembodied minds argue without reference to their corporeal ground may be a utopian fantasy in its purest form," Jay argues in one defense of rational argumentation, "but it still provides a regulative ideal, which we abandon at our jeopardy."[8]

This conception of intellectual argument also shapes Jay's defense of intellectual history as a modern scholarly discipline that should exemplify the traditional, analytical practices of rational discourse. This long-developing, analytical tradition, which has been reaffirmed in the work of contemporary theorists such as Jürgen Habermas, influences Jay's skepticism about a radical "linguistic turn" among intellectual historians and leads toward his (characteristic) argument for a methodological middle position. "Intellectual history," he writes, "is ... filled with unattractive examples of rationally judgmental readings of the past ... and one would certainly not want a revival of Enlightenment historiography at its most naïve. But in turning too eagerly to linguistic philosophy in any of its various guises and making it the sole or even primary source of our method, we risk losing the critical edge that rationalism ... can provide."[9] The hard-earned "critical edge" of rationalism, in other words, should guide the work of intellectual critics and intellectual historians, no matter which side they take in modern cultural debates.

"Synoptic Content Analysis" and Enlightenment Traditions of Rational Communication

As Jay describes it, therefore, the work of past intellectuals and contemporary intellectual historians come together in their shared commitments to historical analysis, critical theoretical perspectives, and the traditions of rational communication. There are extreme poles or tendencies within each of these components of intellectual work (which Jay recognizes and wants to avoid), but all three appear in his approach to intellectual history. He writes historically about past intellectuals, of course, but he also engages their work in a critical, theoretical dialogue and affirms his commitment to Enlightenment-style communicative traditions. To be sure, he understands and even appreciates the significant themes in linguistic and postmodernist critiques of Enlightenment rationalism. Yet, he identifies more with the rationalist tradition than with theoretical critiques of rationalism's tendency to promote categorical "unities" over the play of "difference" or to overlook the linguistic constructions of truth. Stressing what he calls "the extraordinarily rich and fecund tradition of rationalism," Jay has never really broken with an early warning to intellectual historians, who "ignore at their peril its power to give our intercourse with the past a valuable critical dimension."[10] Although he has frequently acknowledged the critical value of the "linguistic turn" in intellectual history, Jay has responded to the methodological debates among intellectual historians by insisting that rationality should still be defended and that "the opposition between a linguistically informed intellectual history and one indebted to traditional ... concepts of rationality is unnecessarily extreme."[11] He thus seeks to avoid these possible extremes by calling for a "dialogic play between them," because a one-sided method means that intellectual historians "remain either anachronistic, in the sense of being indifferent to the liveliest philosophical currents of our day, or, what is worse, incapable of providing a critical [rational] perspective on the past and present in the name of a more attractive future."[12] All of Jay's enduring intellectual commitments come together in this support for an intellectual history that rejects theoretical extremes and contributes critical perspectives to contemporary culture.

Jay's major historical studies pursue these methodological strategies through analytical synoptic summaries of major thinkers who belonged to intellectual elites rather than popular cultural movements. His first book, *The Dialectical Imagination*, provides valuable contextual information on "The Institute of Social Research" and on the lives of leading figures such as Max Horkheimer and Theodore Adorno, but Jay's longer historical narratives usually include relatively little biographical or contextual analysis of the writers he discusses. He emphasizes ideas rather than the social or personal experiences that may have shaped an intellectual's thought; he never adds photographs, artwork, or other visual images to his books (even when he discusses a subject such as "vision); and he writes mostly about Europeans rather than intellectuals in non-western cultures. He discusses people who wrote in the past about social or cultural theories, but his books are also filled with wide-ranging references to the recent secondary literature on whatever issue he addresses—Marxist social thought, critiques of "ocularcentrism," conceptions of personal experience, and much more.

Responding to critics who have raised questions about his synoptic narrative style, Jay concedes that synopsis inevitably reduces some of the complexity in an author's original argument. At the same time, however, he argues that the synoptic work of historians who paraphrase another thinker's ideas "cannot be seen simply as the betrayal of the irreducibly complex and uniquely heterogeneous nature of the texts whose meaning they seek to paraphrase."[13] It would in fact be impossible for historians to write about past thinkers without paraphrasing their ideas, because the intellectual task of identifying patterns and structures in an author's work requires a rephrasing and interpretation of the original texts. A good work of intellectual history, as Jay describes it, provides an interpretive framework that should both enable and encourage readers to go back to the original texts themselves. This kind of critical engagement with original texts becomes the goal of a sophisticated "communicative rationality" that differs from what Jay calls "the naïve synoptic approach." In contrast to a one-dimensional synopsis, a good, critical synoptic method conveys a "dialogic" process of "linguistic give and take between the original text and its parallel restatement in our terms."[14] Careful explications of a complex thinker's ideas therefore pose an intellectual challenge for both historians and their readers—a challenge for which Jay makes no apology.

Jay's synoptic method can be compared to the work of his own academic mentor, the historian H. Stuart Hughes (1916–1999). Teaching at Harvard in the 1960s, Hughes trained a large cohort of talented intellectual historians and helped to define the evolving sub-discipline in a classic study of European cultural transitions, *Consciousness and Society: The Reorientation of European Social Thought, 1890–1930* (1958).[15] This influential book examined the early twentieth-century revolt against European Positivism and provided concise intellectual biographies of social theorists such as Durkheim, Bergson, Freud, Croce, Sorel, and Weber. Hughes wrote intellectual history before the linguistic turn or the methodological debates that would reshape the discipline between the 1970s and 1990s, so Jay's more recent theoretical concerns, historical methods, and writing style obviously differ significantly from the work that Hughes did in the 1950s. Yet, there are also some notable similarities in the synthetic methods that Hughes and Jay use in their synoptic analyses of prominent European thinkers. Both Hughes and Jay approach modern intellectual history by focusing on themes that attracted the shared interest of otherwise diverse intellectuals—for example, the revolt against positivism or the preoccupation with "experience" in personal and social life. Their books thus develop analytical unity through an emphasis on specific intellectual problems rather than through accounts of shared social contexts (e.g., a city) or shared historical events (e.g., the French Revolution). Both Hughes and Jay examine diverging interpretations of their particular themes by providing roughly a chapter on each thinker they describe, and they both discuss movements that challenged or criticized Enlightenment traditions. They both recognize the historical significance of these critiques, and they criticize naïve defenses of objective knowledge or overly optimistic Enlightenment beliefs in the social value of rationalist thought. They nevertheless emphasize the enduring value of the Enlightenment's rationalist and clarifying methods of intellectual analysis, which they link to the nuanced practice of "synoptic content analysis" and to the historical purpose of their own analytical, synthetic projects.

Hughes explicitly connected the historical perspective of *Consciousness and Society* to a "humane" Enlightenment tradition that "civilized" critics should still draw upon as they analyze the history of modern social and political movements. He praised the Enlightenment's "open, undogmatic" forms of thought and its "flexible use of the concept of reason," even as he acknowledged that later critics had rightly pointed to various problems in Enlightenment epistemology and psychology. In general, Hughes insisted that the commitment to the "rational solutions" and "humane behavior" of eighteenth-century *philosophes* had given intellectuals a framework for future critical thinking, and, he stressed, "as guides to conduct and intellectual investigation we can reject the principles of the Enlightenment only at our peril."[16]

Jay's support for Enlightenment thought is somewhat more muted, perhaps because thinkers such as Bataille, Foucault, and Derrida have pushed intellectual historians toward a more critical view of the dangers in one-dimensional, instrumental uses of rational knowledge. Yet Jay also places himself firmly within the Enlightenment tradition whenever he sets out to identify his own intellectual allegiances. "I remain unrepentantly beholden to the ideal of illumination that suggests an Enlightenment faith in clarifying indistinct ideas," he writes in the introduction to *Downcast Eyes*.[17] Describing his historical method as a "synoptic survey" of thinkers who often challenged such forms of synthetic writing, Jay notes that, "the traditional intellectual historian's tool of synoptic content analysis, when complicated by a healthy distrust of reductive paraphrase, is indispensable in making sense of the past. For it expresses a certain cautious optimism about the potential for a communicative interaction between the historian and his subject matter"[18]—the communicative process that Jay defines as the "dialogic" approach to intellectual history.

This dialogical method reaffirms Hughes's earlier emphasis on a nondogmatic view of intellectual truths, though Jay turns to German predecessors such as Gadamer and Habermas (rather than Hughes) to support his conceptions of knowledge and human experience. The themes in Jay's recent books would have seemed familiar to his late graduate mentor, however, especially when he endorses this kind of open-ended Gadamerian description of knowledge in the last pages of *Songs of Experience*: "being experienced does not mean that one knows something once and for all and becomes rigid in this knowledge," Gadamer explains; "rather, one becomes more open to new experiences. A person who is experienced is undogmatic.... In our experience we bring nothing to a close; we are constantly learning new things from our experience ... this I call the interminability of all experience."[19] Such themes come back to Hughes's account of the "undogmatic" qualities of Enlightenment thought, but they also point toward the dialectical exchanges that run through all of Jay's own descriptions of intellectual life. Synoptic content analysis, as Jay practices the method, clarifies the ideas of complex thinkers and summarizes the evolving, critical possibilities that emerge dialectically from opposing poles of thought (or experience) in every historical era and every intellectual debate.

Dialectical History and the Critical "Middle Way"

Although I cannot possibly summarize all of the subjects or themes in Jay's books, a brief survey of the arguments in his four major historical studies can show how his synoptic method consistently provides a careful analysis of dialectical alternatives. Jay's methodological tendency to look at all intellectual debates as an on-going dialogue between such alternatives emerged in his first book, *The Dialectical Imagination*, and his subsequent historical work could be described as a "working out" of intellectual perspectives that he first identified in the texts of the Frankfurt School Critical Theorists. He began his still-important first book by noting how the Frankfurt School critics had navigated between the conflicting impulses of an elite intellectual life and various forms of social or political activism. Critical theorists wanted to affirm their solidarity with reform movements outside the academic world and yet retain a rigorous, intellectual independence, but this complex mediation between two cultural worlds posed a constant challenge for critical-minded intellectuals. "Between the Scylla of unquestioning solidarity and Charybdis of willful independence, he [the critical intellectual] must carve a middle way or else fail," Jay wrote in the introduction. "How precarious that middle path may be is one of the chief lessons to be learned from the radical intellectuals who have been chosen as the subjects of this book."[20]

Beginning with this view of the radical intellectual's complex cultural role, Jay goes on to explain how the critical theorists rightly understood that "the ideal of a 'free-floating' intellectual above the fray was a formalistic illusion, which should be discarded. At the same time, it would be equally erroneous to see the intellectual as entirely ... rooted in his culture or class.... Both extremes misconstrued subjectivity as either totally autonomous or totally contingent."[21] Intellectual identities, in short, cannot be reduced to simple categorical explanations. It would thus be simplistic to say that Jay learned the "lesson" of the "precarious middle path" from the Frankfurt School and then went on to follow that path in all of his later work, but the "middle path" definitely became one of the key themes that he drew from the Frankfurt School intellectuals. Take, for example, his description of Max Horkheimer's thought in a chapter on the "genesis of critical theory." According to Jay, "Horkheimer consistently rejected the Hobson's choice of metaphysical systematizing or antinomian empiricism. Instead, he argued for the possibility of a dialectical social science.... It was in large measure this refusal to succumb to the temptations of either alternative that gave Critical Theory its cutting edge."[22] This concise account of Horkheimer's "dialectical social science" might be applied to Jay's own conception of "dialectical" intellectual history, because (like Horkheimer) he always stresses the interaction between opposing categories. "Dialectics," as Horkheimer conceived the process, "probed the 'force field,' to use an expression of Adorno's, between consciousness and being, subject and object.... It rejected the extremes of nominalism and realism and remained willing to operate in a perpetual state of suspended judgment."[23]

This rejection of both radical empiricism and radical linguistic determinism—already part of the Frankfurt School's Critical theory—becomes the "Martin Jay approach" to intellectual history. Discussing Adorno's analysis of the relation between individuals and the social world, for example, Jay summarizes a balanced response to the opposing theoretical poles of radical individualism and social determinism. "Against those who stressed an abstract individualism, he [Adorno] pointed to the social component through which subjectivity was inevitably mediated. He just as strongly resisted the temptation to acquiesce in the dissolution of the contingent individual into a totality, whether of the *Volk* or class."[24] The key intellectual insight of Critical Theory, as Jay describes it, evolved through its dialectical engagement with alternatives that never settled into static, one-dimensional conclusions. The fluidity of this open-ended, intellectual perspective made it difficult to pin down and notoriously difficult to read, but the Frankfurt School's dialectical method pointed toward the "precarious middle path" that can still guide the analytical work of modern intellectual historians.

The Frankfurt School theorists thus developed a subtle, historical-minded approach to cultural or political problems, which enabled them to affirm the value of elite philosophical, literary, and musical traditions without lapsing into a "hypostatization of those values as something apart from and superior to material interests."[25] The legacy of this influential, twentieth-century form of Marxist thought emerged from its critique of both "vulgar materialism" and radical idealism. "Critical theory," Jay concludes, "was rooted in a dialectical overcoming of the traditional idealism-materialism dichotomy;"[26] and this theoretical achievement suggests why Jay also employs a dialectical method to challenge the dichotomous poles in modern historiography and contemporary critical theory.

The quest for a theoretical middle path reappears in Jay's comprehensive study of modern Marxist theory, *Marxism and Totality* (1984). Departing from the emphasis on an institutional context in *The Dialectical Imagination*, Jay's second major book introduced his method of studying a single concept or idea as it evolved across changing historical contexts and in the texts of numerous, contrasting thinkers. This method stresses the multiple meanings of key concepts, such as "totality," and also engages contemporary theoretical debates. It might be compared in some ways with an older "history of ideas" (as practiced, for example, by Arthur Lovejoy), which also traced the intellectual evolution of key concepts, such as the "great chain of being," but this older "internal" analysis of ideas generally ignored changing social-political-cultural contexts and the present-day concerns of critical theorists—both of which are important for Jay's approach to intellectual history.[27]

Jay begins his comprehensive account of modern Marxist theory with a brief survey of how premodern and Enlightenment philosophers used the concept of totality and then he carries the history of Marxist debates down to the late twentieth-century work of Jürgen Habermas. This long narrative shows how the belief in "totalizing history" gradually broke down as thinkers rejected Positivist conceptions of Marxism and came to recognize that a "total" program of social transformation was historically impossible. *Marxism and Totality* may well be Jay's most challenging work, in part because Marxist thinkers often wrote difficult books and in part because the concept of totality has fallen out of favor in contemporary intellectual culture. Jay returns to various thinkers who also appeared prominently in *The Dialectical Imagination*, but he places his key figures in new cultural contexts that show how the significance of these thinkers evolves in relation to changing debates and political conflicts. Adorno's importance in *Marxism and Totality*, for example, derives from his incisive critique of older conceptions of totality rather than from his dialectical analysis of individualism and social class. "No longer could history itself be seen as a coherent whole with a positive conclusion as its telos," Jay notes in one explanation of Adorno's critical project. "And no longer could the totalizing epistemology of the Hegelian tradition be invoked with confidence against the antinomies of bourgeois thought."[28] Adorno's critical demolition of Marxist "totality" led toward the wider critique of all holistic or grand theories in later intellectual movements, such as Italian Marxism and French poststructuralism.

According to Jay, the aspiration for a totalizing social and cultural theory gradually gave way to its dialectical opposite: a vehement poststructuralist critique of the repressive tendencies in all totalizing "grand theories." This critique of "totality" may have been a useful corrective to holistic theories, but it drifted into the kind of extreme position that Jay steadfastly resists in all of his intellectual histories. In this case, however, he turns to Habermas rather than Adorno or Horkheimer to identify a possible "middle way" between the (deadend) extremes of totality and radical deconstruction. Habermas recognized the force of neo-Nietzschean, linguistic attacks on totality, yet he did not want to give up the critical possibilities of the "totalizing," critical tradition. He thus sought "a way to escape the relativistic implications of pure hermeneutics without ... regressing to a discredited Hegelian rationalism,"[29] thereby making a valuable theoretical contribution to Jay's own search for an intellectual middle path that leads beyond the flawed Marxist idea of historical totality.

The Marxist tradition, as Jay explains it, did not give enough attention to the linguistic or cultural construction of "instrumental reason," which also lost credibility for other reasons in the repressive "totalizing" systems of twentieth-century communist states. But Jay insists that rejecting the dangers of Marxist "totality" should not lead to the simple embrace of its dialectical alternative. "[E]ven after one acknowledges all of these reasons why the discourse of totality is now so much in disfavor, it is precisely because of one of contemporary history's most frightening realities [threat of nuclear annihilation] that it is both impossible and unwise to abandon it entirely." Intellectuals should continue to engage the idea of "totality" as they examine the "complex interrelatedness of our planetary existence"; and the "search for a viable concept of totality ... should not therefore be written off."[30] Jay thus assumes that dialectical life can still be drawn from a concept that too many theorists have simply dismissed. If the Marxist concept of totality has gone into a radical, dialectical decline—and Jay recognizes this historical reality—it nevertheless retains its theoretical status as a starting point for future critical debates: "is it too much to hope," asks Jay, "that amidst the debris there lurks, silent but still potent, the germ of a truly defensible concept of totality—and even more important, the potential for a liberating totalization that will not turn into its opposite?"[31] This concluding question reaffirms Jay's interest in the continuing interaction of theoretical oppositions and also exemplifies his desire to end every survey of intellectual history with questions that help sustain or revitalize the next phase of intellectual debate. *Marxism and Totality* concludes that the older Marxist concept of totality has lost its former significance in modern critical discourse, but this story of decline also leaves readers with a challenge to their own guiding intellectual assumptions (for example, the belief that concepts of "totality" no longer carry critical value in contemporary intellectual life).

Jay's interest in restoring the critical force of apparently discredited ideas also influences his more recent books. His detailed studies of the "denigration of vision" in modern French thought (the historical subject of *Downcast Eyes*) and of the concept of "experience" in modern Western cultures (the theme in *Songs of Experience*) both seek to revive the significance of ideas that poststructuralist theorists have criticized or vehemently rejected. These important books begin with historical overviews of the evolving idea—vision or experience—from the time of the ancient Greeks to the early modern era (roughly from Plato to Montaigne and Descartes). This *longue durée* of early intellectual history provides the backdrop for Jay's main interest, which focuses on cultural debates that gradually transformed Enlightenment-era beliefs in the epistemological value of "vision" or "experience" into a prolonged twentieth-century critique of these earlier intellectual categories. Modern thinkers, in short, criticized the eighteenth-century assumption that what we see or experience with our senses can provide a stable foundation for knowledge. Many of the authors whom Jay discusses in his earlier studies of Marxism and Critical Theory receive further analysis in these later books, but he comes back to authors such as Adorno, Benjamin, Althusser, Sartre, and Foucault with new questions and new intellectual themes.

Jay's frequent return to the same theorists shows how important intellectuals participate simultaneously in different cultural debates and offer themes for the possible extension of quite diverse dialectical exchanges. His more recent books follow the familiar narrative style in which Jay describes opposing positions on each question, notes the critiques of each "dialectical pole," and then moves toward the defense of a critically informed middle path. After showing how Foucault, Derrida, and Lyotard developed "anti-ocular" critiques of the Enlightenment's faith in the epistemological validity of vision, for example, he stresses both the insights of their poststructuralist critiques and the continuing value of what they attacked. To be sure, he does not accept a simple empirical belief in the unproblematic reliability of what we "see" when we observe objects, images or social realities in the world around us. In contrast to naïve "ocularists," Jay recognizes that languages shape what we see and that the "antiocularcentric discourse has successfully posed substantial and troubling questions about the status of visuality in the dominant cultural traditions of the West."[32] Yet, he also insists (as with Marxist ideas of totality) that earlier beliefs in the truthfulness of visual evidence should not simply be dismissed as delusions. "If … the still faintly visible positive side [of ocular traditions] is not forgotten," he writes, "it may be possible to salvage something from the debris."[33] The notion of salvageable debris thus reappears in a conclusion that resembles Jay's language at the end of *Marxism and Totality* and offers a comparable defense of a much-criticized idea: despite the recent assaults on ocularism, surveillance, and the spectacle, the "power of visuality has certainly survived the attack." This continuing appreciation for the visual is not a bad thing, as Jay describes it, because we need to "see" that "vision and visuality in all their rich and contradictory variety can still provide us mere mortals with insights and perspectives, speculations and observations, enlightenments and illuminations, that even a god might envy."[34] A dialectical exchange between an older confidence in "vision" and the postmodern skepticism about what we actually "see" thus becomes essential for a balanced, critical perspective that can open the next historical phase of an ongoing debate.

Jay has extended his dialectical, historical method to the systematic analysis of another specific intellectual debate in *Songs of Experience: Mod-*

ern American and European Variations on a Universal Theme. This wide-ranging survey resembles his other major books by providing an overview of ancient Greek, medieval, and early conceptions of experience—stressing the influential work of Montaigne, Bacon, Descartes, Locke, and others who laid the intellectual foundations for modern empiricism and idealism. But Jay's principal interest lies (as usual) in the period between the mid eighteenth and late twentieth centuries, when European and American thinkers developed new philosophical, religious, aesthetic, political, and historical accounts of human experience. The book begins and ends, however, with Jay's response to poststructuralist critiques of "experience." Developing themes that also shape their critiques of "ocularism" and "totality," the poststructuralists have described a linguistic construction of "experience" that challenges older beliefs in transparent experiential realities. Much of Jay's critical work since the 1980s has evolved as a dialogue with poststructuralist critics, and *Songs of Experience* continues this pattern by placing poststructuralism on one of the dialectical poles in recent debates about experience. Jay again refers to an extraordinary number of writers, theorists, and texts to show how an intellectual debate has moved between extreme positions—neither of which is entirely convincing. On one side, Jay notes, religious thinkers, artists, and poets have often used the concept of "experience" to describe "precisely that which exceeds concepts and even language itself" and to indicate a complex reality that "is so ineffable and individual (or specific to a particular group) that it cannot be rendered in conventionally communicative terms to those who lack it."[35] Mystical advocates of this view therefore suggest that experience is a sensory or spiritual reality defying all linguistic attempts to describe it. On the other side, however, the linguistic theorists have challenged the "assumption of absolute experiential self-sufficiency" and stressed that no human "experience" or reality "can appear outside the boundaries of linguistic mediation."[36] The inescapable linguistic construction of experiences means that culture, history, and words always shape what people commonly describe as their distinctive "personal experiences."

These opposing conceptions of experience form the historical alternatives in cultural debates that extend from Christian and Jewish religious thought to modern historiography, literary criticism, and radical political movements. Jay examines all of these cultural spheres, but he leads readers into the debates via his usual middle path. "Neither of these alternatives [pure personal experience vs. the discursive production of "experience"] ... is fully convincing," he explains in the introduction to *Songs*. The careful historian, however, does not have to embrace a single side of the argument. "It would be more fruitful to remain within the tension created by the paradox. That is, we need to be aware of the ways in which 'experience' is both a collective linguistic concept, a signifier that yokes together a class of heterogeneous signifieds located in a diacritical force field, and a reminder that such concepts always leave a remainder that escapes their homogenizing grasp."[37] As Jay describes it, experience is embedded in the inescapable linguistic and cultural traditions of one's culture, yet individuals can have the "experience" of encountering others who transform the meaning of these traditions or the language that defines social reality. "Whether a 'fall' from innocence or a gain of new wisdom, an enrichment of life or a bitter lesson in its follies, something worthy of the name 'experience' cannot leave you where you began."[38] The complexity of human experience, in other words, exceeds the limits of conventional language because something that might be called "experiential transformation" emerges from the ongoing exchanges between subjects and objects, the self and others.

This interaction between self and others shapes the meaning of "experience" and drives a debate that extends from antiquity, the Enlightenment, and early Romanticism down to the quest for "limit experiences" in radical twentieth-century writers such as Bataille, Foucault, and Roland Barthes. Opening another dialogue with thinkers who regularly enter his intellectual "conversations" (e.g., Kant, Benjamin, Adorno, Foucault) and introducing others who have contributed specifically to the modern debate on experience (e.g., William James, John Dewey, Richard Rorty, Joan Scott, F.R. Ankersmit), Jay again rejects both the simple synthesis and endless dualisms of opposing theoretical categories. A creative intellectual tension keeps the competing theoretical accounts of "experience" apart, but it also avoids the frozen dualities of radical extremes. Jay concludes that "experience" cannot be understood as a personal reality that lies entirely within the subject or as an unmediated response to realities that exist entirely outside the self (art, God, objects in the world). "If the subjective case is pushed to an extreme, it can allow the inappropriate slippage that turns anything into, say, an aesthetic experience, no matter what its precipitating object might be."[39] Extreme subjectivism—if one could actually live in such a self-referential mode—blocks the kind of change or learning that comes through encounters with otherness. Yet Jay also insists that the "opposite extreme, turning the subject into a totally passive receptacle of external influences ... short-circuits the constructive moment that allows experience to transcend mere sensual stimulation."[40] Human subjects usually shape their sensory encounters into some kind of intellectual structure, which means that Jay follows Kant in stressing that the idea of "experience" indicates "a mixture of passivity and activity, of allowing the world to impinge, but on a mind that is not a blank recipient of stimuli from without."[41]

Jay's most recent "big book" thus reiterates his respect for Enlightenment traditions (Kant plays the role here that Habermas plays in the last sections of *Marxism and Totality*), but it also shows that the debate about experience did not end in the eighteenth century or with Kant or with any other thinker Jay examines. He pointedly criticizes the advocates of "identity politics" for "essentializing" the experiences of certain groups or claiming that others can never understand their distinctive experiential history (a claim that can stop conversations); and he concludes with a Kantian reminder that experience is "a delicate interplay between subjectivity and intersubjectivity, bodily sensations and the assent of all who share the same capacity for appreciating beauty." In short, experience is "at once deeply personal and yet to a significant extent capable of being shared with others."[42] Jay's "middle path" takes readers back to the assumption that "experience" remains a useful category of thought because the critically informed understanding of the concept carries "a willingness to open the most seemingly integrated and self-contained subject to the outside, thus allowing the perilous, but potentially rewarding [intellectual] journey to begin."[43]

All of the familiar components of Jay's approach to intellectual history come together again in *Songs of Experience*: the synoptic content analysis; the exploration of a specific theme in long chapters on different thinkers; the defense of a "middle path" between dialectical extremes; the respect for Enlightenment traditions—tempered by a thoughtful engagement with modern linguistic critiques of these traditions; and the belief that past debates have given us a fluid theoretical inheritance that we can now carry forward in our own intellectual conversations. These methodological patterns and intellectual commitments reappear throughout Jay's work, including the many essays and occasional pieces that cannot be discussed in a brief, "synoptic" summary of his constantly expanding contributions to historical scholarship. It should nevertheless be emphasized that the shorter essays also constitute an important aspect of Jay's work as an intellectual historian, and I want to note how he uses this genre to engage controversial issues in contemporary academic and public culture.

Writing for Wider Intellectual Audiences

In the late 1980s, Jay became a contributor to the journal *Salmagundi*, where he published a regular column called "Force Fields" (the concept he draws from Adorno) and where he sought to interpret arcane academic debates for readers who lived happily outside the realm of professional intellectual historians. He has republished many of his *Salmagundi* columns in books such as *Cultural Semantics: Keywords of Our Time* (1998), an important collection that exemplifies Jay's analytical approach to concepts that have shaped recent scholarship and cultural studies.

His method in these essays follows his intellectual inclination to define cultural debates as a dialogue between contending theoretical positions, and then to stake out a balanced critical position that becomes the synthetic starting point for further discussion. Although this method evokes Hegelian philosophical traditions, Hegel himself is not usually mentioned as an intellectual reference point.[44] My reference to Hegel may therefore suggest a high level of abstraction for Jay's "occasional pieces," but I want to show how this method works in specific essays with an example from his analysis of the term "theory," which is one of his "keywords." In an essay entitled simply "For Theory," Jay uses Alvin W. Gouldner's book *For Sociology* (1973) to reflect on how an earlier intellectual praise for "grand theory" has given way to recent critiques (or negations) that find such theories repressive and dangerous. On one side of the debate, Jay finds a small group of theorists who agree with Gouldner in believing that "a community of theorists, following the rules of rational deliberation" can still establish universal principles and provide theoretical directions toward "human liberation."[45] On the other side of this debate, however, a much larger group of intellectuals now sees "grand theory" as a "game of mastery, tainted by its association with the evils of transcendentalism, foundationalism, essentialism, and the vain search for a metalanguage" that serves the "privileged position of those who arrogantly pretended to speak for the whole."[46] The grand theorists, as their critics describe them, claim a God-like view of the world that ignores the differences and experiences of real people on the ground.

Jay responds to this critique by affirming the value of "grand theory," but he also carefully and respectfully summarizes the main themes of the critics: complaints about the use of abstractions to efface the particularity of different people or objects; complaints about intellectual elitism and the privileged positions of theorizing elites; complaints about the many gaps between theory and practice; and complaints about the different forms of knowledge that derive from experience and theory. Following his usual analytical strategy, Jays notes the importance of these critiques and stresses that no social or philosophical theory can emerge outside of historical contexts, power relations, and social institutions. Theory is always connected to social and material realities that often defy or challenge the theories that claim to describe them. Great works of art, for example, may express the "theories that generate them," but they also "exceed those theories"; and the material components of history and social life that gain their meaning through theories also "resist reduction to theory alone."[47]

If theories face this inevitable material challenge, however, it is also true (in Jay's view) that people cannot understand their social world without theories. Here again we find a middle path beyond the debates between the defenders and critics of theory, because in fact both "theory" and "experience" evolve in a dialectical interaction. Theory must refer to a material world of objects in order to make sense, yet "even the most everyday of everyday languages contains conceptual homogenizations, tropic displacements, and rhetorical ambiguities" that depend on (usually unexamined) theories.[48] Intellectuals who want to explore the historical or critical uses of "grand theory" thus have good reasons to pursue their theoretical work, even as they recognize the inevitable limitations and problems in theories that promise universal truth and human liberation. This is the balanced approach to theory that Jay advocates for intellectual historians and for other intellectuals who continue to develop theoretical critiques of the existing social world. Placed in the broader context of other intellectual debates and "keywords," Jay's analysis of theory also points toward the middle path that connects his *Salmagundi* columns with his historical scholarship. But this search for a "middle way" evokes the kind of criticism which Jay answers in dialogic exchanges that have become another example of his continual engagement with contemporary intellectual debates.

Dialogues with Critics

Jay's books and articles examine a very wide range of controversial ideas and influential authors, so it is not surprising that his analysis of such subjects attracts mixed reviews. Criticisms have come from Marxists who disagree with his interpretations of the Frankfurt School or modern Marxist theory, from poststructuralists who challenge his Habermasian conception of rational communications, from anthropologists, art historians, and literary theorists who complain about his lack of attention to key themes in their disciplines, and even from the subjects of his own books—one of whom (Adorno) commented angrily in a posthumously published letter that Jay had "an unerring instinct to direct himself to dirt."[49] It would therefore be impossible to provide a comprehensive summary of the diverse reactions to Jay's writings, but I will refer briefly to several recurring themes in the critical assessments of his work and in his responses to these critiques.

Critics have questioned Jay's historical method of "synoptic content analysis" (as noted earlier), but these questions also carry the methodological debates of intellectual historians into larger issues of disciplinary language and politics. The criticism of his writing, in other words, extends to broader criticisms of "communicative rationality" and of Jay's apparent reluctance to make forceful political judgments on the historical figures or subjects he discusses. Responding to these criticisms, Jay has attempted to practice his theory of dialogic communication in self-conscious, reflexive commentaries on his own scholarship and in repeated critical engagement with the significant questions his critics have raised.

The critique of Jay's "synoptic" writing style has often emerged in poststructuralist arguments that describe synthetic narratives as inherently hostile to ideas and subjects lying outside the narrative's dominant discursive perspective. Although paraphrase and synopsis are more or less essential to all coherent, historical writing, critics such as the literary theorist Michael Ryan argue that synoptic prose follows an exclusionary "pattern of conceptualization as it is found in Western rationality." According to Ryan, the problem with this "pattern" develops in a "rational operation of theoretical exclusion, hierarchization, and marginalization [which] translates fairly consistently into a questionable political practice." Authors who write a synopsis of intellectual traditions may not intend to exclude the "other" from their narratives, but "it is in the nature of the 'natural,' rational method to assume legislative authority in the knowledge and management of the world."[50] Other voices (including the voices of women and non-western people) frequently disappear from this kind of history, and the story of Western intellectual life is reduced to certain thinkers who have worked within the cultural framework of a particular rationalist tradition.

Critics in other disciplines have restated Ryan's complaints by calling Jay an "academic policeman" who cannot understand writing that differs from his narrow conception of reasonable discourse. This theme appears, for example, in an angry letter from the anthropologist Michael Taussig, who was the subject of a highly critical review that Jay published in the *Visual Anthropology Review*. Summarizing the scholarship and prose in two of Taussig's books, Jay concluded that his work "willingly abandons the traditional scholarly mode of reasoned explanation in favor of poetic evocation based on Dada and Surrealist principles of montage," all of which suggested the "illusion of profundity produced by the deliberate repudiation of clarity." Jay specifically criticized Taussig's interpretations of Adorno and Benjamin as well as a writing style that "careens erratically from topic to topic," and he stressed that Taussig's sympathetic account of non-Western magic and shamans could not offer a plausible theoretical foundation for reforming modern social and political systems.[51] Taussig vehemently rejected this assessment, of course, and charged that Jay had approached his work "like the police" rather than like a poet. The review's "cop-like" response to Taussig's original writing style (according to the author himself) showed the anxiety of an unoriginal, "exegetical" critic who could not tolerate challenges to his own limiting definitions of Reason and Unreason. Another anthropologist, Paul Stoller, also reacted to Jay's critique of Taussig in a commentary that described Jay as "a gatekeeper of academic standards. Like the wise and erudite philosopher king," Stoller complained, "Jay defends reason and reflection and warns readers to beware the beguilements and trickery of would-be poets and other innovators."[52]

This view of Jay's rationalist "gatekeeping" reappears in a subsequent anthropological critique of *Downcast Eyes* by Peter Pels. Referring to Jay's criticisms of Taussig's work, Pels suggests that Jay's history of the "vision debate" exemplifies the traits of an "academic policeman" who prefers science and Enlightenment "ocularcentrism" over anti-ocular critics, "pays no attention to the role of the primitive and exotic, that is, of ethnography" in avant-garde movements such as Surrealism, and downplays the ways in which scientific surveillance serves "policing as much as democracy."[53] More generally, Pels and other critics argue that Jay's approach to European intellectual history overlooks the influence of non-European cultures on the development of modern thought—an influence that often challenged Enlightenment ideologies as it entered into the arts, social theories, and political movements during and after the colonial era.

The poststructuralist and anthropological criticisms of Jay's support for European rationalist traditions carry an implicit suggestion that his intellectual methods have political consequences (e.g., the exclusion of non-Western cultural traditions that use different methods to establish their truths). But Jay has also been criticized for giving insufficient attention to the politics of thinkers *within* Western culture and for failing to provide more explicit or provocative statements about his own political positions. The sociologist Craig Calhoun, for example, argues that *Downcast Eyes* is a "very intellectualistic intellectual history" that should have included more analysis of the social and political aspects of debates about ocularcentrism. Understanding the "political intent" of French intellectuals, Calhoun suggests, "may require an analysis of what was at stake politically," but Jay's approach to intellectual history lacks a sustained consideration of "political action."[54]

This criticism of a "missing politics" emerges also in a review of *Songs of Experience* by the Marxist literary critic Terry Eagleton. Although he praises Jay's "absorbing" analysis and "formidably erudite" knowledge of intellectual history, Eagleton argues that Jay should say more about how gendered languages shape the cultural meaning of experience and how Freudian conceptions of the unconscious transformed the modern understanding of subjectivity. But he especially complains about Jay's resistance to straightforward political interpretations of the whole subject. Indeed, Eagleton finds *Songs of Experience* to be "perversely shy of advancing a case of its own, least of all a controversial one," and so he wants Jay to develop a more explicit political analysis. Eagleton compares Jay's "synoptic sweep" to the work of intellectual historians such as Arthur Lovejoy and Ernst Cassier, but he does not come upon enough "conceptual daring" in *Songs of Experience* because "when [Jay] spots a polarity, he steers right down the middle." To be sure, Jay's scholarship leads to careful, "judicious" arguments, yet Eagleton wonders about the political implications of the middle way. "It is possible," he writes, "... to be hopelessly well-balanced as well as admirably judicious.... Like most liberals, Jay prefers questions to solutions." Eagleton would like to see more "capacity for invective" in Jay's books, which are filled with the footnotes of academia rather than the passion of polemics.[55]

Jay responds to such criticisms with vigorous defenses of his own approach to intellectual history, even when he concedes that some of his critics have brought attention to important issues. Writing in response to the poststructuralist critique of synopsis and paraphrase, for example, he stresses that critics such as Dominick LaCapra have rightly shown intellectual historians "the inevitable obstacles in any attempt to render or reproduce a thought transparently without linguistic mediation."[56] He also concedes that Michael Ryan's description of certain "exclusions" in intellectual debates might be at least partly accurate, insofar as scholarly communities that rely on rational communication may well exclude people "who claim a privileged right to suspend the procedures of the speech community in the name of a higher claim to truth."[57] Jay obviously wants to include women, men, and persons of every racial or national group within the community of intellectual debate. He also argues, however, that people who join the academic "speech community" should recognize that paraphrase and synopsis make a constructive contribution to the communicative rationality that is needed for both scholarship and public conversations. This method of writing, as Jay defends it, promotes a "kind of communicative rationality that is so different from the coercive, totalizing reason rejected by Ryan and other deconstructionists," because it seeks to achieve "an intersubjective consensus" or "common ground" or "fused horizon" that connects the "past and present." Where his critics see exclusion, Jay sees a crucial link between "paraphrastic intellectual history" and "communicative rationality"—which means (for Jay) that such work carries a positive political significance.[58]

Synopsis and paraphrase, in short, provide a foundation for the dialogic communications that are essential for open human societies. "We have become increasingly sensitive to the ways in which language erodes meaning, disperses intentionality, and frustrates understanding," Jay writes in response to his poststructuralist critics. "It is perhaps time to be equally open to those aspects of it that preserve hope for a very different kind of human solidarity. In its very modest way, synoptic content analysis, in its sophisticated rather than naïve form, may justifiably be defended as a prefiguration of such an outcome."[59] Despite what the critics may claim, synopsis provides a starting point for the thoughtful engagement with "others" that must be present in all successful social and political struggles for "human solidarity."

Jay's response to the poststructuralists expresses agreement with certain aspects of their argument, but he makes few such concessions in his exchanges with Michael Taussig and the critical anthropologists. Replying to Taussig's criticism of his unoriginal, "exegetical" work, Jay sarcastically notes "how hard it must be for people lucky enough to be on your side of the original poet/exegetical police divide to tolerate the obsessive insistence of lumbering dolts like myself on making sense, rather than noise." Yet, it is precisely the need to "make sense" of thinkers such as Adorno and Benjamin that Jay reiterates in his criticism of Taussig's "substantive confusion" and "stylistic bombast." Even in this case, however, Jay makes one modest concession on his way to the final point: "You are right, I would be the first to concede, that I am more a humble commentator than an original thinker, more an exegete than a poet, but at least one thing that a career of plodding commentary has given me is the ability to distinguish real turtle soup from the mock."[60] The passion that Eagleton finds missing in Jay's books definitely emerges here and in other responses to his critics, so anyone who yearns for a sharper edge in Jay's prose might well come upon what they are looking for in his essays and occasional pieces.

Jay's debate with the anthropologists continues in a later exchange with Peter Pels, the critic who questions what Jay (summarizing the critique) calls the alleged political agenda of "an ethnocentric, Enlightenment policeman anxious to suppress the libertarian impulses coming from non-Western traditions of shamanistic magic and the occult." Although he changes the tone of his earlier exchange with Taussig, Jay again questions the idea that esoteric cult leaders can offer guidance for modern social or political reforms: "how does shamanistic magic avoid the preserve of an elite that keeps the rest of us in a state of necessary ignorance?"[61] The charge of elitism, which critical readers tend to direct at the "rationalist" intellectuals whom Jay often endorses, turns out to be a two-edged sword that Jay is more than willing to swing at some of his ethnographic critics.

The political argument within Jay's response to the anthropologists comes back to his Habermasian belief in the democratic value of communicative rationality, which is why Jay seems mystified by charges that he has ignored the political implications of historical analysis. He argues in answer to Calhoun's critique of the "missing politics" in *Downcast Eyes*, for example, that he regularly examines the political implications of a thinker's views when the politics become relevant. The politics of "ocularist" and "anti-ocularist" intellectuals are by no means self-evident or consistent, however, and Jay therefore refuses to give the thinkers in any theoretical camp "a one-directional political spin." Here, too, his response to critics emphasizes the complexity, contradictions, and interplay of opposing positions, which (Jay argues) make it "foolish for me to arrive at some self-assured conclusion concerning the political implications of ocularcentrism or its critique *tout court*."[62]

This resistance to "self-assured" conclusions shows the kind of judicious balance that dismays polemical critics such as Terry Eagleton, but it also explains why Jay's intellectual history is important for a wide range of academic disciplines and political perspectives. Jay approaches past thinkers and his contemporary critics with a strong intellectual and political commitment to dialogic exchanges, which he has summarized (among other places) in response to an interdisciplinary forum on *Downcast Eyes*. "The point, after all, is to keep the discussion going, not to end it prematurely," Jay argues. "The uncompleted (and uncompleteable) project of enlightenment is not ... an act of police brutality but, rather, an invitation to all who wish to participate to bring their arguments to the table, where they can be weighed in the full glare of a light that refuses to dazzle or blind."[63] This invitation to continue the "uncompleted" discussion concisely conveys Jay's approach to intellectual life, historical studies, and the political challenges of a democratic society.

Critical Intellectual Journeys along the "Middle Path"

This overview of Martin Jay's historical and theoretical writings has described one of the methods that intellectual history provides for historians who seek a critical engagement with contemporary academic and public culture. Intellectual historians, as Jay repeatedly asserts, can use "synoptic content analysis" and "paraphrase" to develop analytical insights that help sustain public conversations and democratic political cultures. In addition to its descriptions of past thinkers and ideas, intellectual history offers a scholarly method for placing contemporary conflicts in a broad historical context and for developing theoretical arguments that can reshape intellectual traditions or reigning cultural assumptions. Jay pursues these broad intellectual goals by writing for scholars and by interpreting scholarly debates for readers who may not be familiar with the jargon of contemporary academic culture.

Theorists who work within this academic culture, however, may well question how one derives critical perspectives from Jay's historical method of synoptic content analysis or from his tendency to move toward a middle path in all of the intellectual debates he examines. Although the most radical positions in intellectual debates often seem to carry the sharpest critical edge, Jay's emphasis on the constant intellectual flow between dialectical alternatives also carries important critical implications. The continual analysis of this fluid, dialectical process pushes both historians and theorists to remain open to the widest range of possible explanations for every social problem or political conflict. Resisting closure, Jay argues for the democratic value of open-ended debates and sees the often-maligned "middle path" as a winding, dialogic road toward future cultural changes.

Jay also demonstrates that the careful explication of complex thinkers makes an important contribution to cultures lacking historical consciousness or the memory of past intellectual debates. His long scholarly books thus become historical interventions in contemporary debates about issues such as the nature of Marxist theory or the meaning of vision or the complexity of human experience—debates that tend to remain all too presentist in most academic disciplines (not to mention the wider public culture). Jay reaffirms the scholarly value of synthetic summaries and shows historians how they might write intelligently about both the Enlightenment and its modern critics. His work exemplifies his own commitment to the Enlightenment legacy of "rational communications," but it also provides insightful accounts of the radical, anti-Enlightenment critiques that have shaped much of modern intellectual life.

Jay's synoptic prose style brings the obscure or forgotten themes of traditional Western thought into a dialectical exchange with recent critical theories. He reminds contemporary theorists that Western cultural traditions still carry critical vitality, but he also shows historians why they need to understand the intellectual insights of modern French theorists, such as Foucault, Barthes, or Bataille, and German theorists, such as Adorno and Habermas. To summarize the significance of his wide-ranging scholarship, one might say simply that Jay offers analytical distance and historical perspectives for present-minded cultural theorists and theoretical perspectives for empirical-minded historians. He defends the still-liberating potential of Enlightenment-style rational thought and even the potential value of universalizing theories, but he also knows that Enlightenment traditions must be approached with a critical reassessment of their many blind spots, cultural exclusions, and possible political dangers. The dialectical study of past thinkers flows between a sympathetic understanding and rigorous critique, both of which are essential for intellectual history.

Jay's work therefore affirms the value of an historical method that combines synthetic, synoptic summaries of difficult authors and texts with careful analysis of their interactions and exchanges. As he has shown throughout his many books and articles, critical thinking remains a vital component of cultural life when it moves freely across the shifting ground of complex "force fields" that evolve historically along the fault lines of opposing intellectual positions. This open-ended perspective recognizes the flaws in modern societies and scholarship, but it also expresses optimism about the possibilities for social change and gives Jay's work its enduring significance for the systematic analysis of modern cultures as well as the academic study of modern intellectual history.

Notes

1. The full bibliography of Jay's publications is too long to list here, but the major books include the following: *The Dialectical Imagination: A History of the Frankfurt School and the Institute of Social Research* (Boston, 1973; Berkeley and Los Angeles, 1996); *Marxism and Totality: The Adventures of a Concept from Lukács to Habermas* (Berkeley and Los Angeles, 1984); *Downcast Eyes: The Denigration of Vision in Twentieth-Century French Thought* (Berkeley and Los Angeles, 1993); and *Songs of Experience: Modern American and European Variations on a Universal Theme* (Berkeley and Los Angeles, 2004). Among his many other publications, one finds excellent examples of his approach to intellectual history in *Adorno* (London, 1984), a concise intellectual biography of a figure who has influenced Jay's own views of modern culture, and in the numerous articles, papers, and commentaries that he has republished in books of collected essays. See, for example, *Permanent Exiles: Essays on the Intellectual Migration from Germany to America* (New York, 1985); *Fin-de-Siècle Socialism and Other Essays* (New York and London, 1988); *Force Fields: Between Intellectual History and Cultural Critique* (New York and London, 1993); *Cultural Semantics: Keywords of Our Time* (Amherst, MA, 1998); and *Refractions of Violence* (New York, 2003). The essays in these collections merit careful analysis, but I will not examine them in detail here. My analysis in this chapter draws in several places from my earlier review essays on Jay's work: "Martin Jay and the Cultural Insights of Synthetic Intellectual History," *Comparative Studies in Society and History* 38 (1996): 370–375, and a review of *Cultural Semantics* in *Theory and Society* 29 (2000): 253–261.
2. Jay has described his approach to intellectual history in various essays and in responses to critics. In one such commentary on the method of his book *Downcast Eyes*, for example, he refers to the "dialogic" aspect of historical writing, a theme (as Jay notes) that appears often in the work of the intellectual historian Dominick LaCapra. Jay explains that, "we are always putting questions to the past that reflect 'a vantage point in the present.'" He concedes that there is no single "present" from which all writers begin, but he also insists that "we can have no dialogue with

[the past] unless we first admit our own historical situatedness." Jay argues that his method in *Downcast Eyes* "tries to perform, rather than merely espouse, a dialogic interaction" with diverse thinkers who wrote about the meaning of vision. See Jay, "Disciplinary Prisms: Responding to My Critics," *Comparative Studies in Society and History* 38 (1996): 390.

3. Jay draws the term "force field" from Theodor Adorno, who used this metaphor to describe a "relational interplay of attractions and aversions that constituted the dynamic, transmutational structure of a complex phenomenon." Intellectual debates are thus one of the cultural spheres in which such "relational interplay" occurs. Adorno also referred to a constellation (a term that was drawn from Walter Benjamin), and Jay borrows this word to think critically about "a juxtaposed rather than integrated cluster of changing elements that resist reduction to a common denominator, essential core, or generative first principle." Jay, *Adorno*, 14–15. These concepts become useful for Jay's view of intellectual history, which he describes as an academic discipline that "can itself be fruitfully understood as a force field," because it "functions at the shifting intersection of different, often conflicting discourses." Jay, *Force Fields*, 2. The introduction to this collection of essays includes Jay's brief, but insightful, self-portrait of his position amid the different themes and methods of contemporary intellectual history.
4. Jay, "Educating the Educators," in *Cultural Semantics*, 105.
5. Ibid., 106.
6. Jay, *Songs of Experience*, 231. This quotation appears in a summary of Wilhelm Dilthey's view of history, but it also conveys a theme in Jay's own view of history and experience.
7. Jay, "For Theory," in *Cultural Semantics*, 28.
8. Jay, "The Academic Woman as Performance Artist," in ibid., 143.
9. Jay, "Should Intellectual History Take a Linguistic Turn? Reflections on the Habermas-Gadamer Debate," in *Fin-de-Siècle Socialism*, 35. In this same essay, Jay praises Habermas for reaffirming the value of intellectual themes that modern critics drew from the Enlightenment: Habermas "has remained true to the classical Frankfurt School insight that critique and rationality are intimately linked"; and Jay argues that there is an "indisputable" need for intellectuals to continue exploring this link between rationality and criticism. Ibid., 34.
10. Ibid., 35.
11. Ibid., 35–36.
12. Ibid., 36.
13. Jay, "Two Cheers for Paraphrase: The Confessions of a Synoptic Intellectual Historian," in ibid., 58. This essay responds to criticisms of Jay's "synoptic content analysis" that appear in Dominick LaCapra, *Rethinking Intellectual History: Texts, Contexts, Language* (Ithaca, NY, 1983), 33, and in Michael Ryan, *Marxism and Deconstruction: A Critical Articulation* (Baltimore, MD, 1982), 144. Ryan complains that synopsis "abridges and reduces a complicated, heterogeneous mass to an abstract, homogeneous form" in a "rational operation that is normative and hierarchical," because "it must create marginal spaces for elements that do not contribute to the efficiency of synopsis." In other words, Ryan claims that the synoptic method excludes dissonant voices from its narrative (this criticism does not refer to Jay by name, but describes a conference at which Ryan questioned Jay's synoptic method). LaCapra describes "synoptic content analysis" as "both necessary and limited" in its approach to texts, but he praises Jay's work as "one of the most successful and perspicacious" examples

of the genre. He also notes in another book that Jay offers a "cogent defense of synopsis," though LaCapra warns that synopsis may reduce the "play" and complexity of creative texts "insofar as it inhibits or invalidates more insistently interpretive or speculative ventures." Dominick LaCapra, *History and Reading: Tocqueville, Foucault, French Studies* (Toronto, 2000), 37.
14. Jay, "Two Cheers for Paraphrase," in *Fin-de-Siècle Socialism*, 58, 60.
15. H. Stuart Hughes, *Consciousness and Society: The Reorientation of European Social Thought, 1890–1930* (New York, 1958).
16. Ibid., 27–28.
17. Jay, *Downcast Eyes*, 17.
18. Ibid., 18.
19. Jay, *Songs of Experience*, 402. Jay draws Gadamer's comments from Hans-Georg Gadamer, *Gadamer in Conversation: Reflections and Commentary*, ed. and trans. Richard E. Palmer (New Haven, CT, 2001).
20. Jay, *Dialectical Imagination*, xv.
21. Ibid., 81.
22. Ibid., 48.
23. Ibid., 54.
24. Ibid., 70.
25. Ibid., 294.
26. Ibid.
27. Arthur Lovejoy analyzed what he called "unit-ideas"—concepts that are reused through the centuries, but gradually gain new meanings as they recombine (somewhat like chemical elements) in recurring intellectual configurations. Lovejoy's best-known studies of such ideas appear in *The Great Chain of Being* (Cambridge, MA, 1936) and in *Essays in the History of Ideas* (Baltimore, MD, 1948). Jay's method of intellectual history is closer to the work of H. Stuart Hughes than to Lovejoy, and his interest in political-social contexts goes well beyond Lovejoy's "internalist" approach to the "history of ideas." Jay also gives greater emphasis to changes that occur in the rethinking of older ideas, and his commentaries on notable thinkers show much more engagement with contemporary interpretations of the past. In the wake of the "linguistic turn," he is also more alert to the play of language, which challenges the coherence of "unit-ideas." Jay's books on concepts such as totality, vision, and experience, however, resemble the Lovejoy tradition in their careful attention to the evolution of key ideas across time.
28. Jay, *Marxism and Totality*, 274.
29. Ibid., 477.
30. Ibid., 536.
31. Ibid., 537.
32. Jay, *Downcast Eyes*, 589.
33. Ibid., 593.
34. Ibid., 594.
35. Jay, *Songs of Experience*, 5.
36. Ibid., 6.
37. Ibid.
38. Ibid., 7.
39. Ibid., 405.
40. Ibid., 406.
41. Ibid.

42. Ibid.
43. Ibid., 408.
44. Hegel discusses history in an Idealist philosophical language that Jay does not use, but Hegel's concept of dialectical change refers to patterns of negation that also interest Jay. "World history," Hegel explains, "presents the development of consciousness … and the [material] actualization that is produced by that consciousness. This development entails a gradual process, a series of further determinations of freedom, that arise from the concept of world history. The logical nature, and moreover the dialectical nature of the concept in general is that it is self-determining: it posits determinations in itself, then negates them, and thereby gains in this negation (*Aufheben*), an affirmative, richer, and more concrete determination." G.W.F. Hegel, *Introduction to the Philosophy of History*, translated, with introduction, by Leo Rauch (Indianapolis, IN, 1988), 67. This evolution of ideas through negations that challenge and/or enrich the meaning of earlier concepts is the "dialectical" process that attracts Jay's historical analysis.
45. Jay, "For Theory," in *Cultural Semantics*, 16.
46. Ibid.
47. Ibid., 28.
48. Ibid., 29.
49. Jay responds to Adorno's "withering rant" in an essay about the challenges of writing the history of contemporary subjects, "The Ungrateful Dead," in *Refractions of Violence* (New York, 2003), 39–46. Adorno was unhappy with Jay's research on the Frankfurt School, but Jay uses Adorno (and the hostile references to him by another deceased author, Gershom Scholem) to reflect on how historians bring their personal "psychological processes" and various "identifications, idealizations, and demonizations" to the people they study.
50. Ryan, *Marxism and Deconstruction*, 144–145.
51. Martin Jay, "Unsympathetic Magic," Review of Michael Taussig, *The Nervous System* (New York, 1992), and Taussig, *Mimesis and Alterity: A Particular History of the Senses* (New York, 1993), *Visual Anthropology Review* 9 (Fall, 1993): 79.
52. "Michael Taussig Replies to Martin Jay," in ibid., 10, 1 (Spring, 1994): 154; and "Double Takes: Paul Stoller on Jay on Taussig," in ibid., 155.
53. Peter Pels, "Visions of Anthropology," *Comparative Studies in Society and History* 38 (1996): 376–379; quotations on 379. Pels contributed this review essay to a forum on *Downcast Eyes*, which concluded with Jay's response to his critics.
54. Craig Calhoun, "What Do We See in the Discourse of Vision," in *Comparative Studies in Society and History* 38 (1996): 384, 387.
55. Terry Eagleton, "Give Me a Fiver" [Review of *Songs of Experience*], in *London Review of Books* 27, no. 12 (23 June 2005): 23–24.
56. Jay, "Two Cheers for Paraphrase," in *Fin-de-Siècle Socialism*, 63.
57. Ibid., 55
58. Ibid., 60.
59. Ibid., 63.
60. "Martin Jay Replies to Michael Taussig and Paul Stoller," *Visual Anthropology Review* 10, 1 (Spring, 1994): 163–164.
61. Jay, "Disciplinary Prisms: Responding to my Critics," in *Comparative Studies in Society and History* 38 (1996): 393–394.
62. Ibid., 389.
63. Ibid., 394.

Bibliography

Calhoun, Craig. "What Do We See in the Discourse of Vision." In *Comparative Studies in Society and History* 38 (1996): 383–387.
Eagleton, Terry. "Give Me a Fiver" [Review of *Songs of Experience*]. In *London Review of Books*, no 12. 23 June 2005.
Gadamer, Hans-Georg. *Gadamer in Conversation: Reflections and Commentary.* Edited and translated by Richard E. Palmer. New Haven, CT, 2001.
Hegel, G.W.F. *Introduction to the Philosophy of History.* Translated by Leo Rauch. Indianapolis, IN, 1988.
Hughes, H. Stuart. *Consciousness and Society: The Reorientation of European Social Thought, 1890–1930.* New York, 1958.
Jay, Martin. *Adorno.* London: Fontana [Modern Masters]; Cambridge, MA: Harvard University Press, 1984.
———. *Cultural Semantics: Keywords of Our Time.* Amherst, MA: University of Massachusetts Press, 1998.
———. *The Dialectical Imagination: A History of the Frankfurt School and the Institute of Social Research.* Boston: Little, Brown and Co., 1973; Berkeley: University of California Press, 1996.
———. "Disciplinary Prisms: Responding to My Critics." In *Comparative Studies in Society and History* 38, no. 2 (1996): 388–394.
———. *Downcast Eyes: The Denigration of Vision in Twentieth-Century French Thought.* Berkeley: University of California Press, 1993.
———. *Fin-de-Siècle Socialism and Other Essays.* New York and London: Routledge, 1988.
———. *Force Fields: Between Intellectual History and Cultural Critique.* New York and London: Routledge, 1993.
———. "Martin Jay Replies to Michael Taussig and Paul Stoller." In *Visual Anthropology Review* 10, 1 (Spring, 1994): 163-164.
———. *Marxism and Totality: The Adventures of a Concept from Lukács to Habermas.* Berkeley: University of California Press; Cambridge, England: Polity Press, 1984.
———. *Permanent Exiles: Essays on the Intellectual Migration from Germany to America.* New York: Columbia University Press, 1985.
———. *Refractions of Violence.* New York: Routledge, 2003.
———. *Songs of Experience: Modern American and European Variations on a Universal Theme.* Berkeley: University of California Press, 2004.
———. "Unsympathetic Magic," Review of Michael Taussig, *The Nervous System* and *Mimesis and Alterity.* In *Visual Anthropology Review* 9, 2 (Fall, 1993): 79-82.
LaCapra, Dominick. *History and Reading: Tocqueville, Foucault, French Studies.* Toronto, 2000.
———. *Rethinking Intellectual History: Texts, Contexts, Language.* Ithaca, NY, 1983.
Lovejoy, Arthur. *The Great Chain of Being.* Cambridge, MA, 1936.
———. *Essays in the History of Ideas.* Baltimore, MD, 1948.
Pels, Peter. "Visions of Anthropology." In *Comparative Studies in Society and History* 38 (1996): 376–379.
Ryan, Michael. *Marxism and Deconstruction: A Critical Articulation.* Baltimore, MD, 1982.
Taussig, Michael. *Mimesis and Alterity: A Particular History in the Senses.* New York, 1993.
———. "Michael Taussig Replies to Martin Jay." In *Visual Anthropology Review* 10, 1 (Spring 1994): 154.

Part I

Intellectual History

"THE KISS OF LAMOURETTE"
"Possibilism" or "Christian Democracy"?

David Sorkin

> The sense of boundless possibility—"possibilism" one could call it—was the bright side of popular emotion, and it was not restricted to millenarian outbursts in the streets. It could seize lawyers and men of letters sitting in the Legislative Assembly. On July 7, 1792, A.-A. Lamourette, a deputy from the Rhône-et-Loire, told the Assembly's members that their troubles all arose from a single source: factionalism. They needed more fraternity. Whereupon the deputies, who had been at each other's throats a moment earlier, rose to their feet and started hugging and kissing each other as if their political divisions could be swept away in a wave of brotherly love.
> —Robert Darnton, *The Kiss of Lamourette*

With an essay entitled, "The Kiss of Lamourette," and the volume in which it appeared bearing the same title,[1] Robert Darnton has made this obscure incident of the French Revolution so widely known that other historians have begun to repeat his account of it.[2] Yet the one engaging paragraph devoted to the incident reduces the "kiss of Lamourette" to a curiosity that allegedly reveals the French Revolution's excesses and eccentricities ("possibilism"). Darnton rightly insists that we should prefer the voices and thoughts of historical participants to the theories of contemporary historians.[3] In this essay, I will attempt to let Lamourette speak for himself. I will offer an alternative understanding of the incident by providing a detailed account of Lamourette's life and thought. My contention is that we need to employ the methods of narrative intellectual history to comprehend this event as did the historical participants themselves.

Lamourette, whom Darnton identifies only as a "deputy from the Rhône-et-Loire," was not only an Abbé, a serious theologian, a Constitutional Bishop, and a deputy, but one of the patriotic clergy who understood enlightened Catholic belief and the Revolution to be mutually fulfilling. His "kiss" was located at the heart of the Revolution's conflicts: it was intended as a defense of what he significantly called "Christian democracy." This essay will revisit the "kiss" by employing the methods of narrative intellectual history to look closely at what the sources say first about Lamourette and next the kiss itself.

Who was "A.-A. Lamourette"?

Adrien Lamourette (1742–1794) was a member of the Lazarist order, a sometime seminary Professor, Seminary Director, and parish priest.[4] Born in 1742 as the oldest of five children to a humble family in the market town of Frévent (in the northwest, now the Department of Pas-de-Calais) where his father was a comb-maker, he showed an early aptitude for study and his parents dedicated him to the Church. He entered the Lazarist order at the age of seventeen (1759) and was ordained a Priest ten years later (1769).[5] Lamourette attended the Order's central seminary at its Paris headquarters, known as the Maison Saint-Lazare (hence the Order's name), where he likely followed a twelve-year curriculum for the training of Lazarist seminary professors.[6] His first teaching post was at Metz (1769–1772), where he taught philosophy, and the Abbé Grégoire (1750–1831) was one of his students. Beginning in 1773, he was a Professor at the Lazarist seminary in Toul (west of Nancy) in the province of Lorraine. He served for two years (1776–1778) as Director of the Seminary of Toul, a placeholder during the reorganization of the institution.[7] Lamourette then became a parish priest in Outremcourt (Haute-Marne), where he spent five formative years (1778–1783). Lamourette returned to the Congregation of Saint Lazare in 1784, and in 1785 went home to his parish of origin, where he was appointed a member of the Academy of Arras.

Lamourette's first book appeared in 1785 and he published three more by the time of the Revolution (1786, 1788, 1789). This torrid pace says something about the 1780s as a crucial juncture in France's history: the accession of Louis XVI brought an end to the era of *Unigenitus* (1713). By enforcing this papal bull prohibiting Jansenism, Louis XV's government had created the conditions for a tripartite struggle (Jansenists vs. *parti dévot* vs. *philosophes*) that largely determined the shape of French religious and political culture throughout his long reign (1715–1774).[8] The Jansenist-*parti dévot* divide began to dissolve with the suppression of the Jesuits in 1764. Louis XVI's restoration of the Parlement at the conclusion of the Maupeou controversy (1774) signaled the end of the monarchy's alliance with the *parti dévot* and its heretofore implacable dispute with Jansenism.[9] A political realignment ensued, in which the clergy and the Bishops began to ally with the Parlement, Jansenist thinkers opened to new cultural possibilities, and the government began to implement reforms, the most salient being the limited toleration granted to Protestants (1787).[10]

The 1780s were thus conducive to new directions in thought. In his four books, Lamourette attempted to offer a version of Catholic Enlightenment. Most famously associated with Joseph II's reforms, Bishop Hontheim, the Punctation of Ems (1786), and Bishop Scipio de Ricci and the Council of Pistoia (1786), Catholic Enlightenment was an attempt to articulate Catholic faith in the categories of Enlightenment science and philosophy. Catholic Enlightenment also included an effort to recover neglected aspects of Catholic tradition (e.g., study of Scripture, Patristics) and a program of Church reform (usually inspired by the ideal of the primitive Church, conciliarism, and some variant of Jansenism or neo-Jansenism). Its proponents generally adopted the key ideas of reasonableness and natural religion, natural law and toleration. Other theologians in France began to move in this same direction prior to the Revolution: the Abbé Grégoire applied natural law theory to the issue of the Jews' civil status (*Essai sur la Régénération physique, morale et politique des Juifs*, 1789), while the Abbé Claude Fauchet (1744–1793) applied it to the reorganization of the Church (*De la Religion nationale*, 1789).[11]

Lamourette broke new ground in endeavoring to devise a Catholic Enlightenment theology. His theology is distinctly apologetic. The *philosophes* are his partners in dialogue to the degree that on every fundamental issue, he developed his own position by criticizing theirs: the role of reason and sentiment (inspired by Rousseau) in faith; the relationship between revealed and natural religion; and Christianity as a political philosophy and a social ethics.

In general, Lamourette aimed to make a fresh theological start. He referred neither to medieval scholastic theology nor to the vast and acrimonious theological literature of the eighteenth century, but rather turned to the great figures of the seventeenth century (Bossuet, Fénelon). As his biographer aptly observed, Lamourette was trying to avoid the extremes of Jansenism, whose aridity destroyed the sources of piety, and of philosophy, which sapped the basis of faith.[12]

Lamourette's version of Catholic Enlightenment consisted of a moderate skepticism, well established in French Catholicism (Pascal), which he wielded against the *philosophes'* claims. By considering such words as "revelation, miracle, mystery, and prophecy" incompatible with truthful analysis, the *philosophes* deluded themselves, Lamourette believed, into thinking that they are able to decipher everything but religion. In fact, they found nature impenetrable and cannot even explain the true character of a drop of water. The theologian's belief in the trinity had the same basis as the philosopher's in geometry: perception, *"bon sens,"* and reason. Theology qualifies as philosophy since it rests on true perception and reason: "everywhere philosophy consists in heeding reason and submitting to truth." It is "anti-philosophical" to cite as grounds for incredulity the obscurity of miracles and mysteries.[13]

Lamourette's skepticism restricts his notion of reason, and especially, science. While admiring two centuries of scientific achievement (Copernicus, Galileo, Cassini, Torricelli, Pascal, Malphighi), he insists that it remains on the surface of phenomena. The essence or final cause of nature is as impenetrable as the divine mysteries: "it is ... only in the Infinite that the true principles of differences that distinguish created substances are to be found hidden away." Man's task is to act, not to understand.[14]

From this skeptical restriction of science and equation of theology and philosophy, Lamourette made a fideist leap, redefining "enlightened man."

> For the enlightened man [*l'homme éclairé*] of good faith the collection of human knowledge carries a preconceived disposition to believe without understanding; and the reluctance to recognize as truth that which cannot be explained is an absurd ostentation which decisively proves mediocrity and ignorance.[15]

Lamourette then turns on its head the *philosophes'* claim that "Christianity is a cruel and seditious religion" and a form of "religious fanaticism." The *philosophes* are the true fanatics since they aim to create "discord in the hearts of all peoples and combustion in the entire universe" by making "the philosophical spirit ... as much the ruin of reason as the tomb of all virtue."[16]

Lamourette strove to overcome the polarity between religion and reason: "the *philosophes* of our century have shown themselves to be too *anti-Theologian*, and our other theologians have perhaps been a bit too *anti-Philosophes*." This polarity is a human invention—people mistakenly confound reason and revelation's fundamental compatibility.[17] This false polarity can be avoided by finding a middle ground in which "the masters of theology would reduce less severely the rights of reason, and ... the *philosophes* show more respect and consideration for those of revelation." Philosophers should recognize not only that there are truths beyond reason, but that the very fact of being beyond reason attests to their divine source.[18]

Lamourette proposed to undo this polarization in France by recapturing the University and the Republic of Letters for belief.[19] He wanted the Republic of Letters to promote belief and piety, and the Universities to allow pious writers to teach religion.[20]

Within this skeptical structure, Lamourette made sentiment a source of belief alongside reason. Lamourette began to exhibit traces of Rousseau's sentimental understanding of religion in his second book (*Thoughts on the Philosophy of Unbelief or Reflections on the Spirit and Design of the Irreligious Philosophers of our Century*, 1786), where he wrote repeatedly of the "sentiment of faith" and asserted that Catholicism not only elevated the spirit but also "contents the most capacious heart."[21] In his third book, *The Pleasures of Religion, or the Power of the Gospel to make us Happy* (1788), he elevated sentiment to a source of religious knowledge equal to reason. He combined the argument of reasonable religion with that of belief from sentiment, aiming "to enlighten reason and interest feeling," as his treatment of the Gospel demonstrates: "our intimate sense [*sens intime*] is the first proof of the beauty of the Gospel and the strongest conjecture of its truth." The same holds for our perception of Jesus, which has all the persuasive proof of science.

> It is not the demonstration of the internal truth of the *miracles* of Jesus Christ that determines my adoration and belief; but it is a proof of sentiment that draws its strength from the knowledge that I have of his character, the tissue of his actions, the infinity of local circumstances and persons, whose combination victoriously produces conviction in a healthy and reasonable mind, like all the evidence of a geometric proof.[22]

Since reason is equally a source of belief, Lamourette argued that we must disengage ourselves from the "realm of passions" and submit to "reason" which is the "realm of God": "Therefore we see reason everywhere beginning the work of faith, and we are transported by the most natural gradations to the great wisdom of the Gospel."[23]

Whereas in his third book Lamourette had explicitly associated natural religion with rank unbelief ("the disciple of natural religion, the impious person who no longer sees God in the universe"), in his last book he linked it to reason in a manner characteristic of Catholic Enlightenment: natural religion is identical with Christianity since there is no such thing as theism without revelation.[24] True natural religion "pushes and inclines toward the Gospel."[25]

Lamourette vehemently attacked the *philosophes'* political philosophy, unmasking them as "a dark and malicious sect which ... makes a study of corrupting men and freeing them of every sort of duty" as well as subverting all authority and undermining morality because there is no "middle route ... between Christianity and atheism."[26] Lamourette discerns similar "malignity" in the *philosophes'* view of society: by positing that men are originally solitary beings who wish to devour each other, they promote an "egoism destructive of all social virtue" that removes all sense of obligation.[27] The *philosophes* are, therefore, "as much an enemy of throne as of altar."

Lamourette had two political-social ideals. He examined an idyllic, penurious rural parish (which he had presumably experienced first hand in his years at Outremcourt, but which was also a trope of eighteenth-century Jansenist literature), which is led by a dedicated priest and is imbued with faith.

> [A] rural parish becomes, through a virtuous and sensible pastor, the most beautiful and delightful spectacle that the entire grand theater of the world can offer. There one can see religion shining in all the glory of its triumph.[28]

In his third book, he construed this rural parish in terms of sentiment, idealizing the poor as its true repository. He then combined it with his second ideal, the property-less primitive Church. "[N]ever were the virtues of Christianity known and practiced to such an amazing and sublime extent" as in the early Church.[29]

Lamourette sketched an alternative social philosophy.[30] He took issue with social contract theory, attacking its "first principle," namely, that there is a "natural man" or "state of nature." This is "an abstraction and a pure hypothesis," a "geometric *postulatum*" that is the equivalent in the social world of being emerging out of chaos in the physical world, namely, that, "*matter is originally indifferent to everything*." The underlying problem for philosophers is that they "cannot explain anything without chaos."

He posited instead that society, not the so-called "state of nature," is the "first state of humankind." Man is born into a "double relationship" with God and society, in which his relations with God yield religion, those with his fellowmen yielding morality. Both of these are embodied in the ideas of the Gospel. The Gospel teaches the "lessons of respect and submission to the powers that be," which makes Christians the "true and excellent *philosophes*."[31] Thus, "society is the natural state of the human species [genre]." God creates man in society from the start.[32] "The state of society is therefore a work of creation; it is a mode of human nature that does not rest at all on what one calls a pact or a contract."[33]

Christian society derives directly from its Creator and is invested with an authority that is neither man-made nor subject to man's approval.[34] Christianity inculcates performance of obligations as the first step toward the "mystery of God's kingdom."[35] Christianity also indicates a conservative acceptance of the established order, with divine society serving as the template for human society: "the infinitely perfect society of eternity is the origin and model of the profound idea that God used in conceiving and fashioning temporal society."[36] In this divinely ordained Christian social order, in which authority and obedience are foremost, the ideal form of government would be "a *theocratic regime*," but barring that, "a monarchical regime ... is the most perfect of all the social forms."[37]

Christianity creates not only the best government, but also the best society: it is "the unique system which is able to form a perfect society, and people the empire with true and incorruptible citizens," because it corresponds to the infinite's unity within plurality.[38] In his fourth book, *Thoughts on the Philosophy of Faith, or the System of Christianity* (1789), Lamourette in fact attempted to formulate a systematic theology of the infinite in which reasonableness and sentiment were equal sources of belief.[39] The ideal of the primitive Church fortifies this notion of a Christian social order since, based on communal property and a life devoted to prayer, it represented "all the characteristics of the most perfect and happiest society that could establish itself on earth," embodying the ideals of "equality" (*égalité*) and "sociability" (*sociabilité*).[40]

Lamourette's idea of the infinite is also the basis of his social ethics. Man's very Christian potential depends upon it: "a man is so great a being through the excellence of his nature and entirely by his capacity to know and to possess the Infinite."[41] In contrast, Lamourette discerned the "false" infinity of the impious who, rather than looking to the true infinity of God, pursue luxury and sensual experience. Luxury is none other than the inarticulate and confused search for the infinite that religion gives us. It is the sterile and deceptive supplement to the great force in which Jesus Christ comes to incorporate all of humankind.[42]

Lamourette's ethics were, then, in clear opposition to the *philosophes*', which he derisively labeled the "regime of the passions." Based on the desire for the "false infinity" of objects, its ideal is "passionate man" (*l'Homme passionné*) who, acting solely from physical needs and "self-love," is incapable of the benevolence and solidarity society requires. Lamourette pits against "passionate man" the "moderate man" (*l'Homme modéré*) who understands that he is born into society, has an indissoluble solidarity with his fellow men, subjects himself to the true infinity of Christ, and acts in ways that are "profoundly reasonable."[43]

This combination of "moderation" and "reasonableness" was an epitome of Lamourette's conception of Catholic Enlightenment in the 1780s. He opposed the radical *philosophes* by trying to invent a theological middle ground that reconciled major features of Enlightenment thinking—including reasonableness, natural religion, moderation, and Rousseauist sentiment—with the Gospel. While he embraced ideas of equality and sociability that presaged the Revolution, he also held to notions of authority and obedience manifestly at odds with it.

What are the implications of Lamourette's Catholic Enlightenment for our understanding of his "kiss"? We need to examine the direction of his thought and actions during the early Revolution.

"Lawyers and Men of Letters"

In the early years of the Revolution (1789–1791), Lamourette emerged as one of the "patriotic" and "enlightened" clergy. These were priests who understood the Revolution and Christianity in the terms of the Enlightenment and held the two to be not just compatible, but mutually fulfilling: the Revolution realized the central ideas of the Gospel, while the Gospel was indispensable to the Revolution's success. The "patriotic" or "enlightened" clergy were not a party or even a coterie, but a group who professed equal loyalty to Christianity and the Revolution.[44]

While Lamourette held no office in the first two years of the Revolution (1789–1791), he publicly articulated his position in a number of ways. He frequented the salons of Madame Genlis (1746–1830) and Madame Helvétius (1719–1800), both of which were identified with the Revolution and constitutional monarchy. Through the latter, Lamourette became acquainted with Mirabeau, for whom he later ghostwrote two important speeches.[45] He was a member of the Directory of the *Cercle Social* (1789–1791), the group of thinkers and politicians around Nicolas Bonneville (1760–1828) (first a faction in Paris' municipal politics, then a political club, *Confédération des Amis de la Vérité* (1790), and finally a publishing house, *Imprimerie du Cercle Social*, 1791–1793), which eventually became the most important base of the Parisian Girondins. Fauchet, the "preacher of the Paris Commune," and a leader of the early *Cercle Social* (1789–1791), delivered to the meetings of the *Confédération* his famous lectures on Rousseau's *Social Contract*, trying to reconcile the Gospel and the Revolution.[46] Finally, Lamourette published pamphlets and a journal in which we can trace his views on key issues.

Lamourette's articulation of his double loyalty to the early Revolution and Christianity helped him to extend and deepen his version of Catholic Enlightenment. He understood the question of the Jews' admission to civil equality as a legal and constitutional question (December, 1789), that is, "a manifest consequence of the principles adopted by the nation."[47] This stand allowed him to appropriate the idea of "natural right" and connect it with citizenship. Joining other patriotic clergy as advocates, Lamourette abandoned his denigration of "liberty" to espouse this key ideal of the Revolution (he had already embraced equality and fraternity in *Thoughts on the Philosophy of Faith*).[48]

Lamourette supported the Civil Constitution of the Clergy (July, 1790) by drawing on his idealization of poverty and the primitive Church, as well as his Catholic Enlightenment view of church-state relations. A Catholic Enlightenment restructuring of the *ancien régime* Church, the Civil Constitution was perhaps the most radical package of erastian or state-led Church reform (Gallicanism, *Staatskirchentum*) Europe had seen. It was additionally controversial because it was proposed not by a "legitimate" ruler, but by a legislature in the name of a sovereign nation.[49] Lamourette deemed it as being "as necessary to the regeneration of the church as to that of the state," and as "… the sole revolution which can put an end to the ills of religion, and restore it to [its] ancient and austere majesty."[50] In support of the Civil Constitution, for the first time Lamourette voiced the revolutionary ideal of the "sovereignty of nations" and "their legislative power."[51] Like other patriotic clergy, he was enraptured with the Revolution and its millenarian visions. In its "equality and unity in plurality," revolutionary society would emulate the "infinity" that stands as the model for human society ("harmony, unity, and equality").[52] Revolutionary society would also erase the polarity between religion and philosophy—one of his fondest wishes—so that the "two torches [will] unite to enlighten men and make them good and happy," thereby establishing an "eternal alliance of temple and school [*lycée*]."[53]

In a journal addressed to fellow clergy, *Civic Instructions, or the Patriotic Pastor* (1791), in which he offered his most radical version of a revolutionary Catholic Enlightenment, Lamourette rewrote the history of Christianity according to the Revolution's ideals. Jesus championed the "principles of fraternity and equality" and "died a victim of the despots of the synagogue and the tyrants of Rome."[54] Christianity embodied the ideas of 1789; it infused the "principles of reason and nature" and the ideas of "the eternal laws of equality and egalitarianism [*l'équité et l'égalité*]" into every society.[55] He fundamentally revised his understanding of the Enlightenment, recasting the radical *philosophes* as defenders of liberty and freedom against an *ancien régime* despotism which, by including the Church ("that aristocratic theology, source of all the scandals that dishonored Christianity and of all the evils that have tortured the bosom of France"), was responsible for the growth of unbelief: "the history of the entrance of unbelief in France … is, like so many other evils, an effect of despotism."[56]

His effort to promote "enlightened Christianity" as a viable platform for a regenerated France culminated in his ghostwriting two critical speeches for Mirabeau. In a speech of 27 November 1790, in the tense period after the Assembly had enacted the Civil Constitution (July 12), Mirabeau/Lamourette deplored the danger of a mounting "counter-revolution" that could result in a "schism" between "Catholic France and free France." If the clergy were to accept "the spirit of revolution and liberty," they could play a positive role in the new France, whereas if they persist in "decry[ing] liberty in the name of the Gospel," they risked the "horrors of a religious war."

Two months later (14 January 1791; the King sanctioned the clerical oath on 26 December 1790, administration began on 2 January 1791), France appeared to be even closer to a dangerous division. Mirabeau/Lamourette did their utmost to explode the notion that the fundamental "alternative" facing France was between "being Christian or [being] free."[57] They endeavored to establish the middle ground of Catholic Enlightenment and constitutional monarchy by finding a mediating group, which they significantly called "enlightened Christians [chrétiens éclairés]."[58]

Mirabeau/Lamourette vehemently attacked the *ancien régime* church and government, echoing the *Prônes civiques*.

> Enlightened Christians [*les chrétiens éclairés*] asked, whither had fled the august religion of their fathers, and the true religion of the Gospel was nowhere to be found. We were a nation without a country, a people without government and a church without character and discipline.[59]

They visibly alienated most of the clergy sitting on the right side of the Assembly, as the majority rose in protest and departed the chamber. At the same time, the pro-revolutionary anti-clerical party on the left rejected with catcalls the very notion of an "enlightened Christian."[60] Aside from the patriotic clergy, there was no distinct pro-revolution, pro-Christian party that actively identified with the Enlightenment. There could not, then, be a more striking rebuff of the middle ground of Catholic Enlightenment. The Civil Constitution had so radicalized the parties that there was virtually no place for a mediating position.

Lamourette's attempt to defend the middle ground of the Civil Constitution and constitutional monarchy was the background to his "kiss." His proposal was not a curiosity, but part and parcel of his highly informed theological and political agenda.

"A Wave of Brotherly Love"?

In 1791, Lamourette became a public official of the Revolution when he was elected Bishop of Lyon.[61] He was immediately embattled since the former Archbishop, Yves-Alexandre de Marbeuf (1734–1800), was a non-juror who rejected the Civil Constitution, refused to relinquish his seat, and with the help of his Vicar general, organized opposition among the numerous non-juring clergy. Whether the clergy would accept a Constitutional Bishop was a critical test of the Civil Constitution: at one of Lyon's churches (Saint Nizier, 13 March 1791), the priest insisted in his instruction that Lyon had an Archbishop (Marbeuf), but not a Bishop (Lamourette), inciting a brawl which the civil authorities had to quell (the offending priest was jailed).[62]

There was also a pamphlet war. Lamourette at first stoutly defended his integrity, his election, and the Civil Constitution (it did not impinge on "dogma or immutable belief"; the state was entirely within its rights in altering "points of discipline" or the "exterior order"; the reforms were a "return to the spirit and, even more, the practice of the ancient Church").[63] Later, desperate to salvage a functioning Church in the face of the growing polarity of "patrie" and "church," he adopted a more conciliatory tone.[64] In yet another round of pamphlets, Lamourette (16 July 1791) attacked the "ultra-montane" view of the Church as a Papal monarchy and presented the conciliarist conception of a Church governed by bishops and a council that also embodied the ideals of the primitive Church and the Gallican liberties.[65] Despite, or perhaps because of the concerted opposition he faced, Lamourette reiterated his millenarian dreams, professing his confidence in the providential nature of the Revolution: "the establishment of the reign of faith by establishing the reign of liberty."[66]

Lamourette took another step in his revolutionary career when the Department of Saône-et-Loire elected him a delegate to the Legislative Assembly (30 August to 4 September 1791). The large number of votes Lamourette received indicated the esteem the "moderate" and "enlightened" part of the populace had for him as a result of the "indulgence, wisdom, and dignity" with which he conducted himself in the conflict over the Civil Constitution.[67]

Lamourette returned to Paris with some grounds for optimism. The delegates to the Legislative Assembly he joined on 1 October 1791 had been elected by a limited property franchise. The majority comprised a moderate center; the groupings at the extremes were small; and the factions that were later to dominate the Convention (Girondins and Montagnards) had yet to emerge, although most of the salons and clubs that shaped them already existed. For most of the Legislative Assembly's fifty-one weeks, their future members were more likely to cooperate than to clash.

Nevertheless, the grounds for optimism quickly dissipated. The Legislative Assembly was part of a profoundly flawed Constitutional monarchy in which the indecisive and ever more recalcitrant Louis XVI appointed ministers and had veto power over legislation. The Legislative Assembly tried various means to make this imperfect arrangement work. Unsuccessful and increasingly frustrated, especially given the mounting pressures of war and the threat of counterrevolution, the Assembly was forced, by a massive uprising, to take the radical option of deposing the King (10 August 1792).[68]

The Legislative Assembly was also more anti-clerical than its predecessor. The Constituent Assembly had contained large numbers of clergy to whom it was heavily indebted: for the "revolt of the curés" that brought it into existence, for the "core" of the Constitutional Party, and for much of its leadership.[69] Its successor, which by law was an entirely new body, included only twenty clergy (sixteen were Constitutional Bishops), all of whom had taken the oath to the Civil Constitution, and none of whom could offer the kind of leadership that distinguished the earlier body. The declaration of war and the fall of the throne, the growing numbers of emigrés and the failure of the Civil Constitution, plus the treatment of refractory clergy as a "fifth" column combined to propel the polarization of the Revolution and religion by increasingly branding as anti-revolutionary the Church, the clergy, and Catholicism itself. In its last month, the Legislative Assembly enacted this polarization by laicizing the registry of births, deaths, and marriages (état civil) and permitting divorce (20 September 1792). Not surprisingly, the Constitutional clergy protested these measures. The polarization also found expression in public celebrations. All of the early celebrations of the Revolution (1789–1790) had contained salient religious elements, including the mass. In contrast, Voltaire's burial in the Pantheon (11 July 1791) marked a decided turn to the secular. This trend would culminate in the fête for the Constitution (10 August 1793) and the deistic "Cult of Reason."[70]

When Lamourette entered the Legislative Assembly, he faced an uphill struggle in trying to maintain his Catholic enlightenment fusion of the Constitutional Church and the Revolution. Before the end of its first month (21 October 1791) the Legislative Assembly began a five-week debate over church-state relations that pitted anti-clerical deputies against the Constitutional Bishops. Toward the end of that debate, a deputy proposed eliminating the Civil Constitution of the Clergy. He voiced the sentiment, widely held across the Legislative Assembly's aisles, that the

Constituent Assembly had been mistaken in adopting that legislation.[71] Lamourette understood the proposal to have two aims: to create "theism," which the deputy obviously regarded "as the perfection of the French revolution," and to reconcile the refractory clergy to the Constitution.[72]

Lamourette found both of these aims so repellent that he was challenged to produce his most trenchant formulation of the fusion of Christianity and the revolution. The Gospel is the "ancient and unfailing root" of "unity, liberty and equality." "[T]he religion of the gospel ... is more democratic than even the constitution of the French." What "the Sage of Nazareth, the true friend of the people" voiced was "the luminous principles of Christian democracy [*démocratie chrétienne*]."[73] Lamourette had now given an enduring label to the agenda of the patriotic clergy.

Lamourette's "kiss" was his last effort to prevent the polarization that threatened to undo his vision of "Christian democracy." He made his proposal after Roland's ministry had been dismissed (13 June); demonstrators had invaded the Tuilieres (20 June); and heated discussions over further restrictions on the Church (suppression of teaching and missionary orders, prohibition of clerical dress, 6 April 1792; a substitute religion for Catholicism, 20–21 April; and the deportation of non-juring clergy, 26 May). Lamourette's motion (7 July 1792) was intended to defend the status quo of constitutional monarchy and the Civil Constitution.

Lamourette identified France's current malady as the "disunion of the Assembly." He asserted that, "the position of the legislative body is the true barometer of the state of the nation. ... Here resides the lever that can drive the great machine of the State in the sense of unity and harmony, or which produces the complications and opposition to movements which destroy it." The truest benefactor of the state and his fellow citizens is he who creates unity among the legislators. Convinced that "schism is never irremediable," he endeavored to find underlying points of consensus and commonality by appealing to "unity of purpose" and "virtue" among "men of goodwill." He asked his fellow delegates to make a show of "unity of national representation" in the face of a deep divide. "One section of the Assembly attributes to the other a seditious plan to undermine the monarchy and establish a republic; and the second ascribes to the first the crime of wanting the destruction of the egalitarian constitution by striving for the creation of two chambers." To restore unity and to safeguard the revolution, he proposed "an irrevocable oath, striking down the republic and two chambers"—in other words, rejecting two ominous challenges to the status quo. The Assembly accepted this proposal. The delegates swore the oath and celebrated by embracing and kissing.[74] In the next two months, many of them would vote first to depose the King (10 August) and then to abolish the monarchy (21 September 1792).

The "kiss of Lamourette" was, then, a last ditch effort by a member of the "enlightened" and "patriotic" clergy to defend the fusion of Christianity and the Revolution. It was not a matter of "possibilism," "the bright side of popular emotion," or misplaced faith "in a wave of brotherly love." It was rather the desperate attempt of a Bishop and delegate to hold a middle ground position that had appeared to triumph during the Revolution's early consensus yet quickly lost support during the divisive controversy over the Civil Constitution. Lamourette's proposal to foreclose the extremes of a (more radical) republic or (more conservative) two chambers was sufficiently serious and realistic, emerging out of the political process of the Legislative Assembly, to gain the chamber's assent. That it was superseded within a month or two testifies, perhaps, to Lamourette's prestige and persuasive powers as well as to the accelerating tempo of events.

A serious theologian, Bishop, and delegate, Lamourette was a respected figure who advocated "Christian democracy." He was as much a part of the Revolution as the "lawyers and men of letters" who usually populate the textbook accounts and even an article entitled "the kiss of Lamourette." In mentioning Lamourette and in naming his essay and volume after him, Darnton in particular missed an opportunity to complicate the notion of "de-sacralization" that is so central to his account of the causes of the revolution and the revolution itself.[75] At bottom, Lamourette and his kiss remain incomprehensible so long as historians treat the Revolution primarily as a secular political event ("possibilism") bereft of religious dimensions. In his essay marking the bicentenary of the French Revolution, François Furet suggested the need to see the Revolution as having a "plural heritage"; yet in his own account, he focused on the revolution's "secular messianism." "Christian democracy," however transient and precarious it might have been in 1789–1791, strikingly does not figure as one possible heritage.[76] When referring to "the kiss of Lamourette" in the future, historians should allow Lamourette, and the historical possibility he represented, to speak for themselves and thereby attain their rightful place in our understanding of the French Revolution.

Notes

1. Robert Darnton, *The Kiss of Lamourette* (New York, 1990), 17
2. For the repetition of Darnton's account, see Nigel Aston, *Religion and Revolution in France, 1780–1804* (Washington, D.C., 2000).
3. For critical discussions of Darnton's work, see the essays in Haydn T. Mason, ed., *The*

Darnton Debate: Books and revolution in the Eighteenth Century (Oxford, 1998), esp. Jeremy D. Popkin, "Robert Darnton's Alternative (to the) Enlightenment," 105–128; Daniel Gordon, "The Great Enlightenment Massacre," 129–156; and Elizabeth L. Eisenstein, "Bypassing the Enlightenment: Taking an Underground Route to Revolution," 157–178. On "trivialisation," see Gordon, "The Great Enlightenment Massacre," 144.
4. On Lamourette, see F.Z. Collombet, "L'Abbé Lamourette," *Revue du Lyonnais* 2 (1835): 195–212; Abbé Liebaut, *Prêtre et Évêque Assermenté* (Nancy, 1894); André Monglond, *Le préromantisme française*, 2 vols. (Paris, 1966), 2: 86–98; Daniele Menozzi, *"Philosophes" e "Chrétiens éclairés": Politica e religione nella collaborazione di G.H. Mirabeau e A.A. Lamourette (1774–1794)* (Brescia, 1976); Norman Ravitch, "Catholicism in Crisis: The Impact of the French Revolution on the Thought of the Abbé Lamourette," in *Cahiers internationaux d'histoire économique et sociale* 9 (1978): 354–385; William R. Everdell, *Christian Apologetics in France, 1730–1790: The Roots of Romantic Religion* (Lewiston, KY, 1987), 213–224.
5. Menozzi, *"Philosophes" e "Chrétiens éclairés,"* 96n4.
6. A. Degert, *Histoire des séminaires français jusqu'à la Révolution*, 2 vols. (Paris, 1912), 1:331; 2:97–208; John McManners, *Church and Society in Eighteenth-Century France*, 2 vols. (Oxford, 1998) 1:199–202; L.W.B. Brockliss, *French Higher Education in the Seventeenth and Eighteenth Centuries* (Oxford, 1987), 231–232. For the training of seminary professors, see Raymond Darricau, *La Formation des professeurs de séminaire au début du XVIIIe siècle d'après un directoire de M. Jean Bonnet (1664–1735), Supérieur général de la congrégation de la mission* (Piacenza, 1966).
7. Inordinately large, the diocese of Toul was divided in 1778 into three—Toul, Nancy and Saint-Dié, and the Seminary was associated with the new University of Nancy. See Eugene Martin, *Histoire des diocèses de Toul, de Nancy & de Saint-Dié*, 3 vols. (Nancy, 1900–1903), 3:52; and Gérard Dessolle, *Étienne, François-Xavier des Michels de Champorcin (1721–1807): Prêtre provençal, évêque de Senez, évêque-comte de Toul, prince due Saint-Empire* (Association pour l'étude et la Sauvegarde, du patrimoine religieux de la Haute-Provence, 2001), 65–66.
8. The "eighteenth century may be as plausibly christened the century of *Unigenitus* as of *lumières.*" William Doyle, *Jansenism* (Basingstoke, 2000), 87.
9. Dale Van Kley, *The Religious Origins of the French Revolution* (New Haven, CT, 1996), 294.
10. Dale Van Kley, "The Abbé Grégoire and the Quest for a Catholic Republic," in *The Abbé Grégoire and His World*, ed. Jeremy Popkin and Richard Popkin (Dordrecht, 2000), 79; McManners, *Church and Society in Eighteenth-Century France*, 2:644–744. For the clergy's opposition, see Nigel Aston, *The End of an Élite: The French Bishops and the Coming of the Revolution, 1786–1790* (Oxford, 1992), 90–98, 109.
11. On Grégoire see Alyssa Sepinwall, *The Abbé Grégoire and the French Revolution: The Making of Modern Universalism* (Berkeley, CA, 2005); Popkin and Popkin, *The Abbé Grégoire and His World* (Dordrecht, 2000); Rita Hermon-Belot, *L'Abbé Grégoire, la politique et la vérité* (Paris, 2000); Bernard Plongeron, *L'Abbé Grégoire (1750–1831) ou L'Arche de la Fraternité* (Paris, 1989). On Fauchet see J. Charrier, *Claude Fauchet, Évêque constitutionnel du Calvados, Député à l'Assemblée Législative et à la Convention (1744–1793)*, 2 vols. (Paris, 1909); Norman Ravitch, "The Abbé Fauchet: Romantic Religion during the French Revolution," *Journal of the American Academy of Religion* 42 (1974): 247–262; Monglond, *Le préromantisme français*, 2:106–113; and Hans Maier, *Revolution and Church: The Early History of Christian Democracy, 1798–1901* (South Bend, IN, 1969), 105–131.

12. Liebaut, *Prêtre et Évêque Assermenté*, 43.
13. *Pensées sur la Philosophie de l'Incrédulité, ou Reflexions sur l'esprit et le dessein des philosophes irréligieux de ce siècle* (Paris, 1786), 283, 14–15, 21–22. On Catholic skepticism see Richard Popkin, *The History of Scepticism: From Erasmus to Descartes* (New York, 1964). On Grégoire's frequent reference to Pascal see Rita Hermon-Belot, *L'Abbé Grégoire, la politique et la vérité* (Paris, 2000), 29.
14. *Pensées sur la Philosophie de la foi, ou Le Systeme du Christianisme. Entrevu dans son Analogie avec les Idées naturelles de l'entendement humain* (Paris, 1789), 100. Cf. 93–95, 98–99, 339, 103, 112–115.
15. *Pensées sur la Philosophie de l'Incrédulité*, 16.
16. *Pensées sur la Philosophie de l'Incrédulité*, 201, 208. Cf. 206–207.
17. *Pensées sur la Philosophie de la foi*, xviii–xix. Cf. *Pensées sur la Philosophie de l'Incrédulité*, 253, 263; and *Les Délices*, ix.
18. *Pensées sur la Philosophie de la foi*, xviii, xx–xxi.
19. *Pensées sur la Philosophie de l'Incrédulité*, 13: "the singular idea that … the discredit of religion is a necessary consequence of the progress of enlightenment [*lumières*] and the perfection of philosophical knowledge." Cf. 263: "the interests of religion have been estranged from the design of academic institutions; … an academic and a theologian [are regarded as] the two extremities of philosophy and madness [*dérasion*]."
20. *Pensées sur la Philosophie de l'Incrédulité*, 250, 267–268.
21. *Pensées sur la Philosophie de l'Incrédulité*, 26–27, 78, 137.
22. *Les Délices de la Religion, ou le pouvoir de l'Évangile pour nous rendre heureux* (Paris, 1788), iii–iv, 8, liv, 124. Cf. v, vii–viii, liv, 27, 78–80, 247, 350.
23. Ibid., 272.
24. *Pensées sur la Philosophie de la foi*, 2–3, 10–11. For his earlier view see, *Les Délices de la Religion*, 105.
25. *Pensées sur la Philosophie de la foi*, 272, 288, 291, 293.
26. *Pensées sur la Philosophie de l'Incrédulité*, 5–6, 30–31, 42. For the *philosophes* as a "sect" or "cabal" see 22–23, 42, 51, 55, 90, 105, 115, 124, 238, 244. For morality see 99, 112–116, 151, 90–95.
27. *Pensées sur la Philosophie de l'Incrédulité*, 243 (Italics in original). Cf. 48–49, 60–63, 75, 78–79.
28. *Pensées sur la Philosophie de l'Incrédulité*, 184. Idealization of the poor and the rural parish were common Jansenist tropes. See Monique Cottret, *Jansénismes et Lumières: pour un autre XVIIIe siècle* (Paris, 1998), 244–250.
29. *Les Délices de la Religion*, 191–192. On Lamourette's idealization of the early Church see Menozzi, *"Philosophes" e "Chrétiens éclairs,"* 95–104.
30. In a letter to Grégoire (7 September 1789), then a delegate to the "National Assembly," Lamourette wrote that the work contained "the elements of a political philosophy." See Leon Berthe, "Grégoire, élève de l' Abbé Lamourette," in *Revue du Nord* 44 (1962): 43.
31. *Pensées sur la Philosophie de l'Incrédulité*, 70–71, 63, 70–72.
32. *Pensées sur la Philosophie de la foi*, 3, 17–18.
33. *Pensées sur la Philosophie de la foi*, 30–31.
34. *Pensées sur la Philosophie de la foi*, 29: "it can never be salutary when the subjects of a power, contrary to the evidence of the established order, regard the authority which governs them as their own work [*propre ouvrage*], and as the result of an arrangement that circumstances produced and which other circumstances might change or destroy."
35. *Les Délices de la Religion*, 178–181, 112, 100.

36. *Les Délices de la Religion*, 250, 261, 147–148.
37. *Pensées sur la Philosophie de la foi*, 121, 19, 29.
38. *Pensées sur la Philosophie de la foi*, 221, 23. Cf. 85, 186.
39. *Pensées sur la Philosophie de la foi*, 272.
40. *Pensées sur la Philosophie de la foi*, 223, 233–236.
41. *Les Délices de la Religion*, 183, 55–58, 346–347. Cf. xxxvii, 345, 159–160.
42. *Les Délices de la Religion*, 259. Here are the lineaments of a counterargument to the important Enlightenment view that trade and goods have a civilizing impact ("*doux commerce*"). Proposed in a variety of forms by such diverse thinkers as Montesquieu and Hume, this doctrine held that free trade had a decidedly positive effect on society: it fashioned a "commercial humanism" through a new sociability that cultivated either the arts and sensibility or manners and morals.
43. *Pensées sur la Philosophie de la foi*, 204–211.
44. Mona Ozouf, "La Révolution française et l'idée de fraternité," in *L'Homme Régénéré: Essais sur la révolution française* (Paris, 1989), 158–182, esp. 164; Rita Hermon-Belot, *L'Abbé Grégoire, la politique et la vérité* (Paris, 2000), 63–129; 183–226. Hermon-Belot identified as "clergé patriote" or "éclairé" Grégoire, Fauchet, Lamourette, Bertolio, Jumel, Mulot, Chaix, Le Conte, and Delehelle. Her definition is on p. 72. Daniele Menozzi labelled the precursors "chrétiens éclairés." See, *Les Interprétations politiques de Jésus de l'Ancien régime à la Révolution* (Paris, 1983), 92–114. Bernard Plongeron used the term "philosophe chrétien." See, *L'Abbé Grégoire (1750–1831) ou L'Arche de la Fraternité* (Paris, 1989), 40–41.
45. On Mirabeau and Lamourette see Menozzi, *"Philosophes" e "Chrétiens éclairés,"* 183–187. On the Helvétius salon see Antoine Guillois, *Le Salon de Madame Helvétius: Cabanis et les idéologues; ouvrage orné de deux portraits d'après des originaux inédits* (Paris, 1894), 76–77. On Mirabeau's atelier see Oliver J.G. Welch, *Mirabeau: A Study of a Democratic Monarchist* (London, 1951), 211. The other major Parisian salons were Geoffrin, Lespinasse, d'Holbach, Necker. See Dena Goodman, *The Republic of Letters: A Cultural History of the French Enlightenment* (Ithaca, NY, 1994), 75, 145, 227.
46. *Journal des Amix* (1 January 1793): 6, quoted in Charrier, *Claude Fauchet*, vi. See Gary Kates, *The Cercle Social, the Girondins, and the French Revolution* (Princeton, NJ, 1985).
47. *Observations sur l'état civil des juifs; adressées à l'assemblée nationale* (Paris, 1790), 19.
48. The others were François Mulot, Antoine Bertolio, Fauchet, and Grégoire. See Ozouf, "La Révolution française et l'idée de fraternité," 164; and Rita Hermon-Belot, *Les émancipation des juifs en France* (Paris, 1999), 55. *Pensées sur la Philosophie de la foi*, 233–236.
49. Albert Mathiez, *Rome et le Clergé français sous la Constituante: La Constitution civile du Clergé, L'Affaire d'Avignon* (Paris, 1911), 78–79. For the aspirations to a "national Church" see J. Tresal, "Le débat sur la constitution civile du clergé à la Constituante," in *Revue du clergé français* 36 (1903): 472–488; and Maurice Vaussard, "Éclaircissements sur la constitution civile du clergé," in *Annales historiques de la Révolution française* 42, no. 200 (1970): 287–293.
50. *Le Décret de l'Assemblée nationale sur les biens du clergé, Considéré dans son rapport avec la nature et les lois de l'institution ecclésiastique* (Paris, 1790), 2.
51. Ibid., 19–20; 11, 13–14, 19; 2–4; 68. For divine right monarchy see *Pensées sur la Philosophie de la foi*, 19, 29. For the patriotic priests' rejection of divine right monarchy see Hermon-Belot, *L'Abbé Grégoire, la politique et la vérité*, 200–201.
52. *Le Décret de l'Assemblée nationale sur les biens du clergé*, 15-17. Cf. *Pensées sur la Philosophie de la foi*, 223–226. For these ideas among the "patriotic clergy" see Hermon-

Belot, *L'Abbé Grégoire, la politique et la vérité*, 74–75. For the Constitutional Church see Aston, *Religion and Revolution in France, 1780–1804*, 203.
53. *Le Décret de l'Assemblée nationale sur les biens du clergé*, 59–60. Cf. *Pensées sur la Philosophie de l'Incrédulité*, 13, 253, 263.
54. *Prônes Civiques, ou le Pasteur patriote par M. l'Abbé Lamourette, Docteur en Théologie, et membre de l'Académie royale des Belles-Lettres d'Arras* (Paris, 1791), i–ii. For reviews see Kates, *The Cercle Social, the Girondins and the French Revolution*, 87n23; and Menozzi, "Philosophes" e "Chrétiens éclairs," 261f. Fauchet made a similar argument in his *Sermons sur l'accord de la Religion et de la liberté*. See Plongeron, *L'Abbé Grégoire (1750–1831) ou L'Arche de la Fraternité*, 55; and Menozzi, *Les Interprétations politiques de Jésus de l'Ancien régime à la Révolution*, 136–140. Rita Hermon-Belot treats the *Prônes Civiques* as "patriotic sermons" alongside those of Fauchet and Bertolio. See *L'Abbé Grégoire, la politique et la vérité*, 63–68.
55. *Prônes Civiques* no. 3, 27.
56. Ibid., no. 3, 33–36.
57. "Séance du 14 Janvier," in M. Mérilhou, ed., *Oeuvres de Mirabeau*, 9:14–46, here 9:37. English translation in *Speeches of M. de Mirabeau the Elder, pronounced in the National Assembly of France*, trans. James White, 2 vols. (London, 1792): 2:265–331. I cite White's translation. On this speech see Menozzi, "Philosophes" e "Chrétiens éclairs," 289–301.
58. This was the only time Lamourette used the term. For the term being used since mid century see Menozzi, *Les Interprétations politiques de Jésus de l'Ancien régime à la Révolution*, 92f.
59. *Oeuvres de Mirabeau*, 9:43. Cf. *Prônes Civiques*, no. 2, 34–35.
60. Menozzi, "Philosophes" e "Chrétiens éclairés," 294–300. For the missing middle ground see Bonnel, "Ecclesiological Insight at the 1790 National Assembly," 54–55.
61. Members of the *Cercle Social* sponsored Lamourette. See Kates, *The Cercle Social*, 135; for local journals and correspondence see Menozzi, "Philosophes" e "Chrétiens éclairés," 304–308; for the election see Maurice Wahl, *Les premières années de la Révolution à Lyon, 1788–92* (Paris, 1894) 304–305; and A. Kleinclausz, *Histoire de Lyon*, 3 vols. (1939–1952) 2:265–266, 277.
62. For Marbeuf's position see *Déclaration de M. l'archevêque de Lyon, primat des Gaules, en réponse à la proclamation du département de Rhône-et-Loire concernant l'exécution des décrets sur la constitution civile du clergé* (Paris, 1790). Cf. Wahl, *Les premières années de la Révolution à Lyon*, 291f.; and Kleinclausz, *Histoire de Lyon*, 2:274–279.
63. *Lettre pastorale de M. l'évêque du département de Rhône et Loire. Métropolitain du Sud-Est, A tous les fidèles de son diocèse* (Lyon, 1791), 15–16. Cf. *Instruction pastorale de M. l'évêque du département de Rhône et Loire. Métropolitain du Sud-est, A MM. les curés, vicaires et fonctionnaires ecclésiastiques de son diocèse* (Lyon, 1791).
64. *Avertissement pastoral de M. l'évêque du département de Rhône et Loire, Métropolitain du Sud-Est, aux ecclésiastiques qui exercent dans son diocèse, le ministère de la Confession* (Lyon, 1791), 2–3, 9, 12.
65. *Instruction pastorale de M. l'évêque du département de Rhône et Loire, Métropolitain du Sud-Est, au clergé et aux fidèles de son diocèse* (Lyon, 1791), 42. Menozzi, "Philosophes" e "Chrétiens éclairés," 331–346, sees this publication as Lamourette's answer to the Pope.
66. *Instruction pastorale*, 10.
67. Georges Guigue, ed., *Procès-verbaux des séances du Conseil Général du département de Rhône-et-Loire, 1790–93* (Lyon, 1895), 412; his acceptance speech is at 427. Cf. Wahl, *Les premières années de la Révolution à Lyon*, 425; and Kleinclausz, *Histoire de Lyon*, 2:283.

68. C.J. Mitchell, *The French Legislative Assembly of 1791* (Leiden, 1988).
69. Nigel Aston, *The End of an Élite*, 3.
70. John McManners, *The French Revolution and the Church, 1789–95* (New York, 1969), 63–79. For the mediocrity of Lyon's deputies see Wahl, *Les premières années de la Révolution à Lyon*, 424n1.
71. The deputy was François de Neufchâteau (1750–1828), a poet whom Lamourette either knew personally or by reputation, since he had contributed to the turmoil at the Toul Seminary (1771). See Pierre Marot, *Recherches sur la vie de François de Neufchâteau à propos de son lettres à son ami Poullain-Grandprey* (Nancy, 1966), 52–54; and Mitchell, *The French Legislative Assembly of 1791*, 51.
72. *Observations contre l'Article XV du Projet de décret du comité de législation sur les troubles religieux; Prononcées le 21 novembre 1791, par M. Lamourette, évêque du département de Rhône et Loire*, 3, 7. Menozzi emphasizes Neufchâteau's desire for secularization; see, "Philosophes" e "Chrétiens éclairs," 347–364. Mitchell emphasizes the tactical maneuvers; see, *The French Legislative Assembly of 1791*, 53.
73. *Observations contre l'Article XV du Projet de décret du comité de législation sur les troubles religieux*, 4–5.
74. *Projet de Réunion entre les membres de L'Assemblée nationale, par M. Lamourette, Député du Département de Rhône-et-Loire*. For earlier views of this motion see Sydenham, *The Girondins*, 112; Mitchell, *The French Legislative Assembly of 1791*, 57–60, 247; Everdell, *Christian Apologetics in France*, 237–8.
75. On Darnton's notion of de-sacralisation see Gordon, "The Great Enlightenment Massacre," 145–154.
76. François Furet, *L'héritage de la Révolution française* (Paris, 1989), 13–31.

Bibliography

Aston, Nigel. *The End of an Élite: The French Bishops and the Coming of the Revolution, 1786–1790*. Oxford, 1992.

———. *Religion and Revolution in France, 1780–1804*. Washington, DC, 2000.

Berthe, Leon. "Grégoire, élève de l' Abbé Lamourette." In *Revue du Nord* 44 (1962).

Brockliss, L.W.B. *French Higher Education in the Seventeenth and Eighteenth Centuries*. Oxford, 1987.

Charrier, J. *Claude Fauchet, Évêque constitutionnel du Calvados, Député à l'Assemblée Législative et à la Convention (1744–1793)*. 2 vols. Paris, 1909.

Collombet, F.Z. "L'Abbé Lamourette," *Revue du Lyonnais* 2 (1835): 195–212.

Cottret, Monique. *Jansénismes et Lumières: pour un autre XVIIIe siècle*. Paris, 1998.

Darnton, Robert. *The Kiss of Lamourette*. New York, 1990.

Darricau, Raymond. *La Formation des professeurs de séminaire au début du XVIIIe siècle d'après un directoire de M. Jean Bonnet (1664–1735), Supérieur général de la congrégation de la mission*. Piacenza, 1966.

Déclaration de M. l'archevêque de Lyon, primat des Gaules, en réponse à la proclamation du département de Rhône-et-Loire concernant l'exécution des décrets sur la constitution civile du clergé. Paris, 1790.

Degert, A. *Histoire des séminaires français jusqu'à la Révolution*. 2 vols. Paris, 1912.

Dessolle, Gérard. *Étienne, François-Xavier des Michels de Champorcin (1721–1807): Prêtre*

provençal, évêque de Senez, évêque-comte de Toul, prince due Saint-Empire. Association pour l'étude et la Sauvegarde, du patrimoine religieux de la Haute-Provence, 2001.
Doyle, William. *Jansenism*. Basingstoke, 2000.
Everdell, William R. *Christian Apologetics in France, 1730–1790: The Roots of Romantic Religion*. Lewiston, KY, 1987.
Furet, François. *L'héritage de la Révolution française*. Paris, 1989.
Goodman, Dena. *The Republic of Letters: A Cultural History of the French Enlightenment*. Ithaca, NY, 1994.
Guigue, Georges, ed. *Procès-verbaux des séances du Conseil Général du département de Rhône-et-Loire, 1790–93*. Lyon, 1895.
Guillois, Antoine. *Le Salon de Madame Helvétius: Cabanis et les idéologues; ouvrage orné de deux portraits d'après des originaux inédits*. Paris, 1894.
Hermon-Belot, Rita. *L'Abbé Grégoire, la politique et la vérité*. Paris, 2000.
———. *Les émancipation des juifs en France*. Paris, 1999.
Instruction pastorale de M. l'évêque du département de Rhône et Loire. Métropolitain du Sud-est, A MM. les curés, vicaires et fonctionnaires ecclésiastiques de son diocèse. Lyon, 1791.
Kates, Gary. *The Cercle Social, the Girondins, and the French Revolution*. Princeton, NJ, 1985.
Kleinclausz, A. *Histoire de Lyon*. 3 vols. 1939–1952.
Lamourette, A.-A. *Avertissement pastoral de M. l'évêque du département de Rhône et Loire, Métropolitain du Sud-Est, aux ecclésiastiques qui exercent dans son diocèse, le ministère de la Confession*. Lyon, 1791.
———. *Docteur en Théologie, et membre de l'Académie royale des Belles-Lettres d'Arras*. Paris, 1791.
———. *Observations contre l'Article XV du Projet de décret du comité de législation sur les troubles religieux; Prononcées le 21 novembre 1791*.
———. *Observations sur l'état civil des juifs; adressées a l'assemblée nationale*. Paris, 1790.
———. *Pensées sur la Philosophie de la foi, ou Le Systeme du Christianisme. Entrevu dans son Analogie avec les Idées naturelles de l'entendement humain*. Paris, 1789.
———. *Prônes Civiques, ou le Pasteur patriote par M. l'Abbé Lamourette, Docteur en Théologie, et membre de l'Académie royale des Belles-Lettres d'Arras*. Paris, 1791.
Le Décret de l'Assemblée nationale sur les biens du clergé, Considéré dans son rapport avec la nature et les lois de l'institution ecclésiastique. Paris, 1790.
Lettre pastorale de M. l'évêque du département de Rhône et Loire. Métropolitain du Sud-Est, A tous les fidèles de son diocèse. Lyon, 1791.
Liebaut, Abbé. *Prêtre et Évêque Assermenté*. Nancy, 1894.
Maier, H. *Revolution and Church: The Early History of Christian Democracy, 1798–1901*. South Bend, IN, 1969.
Marot, Pierre. *Recherches sur la vie de François de Neufchâteau à propos de ses lettres à son ami Poullain-Grandprey*. Nancy, 1966.
Martin, Eugene. *Histoire des diocèses de Toul, de Nancy & de Saint-Dié*. 3 vols. Nancy, 1900–1903.
Mason, Haydn T., ed. *The Darnton Debate: Books and Revolution in the Eighteenth Century*. Oxford, 1998.
Mathiez, Albert. *Rome et le Clergé français sous la Constituante: La Constitution civile du Clergé, L'Affaire d'Avignon*. Paris, 1911.
McManners, John. *Church and Society in Eighteenth-Century France*. 2 vols. Oxford, 1998.
———. *The French Revolution and the Church, 1789–95*. New York, 1969.
Menozzi, Daniele. "Philosophes" e "Chrétiens éclairés": *Politica e religione nella collaborazione di G.H. Mirabeau e A.A. Lamourette (1774–1794)*. Brescia, 1976.

Mitchell, C.J. *The French Legislative Assembly of 1791*. Leiden, 1988.
Monglond, André. *Le préromantisme française*. 2 vols. Paris, 1966.
Ozouf, Mona. "La Révolution française et l'idée de fraternité." In *L'Homme Régénéré: Essais sur la révolution française*. Paris, 1989.
Plongeron, Bernard. *L'Abbé Grégoire (1750–1831) ou L'Arche de la Fraternité*. Paris, 1989.
Ravitch, Norman. "The Abbé Fauchet: Romantic Religion during the French Revolution." In *Journal of the American Academy of Religion* 42 (1974): 247–262.
———. "Catholicism in Crisis: The Impact of the French Revolution on the Thought of the Abbé Lamourette." In *Cahiers internationaux d'histoire économique et sociale* 9 (1978).
Sepinwall, Alyssa. *The Abbé Grégoire and the French Revolution: The Making of Modern Universalism*. Berkeley, CA, 2005.
Speeches of M. de Mirabeau the Elder, pronounced in the National Assembly of France. 2 vols. Trans. James White. London, 1792.
Tresal, J. "Le débat sur la constitution civile du clergé à la Constituante." In *Revue du clergé français* 36 (1903).
Van Kley, Dale. "The Abbé Grégoire and the Quest for a Catholic Republic." In *The Abbé Grégoire and His World*, edited by Jeremy Popkin and Richard Popkin. Dordrecht: Kluwer, 2000.
———. *The Religious Origins of the French Revolution*. New Haven, CT, 1996.
Vaussard, Maurice. "Éclaircissements sur la constitution civile du clergé." In *Annales historiques de la Révolution française* 42, no. 200 (1970): 287–293.
Wahl, Maurice. *Les premières années de la Révolution à Lyon, 1788–92*. Paris, 1894.

Selves without Qualities?
Duchamp, Musil, and the History of Selfhood

Jerrold Seigel

Recent writers about the self, whether philosophers, historians, or critics, have often sought escape from a conception of personal identity said to be characteristic of the modern West. The notion they target posits the self as coherent, stable, autonomous, and turned inward in a way Charles Taylor calls "punctual" or "disengaged." In its place, post-modernists, Nietzscheans, Heideggerians, communitarians and others all propose an image of the self that is shifting and fluid, divided or fragmented, and bound up in the power of its exterior attachments and connections. I want to consider the relationship between these two figures of the self, asking to what degree we should regard them as distinct alternatives, historically and theoretically. I approach this question first by comparing two well-known advocates of a fluid and unsettled manner of individual existence, and second by looking at a recent historical account of modern selfhood's emergence, one that argues for the prevalence of the second mode of selfhood before the end of the eighteenth century.

The two figures are Robert Musil and Marcel Duchamp. They were near contemporaries (born respectively in 1880 and 1887) and had a number of things in common, one of which offers an illuminating starting point for comparison: each was the author of a remarkable unfinished work. Musil's was his signature novel, *The Man Without Qualities*, on which he labored throughout the 1920s and 1930s; Duchamp's was the Large Glass, entitled *The Bride Stripped Bare by her Bachelors, Even*, conceived in 1912 and declared "definitively unfinished" in 1923. Each work was part of a sustained attempt by its author to arrive at a satisfying understanding of, and relationship to, the self in general, and his own in particular.

Musil's way of pursuing this goal is—or seems to be—encapsulated in his book's title, which refers to its partly autobiographical hero, Ulrich, a person unwilling to settle on any single professional identity, and who devotes himself instead to a life of constant experimentation with his own personal being and his relations to the world. Musil considered the reasons for Ulrich's dedication to such a life, and its implications, in his other writings and notebooks, as well as in essays interspersed throughout his novel. Duchamp's way of theorizing such a condition was less sustained and explicit, but he did write about it, and he clearly aimed to embody it, substituting a fluid persona constructed out of masquerade, mystery, and caprice for the traditional role of the artist as a maker of aesthetic objects. To preserve himself from the marks of a stable identity was one reason Duchamp gave for offering his famous readymades, ordinary everyday objects such as a bicycle wheel, a bottle drying rack, and most famously a porcelain urinal, in the place of traditional objects of art. The virtue of such a series, he once explained, was that the objects comprising it had no common visual or stylistic features; hence he could "produce" them without tying himself to any single style or taste; and taste, he proclaimed, was merely a habit, "the repetition of something already accepted." Artists who operated with a consistent style exhibited the ties that bound them to a distinct and persisting personality in each new work, but the artist of readymades was free to find himself anew in each unconnected object and at any moment.[1] Such a strategy for eluding consistent self-definition shared ground with Musil, who compared the effects of having a stable social identity to flies stuck in flypaper, condemned to a struggle that only sapped their vital energy. In contrast, the man without qualities escaped subjection to such debilitating attachments, retaining the potential to expand and renew his life.[2]

These are not the only similarities to be recognized between the French artist and the Austrian writer; we shall come upon even closer ones below. Despite all of them, however, I think it can be shown that Duchamp and Musil were in search of very different kinds of selves, and that the contrast between them has much to teach us about what it may mean to acknowledge the fluidity and external dependency of the self. This in turn helps us to consider the relative place of different images of the self at certain historical moments. Because the account of Duchamp I give here is based on one I provided a few years ago in a book about him, it will be presented rather summarily.[3] The reading of Musil, not offered before, will be more extensive.

Duchamp's desire to be without qualities was part of his hunger to be free from the limits imposed by ordinary physical and temporal existence.

He cited those limits as one reason for abandoning painting, contrasting the pure idea of a picture in his mind with the debased form that material expression imposed on it: the image in the head "always loses something when it is turned into paint. I prefer to see my pictures without that muddying."[4] The same liberation from the obligation to produce objects gave him a still more intense release from everyday limitations by allowing him to live each moment as it came. As he explained to Pierre Cabane: "I like living, breathing, better than working ... Each second, each breath is a work which is inscribed nowhere, which is neither visual nor cerebral. It's a kind of constant euphoria."[5] Duchamp sought to cut the ties between some inner essential being and the world in other ways, among them a series of linguistic "works" and experiments to which we cannot give attention here.[6] Some of his reasons for disrupting such relations appears from one of the notes he published in connection with the Large Glass. It was about shop windows, which he enigmatically described as providing "proof of the existence of the outside world." Here is the passage:

> When one undergoes the interrogation of shop windows, one also pronounces one's own sentence. In fact, one's choice is "round trip." From the demand of shop windows, from the inevitable response to shop windows, the fixation of choice is determined (*se conclut l'arrêt du choix*). No obstinacy, ad absurdum, of hiding the coition through a glass pane with one or many objects of the shop window. The penalty consists in cutting the pane and in gnawing at your thumbs (*s'en mordre les pouces*) as soon as possession is consummated. Q.E.D.[7]

As in many places, Duchamp's words are cryptic and difficult to decipher, but clearly the world whose existence was demonstrated was anything but nurturing. The sentence pronounced on oneself in the first sentence is the "round trip" of the second: drawn outward into the world of desired objects by seeing them displayed, we will be sent back into ourselves once our desire seeks fulfillment by fixing itself on certain ones. Until that moment, Duchamp seems to say, desiring carries us outward toward a still-imagined state, promising an altered and expanded form of existence. But to possess the chosen object puts an end to the desire and what it promises, leaving us in a state of disappointment and regret. The world's externality was a barrier to the fulfillment it promised to the self.

These ideas were often the subject of Duchamp's art, for instance in an early picture called *Paradise* (Figure 1). It shows a sitting woman and a standing man in a grassy, wooded setting. The male figure's gesture of hiding his sex tells us what moment we have happened upon, the one that follows on the couple's loss of innocence. Their unmeeting eyes and blank, anxious faces suggest the same kind of disillusionment described in the

Figure 1. Marcel Duchamp, "Paradise (Adam and Eve)," 1910–11. The Philadelphia Museum of Art/Art Resource, NY © 2007 Artists Rights Society (ARS), New York/ADAGP, Paris/Succession Marcel Duchamp.

note on shop windows. Physically, the couple may be in the Eden of the title, but psychologically they have banished themselves from it by seeking to realize the satisfaction it seemed to promise.

The themes sounded in this note and picture are central to Duchamp's most famous pictorial construction, the Large Glass (Figure 2).[8] Put simply and directly, what the picture calls up is a moment in which the story of possession and disillusionment told in *Paradise* and the note on shop windows does not and cannot take place. *The Bride Stripped Bare by Her Bachelors, Even* came with a subtitle, "delay in glass." A delay is a space of time in which some expected occurrence does not arrive—in this case the stripping called up in the title. The bride is never physically unclothed by her bachelors, whoever they are; indeed, they can never enter into the space she occupies, much less touch her, because they (symbolized by the odd assemblage of mostly mechanical apparatus that occupies the lower

Figure 2. Marcel Duchamp, "The Bride Stripped Bare by Her Bachelors, Even," 1915–23. The Philadelphia Museum of Art/Art Resource, NY © 2007 Artists Rights Society (ARS), New York/ADAGP, Paris/Succession Marcel Duchamp.

half of the picture) exist in the ordinary three-dimensional universe we all inhabit. She, on the contrary, floats inside a mysterious four-dimensional world, to which they can have no entry. Duchamp's notes speak about the way that mere three-dimensional objects would lose their substantiality in a four-dimensional world, just as a genuinely two-dimensional line would be without thickness in three-dimensional space such as ours. The three-dimensional "bachelors" can have no purchase on a four-dimensional being, which we are able to see only as a mysterious presence when we try to represent it.

To what then does the stripping of the title refer? The action of the picture takes place not in the physical universe of ordinary time and space, but in the imagination of the scene's *personae*. The bride imagines the bachelors fantasizing about her nudity, but it is frozen in its still virginal state by the delay that the picture makes permanent. Duchamp describes her condition as "an apotheosis of virginity." To be sure, this exaltation was not religious. What gives glory to virginity is that in it sexuality is known only by way of imagination and anticipation. The drama of the Large Glass is a play of perpetuated desire; it transpires in a moment outside time, where erotic longing has been, as Walter Benjamin said in reference to Baudelaire, "spared rather than denied fulfillment."[9] The bride of the Large Glass inhabits a timeless world of pure imagination, a kind of utopia of pure possibility.

The same themes often resound in Duchamp's readymades. Indeed, I believe that the first objects later subsumed under this title, as well as some of the later ones, appealed to him because they could stand as secret symbolizations of these notions, making them a kind of private language. We can see these connections by looking briefly at two of these works. The first he called *Air de Paris* (Figure 3), a glass ampoule containing 50 cc of Paris air. Like others in the category, it was not

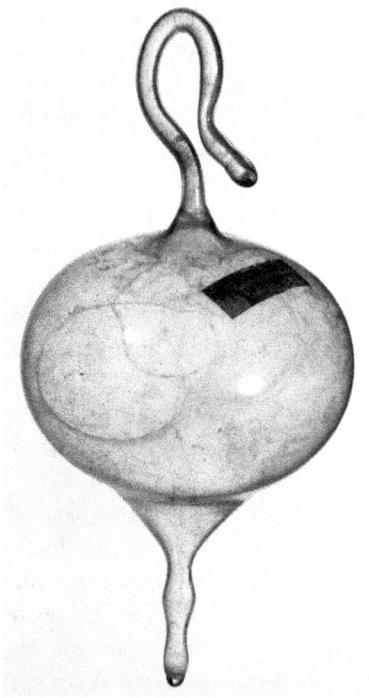

Figure 3. Marcel Duchamp, "Sculpture (50 cc of Paris Air)," 1919. The Philadelphia Museum of Art/Art Resource, NY © 2007 Artists Rights Society (ARS), New York/ADAGP, Paris/Succession Marcel Duchamp.

wholly a found object, since Duchamp produced it by having a pharmacist in Paris seal up its opening. Transported to New York, the Paris air could then work its attraction on anyone in its presence, but only so long as the beholder agreed to renounce the actual experience it seemed to promise; to open or break the glass so as to gain access to the desirable substance it contained was to lose it. The air occupies exactly the position of the objects displayed in the shop window before we try to take possession of them, making the readymade a kind of miniature emblem for, or visual pun on, the Large Glass. Duchamp passionately loved puns, in part no doubt because one of their qualities is the ability to disrupt what seems to be a stable connection between words and referents (just the result he sought in his linguistic works and experiments). Others of the readymades also served as punning references to the bride and her bachelors. Among these was one of the earliest ones, the bottle rack (Figure 4). To describe the prongs as phallic may elicit some skepticism in a world over-saturated with Freudian readings, but according to Arturo Schwarz, a biographer and friend of Duchamp, the latter accepted it, and not surprisingly given both his love of sexual symbolism and his just-mentioned fascination with puns.[10] But it is not the phallic quality of the prongs alone that gives the rack its close thematic relationship to the Large Glass. What sets up the echo is the nonappearance of the bottles for whose sake the prongs exist (easy enough to provide some); here as before the expected action is consigned to a space of permanent delay, so that it can only take place in a sphere of pure imagination. In the world of material existence, which the rack (like the bachelor figures of the Glass) cannot escape, male and female are denied, or spared, physical contact, casting their relations into a realm of imagination and pure possibility.

This is the undeterminable space Duchamp sought to inhabit, by representing himself as an artist whose character inhered in having abandoned making objects, including the "definitively unfinished" Glass. The identity he sought was one that constantly destabilized itself, forever disengaged from any form of definite constitution. Even as a young painter, he exhibited a self-conscious fluidity in the rapid moves he made between modernist styles; in 1915, he told an interviewer in New York that his methods were always in flux and that his most recent work was "utterly unlike anything that preceded it … in the midst of each epoch I fully realize that a new epoch will dawn." Later in life, when this phase in his history was behind him, he told Pierre Cabanne that, "I force myself to contradict myself, so as to avoid conforming to my own taste."[11] By then he had also injected a different kind of fluidity into his self-conception by taking on a second persona as Rrose Sélavy (*eros, c'est la vie*, life is eros), signing works with her name and arranging to have himself photographed

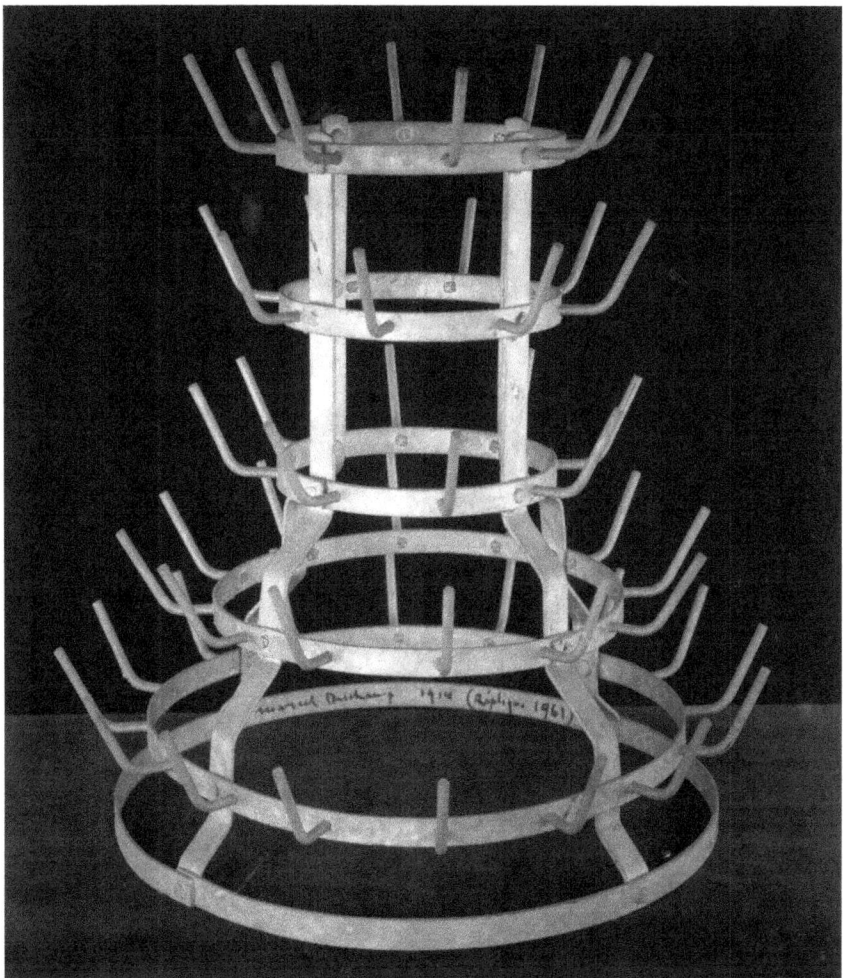

Figure 4. Marcel Duchamp, "Bottlerack," 1961 (replica of 1914 original). The Philadelphia Museum of Art/Art Resource, NY © 2007 Artists Rights Society (ARS), New York/ADAGP, Paris/Succession on Marcel Duchamp.

in the guise of his transgendered alter ego (Figure 5). Not only did the mix of masculine and feminine identities destabilize his public character, it also joined him to a figure who embodied the perpetuated desire to which he appealed in many of his works: as the passionate energy that corresponded to life itself, Rrose would never betray her lovers by granting them the possession that stilled erotic longing. By presenting himself as Rrose, Duchamp made his own body into a kind of readymade, a found object (suitably altered, like some of the others) capable of serving as a

Figure 5. Marcel Duchamp, "Marcel Duchamp as Rrose Sélavy," ca. 1920–21. The Philadelphia Museum of Art/Art Resource, NY © 2007 Artists Rights Society (ARS), New York/ADAGP, Paris/Succession Marcel Duchamp.

metaphor for the relations figured in the Large Glass. And it was this infusion of his own self with ever-flowing desire that made it possible for him to think of the passing seconds of his existence, in terms we noted above, as moments in a life of "constant euphoria." Duchamp sought similar results in his dealings with scientific ideas, to which he sometimes made

Selves without Qualities? Duchamp, Musil, and the History of Selfhood • 33

reference in his work. Typical was his construction of "Three Standard Stoppages" (Figure 6), meter-long strings dropped from a height so as to fall into distorted shapes that allowed each one to represent "meters" of different lengths. The purpose was to infuse the aspiration to precision

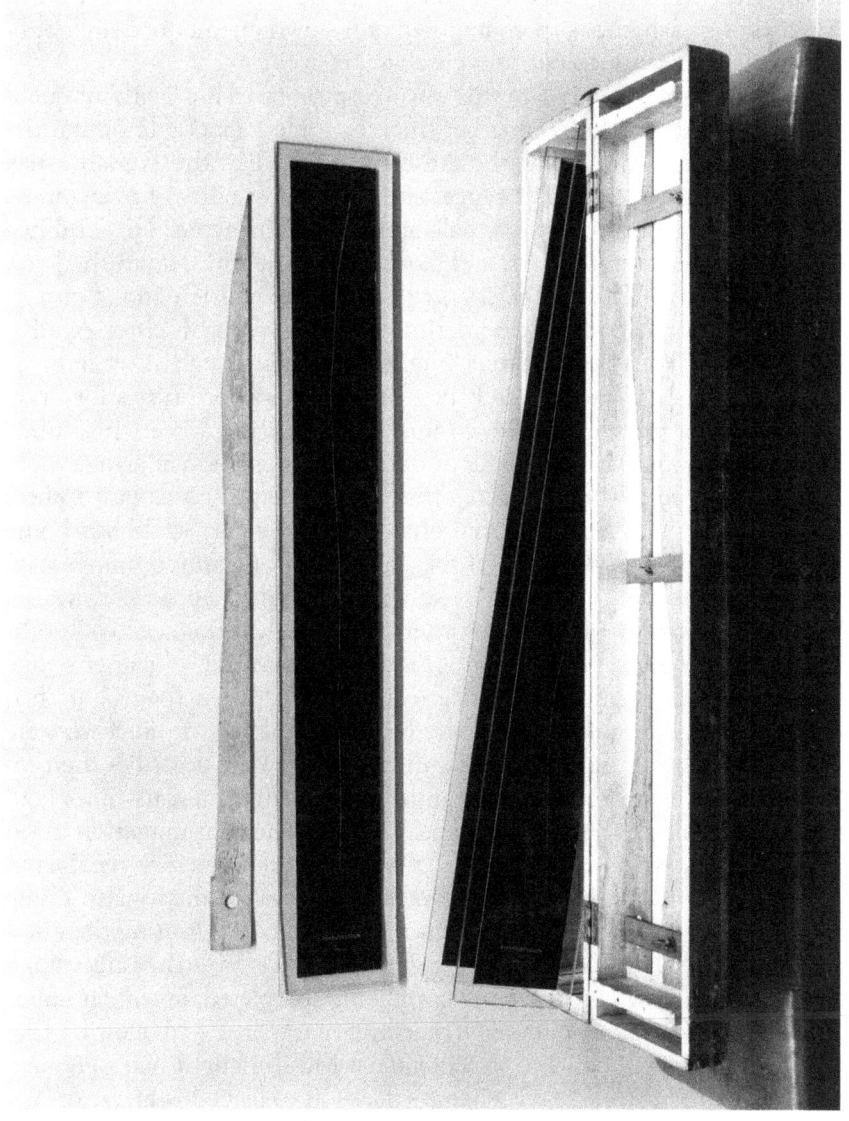

Figure 6. Marcel Duchamp, "3 Stoppages Étalon," 1913–14. Digital Image © The Museum of Modern Art/Licensed by SCALA/Art Resource, NY © 2007 Artists Rights Society (ARS), New York/ADAGP, Paris/Succession Marcel Duchamp.

with the vagaries of chance, and thus (as he said) "to strain the laws of physics just a little." That little was enough to deprive standards of what made them generally applicable, providing Duchamp with an illustration of the kind of science that Alfred Jarry (whom he invoked and admired) called "'pataphysics," a science whose laws consisted entirely of exceptions.[12] In such a universe, individual existence reigned supreme, but it was a kind on which, as Duchamp said of his own manner of being, ordinary consistency was to have no purchase.

If we now seek to compare this way of aspiring to a life "without qualities" to Musil's, we should first be struck by some remarkable similarities between them. One is that the Austrian writer, like the French artist, was fascinated by sexual difference, and by the possibility of overcoming it through effecting a union of male and female characters. He exhibited this interest in his notebooks, and most fully in the third, unfinished volume of *The Man Without Qualities*, where the hero Ulrich enters into an intense relationship, closely bordering on incest, with his sister Agathe. In his notes, Musil insisted that "the love of brother and sister must be strongly defended"; it provided "one of the few opportunities for unity that are given to" Ulrich. Grown up, Ulrich became a "very masculine man" and "conqueror and hunter of women," but as a boy, at an age when he still sometimes wore female clothes, he had felt a secret wish to be a girl, a sign perhaps that "the soul of a girl that he may well have borne inside him still, was yearning for the boy-soul in him and for minutes on end submerged the other one."[13] When Agathe first appears in Musil's novel, after many years when brother and sister had not seen each other, she is by "chance" clothed in a Pierrot costume that blurs her sexual identity, accentuating the physical similarities between them. Ulrich is struck by the resemblance, and she bursts out, "I had no idea we were twins." Musil plays on this likeness-in-difference as he describes their increasingly intimate relationship, and the moments when its incestuous potential seems on the verge of being realized. The consummation never takes place, however, and students of Musil's work have disagreed about whether, had the novel been finished, it would have come to pass. Philip Payne thinks it likely that Musil changed his mind, answering the question affirmatively at first and negatively later.[14] Perhaps the uncertainty was one thing that kept the book from being completed; leaving it unfinished was the only way to fend off a definitive response to a question that (for reasons we will come to in a moment) Musil thought had to remain open. If so, the parallel to Duchamp's decision to leave his image of "delay" unfinished (and to represent the fantasized union of male and female desire as a union of his own person with its feminine side in becoming Rrose Sélavy) seems eerily close.

The possibility even of a kind of occult interconnection between the two artists is one that might have stirred the interest of both, since each was drawn in some way to mystical ideas and experiences. Duchamp once described the artist as "like a mediumistic being who, from the labyrinth beyond time and space, seeks his way out to a clearing."[15] Musil's persisting interest in mystical states was part of his abiding fascination for what he called "the other condition" (*der andere Zustand*), a mode of relating to people and things foreign to everyday experience. Mysticism was an exemplary form of this other condition because its sense of direct union with powerful forces at the center of the universe draws people into a more intense conjunction with their own deep energies, and with those that may animate other people and objects. Other instances include erotic arousal and passionate love, sudden intuitive understanding of a complex problem, the "holy simplicity" of saintly deeds, and the spectrum of exceptional mental states that runs from enthusiasm to mild and serious forms of madness. In this condition, lasting (as Musil wrote in one essay) sometimes only for an instant and sometimes for days on end, our everyday way of being "melts in the glow of a different attitude toward the world and people. One becomes a straw and a breath, the world a trembling soap bubble. In every such moment all things arise anew; one recognizes that to regard them as fixed entities is inner death."[16] Such language recalls the world beyond physical limits to which Duchamp was also seeking access. But a closer look at Musil's interest in such states, and in their bearing on his thinking about the self, will bring the contrasts between them into relief.

The basic difference can be simply stated. Duchamp's interest in a kind of "other condition," the utopia of possibility figured in the Large Glass and echoed in some of his readymades, was fundamentally aesthetic; it had to do with what it meant to be an artist, with the kind of untrammeled life that artistic creativity promised, and to which it might provide an entry. Musil's interest in these things had an aesthetic dimension to be sure, but it was basically moral and ethical, pursued for the light it reflected on conduct and behavior more generally. Despite the expectations some of his writings arouse, that he was in search of a wholly fluid mode of existence infused with something like the "constant euphoria" to which Duchamp aspired, a number of things separated him from such a quest. Beyond his concern to develop a moral and ethical position relevant to everyday life and human relations generally, these included his commitment to scientific understanding and the limits imposed by its dedication to precision, and his devotion to an ideal of personal balance and equilibrium to which persisting elation or rapture was alien.

Both the potential radicalism and the actual moderation of Musil's stance appear in his views about moral systems and how people live inside them. He reported in a notebook entry that one of his "earliest ... attempts at thinking was to distinguish between a moralist and an ethicist." The distinction was between those ("moralists") for whom values are part of a fixed and systematized order of precepts or principles, to which they conform without adding anything to them, and those ("ethicists") who sustain or go through "new ethical experiences." The latter were "'other' people," and it was they who brought new moral perspectives into the world. Examples included Confucius, classical Stoics and Epicureans, Christ, Nietzsche, and the mystics; to them "belong, finally, all anonymous forces that transform morality."[17] These "anonymous forces" appear in another diary passage as a kind of life force, given form in particular social and cultural systems, but always in ways that fail to embody its full creative vitality, so that the self-conscious ethicist feels hemmed in and oppressed by them, and justified in rejecting the limits they impose.

> The social mores, the morals, etc. are totalities in which individual things appear to be determined. In world-historical terms, however, these are "Gestalt" forms shaped by the trial-and-error that is life, in just the same way that it has shaped the dinosaurs, etc., that succeed each other like failed experiments. When one looks at life in this way, one arrives at an absolute (religious) lack of respect.[18]

That the lack of respect was "religious," however, gives a hint that Musil did not think it possible to establish, in Nietzschean fashion, a wholly different kind of morality based on the perpetuation of life's deeper creative impulse. One reason why it was not possible was that the process by which new ethical attitudes become active in the world is through embodiment in generalized formations that rob them of their original vitality. This passage was simply part of the inevitable rhythm of cultural development, bound to repeat itself for every new inspiration, so that people could never finally liberate themselves from its effects. The "pulsating ideas" that carry us beyond everyday limits and make "all things arise anew" were subject to this fate because such notions were rooted in highly individualized feelings and experiences that everyday discourse cannot communicate. To transmit them from one person to another would "require identical mental conditions," whereas "in reality at most only analogous dispositions of the soul are present." What forever prevents generalized social experience from embodying the energies that flow inside "the other condition" are the ineradicable differences between the individuals whose life together constitutes society and culture. The weight of these variations mounts up as populations expand, which explained in part "why late periods are so fragmented, and why in such civilized eras cultures decay like mountains."[19]

Beyond these considerations, Musil stood apart from attempts to make some kind of "other condition" the basis for a different form of life by virtue of his well-known commitment to the spirit and the procedures of modern science, a loyalty rooted in his early training in engineering, mathematics, and physics. To be sure, he saw excessive intellectualism and the sheer weight of the technical means required by modern production and communication as responsible for some of the ills of contemporary life. But he also regarded science as one of the chief modes of human creativity, as powerful a force for liberating people from outdated ideas and rigidified attitudes and beliefs as the ethical innovations of "other" people. Those who set themselves against science failed to see that reason was a necessary part of every instance of human perception and thinking, including their own; thus, they opened themselves up to forms of irrationality that gave entry to chaos and madness. Modern culture was enriched by the many attempts made within it to recover something of what the other condition promised, beginning with romanticism, but even those who brought these gifts needed to employ reason in order to convey what they sought beyond it. Musil was especially harsh on those in his own time who sought to enclose art in a pure inner space where spontaneous feeling could gush forth, free of the limitations of ordinary life. "All these hypersensitive types leave the impression of debilitated drug addicts or old drunks, who have nothing to hang onto when they are sober."[20] In *The Man Without Qualities*, Ulrich often invokes the ideal of precision, and at one point (in regard to plans to celebrate the jubilee of the Habsburg emperor), he gives voice to a duality that captures much of Musil's personality, when he proposes to establish "a world secretariat for precision and soul."[21]

It is inside this frame that we can understand his exploration of the relationship between Ulrich and Agathe in *The Man Without Qualities*. The frank willingness of brother and sister to allow the possibility of incest to arise between them, even to let it drive their fascination for each other, calls up the "absolute (religious) lack of respect" for established moral conventions and limits that the "ethical" attitude carried with it. And yet, both Musil's failure to resolve the question, and his treatment of it in unpublished draft chapters, point to his conviction that one should not seek to make the other condition lasting. Paradoxically or not, the means that seem to promise its permanence end up dissolving our ability to encounter it, thus shutting out the possibilities it opens up for us.

Consider the conclusion of the scene when the love between the siblings comes closest to being physically consummated. "When their glances met, nothing was so certain as that the decision had been made and all prohibitions were now a matter of indifference to them." They had reached agreement finally to "redeem themselves from the ill humor of longing." In imagination they were already united, driven by waves of desire.

> But a still greater desire bade them be calm, and they were incapable of touching each other again. They wanted to begin, but the gestures of the flesh had become impossible for them, and they felt an ineffable warning that had nothing to do with the commandments of morality. It seemed that from a more perfect, if still shadowy union, of which they had already had a foretaste as in an ecstatic metaphor, a higher commandment had marked them out, a higher intimation, curiosity, or expectation had breathed upon them.

Many questions might be asked about what Musil means in this passage, but it seems clear that "the more perfect, if still shadowy union" for the sake of which they draw back from a sexual one requires the continuation of the relationship they already have. That relationship is full of uncertainty, involving as it does their rejection of the prohibition on incest in principle (they give no care to the rumors and suspicions swirling around them, that their bond is already incestuous, based on their living together and being always in each other's company), since accepting it would set a conventional limit to what they can be to each other; but they pull back from the act itself, since its occurrence would put a definite physical and moral stamp on their relations. Despite the superficial resemblance this account bears to the drama of perpetuated desire in the Large Glass, it is "calm" to which the "greater desire" calls the two siblings, not any dream of "constant euphoria." Nor do they draw back in order to avoid the disillusionment of Duchamp's shop windows or *Paradise*. Sexual craving is not provided with a space where it survives unfulfilled, but yields to a "higher commandment ... a higher intimation." It is hard to say at this point which of the two "conditions" Musil values more highly, but we cannot understand his views about them unless we recognize—as superficial readings do not—that it is only the normal one that offers a frame for the continuing presence of both. Only if the "other" world refrains from imposing itself on the one from whose limits it seems to offer release can it retain the promise that makes it valuable to us.[22]

Musil's explicit dealings with the self exhibit a concern to preserve the same duality. In some of his notebook entries, he appears to exalt the self that is "without qualities" over one imprinted with definite features, but he always draws back from seeking to replace the second with the first. He seems at one point to locate all of the self's vital possibilities in its ability to be the bearer of an "unformed energy" that dies when the personality takes on features from the world outside. À propos of the self we bear inside the world, he asks at one juncture: "What is the point of cultivating an 'I' on which we have almost no influence whatsoever?" But formlessness would be a kind of death too, so that the self's survival demands it balance fluidity with form: "On the path between the world as active agent and the world as passive object of activities (even if only through locomotion) lies the 'I'; switching apparatus with a dark glow from her (?) [sic]. If one of the two parts is in the ascendant, then the 'I' is sucked up and blotted out." The passage is incomplete, to be sure, but it clearly requires that the self be both passive and active, at once a denizen of the material world and an avatar of what never genuinely belongs to it; were it wholly one or the other, it would lose either its vitality or its objective existence. As he says in a nearby place, "There is something dynamic about it, one simply has to continue moving forward to keep one's balance."[23]

In *The Man Without Qualities*, the subject of the self comes up many times, both explicitly and implicitly. We cannot attend to all of these instances here, but three major ones, taken together, give a good sense of how Musil dealt with the issue in the published parts of the book. The first, and most-often quoted place provides a good point of entry:

> It is always wrong to explain what happens in a country by the character of its inhabitants. For the inhabitant of a country has at least nine characters: a professional, a national, a civic, a class, a geographic, a sexual, a conscious, an unconscious, and possibly even a private character to boot. He unites them in himself, but they dissolve him, so that he is really nothing more than a small basin hollowed out by these many streamlets that trickle into it and drain out of it again, to join other such rills in filling some other basin. This permits a person all but one thing: to take seriously what his at least nine other characters do and what happens to them; in other words, it prevents precisely what should be his true fulfillment. This interior space—admittedly hard to describe—is of a different shade and shape in Italy from what it is in England, because everything that stands out in relief against it is of a different shade and shape; and yet it is in both places the same: an empty, invisible space with reality standing inside it like a child's toy town deserted by the imagination.[24]

Inside this seemingly casual and informal account, Musil sets up a subtle dialectic that alternately affirms and undermines the ability first of the "inner," and then the "outer" elements of personal existence to determine the other. To begin with, people have no stable character because a series of unconnected and diverse social and physical elements of identity enter into each one's being, dissolving the self into a "hollow basin" that is merely the residue of their action on it. But in order for them to have this effect, the person who undergoes it must "unite them in himself," and the consequence of their dissolving him in turn is not to give them greater substance than he has but instead less, since all of them lose their power to serve as matters of concern and sources of fulfillment. The same dialectical dissolution of terms then recurs in the last sentence: the interior space takes on the "shade and shape" of the particular milieu an individual inhabits, but in every case the substance that makes up this milieu turns out to be "empty and invisible" because the extra-individual "reality" it represents is abandoned by the consciousness and agency, without which it becomes merely inert. Every human group has its own way of giving "no respect" to the reality that constitutes its existence, but all are alike in doing so. It is this constant shifting of the relations between extra-individual and "inner" agents of being that makes the self constantly dissolve and reform itself. There was one country in particular that represented this dialectical insubstantiality of world and self in the most exemplary way, namely his own Austria-Hungary. The "negative freedom" enjoyed there, by virtue of the slapdash arrangements that kept the empire's competing nationalities inside "a state just barely able to get along with itself," left each inhabitant with a "sense of insufficient grounds for one's own existence, and lapped around by the great fantasy of all that had not happened or at least not yet happened irrevocably as by the breath of those oceans from which mankind had once emerged."[25] Austria here appears as a place where glimmerings of the other condition are especially easy to obtain (although the term is not used, we recognize the language that describes it from other places), precisely because its character is so unstable, but what made this to be the case was a set of qualities that gave the place a very particular character indeed.

The same dialectic defined Ulrich's own being, as we learn most explicitly at a moment when he looks back on his inability to settle on a single occupation, and attributes his living "in a dim and undecided fashion" to the way "every possibility beckoned him, but something stronger kept him from yielding to the attraction." "Obviously," he told himself,

> what was keeping him spellbound in this aloof and nameless way of life was nothing other than the compulsion to that loosening and binding of the world that is known by a word we do not care to encounter by itself: spirit, or mind. Without knowing why, Ulrich suddenly felt sad, and thought: "I simply don't love myself." Within the frozen, petrified body of the city he felt his heart beating in its innermost depths. There was something in him that had never wanted to remain anywhere, had groped its way along the walls of the world, thinking: There are still millions of other walls; it was this slowly cooling, absurd drop "I" that refused to give up its fire, its tiny glowing core.

One thing that speaks clearly out of this passage is the inspiration Musil found for the idea of being "without qualities" in mystical literature. For the mystics, to be "âne Eigenschaften" (to employ the thirteenth-century spelling of Meister Eckhart, in whose writings Musil probably first encountered the term) was to be in a state of grace, free of self-love, and of the connections to the world that it powered. The "tiny glowing core" of spirit was for the mystics the spark of divine being that persisted in human souls even in the face of sin, inspiring them at once to withdraw from the world and to love it wholly and selflessly, as God was thought to do. Ulrich finds this perpetual "loosening and binding of the world" to the self in his manner of being, since what keeps him from a settled way of life is what he calls the attraction of the walls not yet encountered, the sense of being able to seek his never-realized selfhood in connection with the endless range of things that give the world solidity and limits. As in the passage about the nine characters, people naturally seek satisfaction in their connections to the world they inhabit, but the same power that pushes them to make such ties urges them ever away from them and toward new ones. (Musil had originally thought to call Ulrich "Anders," which perhaps best translates as "otherwise.") This power is the "I," for whom worldly connections and attachments are at once essential and without substance.[26]

The metaphor of "balance" briefly invoked in the notebooks appears more fully developed in the novel, in connection with the morality appropriate to Musil's kind of self-understanding. It makes its appearance in the chapter (62) devoted to "essayism," an intellectual and moral attitude that we are told is not Ulrich's final position, but in which one might argue that Musil persists all the same, since it is a way of thinking and living that never remains at a settled point, constantly shifting perspectives, and exploring each thing "from many sides without wholly encompassing it." Such a shifting point of view reveals the world as "an open-ended series of relationships" to which no fixed and stable meanings or judgments can be attached; within it, "man as the quintessence of his possibilities, potential man, the unwritten poem of his existence, confronts man as recorded fact, as reality, as character." Ulrich is drawn to this position through recognizing in himself a "drive of his own nature to keep developing [that] prevents him from believing that anything is final and complete," despite the claims things make to the contrary. The concomitant of this self-understanding is a view of life as "in the long run" revoking "everything it has done, to replace it with something else; what it used to regard as a crime it regards as a virtue, and vice versa; it builds up impressive frameworks of meaningful connections among events, only to allow them to collapse after a few generations." A conscious essayism, we learn, would "face the task of transforming the world's haphazard awareness [of its essential mobility] into a will," and such a will would establish for itself a "moral norm" that would no longer appear as "a set of rigid commandments but rather as a mobile equilibrium that at every moment requires constant efforts for renewal."[27]

In this chapter, as in other places, Musil sometimes seems to envisage a self alienated from its external connections and the stability they can impart (at the end, Ulrich describes himself as waiting and hiding "behind his person, insofar as this word characterizes that part of a human being formed by the world and the course of life"),[28] but interspersed with such images are others that project a different form of personal existence. One reason that Musil said traditional notions of a stable self no longer spoke to people in the present was that the complications of modern life, the sheer weight and power of the institutions and arrangements within which people live, overpower mere individual will, leading people to act in ways they neither choose nor wholly approve. But a certain deepening of self-understanding resulted from this situation:

> We are learning to recognize the interplay between inner and outer [just the interaction Musil often examined, as we have seen], and it is precisely our understanding of the impersonal elements in man that has given us new clues to the personal ones, to certain simple patterns of behavior, to an ego-building instinct that, like the nest-building instinct of birds, uses a few techniques to build an ego out of many various materials.[29]

Musil went on to suggest that this understanding of how the self was built up out of elements originally external to it promised ways to mitigate certain "pathological conditions," for instance, through altering the circumstances that turned some people into criminals (one criminal, the homicidal maniac Moosbrugger, draws a great deal of public attention in the novel, bringing an exemplary instance of the other condition into awareness for people whose domination by rigid moral systems otherwise kept them from acknowledging its remnants in themselves, and thus, as Musil put it in his Diary, setting "various reference bells ringing at once"). Comparing the way humans combine a variety of materials into an ego with birds who build nests out of bits and pieces of what they find around them certainly suggests a self whose "instinct" to provide itself with stability and shelter works and persists in the face of the need to be constantly remaking its own structures.

Musil's way of appealing to the image of a "man without qualities" stands out in clear relief when we compare it with Duchamp's quest for a kind of existence shot through with fluidity. Musil would never have described his manner of life as achieving or aspiring to a "constant euphoria," nor would Duchamp have pictured his in terms of a "mobile equilibrium" requiring "constant efforts for renewal." For the maker of the Large Glass, the themes of "delay" and perpetuated desire were aspects of an aesthetic aspiration to infuse life as much as possible with a mode of existence on which material limitations and objective determinations had no purchase. For the author of *The Man Without Qualities*, however, exploring the other condition was a way to restore to the self the often hidden or suppressed powers it needed in order to reorient itself intellectually and morally in a world from which traditional forms of stability were draining away. For Duchamp, the contrast between a fluid self and one whose existence required some degree of stability was between a superior and an inferior mode of existence; one settled for the latter as little as one could. For Musil, the two modes of self-existence were the poles of a dialectical field from which there was no satisfying escape, and within which one had to learn to live with as much awareness and vitality as human will and imagination could muster, accepting the risks this entailed. We are fluid creatures, to be sure; and persisting, formed and limited ones, too.

The distinction between a view of the self as enduring and coherent and one that pictures it as changing and diffuse has become a central point of reference for influential historical and theoretical accounts of modern self-existence. But the question of how we should understand the relations between these two contrasting images, whether one excludes the other, and whether the strong presence of one in a given time and place means some absolute or relative absence of the other, is often left unposed. This situation and its consequences can be illustrated, I think, by considering Dror Wahrman's recent book, *The Making of the Modern Self*. Wahrman proposes a narrative based on a contrast between two distinct "regimes of identity," one "old" and one "new," which divide history into an era "before the self" and one (which we still inhabit, and which we falsely universalize) that gave to personal identity the lineaments we commonly find in it. The breaking point comes at the end of the eighteenth century, at the time when the American Revolution forced the defeated British to reconsider their basic ways of living in the world.

Wahrman takes his understanding of modern selfhood from a justly famous formulation by Clifford Geertz, which delineates the notion of the self particular to the modern West as "a bounded, unique, more or less integrated motivational and cognitive universe, a dynamic center of awareness, emotion, judgment, and action, organized into a distinctive whole and set contrastively against other such wholes."[30] Such an understanding of the self was not part of Wahrman's "*ancien régime*," within which people commonly regarded identity and its elements as "mutable, malleable, unreliable, divisible, replaceable, transferable, manipulable, escapable, or otherwise fuzzy around the edges."[31] Wahrman supports and illustrates his claim with a richly detailed reading of eighteenth-century accounts about women, sex, and gender, the theater, and the widespread enthusiasm for masquerades that marked mid century London. In each case (and in some others we can leave aside here), forms of understanding and behavior that assumed the permeability of male and female gender markers and roles and what he calls "the protean mutability of identity" all flourished and declined in the same temporal rhythm. These accounts are often fascinating and sometimes convincing. Some significant sea change in the way people understood gender identity in particular, and perhaps other social identities as well, came about in the period he discusses. (As he acknowledges, this is not a wholly new observation, and it might be noted that there is evidence about it from sources outside Britain to which he does not refer.) It may even be that, in the English case, the impact of the American Revolution was significant in the way and on the scale he argues.

But what of his claims (the aspect of his book at issue here) about "regimes" of identity and selfhood, and in particular that mid century Britons experienced the self as mutable and malleable in a way that distinguished it clearly from the stable and coherent mode of personal existence that replaced it? One way to approach this question is to ask whether an ongoing social life is possible between people whose selves have such a broad absence of persisting form and definition. One philosopher constructed his negative answer to this question by starting from the observation that "the mutual dependence of men is so great, in all societies, that scarce any human action is entirely compleat in itself, or is performed without some reference to the actions of others, which are requisite to make it answer fully the intentions of the agent." Because of this mutual reliance of individuals on the actions and responses of their fellows, people "take their measures from past experience, in the same manner as their reasonings concerning external objects; and firmly believe that men, as well as all the elements, are to continue, in their operations, the same, that they have ever found them." If they did not regard themselves and others in this way, neither individual projects nor social relations could survive. The same writer continues a few lines later:

> Where would be the foundation of *morals*, if particular characters had no certain or determinate power to produce particular sentiments, and if these sentiments had no constant operation on actions? And with what pretence could we employ our *criticism* upon any poet or polite author, if we could not pronounce the conduct and sentiments of his actors, either natural or unnatural, to such circumstances?

One might perhaps argue against such a view (for myself I admit I find it quite persuasive), but what concerns us here is less its truth than the evidence it provides about mid-eighteenth-century British attitudes toward the self. For, as some readers will already know or have guessed, the author in question is David Hume, who developed these views in *An Enquiry Concerning Human Understanding*, published in 1756.[32] Hume died in 1776, but he clearly did not belong to Wahrman's "old regime" of the self.

This is not to say that Hume was unaware of a side of the self that was fluid and without stability. Indeed, the passage just quoted is less often brought forward in connection with Hume's view of the self than is one from his earlier work, *A Treatise On Human Nature*. In that book, Hume dismissed the views of certain philosophers who held that "we are every moment intimately conscious of what we call our SELF; that we feel its existence and its continuance in existence; and are certain, beyond the evidence of a demonstration, both of its perfect identity and simplicity." That we have such a certainty was evidently false, Hume maintained, because all of our ideas come from sense impressions, and "every real idea" comes from some "one impression."

> But self or person is not any one impression, but that to which our several impressions and ideas are suppos'd to have a reference. If any impression gives rise to the idea of self, that impression must continue invariably the same, thro' the whole course of our lives; since self is suppos'd to exist after that manner. But there is no impression constant and invariable. Pain and pleasure, grief and joy, passions and sensations succeed each other, and never all exist at the same time. It cannot, therefore, be from any of these impressions, or from any other, that the idea of self is deriv'd; and consequently there is no such idea.

Hume went on to conclude that humans in general "are nothing but a bundle or collection of different perceptions, which succeed each other with an inconceivable rapidity, and are in perpetual flux and movement." The mind was "a kind of theatre, where several perceptions successively make their appearance," and we have no notion at all "of the place, where these scenes are represented, or the materials, of which it is compos'd."[33]

Even in the *Treatise*, however, Hume did not think this ended the discussion about the self. He made this argument in Book One, which was devoted to "the understanding." But he dealt very differently with the question in Book Two, whose subject was "the passions." In this connection, the self no longer appeared as an idea without any object. On the contrary, here "'Tis evident, that the idea, or rather impression of ourselves is always intimately present with us, and that our consciousness gives us so lively a conception of our own person, that 'tis not possible to imagine, that any thing can, in this particular go beyond it."[34] In other words, the mind and its operations cannot provide us with a solid idea of the self, but the passion and concern that constitutes the life of individuals can and does. We cannot pause here to consider how Hume reconciled these apparently contradictory declarations (one motive behind the first one was to cut the ground from under scholastic and Cartesian pretensions to prove the immateriality and immortality of the soul, based on the "perfect identity and simplicity" to which Hume refers),[35] but that he expressed them suggests that he did not regard fluidity and stability as mutually exclusive forms of self-existence. Hume thought people should aspire to a kind of character in which a constant disposition to virtue ruled their actions, since such a way of being "steels the heart against the assaults of fortune." He recognized all the same that people were seldom so stable as such a Stoic formula prescribed, and that many saw certain attractions in a more fluid personal style: "No man would ever be unhappy, could he [constantly] alter his feelings. PROTEUS-like, he would elude all attacks, by the continual alternations of his shape and form. But of this resource nature has, in a great measure, deprived us."[36] Hume's protean kind of character was not far from the one Duchamp aspired to develop for himself, but his own view, closer to Musil's (albeit on different premises), identified fluid and stable selfhood as poles inside a more complex field of experience.

Wahrman mentions Hume a few times, but makes no real effort to establish his relation to the two "regimes." He does however present Hume's good friend Adam Smith as belonging to the older, pre-modern regimen. Smith was much interested in the theater as a metaphor for social relations, noting that our need for sympathy with others leads us to imagine ourselves as somehow inside their skin, so that if one of my friends suffers a deep personal loss, "I consider what I should suffer *if I was really you*, and I not only change circumstances with you, but *I change persons and characters*." For Wahrman, this theatrical metaphor locates Smith close to contemporary writers on drama, who considered that a good actor ceases to be the person he or she is when on the stage, and actually becomes the character for which the drama calls, thus demonstrating the self's mutability. In other places, Smith referred to the times when a person exercises judgment over his or her own character as creating a situation in which "I *divide myself, as it were, into two persons*; and that I, the examiner and judge, represent a different character from the other I, the person whose character is examined into and judged of."[37] Such statements might well place Smith inside the supposed *ancien régime* were they sufficient to convey his thinking on the subject. But Wahrman does not mention that all of Smith's discussions of sympathy, role-playing, and self-observation in *The Theory of Moral Sentiments* were part of his account of how human beings develop what Smith called "self-command," the power to impart a consistent direction to our actions. It is through sympathy with others, and the desire to live in stable relations with them, that we are moved to mitigate and restrain our passions and impulses, learning to judge them at a distance, and thus gaining a degree of coherence and stability that only a long process of education can effect. Smith understood and valued the permeability of personal boundaries, together with the human proclivity to identify strongly with others and to look on our own sentiments and actions from a distance, precisely because people dedicated these powers of malleability to the development of a stable personal and moral existence. It is true that he (as I have argued in a recent discussion of him) regarded this process of self-development as never complete. Indeed, he thought it necessary that individuals preserve the openness to others that makes them susceptible to outside influences, even though this sets limits to self-command, since our very ability to control our passions and impulses depends on continuing to respond to the feelings of others.[38] But that is just the point: the process of developing a stable self on the ground of its original mutability was never-ending, and the two "regimes of the self" were thus not opposites, but part of a larger and enduring configuration that comprehended them both.

Hume and Smith approached the self partly on grounds opened up by their predecessor John Locke, and Wahrman wants to locate Locke inside his old regime as well. There would appear to be good reasons for doing so, since students of Locke have long recognized in his thinking a set of implications that point toward modern images of self-dissolution, in romanticism, in the positivism of Ernst Mach, and even in poststructuralist notions of the "death of the subject."[39] The kinship between Locke's account of the self and these later ones descends from his famous metaphor that likened the mind as it came into the world to a *tabula rasa* or blank slate, deriving its contents from experience, and thus from the shifting external situations and influences to which life subjected it. Locke offered this account as a replacement for classical and scholastic ones attributing a permanent substantial form to the soul; to him, such claims to know the essence of anything drew human beings beyond the limits of their possible knowledge (which could only have its roots in experience), so that improving our understanding required first of all that we abandon them. That such an approach left the self without any stability or continuity was the view of a number of his contemporary critics, notably Bishop Joseph Butler, who summarized what many feared to be the implications of Locke's views in these terms: "That personality is not a permanent, but a transient thing: that it lives and dies, begins and ends continually: that no one can any more remain one and the same person two moments together, than two successive moments can be one and the same moment."[40] Butler knew that Locke himself did not draw these conclusions from his premises, but he argued that the basis on which Locke sought to establish a continuing self-identity in the face of this changeability, namely the consciousness that tied an individual to the memory of deeds done in the past, and to concern about the future, with its possible rewards and punishments, did not provide a sufficient barrier against them. Only an understanding of the self that rooted it in a soul whose being survived bodily death, retaining its self-identity to the end of time, could justify the Christian insistence on individuals' eternal responsibility for their own fate and the righteousness of divine judgment.

Without sharing Butler's theology, Wahrman offers a very similar view of Locke. In the chapter on personal identity in *An Essay Concerning Human Understanding*, Locke proposed a series of thought experiments, imagining for instance that a single soul could occupy different bodies, in the same or different historical moments, or two souls inhabit a single one, all in order to point up the absurdities that arose from such ways of thinking, and to justify his argument that neither body nor soul nor any combination of them can provide a basis for the sense of oneness that makes the self be "self to itself." Only the conscious connection we feel to our personal existence, to what we have done in the past and to what may happen to us in the future, gives to human beings as we can know them the continuity of identity that makes them selves, and thus creatures who are morally responsible for their actions. Locke acknowledged that this perspective cannot easily resolve all the difficult cases involving forgotten actions, things done under the influence of alcohol or psychic weakness, but he thought it provided the best account of the self human beings, with their limited knowledge, can obtain, leaving us to deal with the difficult instances as they come up, one by one. Locke's aim was to show that this understanding of selfhood provides a sufficient ground for personal identity and moral accountability, while remaining outside the metaphysical swamp of soul and substance.

But Wahrman, in order to squeeze Locke into the straightjacket of his two "regimes," takes the situations Locke dreams up in the thought experiments, which make it appear as if two people could be the same person or a single one be two, as showing the implications of Locke's own views. "In short, as Locke spins out the consequences of his reflections on personal identity, we find insubstantiality, mutability, and doubleness; precisely those fluid aspects of the *ancien régime* with which we are now familiar." In the *Essay*, however, these are the consequences of the views Locke rejects, not of his attempt to show how a being, which is in many ways fluid and unstable, all the same can be sufficiently coherent to know itself over time, and be responsible for its actions. Still worse, a few pages later Wahrman briefly takes up Locke's distinction between identity "as a man," by which he means the vital continuity of a living, physical being that remains the same over its lifetime whether aware of it or not, and identity "as a person," which involves the kind of subjective and moral continuity just discussed. Somehow he manages to read this distinction (just how the trick is turned remains unclear to me) to make "the thrust of Locke's argument" be "that personhood, or selfhood, can in certain cases roam away from the man, move to another man, or be superseded by another self within the same man." This is simply absurd as an account of Locke's views or of implications that can legitimately be drawn from them; certainly it cannot be derived from the contrast between the two kinds of identity Locke distinguishes.[41]

It might be argued that these strictures against Wahrman's book are unfair to it, since they concentrate on matters that belong to intellectual history, to formal texts by thinkers, whereas *The Making of the Modern Self* is concerned primarily with cultural history, drawing most of its evidence from more popular accounts and public practices. To this, the first reply is that if the putative regimes ever had any real existence then their effects should be visible in Hume and Smith and Locke no less than in theatrical performances and masquerades, as Wahrman's own attempts to draw these writers into his account acknowledge. But the claim that mid-eighteenth-century people experienced their identities as fluid and unstable in ways that excluded their recognition of the opposite qualities in themselves is just as dubious in the public and popular arena as in the more strictly intellectual one. Take Peg Woffington, an actress famous in the 1740s and 1750s for her "pants" roles, and her ability to make audiences believe that the figure before them was indeed male. About one of these characterizations a critic enthused that "*there was no trace of the woman*. The audience beheld only a young man of faultless figure, distinguished by an ease of manner, polish of address, and nonchalance that at once surprised and fascinated them." Other observers praised her power to make women react to her as they did to attractive men, so that in her presence "*both sexes* vanquished lie."[42] These comments testify that Woffington was a remarkable actress, and also that her audiences were willing to accept her gender-bending impersonations as exercising real power over them. But did this ability mean that she and they regarded her personality to be fluid and plastic in a way that excluded its simultaneous permanence, or just the opposite, that these powers were the properties of a particular and highly unusual individual, whose persisting identity was heightened and underlined by her ability to control its manifestations? Exactly the same question arises in regard to the masquerades. If on these occasions "people were so disguised, that without being in on the secret, none could distinguish them," and if they "may possibly forget their own selves" until the party was over, is this a sign of the mutability of identity or of its persistence, even a testimony to the strength required to engage in such disguises without impairing ones ability to return to ordinary life afterward?[43] To every claim that such behavior indicated the presence of a self "without depth," there is bound to arise its dialectical opposite, that only selves with considerable depth can successively enter into such relations and exit from them. Only if a Peg Woffington could indeed become someone else, or masqueraders regularly pass through the excitement of their revels into a different life, could Wahraman's claim that they belonged to a regime where protean selves without depth acquired and cast off personal identities like costumes be validated.

Considering the problems that arise in such a project as Wahrman's suggests that the contrast between Duchamp's and Musil's ways of appealing to a self without qualities possess a relevance that extends well beyond their personal differences. To regard a self conceived in terms of fluidity and malleability as excluding one understood as constant and stable is to line up with Duchamp rather than Musil. And to project such a view onto the history of selfhood cannot escape distorting what modern thinkers, beginning with Locke, Hume, and Smith, in fact understood about the dialectic of mobility and persistence that constitutes personal existence. The historians and theorists who take such a stance (since Wahrman is not alone in doing so) may not aspire to live in the kind of aesthetic utopia Duchamp envisioned, but the temptation to imagine a human nature so malleable that it can only appear inside successive and antithetical regimes of the self lands them in a position that shares much with it. It is no accident that Duchamp foreshadowed many ideas and attitudes that have blossomed in the self-consciously postmodern thinkers and currents where such ways of thinking about history have arisen and been developed. In arguing against them, and against him, here, I hope to have shown that modern European intellectual history can provide us with points of observation from which to clarify issues of wide import. If I have succeeded in some degree, then this essay should provide a suitable tribute to Martin Jay, a historian for whom studying the history of thought has always gone hand in hand with both recognizing and criticizing the claims of theory.

Notes

1. Pierre Cabanne, *Dialogues with Marcel Duchamp*, trans. Ron Padgett (London, 1979; New York, 1987), 48; Michel Sanouillet and Elmer Peterson, eds., *The Writings of Marcel Duchamp*, trans. Elmer Peterson (New York, 1989), 32. I have discussed Duchamp's readymades in *The Private Worlds of Marcel Duchamp: Desire, Liberation, and the Self in Modern Culture* (Berkeley and Los Angeles, 1995), 115–128 and 131–139, where other literature is cited.
2. For the image of the fly and the flypaper see Robert Musil, *The Man Without Qualities*, 2 vols. (with consecutive pagination), trans. Sophie Wilkins and Burton Pike (New York, 1995), 137.
3. Seigel, *The Private Worlds of Marcel Duchamp*.
4. A remark reported by Walter Pach in *Queer Thing, Painting* (New York, 1938), 155; also cited by Anne d'Harnoncourt in her introduction to *Marcel Duchamp*, ed. by her and Kynaston McShine (Philadelphia, PA, 1973, 1989), 39.
5. Cabanne, *Dialogues*, 72.
6. See *The Private Worlds of Marcel Duchamp*, chap. 6.
7. This note was not published in the *Green Box* of 1934, but later on in the *White Box*, also called A *L'infinitif*, of 1966; *Writings*, 74. I have altered the translation found there, using the original in *Duchamp du signe*, ed. Michel Sanouillet and Elmer Peterson (Paris, 1975, 1994), 105–106. "Interrogatoire" is not just an examination, but a judicial interrogation, and it is not enough to translate "se conclut l'arrêt du choix" as "my choice is determined."
8. What follows is a brief summary of the reading I give in *The Private Worlds of Marcel Duchamp*, chap. 4.
9. Walter Benjamin, "On Some Motifs in Baudelaire," in *Illuminations*, ed. Hannah Arendt, trans. Harry Zohn (New York, 1969), 170. The motif was of course common in romanticism. See for instance Gerald N. Izenberg's discussion of Chateaubriand in *Impossible Individuality: Romanticism, Revolution, and the Origins of Modern Selfhood* (Princeton, NJ, 1992).
10. For Schwarz's reading see his book, *The Complete Works of Marcel Duchamp* (New York, 1969), 449; he notices the absence of the bottles, but can only see in it a reference to Duchamp's bachelorhood. The information that Duchamp accepted the reading was conveyed by Schwarz to William A. Camfield, who reports it in his article "Marcel Duchamp's *Fountain*: Its History and Aesthetics in the Context of 1917," in *Marcel Duchamp: Artist of the Century*, ed. Rudolf E. Kuenzli and Francis M. Naumann (Cambridge, MA, 1989), 94n60.
11. The first interview is reprinted in *New York Dada*, ed. Rudolf E. Kuenzli (New York, 1986), 134. For the second, Cabanne, *Dialogues*, 48.
12. I discuss this work and Duchamp's relationship to Jarry in *The Private Worlds*, 162–167.
13. Robert Musil, *Diaries, 1899–1941*, selected and trans. by Philip Payne, from the original German version by Adolf Frisé, ed. and intro. by Mark Mirsky (New York, 1998), 295–296.
14. Philip Payne, *Robert Musil's "The Man Without Qualities": A Critical Study* (Cambridge and New York, 1988), 189–191, 197–198. That the relationship was not to be consummated was also the view of Denis de Rougemont, whom Payne discusses here.
15. The statement is from "The Creative Act," a lecture first delivered in 1957, and reprinted in *Writings*, 138–140. The portrait is "Portrait of Dr. Dumouchel" (1910).

16. "Mind and Experience: Notes for Readers who have Eluded the Decline of the West," in *Precision and Soul: Essays and Addresses*, ed. and trans. Burton Pike and David S. Luft (Chicago and London, 1990), 144–145.
17. *Diaries*, 312.
18. Ibid., 302.
19. "Mind and Experience," 145–147. Musil refers here to Bergson (144), rejecting the connection some posited between him and Spengler, but without discussing the French philosopher further.
20. "Toward a New Aesthetic: Observations on a Dramaturgy of Film," in *Precision and Soul*, 202.
21. Musil, *The Man Without Qualities*, e.g., 233, 268, 272.
22. Ibid., 1178. For a somewhat similar formulation, see Payne, *Robert Musil's "The Man Without Qualities,"* 206. In a rather enigmatic notebook entry that has, so far as I know, been little discussed by students of his work (neither Luft nor Payne mentions it), Musil compared coitus to the trance states entered into in Balinese medical rituals, and in which people caught up in the excitement were reported as seeking to injure themselves. Musil seems to attribute this behavior to the participants' belief that spiritual powers have entered into their bodies, i.e., to a breach of the separation between the two worlds; describing coitus as "a remnant of the trance," he concludes: "Thus it is logical that Ag[athe] and U[lrich] do not want coitus." See *Diaries*, 400, for a truncated version of this entry. The complete entry on it is in Musil, *Tagebücher, Aphorismen, Essays und Reden*, ed. Adolf Frisé (Hamburg, 1955), 434–435. I take this to mean that what they do not want is to be caught up in the confusion of the two spheres, which is just the condition he attributes to the characters in the novel he treats negatively, including Walter and Clarisse, and Diotima and Arnheim.
23. *Diaries*, 290–291, 319, 316.
24. Musil, *The Man Without Qualities* (hereafter *MwQ*), 30.
25. Ibid., 30–31.
26. Ibid., 162. Meister Eckhart's language is cited by Mark Jay Mirsky in his introduction to Musil's *Diaries* (in the edition cited above), L. Mirsky refers to a forthcoming book by Genese Grill on Musil and mysticism; so far as I have been able to determine, the book is not yet published.
27. *MwQ*, 269–272.
28. Ibid., 276.
29. Ibid., 272.
30. Dror Wahrman, *The Making of the Modern Self: Identity and Culture in Eighteenth-Century England* (New Haven, CT, 2004), 2; quoting Geertz, "'From the Native's Point of View': On the Nature of Anthropological Understanding," in *Cultural Theory: Essays on Mind, Self, and Emotion*, ed. R.A. Shweder and R.A. LeVine (Cambridge, 1984), 126.
31. Wahrman, *The Making of the Modern Self*, 198.
32. David Hume, *An Enquiry Concerning Human Understanding*, ed. Tom L. Beauchamp (Oxford, 1999), 254–255.
33. David Hume, *A Treatise of Human Nature*, ed. Ernest G. Mossner (London and New York, 1969, 1985), 299–301.
34. Ibid., 368.
35. For an extended attempt to do so see chapter four of my book, *The Idea of the Self: Thought and Experience in Western Europe since the Seventeenth Century* (Cambridge and New York, 2005).

36. "The Sceptic," in Hume, *Essays Moral, Political, and Literary*, ed. Eugene F. Miller (Indianapolis, IN, 1985), 168–169.
37. Wahrman, *The Making of the Modern Self*, 174 and 189.
38. I discuss Smith in chapter five of *The Idea of the Self*.
39. The connection was noted by Ernest Lee Tuveson, *The Imagination as a Means of Grace: Locke and the Aesthetics of Romanticism* (Berkeley and Los Angeles, 1960; reprinted, New York, Gordian Press, 1974), 29.
40. See "A Dissertation on Personal Identity," in *The Works of the Right Reverend Father in God Joseph Butler, D.C.L, Late Lord Bishop of Durham*, with a preface by Samuel Halifax, D.D., 2 vols. (Oxford, 1859), 307–308.
41. Wahrman, *The Making of the Modern Self*, 191, 197. I discuss Locke on selfhood and personal identity in chapter three of *The Idea of the Self*.
42. Wahrman, *The Making of the Modern Self*, 48–49.
43. Ibid., 161.

Bibliography

Benjamin, Walter. "On Some Motifs in Baudelaire." In *Illuminations*, edited by Hannah Arendt, translated by Harry Zohn. New York, 1969.

Butler, Joseph. "A Dissertation on Personal Identity." In *The Works of the Right Reverend Father in God Joseph Butler, D.C.L, Late Lord Bishop of Durham*, with a preface by Samuel Halifax, D.D. 2 vols. Oxford, 1859.

Cabanne, Pierre. *Dialogues with Marcel Duchamp*. Translated by Ron Padgett. London, 1979; New York, 1987).

Camfield, William A. "Marcel Duchamp's Fountain: Its History and Aesthetics in the Context of 1917." In *Marcel Duchamp: Artist of the Century*, edited by Rudolf E. Kuenzli and Francis M. Naumann. Cambridge, MA, 1989.

Duchamp, Marcel. *Duchamp du signe*. Edited by Michel Sanouillet and Elmer Peterson. Paris, 1975, 1994.

———. *The Writings of Marcel Duchamp*. Edited by Michel Sanouillet and Elmer Peterson and translated by Elmer Peterson. New York, 1989.

Hume, David. *An Enquiry Concerning Human Understanding*. Edited by Tom L. Beauchamp. Oxford, 1999.

———. "The Sceptic." In Hume, *Essays Moral, Political, and Literary*. Edited by Eugene F. Miller. Indianapolis, IN, 1985.

———. *A Treatise of Human Nature*. Edited by Ernest G. Mossner. London and New York, 1969, 1985.

Izenberg, Gerald N. *Impossible Individuality: Romanticism, Revolution, and the Origins of Modern Selfhood*. Princeton, NJ, 1992.

Kuenzli, Rudolf E., ed. *New York Dada*. New York, 1986.

Musil, Robert. *Diaries, 1899–1941*. Edited and introduction by Mark Mirsky, selected and translated by Philip Payne. New York, 1998.

———. *The Man Without Qualities*. 2 vols. (with consecutive pagination). Translated by Sophie Wilkins and Burton Pike. New York, 1995.

"Mind and Experience: Notes for Readers who have Eluded the Decline of the West."

In *Precision and Soul: Essays and Addresses*. Translated and edited by Burton Pike and David S. Luft. Chicago and London, 1990.

———. *Tagebücher, Aphorismen, Essays und Reden*. Edited by Adolf Frisé. Hamburg, 1955.

Pach, Walter. *Queer Thing, Painting*. New York, 1938.

Payne, Philip. *Robert Musil's "The Man Without Qualities": A Critical Study*. Cambridge and New York, 1988.

Schwarz, Arturo. *The Complete Works of Marcel Duchamp*. New York, 1969.

Shweder, R.A. and R.A. LeVine, eds. *Cultural Theory: Essays on Mind, Self, and Emotion*. Cambridge, 1984.

Seigel, Jerrold. *The Idea of the Self: Thought and Experience in Western Europe since the Seventeenth Century*. Cambridge, 2005.

———. *The Private Worlds of Marcel Duchamp: Desire, Liberation and the Self in Modern Culture*. Berkeley and Los Angeles, 1995.

Tuveson, Ernest Lee. *The Imagination as a Means of Grace: Locke and the Aesthetics of Romanticism*. Berkeley and Los Angeles, 1960; Reprint New York, 1974.

Wahrman, Dror. *The Making of the Modern Self: Identity and Culture in Eighteenth-Century England*. New Haven, 2004.

LIBERTY AND THE "COMING-INTO-BEING" OF NATURAL LAW
Hans Kelsen and Ernst Cassirer

Gregory B. Moynahan

In an overview of Ernst Cassirer's Weimar career, Jürgen Habermas comments on a central contradiction. "In the realm of the German Mandarins, [Cassirer was] one of the few courageous exceptions who defended the Weimar Republic against its despisers among the intellectuals," yet it is "all the more astonishing" that nowhere in Cassirer's key writings on symbolic forms from the Weimar Period does the concept of right and morality, and with it the realm of politics, find a clearly defined place.[1] In this, Habermas voices a disappointment common to many readers of Cassirer: even as Cassirer was clearly aware of the perils of his era, his philosophy appears to have retained a "Mandarin" distance from politics. Habermas responds to this lacuna by noting the continuity and importance of Cassirer's concept of symbolic form with a "theory of civilizational processes," an argument that has been developed from a different perspective by Drucilla Cornell's recent work on Cassirer.[2] If we look further back in Cassirer's career to his work in the Wilhelmine period, however, we find the outlines of a surprisingly robust theory of law and the state that greatly strengthens Habermas' reading of Cassirer. Indeed, Cassirer's theory of law and ethics prove integrally related to his later work, and only by placing these aspects of his project together can we understand the political meaning of his philosophy.

Cassirer's early theory of the relation of ethics, law, and the state developed from his teacher Hermann Cohen's (1842–1918) philosophy, and was articulated largely through their mutual reading of the German intellectual tradition from Nicholas of Cusa to G.W.F. Leibniz. Cassirer saw Cohen's philosophy of origin, or *Ursprung*, as anchored in a reading of the negative theology of Cusa, as well as Moses Maimonides, which Cassirer's own work developed and attempted to popularize.³ Politically, this reading resulted in what we might term a "negative anthropology" in which the essence of humanity can never be defined directly and in which the basis of liberty is not the commonsense free person of Mill, but the conditions for the possibility of such freedom in social, intellectual, and cultural form. Like the negative theology of Cusa, political form strives to define its object as infinite and knowable only in relation to what it is not.⁴ Developed in its fullest form through a reading of Fichte on the basis of Solomon Maimon, Cassirer held that the individual can only be understood as a limit case, and that this limit case can only be defined negatively in law, state constitution, and social form.⁵ Cassirer understood form through a highly practical definition based on Dilthey's definition of "objective spirit" as concrete historical institutions and through a highly abstract definition based on group theory in mathematics and a Goethean philosophy of science.⁶ It is in this spirit that Cassirer termed his key text on this theme *Freedom and Form: Studies in German Intellectual History* (*Freiheit und Form: Studien zur deutschen Geistesgeschichte*) (1916), since the proper corollary of freedom was a critique of form carried out through the social, juridical, and natural sciences: "true freedom is directed at the cultivation [*Erzeugung*] of rules of form [*Gesetzform*]."⁷

Just as Norbert Ihmig and others have noted that the crux of Cassirer's later work must be approached first by understanding his philosophy of science from the Wilhelmine period, so here Cassirer's early understanding and critique of law as science is central for understanding his vision of a liberal democracy based on a "critical idealism" and the "critique of knowledge."⁸ Cassirer's understanding of critical idealism is rooted, as most clearly outlined in his *Substance and Function* (1911), in a process philosophy that avoids any substantive definitions, particularly—following Ernst Mach—any substantial definitions of the empirical ego or objective "thing."⁹ Instead, Cassirer places a priority on process over static definition, and difference over similarity. Neither object and subject exist except as "the identity of functional orders and correlations. These functional correlations, however, do not exclude diversity and change, but are determined only in it and by it."¹⁰ This determination "only in … and by change" occurs through a sort of metastructuralism in which every particular phenomenon is determined through a play of relations—which Cassirer defines as "functions" in the sense of a mathematical function as pure relation. Structure is modeled in its complexity and radical permutability on mathematical group theory; in its relation to the immediacy of phenomenal perception, it is grounded, following Wilhelm von Humboldt, on the function of language.[11]

Whereas for Mach all of experience could be reduced to "elements of sensation," Cassirer removes even this aspect of substantialism from his philosophy by developing Cohen's use of the concept of the limit and the infinitesimal as a means of describing all elements of determination (*Bestimmung*) as purely relational, whether these are of immediate perception, reality itself (*das Real*), or temporality.[12] Summarizing this project in the 1920s, Cassirer writes: "All being, whether we regard it as 'objective' or 'subjective' being, depends upon an act of determination and on certain forms in which this can take place ... we have not a finished, closed world of the ego emerging from itself but rather the formation of this world in and through these forms."[13] Any form of presentation or representation is based not on a "copy theory of knowledge," but on the determination of the particular by the whole in which the "particular appears as a differential, that is not fully determined and intelligible without reference to an integral."[14]

Both *Leibniz' System* and Cassirer's early project as a whole culminates in the application of this system to law and state theory.[15] In this context, it is immediately evident that Cassirer was not advancing a "traditional" form of Western liberalism in Germany, as has been assumed by David Lipton and others.[16] Rather, as most concisely argued in his 1916 *Freedom and Form*, Cassirer saw his own work as developing Leibniz's initial insights to form a definition of right and law that was "more sharply argued and more consequently executed than by Locke, Montesquieu, or Rousseau," and which could be used to recast the history of German thought and develop a new form of liberalism.[17] It was from this strong viewpoint that Cassirer later sought to defend the "idea of a Republican constitution" in his 1928 *Rektorsrede* on Constitutional Day as, in words Habermas quotes, "in no regard a foreign concept, but rather [grown] from our own ground and through its fundamental power, and nourished through the power of idealistic philosophy."[18] In light of his early work, Cassirer did not consider this as a secondary defense of the embattled Republic, but as part of a new understanding of state and law that would work in combination with a thoroughgoing critique of form across the sciences.

Cassirer largely underplayed his subtle early theory of liberalism in the Weimar period due not only to the tenuous success of the fragile Republic—and its consequent need for clear rhetorical support—but also because Cassirer's argument depended upon a definition of science and knowledge for which he found the Weimar generation had little patience. Nonetheless, Cassirer never abandoned his early position. He clearly understood it as the basis for a more durable form of liberalism for a future of permanent epistemic change of the sort outlined in *Substance and Function*.

Liberal Theory Between Mill and Humboldt

Whereas classical liberalism, notably in the form of John Stuart Mill's *On Liberty* (1861), developed from a commonsense definition of the person and from an "enclave theory" of rights protecting this person, Cassirer's Leibnizian position undermined both assumptions. Following both Hermann Cohen and Leibniz, Cassirer argued that the individual was unfathomable even to themselves (as monadic Kantian transcendental ego) and radically shaped through forms of sociation and knowledge (as Kantian empirical ego). Cassirer held that the individual was paradoxically both ineffable yet potentially presented through form as an immanent infinity. The model within idealist tradition was Nicholas of Cusa's *De Visione Dei*, where the initial figure of the face-to-face relation of Christ and humanity ultimately is applied to the immanent infinity of any form properly understood.[19]

The form of liberalism advanced by John Stuart Mill, Cassirer's reading suggests, represents a fundamental mistranslation into Anglo-American terms of Mill's principle source, Wilhelm von Humboldt. Mill had of course emphasized his debt to Humboldt in *On Liberty* (1861). "Few persons outside of Germany," Mill wrote, "even comprehend the meaning of the doctrine which Wilhelm von Humboldt put forth ... [which would yield] 'individual vigor and manifold diversity,' which combine themselves in 'originality.'"[20] The epistemological underpinning of Humboldt's idea of individual development was not Locke or Newton but Leibniz, however, and the concept of the individual at play was not an insular individual derived from the state of nature, the liberties of the Englishman, or the person of common law, but was the monad radically co-defined through the relations (harmonies) of its environment in society. Humans are not social animals in the sense of other animals, for "defense, help, and for rearing," but, Cassirer writes of Humboldt, "in the deeper sense, that it is only through others that one is raised to *consciousness* of oneself and an 'I' without a 'You' for its understanding and its perception is an impossibility [*ein Unding*]."[21] For this reason, it is always the concept of "form and spiritual energy [*geistigen Energie*] that is at the center of Humboldt's thought," since the forms or "organization" of sociation determine the individual.[22]

By "energy," Cassirer here has in mind the model of Humboldt's concept of language as a force that, in the manner later popularized through the Sapir-Whorf thesis, *defines* reality rather than simply reflects it. "By the same spiritual act," as Cassirer later summarizes this concept, "through which man spins language out of himself he spins himself into it. In the end he communicates and lives with intuitive objects in no other manner than that shown him by the medium of language."[23] In Humboldt's reading, the basis of individual worth is the "fine web" of interpersonal perceptions, which is beyond comprehension by any one actor and destroyed once the "person" is defined in any substantial manner by the state or society.

> The more individual the foundation of the relations are, ever more comprehensive and general is the affect that goes out from it. This inner wealth of giving and taking is immediately destroyed, however, in so far as it is placed under the tutelage of an outer instance.[24]

The state is, of course, the principle form of this "outer" instance and, in a manner similar to Edmund Burke, Humboldt holds that the mechanisms of the state can only encumber this process of exchange. "It is enough," as Cassirer summarizes Humboldt's view, that "[the state] creates and defends the material foundations on which this spiritual relation can be developed as the free work of individuals."[25] Unlike Burke, however, Humboldt held that tradition itself was also potentially an "outside instance" so that the forms of sociation had to always be redefined and revivified. The danger of the state, and indeed of any objectification of humans, is not merely to make people into a means rather than an end, but not to recognize the creative power that all people exercise simply in interacting. Not only is this to "misidentify humanity and make of humans machines," but to block a creative social power and reduce the "infinitely greater" power of human passions to those organized from the outside. It is the difference, Humboldt states, "between war games and actual war, between rented soldiers and actual soldiers."[26] The immediacy of individuality is, like the apperception of consciousness itself, a limit situation beyond the boundaries of representation. Yet precisely as such, it is pervasively shaped—like the existential fear of the soldier in war—precisely by the forms of conflict and meaning of which it is a part.

It is in this sense that Cassirer sees Humboldt arguing that, "The grounding and foundational right of the individual, which is to defend it against both [state and society], is no longer simply the right to freedom inside a specific walled off individual sphere, such as was the case in freedom of consciousness or freedom of thought. It is the right to particularity [*eigentumlichkeit*] altogether."[27] In this regard, "the basic poverty of the state mechanism consists in this tendency to level the particularity, this inner difference of the individual, and thereby to sublate it."[28] For Humboldt, Cassirer emphasizes: "It is not the disturbance of this possession [of the individual sphere] which serves as the point of attack, but the fixing and approbation [*bestätigung*] which the state gives the subject. Through this fixing, something is changed into a completed good that should only be the result of a free self-activity."[29]

What Mill understood as a commonsensical "variety of situations," was for Humboldt more fully defined as the defense of radical differences of forms of experience and knowledge, and with them forms of individuality.[30] Any pre-established substantive definition of the "person" and their boundaries, whether from the state or from culture, whether at the level of the individual or through the "personality" or state or race, was in Cassirer's reading a threat to this development. The goal of liberal theory was to develop new forms through which individuals could interact and more richly understand themselves through these actions. Humanity was a permanently unfinished and open project, and the goal of law and society was to productively amplify this fundamental reality.

For Cassirer, the development of the modern idea of the individual and state represented one model for such a development, in which the successive struggles for religious, intellectual, and, beginning with Humboldt, "aesthetic freedom" in the modern period "dialectically confront and demarcate each other."[31] They gradually reveal the viability of a definition of the individual—whether understood as an individual human, association, or any other form of objective spirit—defined purely formally. Humboldt's concept of "aesthetic individuality" introduces a defense of radical "particularity in itself," which steps well beyond earlier legal or political protections of spiritual belief or freedom of thought in the Reformation and Enlightenment.[32] Both legal constitutions (*Verfassungen*) and the constitution of different forms of knowledge establish dynamic rules of action through which subjects and objects are themselves constituted, within a certain epoch.[33]

The Two Legal Receptions of Cassirer: Abstract "Functionalist" and Liberal Humanist

Cassirer's understanding of law and liberalism developed largely in relation to contemporary circumstances. Cassirer's political theory was intended to redefine two largely opposed extremes of turn of the century legal and political debate. On the one hand, law and politics were increasingly approached through positivistic, technocratic, and systemic means. This development began with Christian Wolff's popularization and systemization of Leibniz's work and culminated in the German Civil Code of 1900. On the other hand, often under the banner of the "personality of the state," law and politics were increasingly approached as affective, symbolic, and, in Cassirer's preferred term, "physiognomic." Leibniz provided Cassirer with the initial template for understanding how to criticize this concept of "personality," by demonstrating how all "physiognomic wholes" could be defined through functions, and how a critical system could develop into a critique of reality.

In this way, Cassirer saw Leibniz's work as initiating a movement that would culminate in Kant and Cohen, and would open for critique all areas in which "one dresses certainty in the intuition of objects" as a problematic continuity of medieval notions of substance as what is *in se et per se esse* (in and of itself).[34] Ultimately, this allowed Cassirer to claim that the putative opposition of quantitative and qualitative individuality, derived from Humboldt and Mill, was a false dichotomy. Qualitative individuality in the sense of the aesthetic individual put forth by Humboldt can only come into existence through the *most* abstract "quantitative" form of defining the individual, as epitomized by the fully abstract concept of the legal individual.

Within this argument, Cassirer's understanding of law, as developed through his reading of Leibniz, occupies the key position as the mediating form between function and appearance, quantitative and qualitative experience. "The link between general ethical rules and the reality of history," Cassirer writes,

> occurs principally through the development of forms of empirical communal life [*empirischen Gemeinschaftslebens*]. Within these forms the most important factor is positive law, which on one hand in its foundations refers back to the principal questions [*Prinzipienfragen*] while on the other it brings to representation [*zur Darstellung bringt*] in the manifold of its development the transformation of individual historical determinations.[35]

The focal point of liberal theory is again not the "person" *per se*, but the forms of objective spirit and law that negatively allow individuality and sociation to fully develop. *Freedom and Form* takes apart the concept of substantial personality, whether of the individual or the state, and demands a critique of the forms of life, particularly the institutions of law as "objective spirit" in Hegel's view, so as to "place us in the middle point of the active and productive forces on which will affect the future formulation [*Gestaltung*] of our being [*Dasein*]."[36] Curiously, Cassirer's reception in the 1920s was dominated by two completely opposed receptions of his argument—one emphasizing his quantitative and functional emphasis on system, the other his qualitative and "physiognomic" emphasis on experience—neither of which alone grasped his unified response to the crisis of law at the turn of the century.

The Pure Theory of Law and Cassirer's Functionalism

That Leibniz's work is both the foundation of modern German legal jurisprudence and a modern technocratic definition of law itself has recently been persuasively argued in several texts. As summarized in Roger Berkowitz's recent *The Gift of Science: Leibniz and the Modern Legal Tradition*, "Leibniz presided over the birth of positive law" in Germany leading up to the *Bürgerliches Gesetzbuch* (1900), and Leibniz's understanding of law as a science was dominant throughout the modern period.[37] Cassirer similarly saw Leibniz's concepts as the beginning of a distinctly modern form of law based on human will understood through a science that "had no recourse to a law-giver, whether human or godly" and that was thus for the first time, along with Grotius, "removed in principle from the question of the existence of God."[38]

Law for Leibniz is principally a means of structuring community (*empirisches Gesellschaftslebens*) as a system of norms, of relations of "*sollen*," (should) and was not to be confused with relations of being.[39] Law is thus an organized system of statements; if *x* occurs, than *y should* result, both in the relation of expectations between legal actors and in the relation of crime to punishment. In this regard, Leibniz saw Hobbes' work in particular as fundamentally incorrect. Although it was well founded in trying to develop an interconnected *system* of rules for human society, it replaced the actual form of law as based on *sollen* relations with a reading, indeed a political physics, of *being* relations. "The leveling of law and power is indeed," Cassirer notes of Leibniz's critique, "generally expressed, a symptom of a fundamental misrecognition of the relation of *sein* [being] and *sollen*."[40] The relation of *sollen* statements is not based on what is given, but rather functions *regulatively* and guides the creation of positive law. For Leibniz, however, the overall relation of *sollen* statements itself formed a unified system, and thus a science.

In this regard, the purist modern exemplar of Leibniz's system at first appears to be the enormously influential jurist Hans Kelsen, who attempted to develop a "pure theory of law" purged of any "substantial" definitions of the legal subject or the state. Kelsen is often held to be a close student of both Cohen and Cassirer. Kelsen's goal was to define law solely as a play of functional relations or "norms." In theory, these relations could define any state, and one need not enter into any sociological or empirical study of society to understand its system of law. Kelsen describes his work in relation to Cassirer as follows: "As with every personification, so that of the state is accomplished in order to make a multiplicity of relations simple and intuitively concrete [*Veranschaulich*] for thought.... This is simply a particular case of the 'general tendency of thought to transform the pure means of knowledge into ever so many objects of knowledge. (Cassirer)'"[41] As Samuel Paulsen and others have argued, although Kelsen was certainly influenced by Hermann Cohen, Cassirer's functionalism appears to be the root of his system.

Kelsen proposed a radically nominalistic legal theory, in which all "fictional" aspects of the law would be debunked and replaced with a pure study of relations. "The idea of the state has the same place as the idea of 'force' in physics, of the idea of the 'soul' in psychology, and generally of the idea of 'substance' in natural science."[42] All of these are "fictional" concepts that lend intuitive immediacy to what upon analysis proves to be pure systems of relations. As long as one can assume one "grounding norm" of a system of law, the entirety of its functioning can be considered purely relational. As critics have long noted, however, Kelsen's theory had no ready means of defining this grounding norm in itself, and thus it could apply to nearly any political system.

Kelsen was part of a general movement emphasizing relations over substance which contemporaries often linked with Cassirer's "functional" definition of science. Thus, when the philosopher Siegfried Marck wrote an overview of the state of German legal philosophy in 1925, he summarized the basic issues of dispute in his title by referring back to Cassirer's earlier work, *The Substance and Function Idea in the Philosophy of Law*.[43] Marck described the development of law in the previous thirty years as generally characterized by a movement from "the idea of substance to the idea of function."[44] The terms, he noted in a preface, are derived from Cassirer's *Substance and Function*. "Considering the present setting of problems in the current philosophy of law," Marck writes, "making use of this terminology appears to be the most pregnant means of expressing its present oppositions and questions of contention." Only through this functionalist approach to the problem does Marck think that he can survey the wide expanse of problems linking representation with the problem of personality, a subject to which Marck turns in his penultimate chapter on "the problem of personality in law," which serves as a prelude to a "general theory of the state."[45]

Humanism and the Coming-Into-Being of Natural Law

At odds with Cassirer's reception as an important source of a critical functional definition of law is his widespread reception as the quintessential liberal humanist. To understand the bridge between these two designations, we could begin with Cassirer's own defense of the concept of natural law and its relation to norms in society in an essay to the Hamburg jurists in

1932, entitled "On the Nature and Coming-into-Being of Natural Law." Despite the late date of the lecture, Cassirer's views were deeply interwoven with his earliest work and only fully comprehensible in reference to it.

Cassirer begins his essay by noting the extreme disfavor into which the concept of natural law has fallen in the modern world. Indeed, from Kelsen at one extreme to Carl Schmitt at the other, natural law had by the late Weimar period largely ceased to be a topic in German jurisprudence. Cassirer's lecture suggests that the concept of natural law has to be understood as a developmental concept, focused *prospectively* on future human development. By natural law, Cassirer here means the concept that certain rights and privileges are inherent to human beings independent of their place in civil society. Cassirer's argument hinges on the definition of nature in his philosophy of science, which held that there is no difference between nature and culture. Again, Leibniz is the original source of this definition, since his work forms the basis for Kant's conclusion that community understood ethically "is no second nature, but the means of a new viewpoint of judgments, over which we can relate to this [one] nature."[46] In many ways, forms of sociation construct and reveal invariants in the world in a manner effectively just as free from, and for, human volition as do forms of knowledge about the natural world.

Although Cassirer would later put great effort into distinguishing the particularities of the field of "culture" from that of nature, he never failed to insist on the importance of tracing both back to a single origin, in Cohen's original sense of *arché* and along the lines first outlined by Leibniz.[47] Natural law in this context is an ideal that guides positive law to approach those structures that allow human beings to perceive each other—much in the early Renaissance sense of Cusa or Della Mirandola—as protean, infinitely complex creatures, capable for better and for worse of changing the forms in which they perceive themselves and others.

In his lecture, Cassirer begins with the foundation of modern natural law by Hugo Grotius, who attempted to develop a "rational" idea of law based on mathematics. At first, this appears to suggest law as a form of science in the manner that will come to dominate the German legal code. But Cassirer's point here is the necessary interrelation of law with broader questions of ethics and other forms of objective spirit. Cassirer notes the apparent absurdity of Grotius' rational model of law, but is also careful to say that the form of rationality Grotius had in mind was not necessarily the same as that of mathematics. "Rationality" is not an "abstract" principle, but becomes a tacit "reality" of our sense of other people in the fullest sense—and this rationality is precisely what allows it to take on the name "natural."

Cassirer understands Grotius as arguing that through *use*, certain patterns or rules in society reveal larger forms of order and more complete definitions of what "humans" are. For Grotius, as for Leibniz, this does not lead to empiricism, but to a quest for the rules that first allow order to come into being in the first place. As Leibniz puts it: "The science of right and not-right does not have its foundation in experience and details, just as little as does that of logic, metaphysics, arithmetic, geometry or dynamics. Rather it serves to make details themselves calculable [*von den Thatsachen selbst Rechenschaft zu geben*] and to regulate them in advance."[48] To take a trivial example, it is through having a sense of "forming a queue" that one can understand certain rules of fairness ("going in order," "first come, first serve") and with them understand other people in a particular manner. In the context of the argument in *Freedom and Form*, Cassirer's broader point is that the "rational" principles of law are what first allows us to "see" the rights inherent to a person—indeed, to even understand what a person is—in the first place. The battles over religious freedom, political opinion, and the inviolability of individual perception were plays of forces that in time revealed broader ideals of law culminating in the "open" or "empty" definition of the individual in the modern state.[49] Freedom of conscience defines both the person and "religion" in a new manner in which any particular belief is defined negatively against the spectrum of belief in general. Civic freedoms first allowed for the possibility of imagining a political space in which others are considered "equal" as defined negatively against the (Kantian) infinite ideal of "human," which in turn becomes a "rational" principle for the founding of a constitution and system of law based on identical civic subjects.

In a curious parallel to Kelsen's concept of a "fundamental norm," Cassirer writes that there is an "inescapable basic moment" (*unentbehrliche Grundmoment*) of the ideal structure of natural law that exists as the horizon of any community. Whereas for Kelsen the "founding" norm is an ideal or judgment, for Cassirer it is clearly something like the "asymptotic" point of humanity suggested by Kant, but developed solely, as in Kant's "cosmopolitan ideal of history," through the progressive unfolding of new structures of society.[50] Being in any communicative community at all presupposes, as the basis of communication itself, a minimal definition of the "coming-into-being" of natural law that provides the underlying structure of community. The horizon of human activities always suggests some means of triangulating with a new more foundational definition of "human," and thus of nature.

Cassirer developed this reading at greater length in other treatments of Grotius, whose work he saw as most fully developed by Leibniz.[51] Thus, he writes concerning Grotius a year after his discourse to the Hamburg Jurists in *The Philosophy of the Enlightenment* (1932):

> Law is not simply the sum total of that which has been decreed and enacted; it is that which originally arranges things. It is "ordering order" (*ordo ordinans*), not "ordered order" (*ordo ordinatus*). The perfect concept of law presupposes without doubt a commandment affecting individual wills. But this commandment does not create the idea of law and justice; it is subject to this idea; it puts the idea into execution, though the execution must not be confused with the justification of the idea of law as such … The assertion that there can exist and must be a law even without the assumption of divine existence, is therefore not understood as a thesis but a hypothesis.[52]

Far from being restrained by a concept of "nature" in the sense of natural science, divine nature, or even a stable anthropology, natural law in Cassirer's sense is similarly a "hypothesis" based on the ideal of a radically heterogeneous individuality. As law, however, all forms of rights operate to amplify what Georg Simmel defined as a "social *a priori*," the conditions of the possibility of social action. Natural law is always "coming-into-being," rather than simply given, since this process is always developmental, and can, for Cassirer, be destroyed by "outside instances of power." In this regard, law is just one form of objective spirit among others, and is defined in part as a reflection or concrescence of all of the other struggles of society.

The background of Cassirer's understanding of this problem, and the realistic context of his placement of it, only comes out in the last paragraph of the essay to the Hamburg jurists. Here, Cassirer suggests a "personal reflection" on the problem of natural law that occurred to him and that contains a "typical meaning and a symbolic value."[53] Cassirer notes an observation he made during the Dreyfus-Trial, the trial of a French-Jewish Captain that acted as a lightning rod for anti-Semitism in its time. Cassirer recalls a jurist asking a long line of questions pertinent to the case in which the defense replied, "*cette question ne sera pas posée*"—since the question stood outside of what could legally be asked, it was not admissible. Cassirer says he is sure that at the time, the lawyer in charge believed that these questions were technically inadmissible, and that they were operating within the proper ambit of these laws. Yet as Cassirer notes, these same questions—which presumably were those having to do with the justice of the Dreyfus case, the fact that he was a Jew being tried for military espionage, etc.—were asked everywhere outside of the court and ultimately led to the case's ongoing trial and retrial.

Natural law develops in conjunction with those "unwritten laws" structuring how people imagine themselves and their society.[54] These "unwritten laws" develop through all of the forms of objective spirit in society, which is why Cassirer's philosophy culminated in an historical critique of forms of objective spirit in society and nature. Law, however, provides an axis for the interrelation of these forms based on the maximal definition of individual difference and human future potential. The very idea of the constitution epitomizes this idea, since a constitution is only ideally valid when it expresses the will of the people.[55] In Cassirer's view, the best route to this goal was to define civilization as a complex and heterogeneous process, and law as a minimal defense of "natural" human rights and an open structure for debate.

The basis of Cassirer's reading is Cohen's concept of origin, which suggests that behind the relations of any two or more given statements or propositions, a certain "next lower" level of transcendental logic must exist which supports their coherent connection. The form of logic and concept are not based on the Aristotelian notion of "abstraction," but on a complex form of "limitative judgement" in which each statement is based on a certain horizon of assumptions, "a connection by implication," with others.[56] Thus, in a manner anticipating Habermas' later theory of communicative action, any cultural form that allows for communication suggests a certain logic that can be considered reflective of a broader rule. In human interaction, this rule reflects on some level the nature of "humanity" and thus gradually comes to define human or "natural" rights. Any particular law or communicative act in the present is similarly based on an ideal of difference, which always resolves into an infinite horizon of past acts and toward an infinite future horizon of ethics that determines what "human" might be.

For Cohen, a guarantee of this infinity was God. For Cassirer, following Leibniz's definition of a fully immanent and ultimately secularized notion of God, this infinity is revealed in the infinite coordination or ordering of the world on ever more subtle and surprising levels.[57] As Cohen put it in an earlier essay: "The irreplaceable, very deep ground of the ethics of humanity can no longer lie in the prophetic *hope* of the future, but, in accordance with its method, in the *reality of the future*. This reality is an ethical idea: the idea where the idealism of ethics separates from the utopia of a transcendent bucolic world."[58]

Cassirer's Synthetic Position Between Technocracy and the Personality of the State

The foundation of Cassirer's synthetic position lies with Leibniz, and it is by returning to Leibniz's philosophy that we can grasp the distance of

Cassirer's ultimate position from Kelsen's purely functionalist understanding of law. The broadest feature of Leibniz's work is its contrast of discursive and intuitive knowledge, that is, knowledge gained through signs and symbols and that which is given immediately. The opposition was again picked up in a more refined manner in Kant, who defined it as the opposition of *intellectus ectypus*, "which needs images," and *intellectus archetypus*, which does not.[59] For humanity, only the former is possible. "For us human beings," Cassirer writes, "'knowledge' is given in no other way but in this form, only through the power and function of 'signs.'"[60] Similarly, this split suggests the antinomy of freedom at the basis of Leibniz's project: for God, the interaction of monads is fully determined, whereas for humans and other conscious monads, it is pure spontaneity.

In relation to law, this split in Leibniz's work had profound implications, particularly once it was received and transformed by Kant. Kant's work refined Leibniz's understanding of the monad to form the basis of the famous distinction of the transcendental and empirical ego. In Cassirer's reading, this tradition meant that there is no stable definition of the ego that is accessible to the subject or between subjects. The "transcendental ego" represents simply the mysterious *factum* of connection in the world at all (and is thus equivalent to Leibniz's monad as a unity of apperception), while the "empirical ego" is always shaped by contingent forces and accessible only within the mediation of these forces. "The self thus always comprehends and constitutes itself only in some form of activity."[61] The transcendental ego cannot be known intuitively, since even as it is directly given, it correlates with no object or delimitation; the empirical ego, on the other hand, can be known only as a functional determination of signs. A liberal society has to be based foremost on the historical critique of the forms through which these relations are developed.

This problem also suggests that the *relations* between individuals can also not be perceived in their true individual form, but only through signs, that is, through form. For Leibniz, following medieval definitions of reality and virtuality, other individuals cannot be directly perceived as "true" individuals other than intuitively—a feat possible only by God or, in the medieval definition, after death in heaven by "beatific vision," where the infinite difference of individuals can be seen. In human knowledge, one can only perceive relative individuality and aesthetic infinity through comparison and form. The culmination of Leibniz's basic insight thus occurs, for Cassirer, with Humboldt's philosophy. Here, the more it is assumed that the "fine web" of individual communication *exceeds* what is perceived, and the more it is protected from outside simplification, the better.

The import of Humboldt's philosophy can only truly be grasped by linking it with Leibniz's theory of natural right, which will in turn be the basis for Cassirer's understanding of the "Coming-Into-Being of Natural Right." For Leibniz, the basis of the "scientific knowledge of the natural law" is an infinite horizon that is in itself rationally unknowable to humans. In its complexity and in the infinite terms at its basis, it is not accessible to discursive thought—it is only perceivable through God's intuitive thought. Nonetheless, within discursive thought, the movement *toward* natural law structures the "experiential knowledge of positive law" which we have access to.[62] For example, Leibniz "could not have had the inventory of general and unchangeable rights develop from the original 'equality' of all subjects: because for him this 'equality' is a purely abstract concept, that doesn't have any reality in the world."[63]

Ironically, however, it is the quantitative definition of the individual that was most immediately developed from Leibniz, and indeed became in Cassirer's reading the unfortunate centerpiece of the Western definition of the individual. The basis of this development was the popularization of Leibniz's work by Christian Wolff, who immediately systematized Leibniz's reading of the individual as one in which there are inherent "equal" rights. Equivalence is defined in the sense of identity. Cassirer is unambiguous about the gravity of this mistake. "Whereas Wolff takes the original equality of right to develop ontologically from the similar being of the individual [thing], for Leibniz it constructs the universal society [*Gemeinschaft*] of ethical organization."[64] The two are contradictory: if one assumes rights inherent to the similar being, then there can be no ethics in Leibniz's sense. For Leibniz, it is through ethics and human activity that this equivalence can first be perceived as a limit case. Cassirer observes that Wolff's systematization of Leibniz's ideas was developed and further popularized by William Blackstone (1723–1780) in his *Commentaries on the Laws of England*. These in turn played a key role, as argued by Georg Jellinek (1851–1911), in both the development of the Virginia constitution and, through this, the French and American declaration of rights.[65]

Leibniz's broader theory of truth is pivotal for understanding the very different basis of his juridical philosophy from the popular reception, since this theory will demonstrate that law is not a copying of one reality, or an identification of substantive similarities between people, but a process for discovering invariables that come to define these subjects themselves. If Leibniz's theory of truth is for Cassirer "the basis of his system," nowhere will this be truer than in his system of law.[66] The rules for determining "truth" are similar to constructing hypotheses in the natural world. Thus, Leibniz held that one and the same idea of a truth could be:

> grasped by various subjects under the most varied of material symbols, but it remains nonetheless identical with itself in so far as in all of these differ-

ences of symbols a particular invariable rule is followed. Every individual has in this, when we consider the content of their representations [*Vorstellungen*], their own world, indeed they have their own "truth"; their unity with the whole will nonetheless be established through the form of connection which is given by these representations.[67]

As Norbert Ihmig has shown in depth, Cassirer's reception of this "invariant theory of truth" uses later mathematical models, particularly Felix Klein's group theory, to create perhaps the most sophisticated form of structuralism and definition of truth statements in the philosophy of science in the twentieth century.[68] Invariants need not, and indeed cannot, directly map reality; they need only approach forms of consistency. In order for a statement to be true, as Cassirer puts it in describing Leibniz's break with scholastic logic, it is not necessary that the predicate "perfectly and without remainder resolves into the subject, but only that a general rule of development can be perceived so that we can grasp with certainty that the difference between the two becomes ever smaller."[69] Similarly, "natural law" is always being approximated and revealed in "positive law" as it allows us to see the complexity and difference of others.

Knowledge is not a "copy" of reality, but rather invariants can be reinscribed in different permutations in the sense later popularized by Ludwik Fleck and Thomas Kuhn as paradigm shifts.[70] Law is a process of finding ever more elegant invariants, forming an ordered and harmonious system, and being continuously oriented toward possible future permutations. Just as in projective geometry point and line were revealed as definitionally equal in some cases, so in law surprising links might lead to the postulate of equality being developed in ways never originally contemplated—as Cassirer's *Freedom and Form* demonstrated for earlier struggles for religious, intellectual, and aesthetic individuality. Contemporary examples might be found in the changing of the meaning of equality provided by access to buildings and services in the 1990 Americans with Disabilities Act, or the emphasis on radical individuality in the Lesbian, Gay, Bisexual, and Transgender Movement.

In Cassirer's reading, law effectively forms rules of invariance through which individuals can come to see each other as infinite and in which the relations among individuals can be allowed to develop with maximum complexity. It is in this context that Cassirer can write at the conclusion of *Freedom and Form*, in relation to Fichte, that "the stability of law doesn't follow from the being [*Dasein*] of various different subjects, but from the recognition that the necessary validity of a norm of law is itself the *condition* [*Bedingung*] for the [possibility] that the 'I' will take itself not as an empirical thing, but as a free, self-determining [*sich selbst bestimmende*] reasonable being." For Leibniz, taking oneself as a "reasonable being" implies not similarity with other reasonable beings, but infinite difference from them mediated by invariants of law.

The distinction Leibniz drew between discursive and intuitive knowledge, between an invariant and "copy" theory of truth, meant that law had to acknowledge its inability to grasp its object as a totality and acknowledge its incapacity of making final definitions of its objects. Similarly, the provisional science of law has to always be complemented by ethics and aesthetics, which will outline humanity's relation to both other forms of society and to the infinite plenum of human relations. It is precisely this issue that Cassirer raises at the end of his "coming-into-being of natural law" essay, and it is indeed this aspect that fundamentally separates Cassirer's interest in the "inescapable basic moments" that ethically structure a community from the "grounding norms" that form the structural pivot of Kelsen's pure law.

The dichotomy of intuitive and discursive understanding suggests a radical disjunction between the sort of calculation that can be done by the system of law and the actual moment of decision contained in ethical action. The first is by definition based on the asymptotic limit suggested by the interactions of all forms of objective spirit, codified and organized within the particular form of "positive law" so as to best approximate the "natural law" that reveals human society in its greatest complexity. The second, however, is a moment beyond discursive knowledge, even as it, like individuality itself, is thoroughly informed by it. Here a choice cannot be simply "calculated" because it actually occurs in an infinity of relations.

This infinity of relations, however, would pose an "absolutely insoluble labyrinth" if it were taken, in the manner of Schopenhauer, as "the willing subject" giving itself "in its determinate essence once and for all in a primitive act underlying its empirical existence."[71] Rather, this infinity can only connect the "in itself" of actual infinite complexity with our discursive knowledge through its orientation to the future, and indeed, the future not of the subject, but of humanity as an unknowable whole. "One and the same act stands on the one hand under the compulsion of causes that are past and gone, while on the other hand it is seen from the point of view of future ends and their system unity."[72] It is in this sense that Kant's second critique asks that the individual consider the categorical imperative as bidding "the will to act as if the maxim of its action were through it to become a law of nature." As Cassirer emphasizes, however, the nature Kant has in mind "is not the sensuous existence of objects, but the systematic interrelation of individual ends and their harmonious composition in a 'final end.'"[73]

Even as positive law contains its own organizational structural and norms, its relation to present and future forms that could define "humanity" will always inform it through ethics. The immediate objective of "humanity" as a topic of law is, as Leibniz and Kant insisted, never immediately given even in theory. It is defined in relation to both a future and a potentially infinite transformative idea in a manner that forces positive law to always have reference to the ideal, and that explicitly demands the transcendental imagination as the means for matching schema to intuition.[74]

It is on this ground that we can understand why for Cassirer the basis of politics and law is not the individual, the state, or even the constitution, but the concept of form itself, which is our best means of grasping the various and interrelating formation processes of "humanity." The hermeneutics of understanding how we are shaped by, and how we shape, forms of objective spirit express the principal mode of freedom available to humans. Cassirer redefined the Kantian notion of autonomy so that far from relating to an "autonomous subject," it is always understood as only coming into being through the social phenomenon of form, and through this balance "overcomes the contradictions between freedom and form … true freedom is directed at the development [*Erzeugung*] of rules of form [*Gesetzform.*]"[75] The historical and aesthetic study of "the development of rules of forms" is directly implicated in the issue of ethics and law, for it is from the invariants of these forms that the law can best approach "natural law." Close readers of Cassirer such as Hans Blumenberg, Norbert Elias, Michel Foucault, and Erwin Panofsky more concretely applied the historical critique of all forms of society and the constant questioning of the form of "human" itself.

Cassirer's early understanding of the necessary correlation of such modes of historical critique with the development of positive law is the deeper basis for Habermas' description of Cassirer's project as a theory of "civilizational processes." Only by understanding the forms through which individuation is determined, and anchoring the most important of these in positive law and constitution, can a creative advancement of present politics and future human development occur. Cassirer summarized his project at the end of *Freedom and Form* by writing in relation to Fichte that the "constitutional moment isn't the past of a country, but its future."[76] It is only in the prospective ideal of humanity, and the present sense of the infinite complexity of political actors, that true politics can be developed. The goal of the constitution and law is to allow human beings to perceive ever more clearly this mutual complexity and, as in Humboldt, the far greater level of subtlety of communication and meaning than could be perceived from any "outside instance." Kelsen's pure law developed only the scientific aspect of Cassirer's theory of law, whereas the historicist and humanist reception of Cassirer's Wilhelmine project tended conversely to overlook its integral critique of law and science. Cassirer's own notion of a "coming-into-being of natural law" suggests the relation of the system of law with the "foundational norms" that generally structure society. The state is never a totality, but rather a plenum whose unlimited horizons can only be grasped in ethics, not science, even as it is only through the sciences, and particularly the science of law, that ethics can first locate its modes of activity.

Notes

1. Jürgen Habermas, "Die befreiende Kraft der symbolischen Formgebung: Ernst Cassirers humanistisches Erbe und die Bibliothek Warburg," in *Vom sinnlichen Eindruck zum symbolischen Ausdruck* (Frankfurt am Main, 1997), 9.
2. Drucilla Cornell, "Symbolic Form as Other: Ethical Humanism and the Vivifying Power of Language," in *Moral Images of Freedom: A Future for Critical Theory* (London, 2007).
3. Notably the early volumes of Cassirer's *Das Erkenntnisproblem in der Philosophie und Wissenschaft der neueren Zeit*, 4 vols., 2nd ed. (Darmstadt, 1994), particularly 1: 21–72, 2: 126–190 (hereafter *The Knowledge Problem*); and *Leibniz' System in seinen Wissenschaftlichen Grundlagen* (Marburg, 1902) (hereafter *Leibniz' System*).
4. Cassirer extensively develops Cusa's work in the first volume of his *The Knowledge Problem*, culminating in a section on the "The Contradictions of the Aristotelian Concept of Substance," 1: 21–72. Cassirer returns to Cusa extensively in *The Individual and the Cosmos in Renaissance Philosophy*, trans. Mario Domandi (Mineola, 1963), 7–72.
5. Cassirer, *Knowledge Problem*, 3: 80–126, 126–129; Ernst Cassirer, *Freiheit und Form: Studien zur Deutschen Geistesgeschichte* (Darmstadt, 1994), 336–337 (hereafter *Freedom*).
6. "We cannot treat," Dilthey writes, "the objective spirit as an ideal construction: rather we must take as our basis its reality in history." In Wilhelm Dilthey, *Introduction to the Human Sciences: An Attempt to Lay a Foundation for the Study of Society and History* (Detroit, MI, 1988), 183.
7. Cassirer, *Freedom*, 150.
8. Karl-Norbert Ihmig, *Cassirers Invariantentheorie der Erfahrung und seine Rezeption des "Erlanger Programs"* (Hamburg, 1997).
9. Ernst Cassirer, *Substance and Function & Einstein's Theory of Relativity*, trans. William Curtis Swabey, Marie Collins Swabey (1911; reprint New York, 1953), 314–325.
10. Cassirer, *Substance*, 324.
11. Ibid., 86–100; 253–271; Ernst Cassirer, *The Philosophy of Symbolic Forms*, trans. John Michael Krois, ed. J.M. Krois and D.P. Verene, 4 vols. (New Haven, CT, 1996), 3: 50–51.
12. Hermann Cohen, *Das Prinzip der Infinitesimalmethode und seine Geschichte: Ein Kapitel zur Grundlegung der Erkenntniskritik* (Frankfurt am Main, 1968), 171, 206–215; Cassirer, *Substance*, 165–170.

13. Cassirer, *The Philosophy of Symbolic Forms*, 4: 85.
14. Cassirer, *Substance*, 300.
15. Cassirer, *Leibniz*, 401–487.
16. David R. Lipton, *Ernst Cassirer: The Dilemma of a Liberal Intellectual in Germany, 1914–1933* (Toronto, 1978); John Michael Krois, "David R. Lipton, Ernst Cassirer: The Dilemma of a Liberal Intellectual in Germany, 1914–1933," *Journal of the History of Philosophy* 20, no. 2 (1982): 209–212.
17. Cassirer, *Freedom*, 315.
18. Ernst Cassirer, *Die Idee der Republikanischen Verfassung: Rede zur Verfassungs Feier am 11. August 1928* (Hamburg, 1929).
19. Cassirer, *Knowledge Problem*, 1: 60–61; Cassirer, *Individual*, 31–46.
20. John Stuart Mill, *On Liberty* (London, 1921), 33.
21. Cassirer, *Freedom*, 335.
22. Ibid., 336.
23. Cassirer, *Philosophy of Symbolic Forms*, 1: 15.
24. Cassirer, *Freedom*, 330.
25. Ibid.
26. Ibid., 330–331.
27. Ibid., 329.
28. Ibid., 329.
29. Ibid., 330.
30. Mill, *On Liberty*, 43.
31. Cassirer, *Freedom*, 311.
32. Ibid., 327.
33. Cassirer, *Knowledge Problem*, 7.
34. Cassirer, *Freedom*, 154.
35. Cassirer, *Leibniz*, 449.
36. Cassirer, *Freedom*, xi.
37. Roger Berkowitz, *The Gift of Science: Leibniz and the Modern Legal Tradition* (Cambridge, MA, 2005), 7.
38. Cassirer, *Leibniz*, 449.
39. Ibid.
40. Ibid., 452.
41. Hans Kelsen, "Das Verhältnis von Staat und Recht im Lichte der Erkenntniskritik," in *Die Wiener Rechstheoretische Schule*, ed. R.M.H. Klecatsky and H. Schambeck (Vienna, 1971), 101.
42. Kelsen, "Verhältnis," 101.
43. Siegfried Marck, *Substanz- und Funktionsbegriff in der Rechtsphilosophie* (Tübingen, 1925), 23–25, 83–147; on von Gierke, 92–104.
44. Marck, *Substanz*, Vorwort.
45. Ibid., 83–147, 148.
46. Cassirer, *Freedom*, 154.
47. Hermann Cohen, *System der Philosophie—Erster Teil: Logik der reinen Erkenntnis*, 4th ed., in Hermann Cohen, *Werke*, 20 vols. (New York, 1997), 6.1: 1.
48. Cassirer, *Leibniz*, 452.
49. Cassirer, *Freedom*, 317.
50. Ibid., 324–325; Ernst Cassirer, *An Essay on Man: An Introduction to a Philosophy of Human Culture* (New Haven, CT, 1965), 38.
51. Cassirer, *Leibniz*, 450.

52. Ernst Cassirer, *Philosophy of the Enlightenment*, trans. F.C.A. Koelln, J.P. Pettegrove (New Haven, CT, 1961), 240.
53. Ernst Cassirer, "Vom Wesen und Werden des Naturrechts," *Zeitschrift für Rechtsphilosophie in Lehre und Praxis* 6 (1932): 26.
54. Cassirer, "Vom Wesen und Werden," 27.
55. Ibid., 22.
56. Cassirer, *Substance*, 16, 24.
57. Cassirer, *Knowledge Problem*, 2: 455.
58. Hermann Cohen, "Religion und Sittlichkeit. Eine Betractung zur Grundlegung der Religionsphilosophie" (1907), in Herman Cohen, *Jüdische Schriften*, 3 vols. (Berlin, 1924), 3: 148.
59. Citing Kant, *Critique of Judgment*, trans W. Pluhar (1790; reprint Indianapolis, IN, 1987), 291–293 [Section 77, Paragraph 408].
60. Cassirer, *Philosophy of Symbolic Forms*, 4: 229.
61. Cassirer, *Substance*, 342.
62. Berkowitz, 49, citing Leibniz, letter to Conring, 13/23 January 1690.
63. Cassirer, *Freedom*, 317.
64. Ibid., 318.
65. Georg Jellinek, *Die Erklärung der Menschen und Bürgerrechte: Ein Beitrag zur modenen Vergassungsgeschichte* (Leipzig, 1895), cited in Cassirer, *Freedom*, 315.
66. Cassirer, *Freedom*, 25.
67. Ibid., 277–278.
68. Ihmig, *Cassirers Invariantentheorie*.
69. Cassirer, *Knowledge Problem*, 2: 181.
70. Cassirer, *Substance*, 321–322.
71. Cassirer, *Knowledge Problem*, 3: 425.
72. Cassirer, *Freedom*, 257.
73. Cassirer, *Kant's Life and Thought*, trans. James Haden (1918; reprint New Haven, CT, 1981), 259.
74. Cassirer, *Freedom*, 148, 325; Cassirer, *Leibniz*, 134.
75. Cassirer, *Freedom*, 150.
76. Ibid., 325.

Bibliography

Berkowitz, Roger. *The Gift of Science: Leibniz and the Modern Legal Tradition*. Cambridge, MA, 2005.

Cassirer, Ernst. *Das Erkenntnisproblem in der Philosophie und Wissenschaft der neueren Zeit*. 4 vols. 2nd ed. Darmstadt, 1994.

———. *An Essay on Man: An Introduction to a Philosophy of Human Culture*. New Haven, CT, 1965.

———. *Freiheit und Form: Studien zur Deutschen Geistesgeschichte*. Darmstadt, 1994.

———. *Die Idee der Republikanischen Verfassung: Rede zur Verfassungs Feier am 11. August 1928*. Hamburg, 1929.

———. *The Individual and the Cosmos in Renaissance Philosophy*. Translated by Mario Domandi. Mineola, 1963.

———. *Kant's Life and Thought*. Translated by James Haden. 1918; Reprinted New Haven, CT, 1981.
———. *Leibniz' System in seinen Wissenschaftlichen Grundlagen*. Marburg, 1902.
———. *The Philosophy of Symbolic Forms*. 4 vols. Translated by John Michael Krois. Edited by J.M. Krois and D.P. Verene. New Haven, CT, 1996.
———. *Philosophy of the Enlightenment*. Translated by F.C.A. Koelln and J.P. Pettegrove. New Haven, CT, 1961.
———. *Substance and Function & Einstein's Theory of Relativity*. Translated by William Curtis Swabey and Marie Collins Swabey. 1911; Reprinted New York, 1953.
———. "Vom Wesen und Werden des Naturrechts." *Zeitschrift für Rechtsphilosophie in Lehre und Praxis* 6 (1932).
Cohen, Hermann. *Das Prinzip der Infinitesimalmethode und seine Geschichte: Ein Kapitel zur Grundlegung der Erkenntniskritik*. Frankfurt am Main, 1968.
———. "Religion und Sittlichkeit. Eine Betractung zur Grundlegung der Religionsphilosophie" (1907). In *Jüdische Schriften*. 3 vols. Berlin, 1924.
———. *Werke*, 20 vols. (New York, 1997).
Cornell, Drucilla. "Symbolic Form as Other: Ethical Humanism and the Vivifying Power of Language." In *Moral Images of Freedom: A Future for Critical Theory*. London, 2007.
Dilthey, Wilhelm. *Introduction to the Human Sciences: An Attempt to Lay a Foundation for the Study of Society and History*. Detroit, MI, 1988.
Habermas, Jürgen. "Die befreiende Kraft der symbolischen Formgebung: Ernst Cassirers humanistisches Erbe und die Bibliothek Warburg." In *Vom sinnlichen Eindruck zum symbolischen Ausdruck: philosophische Essays*. Frankfurt am Main, 1997.
Ihmig, Karl-Norbert. *Cassirers Invariantentheorie der Erfahrung und seine Rezeption des "Erlanger Programs."* Hamburg, 1997.
Jellinek, Georg. *Die Erklärung der Menschen und Bürgerrechte: Ein Beitrag zur modenen Verfassungsgeschichte*. Leipzig, 1895.
Kant, Immanuel. *Critique of Judgment*. Translated by W. Pluhar. 1790; reprinted Indianapolis, IN, 1987.
Kelsen, Hans. "Das Verhältnis von Staat und Recht im Lichte der Erkenntniskritik." In *Die Wiener Rechstheoretische Schule*, edited by R.M.H. Klecatsky and H. Schambeck. Vienna, 1971.
Krois, John Michael. "David R. Lipton, Ernst Cassirer: The Dilemma of a Liberal Intellectual in Germany, 1914–1933." *Journal of the History of Philosophy* 20, no. 2 (1982): 209–212.
Lipton, David R. *Ernst Cassirer: The Dilemma of a Liberal Intellectual in Germany, 1914–1933*. Toronto, 1978.
Marck, Siegfried. *Substanz- und Funktionsbegriff in der Rechtsphilosophie*. Tübingen, 1925.

The Artwork beyond Itself
Adorno, Beethoven, and Late Style

Peter E. Gordon

> One can no longer compose like Beethoven, but one must *think* as he composed.
> —T.W. Adorno, from the fragmentary notes to
> *Beethoven: The Philosophy of Music*

Introduction

The question of how music relates to the social order continues to perplex and inspire a great many scholars in various disciplines, not only musicologists but also intellectual historians, sociologists of culture, and (most famously, perhaps) those who in some fashion or another have not ceased to align themselves with the Frankfurt tradition of critical theory. The question posed a special challenge to Theodor W. Adorno, not least because as a theorist schooled in Marxism, he resisted the bourgeois and Schopenhauerian-mystical notion that music is "absolute" and therefore beyond all social determination, even while as a musician himself—he studied composition (intermittently from 1925 onward) in Vienna with Alban Berg—he found the materialist's wholesale reduction of musical value to social being not only vulgar, but ultimately futile insofar as it involved a basic misrecognition of the aesthetic realm.[1] One could even argue that music became for Adorno *the* paradigm for any properly mediated (i.e., non-reductive, but also non-idealistic) theory of culture. As Max Paddison has indicated, Adorno's own writings on music fill up a full half of the twenty volumes of his collected works.[2] Indeed, the question as to how one can pass in a critical idiom between music and society was not simply one question among many. For Adorno it was perhaps the most urgent of all of the philosophical problems since it offered a test case for the difficult task of mediating between transcendence and immanence, freedom and necessity, spirit and social need.

Given the centrality of this question not only within Adorno's own thinking, but also within the larger tradition of critical theory, it is perhaps unsurprising that he could never arrive at a satisfactory solution. In fact, the key text remained unwritten. Notwithstanding his prodigious contributions to musicology and sociology and his shorter musical "physiognomies" of Mahler, Berg, and Wagner, Adorno conspicuously failed to complete what he believed would be the single most important work of his life: the Beethoven-study. As his biographer Stefan Müller-Doohm reminds us, Adorno had been planning and then deferring this project since at least 1940, when he had first announced to his parents: "the next major piece of work I shall undertake will be the book on Beethoven."[3] In late 1943, in a letter sent from his California exile, he wrote of "my long-planned book on Beethoven." And by 1956 one could have sensed his increasing despair: "If only I could get on with writing my book on Beethoven, on which I have copious notes. But heaven alone knows when and whether I shall be able to complete it." The following year Adorno achieved a partial breakthrough by writing the short essay, "Alienated Masterpiece" ("*Verfremdetes Hauptwerk*") on Beethoven's *Missa Solemnis*.[4] But the larger and more capacious study—the monograph that was supposed to set the entirety of Beethoven's music within an adequate theoretical framework—remained unfinished. Müller-Doohm tells us that Adorno died leaving behind "over forty notebooks" for the Beethoven-study.[5] In 1993, the extant materials were eventually gathered together and edited with scrupulous care by Rolf Tiedemann in an indispensable volume under the title, *Beethoven: The Philosophy of Music*. But it is a work in fragments, replete with digressions, repetitions, and reminders that the author hoped to revisit when it finally came time to compose the book. Everywhere there are comments such as: "possible epigraph for the last chapter." "All this needs to be pursued in detail." And: "take this further."[6] One could argue that this was the most appropriate form for a book that would most likely have concluded with an excursus on the fragmentary and non-identical character of Beethoven's "late style." Yet this would be to infer theoretical significance from a personal difficulty. The fact remains that Adorno's own *Hauptwerk* is not truly an alienated masterpiece, but simply an unrealized one.

Yet even today the centrality of Beethoven to Adorno's overall theoretical project is rarely acknowledged, and it is not hard to explain why.

Since its earliest reception, Adorno's work and critical theory in general have been understood primarily within the tradition of Western Marxism, for which a driving concern was to repair the broken relation between the dominant idioms of mass culture and the prevailing tendencies in proletarian life. Accordingly, the initial impulse for cultural criticism was to explain the potential *obstructions* to the formation of working class consciousness, whether these were understood after Lukács as "reification," or after Gramsci as one component within a larger problem of bourgeois cultural "hegemony." Given this interpretive emphasis on the supposed pathologies of class formation, it was perhaps natural that scholars within the tradition of Western Marxism or critical theory devoted a disproportionate share of their attention to the Frankfurt School's theory of the so-called "culture industry." This was especially the case in the United States, where the very name of critical theory came to be associated most of all with certain trends in "popular culture" studies or cultural criticism, which encouraged the focus on pathological features of mass cultural production (e.g., the theory developed in *Dialectic of Enlightenment* concerning patterns of internalized censorship in the Hollywood film studios) or of pseudo-rebellious fashions of popular taste (e.g., Adorno's controversial remarks on jazz). But such interpretations could only function by suppressing the decidedly non-Marxist elements in Adorno's work. Inevitably, this very suppression resulted in reflexive gestures of outrage when it was "discovered" that an ostensibly Marxist theoretician could have harbored such decidedly un-Marxist or elitist tastes. Since the collapse of Eastern bloc Marxist-Leninist regimes, such patterns of misrecognition may be coming slowly to an end. The space was cleared for newer and more elastic interpretations, both neo-Marxist and postmodern.[7] But the basic impression of Adorno as a theorist caught in an apparent contradiction between his cultural preferences and his social program had remained a commonplace of his reception.

An early exception is Martin Jay's 1984 study, *Marxism and Totality*, which devotes little room to the assessment of Adorno's critique of the culture industry, yet takes special care to acknowledge the paradigmatic centrality of Beethoven (and Schoenberg) within Adorno's larger philosophical project. As Jay reminds us, Adorno was "the only Western Marxist who commented extensively upon music as part of his cultural criticism." And "perhaps more important," Jay adds, "*he was the only one who drew from the principles of composition inspiration for this theorizing*" (my emphasis).[8] This is a crucial point, although its significance might easily be missed given that the book's primarily goal was to recapture even the more eccentric themes in Adorno's work within a broader, developmental narrative concerning the Western Marxist discourse of totality. It might be argued, incidentally, that even this larger and highly flexible framework imposed a certain expectation of political *realizability* upon Adorno's thought: it therefore seemed justifiable for Jay to conclude by noting that "Adorno's work inevitably led into a kind of cul-de-sac, at least from a political point of view."[9] But even while this emphasis on the political realization of theory may have reinforced a persistently Marxian subordination of theory to practice, the fact remains that Jay was among the first readers to appreciate the significance of Adorno's musicological work as a privileged laboratory for the *development* of theoretical principles, and not as an *application* of a prior theory. More recently, scholars in musicology such as Rose Rosengard Subotnik and Max Paddison have taken up this same insight to create a truly integrated portrait of Adorno as both philosopher *and* musicologist.[10] But Paddison's 1993 study, *Adorno's Aesthetics of Music*, does not address the Beethoven-book, which Tiedemann published the very same year. An urgent question today is whether a careful study of the Beethoven-book might eventually compel us to revise some of our most fundamental convictions about Adorno's philosophy overall.

The Origins of Late-Style: Adorno in the 1930s and 1940s

According to Adorno, Beethoven's music came into its fullest realization only in the works from the final decade of the composer's life (*circa* 1815 to 1827), which exhibit what Adorno termed "late-style" (*Spätstil*). The term embraces some of Beethoven's most effective compositions: e.g., the "Hammerklavier" Piano Sonata (Opus 106) and the Ninth Symphony (Opus 125), but also those late works in which Beethoven gave himself over to his most experimental or even erratic tendencies, e.g., the Eleven Bagatelles (Opus 119), the Six Bagatelles (Opus 126), the song "An die Hoffnung" (Opus 94), the song cycle, *An die ferne Geliebte* (Opus 98), and, most important of all, the six late String Quartets (Opus 127 and Opoi 130 through 135). It can even be argued that the term provides the best means for categorizing the uncategorizable *Missa Solemnis* (the Mass in D minor, Opus 123).

Throughout his life, a precise characterization of the late-style remained an issue of key importance for Adorno. His first attempt at a definition can be found in the short essay, "Beethoven's Late-Style," written in 1934 and published in a Czechoslovak journal in 1937 shortly before his American exile.[11] In a 1934 letter to Walter Benjamin, Adorno declared with evident satisfaction that the essay, along with a shorter, then unpublished commentary on the Six Bagatelles, Opus 126, stood as "my *very first* works on Beethoven."[12] The two essays clearly mark the very beginning of Adorno's lifelong struggle to develop a coherent assessment of Beethoven's achievements. But their contents also indicate that these were not simply a musicological commentaries, but rather *philosophical meditations on basic problems of aesthetic form*. An essential feature of the late-style, Adorno notes, is that the composition no longer obeys the basic law of compositional unity. Instead, its "fissures and rifts" (*Risse und Sprünge*) are the only remaining evidence of a creative subject who can no longer unify and claim mastery of his material. In this sense, Adorno argues that "late-style" might be a useful category for understanding not only Beethoven, but other artists as well: "The maturity of the late works of important artists," he writes, "is not like the ripeness of fruit. As a rule, these works are not well rounded, but wrinkled, even fissured [*Sie sind gemeinhin nicht rund, sondern durchfurcht, gar zerrissen*]." They are not easily consumed insofar as "they are apt to lack sweetness." They violate the classical ideal of proportion and harmony and display "more traces of history than of growth."[13]

In the 1934 commentary on the Six Bagatelles (Opus 126), Adorno further elaborated the idea that Beethoven's late-style involved a principled rejection of formal unity and a recourse to aesthetic fragmentation. The last Bagatelle (*Andante amabile e con moto*) was an especially striking case, in that its first theme, notwithstanding its lyricism, seemed "haltingly composed of motif fragments." Its overall structure was remarkable, especially for its beginning and closing bars in *presto*, which were "among the strangest and most enigmatic left behind by the late Beethoven." These enigmatic moments were hardly anomalous, but were instead the very key to the late-style in which one could say *"his form itself tends towards the fragment."* Thus, while technical and interpretive difficulties placed many of the larger late works beyond the reach of most amateur players and listeners, smaller compositions such as the Bagatelles afforded object lessons in the general character of late-style:

> Unsociably, the very late Beethoven makes no concessions to domestic music-making. Faced with the last quartets the amateur violinist is completely out of his depth.... No easy path leads into that petrified landscape. But when Beethoven made the stone speak by carving figures in it with his chisel, the splinters flew under the terrible impact. And as the geologist can discover the true composition of whole strata from tiny, scattered particles of matter, the splinters bear witness to the landscape from which they come: the crystals are the same. Beethoven himself called them bagatelles. Not only are they splinters and documents of the mightiest productive process in music, but their strange brevity reveals at the same time the curious contraction, and the tendency toward the inorganic, which give access to the innermost secret not only of the late Beethoven but perhaps of every great late style.[14]

Adorno thus conceived of "late-style" as a formal category applicable to a wide variety of aesthetic objects (a point that would later inspire Edward Said, among others). But Adorno himself was clear from the beginning that Beethoven's late compositions stood as the supreme paradigms for late-style as such. And they were accordingly the privileged examples for working out essential issues in both aesthetics *and* social philosophy.

To comprehend this exemplary status, one must recall that Adorno understood Beethoven's music as providing something like documentary evidence for the vicissitudes of modern subjectivity. The development of thematic material in particular was interpreted as a personal narrative of education and fulfillment, analogous to the bourgeois novel of self-formation, or *Bildungsroman*. This was especially true of the so-called "heroic" style of Beethoven's middle period, e.g., the Symphony #3 in E-flat Major with its explicit references to Napoleon, and the Symphony #5 in C minor (about which Adorno wrote in an 1941 entry that its "monumental" character outstripped its "truth").[15] Adorno was therefore most especially interested in the transformation of Beethoven's style from the middle to late period, a shift which Adorno interpreted as a fundamental crisis in bourgeois subjectivity:

> The force of subjectivity in the late works is the irascible gesture with which it leaves them. It bursts them asunder, not in order to express itself but, expressionlessly, to cast off the illusion of art. *Of the works it leaves only fragments behind, communicating itself, as if in ciphers, only through the spaces it has violently vacated.*[16]

The notion of late-style therefore emerged in explicit contrast to Beethoven's middle period.[17] If the earlier works exhibited a formal unity corresponding to the Hegelian ideal of an expressive totality, in the later works this ideal was abandoned, often with such finality that the most paradigmatic late compositions sounded simply "expressionless" (*ausdruckslose*). In place of an "individualistic" style that had permitted the subject to express his aims and achieve fulfillment through an almost exhaustive exploration of musical materials, the late-style now appeared dominated by impersonal conventions: decorative trills, cadences, and *fioriture*, or written embellishments. Such mindlessly conventional and even cliché tactics recurred with notable frequency, lending late works such as the Bagatelles an "unconcealed, untransformed bareness." Lacking sovereign or unified intent, the late works were rife with conventions and fragmentary or undeveloped themes that figured as remnants of a no longer heroic consciousness. Thus, the conventions were "no longer imbued and mastered by subjectivity." But the irony of the late works was that this bareness and apparent paucity of expressive material became itself the foundation of a new style. The conventions were turned against convention: The "fissures and rifts" within the last works bore poignant witness to "the ego's finite impotence before Being." The result was the paradox of a style built upon the fragments of a previous style that had been exploded from within: Beethoven "no longer draws together the landscape, now deserted and alienated, into an image." Extremes were not united, but instead were allowed to persist without mediation or development. Phrases were not concluded, but contrasted and broke off suddenly without resolution. The "caesurae" or abrupt stops in the music were "monuments" to a subjectivity that had struggled to break free of the artwork's self-contained totality. "As splinters, derelict and abandoned, they finally themselves become expression."

> The work falls silent as it is deserted, turning its hollowness inwards. Only then is the next fragment added, ordered to its place by escaping subjectivity and colluding for better or worse in what has gone before.... *The fragmented landscape is objective, while the light in which alone it glows is subjective. He does not bring about their harmonious synthesis. As a dissociative force he tears them apart in time, perhaps in order to preserve them for the eternal. In the history of art, late works are the catastrophes.*[18]

Such remarks furnish clear evidence that, already in his earliest musicological studies of Beethoven, Adorno was developing the critique of identity theory he would later articulate in more properly philosophical works as the 1966 *Negative Dialectics* and the late essay "Subject and Object."[19] As early as 1939, he had drafted notes for himself under the title, "Towards a Theory of Beethoven," in which he observed that "Beethoven's music is, in a sense, a means for putting to the test the idea that the whole is the truth." In middle period Beethoven, one could recognize something like a musical realization of Hegelian principles: "The Beethovenian form is an integral whole," Adorno wrote, "in which each individual moment is determined by its function within that whole only to the extent that these individual moments contradict and cancel each other, yet are preserved on a higher level within the whole."[20]

But while the affinity between Hegelian reconciliation and Beethoven's technique of musical "mediation" seemed self-evident, the apparent analogy between them immediately suggested the further thought that *musical form itself* could be used to criticize *the inadequacies of the philosophy*. This was in Adorno's view the signal achievement of late Beethoven works. For while Hegel had fallen into the affirmative thesis that society is a self-identical whole, the late Beethoven had succeeded in criticizing *precisely* this ideological presupposition through the deployment of new compositional techniques. The denial of an expected recapitulation, for example, is both a signal that "formal identity is insufficient," and a confirmation that a more substantive identity remains as *"the possible"* that *"lies outside identity."*[21] This was the case not only for recapitulation, but also for a whole repertoire of "affirmative" gestures characteristic of the classical style, such as transition and harmonic resolution:

> The key to the very late Beethoven probably lies in the fact that in this music *the idea of totality as something already achieved had become unbearable to his critical genius*. The material path taken by this realization within Beethoven's music is one of contraction. The developmental tendency in those works of Beethoven which precede the late style itself is opposed to the principle of transition. The transition is felt to be banal, "inessential"; that is, the relation of disparate moments to the whole which holds them together is seen as no more than a prescribed convention, no longer tenable.[22]

Adorno's verdict was striking: Beethoven's music contained an intrinsic protest against the Hegelian principle that "the whole is the truth." The formal principles of Beethoven's late style therefore exposed the inadequacy of Hegel's philosophy: "Beethoven's music is Hegelian philosophy," Adorno concluded, *"but at the same time it is truer than that philosophy."*[23]

It would be easy to misunderstand this conclusion as an opportunistic recourse to musicological analysis for the sake of an essentially conceptual argument. On the contrary, it is crucial to recognize that according to Adorno, music *itself* through its very *form* articulated a critique of ideological totalization that succeeded *only* thanks to the difference between art and philosophy. Philosophical reflection constructed a reality wholly immanent to its own concepts and it therefore sought to arrive at an affirmative unity of subject and object. By contrast, a work of art depended for its very reality upon the dualism between the art object and the subject who experienced it. Art was therefore in its very form less affirmative and "more critical" than any philosophical reflection. Hence Adorno's notes from 1940:

> The gaze of the work of art, which is manifested in this theme, and wants, through its meaning, to be gazed upon in turn, has something withstanding, resistant about it which is really unknown to idealistic philosophy—for which everything is its own work. In this way the work of art, in the dualism constituted between itself and the beholder (a dualism posited by the art-work itself), *is more real, more critical, less "harmonistic" than philosophy.... The Ninth Symphony puts less faith in identity than does Hegel's philosophy. Art is more real than philosophy in that it acknowledges identity to be appearance.*[24]

By the later 1940s and well into the 1950s, Adorno returned on numerous occasions to the critical potential he had associated with the "cracks and fissures" of Beethoven's late-style. In several of the notebooks, Adorno seems to recall Benjamin's "angel of history" with its backward gaze upon the ruins of human achievement. Late works (which Adorno had previously termed "catastrophes" in the history of art) bespoke the objective "truth" about the world in that their formal fragmentation mirrored the catastrophes of history itself. But this suggests that music was itself analogous to the angel insofar as it afforded a critical perspective upon the world. Yet this criticism, Adorno warned, was itself prone to destruction. Because music was itself irredeemably temporal, it could never fall into the error of unqualified transcendence. In an entry from 1942, Adorno reminded himself of this double-bind: "Relate the end of my study to the teaching of Jewish mysticism about the grass angels, who are created for an instant only to perish in the sacred fire. Music—modeled on the glorification of God, even, and especially, when it opposes the world—resembles these angels. Their very transience, their ephemerality, is glorification." Music was therefore analogous to the grass angels because its temporal form mirrors the "incessant destruction of nature" and can never be reified as pure thought. Beethoven, Adorno concluded, "*composed to its end the absolute transience of music.*"[25]

Such remarks reinforce the impression that for Adorno, the fragmentary character of Beethoven's late-style was not a matter of purely aesthetic concern, but in fact held a special and perhaps even central place within his overall conception of critique. Indeed, the thematic imagery of "fissures and rifts [*Risse und Sprünge*]" (mentioned as early as the 1934 essay on Beethoven's late-style) recurs with variations throughout Adorno's later writing. The memorable "Finale" to *Minima Moralia*, written in 1947, builds upon Benjamin's metaphors of redemptive criticism to suggest that such rifts are not merely marks of aesthetic disunity, but are the signs of a worldly negativity which it is the duty of the critic to expose: "The only philosophy which can be responsibly practiced in the face of despair," Adorno wrote, "is the attempt to contemplate all things as they would present themselves from the standpoint of redemption." But since actual redemption is not at hand, the world cannot yet be contemplated as a seamless totality (as Hegelian identity-theory would require); the critical anticipation of an unrealized utopia actually *demanded* that one pay attention to the world's present disunity. The task of criticism was therefore to "displace and estrange the world, reveal it to be, with its *rifts and crevices* [*Risse und Schründe*], as indigent and distorted as it will appear one day in the messianic light."[26]

Adorno in the 1950s and Beyond: Late Works on Late-Style

Given the pivotal status of Beethoven's late-style within Adorno's philosophy, it is perhaps unsurprising that by the late 1950s, the ambition of writing a unified monograph on all of Beethoven's music began to yield to more modest and more occasional efforts such as the 1957 essay, "Alienated Masterpiece" on the Missa Solemnis. While the forbidding and virtually uncategorizable Missa Solemnis was distinct in many ways from other late compositions such as the final string quartets or the Bagatelles, it nonetheless warranted inclusion under the category of late-style because of what Adorno termed its "aesthetically fractured quality."[27] If it seemed anomalous, then this had to do most of all with its archaism, i.e., its recourse to liturgical forms such as scale steps that resembled "old church music," but were wholly unlike almost anything found in Beethoven's other works. Most of Beethoven's characteristic techniques—the economic use of motive, the muscularity of initial statement and recapitulation, the overall unity of composition, even the basic techniques of development—seemed largely absent.

It was therefore not surprising that listeners often failed to identify its composer. Most of all, it was a work that seemed to lack Beethoven's expressive individualism, that quality that marked him unmistakably as the "prototype of the revolutionary bourgeoisie."[28] "[W]hat is expressive in the Missa is not the modern," Adorno declared, "but the very ancient."[29] Yet despite these many differences, Adorno hastened to add that the Missa Solemnis was nonetheless a specimen of the late-style since it too denied the affirmative and premature reconciliation of the subject with its materials:

> The late Beethoven's demand for truth rejects the illusion of such identity of subjective and objective, which is almost the same thing as the classicist idea. A polarization results. Unity is transcended, yielding fragmentariness. In the last quartets this is achieved by the abrupt, unmediated juxtaposing of bare axiomatic motifs and polyphonic complexes. In its way the Missa, too, sacrifices the idea of synthesis, but it does so by peremptorily debarring from the music a subject which is no longer ensconced in the objectivity of the form but is also unable to generate this form intact from within itself.[30]

The Missa resorted to archaic forms only to better effect its "permanent renunciation" of the classical ideal of expressive subjectivity. But because these forms were lifted out of the past, they remained dislocated from the present such that the entire work functioned as a "sacrifice to the future." In an unpublished note from 1957, Adorno concluded on a familiar theme: "The *aesthetic* fragmentariness of the *Missa* corresponds, despite the closed surface, to the *cracks and fissures* [*Schründen und Rissen*] in the texture of the last string quartets."[31]

By the 1960s, Adorno had produced so many notes and drafts for the much-planned Beethoven-study that it seemed perhaps redundant at that point to gather them into a finished work. The one exception was a speech on late-style for German radio.[32] He turned instead to projects of equally if not more ambitious scope: the *Introduction to the Sociology of Music* (published in 1962), *Negative Dialectics* (1966), and, at the very end of his life, the forbidding manuscript *Aesthetic Theory*, which appeared posthumously and unrevised in 1970. But it would be wrong to conclude that Adorno had left Beethoven wholly behind. In fact, the most perplexing problems in both the sociology of music and the aesthetic theory were a continuation of themes that had first emerged in Adorno's early reflections on Beethoven. Thus, the sociology of music confronted a basic methodological question: how can an apparently nonrepresentational art form such as music bear any relation to social reality? If Adorno emphasized that this was a problem applicable to all modes of musical production, both popular and elite, the reader could hardly fail to notice that Adorno seemed especially concerned to address the relation between sociology and what he called "fully autonomous music." Popular modes of musical expression such as jazz remained (on Adorno's view) bound, explicitly and without mediation, to both their social origins and their social utility, and in such cases the task confronting a musical sociology was relatively straightforward: to decrypt such expression back into the language of instrumental reason. But this was not the case for those higher forms of musical production that had attained greater distance from the social order and therefore embodied a freedom *opposed* to social need: "While autonomous music … also has a place in the social totality and bears its mark of Cain, the idea of freedom lives in it at the same time." To be sure, the emancipatory message inscribed in higher music itself had its social origins in bourgeois emancipation and was therefore traceable to the "infrastructure." But to reduce this message wholly to its social foundation would be to ignore the complexity of the music itself. The sociologist would thereby succumb to "the arbitrariness of political slogans." Whereas popular music was itself absorbed in the social totality, in the case of autonomous music, the distance was simply too pronounced:

> The first social characteristic of autonomous music, as of all modern art, is its distance from society; our job is to recognize, and, if possible, to deduce this distance, not sociologistically to feign a false proximity of what is distant, a false immediacy of what is indirect.[33]

This "distance" was not merely an obstruction to sociological reduction; it was also a negation of the social present. Paradoxically, the bourgeois ideal of useless aesthetic pleasure was therefore not an abstract negation of society (in which case one could rightly condemn it as an ideological opiate, as "absolute music" or "*l'art pour l'art*"), since it retained its social truth as a preserve for critical negativity. The sociology of music must take care to acknowledge that negativity so as to avoid vulgar reductionism. Autonomous music therefore marked something like a limit-case for sociological explanation:

> This is the limit that the social theory of the sociology of music prescribes regarding its proper objects: the great compositions. In fully autonomous music, society in its existing form is opposed ... What society might chalk up to great music as a negative quality, its inutility, is at the same time a negation of society and as such concrete, in keeping with the state of what is negated. This is why musical sociology is forbidden to interpret music as if it were nothing but a continuation of society by other means.[34]

Adorno was ready with many musical cases that could serve to illustrate music's "negative" or critical potential. But one case received special emphasis: the music of Beethoven. The concluding chapter of the *Introduction to the Sociology of Music* (entitled "Mediation") contained an extensive methodological commentary as to how the musical sociologist should develop a non-reductive or *mediated* theory of the relation between music and society. Such a theory was needed if the sociologist did not wish to erase the critical power of autonomous music and thereby collude with the imperatives of affirmative society. For any such theory, Beethoven appeared to offer a supreme test: "If he is the musical prototype of the revolutionary bourgeoisie, he is at the same time the prototype of a music that has escaped from its social tutelage and is esthetically fully autonomous, a servant not longer. His work [therefore] explodes the scheme of a complaisant adequacy of music and society."[35]

Beethoven's music was not only the earliest historical illustration of the emancipatory moment in autonomous music. It was actually the most instructive model of *how* that meaning could be said to inhere in musical form *itself*: its very structure thus allowed it to be at once external to society *and* its immanent negation. On the one hand, any composition by Beethoven was itself a "totality" in that it achieved a compositional structure formally independent of its social origin. On the other hand, precisely because it was a social product, that structure necessarily referred back to its social beginnings. The principle mediating these two imperatives was that of an "imageless" relation between music and society. No musical sociologist could hope to trace discrete elements of the musical structure to its social point of origin since the very ideal of social freedom inherent in that structure blocked any such reduction: "The kinship with that bourgeois libertarianism which rings all through Beethoven's music is a kinship of the dynamically unfolding totality. It is a fitting together under their own law, as becoming, negating, confirming themselves and the whole without looking outward, that his movements come to resemble the world whose forces move them; they do not do it by imitating the world." The social meaning of the compositions therefore *itself* obstructed any mimetic relation between society and musical form: "In Beethoven's music," Adorno concluded," society is conceptlessly known, not photographed."[36]

Yet within the bounds of his musical sociology, Adorno paid little notice to the differences between the compositions of Beethoven's middle and late period. He seemed content to celebrate Beethoven's achievement as an "emancipatory" composer for whom "the category of totality still preserves a picture of the right society."[37] More or less forgotten was the notion, developed as early as the first notebooks and the essay on late-style, that only Beethoven's late compositions provided a "truthful" knowledge of the social whole precisely because they *rejected* the ideological consolations of formal unity. There was no mention of those "rifts and fissures" in the late-style works that were supposed to function as negations against false totality and, therefore, as anticipations pointing beyond the artwork to an unrealized social whole. The music had performed the task of criticism as an internal function of its own form. But in the *Sociology of Music*, this internal claim was momentarily forgotten. What had once been a formal and immanent feature of Beethoven's music itself was now presented as a task for the *social critic* whose charge it was to make structural negativity explicit:

> Music is not an ideology pure and simple; it is ideological only insofar as it is a false consciousness. Accordingly, a sociology of music would have to set in at the *fissures and fractures* of what happens in it, unless those are attributable merely to the subjective inadequacy of the individual composer. Musical sociology is social critique accomplished through that of art.[38]

The critical and anticipatory significance of aesthetic fragmentation was to return as a central theme in Adorno's *Aesthetic Theory* (published posthumously in 1970). Adorno now embraced the universal principle that an artwork can achieve truth only if it has internalized social disunity as its formal law. And the privileged example of aesthetic negativity was Beethoven's late-style. This point may strike some readers as controversial. Many assume that Adorno was most responsive to the critical potentials of aesthetic *modernism* and that his aesthetic theory therefore reserved its highest esteem only for those works of modernist art (by, e.g., Schoenberg, Beckett, Celan) created in the shadow of twentieth-century catastrophe. J.M. Bernstein, for example, reasons that for Adorno, modernist works of art were "ideal candidates" for the fugitive or metaphysical experiences of ethical possibility in an otherwise unethical world.[39] And Raymond Geuss reiterates a common misperception that for Adorno critical resistance against the catastrophes of modernity were to be found *only* in the avant-guarde artworks of the early twentieth century (especially those of the "second" Vienna School).[40] It is therefore crucial to recognize that modernist artworks could be assigned this seemingly privileged status in Adorno's thought only because they exhibited formal characteristics *already anticipated by the artworks of the previous century*. The point is especially instructive as it signals Adorno's dissent from the contextualist historicism implicit in the Marxian principle that each epoch must possess its own unique modes of expression. Against this historicist principle, Adorno seemed ready to admit that certain formal characteristics inhered in the very nature of the aesthetic, notwithstanding any mechanistic laws that might refer the artwork back to its social-historical point of origin. Yet, even while such characteristics belonged to the *essence* of aesthetic expression, Adorno still insisted that aesthetic transcendence as such would always bear traces of the damaged social landscape it transcends: "The basic levels of experience that motivate art," he explained, "are related to those of the objective world from which they recoil." But this was true in principle of *all* aesthetic experience and not of modernism alone: since all works of art emerged as products of an unresolved social reality, aesthetic unity *as such* now stood condemned as ideological falsification. By contrast, the internally broken character of an artwork was a mark of its social truth: hence Adorno's guiding interpretative principle in the *Aesthetic Theory*: "The unresolved antagonisms of reality return in artworks as immanent problems of form."[41]

Adorno's aesthetic principles thus appear to be axiomatic rather than an historical or sociological reflex. Thus, even if one accepts, for example, the art historian Serge Guilbaut's claim that postwar modernism in North America received its imprimatur of cultural validity *because of* its apolitical (and politically anti-Marxist) reputation as the aesthetic of heroic individualism, such efforts to historicize modernist tastes as Cold War fashion would still leave unexplained any *immanent* continuities between modernism and prior aesthetic styles.[42] Such continuities mark the limits of Marxian historicism. And they may prompt us to question whether the critical reception of Adorno's aesthetics under the customarily sociopolitical couplet—"modernism" and "late-capitalism"—still merits our assent.[43]

It seems clear in any case that Adorno's aesthetic of fragmentation was not just a development "after Auschwitz" or particular to the horrors of the twentieth century. Citations to "catastrophe" notwithstanding, its application can hardly be limited to, for example, the ruinous spectacles of Anselm Kiefer.[44] The aesthetic appeal to "rifts and crevices" is traceable to Adorno's earliest commentary on Beethoven, but it came to be axiomatic for all works of art. But this meant that late-style itself now enjoyed a transhistorical validity and was conceived as synonymous with aesthetic truth:

> If there is something like a common characteristic of great late works, it is to be sought in the breaking through of form by spirit. This is no aberration of art but rather its fatal corrective. Its highest products are condemned to a fragmentariness that is their confession even that they do not possess what is claimed by the immanence of their form.[45]

Although "late-style" was originally a category confined in its application to Beethoven's late compositions, the term as Adorno used it in his own later years had swelled in significance: it now described the formal law of antagonism governing *all* genuine art. "Aesthetic experience must overstep itself," wrote Adorno in the draft introduction to *Aesthetic Theory*. Any phenomenon of aesthetic value was necessarily caught irredeemably between the "antithetical extremes" of its social genesis and its own immanent structure: "It traverses its antithetical extremes rather than settling peacefully into a spurious median between them. It neither renounces philosophical motifs, which it transforms rather than drawing conclusions from them, nor does it exorcise from itself the social element." Although this was perhaps the case of all artistic production, it became the immanent sign of "truth" only where the artwork registered its own self-contradiction between genesis and immanence in purely aesthetic terms:

> One is no more equal to a Beethoven symphony without comprehending its so-called musical course than if one is unable to perceive in it the echo of the French Revolution; how these two aspects are mediated in the phenomenon belongs to the obstinate and equally unavoidable themes of philosophical aesthetics.... *Consciousness of the antagonism between interior and exterior is requisite to the experience of art.*[46]

Here, then, was Adorno's conclusion after decades of musical and philosophical reflection: for aesthetic experience to "overstep itself" required that the antagonism between aesthetic pleasure and social need—between interior and exterior—must *become internal*, a formal characteristic within the artwork that pointed beyond the artwork itself; thus Adorno's conclusion: "The spirit of artworks is bound up with their form, but spirit is such *only insofar as it points beyond that form.*"[47]

But this could only mean that the artwork—and here Adorno seemed to mean *any artwork as such*—must exhibit the internal fragmentation previously identified as a distinctive feature of late-style. The argument was striking and no doubt controversial: since the very beginning of his career, Adorno had struggled to articulate the larger significance of the late-style he had first discovered in Beethoven's compositions. By the end of his career, he seems to have concluded that late-style was not merely a preferential option amongst many aesthetic possibilities; it was quite simply the highest realization of autonomous art.

Conclusion

After this brief excursion through Adorno's various writings on musical aesthetics, the question arises: was Adorno a social theorist whose chief object was music, or a musical theorist whose chief object was society? It may seem fruitless to choose between these alternatives. But it is hard to suppress the idea that notwithstanding his commitment to social criticism, Adorno cleaved throughout his life to an ideal of thinking that was primarily *aesthetic*, even if this thinking was then directed toward questions of social life. In a 1948 entry in the notebooks, he condensed this ideal into the dictum that "One can no longer compose like Beethoven, but one must *think* as he composed."[48]

Whether Adorno was successful in realizing this ideal is disputable. There is admittedly a great deal of creativity and perhaps even arbitrary interpretation in the manner Adorno understood Beethoven's compositions. The *Missa Solemnis* (especially the lyrical *Benedictus*) is not nearly so alien a presence within Beethoven's overall physiognomy as Adorno claimed it to be. Nor is "late-style" always evident in all of the later compositions. The first movement of the String Quartet in E flat Major (Opus 127) is as "bourgeois" and "heroic" as the Third Symphony (Opus 55), also in E flat Major. The Piano Sonata in B flat Major (Opus 106, the *Hammerklavier*) exhibits a stylistic unity over long stretches of melody that qualifies any talk of aesthetic fragmentation. And from the other end, much of what Adorno saw as the breakdown of unity already belongs to the "playful" interruptions intrinsic to Haydn, Beethoven's predecessor in the classical style.[49] Nor should we resist asking more basic methodological and metaphysical questions about Adorno's overall manner of interpretation: why, after all, should we *accept* the claim that musical fragmentation points to a social reality beyond the music itself? Social decryption of formalism is only one mode of musicology and hardly the most obvious. If this claim remains enigmatic, however, its truth is nonetheless presupposed in everything Adorno wrote concerning the social-critical import of late-style.

The fact remains that music—and, most especially, Beethoven's music—was for Adorno the very model of what it is like to *think*.[50] The analogy may help us to understand the notorious difficulty of Adorno's own written style. Returning to Adorno's philosophical texts after reading his notebooks on Beethoven, one cannot fail but notice the recurrence of certain stylistic idiosyncrasies: fragmentation, paradox, and a habit of statement that reverses its own manifest meaning for the sake of an unrealized alternative. In the 1969 radio lecture, "Resignation," Adorno went so far as to claim that this anticipatory gesture belonged to the very essence of *thinking as such*:

> As long as thinking is not interrupted, it has a firm grasp on possibility. Its insatiable quality, the resistance against petty satiety, rejects the foolish wisdom of resignation. The utopian impulse in thinking is all the stronger, the less it objectifies itself as utopia—a further form of regression—whereby it sabotages its own realization. *Open thinking points beyond itself.*"[51]

Critical theory was therefore by definition an *anticipatory* mode of thought. Martin Jay includes this passage in *Marxism and Totality* to demonstrate that Adorno (notwithstanding his troubled relation to the German New Left) remained forever faithful even in his final years to the ideal of an unrealized utopia. But it deserves notice that Adorno's definition makes no reference to any particular thought *content*. What Adorno called a "firm grasp on possibility" was a *formal* characteristic of thought unconditional upon any substantive concepts or doctrines. This emphasis on form itself would seem to imply that his commitment to possibility was grounded as much in purely *aesthetic* considerations as in the utopian energies of Western Marxism.[52] Aesthetic form, particularly musical form, may have furnished Adorno with the initial template for critical theory.[53]

It is therefore instructive to recall that throughout the later 1920s, the young Adorno still entertained the hope of becoming a composer.[54] Although eventually he abandoned this ambition (when he realized, perhaps, that his hopes outstripped his talents), he was still determined to think as Beethoven had composed. The essential requirement was to preserve for reflection itself the autonomy and possibility that had initially attracted his notice as immanent characteristics of musical form.[55] In a 1962 essay (which Adorno dedicated to his friend and teacher Walter Benjamin), Adorno observed that:

As a temporal art, music is bound to the fact of succession and is hence as irreversible as time itself. By starting it commits itself to carrying on, to becoming something new, to developing. What we may conceive of as musical transcendence, namely, the fact that at any given moment it has become something and something other than what it was, that *points beyond itself*—all that is no mere metaphysical imperative dictated by some external authority. It lies in the nature of music and will not be denied.[56]

The above considerations may prompt us to conclude that for Adorno critical reflection and utopia were *modeled after musical form*. Theological imagery such as inspired Benjamin could be considered mere surplus if redemptive inspiration could be found in music alone. As Adorno observed: "Freedom is an intrinsic necessity for music." Formalism therefore culminated in normative content. If freedom always stood as the unrepresentable to any totality, it is perhaps unsurprising that Adorno discovered the "imageless image" of freedom in the most non-representative of the arts.

Notes

1. This basic problem—that music *must somehow* relate meaningfully to the social order—stands at the center of Adorno's writing. For an alternative view suggesting Adorno's commitment to the German tradition of absolute music, see Michael Steinberg, "The Musical Absolute" *New German Critique*, no. 56, Special Issue on Theodor W. Adorno (Spring–Summer, 1992): 17–42.
2. Max Paddison, "Immanent Critique or Musical Stocktaking? Adorno and the Problem of Musical Analysis," in *Adorno: A Critical Reader*, ed. Nigel Gibson and Andrew Rubin (Malden, MA, 2002), 210.
3. Stefan Müller-Doohm, *Adorno: A Life*, trans. Rodney Livingstone (Cambridge, 2005), 482.
4. These facts from Rolf Tiedemann, "Editor's Preface," in Adorno, *Beethoven, The Philosophy of Music: Fragments and Texts*, ed. Tiedemann, trans. Edmund Jephcott (Stanford, 1998), vii-viii.
5. Müller-Doohm, *Adorno: A Biography*, 482.
6. Adorno, *Beethoven*, 162, 50, 165.
7. See Hohendahl, "Introduction: Adorno Criticism Today," *New German Critique*, no. 56. Special Issue on Theodor W. Adorno (Spring–Summer, 1992): 3–15.
8. Martin Jay, *Marxism and Totality, The Adventures of a Concept from Lukács to Habermas* (Berkeley Los Angeles, 1984), 252.
9. Ibid., 274.
10. Max Paddison, *Adorno's Aesthetics of Music* (New York, 1993); Rose Rosengard Subotnik, *Developing Variations: Style and Ideology in Western Music* (Minneapolis, MN, 1991). Also see the crucial essay by Subotnik, "Adorno's Diagnosis of Beethoven's Late-Style: Early Symptom of a Fatal Condition," *Journal of the American Musicological Society* 29, no. 2 (Summer, 1976): 242–275. Also see the essays in *Adorno: A*

Critical Reader, especially Subotnik, "Adorno and the New Musicology," 234–254; Paddison, "Immanent Critique or Musical Stocktaking?," 209–233; and Edward Said, "Adorno as Lateness Itself," 193–208.

11. "Spätstil Beethovens" originally published in *Der Auftakt: Blätter für die tschechoskowakiche Republik*, 17, nos. 5/6 (1937), reprinted in *Moments musicaux* (Frankfurt, 1964), and in Adorno, *Gesammelte Schriften*, 20 vols., ed. Tiedemann (Frankfurt, 1997), 17: 13–17. In English in Adorno, *Beethoven*, 123–126.
12. Theodor W. Adorno and Walter Benjamin, *The Complete Correspondence, 1928–1940*, ed. Henri Lonitz, trans. Nicholas Walker (Cambridge, MA, 2001), 38 (letter dated 5 April 1934).
13. "Beethoven's Late Style," 123–126.
14. Adorno, "Ludwig Van Beethoven: Six Bagatelles for Piano, op. 126," in English in Tiedemann, *Beethoven*, 130–132; in German in *Gesammelte Schriften*, 18: 185–189.
15. Adorno, *Beethoven*, 109. On the "heroic" style as found in the middle period works see Scott Burnham, *Beethoven Hero* (Princeton, NJ, 2000).
16. "Beethoven's Late Style" in Adorno, *Beethoven*, 123–126; 125, my emphasis.
17. Frederic Jameson, otherwise so attentive to the ways that Adorno conceived aesthetic *form*, tells us that Beethoven's music represented for Adorno the possibility of "synthesis," "totality," and "reconciliation." But this is *only* true of middle period Beethoven, and it altogether fails to acknowledge Adorno's higher esteem for the later works. See Jameson, *Marxism and Form: Twentieth-Century Dialectical Theories of Literature* (Princeton, NJ, 1971), 38–51.
18. "Beethoven's Late Style" in Adorno, *Beethoven*, 126, my emphasis.
19. Adorno, "Subject and Object," *The Essential Frankfurt School Reader*, ed. Andrew Arato and Eike Gebhardt (Oxford, 1978), 497–511.
20. "Towards a Theory of Beethoven," in Adorno, *Beethoven*, 13.
21. Ibid., 14, my emphasis at "truer than that philosophy" and "the possible which lies outside identity."
22. Ibid., written in 1939.
23. Ibid.
24. Ibid., fragment 31; written 1940; my emphasis.
25. Ibid., 176–177; originally written 1942.
26. Adorno, "Finale," from *Minima Moralia, Reflections from Damaged Life*, trans. E.F.N. Jephcott (London, 1978), 247, my emphasis.
27. Adorno, *Beethoven*, 153.
28. Adorno, *Introduction to the Sociology of Music*, trans. E.B. Ashton (New York, 1976), 209.
29. Adorno, *Beethoven*, 148.
30. Ibid., 152.
31. Ibid., 141, this entry dated 1957. German Edition: Theodor W. Adorno, *Beethoven: Philosophie der Musik. Fragmente und Texte*, ed. Rolf Tiedemann (Frankfurt am Main, 1993). "Das *ästhetisch* Brüchige der Missa entspricht, bei geschlossener Oberfläche, den *Schründen und Rissen* in der Faktur der Letzten Quartette"), 203, my emphasis.
32. On radio he offered the following remarks (occasioned by the F major Quartet) that
    in the latest Beethoven, the fabric, the interweaving of voices to form something harmoniously rounded, is deliberately cut back. In Beethoven's late style there is altogether something like a tendency towards dissociation, decay, dissolution, but not in the sense of a process of composition which no longer holds things together: the dissociation and disintegration themselves become artists means, and works which have been brought to a rounded conclusion take on

through these means, despite their roundedness, something spiritually fragmentary. Thus, in the works which are typical of the true late style of Beethoven, the closed acoustic surface which is otherwise so characteristic of the sound of the string quartet with its perfect balance, also disintegrates.

Quoted from Adorno, "Beethoven's Late Style" in Adorno, *Beethoven*, Appendix 3, Text 9, 189.

33. Adorno, *Sociology*, 204.
34. Ibid., 204–205.
35. Ibid., 209.
36. Ibid., 209. Similar claims can be found in the Beethoven-notebooks: e.g., "Beethoven may not represent an attempt to *circumvent* the ban on images. His music is not an image of anything, and yet is an image of the whole: an imageless image." Tiedemann, *Beethoven*, 8.
37. Ibid., 64.
38. Ibid., 63.
39. J.M. Bernstein, *Adorno: Disenchantment and Ethics* (Cambridge, MA, 2001), 38.
40. Raymond Geuss, "Art and Criticism in Adorno," in Geuss, *Outside Ethics* (Princeton, NJ, 2005), 161–183.
41. Theodor W. Adorno, *Aesthetic Theory*, ed. Gretel Adorno and Rolf Tiedemann, trans. Robert Hullot-Kentor (Minneapolis, MN, 1997), 6.
42. Serge Guilbaut, *How New York Stole the Idea of Modern Art: Expressionism, Freedom, and the Cold War*, trans. Arthur Goldhammer (Chicago, IL, 1983).
43. See, e.g., Eugene Lunn, *Marxism and Modernism: An Historical Study of Lukács, Brecht, Benjamin, and Adorno* (Los Angeles and Berkeley, CA, 1984); and Frederic Jameson, *Late Marxism: Adorno, or, The Persistence of the Dialectic* (London, 1990).
44. Lisa Saltzman, *Anselm Kiefer and Art after Auschwitz* (Cambridge, 1999).
45. Adorno, *Aesthetic Theory*, 90.
46. Ibid., 349.
47. Ibid., 89.
48. Adorno, *Beethoven*, 160.
49. On the Hammerklavier and its unity, see Charles Rosen, *The Classical Style: Haydn, Mozart, Beethoven* (New York, 1972), e.g., 34–35, and passim.
50. This may be the deeper import behind Edward Said's observation that late-style was not simply a topic for aesthetic criticism, but that Adorno *as a critic* was "lateness itself." See Said, "Adorno as Lateness Itself," in Gibson and Rubin, *Adorno, A Critical Reader*.
51. Adorno, "Resignation," as quoted in Jay: *Marxism and Totality*, 264 (emphasis added). Jay quotes from Adorno's essay, originally composed in 1969, a year before his death.
52. This point has been made in different ways by both Jürgen Habermas and Seyla Benhabib. Both authors conclude (in a rather preemptive fashion) that because Adorno's grounding for utopia is *aesthetic rather than discursive*, it fails the test of rational justification. But this conclusion denies in advance Adorno's unusual notion that the aesthetic is in itself a preserve of critical consciousness. To identify Adorno's argumentation as "aesthetic" does not yet prove it is indefensible. See Habermas, *The Philosophical Discourse of Modernity*, trans Frederick G. Lawrence (Cambridge, MA,1987), and Benhabib, *Critique, Norm, Utopia: A Study of the Foundations of Critical Theory* (New York, 1986).
53. Hence Frederic Jameson's insightful comments on form, and the form of the essay as "the fragments of or footnotes to a totality which never comes into being." He fur-

ther remarks that "dialectical thinking" for Adorno demands "dialectical sentences" in Jameson, *Marxism and Form*, 52–53.
54. See Müller-Doohm, *Adorno, A Biography*, 107.
55. For a similar point, see J.M. Bernstein's remark that for Adorno art "systematically thematizes" our special and "fugitive" experiences of metaphysical possibility. The question thus arises whether philosophy must render such possibility in concepts or whether "the works themselves" might be considered (quite independent of philosophical elaboration) "the demonstration of possibility." Bernstein, 440–441.
56. From Theodor W. Adorno, "Stravinsky: A Dialectical Portrait," in *Quasi una fantasia: Essays on Modern Music*, trans. Rodney Livingstone (New York, 1998), 150–151.

Bibliography

Adorno, Theodor. *Aesthetic Theory*. Edited by Gretel Adorno and Rolf Tiedemann. Translated by Robert Hullot-Kentor. Minneapolis, MN, 1997.
———. *Beethoven: Philosophie der Musik: Fragmente und Texte*. Edited by Rolf Tiedemann. Frankfurt, 1993.
———. *Beethoven, the Philosophy of Music: Fragments and Texts*. Edited by Rolf Tiedemann. Translated by Edmund Jephcott. Stanford, 1998.
———. "Finale." In *Minima Moralia: Reflections from Damaged Life*. translated by E.F.N. Jephcott. London, 1978.
———. *Gesammelte Schriften*. 20 vols. Edited by Rolf Tiedemann. Frankfurt, 1997.
———. *Introduction to the Sociology of Music*. Translated by E.B. Ashton. New York, 1976.
———."Stravinsky: A Dialectical Portrait." In *Quasi una fantasia: Essays on Modern Music*, translated by Rodney Livingstone. New York, 1998.
———."Subject and Object." In *The Essential Frankfurt School Reader*, edited by Andrew Arato and Eike Gebhardt. Oxford, 1978.
——— and Walter Benjamin. *The Complete Correspondence, 1928–1940*. Edited by Henri Lonitz. Translated by Nicholas Walker. Cambridge, MA, 2001.
Benhabib, Seyla. *Critique, Norm, Utopia: A Study of the Foundations of Critical Theory*. New York, 1986.
Bernstein, J.M. *Adorno: Disenchantment and Ethics*. Cambridge, MA, 2001.
Burnham, Scott. *Beethoven Hero*. Princeton, NJ, 2000.
Geuss, Raymond. "Art and Criticism in Adorno." In *Outside Ethics*. Princeton, NJ, 2005.
Guilbaut, Serge. *How New York Stole the Idea of Modern Art: Expressionism, Freedom, and the Cold War*. Translated by Arthur Goldhammer. Chicago, 1983.
Habermas, Jürgen. *The Philosophical Discourse of Modernity*. Translated by Frederick G. Lawrence. Cambridge, 1987.
Jameson, Frederic. *Late Marxism: Adorno, or, The Persistence of the Dialectic*. London, 1990.
———. *Marxism and Form: Twentieth-Century Dialectical Theories of Literature*. Princeton, NJ, 1971.
Jay, Martin. *Marxism and Totality: The Adventures of a Concept from Lukács to Habermas*. Los Angeles and Berkeley, 1984.
Lunn, Eugene. *Marxism and Modernism: An Historical Study of Lukács, Brecht, Benjamin, and Adorno*. Berkeley, CA, 1984.

Müller-Doohm, Stefan. *Adorno: A Life*. Translated by Rodney Livingstone. Cambridge, 2005.
Paddison, Max. *Adorno's Aesthetics of Music*. New York, 1993.
———. "Immanent Critique or Musical Stocktaking? Adorno and the Problem of Musical Analysis." In *Adorno: A Critical Reader*, edited by Nigel Gibson and Andrew Rubin. Malden, MA, 2002.
Rosen, Charles. *The Classical Style: Haydn, Mozart, Beethoven*. New York, 1972.
Saltzman, Lisa. *Anselm Kiefer and Art after Auschwitz*. Cambridge, 1999.
Steinberg, Michael. "The Musical Absolute." *New German Critique*, no. 56 (1992): 17–42.
Subotnik, Rose Rosengard. "Adorno's Diagnosis of Beethoven's Late-Style: Early Symptom of a Fatal Condition." *Journal of the American Musicological Society* 29, no. 2 (Summer, 1976): 242–275.
———. *Developing Variations: Style and Ideology in Western Music*. Minneapolis, MN, 191.

MARXISM AND ALTERITY
Claude Lefort and the Critique of Totality

Samuel Moyn

On 3 May 1961, in the evening, as he prepared his lesson for the next day at the Collège de France, the institution at the summit of French intellectual life where he had taught for almost a decade, Maurice Merleau-Ponty's heart stopped.[1] He was fifty-three years old. Though devastated by his teacher's untimely death, Claude Lefort, who became Merleau-Ponty's literary executor and editor as well as a fundamentally important philosopher himself, offered a memorial essay in *Les Temps modernes* that has not been recognized as a pivotal document in twentieth-century French thought. Yet it is, in retrospect. From the constant self-revisions he witnessed as a student, and the complex and interrupted departure from Merleau-Ponty's early thought that his final work represented, Lefort argued that the thinker's famous break with his early Marxist politics also involved a shift to *a post-holist ontology*. In offering this interpretation, Lefort not only provided a crucial early instance of the sea change that—for better or worse—would come to inform so much contemporary thought; he also laid the foundations for his own project in political theory.[2]

Yet something remains basically curious, perhaps even questionable, about Lefort's interpretation of Merleau-Ponty, intellectually fecund as it may have been. In his classic history of the tradition that Merleau-Ponty labeled "Western Marxism," Martin Jay also argued—in a strikingly and usefully opposite reading—that Merleau-Ponty's career was best understood as a long and difficult attempt to fuse Marxism and holism. But in Jay's account, Merleau-Ponty's flirtation with Marxist theory and practice eventually fell, not because he finally relinquished his holist philosophical principles, but thanks to his dogged allegiance to them. "Merleau-Ponty's philosophy, indeed his entire outlook on the world, was deeply holistic from the beginning, so much so that when he finally abandoned Marxism, he did so in the name of a competing holism," Jay reported. Much finally separated Merleau-Ponty, therefore, from the poststructuralist challengers to the combination of Marxism and holism whose main rallying cry, as Jay reconstructed it later in the same book, was the opposition to plenitude and thus to any such synthesis.[3] The strength of Jay's alternative reading prompts the questions—which I will try to explore in this chapter—of how Lefort made his very different argument work and why he made it.

Lefort had been activated as a thinker and inducted into political theory specifically by his teacher in the prewar era, and he remained in Merleau-Ponty's orbit as the latter became a founder of the famous postwar journal, *Les Temps modernes*, and, finally, in his last period, a Collège de France luminary. Curiously, in the emerging scholarship on Lefort, and indeed in the monumental literature on Merleau-Ponty, there has been no attention paid to their relationship, which was as essential for founding the project of the former as for shaping the reception of the latter.[4] The position Lefort staked out is not merely of historical interest, for Lefort's interpretation of Merleau-Ponty provided the ground for the turn to democratic theory that has come to define much of the most important contemporary French thought. At the time, Jay saw Claude Lefort's attempt to further Merleau-Ponty's project as one that fizzled out, falling before the fashion of Louis Althusser's structuralism. The passage of time shows that judgment, understandable then, to have been premature. But Lefort's original interpretation, no less than his theoretical reemergence, ratify Jay's own insistence that much rode on the choice between founding social thought not on plenitude, but on what escaped it—not on Marxist holism, but on the claim of alterity that led social theory not simply beyond Marxism, but toward a new interpretation of democracy.

Lefort's powerful depiction of politics as the foundation of social cohesion, and democracy as experiential and experimental, interestingly exploited by his direct followers, remains an important source for contemporary theory. Even so, in spite of proliferating attention, Lefort remains little known and less studied in the Anglo-American world. Eventually a theorist of democracy who taught at the École des Hautes Études en Sciences Sociales, Lefort exercised considerable influence not just on his colleagues such as François Furet, but also on a network of associates and students who have become some of the most prominent theorists in social and historical study of the present time. The political theory of Marcel Gauchet—addressed later in this essay—as well as the work of Pierre

Rosanvallon flow out of this tradition. The formative moment in the school of thought Lefort founded, I argue, was in a recondite but revealing interpretation of his own teacher's work.

Philosophy and Politics

It can be said in a general way that Merleau-Ponty's mission all along, together with a host of other French phenomenologists, had been to explore what it might mean to replace the philosophy of consciousness they had inherited as students, when it ruled the Third Republic's departments of philosophy. Throughout, Merleau-Ponty's thought involved (as Lefort later put it) "a critique of the Cartesian démarche, which required a new idea of philosophy."[5] The stages of Merleau-Ponty's experimentation with a non-Cartesian philosophy, with subjectivity rooted in the body and isolated perceptual acts dependent on prior community, have been endlessly discussed, of course. But it remains evident that beginning with his classic *Phenomenology of Perception* of 1945, Merleau-Ponty adopted the holistic commitment perhaps most definitional of the twentieth-century philosophy. Cartesianism, notably that promoted by prior French thought, promoted a model of disengaged knowing. Holism, now permanently associated with Martin Heidegger's innovations, criticized the epistemological focus of much modern philosophy by holding that knowing is dependent on practice; the implication for philosophy is that it must, as Merleau-Ponty constantly admonished, give up the model of high-flown spectatorship and see from within the world, replacing a quest for certainty with a respect for ambiguity, with knowledge even at its most theoretical bound to its framing and holistic conditions of possibility. There is no transcending the whole, constituting it from without, as opposed to being situated from within.[6]

Such implications were hardly absent from Merleau-Ponty's early work; on the contrary, they were there from the start. "Radical reflection," he said, for example, in his famous preface to *Phenomenology of Perception*, "amounts to a consciousness of its own dependence on an unreflective life which is its initial constant, and final situation."[7] Yet Merleau-Ponty went on in the same book to reinstate in "tacit" form the *cogito* he began the book by claiming to topple, and this fact prepared the ground for the view later advanced by Lefort that the realization of his program required a full-scale break from his early masterpiece. In the contribution to a special issue of *Les Temps modernes* commemorating Merleau-Ponty's life and work (in spite of his acrimonious departure from the journal a few years before), Lefort began by citing his teacher's comment that Edmund Husserl's last manuscripts alone illustrated how radically he intended to break with idealism. "The more phenomenology develops," Merleau-Ponty had written of the discipline's founder, "the more accurately philosophers are distinguishing it from the new philosophy of consciousness in whose guise it originally presented itself." Lefort added: "Speaking of Husserl, Merleau-Ponty is speaking about himself."[8] The true novelty of Merleau-Ponty's philosophy had to be extracted from his career through emphasis on his final manuscripts—on the model of Merleau-Ponty's interpretation of Husserl before him.

Above all, of course, Lefort referred to Merleau-Ponty's most important *opus postumum*, which appeared three years later as *The Visible and the Invisible* under his editorship. But Lefort's pivotal essay also introduced the kernel of a decisively important interpretation of Merleau-Ponty's political itinerary (one he would expand in an equally important article dating from this same early 1960s moment). And it is clear that Lefort's reading of Merleau-Ponty's overall trajectory was always refracted though the student's reading of the teacher's political evolution. This linkage of Merleau-Ponty's speculative itinerary to his political conversion—a controversial choice at the opposite pole from Anglo-American interpretations that typically view the former in isolation from the latter—has to be examined as a frame for Lefort's argument for the departure from holism.[9]

Marxism and Existentialism

It is true that Merleau-Ponty's self-interpretations always searched for a way to see consistency between his theoretical and his political positions. Especially since it seems so unlikely that the theoretical shifts exactly matched—much less motivated—his political journey, it was an additional act of filial piety for Lefort to insist on their congruence in retrospect. "Who would deny," Lefort asked rhetorically in *Les Temps modernes*, "that everything that he wrote on [politics and history] belonging to his work is bound up in it with the rest with such clear self-evidence that when we are in its presence, whatever its diversity, it is as if it were the presence of a person. The secret of his work, like that of all really great works, is that it makes what is scattered in our experience and to be found on all sides hang together without artifice."[10] Yet reading Lefort, it is impressive how seamless he was able to make the fusion of philosophy and politics in his reconstruction of Merleau-Ponty's career seem.

In the beginning, Merleau-Ponty strikingly proposed in a long footnote of *Phenomenology of Perception* to interpret historical materialism as a theory of "interhuman relations as they are actually established in concrete living."[11] In his next book, *Humanism and Terror* (1947), he tried to spell out this unexpected thesis, contending that Karl Marx was in effect a prophet of the very post-Cartesian and socialized existentialism Merleau-Ponty had laid out in his phenomenology. Of course, this argument presupposed that the usual interpretations–especially the scientific ones–of Marx were false. Marx, Merleau-Ponty insisted, never rose above history, like a soul out of the body, in claiming to know its rules and foresee its fate. According to Merleau-Ponty, Marxism could not possibly involve the "adoration of an unknown god," as Arthur Koestler (and later interpreters of the position of Merleau-Ponty's own essay) claimed. Instead, it was part of the point of Marxism that "our understanding of history should be partial since every consciousness is historically situated," and so it claimed to develop its advocacy of revolution based on an analysis of "concrete subjectivity and concrete action."[12] At this stage, of course, Merleau-Ponty saw no need, or had no ability, to distinguish his Heideggerian commitment to human situatedness from his Hegelian commitment to the gathering in history of a drive to the recognition of man by man (as he frequently put it). And so he argued that it was precisely Marxism's critique of subjectivism, its immersion of man in the "interworld" of others and things, that licensed the faith of its adepts in—and their violent wagers on—a humanity reconciled to itself through its historical becoming.

This was a hard argument, to say the least, and one that Merleau-Ponty soon relinquished. Yet in his essays, Lefort claimed to see even in *Humanism and Terror*—especially its more irenic closing sections, which accepted at least some evidence about the shipwreck of the Soviet experiment—the basis on which Merleau-Ponty would ultimately break with his "superficial" commitment to Marxism, to the point that his eventual conversion away from his early politics could be understood as an act faithful to the philosophy that initially led to Marxism's embrace. In *The Adventures of the Dialectic*, his history of "Western" Marxist theory and practice of 1955, Merleau-Ponty concluded that, far from the philosophy of embedded praxis that Georg Lukács had rediscovered at the beginning of the tradition, Marxism ended as a doctrine of the wholly passive objectivity of the workers, who could nonetheless surge in revolution from nothingness, thanks to their guidance from without, both before and after their revolution, by some all-knowing party able like Descartes's ego to abolish its facticity and transcend history. If so, Marxism's original promise had been betrayed, with the outcome of the proletariat in history understanding nothing and the party able to offer a claim of knowledge implausibly transcending the constitutive limitations of human existence. For Merleau-Ponty, it remained a fundamental condition of analysis—if argued far more insistently now—that philosophy, especially of history as a whole, respect its own limitations, which were ones that followed from holist premises. "Thought ... does not constitute the whole but is situated in it," he insisted, in *Adventures of the Dialectic*. "Politics is never able to see the whole directly."[13] The disappointing result of a Marxism that could somehow transcend its situation—disappointing philosophically no less than politically—convinced Merleau-Ponty that Marx's thought, whatever its initial promise, violated the requirement of remaining in an ambiguous history and of respecting an indeterminate being. The subject matter of philosophy was not subjectively "constituted" knowledge, but intersubjectively "instituted" practice.

These were the ultimate reasons, Lefort concluded, that Merleau-Ponty's politics shifted. It bears emphasizing, of course, that this unique reading of Merleau-Ponty's political trajectory has the effect of nearly reversing the verdict famously on offer by the harshest critics of Parisian philocommunism, which treats theory as a fallout of politics rather than the authority for it. On the basis of his reading, however, Lefort could later accord *Humanism and Terror* the status of "a great book" since it "contains the conditions for surpassing" its own politics. Indeed, it introduces "the materials for a reinvention of the concept of history."[14] It was a lacuna of Merleau-Ponty's reception, for Lefort at least, that few understood Merleau-Ponty's late work his way, and reviewing in 1969 the interpretations of it that had accumulated to that point, Lefort could note with regret that "the evolution of Merleau-Ponty's political thought has hardly been interrogated."[15] Needless to say, it has hardly been interrogated in the way Lefort undertook since, either.

Interpreting Merleau-Ponty's Unfinished Masterpiece

This explanation of political conversion had undoubted effects on Lefort's reading of Merleau-Ponty's evolution from *Phenomenology of Perception* to his final torso of a book, *The Visible and the Invisible*. It remains paradoxical, however, that in a sense Lefort's interpretation made the story of Merleau-Ponty's political choices more continuous than tumultuous, in spite of a spectacular break, even as he came to argue that Merleau-Ponty's general philosophy turned out to be far more evolutionary than static, in spite of obvious continuities. For just as Merleau-Ponty placed stress on Husserl's "last manuscripts" to make him out to be a much more subversive figure than the standard image of him suggested, so Lefort came to insist that Merleau-Ponty's own final thinking struck out in a radically new, if now permanently incomplete, direction. The key to his interpretation was Merleau-Ponty's own sense, announced prior to his death and made graphic in a number of posthumous fragments, that the story of his career was a commitment to holism whose full implications he did not originally grasp. His celebrated if enigmatic descriptions of the flesh of the world, like his emphasis on the chiasmatic intertwining of perception and being, suggested he felt the need to strain more resolutely against his philosophical inheritances than he had ever done before. But Lefort precisely did not see this as a final attempt to purify holism: an extrapolation from or working out of an initial holism that finally broke entirely with the Cartesianism the thinker had intended, but had failed, to leave behind from the outset. Instead, Lefort insisted that the later Merleau-Ponty turned his back not just on Marxism, but also on holism, and it is crucial to examine the nature and form of his claim.

In the memorial essay of 1961, Lefort left not just the initial but also the most important evidence of how he proposed to read Merleau-Ponty's final phase. It was a matter now of recapturing what "*Phenomenology of Perception* announced," but only emerged in the last years once Merleau-Ponty—as Lefort phrased it—felt no need to be "faithful to an order of questions formulated by classical philosophy."[16] Drawing heavily, again, on Merleau-Ponty's own self-inscription as Husserl's legitimate follower—as if he were simply bringing to light the "unthought" of his predecessor's project—Lefort in effect suggested that a similar obligation to excavate and extend fell to Merleau-Ponty's own interpreters. "One has to follow most closely the visible surface of the work to feel, at each moment, what is between the thoughts, at their junction, and in their prolongation," Lefort put it, "to discover what has neither form nor name—but in virtue of which what is there has meaning at all. It is awaiting its destination."[17]

Initially, this would imply taking seriously—once and for all, as it were—the impossibility for inquiry of gaining some absolute purchase on being, as if the Cartesian subject whose possibility the philosopher denied could simply reassert itself in the character of his descriptions of the world. But, just as much as the total separation of reflection, the fantasy of the intuitive identity of thought and being, the complete fusion of immersion, would also have to be given up. Such developments suggested that Merleau-Ponty had been wrong, untrue to himself, when he had promised in *Phenomenology of Perception* to allow inquiry access to things in themselves or reflection to take the same form as [*égaler*] the unreflective life that was its continuing ground.[18] So far, Lefort seems to be spinning out the circular lessons of holism: "It is neither allowed to wish to coincide with the unreflective without forgetting the distance that in the same moment reflection involves from it, nor to want to withdraw into pure thought without forgetting that this operation is an event and presupposes something before it."[19]

Now, however, Lefort began to detect consequences of holism that, he claimed, were in effect destructive of holism. There could be "no concern," he argued in a pivotal sentence, "to integrate the diversity of the experience of being in a thought of Totality, for the notion of ... totality surreptitiously reintroduces the belief in being-as-an-object or the temptation of surveying being as a whole."[20] This, Lefort averred, is what Merleau-Ponty had been getting at when, in his later years, he labeled being "wild" (*brut*) and the inquiry aiming at it as "unruly" (*sauvage*). It meant that the constitutive situation of inquiry had to be seen as a "tearing [or heartbreak: *déchirement*] without repair." The problem was not just that "it would be vain to substitute for the imaginary reality of the Totality the ideal of totalization," as Lefort wrote in an obvious allusion to Sartre's own proposal in that year's *Critique of Dialectical Reason* for such a switch (touchingly, Lefort was continuing his teacher's old polemic against his rival's newest position).[21] Merleau-Ponty's model, now presented independently of the negative critique of idealism and empiricism that had been its original vehicle, focused on a positive vocabulary for understanding the inherence of perception in the perceived, one famously enigmatic, but depending, for Lefort, on an unceremonious and complete departure from holism. In his essay, Lefort contended that Merleau-Ponty's final thinking carefully avoided a reversal of classical transparency into a celebration of opacity or a replacement of fantasies of omniscience with a reduction of the world to an endless train of riddles. Nevertheless, Merleau-Ponty made all philosophical possession come along on principle with what he dubbed "dispossession," the presence of things necessarily bound up with estrangement from them, and all intimate proximity with the world featuring a moment of inexpungeable alterity at its heart.[22]

At the time, Lefort was in effect founding a massive literature, still accumulating to this day, on the mysterious finale of Merleau-Ponty's philosophical life.[23] And it is of extreme importance to try to be clear about what Lefort was saying. Here, in fact, Martin Jay's remarks on the later Merleau-Ponty provide a useful counterpoint and allow one to see Lefort's interpretation as in need of either defense or explanation—if not both. While acknowledging a certain "decentering" of man (in relation to language and nature) in Merleau-Ponty's later thought, themes a more "resolutely anti-holistic" later generation of French philosophy would take yet further, Jay argued that his subject's shift ultimately involved a move "from an essentially critical concept [of totality] capable of providing a vantage point from which the present might be judged" to "an essentially descriptive one used to make sense of what was." Thus, Merleau-Ponty only moved away from the "Hegelian Marxist variant" of totality, not "from holism per se."[24] In short, the humanist, reconciliationist holism that coexisted so uneasily with Merleau-Ponty's Heideggerian and interpretive holism from the start finally had to be dropped to make room for its competitor and not some non- or post-holist alternative beyond both.

Lefort's interpretation, however, seems to cover that transition, but attempts to see Merleau-Ponty's self-criticism as forcing a considerable further step. One initial way to put this is that Lefort's interpretation sees Merleau-Ponty insisting on a moment of alterity involved in or generated by holism itself. That a perceptual act takes place thanks to a totality of significance, one never fully legible to the perceiver, meant that something necessarily remained immune to his perception; that inquiry about the world presupposes framing for intelligibility meant that something necessarily remained unintelligible in spite of all inquiry. If so, is even interpretive holism really guilty (as Lefort charged) of "surreptitiously reintroduc[ing] the belief in being-as-an-object or the temptation of surveying being as a whole"? At a minimum, Lefort argued that the temptation to return to some vantage point above things, no matter how often denied, would return unless more active guard was taken against it. Lefort's argument seemed to be that *positing* a holistic context of significance in which perception or inquiry is said to take place itself violates holistic premises, or—put in a positive way—he thought such premises necessarily led beyond holism to an insistence on ineliminable opacity and constitutive difference.

Explaining Lefort's Interpretation

It is true that Lefort gave disappointingly little philosophical defense of the plausibility of this claim about holism's self-qualification, especially for those who do not see the difficulty with holism that Lefort claimed to identify. But an attempt—out of the question in these pages—to verify or contest Lefort's interpretation, of Merleau-Ponty or of holism, is best left aside in favor of consideration of the *historical* problems of why Lefort may have crafted it and what legacy it left. For it is quite striking that in 1961, Lefort, in spite of his own incipient sense of the fundamental continuity of Merleau-Ponty's political thought, did not even recognize the possibility of such a continuous interpretation of his teacher's "metaphysical" turn. Merleau-Ponty's last speculative works had to be scanned, Lefort argued, for "signs of a future achievement" and "the promise of a new beginning."[25] And what is original in Lefort's emphasis is the final break that Merleau-Ponty's thought from holism is said to require. The anticipation of a breakthrough to alterity of Merleau-Ponty's "unthought," not the persisting commitment to totality of his thought, is what mattered.

I want to propose that Lefort's reading flows, in the first instance, out of a personal and political conjuncture. After the Korean War, followed by Sartre's implausible *ralliement* to the Communist Party, Merleau-Ponty had made his break, as shown, not simply with communism but with Marxism, too.[26] While Lefort had beaten Merleau-Ponty to a skepticism about Bolshevism, he came later than his teacher to the departure from Marxism more generally, as a result of his decade-long participation in the famous leftist group *Socialisme et Barbarie* (Socialism or Barbarism). Even Merleau-Ponty's devastating chapter-length critique of Lefort (and his group) in *The Adventures of the Dialectic* had not been enough, by itself, to lead Lefort to change his politics. But when he ultimately left the group late in the 1950s, Lefort justified his choice as an act of allegiance to Merleau-Ponty's principles (in line with his interpretation of Merleau-Ponty's own break with Marxism as an act of fidelity to himself). "I had adopted Merleau-Ponty's critique of any claim to absolute knowledge," Lefort recalled, attempting to explain his pre–1958 position. "But I had forced myself to reconcile it with Marx's thought."[27] For a few years, he was saying, his allegiances to *Socialisme et Barbarie* kept him from turning Merleau-Ponty's core premises against (rather than in favor of) Marxism, at least once Merleau-Ponty's own example made this possibility obvious, and his departure from the group therefore had the consequence of leading him to affiliate with his teacher's own perception of irreconcilable approaches and choice between them. At the time of Merleau-Ponty's death, in short, Lefort was still catching up to him.

To bolster this interpretation, it is important to consider how chronologically specific Lefort's narrative of Merleau-Ponty's political evolution was, and how tightly his evaluation of Merleau-Ponty's holism proved to be tethered to it. In the 1940s, when Lefort was less favorable than Merleau-Ponty toward actually existing socialism, his criticisms of his teacher were biting. And while in the moment in the early 1960s that I have been discussing only a footnote intruded about whether Merleau-Ponty's political meandering might have been much less complicated had he simply taken the facts of Soviet repression more seriously, Lefort's analysis would soon shift in its emphasis. A decade later, Lefort could much more strongly indict his teacher for the philosophical contortions that blinded him to terror and suffering.[28] But no piece of his writing—in light of my concerns in this essay and perhaps in Lefort's entire corpus—is more remarkable than an even more recent article, delivered a quarter century after Merleau-Ponty's death, in which he indicted his teacher for "abstain[ing] from speaking of the totalitarian state." This shortcoming, Lefort argued, counted as far more than a political error, for it reflected a deeper failure, of which Merleau-Ponty never fought free, to make room for alterity in a persistently holistic metaphysics.[29]

It was, in other words, a complete reversal. Where once it seemed that holism had led Merleau-Ponty beyond a politically troubling past, it later appeared to Lefort that his teacher remained always mired in it. And where once it seemed as if Merleau-Ponty might, in the end, have taken his holism so far that it made room for difference, Lefort later took the opposite view in the strongest possible terms, the "reversibility" of perceiver and perceived and the "entwining" of sentience and sensible—the key themes of Merleau-Ponty's late work—allowing "no sense of otherness."[30] If, then, these considerations are correct, the paradox noted before is redoubled, for it is not just that Lefort read Merleau-Ponty's politics as continuous and his phenomenology as evolutionary, but that he did so as a result of political shifts—his own—rather than because the metaphysics were in motion, or at least not because of them alone.

A Turning Point in French Thought

Of course, this political explanation, microscopic as it is, ignores the macroscopic fact that Merleau-Ponty had approached the brink of a full-scale paradigm shift in philosophy, and Lefort was merely the first of many commentators to read his final thought as premonitory of a later postmodernism. How those currents of thought that Americans came to label in this way emerged remains among the most intriguing and contested problems intellectual historians of twentieth-century Europe are called upon to consider. No unified story of that transition is available: postmodernism is an Anglo-American construction and better studied as the hugely differentiated and multiply sourced set of movements it actually was. Yet a pivotal overall moment clearly occurred when philosophers turned to attack the inherited premise of ontological holism—one of the chief legacies of prior European and, especially, of Martin Heidegger's thought—out of a concern that the commitment to plenitudinous unity ruled out (or even suppressed) the "alterity" and "difference" that the new currents came to champion. Now again, this broad if important transition is itself a constructed stereotype, incontestably plural in its real origins and meaningfully different in each of its variations. It mattered whether the siege on unity came as a revision of psychoanalysis in which selfhood came to be seen as bound up with self-loss, for example, or as an appeal to the exteriority of secular revelation against a totalizing philosophy, or as the deconstruction of the metaphysical tradition in the name of political and ontological "difference."³¹ In this essay, then, I have been trying to consider what turns out to be a crucial moment in it, and whether for Merleau-Ponty—or at least in Lefort's interpretation of him—the rise of alterity emerged out of the extension of holism itself.

This development also had a specifically political sequel, which is of course the story of Lefort's later career, and that of the influential movement in political theory he came to found. How closely that sequel remained bound up with the transition I have been examining in this essay is, indeed, a large part of the justification for focusing on it. A decade after Merleau-Ponty's death, Lefort organized a special commemorative issue of the journal *L'Arc*. By then, Lefort had his own students, and the most important of them, Marcel Gauchet, in fact had his philosophical debut in this issue, and—far from coincidentally—on the subject of Merleau-Ponty and alterity.

Gauchet, who has recently recalled that he had begun studying Merleau-Ponty in his own high school philosophy class before even meeting Lefort in 1966 at college, devoted this first published work to an interpretive commentary on *The Visible and the Invisible*, and what he said is highly significant for understanding the philosophical commitments that would ground the democratic theory that, together with his teacher, he would elaborate in the years that followed.³² Dedicated to the difficult last chapter of Merleau-Ponty's posthumous and unfinished ontology, Gauchet, like Lefort before him, focused on the philosopher's decision to take to its final conclusions his own original principle that there is no view from nowhere. The step taken on principle in *The Visible and the Invisible* is a:

> displacement of the place of thinking: not the transfer from one place to another, as if it were simply a matter of varying the point of view from which to perceive the object, but the destitution of all points of view, of that distance through which thought has assured itself of the distinctness [*rassemblement en eux-mêmes*] of its objects. Or better put: a destitution of that distance through which modern philosophy, metaphysics, *believed* that it assured itself of the distinctness of its objects, of the identity of the existent. For as Merleau-Ponty instructs, modern philosophy is a prisoner of the illusion that it can occupy a place that is in fact impossible to occupy.³³

Once reflection found itself inescapably doused in the sea of the unreflective, it had to admit unmasterable division as its central and unsurpassable subject matter. Interpreting Merleau-Ponty's replacement notion of chiasmus, according to which perception and inquiry were bound to constitutive finitude, Gauchet insisted that they begin and remain fastened to "a division and an insurmountable internal alterity [that] turn out to be located at the heart of the world and of thought." Further on, Gauchet described this alterity as "a fracture, with no possibility of pinpointing its limits, an abyss without edges [*béance sans lèvres*], an immeasurable infinity, through which the world comes into being."[34] The conclusion is familiar, though rhetorically inflationary. In other words, Gauchet's early labor is clearly in a direct and willed continuity with Lefort's own reflections on the significance of Merleau-Ponty's late ontology.

To be sure, by 1971 it was unremarkable to pledge allegiance to "alterity." Though Lefort's case is too controversial to examine here, it is clear that Gauchet, especially, is best understood as having been influenced by Jacques Lacan's depiction of psychic discord.[35] More generally, laying stress on different sources of the unraveling of holism works only up to a point, as after a certain moment these sources became mutually interactive. But the fact remains that even at this late date, Gauchet presented the breakthrough to alterity as the outcome of Merleau-Ponty's itinerary, and as the necessary implication of his dethronement of the classical subject, with holism undoing itself. The new interpretation of democracy Lefort attempted to develop with his student explicitly assumed, after Merleau-Ponty's learning process, the unavailability of "the illusory position of claiming to have an overview of being," an insight Lefort would soon say made "the question of being" perforce equivalent to "the question of the other."[36]

In the end, it is perhaps useful to note that these interpretive issues were bound up, not simply with the departure from Marxism, as I argued before, but with the search for a new politics—and a new theory of politics. For at the pivotal moment when Merleau-Ponty died, Lefort chose to emphasize not simply his teacher's past journey, or his recent ambivalences. Instead, he stressed the positive theory of which Merleau-Ponty's life and thought provided an alluring premonition, in spite of his teacher's apparent dedication to other topics. "[L]ike all philosophies, the one I am trying to discover would inspire a politics," Merleau-Ponty hesitatingly acknowledged of his new ontology in an interview not long before his death.[37] But only Lefort followed up this manner of remark out of the belief that continuing Merleau-Ponty's thought necessarily implied the development of a plausible theory of society and history, one that rivaled and ultimately overcame the failed promise of Marxist explanation (and engagement). After a period of years, along with Gauchet and other followers, Lefort would attempt to begin precisely such an approach, in the form of a new theory of democracy. It would only germinate, however, thanks to a preliminary departure from holism. The end of the adventures of the concept of totality meant going beyond more than simply its Marxist variant.

Was such a transition a realization or a betrayal of Merleau-Ponty's impulses? As Lefort himself emphasized (in spite of his own later indictment of his teacher), the question may ignore the possibility that figures can point beyond themselves. "The reading of Merleau-Ponty's final writings teaches that he always sought the annunciation of his own enterprise in the past sources he overthrew," Lefort wrote, "and if his enterprise required the destruction of Tradition, ... its fulfillment nevertheless depended on seeking signs in that tradition of its own surpassing."[38] The same, one might argue, is true of Lefort, *mutatis mutandis*, in relation to his own immediate past: he struck out in a new direction, in claiming to scrutinize something already set down. Unlike philosophers, however, intellectual historians care a great deal about distinguishing anticipation from achievement and telling retroactive attribution from real contribution; they do so in part because it helps restore some of the humanity of philosophical inquiry, including its evolution not simply through books, but in an "interworld" of teaching and learning. Other times, Lefort acknowledged this truth, which he knew so well from his own experience. The difficulty of "building myself on an absent column," a phrase from the poet Henri Michaux that Lefort used to describe the relationship he staked out in relation to his disappeared mentor (*Sur une colonne absente* is the title of the collection of Lefort's essays about Merleau-Ponty, some of whose contents I have been discussing here), created the rare opportunity to be both loyal to a master and fully oneself. Yet even before his tragic death, allowing Lefort to think the unthought by allowing him to think his own thought may have been Merleau-Ponty's greatest gift—but it is that of all of the best teachers—to his student.

Notes

1. This essay focuses on a step in an argument given in full (with far less attention to the step) in my book, *A New Theory of Politics: Claude Lefort and Company in Contemporary France* (New York, forthcoming).
2. The essay is Claude Lefort, "L'idée d'être brut et d'esprit sauvage," *Les Temps modernes* 184–5 (1961): 253–286, rpt. in Lefort, *Sur une colonne absente: Écrits autour de Merleau-Ponty* (Paris, 1978).
3. Martin Jay, *Marxism and Totality: The Adventures of a Concept from Lukács to Habermas* (Berkeley and Los Angeles, 1984), 361–362.
4. This is true even of Bernard Flynn's important recent book, *The Philosophy of Claude Lefort: Thinking the Political* (Evanston, IL, 2005), in which the connection surfaces only sporadically and episodically.
5. Lefort, "Préface" to Merleau-Ponty, *L'Œil et l'Esprit* (Paris, 1964), v.

6. For meaning holism in Anglo-American philosophy, see Jerry Fodor and Ernest Lepore, *Holism: A Shopper's Guide* (Oxford, 1992); for practice holism in Continental philosophy, see for example Hubert L. Dreyfus, "Holism and Hermeneutics," *Review of Metaphysics* 34, no. 1 (September 1980): 3–24, or Charles Taylor, "Overcoming Epistemology," in *Philosophical Arguments* (Cambridge, MA, 1995).
7. Maurice Merleau-Ponty, *Phénoménologie de la perception* (Paris, 1945), ix. For Merleau-Ponty, who developed one of the earliest interpretations of Husserl's later work, this meant that the new philosophy betrayed its purpose when it was thought possible to fully complete the phenomenological reduction and wholly seize essences, just as Husserl's true doctrine as revealed by his last manuscripts and *Lebenswelt* concept undercut any superficial impression of antagonism between Husserl's call to return to the things themselves and Martin Heidegger's depiction of being-in-the-world.
8. The citation is in Lefort, "L'idée d'être brut," 8. The citation is from Merleau-Ponty, preface to Angelo Hesnard, *L'œuvre et l'esprit de Freud et son importance dans le monde moderne* (Paris, 1960). The issue featured Sartre's own mammoth obituary as well as contributions from Jacques Lacan and others.
9. The next section is an abbreviated summary of an interpretation presaged in Lefort, "L'idée d'être brut," 41–42, and given in full in Lefort, "La politique et la pensée de la politique," *Les Lettres nouvelles* 32 (1963), rpt. in Lefort, *Sur une colonne absente*, now partially in English as "Thinking Politics," in *The Cambridge Companion to Merleau-Ponty*, ed. Taylor Carman and Mark B. Hansen (Cambridge, 2005). A similar analysis is provided by Dick Howard's chapter on Merleau-Ponty in *The Marxian Legacy* (New York, 1977), whose detailed textual investigation is in effect an attempt to bear out Lefort's original thesis.
10. Lefort, "L'idée d'être brut," 40.
11. Merleau-Ponty, *Phénoménologie de la perception*, 200.
12. Merleau-Ponty, *Humanism and Terror: An Essay on the Communist Problem*, trans. John O'Neill (Boston, 1969), 18, 22. On the book as a "philosophical case for terror," see Tony R. Judt, *Past Imperfect: French Intellectuals, 1944–1956* (Berkeley, CA, 1992), chap. 6.
13. Merleau-Ponty, *Les aventures de la dialectique* (Paris, 1955, 2000), 10, 282.
14. Lefort, "Introduction," in Merleau-Ponty, *Humanisme et terreur: essai sur le problème communiste*, new ed. (Paris, 1980), 19. Portions of this introduction have been rpt. as Lefort, "D'un doute à l'autre," in *Le temps présent: Écrits 1945-2005* (Paris, 2007).
15. Lefort, "Réflexions sur de premiers commentaires," in *Contemporary Philosophy: A Survey*, ed. Raymond Klibansky (Florence, 1969), rpt. in *Sur une colonne absente*, 106.
16. Lefort, "L'idée d'être brut," 34.
17. Ibid., 9–20 at 16. He referred not so much to Merleau-Ponty's preface to his *Phénoménologie* as to his late essay, "Le philosophe et son ombre," rpt. in *Signes* (Paris, 1960).
18. Lefort, "L'idée d'être brut," 40–41, citing Merleau-Ponty, *Phénoménologie de la perception*, xi.
19. Ibid., 20–31 at 26–27.
20. Ibid., 31.
21. Ibid., 33. Jay's chapter on Sartre in *Marxism and Totality* is in fact entitled: "From Totality to Totalization."
22. Lefort, "L'idée d'être brut," 22, 36; cf. 26, 27–28.
23. This literature stretches, in English, from Remy Kwant, *From Phenomenology to Metaphysics: An Inquiry into the Last Period of Merleau-Ponty's Philosophical Life* (Pittsburgh, 1966) to Renaud Barbaras, *The Being of the Phenomenon: Merleau-Ponty's Ontology*,

trans. Leonard Lawlor and Ted Toadvine (Bloomington, IN, 2004). In this literature, historians will find Jerrold Seigel, "A Unique Way of Existing: Merleau-Ponty on the Subject," *Journal of the History of Philosophy* 29, no. 3 (July 1991): 455–480 especially pertinent.
24. Jay, *Marxism and Totality*, 377–380.
25. Lefort, "Merleau-Ponty: une pensée au-delà de la pensée," *Le Monde*, 18 April 1970, rpt. as "Présence de Merleau-Ponty," *Sur une colonne absente*, 1. In a similar vein, see Lefort's postface to Merleau-Ponty, *Le visible et l'invisible, suivi de notes de travail*, ed. Lefort (Paris, 1964), in English as the introduction to Merleau-Ponty, *The Visible and the Invisible, Followed by Working Notes*, ed. Lefort, trans. Alphonso Lingis (Evanston, IL, 1968).
26. As many will recall, Sartre's *ralliement* set off an acrimonious exchange in the pages of *Les Temps modernes* with Lefort, which helped permanently poison Sartre's relationship with Merleau-Ponty. In Lefort's recollection, in fact, the fate of Marxism in Sartre's "ultrabolshevism" first became clear to his teacher in these polemics. See Pierre Pachet, et al., "Pensée politique et histoire: Entretien avec Claude Lefort," *Savoir et mémoire* 7 (1997): 11.
27. "Entretien avec Claude Lefort," *L'Anti-mythes* 14 (November 1975): 5, in English as "An Interview with Claude Lefort," *Telos* 30 (Winter 1976–77): 176. See the similar testimony to the effect that his allegiance to Merleau-Ponty eventually trumped his belief in Marx in Lefort, "L'image du corps et le totalitarisme," *Confrontations* 2 (Autumn 1979), rpt. in Lefort, *L'invention démocratique: les limites de la domination totalitaire* (Paris, 1981), in English in Lefort, *The Political Forms of Modern Society: Bureaucracy, Democracy, Totalitarianism*, ed. John B. Thompson (Cambridge, MA, 1986), 294.
28. For the footnote, see Lefort, "La politique et la pensée de la politique," 82–83n. For full details of their crisscrossing political trajectories, see the relevant chapter of my aforementioned forthcoming book.
29. Lefort, "Flesh and Otherness," in *Ontology and Alterity in Merleau-Ponty*, ed. Galen A. Johnson and Michael B. Smith (Evanston, IL, 1990), 12 and passim. The paper dates from September 1987.
30. Ibid., 13.
31. See, for example, Carolyn J. Dean, *The Self and Its Pleasures: Bataille, Lacan, and the History of the Decentered Subject* (Ithaca, NY, 1992); Samuel Moyn, *Origins of the Other: Emmanuel Levinas between Revelation and Ethics* (Ithaca, NY, 2005); Peter Eli Gordon, "Hammer without a Master: French Phenomenology and the Origins of Deconstruction (Or, How Derrida Read Heidegger)," in *Histories of Postmodernism*, ed. Mark Bevir, et al. (New York, 2007).
32. Marcel Gauchet, "Le lieu de la pensée," *L'Arc* 46 (1971): 19–30. Lefort contributed an essay entitled "Le corps, la chair" to the forum, which mostly reprises his earlier interpretation. It is rpt. in Lefort, *Sur une colonne absente*. Besides many luminaries of French thought of the era, Lefort also solicited a contribution from his young associate Marc Richir, who would shortly thereafter collaborate with Gauchet in Lefortian political theory of the era. On reading Merleau-Ponty, see Gauchet, *La condition historique: Entretiens avec François Azouvi et Sylvain Piron* (Paris, 2003), 49.
33. Gauchet, "Le lieu de la pensée," 19–20.
34. Ibid., 20, 22.
35. Moyn, "The Assumption by Man of His Original Fracturing: Marcel Gauchet, Gladys Swain, and the History of the Self," *Modern Intellectual History* (forthcoming).

36. Lefort, "Esquisse d'une genèse de l'idéologie dans les sociétés modernes," *Textures* 8–9 (1974): 3–54, rpt. in Lefort, *Les formes de l'histoire: essais d'anthropologie politique* (Paris, 1978), and in English as "Outline of the Genesis of Ideology in Modern Societies," in Lefort, *The Political Forms of Modern Society*, 196, 236.
37. Merleau-Ponty, interview with Madeleine Chapsal, in *Les Écrivains en personne* (Paris, 1960), rpt. in Merleau-Ponty, *Parcours deux, 1951–1961*, ed. Jacques Prunair (Paris, 2000), 299. This interview is available in English in Merleau-Ponty, *Texts and Dialogues: On Philosophy, Politics, and Culture* (New York, 1996). See too his interview with Jean-Paul Weber, "La philosophie et la politique sont solidaires," *Le Monde*, 31 December 1960, rpt. in Merleau-Ponty, *Parcours deux*. Similarly, in the early 1970s, Lefort cited from unpublished notes Merleau-Ponty's assertion that "to understand the state or war is a problem of exactly the same type as the problem of perception; the philosophy of history will never be resolved except as the same time as the philosophy of perception," as if his late metaphysical exercises were also an incipient political theory. Cited from notes in Lefort, "Maurice Merleau-Ponty," in Yvon Belaval, ed., *Histoire de la philosophie*, vol. 3, *Du XIXe siècle à nos jours* (Paris, 1974), rpt. as "Qu'est-ce que voir?," in *Sur une colonne absente*, 143.
38. Lefort, "Le corps, la chair," 127, translation somewhat free.

Bibliography

Barbaras, Renaud. *The Being of the Phenomenon: Merleau-Ponty's Ontology*. Translated by Leonard Lawlor and Ted Toadvine. Bloomington, IN, 2004.
Chapsal, Madeleine. *Les Écrivains en personne*. Paris, 1960.
Dean, Carolyn J. *The Self and Its Pleasures: Bataille, Lacan, and the History of the Decentered Subject*. Ithaca, NY, 1992.
Dreyfus, Hubert L. "Holism and Hermeneutics." *Review of Metaphysics* 34, no. 1 (September 1980): 3–24.
"Entretien avec Claude Lefort." *L'Anti-mythes* no. 14 (November 1975).
Flynn, Bernard. *The Philosophy of Claude Lefort: Thinking the Political*. Evanston, IL, 2005.
Fodor, Jerry, and Ernest Lepore. *Holism: A Shopper's Guide*. Oxford, 1992.
Gauchet, Marcel. *La condition historique: Entretiens avec François Azouvi et Sylvain Piron*. Paris, 2003.
———. "Le lieu de la pensée." *L'Arc* 46 (1971): 19–30.
Gordon, Peter Eli. "Hammer without a Master: French Phenomenology and the Origins of Deconstruction (Or, How Derrida Read Heidegger)." In *Histories of Postmodernism*, edited by Mark Bevir, et al. New York, 2007.
Howard, Dick. *The Marxian Legacy*. New York, 1977.
"An Interview with Claude Lefort." *Telos*, no. 30 (Winter 1976–77): 30–33.
Jay, Martin. *Marxism and Totality: The Adventures of a Concept from Lukács to Habermas*. Berkeley and Los Angeles, 1984.
Judt, Tony R. *Past Imperfect: French Intellectuals, 1944–1956*. Berkeley and Los Angeles, 1992.
Kwant, Remy. *From Phenomenology to Metaphysics: An Inquiry into the Last Period of Merleau-Ponty's Philosophical Life*. Pittsburgh, PA, 1966.
Lefort, Claude. "D'un doute à l'autre." In *Le Temps présent: Écrits 1945-2005*. Paris, 2007.

———. "Esquisse d'une genèse de l'idéologie dans les sociétés modernes." *Textures* no. 8–9 (1974): 3–54.

———. "Flesh and Otherness." In *Ontology and Alterity in Merleau-Ponty*, edited by Galen A. Johnson and Michael B. Smith. Evanston, IL, 1990.

———. *Les formes de l'histoire: essais d'anthropologie politique*. Paris, 1978.

———. "L'idée d'être brut et d'esprit sauvage." *Les Temps modernes*, no. 184–5 (1961): 253–286.

———. "L'image du corps et le totalitarisme." *Confrontations* 2 (Autumn 1979), rpt. in Lefort, *L'invention démocratique: les limites de la domination totalitaire*. Paris, 1981.

———. "Introduction." In Merleau-Ponty, *Humanisme et terreur: essai sur le problème communiste*. New ed. Paris, 1980.

———. "Maurice Merleau-Ponty." In *Histoire de la philosophie*, vol. 3, *Du XIXe siècle à nos jours*, edited by Yvon Belaval. Paris, 1974.

———. "Merleau-Ponty: une pensée au-delà de la pensée." *Le Monde*, 18 April 1970.

———. *The Political Forms of Modern Society: Bureaucracy, Democracy, Totalitarianism*. Edited by John B. Thompson. Cambridge, MA, 1986.

———. "La politique et la pensée de la politique." *Les Lettres nouvelles* 32 (1963).

———. "Préface." In Maurice Merleau-Ponty, *L'Œil et l'Esprit*. Paris, 1964.

———. "Réflexions sur de premiers commentaires." In *Contemporary Philosophy: A Survey*, edited by Raymond Klibansky. Florence, 1969.

———. *Sur une colonne absente: Écrits autour de Merleau-Ponty*. Paris, 1978.

———. "Thinking Politics." In *The Cambridge Companion to Merleau-Ponty*, edited by Taylor Carman and Mark B. Hansen. Cambridge, 2005.

Merleau-Ponty, Maurice. *Les aventures de la dialectique*. Paris, 1955, 2000.

———. *Humanism and Terror: An Essay on the Communist Problem*. Translated by John O'Neill. Boston, 1969.

———. *Parcours deux, 1951–1961*. Edited by Jacques Prunair. Paris, 2000.

———. *Phénoménologie de la perception*. Paris, 1945.

———. "Le philosophe et son ombre." In *Signes*. Paris, 1960.

———. "Préface." In Angelo Hesnard, *L'œuvre et l'esprit de Freud et son importance dans le monde moderne*. Paris, 1960.

———. *Texts and Dialogues: On Philosophy, Politics, and Culture*. New York, 1996.

———. *The Visible and the Invisible, Followed by Working Notes*. Edited by Claude Lefort. Translated by Alphonso Lingis. Evanston, IL, 1968.

———. *Le visible et l'invisible, suivi de notes de travail*. Edited by Claude Lefort. Paris, 1964.

———, and Jean-Paul Weber. "La philosophie et la politique sont solidaires." *Le Monde*, 31 December 1960.

Moyn, Samuel. "The Assumption by Man of His Original Fracturing: Marcel Gauchet, Gladys Swain, and the History of the Self." *Modern Intellectual History* (forthcoming).

———. *Origins of the Other: Emmanuel Levinas between Revelation and Ethics*. Ithaca, NY, 2005.

Pachet, Pierre, et al. "Pensée politique et histoire: Entretien avec Claude Lefort." *Savoir et mémoire* 7 (1997).

Seigel, Jerrold. "A Unique Way of Existing: Merleau-Ponty on the Subject." *Journal of the History of Philosophy* 29, no. 3 (July 1991): 455–480.

Taylor, Charles. "Overcoming Epistemology." In *Philosophical Arguments*. Cambridge, MA, 1995.

THE RETURN OF THE KING
Hegelianism and Post-Marxism in Zizek and Nancy

Warren Breckman

There is a certain irony in the fact that Martin Jay's *Marxism and Totality* appeared in 1984, the year when real historical time overtook George Orwell's dystopian totalitarian future. For all the fanfare with which the media greeted the arrival of Orwell's portentous year, his prophetic vision seemed wide of the mark when measured against the real 1984. Though one would not want to understate the reality of the Soviet bloc's repressive politics at a time when no one yet foresaw communism's imminent collapse, the USSR in the wake of Brezhnev was a far cry from the Stalinist regime that had fueled Orwell's worst fears; the West, contrary to Orwell's expectation, had not devolved into the other half of a totalitarian world. Nor did Orwell look like an adequate guide to the history of the European intellectual Left in the twentieth century. That history must distinguish between the totalitarian vision and the philosophically compelling efforts of Western Marxists to develop a critical theory of the social totality in the service of emancipatory goals. In upholding that distinction and tracing the richness of the Western Marxist concept of totality, *Marxism and Totality* remains unsurpassed. Even if he makes no reference whatsoever to Orwell, Jay's account goes still further in underscoring the discrepancy between Orwell's 1984 and the intellectual climate of 1984. The concluding chapter of *Marxism and Totality* makes amply clear that, by the early 1980s, the Western Marxist tradition had been eclipsed by the rise of French poststructuralism. Preferring Nietzsche to Hegel, and heterogeneity to unity, poststructuralism was a style of thought deeply suspicious of the Hegelian underpinnings of Western Marxism and that tradition's yearning for expressive totality. Despite Jay's final plea that we not entirely abandon the search to see things whole, the book ends with the distinct sense that Western Marxism had reached its terminus.

In the intervening years, there is little evidence to contradict that intuition. Yet there have been developments that could not have been foreseen in 1984, which suggest the adventure of totality is not at an end, even if it has decisively left the tracks of historical materialism. In what follows, I want to trace one such path, that of Slavoj Zizek. Zizek defies the categories established in the final chapter of *Marxism and Totality*, for he is a thinker who took from the outset Hegel and Jacques Lacan for his two intellectual polestars. Zizek's obsessive pairing of Hegel and Lacan requires that both be taken in ways radically at odds with conventional understanding. Zizek's Hegel is not the thinker of expressive totality. He writes, "far from being a story of [antagonism's] progressive overcoming, dialectics is for Hegel a systematic notation of the failure of all such attempts—'absolute knowledge' denotes a subjective position which finally accepts 'contradiction' as an internal condition of every identity." Hegel thereby becomes "the first post-Marxist" who disclosed a field of "difference and contingency" Marxism subsequently sutured.[1] With Lacan, whom *Marxism and Totality* firmly placed with the anti-Hegelian French poststructuralists, Zizek quickly bypasses the obvious influence of the Hegelian dialectic of recognition upon Lacan's thought in the 1930s and 1940s, and insists that the later Lacan's theoretical work is "Hegelian precisely where he himself does not know it."[2]

What concept of totality could issue from Zizek's eccentric coupling of Hegel and Lacan? I want to address this question through one of the least commented upon dimensions of Zizek's thought, namely his repeated use of Hegel's theory of the monarch in the cluster of books that marked his debut as a major international figure.[3] It is surprising to see Hegel's monarch suddenly regain his throne in Zizek's *oeuvre*. For by almost universal agreement, the theory of the monarch is the least persuasive element of Hegel's political philosophy and the least relevant to modern appropriations of Hegelian thought. Yet the figure of the monarch does considerable theoretical work for Zizek; indeed, it provides a privileged vantage point from which to explore this latter-day, post-Marxist adventure—or misadventure—of totality.

This inquiry will proceed through three stages. First, it is necessary to dwell on some aspects of the longer historical reception of Hegel's theory of the monarch so as to have a framework for approaching Zizek. Here, it is the French context that seems really crucial for a figure whose intellectual orientation has been so profoundly shaped by French thought. As a student in Ljubljana, Zizek wrote a 400-page Masters thesis on "The Theoretical and Practical Relevance of French Structuralism." The work caused Zizek to be seen as politically suspicious by the Yugoslavian authorities, but despite the handicaps placed upon him, Zizek deepened his engagement with French thought, particularly the work of Lacan. Between 1981 and 1985, he lived off and on in Paris, studying Lacanian theory with Jacques-Alain Miller, and completing a second doctorate in psychoanalysis in 1985. The second step of the inquiry will involve an exploration of the treatment of the Hegelian monarch in the work of Jean-Luc Nancy, a philosopher profoundly influenced by Heidegger and Derrida. Nancy's lengthy 1982 essay "La jurisdiction du monarch hégélien" emerged from the same general context that shaped Zizek's early concerns, yet Nancy's piece provides a revealing foil to Zizek. Finally, I will examine Zizek's repeated use of the Hegelian monarch in his works of the late 1980s and early 1990s. The figure of the monarch served systematic purposes in Zizek's effort to unite Hegel and Lacan; but that most obsolete of Hegelian constructions became charged with contemporary political significance, a fact that has much to do with circumstances. After all, the book where the theme is most prominent, *For They Know Not What They Do*, was first delivered as lectures in Ljubljana in the winter semester of 1989–1990, in the turbulent period between the General Assembly of the Yugoslav Republic of Slovenia's September 1989 assertion of the right to secede from Yugoslavia and the December 1990 referendum that overwhelmingly supported Slovenian independence. Zizek remembered it as "a time of intense political ferment, with 'free elections' only weeks ahead, when all options still seemed open, the time of a 'short circuit' blending together political activism, the 'highest' theory (Hegel, Lacan) and unrestrained enjoyment in the 'lowest' popular culture—a unique utopian moment which is now, after the electoral victory of the nationalist-populist coalition and the advent of a new 'scoundrel time', not only over but even more and more *invisible*, erased from memory."[4] The disillusionment Zizek registered in 1991 here anticipates the final turn our analysis will follow: conceived in a spirit of radical democratic opposition to totalitarianism, Zizek's reading of the Hegelian monarch actually foreshadows the much more troubling view of democracy that has emerged in Zizek's recent work.

Hegel and the Anti-totalitarian Moment in France

Since the publication of the *Philosophy of Right* in 1819, Hegel's theory of the monarch has satisfied almost no one. Hegel's justification of monarchy seems to be one of those rare instances when his tireless search for mediation looks perilously close to a mere political compromise. On the one hand, Hegel firmly embraces the assumption that the modern values of subjective freedom and self-determination should find objective form in the institutions of the state considered as a whole. From this standpoint, Hegel seems to endorse the deepest impulse of the French Revolution, namely the Revolution's destruction of the logic of personal power, that logic of political incarnation whereby one man could say "*L'état c'est moi.*" Hegel's understanding of the state as a rational totality of impersonal laws and institutions seems to deepen the project of separating politics from its incarnation in persons. On the other hand, however, we encounter Hegel's insistence upon a hereditary monarch who stands at the summit of the constitutional order and embodies the state as such. It seems absurd for the philosopher of absolute Reason to make the edifice of the state depend upon the biological accident of birth.

The ambiguities of Hegel's attempt to unite two apparently different political logics produced sharp disagreements almost immediately. Consider the debate in Prussia during the 1830s and 1840s. For committed monarchists, Hegel's monarch was at best a mere shadow of true kingship. They fixed on the purely formal nature of the role assigned to Hegel's king in the *Philosophy of Right*. According to Hegel's reasoning, if the sovereignty of the state is to move from an abstract idea to a concrete actuality, then it requires a *subjectivity* that is certain of itself and a will that is *ungrounded*, that is, truly capable of self-determination through an act of decision. Subjectivity only attains its truth as a *subject*; therefore, sovereignty requires a subject, a person, to exercise the powers of self-determination and decision. Yet, if the state is a rational totality, then the true locus of deliberation and decision is in the institutions and agents of the state. The king is a mere yes-man. Hence, the conservative thinker Friedrich Julius Stahl denounced Hegel's political philosophy as "ultra-governmentalism"; and once the Left Hegelian movement emerged around 1840, Stahl sharpened his charge by presenting Hegel's monarch as a Trojan horse for the republican argument that sovereignty resides in the people.[5]

Among progressives, the critique ran in the opposite direction. In 1840, Arnold Ruge lumped Hegel in with all of the other conservatives who worshipped the monarch as "the *Staatsperson*," who incarnates the totality of the state in "the immediate unity of his person."[6] Indeed, Ruge found Hegel the worst of all, because reactionaries simply appealed to the brute fact of power, whereas Hegel tried to use reason to defend an indefensible system. Once again, Hegel became a Trojan horse, this time for the counterrevolution. The young Karl Marx followed suit in his lengthy critique of Hegel's philosophy of law, where he attacked Hegel for a double mystification: first, the notion of the state as a determination of the Concept conceals the actual democratic foundation of the state; and second, the monarch becomes a political "God-Man," literally a political Christ, mystically personifying the idea of the state and thereby obstructing the development of human community toward its "true generality."[7]

The French discussion of Hegel's political philosophy took many decades to reach a level of detail sufficient to really register the ambiguities and nuances that were already evident in Germany by the 1840s. Indeed, according to Bernard Bourgeois, the *Philosophy of Right* received little attention before 1870.[8] Although one can find some nuanced readings of Hegel's political philosophy, the dominant tendency well into the twentieth century was to denounce Hegel for a "political pantheism" or panlogicism that absorbed the individual into the totality of the organic state, thereby crushing individual liberty beneath an absolute state. The first French translation of the *Philosophy of Right* came only in 1940, and then, a decade later, came the most detailed study up to that time, Eric Weil's *Hegel et l'État*. With serious engagement, however, the ambiguities of the Hegelian theory of the monarch surfaced again. Hence, Weil attempted to rebut the charge that Hegel had reverted to *ancien régime* political absolutism by emphasizing instead the determining role of the state bureaucracy. But this was at the expense of neglecting the role assigned to the monarch, according to Bernard Bourgeois, whose 1976 study of the "prince hégélien" sought to demonstrate the monarch's central place in Hegel's thought. The point I wish to emphasize in Bourgeois's account is his argument that the monarch's power of decision is not a mere formality. That is to say, the act of decision cannot be reduced to the reasons that organize the content of that act, which in the constitutional order of Hegel's state means that no amount of advice from councilors can produce the sovereign decision.[9] Significantly, rather than accepting the Left Hegelian denunciation of this personal dimension, Bourgeois ends by asserting the bond between the personalization of power and the participation of persons in communal affairs. "Hegelian rationality," he writes, "is not that of an abstract structure, but that of a concrete subject." The pervasive presence of subjectivity in Hegel's model, he concludes, contradicts the hasty and partisan attempts to depict Hegel as a totalitarian thinker.

Bernard Bourgeois must have felt himself in a minority position in 1976, for France was then in the midst of what has come to be called the "anti-totalitarian moment."[10] The anti-totalitarian moment is really the story of the collapse of Marxism as a dominant creed among French intellectuals. Disillusionment in 1968, the fragmentation of the Left in the early

1970s, revelations about the Soviet gulag system: all of these contributed to a widespread retreat from Marxism. Gripped by a newfound antipathy toward totalizing systems of meaning, many intellectuals latched onto the term "Totalitarianism" as the catchword describing both the political experience of the twentieth century and French intellectuals' evident attraction to the dream of totality. The most spectacular manifestation of this new mood was the *Nouveaux Philosophes*, whose rather unsophisticated media pronouncements revived all of the old recriminations against Hegel. So, for example, in *Les Maîtres Penseurs*, André Glucksmann implicated Hegel directly in the Stalinist gulags. Fortunately, there were other, much more subtle and reflective voices in the anti-totalitarian moment. Above all, I have in mind Claude Lefort, who had opposed Soviet communism in the name of radical democracy since his student days in the late 1940s. Beyond the shrill tones of the *Nouveaux Philosophes*, Lefort made a fundamental contribution to the reinvigoration of democratic thought in France. Lefort's claim that with the collapse of the monarchy in the period of democratic revolutions, the place of power became a *lieu vide*—an empty place that no person can truly occupy or personify, has now become something of a commonplace in democratic theory. Around twenty years ago, however, Lefort's depiction of democracy as an unprecedented adventure, a political order that had lost its foundational anchors and entered a contingent and open process of self-invention, galvanized many French intellectuals. The same can be said of Lefort's searching exploration of the temptation within democracy to close that adventure by reinvesting power in some body, reoccupying the empty place of democratic power with a Party or a Leader or the People-as-One.

This brings us back to Slavoj Zizek and Jean-Luc Nancy and their engagement with the problem of the Hegelian monarch. I believe that their interest in the monarch has its roots in the question of totalitarianism as it emerged in France during the 1970s and early 1980s. Of course, with Zizek, this influence operated at a greater remove, not only because he is a younger man than Nancy, but also because the French reflection on totalitarianism merged with Zizek's own experience of Yugoslavian communism and the collapse of the Soviet bloc. Zizek and Nancy were both shaped by the collapse of Marxism and the turn toward the question of democracy; moreover, the critique of totalitarianism put the question of political incarnation or embodiment on their agendas. After all, in the influential view of Claude Lefort, the conflict between democracy and totalitarianism is decided ultimately on whether we resist or succumb to the political metaphor of the body. For both Nancy and Zizek, the monarch poses the general question of how power and social union gain a body, or become incarnated in some sort of figure. For many intellectuals affected by the anti-totalitarian moment, this question led to a defense of liberal individualism; for both Nancy and Zizek, it belonged to the attempt to imagine radical democratic politics in the wake of Marxism. There is, therefore, some common ground between Zizek and Nancy; but in fact, they developed the topos of the monarch in quite different ways.

Deconstructing Hegel's Monarch

Among the major deconstructionist thinkers of the 1980s, Jean-Luc Nancy was arguably the most political. Under the influence of Heidegger and Derrida, Nancy was one of the most strident critics of the philosophy of the subject, and his work during the 1980s was dominated by the effort to articulate a new vision of politics beyond the alleged constraints and dangers of subjectivity. Along with his colleague and frequent co-author Philippe Lacoue-Labarthe, Nancy established the "Centre de recherches philosophiques sur le politique" at the École Normal Supérieure in November 1980. The Centre lasted only two years, but it generated numerous interesting contributions from Nancy and Lacoue-Labarthe, as well as from guests such as Claude Lefort, Étienne Balibar, and Jacques Rancière.[11] Most of these texts were published in two volumes, *Rejouer le politique* and *Le retrait du politique*, and among Nancy's contributions, the lengthiest and arguably the most important was "La jurisdiction du monarch hégélien" (1982).[12] That essay reveals the importance of the anti-totalitarian sensibility on its first page, where Nancy agrees in general with the claim that Hegel's *Philosophy of Right* is the "thought of the totalitarian State itself, in that it is the thought of the social totality as an organism or as the organic character of the life of the Subject, which is the mind of the people, which in its turn is the fulfillment, according to history, of the 'self-consciousness of the world mind.'"[13] Nancy's intention is not simply to repeat this cliché, however. Instead, his reading moves beyond the cliché in two different directions: on the one hand, toward the demonstration that the question of "union" or "relation" is a limit-question for any philosophy that presupposes the subject; and on the other hand, toward a new thinking of relation and community opened by a deconstruction of the Hegelian monarch.

Nancy's analysis centers on the impasse created by Hegel's attempt to present the monarch as the fulfillment of the state's true content and aim, namely "*Vereinigung als solche* (union as such)."[14] The monarch does not fulfill union as one element within the whole, but rather, by his unique, singular capacity to present the whole in his person. He literally *is* the state, but as something extra, not one individual among others, but that individual whose personal unity causes their union to exist as a unity. As Nancy writes, "The monarch *is* the fulfillment of relationship—as a relationship to itself."[15] Far from resolving the problem of relation, however, the notion that the relation of all is fulfilled in the singular self-relation of the monarch simply makes the problem more visible, making more visible the "mystery of the incarnation of relation."[16]

Hegel forecloses on this question of relation, however, and instead he substitutes the figure of the monarch, the consummate embodiment of subjectivity, as the truth of union. Thus, the logic of Hegel's theory is to be understood "above all as the totalization in the Subject of subjects and of their union." From this assertion, Nancy makes a more universal claim that a politics of subjectivity will always try to assign a figure or body to the community; assign it an identity that constrains heterogeneity. "By this account," writes Nancy, "whether monarch, Party or Anführer (the term is in §280), it is all the same: the essence of the totalitarian State is in subjectivity, and in the organicity that makes up its structure and its process. The monarch is the organ or the superorgan of organicity itself, of the '*Grund* determining itself' of §278, which is thus finally (dialectically) the *Grund* of *Grundlosigkeit* itself."[17] Nancy extends this critique even to liberal democracy, and in the process, criticizes Claude Lefort for underestimating the "soft" totalitarianism of the western democracies.[18] Strikingly, Nancy inverts the long-standing accusation that the Hegelian state is an impersonal totality that overwhelms the individual, the charge that Bernard Bourgeois in 1976 tried to answer by demonstrating the importance of the subjective dimension in Hegel's theory of the monarch. Now, in the hands of Nancy, it is precisely the attempt to actualize union as such in the figure of the subject that leads him to implicate Hegel in the totalitarian impulse.

Nancy is not content to end with the cliché that Hegel is a totalitarian thinker. Rather, he concludes by arguing that the Hegelian monarch opens the possibility of a "*dis-organization* of totalitarian politics." For between the totality of subjectivity and the monarch's individuality, "there is as much dialectical linkage as absolute rupture." The monarch in his singularity is something extra; in the organic totalization of the Hegelian State, the monarch is lacking; as an individual, he is exempted from the totality, he exceeds it or remains withdrawn from it. The individuality of the monarch should accomplish union, but this happens only in the form of separation. The closure of individuality thus brings about the incompleteness of relation. Yet, as Nancy says, the incompleteness of relation *is* relation itself, because completion would no longer be relation, but simply identity. Unexpectedly, behind the figure of the monarch as the completion of social union emerges the figure of a separation that embodies the incompletion of relation, that is, the very possibility of relation. In short, in the consummate expression of a politics totalized by the Subject, Nancy glimpses an impossibility that suggests a different way of thinking about relation and community, beyond fantasies of fusion and identity and beyond submission to the Subject.

Nancy's essay ends with a utopian, even prophetic call for such a thinking, which his most widely read book, *La communauté désoeuvrée* (1986), tries to answer. Seeking an adequate concept of relation, Nancy rejects the concept of "intersubjectivity" as already too rooted in the subject and turns instead to what he calls "compearance" (*comparution*) to describe a more originary phenomenon of communication and exposure that forms a human being as a "being-the-one-with-the-other." Depicted as a radicalization of Heidegger's *Mitsein*, Nancy's conception pits the spontaneous presentation of relation against the politics of the subject, that is, the politics of unity, essence, and domination. Facing what he describes as the exorbitant expansion of the subject's claim, Nancy seeks a *"retrait"* of the political, both in the sense of a "revaluation" of the complicity of the political with the philosophy of the subject and a "retreat" of the political, a rolling back in the name of compearance. In place of a politics of projects and actions, Nancy offers the paradoxical notion of an "inoperative community," a *being-in-common* that only works so long as it does not work. That is to say, community fails the moment it becomes an object, a site of production, a target, or a goal. The suspension of "work" on community allows community to work, that is, to emerge as the opening and exposure of relation.

With this rather tremulous conception, Nancy sought nothing less than to revive the Left. He believed twentieth-century Leftism was hopelessly enmeshed in the politics of subjectivity, as Leftism was based on a humanistic conception of man as subject and object of history. So, a newly born Left had to return to a primordial awareness of community. At one level, this sense of incompletion and unworking of community might be presented as a moderate counsel, à la Claude Lefort, that democracy should resist the fantasy of the people-as-one. However, Nancy made clear in his next book, *L'Experience de la liberté* from 1988, that he was offering an argument for permanent revolution. That is, if the community can never be the object of a work, then it will always exceed any attempt to give form to the common. A justice adequate to this excess can only reside in the decision to constantly "challenge the validity of an established or prevailing 'just measure' *in the name of the incommensurable.*"[19] In brief, the political task of the Left must be to reopen the framework of every established order. But in the name of what? Here, Nancy empties politics of any normative dimension. Any project, any ideal, will simply throw us back into the problem of transfixing the community as an object or work. In the absence of "representations" (*Vorstellungen*) of goals, a politics of liberation must become each time an act of ontological liberation, that is, the liberation of the originary space of human compearance, the space of an inaugural sharing. Nancy succumbs to the disturbing fantasy of this originary space as a "freedom untainted by any power, though all powers conceal it." Whatever concrete freedoms or rights may be at stake in political struggle, this initial freedom is always before and beyond them. Nancy's politics thus presents us with a pure form of decisionism, a decision each time for a primordial space that offers the freedom of every new beginning.[20] Matters are not helped by the fact that Nancy has essentially banished will from the scene, since it is implicated in the totalitarian impulse. So even if one were to accept Nancy's notion that a claim for any specific exercise of freedom requires an ontological grounding of freedom *as such*, it becomes very difficult to understand how political agents could arrive at concrete goals except as the spontaneously given gifts of our being-in-common. If we return to the question of French receptions of Hegel, we might note that when Nancy tries to co-opt Hegel for this politics in his 1997 book *Hegel: L'inquiétude du négatif*, it can only be a Hegel shorn of two of his most important components: that is, a Hegel presented without any acknowledgement of the function of will in the practice of freedom, and a Hegel without any mention of the role that institutions might play in the realization of our freedom.

The Return of the King

In 1982, Nancy depicts Hegel as playing an unintended role in deconstructing the politics of totality because the paradoxical effect of his attempt at totalization through the figure of the monarch was to demonstrate the impossibility of union; by the late 1990s, Nancy's Hegel emerges as a full-fledged deconstructive thinker. Nancy thus remains within the terms laid out in the final chapter of Martin Jay's *Marxism and Totality*, whereby French poststructuralism squared off against the concept of totality. What Jay could not have foreseen is Hegel's move into the camp opposing ... Hegelianism. Nancy's heterodox reading of Hegel seems to converge with Zizek's, and it is not surprising that one of the admirers of *L'inquiétude du négatif* is Slavoj Zizek, who describes it as "perhaps the best formulation of [the] vertiginous abyss in which the Universal is caught in the Hegelian dialectical process."[21] Yet Zizek's praise of Nancy in fact conceals a profoundly different orientation. Nancy's deconstructive reading of monarchy displays a basic feature of deconstruction. That is, deconstruction presupposes a constituted field of identity in order to set to work on subverting it. As Zizek writes of Jacques Derrida, "Derrida remains prisoner of the ... conception which aims at freeing heterogeneity from the constraints of identity."[22] Here, we have a way to pinpoint the difference between Zizek and deconstructionists like Derrida or Nancy: where the deconstructionist struggles to dissolve the inert solidity of identity, Zizek reverses the procedure to demonstrate the way in which the fluidity of being passes into a point of inert, fixed identity-with-itself. That can be rephrased in terms that are more relevant for the concerns of this essay, namely in terms of the relationship between "universals" and "particulars." The deconstructionist starts with the presupposition of a universal and then demonstrates its impossibility by showing that it is in fact only one term within a chain of terms. No element can dominate, because the meaning of each element is recoded by all of the elements in a movement of endless deferral. Zizek, by contrast, maintains that the universal is always a particular element within a series, elevated to fill the empty place of the series itself. An empty place, it must be emphasized, because the "universal" as such, as the true totality of all the elements in a series, does not exist.

To formulate this in Lacanian terms, Zizek rejects the pluralist and relativist position of postmodernism, and fully endorses Lacan's insistence that "in every concrete constellation, *truth is bound to emerge* in some contingent detail."[23] Or, to put it in Hegelian terms, Zizek embraces the Hegelian idea of the "concrete universal," that is, a universal that is not distinct from and merely externally related to the particular, but rather, a universal that finds embodiment in the particular. Of course, a strict interpretation of Hegel would likely suggest, as Charles Taylor does, that the concrete universal is the "manifestation of the necessity contained in the idea concerned, and it is moreover a necessary manifestation, that is, [it] can be seen as posited by [the idea]."[24] To recall a point made earlier in this essay, this was precisely what Karl Marx had objected to when he attacked Hegel's monarch, including Hegel's entire conception of the state as a mystical derivation from the idea. Zizek's use of Hegel departs from the strict letter of Hegelian philosophy: first, by rejecting the notion that an "abstract universal" could exist as such, and, second, by insisting that all concrete universals are such only through a contingent and arbitrary process.

In Zizek's work of the late 1980s and early 1990s, Hegel's monarch serves as a privileged example of the process whereby a particular element within a series creates the universal. Critics have long attacked Hegel for placing a non-rational, biologically determined man at the head of the rational state. But, according to Zizek, the crucial point is precisely the abyss separating the State as an organic rational totality from the "'irrational' *factum brutum* of the person who embodies supreme power."[25] As the political actor who has only to "say 'yes' and dot the 'i'," the monarch has often nothing more to do "than sign his name." Yet as Hegel emphasizes, "But this name is important: it is the last word beyond which it is impossible to go."[26] The monarch's entire authority and actuality thus consists in his Name, in a signifier. So, states Zizek, "The monarch thus embodies the function of the Master-Signifier at its purest; it is the One of the Exception, the 'irrational' protuberance of the social edifice which transforms the amorphous mass of 'people' into a concrete totality of mores."[27] Zizek treats this as a specific instance of a more general process, which finds its clearest formulation in *The Sublime Object of Ideology*: "it is the universal itself which is constituted by way of subtracting from a set some Particular designed to embody the Universal as such: the Universal arises ... in the act of radical split between the wealth of particular diversity and the element which, in the midst of it, 'gives body' to the Universal."[28] The way the monarch fulfills this process becomes clearer if we consider that the monarch is, in fact, the only *natural* person in the community. He is, as Hegel writes, the place where "*nature took refuge; he is its last remainder, as a positive remainder*—the family of the prince is the only positive family—all other families must be left behind—other individuals *have value only in so far as they are dispossessed*, in so far as they have made themselves."[29] The monarch is thus a singular coincidence of pure Culture and the residue of Nature. By the unique consubstantiality of Culture and Nature in his person, the monarch drives a wedge between Nature and Culture in everyone else. The figure of the monarch thus propels all others out of the organic, natural ties of family and tradition into a community of self-made subjects.

Hence, the monarch operates as a Master-Signifier that organizes a social field in which "spirit," not nature, is determinate. If we recall Nancy's concern with the monarch as the actualization of union as such, we see just how different Zizek's approach is. For Zizek, it is precisely the fact that the Hegelian monarch exceeds the dialectic, or even better, short circuits the dialectical mediation between "nature" and "spirit" or "individual" and "totality," that allows the dialectic to work. Hence, from the argument that "the State as a rational totality exists only in so far as it is embodied in the inert presence of the King's body," Zizek offers a more general statement about Hegel's dialectic: "the greatest speculative mystery of the dialectical movement is not how the richness and diversity of reality can be reduced to a dialectical conceptual mediation, but the fact that in order to take place this dialectical structuring must itself be embodied in some totally contingent element."[30]

This emphasis on contingency immediately takes on political significance. It will be clear by now that Zizek's appropriation of Hegel, brilliant as it is, has at best a partial relationship to Hegel. That is to say, not only does Zizek emphatically reject the image of Hegel as a monist, but he also suppresses Hegel's explicit preference for closure as the means by which to justify negativity, the *negation of the negation* that portends a final totalization. Indeed, Zizek does not even indicate that there is a tension in Hegel's thought between the resolution of contradictions and restless negativity, between necessity and continency.[31] For Zizek, the value of dialectical procedure lies in its power to reveal moments of genesis whereby a Necessity springs up as the "positivization" or "coagulation" of a "radically contingent decision."[32] Given this view, it should not be surprising to hear Zizek assert that the "true politico-philosophical heirs of Hegel are authors who fully endorse the political logic of the excess constitutive of every established Order."[33] Chief among these is Carl Schmitt, Zizek tells us. Schmitt's influence is evident even in the earliest works of Zizek. Hence, Zizek's description of the contingent transformation of a particular into a universal rests firmly on the Schmittian conception of a founding act of violence. In short, a radically contingent, scandalous act of violence stands at the origin of the new Master-Signifier. And this act "succeeds" the moment it conceals its own past, its own conditions, its scandalous character.[34] Hence, the new Master-Signifier becomes naturalized, necessary, and part of the order of things. As the original violence sinks into forgetfulness, people come to identify with the Master-Signifier. It becomes a fantasy-object that seems to hold some key, some promise of completion, an *objet petit a* in Lacanian jargon. This creates the conditions for the strange transubstantiation of the monarch, whereby the king becomes a Thing, a sublime body; or more precisely, we the subjects act *as if* he is the Thing embodied. The contemporary relevance of this comes forward when Zizek notes that, "within the post-revolutionary 'totalitarian' order, we have witnessed a re-emergence of the sublime political body in the shape of Leader and/or Party." In "postdemocratic" totalitarianism, revolutionaries fully assume the role of an instrument of an objective historical order or law; and by doing so, the body of the revolutionary redoubles itself and assumes a sublime quality. Thus, Stalin's vow of the Bolshevik Party: "We, the Communists, are people of a special mould. We are made of special stuff." Hence the uncanny affiliation between Communism and the mausoleum, and the compulsion to preserve intact the body of the dead Leader. "How," Zizek asks, "can we explain this obsessive care if not by reference to the fact that in their symbolic universe, the body of the Leader is not just an ordinary transient body but a body redoubled in itself, an envelopment of the sublime Thing?"[35]

How does one kill such a body? Regicide is one of the recurring motifs of *For They Know Not What They Do*. It is, significantly, a book first delivered as lectures to a public that had just symbolically overturned an objective order, symbolically killed a Master-Signifier. By the end of 1989, Slovenia's neighbors, the Romanians, had executed their leader after a hastily convened revolutionary court judged him guilty of crimes against the people. Zizek is, in fact, not optimistic that regicide can really achieve its goal. By way of illustration, he turns to Lacan's comments on Hamlet. Why does Hamlet not kill Claudius? Is it not that he wants to strike Claudius in such a way that by striking a blow to his material body, he would hit the "thing" in it, the king's sublime body? "What stays Hamlet's arm?" asks Lacan. "It's not fear—he has nothing but contempt for the guy—it's because he knows that he must strike something other than what's there."[36] The Jacobins recognized this uncanny fusion and rightly refused to distinguish between the empirical person and the symbolic mandate of the king; yet, Zizek judges their regicide negatively. It seems like an "impotent *acting out* which was simultaneously excessive and empty." The decapitation of the king was fundamentally superfluous *and* a terrifying sacrilege confirming the king's charisma by the very means of his physical destruction. Zizek claims that the same effect is at work in all similar cases, including the execution of Nicolai Ceaucescu: "when confronted with the picture of his bloodstained body, even the greatest enemies of his regime shrank back, as if they were witness to excessive cruelty, but at the same time a strange fear flashed across their mind, mixed with incredulity: is this really *him*?"[37]

So how does one kill such a body? Karl Marx's answer was that we must destroy the symbolic system in which some men are kings, but Zizek is too much the psychoanalyst not to believe that an emperor without clothes might still be a fantasmatic object. Ultimately, Zizek's answer lies with Lacanian psychoanalysis, more precisely, with the process of "going through the fantasy." Lacan's later work defines fantasy not as escape, but rather as the way we construct our reality by supplementing the lack in being, the impossibility of our desire, with a fantasy-object. Zizek writes that the "final moment of the [psychoanalytic process] is defined as 'going through the fantasy': not its symbolic interpretation but the experience of the fact that the fantasy-object, by its fascinating presence, is merely filling out a lack, a void in the Other. There is nothing 'behind' the fantasy; the fantasy is a construction whose function is to hide this void, this 'nothing'—that is, the lack in the Other."[38] In short, the Other holds no key to meaning. The political meaning of this seems clear. Going through the fantasy would seem to liberate us from the tyranny of political masters and free us for our own political fabrication.

I want to suggest by way of conclusion that Zizek's democratic commitments are actually more ambiguous. At the very beginning of his career, Zizek enthusiastically embraced the project of "radical democracy" most closely associated with the self-described "post-Marxist" philosophers Chantal Mouffe and Ernesto Laclau. In their important book from 1985, *Hegemony & Socialist Strategy*, Laclau and Mouffe explicitly draw on Claude Lefort's description of the democratic experience.[39] Lefort, we have seen, argued that democracy transformed the symbolic dimension of politics by destroying the logic of embodiment or incarnation, thus creating a *lieu vide*, an empty place, at the center of democratic power. For the radical democrats, Ernesto Laclau and Chantal Mouffe, democracy's loss of foundation translates into the possibility of a contingent, open-ended struggle to extend the meaning and reach of democracy. Zizek, as noted above, associated himself with this political belief system, which could be readily aligned with the basic turn away from the ideal of totality that marked French poststructuralism in the 1970s and early 1980s.

But this reading of a posttotalitarian strain in Zizek's work is too simple. In fact, even in his early books, Zizek follows a different path. Consider his discussion of the Jacobins in the final chapter of *For They Know Not What They Do*. Zizek writes that the "tragic grandeur" of the Jacobins lies in their refusal to occupy the empty place of power. Following Lefort's description of the Jacobin Terror, Zizek notes that the Jacobins set themselves up as the guardians of that empty place. They prevented anybody from occupying the empty center of power, protecting this place against false pretenders. But, asks Zizek, does not the guardian reserve for himself a privileged place, "does he not function as a kind of King-in-reverse…?" That is to say, is not the position from which he acts and speaks the position of absolute Power? "Is not safeguarding the empty locus of Power the most cunning and at the same time the most brutal, unconditional way of occupying it?"[40] At this point, Hegel's monarch makes another return, this time as the speculative resolution to the Jacobin impasse. In other words, both the Hegelian monarch and the Jacobin terrorist protect the empty locus of Power. However, in contrast to the Jacobins, the monarch does so only as an empty, formal agent whose main task is to prevent the current performer of Power from identifying himself immediately with the locus of power. Writes Zizek: "The 'monarch' is nothing but a positivization, a materialization of the *distance* separating the locus of Power from those who exert it."[41] The monarch thus interrupts the vicious circle of "democrats cutting off each other's heads indefinitely."

Someone familiar with Hegel's discussion of the monarch may well protest that the monarch is not nearly so stripped of power as Zizek claims. But my interest is less with the accuracy of Zizek's depiction than with the systematic function of the monarch within Zizek's thought. According to Zizek, every politics aims to totalize its claims and struggles to elevate a contingent particular to a universal status. Every politics aims to organize the social field around a Master-Signifier. Zizek is far from the postmodern champions of an endlessly pluralistic, heterogeneous, relativistic democracy, the kind of position we see in Jean-Luc Nancy's "inoperative community," Jean-François Lyotard's critique of a politics of consensus, or Derrida's *"démocratie à venir."* Zizek's politics demands something in the center, something in the locus of Power. Of course, he explicitly advocates that the Master be separated as much as possible from "effective" governance. In this sense, the dumber the better, although here one may wonder whether his example of Ronald Reagan as a dumb Master supports or contradicts his belief that the symbolic head is separated from the locus of actual governance. A conundrum immediately emerges when we consider that at the same time that Zizek insists on filling the space in the center, his analytical method aims to strip us of our fantasmatic investments in the Other. Just as "going through the fantasy" leaves the psychoanalytic patient "destitute," that is, without the fantasmatic props of his subjectivity, so too, the process of going through the political fantasy would seem to create suspicion toward all Master-Signifiers. What is Zizek's response to this tension between symbolic effect and demystification? In a 1991 essay, "Formal Democracy and Its Discontents," he writes: "We must assume a kind of 'active forgetfulness' by accepting the symbolic fiction even though we know that 'in reality, things are not like that.' The democratic attitude is always based upon a certain fetishistic split: *I know very well* (that the democratic form is just a form spoiled by the stains of 'pathological' imbalance), *but just the same* (I act as if democracy were possible)."[42] Substitute *penis* or *breast* for *democracy* in the formula "I know very well, … but just the same …," and it is obvious why this is a formula for fetishism.

Post-Marxism and Totality

Zizek's position vis-à-vis the topography mapped by *Marxism and Totality* should be clear. On the one hand, he shares the French poststructuralists' rejection of the concept of expressive totality that had animated the emancipatory projects of Western Marxism. On the other hand, he inverts the poststructuralist procedure; his interest does not lie in deconstructing a constituted field of identity, but rather in the process whereby a heterogeneous field becomes totalized. Nor does he share the poststructuralists' celebration of dispersal as a liberating goal in itself. If one of Zizek's impulses is the critical exposure of the contingent and fantasmatic structure of all totalities, his insistence on the power of Master-Signifiers makes it difficult for him to break out of a totalizing style of thought. Hence, his linkage of democracy to the logic of Master-Signifiers forecloses on other ways of conceiving democracy. Or, more precisely, he forecloses on the need to combine different forms and types of democracy. If, as Zizek recognized in his essay on formal democracy, it is impossible to embody fully the elements of democratic society in the empirical institutions of public life, then it is doubly important to acknowledge that all types of democratic institutions involve forms of exclusion, limits on discussion, and sources of asymmetry among participants. However, the forms that non-democracy takes within various types of democracy are significantly different. Thus, as Andrew Arato has argued, in principle, other things being equal, it is highly desirable to combine different types of democratic institutions and processes (direct and representative, centralistic and federal, civil and political) in a given constitutional framework.[43]

In the early 1990s, Zizek seemed little interested in such a conception of a pluralism of practices and institutions, opting instead for a fetishistic investment in one Master-Signifier. This fact may explain why Zizek's political thought took such a disturbing turn during the course of the 1990s. As his opposition to global capitalism has sharpened and he has gravitated back toward Marxism, Zizek has more and more insisted that the Master-Signifier of today's "global capitalist universe" is "democracy."[44] But rather than challenging the hegemonic identification of democracy with the singular meaning of capitalist globalization, Zizek has declared himself an opponent of democracy. One of the more perverse aspects of this anti-democratic posture is his recent call for a return to Lenin, to whom we had just finished saying "goodbye." It would seem that the fetishistic attachment to formal democracy is no longer a convincing option for Zizek. But the fetish structure seems to persist in Zizek's thought. Another formula for fetish comes to mind, this time the old cry of the royalist: "the king is dead, long live the king."

Notes

1. Slavoj Zizek, *The Sublime Object of Ideology* (London, 1989), 6–7.
2. See Martin Jay, *Marxism and Totality: The Adventures of a Concept from Lukács to Habermas* (Berkeley and Los Angeles, 1984), 515; Slavoj Zizek, *For They Know Not What They Do: Enjoyment as a Political Factor* (London, 1991), 94n28.
3. To my knowledge, the only extended discussion of this theme is to be found in Peter Starr, *Logics of Failed Revolt: French Theory After May '68* (Stanford, CA, 1995), 194–202.

4. Zizek, *For They Know Not What They Do*, 3.
5. Friedrich Julius Stahl, *Die Philosophie des Rechts*, 2 vols. in 3, *Rechts- und Staatslehre auf der Grundlage Christlicher Weltanschauung. Teil I: Die Allgemeinen Lehren und das Privatrecht* (Hildesheim, 1963), 2, bk. 1: 80.
6. Arnold Ruge, "Zur Kritik des gegenwärtigen Staats- und Völkerrechts," *Die Hegelsche Linke*, ed. Ingrid and Heinz Pepperle (Leipzig, 1985), 163.
7. Marx, "Zur Kritik der Hegelschen Rechtsphilosophie," *Marx-Engels Gesamtausgabe*, 52 vols. to date (Berlin, 1982), 2: 25–43. I have discussed this early debate about Hegel's monarch in detail in Breckman, *Marx, the Young Hegelians, and the Origins of Radical Social Theory: Dethroning the Self* (Cambridge, 1999).
8. Bernard Bourgeois, *Etudes hégéliennes: Raison et decision* (Paris, 1992), 373.
9. Ibid., 231.
10. See especially Michael Scott Christofferson, *French Intellectuals Against the Left: The Anti-totalitarian Moment of the 1970s* (New York, 2004).
11. The *Centre de recherches philosophiques sur le politique* provides one concrete point of contact between Nancy and Lefort, who are not usually associated with each other and indeed belonged to quite different intellectual circles in the early 1980s. It was in the context of the *Centre* that Lefort presented an important statement of his general views, "La Question de la démocratie."
12. The latter of these volumes appears in English as *Retreating the Political*, ed. Jean-Luc Nancy and Philippe Lacoue-Labarthe, trans. Simon Sparks (London, 1997). Nancy's essay appears in English in *The Birth to Presence*, trans. Brian Holmes, et al. (Stanford, CA, 1993).
13. Jean-Luc Nancy, "The Jurisdiction of the Hegelian Monarch," *The Birth to Presence*, 111.
14. Ibid., 112.
15. Ibid., 116.
16. Ibid., 126.
17. Ibid., 139. Nancy's cryptic formulation of the "ground of groundlessness" underscores his distance from Hegel. Hegel operates according to the logic of incarnation, whereby the monarch's subjectivity is identical with the political organism he embodies. For Nancy, the monarch marks the hiatus between subjectivity and community, so even if his decision acts as a ground, it has no other ground than its own utterance.
18. See Nancy and Lacoue-Labarthe, "The 'Retreat' of the Political," in Nancy and Lacoue-Labarthe, *Retreating the Political*, 128–129.
19. Jean-Luc Nancy, *The Experience of Freedom*, trans. Bridget McDonald (Stanford, CA, 1993), 75.
20. This project continues in Nancy's recent works, such as *La création du monde ou la mondialisation* (Paris, 2002).
21. Zizek, *The Ticklish Subject: The Absent Centre of Political Ontology* (London, 1999), 122n26.
22. Zizek, *For They Know Not What They Do*, 88.
23. Ibid., 196.
24. Charles Taylor, *Hegel* (Cambridge, 1975), 113.
25. Zizek, *For They Know Not What They Do*, 82.
26. Hegel quoted in Zizek, ibid., 82.
27. Ibid., 83.
28. Zizek, *The Sublime Object of Ideology*, 44.
29. Hegel quoted in Zizek, *For They Know Not What They Do*, 83.
30. Zizek, *The Sublime Object of Ideology*, 183.

31. See the comments of Ernesto Laclau, "Identity and Hegemony: The Role of Universality in the Constitution of Political Logics," in Judith Butler, Ernesto Laclau, and Slavoj Zizek, *Contingency, Hegemony, Universality* (London, 2000), 75.
32. Zizek, *For They Know Not What They Do*, 189.
33. Zizek, *The Ticklish Subject*, 113.
34. Zizek, *For They Know Not What They Do*, 189.
35. Ibid., 260.
36. Lacan quoted in ibid., 256.
37. Ibid., 256.
38. Zizek, *The Sublime Object of Ideology*, 133.
39. I discuss Laclau and Mouffe in "The Post-Marx of the Letter," in *After the Deluge: New Perspectives on Postwar French Intellectual and Cultural History*, ed. Julian Bourg (New York, 2004).
40. Zizek, *For They Know Not What They Do*, 268–269.
41. Ibid., 269.
42. Zizek, "Formal Democracy and its Discontents," in Zizek, *Looking Awry: An Introduction to Jacques Lacan Through Popular Culture* (Cambridge, 1991), 168.
43. Andrew Arato, "Dilemmas Arising from the Power to Create Constitutions in Eastern Europe," *Constitutionalism, Identity, Difference, and Legitimacy: Theoretical Perspectives*, ed. Michel Rosenfeld (Durham, NC, 1994), 171–172.
44. Slavoj Zizek, "The Rhetorics of Power," *Diacritics* 31, no. 1 (Spring, 2001): 96.

Bibliography

Arato, Andrew. "Dilemmas Arising from the Power to Create Constitutions in Eastern Europe." In *Constitutionalism, Identity, Difference, and Legitimacy: Theoretical Perspectives*, edited by Michel Rosenfeld. Durham, 1994.

Bourgeois, Bernard. *Etudes hégéliennes: Raison et decision*. Paris, 1992.

Breckman, Warren. "The Post-Marx of the Letter." In *After the Deluge: New Perspectives on Postwar French Intellectual and Cultural History*, edited by Julian Bourg. New York, 2004.

———. *Marx, the Young Hegelians, and the Origins of Radical Social Theory: Dethroning the Self*. Cambridge, 1999.

Christofferson, Michael Scott. *French Intellectuals Against the Left: The Antitotalitarian Moment of the 1970s*. New York, 2004.

Jay, Martin. *Marxism and Totality: The Adventures of a Concept from Lukács to Habermas*. Berkeley and Los Angeles, 1984.

Laclau, Ernesto. "Identity and Hegemony: The Role of Universality in the Constitution of Political Logics." In Judith Butler, Ernesto Laclau, and Slavoj Zizek, *Contingency, Hegemony, Universality*. London, 2000.

Marx, Karl. "Zur Kritik der Hegelschen Rechtsphilosophie." In *Marx-Engels Gesamtausgabe*. 52 vols. Berlin, 1982.

Nancy, Jean-Luc. *The Experience of Freedom*. Translated by Bridget McDonald. Stanford, 1993.

———. "The Jurisdiction of the Hegelian Monarch." In *The Birth to Presence*. Translated by Brian Holmes et al. Stanford, 1993.

———. *La création du monde ou la mondialisation*. Paris, 2002.

——— and Philippe Lacoue-Labarthe, eds. *Retreating the Political*. Translated by Simon Sparks. London, 1997.
Ruge, Arnold. "Zur Kritik des gegenwärtigen Staats- und Völkerrechts." In *Die Hegelsche Linke*, edited by Ingrid Pepperle and Heinz Pepperle. Leipzig, 1985.
Stahl, Friedrich Julius. *Die Philosophie des Rechts*. 2 vols. *Rechts- und Staatslehre auf der Grundlage Christlicher Weltanschauung. Teil I: Die Allgemeinen Lehren und das Privatrecht*. Hildesheim, 1963.
Starr, Peter. *Logics of Failed Revolt: French Theory After May '68*. Stanford, 1995.
Zizek, Slavoj. *For They Know Not What They Do: Enjoyment as a Political Factor*. London, 1991.
———. *Looking Awry: An Introduction to Jacques Lacan Through Popular Culture*. Cambridge, 1991.
———. "The Rhetorics of Power." *Diacritics* 31, no. 1 (Spring, 2001): 73–90.
———. *The Sublime Object of Ideology*. London, 1989.
———. *The Ticklish Subject: The Absent Centre of Political Ontology*. London, 1999.

Paradigm Shift
The *Speculation* of *Downcast Eyes*

Rosalind Krauss

Most commentators on the upheavals wrought by poststructuralism's attack on the determinacy of meaning focused on the impact of postwar deconstructionist discourse, characterized as the onset of epistemic relativism or the pronouncement of an irreducible interpretive undecidability for the act of criticism.

Martin Jay's *Downcast Eyes* shifted this terrain to the rise of what he named "anti-ocularism," subtitling his book "The Denigration of Vision in Twentieth-Century French Thought." Indeed, *Downcast Eyes* pronounced the fact of a twentieth-century "paradigm shift"—the result of a movement of the conceptual tectonic plates that undermined the Renaissance's powerful epistemological model, based on perspective, by replacing it with various forms of an anti-ocular conviction that was being developed in the 1980s, both in Europe and the US, as a scholarly, critical, and aesthetic strategy.

A first version of Jay's work was published as "Scopic Regimes of Modernity," for a conference convened as *Vision and Visuality* (its very title an acknowledgement of Jay's influence),[1] with Jay's work joined to that of Jonathan Crary ("Modernizing Vision"), Jacqueline Rose ("Sexuality and Vision: Some Questions"), and myself (Rosalind Krauss, "The Im/pulse to See"), among others. Crary's drive to displace nineteenth-century art history away from its obsession with the visual and the decorative exemplified by Impressionism and its aftermaths, and instead onto the mechanism of optical machines such as photography and early forms of cinema, led to his path-breaking *Techniques of the Observer*.[2] My own rejection of the story of the exclusively visualist drive of modernist practice issued in *The Optical Unconscious*.[3] Both books are indebted to Jay's work.

Downcast Eyes could easily have appeared as just another theorization of postmodernism, joining the rising chorus of those challenges to the "visual" familiar to the art world since the 1960s. From Conceptual Art's use of language to chase any experience of the "optical" from the visual field, to the strategies of hiding or wrapping that had been developed by certain kinds of performance and body art (particularly in the work of Joseph Beuys), the idea that aesthetic production should be geared to either optical display or ocular pleasure (as in the recently dominant style of "Color-Field Painting") was opened to the severest attack.

And if this break was apparent in the domain of practice, the critical understanding of a break between modernism and postmodernism was being read off from an evolution of the senses—here, the sense of sight—which were themselves no longer taken to be a biological given and thus transhistorical, but were seen to be specifically shaped by history. Thus, in order to analyze the onset of postmodernism, Fredric Jameson first describes the modernist experience of the visual, achieved by the time of Impressionism, as the constitution of what he calls a "semi-autonomous" mode of perception. If Realism's drive was to express the experience of the world as a totality that engages the sensory field of the whole body—touch, hearing, smell, balance, motion, as well as seeing—Impressionism, he says, breaks this one perceptual channel off from the whole and makes it instead into a quasi-abstract source of pleasure that could attain new heights of fullness and purity (*l'art pour l'art*). "The transformation of a drab peasant object world," Jameson writes, "into the most glorious materialization of pure color in oil paint is to be seen as a Utopian gesture, an act of compensation which ends up producing a whole new Utopian realm of the senses, or at least of that supreme sense—sight, the visual, the eye—which it now reconstitutes for us as a semi-autonomous space in its own right."[4] In the postwar period, however, within the conditions of late capital, Jameson argues, this abstract but full visuality is transformed into a new and disorienting form of irreality, a generalized kind of seeing that Jameson names "the hysterical sublime."[5] Still others would read out this sense of an image-world divested of anything real behind it, and thus become "simulacral," as a function of an ever-deepening effect of what Guy Debord named "spectacle."[6]

But *Downcast Eyes* projects the attack on vision as more than a postwar or postmodern phenomenon. Instead, the book's prey is the whole complex of poststructuralist theory as it joins to produce the Denigration of Vision. Thus, from being the culture of En*light*enment thinking, in which vision's capacity to survey and order, to abstract and model the elements within a given field, had made it into the privileged vehicle of reason itself, French conceptual production throughout the whole of the twentieth century is now being seen as covering vision with the utmost suspicion. In Jay's account, this begins with Henri Bergson's repudiation of space as the dominant model of experience to which other orders, such as the temporal (Bergson's *durée*), are subordinated. Contrasting the homogeneity of space—a matrix of repeatable equivalent units, each outside the other—to the heterogeneity of time, in which memory and projection are inextricably telescoped into the present, Bergson formulated the idea of experiential duration as radically inassimilable to space. From Bergson, this opposition continues (although in different terms) to the Surrealists and Georges Bataille, and thence to Jean-Paul Sartre's quasi-paranoia in his *Being and Nothingness* about the other's "gaze," which, by trapping the subject in its beam like a deer caught in headlights, objectifies that subject and limits his or her freedom.[7] This subject has become simply a body that exists on the level of all other objects of the world, a self that has suddenly become opaque to his own consciousness, a self that he therefore cannot *know* but only *be*, a self that for that reason is nothing but a pure reference to the Other. As the roll call of French theorists lengthens to include the psychoanalyst Jacques Lacan, with his idea of misrecognition, the Marxist Louis Althusser, with his concept of interpellation, the philosopher Jacques Derrida, with his formulation of "phallogocentrism," the feminist Luce Irigaray, with her notion of the speculum,[8] and the historian and theorist Michel Foucault, with his ideas of surveillance and discipline,[9] Jay argues that "anti-visual discourse is a pervasive but generally ignored phenomenon of twentieth-century Western thought ... [such that] a great deal of recent French thought in a wide variety of fields is in one way or another imbued with a profound suspicion of vision and its hegemonic role in the modern era."[10] Jay goes so far as to term this new attitude a "paradigm shift."

In the case of twentieth-century art, it may seem counterintuitive to characterize the period of high modernism as "anti-ocular." Wave after wave of modernist artists had followed Impressionism's move to establish a "purified" optical stratum as a semi-autonomous field of experience. From Robert Delaunay's extrapolation of the optical blur of an airplane propeller into an abstract set of circular bands, to Giacomo Balla's Futurist search for the laws of pure iridescence, to Wassily Kandinsky's Expressionist attempt to render the whole field of human emotion through symphonic surges of color, to the Bauhaus desire for a systematic exploration of color married to geometric form (conducted by Johannes Itten, Paul Klee, and Joseph Albers), and in the postwar period, to the phenomenon of "color field painting" and Clement Greenberg's campaign for the idea of "opticality," which he also extended to sculpture, we feel the pressures of visual thinking.[11]

Working counter to this opticalist euphoria, however, was quite another tradition, one given theoretical articulation in Georges Bataille's (anti-)concept of "formlessness." A generation of Surrealist artists embraced this attack on *form* and on the privilege it gives to the visual domination of experience—from Joan Miro's "anti-painting" to Salvador Dali and Luis Bunuel's film, *Chien Andalu* (with its razored eyeball). But they were not alone in this. The Dada artist Hans Arp was also attacking the stability of form through the collages he was making of torn and crumbled paper, arranged by chance. Speaking of the welcome these works held out to a withering away of form through the devastating effects of entropy, he asked:

> Why strive for accuracy and purity if they can never be attained? I now welcomed the decomposition that always sets in once a work is ended. A dirty man puts his dirty finger on a subtle detail in a painting to point it out. That place is now marked with sweat and grease. He bursts into enthusiasm and the painting is sprayed with saliva.... Moisture creates mildew. The work decomposes and dies. Now, the death of a painting no longer devastated me. I had come to terms with its ephemeralness and its death, and included them in the painting.

And for his part, Marcel Duchamp had entered into the phase of his work he mockingly called "precision oculism," signaling its anti-artistic nature by the fact that it was now the scientifico-commercial exploration conducted by his alter-ego "Rrose Sélavy," who invariably defied the idea of art's inherent defense against reduplication by submitting such inventions either to copyright or patent. The ironic turn on opticality wrought by these oculist machines, from the sculpture-like *Rotary Demi-Sphere* (1925), to the film *Anémic Cinéma* (1925–1926), to his visual phonograph records, the *Rotoreliefs* (1935), was the havoc they were able to wreak with form. For as the turning spirals of the "oculist charts" opened onto a pulsatile movement from concavity to convexity and back again, the throb of this motion dizzied and destabilized the field of vision, eroticizing and carnalizing it instead, by filling it with a suggestive play of part objects: now a breast, now an eye, now a uterus.[12]

This idea of an attack on visuality itself continued and even intensified in the postwar period. On the one hand, as was noted above, it involved the kind of inoculation of the work against the optical that occurred at the hands of Conceptual Art, either by filling the field with the nonvisual substance of language as in the case of Lawrence Weiner, or by so banalizing the image as to render it unexploitable by the mass-cultural forces of spectacle. But on the other hand, it went beyond the negative strategy of an avoidance of the visual to the more positive one of an active aggression against the very prerogatives of vision.

One dimension of this organized itself around a reprise of the pulsatile force of the *Rotoreliefs*. Adopting both the medium of film and that of video in the late 1960s, artists such as Richard Serra and Bruce Nauman made works employing a repetitive rhythmic beat, in Serra's case, the opening and closing of a fist in his film *Hand Catching Lead* (1971), in Nauman's, the truncated image of an upside-down lower face and neck with the mouth saying "lip sync" over and over (although out of synchronization) in his video work, *Lip Sync* (1969). In both cases the body part performing the gesture becomes organ-like (as in Duchamp's spirals) and the visual field unstable. In the Serra case in particular, the example of contemporary cinematic practices within the field of avant-garde film was important, particularly the phenomenon of the "flicker film" in which alternations of colored frames with more or less equal amounts of black leader produce rapid-fire flashing lights.[13] While it might seem that the visual dazzle set up by the "flicker" is just another instance of "opticality," in fact the phenomenon sets off a strange bodily, or tactile experience due to the way the light stimulates the viewer's production of an after-image which is then projected onto the empty field of the momentary stretch of blackness. So that what we "see" in those interstitial spaces is not the material surface of the "frame" or screen, nor the abstract condition of the cinematic "field," but the bodily production of our own nervous systems, the rhythmic beat of the neural network's feedback, of its "retention" and "protention," (Bergson's *durée*), as the nerve tissue retains and releases its impressions.

This, indeed, is what James Coleman's *Box (ahhareturnabout)* (1977) takes as the complex of material on which to work.[14] For in it, a filmed boxing match, cut into short bursts of between 3 and 10 frames, interrupted by equally short spurts of black, is turned into a pulsing movement that both breaks apart and flows together over those breaks, which is to say, it emphasizes movement itself as a form of repetition, of beats that are separated by intervals of absolute extinction, even while the urgency of the rhythm promises the return of another and another. The gestures of the boxers, and thus of the representational field of the work—which is spun out of a few minutes of found footage documenting the historic Gene Tunney/Jack Dempsey fight of 1927—would seem to embody this rhythm, with their repeated jabs and feints, and their always threatened dive into oblivion. Further, this field of visual representation is doubled aurally by a voiceover that emphasizes both the drive of repetition—"go on/ go on," "again/ again," "return/ return"—and the ever-waiting possibility of the onset of nothingness—"break it/ break it," "stop/ s-t-o-p i-t," "regressive/ to win/ or to die."

The fact, however, that the viewer's own body, in the guise of its perceptual system and the projected after-images it is automatically "contributing" to the filmic fabric, is also being woven into the work, means that *Box*'s subject matter is somehow displaced away from the representational plane of the sporting event, and into the rhythmic field of two sets of beats or pulses: the viewer's and the boxers'. As it also means that the frequent projections of the sound of breathing—expressed in the track as "ah/ ah," "aha/ ah," "p-a-m/ p-u-m"—is giving voice not just to the boxers' bodily rhythms, but to those of the viewer as well.

In all of these cases, then, the attack on modernism's notion of visual autonomy is thus staged in relation to the invasion of the body and its rhythms into the optical field now robbed of both its purity and its formal stability. But another strategy also developed in the following decade to assault the prerogatives of vision, one that could be called the anti-gaze or the uncanny gaze, by which it was meant to return *against* the controlling system of the "gaze" itself by using its own power, jujitsu-like, to overthrow it.

The theory of the controlling gaze emerged from various analyses of the operations of state power and the way modes of surveillance, for example, cause individual subjects to introject systems of prohibition and thereby reproduce themselves as subjects of disciplinary force (the shopper who fears the closed circuit television camera, for instance, and thus restrains him- or herself from stealing). Imported into the field of artistic practice as a theory of the "male-gaze," visual control—now gendered as a function of patriarchy and therefore as masculine—froze women into the position of fetish-objects, rendered immobilized and mute by the force of male desire.[15] Reorganized as the helpless body made intact in the unity of her own beauty, the object of this gaze is now coerced into functioning as a kind of "proof" that the male body is itself unthreatened, that there is no castrational power that can touch him. And if the theory of the Male-Gaze was developed in relation to the mass-cultural construction of women—within advertising, films, pornography, etc.—it could easily be seen as applying to modernist painting with its reciprocity between the visual object as autonomous unity and the individual viewer as independent cognitive subject.

Cindy Sherman's early work, her *Untitled Film Stills* (1977–1980), had taken on the mass-cultural construction of the woman's image, as the artist photographed herself convincingly posed in a variety of cinematic types (gun moll, dumb blond, career girl) and genres (gangster films, suspense, weepies) and styles (Sirk, Rossellini, Hitchcock). But as her work developed into the 1980s, the idea of a perspective that might fix the identity of the Woman as a focal point controlled by the viewing point of the (male) spectator mutated into a kind of shattered visual field. Sometimes this is the effect of a kind of backlighting that forces a glow to emerge from the ground of the image to advance outward at the viewer and thus to disrupt conditions of viewing, producing the figure herself as a kind of blind-spot or Medusa. In others, this corrosive visual dispersal is the result of a kind of "wild light," the scattering of gleams around the otherwise darkened image as though refracting it through the facets of an elaborate jewel. This is the case in *Untitled #110* (1982), where Sherman has concentrated on creating a sense of the completely aleatory quality of the illumination. For while the lighting plunges three quarters of the field into total blackness, it picks out the arm and draped edge of the figure's garment to create a glowing, knotted complex of near unintelligibility.

In opposition to the stability of the perspective scheme, this recourse to ricocheting light opens onto a very different idea of the "gaze," one that destabilizes its subject, making it the victim rather than the master of vision. This new gaze, theorized by the psychoanalyst Jacques Lacan as the gaze-as-*objet-a*, or the uncanny gaze, is modeled on the idea of the light that surrounds each of us. Such an irradiation beaming at us from everywhere in space cannot be assimilated to the single focus of perspective. Instead, to depict this luminous gaze, Lacan turns to the model of animal mimicry, which Roger Caillois had described in the 1930s as the effect of space at large on a subject(-insect), who, yielding to the force of this space's generalized gaze, loses its own organic boundaries and merges with its surroundings in an almost psychotic act of imitation. Making itself into a kind of shapeless camouflage, this mimetic subject now becomes a part of the "picture" of space in general.[16] "It becomes a stain," Lacan says, "it becomes a picture, it is inscribed in the picture."

Insofar as it is the target of this luminous, uncanny gaze, our body's relation to the world founds our perception not in the transparency of a conceptual grasp of space, but in the thickness and density of a being that simply intercepts the light. It is in this sense that to be "in the picture" is not to feel interpolated by society's *meaning*—is not to feel, that is, whole—but it is to feel dispersed, subject to a picture organized not by form, but by formlessness. None of Sherman's works so captures this idea of entering the field as "stain," perhaps, as does *Untitled # 167* (1986), where the camouflage effect of mimicry is in full flower (Figure 7). The figure, now absorbed and dispersed within the background, can only be picked out by a few remnants still visible, though only barely, in the mottled surface of the darkened detritus that fills the image. We make out the

Figure 7. Cindy Sherman, "Untitled #167," 1985. Courtesy of the artist and Metro Pictures.

tip of a nose, the emergence of a finger with a painted nail, the detached grimace of a set of teeth.

The desire awakened by the impossibility of occupying all of those multiple points of the luminous projection of the gaze, is a desire that founds the subject in the realization of a point of view that is withheld, one(s) that he or she cannot occupy. And it is the very fragmentation of that "point" of view that prevents this invisible, unlocatable gaze from being the site of coherence, meaning, unity, gestalt, *eidos*. Desire is thus not mapped here as the desire for form, and thus for sublimation (the vertical, the gestalt, the law); desire is modeled in terms of a transgression against form. It is the force invested in desublimation.

The paradigm shift Jay plots in *Downcast Eyes*, with its insistence on the historical evolution of the senses—in this work, of vision—does not depend on, but is greatly supported by, the work of Walter Benjamin. In his crucial essay "The Work of Art in the Age of Mechanical Reproducibility" (1936), Benjamin speculates on the way a new mode of production will alter, not only human conceptions about art, but human sensory experiences as well. He speaks of the "changes in the medium of contemporary perception" brought about by the onset of photography, which, he argues, has destroyed the *aura* of the traditional work of art: "To pry an object from its shell, to destroy its aura, is the mark of a perception whose 'sense of the universal equality of things' has increased to such a degree that it extracts it even from a unique object by means of reproduction."[17]

We, who have lived through the phenomenon of the art of Andy Warhol, cannot but feel the prescience of this analysis, which would seem to support Jay's contention that, even in the modality of the visual itself, the visual has suffered a critical undoing. Against this aggression, however, Modernist art has also celebrated vision's capacity for a reflexive double perception, in which vision's capacity to survey and order, to abstract and model the elements within a given field, had made it into the privileged vehicle of reason itself. This reflexive consciousness made it possible to view the gridded surface of a Cubist painting as a representation of a figure on top of a canvas and *at the same time* a representation of the surface itself—its shape, its lateral spread, the weave of its canvas, and its flatness. To see the surface at the same time as bringing the figure into focus is to become conscious of the support or *grounds of possibility* of painting.

To recapture the prerogatives of reason, is, then, to restore the optical against the force of "downcast eyes." This restoration came at the hands of those artists refusing the denigration of the visual in the work and theory of conceptual art. Such artists, working in the first decade of the twenty-first century, demanded that the image field of their works would figure-forth the support for these images themselves.

An example would be the animated films of the South African artist William Kentridge, whose technique is a matter of erasure, a charcoal drawing subtly altered by the erasure of part of its contour with each change captured on one frame of a reel of film. Played through a projector, the run-on frames produce the effect of movement as though the drawing were in a constant state of metamorphosis. Many sequences of Kentridge's films address reason as the images reflexively "figure-forth" their own technique or support. An example is a car driving through the rain, its windshield wipers representing the erasure underlying Kentridge's own process (Figure 8). The beat of the wipers addresses visual reason. It refuses the paradigm of "downcast eyes."

Another poststructuralist Jay uses to buttress his argument for the "denigration of vision," is Jacques Derrida, whose essay "The Parergon" dismisses the idea of the work of art's self-enclosure, meant to gain a reflexive achievement of self identity—the climax of visual reason, or en*light*enment. Derrida's critique examines Kant's notion of external decorative additions to the interior selfhood (or ergon) of a work of art, decorations like the frame on a painting (with its additional gilding) or the columns on a building, all of which Kant dismisses as mere parergona. Derrida's refutation needs to be seen in the light of the modernist summoning of

Figure 8. William Kentridge, "History of the Main Complaint," 1996. Charcoal and pastel on paper. Courtesy of Marian Goodman Gallery, New York.

reason to bring the laws of the inner order of the work into consciousness, like the example of the Cubist grid calling attention to the rectangular frame of the painting. His argument is that the parergon's separation of inside from outside (the frame) is that as in Cubism, a frame is "an outside which is called inside the inside to constitute it as inside." Vision's ability to transcend the physical surrounds of consciousness is thereby "denigrated," a conclusion that lends further credence to Jay's argument.

But there are a great number of other contemporary (but nonetheless twentieth century) modernists who, like Kentridge, are intent on visualizing (or "figuring-forth") the ergon of their works. And such cases might lead us to see yet another way in which modernism has countered antiocular aggression. One of these is the Swiss artist Christian Marclay, whose aesthetic support is sound film. One of the basic syntactical gambits of film editing is called shot-counter-shot. This is when we see the face of an actor reacting to something after which the camera cuts away to what he or she sees, then cuts back to the face of the actor. Marclay's *Telephone* places two video monitors side-by-side, alternating an actor dialing a telephone, which rings in the space of the actor in the neighboring monitor, who answers the phone (like the climactic scene in *Dial M FOR Murder*). *Telephone* is constituted entirely by the fundamental editing sequence of film, made central ever since Pudovkhin to the invention of Soviet cinema. Indeed, his work establishes the sequence as the film's ergon, something available to visual reason only.

In referring to certain exceptions to Jay's position—certain supports for the visual and resistances to its "denigration"—I am not critiquing his persuasive idea of a recent paradigm shift. I am only suggesting that now, in the twenty-first century, we may be able to find "up-beat" eyes, in a continuation of the modernist spirit.

Notes

1. *Vision and Visuality*, ed. Hal Foster, *Dia Art Foundation Discussions in Contemporary Culture*, no. 2 (New York, 1988).
2. Jonathan Crary, *Techniques of the Observer: On Vision and Modernity in the Nineteenth Century* (Cambridge, MA, and London, 1990).
3. Rosalind Krauss, *The Optical Unconscious* (Cambridge, MA, 1993).
4. Fredric Jameson, *Postmodernism, or, The Cultural Logic of Late Capitalism* (Durham, NC, 1991), 7.
5. Ibid., 34.
6. Guy Debord, *Society of the Spectacle* (Detroit, MI, 1977).
7. Jean-Paul Sartre, *Being and Nothingness*, trans. Hazel E. Barnes (New York, 1966), chap. "The Look," 348, 352.
8. Luce Irigaray, *Speculum of the Other Woman* (Ithaca, NY, 1985).
9. Michel Foucault, *Discipline and Punish*, trans. Alan Sheridan (New York, 1977).
10. Jay, *Downcast Eyes*, 14.
11. See Clement Greenberg, *The Collected Essays and Criticism*, ed. John O'Brian, 4 vols. (Chicago, 1993), 4: "Louis and Noland," and "Post Painterly Abstraction."
12. See Krauss, "Im/pulse to See."
13. Yve-Alain Bois and Rosalind Krauss, *Formless: A User's Guide* (New York, 1997), 133–137; 161–165.
14. Ibid., 161–165.
15. See Laura Mulvey, "Visual Pleasure and Narrative Cinema," *Screen* 13 (Autumn 1975): 6–18; republished in Laura Mulvey, *Visual and Other Pleasures* (Bloomington, IN, 1989), 15.
16. Jacques Lacan, *The Four Fundamental Concepts of Psycho-Analysis*, trans. Alan Sheridan (New York, 1978), 96. Sheridan mistranslates the end of the paragraph as "In the depths of my eye, the picture is painted. The picture, certainly, is in my eye. But I am not in the picture." In French it reads: "The picture, certainly, is in my eye. But I, I am in the picture."
17. Walter Benjamin, *Illuminations*, trans. Harry Zohn (New York, 1969), 223.

Bibliography

Benjamin, Walter. *Illuminations*. Translated by Harry Zohn. New York, 1969.
Bois, Yve-Alain and Rosalind Krauss. *Formless: A User's Guide*. New York, 1997.
Crary, Jonathan. *Techniques of the Observer: On Vision and Modernity in the Nineteenth Century*. Cambridge, MA, and London, 1990.
Debord, Guy. *Society of the Spectacle*. Detroit, MI, 1977.
Foucault, Michel. *Discipline and Punish*. Translated by Alan Sheridan. New York, 1977.
Foster, Hal, ed. *Vision and Visuality: Discussions in Contemporary Culture*, no. 2. New York, 1988.
Greenberg, Clement. *The Collected Essays and Criticism*, edited by John O'Brian. 4 vols. Chicago, 1993.
Irigaray, Luce. *Speculum of the Other Woman*. Ithaca, NY, 1985.
Jameson, Frederic. *Postmodernism, or, The Cultural Logic of Late Capitalism*. Durham, NC, 1991.
Krauss, Rosalind. *The Optical Unconscious*. Cambridge, MA, 1993.
Lacan, Jacques. *The Four Fundamental Concepts of Psycho-Analysis*. Translated by Alan Sheridan. New York, 1978.
Mulvey, Laura. "Visual Pleasure and Narrative Cinema." *Screen* 13 (Autumn 1975): 6–18.
Sartre, Jean-Paul. *Being and Nothingness*. Translated by Hazel E. Barnes. New York, 1966.

Part II

Violence, Memory, Identity

MEMORY CULTURE AT AN IMPASSE
Memorials in Berlin and New York

Andreas Huyssen

In the course of the past two decades, memory culture and memory politics have become genuinely transnational, if not global. From South Africa to Argentina and Chile, from Bosnia and Kosovo to Rwanda, historical trauma and human rights violations have emerged as privileged sites of public commemoration in the work of architects, academics, artists, and writers. Truth Commissions have been founded, and in countries such as Argentina and Chile, the courts have recently become active after a prolonged period of quiescence about the state terror of the Cold War period. With increasing frequency, nations have turned to their darker, often repressed, pasts, and some, like Japan and Turkey, confront growing international pressures to face their history.

After the fall of the Berlin wall, global memorial politics crystallized in the 1990s around three major factors: Holocaust discourse and intensifying public debates about the 50th and 60th anniversaries of events related to World War II; the transitions to democracy after the collapse of regimes of state terror in Latin America and apartheid in South Africa; and the recurrence of ethnic cleansing and genocide in the present in the Balkans and in Rwanda. This political dimension of commemoration was accompanied in the West by a more general shift from a dominant belief in the future of modernization to a widespread investment in the past through waves of nostalgia and retro-fashions. To some, this recent obsession with memory marks an increasing need for historicity in a world of planned obsolescence and the ever expanding present of consumer culture. Others fear that the ubiquity of memory discourses in the public and in the media actually threatens objective historical knowledge by wiping out the borders between conjured up pasts and the lived present. Indeed, memory itself can become a commodity to be cycled through a voracious culture industry always in search of new frills.

Many historians are therefore suspicious of the memory boom. Simply to oppose good objective history to unreliable memory, however, is not good enough, as mnemo-historians like Pierre Nora and Jan Assmann have shown.[1] More recently, in his incisive essay entitled "When Did the Holocaust End? Reflections on Historical Objectivity," Martin Jay drew on the extensive debate about memory and trauma to point out how the claims of closure implicit in objective fact-based historiography shipwreck on the very nature of traumatic experience, which denies reconciliation, healing, and closure. Traumatic memory of past violence is thus not only unreliable, as all memory is, but it poses fundamental methodological problems for historians.[2] Memory discourse is here to stay. The understanding and representation of traumatic historical pasts requires the cooperation between historians and what Carol Gluck, with a felicitous neologism, calls memorians.[3]

What we still need, however, is a historical reflection on this hypertrophy of memory in our time, something analogous perhaps to Nietzsche's attempt to understand the nineteenth century's hypertrophy of history.[4] It is fairly evident that the recent memory boom is the flip side of the diminishing trust in the future in Western societies. Compared with the promises of progress of an earlier age, future imaginaries today suffer from anemic confidence. To be sure, after 1989, some celebrated the end of utopia and of history only to launch the neoliberal globalization fantasies of the 1990s. Years after 9/11, however, the horizons have darkened and the exuberant promises of globalization are largely damaged goods. Though memory discourses are still going strong, skeptical voices doubting the effectiveness of public memory are getting louder. The relationship between practices of memorialization and the reality of forgetting, however, remains a bone of contention. The paradox is that practices of commemoration themselves may partake in the detemporalizing processes of instant consumption, waste production, and forgetfulness that mark our culture. The 9/11 memorial debate may be the best example to date of how memorialization and forgetting can enter into an unholy alliance that betrays both past and present—this is what I mean by memory culture at an impasse.

This paradox of memory and forgetting has always been best embodied in the medium of monument and memorial. Robert Musil got it right when he suggested that nothing is ever so invisible in an urban environment as the monument.[5] In addition, there is a long history of monuments being vandalized, toppled, and resurrected, only to disappear again. None of this, of course, inspires much confidence in the capacity of some of today's major memorials—say, the Berlin Monument to the Murdered Jews of Europe and the planned New York memorial to 9/11—to keep memory alive and to keep the past visible within the urban fabric. For some time to come, the Berlin monument and the New York memorial (once it is built) will serve as major tourism sites. But who is to guarantee their longevity in the public mind once the memory boom has faded? Perhaps the difficulties surrounding the planning for the 9/11 memorial already indicate that we are approaching that point. At a time when only about a third of the funds needed to build a much-scaled-back design have been raised, some New Yorkers believe that the memorial will never be built. I do not share this view, but I cannot deny that there is a certain logic to it.

II

For a number of reasons, discussions about the 9/11 memorial have occasionally drawn on the extended memorial debate in Berlin. Thus, I was not surprised when I was recently asked to compare the WTC site and its memorial designs with the Berlin Monument to the Murdered Jews of Europe. My first reaction was entirely negative. To compare the Berlin Monument to the Murdered Jews of Europe and the discourse of its genealogy with the 9/11 memorial debate in New York seemed to be a case of an egregiously misplaced comparison, if comparison is meant to suggest affinity, similarity, and proximity. The events remembered are too different in nature, scale, and historical importance. But as I took up the challenge to relate the finished monument in Berlin to the plans for the New York memorial, an interesting perspective emerged that may have broader significance. The Berlin memorial, despite widespread initial skepticism, has been embraced by its critics and by the public. The New York memorial, despite exuberant hopes for some major memorial construction, already looks like a dismal failure. This, too, is what I mean by memory culture at an impasse.

The Berlin monument was erected by the *Nachgeborenen* of the perpetrators to commemorate the victims of Nazi crimes against humanity, which gave rise to the genocide convention of 1948 and later energized much of the transnational human rights discourse in our time. That is why the debate in Germany, apart from its national importance, did have a powerful international resonance, which is also contained in the European dimension of the monument's name. The *Mahnmal*, together with Berlin's Jewish Museum, has become an international reference point not just in New York, but in the case of memorial projects in other parts of the world where histories of state terror, apartheid, and ethnic cleansing are currently being commemorated. This is what I have described elsewhere as the transnational travels of Holocaust discourse and memory practices.[6] By contrast, the memorialization of 9/11 has become increasingly focused on national politics in relation to the ongoing "war on terror" and on the private needs of the victims' families to commemorate their dead.

Thus, the memorials address very different constituencies. Within Germany, the Berlin monument functions at the civic and national levels, and it addresses victims' families only indirectly and across vast distances of temporality and geography. The New York memorial functions centrally at the personal and familial level, even though the line between the intimate and the political remains extremely diffuse in all 9/11 memorialization. Berlin's memorial is about acknowledging German history to the world, coupled with a national commitment to public memory. The New York memorial is about current politics and private memories, which are in open conflict, and it is also, I would claim, about the avoidance of history.

Actually, memorialization in New York underwent a radical shift from a global focus to a narrow national and local dimension; whereas in Berlin, if anything, the movement was the reverse in the context of the 1990s. Liz Greenspan has described this shift in New York as one from international and vernacular to national and official commemoration.[7] Vernacular commemoration sprang up right after 9/11 all over the city—around the WTC site, at St. Paul's chapel, Union Square, the underground transition space from the West Side subway lines to the Grand Central shuttle at 42nd street, and on many city streets, where message-covered plywood walls were erected to display names and photos of "the missing," children's art, flowers, candles, and tributes of all kinds. This vernacular commemoration had an emphatic international dimension: flags from many countries were a part of these sites; inscriptions appeared in many languages; "we love America," "we support you," and the like was written on many of these spontaneous message walls. This cosmopolitan dimension, which also found full expression in the international press, has been entirely lost in the cantankerous official debates about rebuilding the site and constructing a memorial. Local politics, real estate interests, and national ideology have created a poisonous stew around the WTC site that seems to leave no room whatsoever for any transnational consideration. Not even the many non-American victims of 9/11 form a part of the discourse any longer. At the same time, of course, 9/11 triggered the wars in Afghanistan and Iraq, which quickly broke the spell of international solidarity with the United States.

The main difference in addressing the public between Berlin and New York, however, reflects differing temporalities. The time frames between commemoration and event memorialized are simply too divergent. The Berlin monument was erected over 50 years after the Holocaust and it is embedded in the after-history of unification and the decades-long German struggle to commemorate the victims of the Third Reich. The memorial debate in New York began the day after the event. Years later, it is still immediate, raw, unsettled, and shot through with massively opposing and irreconcilable interests—interests of victims' families, state and city politicians, real estate developers, the Port Authority, and the Washington ideologues of the war on terror. Some would take this as supporting an argument that you need distance from an event before you can properly memorialize it. This luxury was not available in New York, since ground zero is also the very site of death and absent burial—thus the argument about ground zero as sacred or hallowed ground to be honored, rather than developed. Some wanted to leave it as it was after 9/11, with the stark reminder of the remnant of steel girders rising up from the rubble being itself the most adequate memorial. As in the case of Berlin, where some imagined leaving the center of the city from Brandenburg Gate down to Potsdamer Platz as a void filled with the ghosts of history, this view never had a chance and was unrealistic to begin with. Besides, we all remember the images.

But even if there had not been the very real need to honor the dead, it is not surprising that the debate about how to memorialize 9/11 started the next day. For 15 to 20 years, we have been living in a memorial culture in which traumatic histories and victimization discourses of all kinds have taken front billing in the media and in public debate as well as in artistic practices and academic research. This discourse immediately imprinted itself on 9/11 in such a way that it led Hal Foster to speak of the WTC as the World Trauma Center.[8] Foster meant it satirically, but of course it was just that, a WORLD Trauma Center, but only for a brief moment of international solidarity and empathy with New York, before 9/11 became a cipher for a national politics of trauma exploitation, fear mongering, and the mishandled war on terror. 9/11 neither began nor ended on 9/11.[9] The long-term causes as well as the damage and political fallout that followed in the wake of 9/11 internationally and nationally will take years to assess, and I am afraid that the effects of 9/11 especially will burden whatever memorial will have been built some day.

One could, of course, trot out certain superficial links between the Berlin and New York memorials that make a comparison more plausible.

Eisenman goes from New York to Berlin to design the monument. Libeskind comes from Berlin to New York to do the masterplan for the WTC site, which is as much architecture as it is itself a memorial monument. The Freedom Tower as the celebration of American values has, in certain ways, overshadowed the planning and discussion of the 9/11 memorial itself. Here we have another obstacle to a meaningful comparison between Berlin and New York's memorial practices. For who would want to compare Libeskind's triumphalist celebration of freedom, with its spire ascending to 1776 feet and mimicking the upwardly extended arm of the Statue of Liberty, to a monument to the Holocaust? Kafka comes to mind as someone who might have given a different reading to Libeskind's spire. In his novel *Amerika*, after all, he imagined the Statue of Liberty as carrying a sword rather than the torch of freedom. Of course, Libeskind has been sidelined as the architect. But the Freedom Tower is still the Freedom Tower, except that now, after its recent redesign, it looks like a fortress at the bottom with a missile on the top.

The most plausible register of comparison between the two memorials, which commemorate such completely incomparable events, is style. Let me insert here a brief description of the winning entry of the 9/11 memorial competition.[10] Designed by Michael Arad and Peter Walker and entitled *Reflecting Absence*, the memorial consists of two voids representing the footprints of the original towers. Surrounded by oak trees, each void will feature rings of cascading water falling into illuminated reflecting pools. Visitors will descend from the upper plaza along two ramps—each as long as a city block—that will take them 30 feet below ground into a central hall. From this hall, they will walk into the galleries surrounding the perimeter of the pools. The walls around the galleries will carry the names of the victims of 9/11 and 26 February 1993, the day of the first bombing attack on the WTC. Adjacent to the two pools, a Memorial Museum will exhibit artifacts telling the stories of both attacks. Visitors will also have access to a section of the massive slurry wall that held back the Hudson River during the attacks and was featured prominently in Libeskind's master plan.

The issue of style then comes to this: one only needs to look at Libeskind's Garden of Exile at the Jewish Museum and certain formal analogies of the Eisenmann project in Berlin (an analogy I actually find thought provoking, as it offers a visual link between the two sites) to know that both architects are representatives of a prevailing style of contemporary architecture and memorial landscaping that might make comparison plausible; so many memorial projects around the world currently work with geometry rather than figuration, and with stone, water, and landscaping.[11] The plans are developed by architects rather than by artists; add to that Arad's design of the 9/11 memorial and its obvious relation to Maya Lin's Vietnam Veterans Memorial in Washington. Arad, too, goes underground, avoids heroicizing figuration (no statues, no flags), embraces the simplicity of landscaping and materials used, uses space symbolically by putting his pools reflecting absence into the footprints of the towers, and so on. Whatever the differences are between Libeskind and Eisenmann, Lin and Arad, you have here an expanded field of memorial practices and a politics of signification that is by now transnational, highly professionalized, controversial to some, but evidently successful with politicians and much (though not all) of the public. Stylistic comparison, however, carries only so far. It is valid only if one limits one's register of analysis to the stylistic features of memorials, forgetting the content of what is to be remembered by whom, where, and for what purpose.

There were long and acrimonious debates about these questions in both cities. As far as public debate is concerned, we may take note of the influential presence of James Young, specialist for (counter)monuments and memorials, on the juries in both Berlin and New York, and give tribute to his argument that the debates surrounding the design and meaning of memorials may be even more important than the finished memorials themselves.[12] Public debate and controversy could be taken then as proof of comparability. The debate in Berlin went on for over a dozen years. In New York, we are in year six and have several more years of changing plans, designs, and building to look forward to or to get annoyed about. As in Berlin, there was a complete rejection in New York of a first round of proposals for the overall reconstruction of the WTC site, a fate that the competition for the memorial only barely avoided. A choice of memorial was made—beside Young, Maya Lin was another member of the jury who allegedly wielded much influence—but the debate over the final version is still very much in flux. Michael Arad's rather sparse and minimalist design has already been supplemented by the landscaping work of Peter Walker (Berlin worked by subtraction: Richard Serra dropped out when his and Eisenman's original design had to be altered; New York has worked by addition). Given cost overruns and security issues, the Arad/Walker project may still meet the same fate as Libeskind's Freedom Tower: the final version may not much resemble the original plan. Thus, some family members question the location underground, presumably for security reasons. Others do not like the slurry wall way down below. But the arguments are reminiscent of similar arguments against Maya Lin's project: all too funereal, too lugubrious, too depressing. Others quibble about whether and how the inscribed names of the victims are to be separated from the names of the firefighters. Some victims are victims only, others are heroes as well; as if death was not a universal equalizer. Some even want names inscribed in terms of their affiliation with the various firms and businesses of the towers. Yet others understandably find the whole memorial design too bland and too recreational. And the debate goes on.

My own sense is that the muted and delicately tactful design of Arad/Walker's memorial plan (empty spaces, cascading water, walls with inscribed names) provides an acceptable though not scintillating solution to the memorializing task precisely because it dedramatizes, encourages reflection, and provides an uncontroversial space for public and private grief. It also counteracts all of the ideological baggage and excessive signifying demands that came with the Freedom Tower's original master plan. And it separates the realm of commemoration and reflection from Lower Manhattan street life by putting the reflecting pools and the memorial hall down below into the pit. On the other hand, apart from the grounding of the memorial in the footprints, it could be a memorial for anything.

Here, one might want to question the universal validity of Young's emphasis on process and open-endedness of discussion. I certainly would not side with Michael Kimmelmann, art critic of the *New York Times*, who suggested junking the results of the memorial competition altogether and just commissioning some major international artist to parachute in and create the memorial as a masterwork.[13] This was escapist and elitist beyond belief. Public memorials do depend on compromise. Architects are better equipped to acknowledge the need for compromise in such matters than artists: witness Richard Serra's exit in Berlin. It may indeed not be a coincidence that memorials these days are more often designed by architects than by artists. At the same time, compromise and open-endedness of discussion do not always yield acceptable results.

The need to archive and document is another aspect of the public debates surrounding both memorial sites. The issue in Germany was the political acknowledgment of crimes against humanity and the incorporation of this acknowledgment into national identity after unification. Thus, it is significant that a center for historical documentation of the Holocaust has been added to the original memorial design by Eisenman and Serra. The museum that is to be part of the Arad/Walker memorial, on the other hand, will take care not to delve too much into history. Its time frame will in all likelihood remain limited to the morning hours of 9/11—a timeless event not to be located in any political history or broader framework. The absence of "2001" in common parlance speaks for itself. The 9/11 debate is all about national victimization and very real personal loss, genuine emotions which are being crudely instrumentalized for nationalist ideological purposes. The attempt to maintain an international dimension with the planned International Freedom Center as part of site development failed miserably. It was attacked by the right as being un-American because of its anticipated inclusion of freedom struggles elsewhere in the world, and it was attacked by the left as too ideological in its focus on freedom— no wonder it was scrapped. Memories of the ideological critique waged especially by the right on the International Freedom Center will guarantee an antiseptic and unhistorical exhibition practice at the memorial museum.

History and memory are related differently to each other in the two cities. Berlin is a city filled with historically loaded memorial sites: the Topography of Terror, the Bendler Block, the nearby concentration camps of Sachsenhausen and Oranienburg, the train station of Grunewald, the Renata Stih and Frieder Schnock memory project in Bayerisches Viertel, and so forth. This is not to say that New York does not also have monuments and memorial sites, but the point is that they are never as present in the minds of New Yorkers as memorial sites are to Berliners. History and memory, tenuously coupled in Berlin's politics of commemoration, are torn asunder in New York. Maybe this is the function of the different temporalities I have spoken about. Or maybe the events of 9/11/2001 are still too close and too fresh in memory to permit broader historical reflection. Colombian artist Doris Salcedo, in another context of violent disappearances, reminds us of an obligation that seems to have been lost in the New York memorial debate: "It is more and more difficult to find the diffuse boundary between the intimate and the political. The grief of the relatives of desaparecidos—like all grief—is of an intimate nature, but when the essence of these events is political, I believe the society must acknowledge it."[14]

The Arad/Walker memorial does not acknowledge anything of the sort. The absence it reflects is not the absence of history and politics in its design, even though history and politics are central components of 9/11 and its commemoration. In that, it remains, I think, fundamentally different from the Berlin monument and closer to Maya Lin's VVM in Washington, which reconciles irreconcilable views on the Vietnam War in the divergent commemorating practices it permits. Whether or not it will work its desired effects in the end remains to be seen. It is not even certain that the final product will resemble the original design, which may indeed soon be forgotten. In the meantime, for me the most powerful and moving memorial remains the Tribute in Light by LaVerdiere and Myoda—two beams of light shooting up into the night sky where the towers once stood. Fleeting and searching, but still and transitory, they mark the absence on the anniversary of 9/11 alone.

Notes

1. Jan Assmann, *Das kulturelle Gedächtnis* (Munich, 1997); Pierre Nora, *Realms of Memory: The Construction of the French Past*, vol. 1: *Conflicts and Divisions* (New York, 1996).
2. Martin Jay, "When Did the Holocaust End? Reflections on Historical Objectivity," in *Refractions of Violence* (New York, 2003), 47–60.
3. See Gluck's forthcoming book *Past Obsessions: World War II in History and Memory* (New York, forthcoming).
4. See Friedrich Nietzsche, *On the Advantage and Disadvantage of History for Life*, trans. Peter Preuss (Indianapolis, IN, 1980). I have tried to work toward such a historical explanation of contemporary memory culture in relation to temporality in *Twilight Memories: Marking Time in a Culture of Amnesia* (New York and London, 1995) and in relation to space in *Present Pasts: Urban Palimpsests and the Politics of Memory* (Stanford, CA, 2003).
5. Robert Musil, "Monuments," in *Posthumous Papers of a Living Author*, trans. Peter Wortsman (London, 1993), 61.
6. Huyssen, "Present Pasts: Media, Politics, Amnesia," in *Present Pasts*, 11–29.
7. Elisabeth Greenspan, "A Global Site of Heritage? Constructing Spaces of Memory at the World Trade Center Site," *International Journal of Heritage Studies* 11, no. 5 (December 2005): 371–384.
8. Hal Foster, "In New York," *The London Review of Books*, 20 March 2003.
9. This problem of dating traumatic events in terms of causes and effects is cogently explored in Martin Jay's already mentioned essay, "When Did the Holocaust End?"
10. For a good discussion of the competition see Nancy Princenthal, "Absence visible: chosen by a jury from 5,201 submitted proposals, the design for the World Trade Center memorial is both the epitome of tact and a consummate expression of bafflement," *Art in America* (April 2004).
11. Another example of this transnational style is the Parque de la Memoria in Buenos Aires, which I discussed in *Present Pasts*, 94–109. Unfortunately, this is also another example of an ambitious memorial project that, due to hesitant financing and lack of political will, may be destined to survive only as a memorial ruin.
12. James Young, *At Memory's Edge: After-Images of the Holocaust in Contemporary Art and Architecture* (New Haven, CT, 2000), and "The Memorial Process: A Juror's Report from Ground Zero," in *Contentious City: The Politics of Recovery in New York City*, ed. John Mollenkopf (New York, 2005), 140–162.
13. Michael Kimmelmann, "Ground Zero's Only Hope: Elitism," *New York Times*, 7 December 2003, section 2: 1, 47.
14. Marguerite Feitlowitz, "Interview with Doris Salcedo," http://www.crimesofwar.org/cultural/cultural-table.html (Accessed on 1 July 2008).

Bibliography

Assmann, Jan. *Das kulturelle Gedächtnis*. Munich, 1997.

Feitlowitz, Marguerite. "Interview with Doris Salcedo." <http://www.crimesofwar.org/cultural/cultural-table.html> (Accessed on 1 July 2008).

Foster, Hal. "In New York." *The London Review of Books*. 20 March 2003.
Gluck, Carol. *Past Obsessions: World War II in History and Memory*. New York, forthcoming.
Greenspan, Elisabeth. "A Global Site of Heritage? Constructing Spaces of Memory at the World Trade Center Site." *International Journal of Heritage Studies* 11, no. 5 (December 2005): 371–384.
Huyssen, Andreas. *Present Pasts: Urban Palimpsests and the Politics of Memory*. Stanford, CA, 2003.
———. *Twilight Memories: Marking Time in a Culture of Amnesia*. New York and London, 1995.
Jay, Martin. "When Did the Holocaust End? Reflections on Historical Objectivity." In *Refractions of Violence*, 47–60. New York, 2003.
Musil, Robert. "Monuments." In *Posthumous Papers of a Living Author*, translated by Peter Wortsman. London, 1993.
Nietzsche, Friedrich. *On the Advantage and Disadvantage of History for Life*. Translated by Peter Preuss. Indianapolis, IN, 1980.
Nora, Pierre. *Realms of Memory: The Construction of the French Past*. Vol 1: *Conflicts and Divisions*. New York, 1996.
Princenthal, Nancy. "Absence Visible." *Art in America* 92, no. 4 (April 2004): 38–48.
Young, James. *At Memory's Edge After-Images of the Holocaust in Contemporary Art and Architecture*. New Haven, CT, 2000.
———. "The Memorial Process: A Juror's Report from Ground Zero." In *Contentious City: The Politics of Recovery in New York City*, edited by John Mollenkopf. New York, 2005.

AGAINST GRANDILOQUENCE
"Victim's Culture" and Jewish Memory

Carolyn J. Dean

The term post-Holocaust refers to a sixty-year period and an array of debates, theological, autobiographical, and philosophical texts, polemics against the "Shoah business," and theoretical discussions of "postmemory." Over the last few decades, those discussions have been framed by accusations of an alleged "'surplus of talk'—companion to the surfeit of memory" that philosopher Berel Lang argues now characterizes attitudes toward "Holocaust representation."[1] At its best, this discourse thoughtfully asks how Jews and others can most substantively engage the past in the context of "too much" memory; at its worst, it accuses Jewish organizations of fostering a "Holocaust Industry" to exploit the memory of Jewish victimization.[2] But the so-called surfeit of Jewish memory is now articulated primarily as an argument about how Jewish memory exemplifies a pathological cultural attachment to having been or being a victim. Critics argue that Jewish memory voids the substance of history and the value of empathy in pursuit of an identification with Holocaust victims that narcissistically appropriates victims' suffering and focuses on Jews' victimization at the expense of others.

This discourse is most intense in the United States and France and particularly so as a matter of intra-Jewish debate. Indeed, influential scholars and journalists who otherwise hold a variety of political views, including Peter Novick, Esther Benbassa, Michael André Bernstein, Alain Finkielkraut, Gabriel Schoenfeld, and Zygmunt Bauman, have all recently interpreted Jewish memory of the Holocaust in these terms. But in so doing, they refer less to the much denounced commercialization of the Holocaust in Hollywood films and in various museums[3] than to a vast commentary in the United States and France on "victimology," "victimhood," and "victim's culture" that first developed in the late 1980s as a critique of identity politics and multiculturalism.[4] They draw on three decades of rhetoric, which insist that victimization now confers social recognition, and that the desire to "have been" a victim is now so pervasive among proponents of identity politics that the enlightened imperative to care for others as others rather than as members of our own besieged group has collapsed.[5]

When public intellectuals construe Jewish memory of the Holocaust as the most visible symptom of the problems implicit in "victim's culture," they do not only seek an antidote to perceptions of exaggerated claims. The now common assertion that everyone wants to be a victim, that is, is not only an insistence that we must be vigilant about preserving the historical record from distortion or a condemnation of (multi)cultural narcissism. The critics' claim that we live in a "victim culture," however appropriate the designation in some contexts, most importantly derives from their rhetorical fashioning of the distinction between reliable and unreliable memory that remains widely unacknowledged. In short, critics constitute the meaning of reliable memory, and thus the definition of what it means to be a victim, at a historical moment when the appellation appears to apply to everyone and to no one, and when victimization and traumatic experience has become nothing less than the paradigmatic historical experience, thus rendering Jewish victims of the Holocaust, still the paradigmatic historical trauma in the West, paradigmatic victims.[6]

Other scholars who have sought to understand why many victims have embraced their pain as a form of identity are not always helpful in addressing victimization in all of its complexity. Lauren Berlant and Wendy Brown do not blame "everyone's" desire to have been a victim on a historically unspecified collapse of enlightened empathy and also do not cast a suspicious light on victims' claims. They argue in different ways that victims' appropriation of "wounded" identity constitutes a prevalent and yet misguided concession to the dominant culture's self-palliative efforts to feel in place of doing: the victim's embrace of her wounds reveals an "attachment" to the recognition accorded her suffering rather than signifies the claims she does not deserve to make.[7] The victim's trauma defines his subordinate identity, and in so doing confuses what the victim has become (and the social processes by which he has been victimized) with what he is. In Berlant's view, feeling for the presumably traumatized victim thus takes the place of political action and mourning the pain of others paradoxically evacuates their suffering of substance.

However compelling their analyses of the anesthetic effects of mass media appeals to human rights and victims' embrace of their own wounds, Brown still conceives the victim's claims to identity-based rights based on injury, however legitimate, to obfuscate the state's role in using such claims to regulate identity itself. She argues that injury will cease to define victims' identities as they make politically empowering demands based on what they want rather than who they are. But what if, for example, making demands is itself traumatic, or you are unable to clear away your past sufficiently to formulate what exactly you want? The argument that victims are finally empowered only by making demands for substantive social justice rather than engaging in the rhetoric of "wounded identity," begs the question of how traumatized victims might mobilize to make such demands.

Thus, the task set by most if not all critics of victim's culture is to find cultural criteria not to distinguish good victims from bad victims, such those who behaved bravely or those who we judge to be more "innocent" than others, but to separate "real" victims from others who proclaim to have been injured, identify vacuously with the injured, or paradoxically become overly and thus pathologically so attached to their wounds that they unwittingly obscure their own social oppression—obscuring not "real" victims but the real causes of victimization—(a phenomenon Marx and Nietzsche both associated with Christianity). And charges of "victim's culture" now so prevalent emerge with particular intensity when Jewish sufferers, their heirs, and often Jews more generally, transform violated innocence into righteous rhetoric and demands for recognition for suffering they often did not witness. They also emerge when those whose histories of persecution have barely been remembered make similar claims for restitution, as if all claims to injury were intrinsically insatiable and grandiloquent demands.

Whatever the claims of various victim groups, the very act of making those claims now raises questions about the extent to which such demands participate in the putatively pervasive condition of wanting to be or having been a victim. The criticisms of "victim's culture" that now abound both testify to the pervasiveness of victimhood as a new and crucial category of being and seek to address the conundrum of victims who become "too" attached to their wounds. There are those who identify inexplicably with the suffering of others, including their Jewish ancestors. Their fascination with Jewish suffering paradoxically empties the Holocaust of its richer historical meaning. In Alvin Rosenfeld's view, the reduction of Holocaust memory to a "meaningless abstraction, 'man's inhumanity to man,'" is encouraged "within those segments of American culture intent on developing a politics of identity based on victim status and the grievances that come with it."[8] The Holocaust becomes a universal symbol of human evil devoid of specific historical content, and therefore one more particularly exemplary incident in the long history of human malfeasance. Similarly, the conservative critic Gabriel Schoenfeld asked why the "Holocaust exert[s] such great fascination these days outside the Jewish community" and suggests that "[t]he answer ... undoubtedly lies at least in part in the rising culture of victimhood, visible in our society at large ... As the ultimate in victimization, the Holocaust is simply assuming pride of place."[9] For Dagmar Barnouw, Holocaust remembrance has suffocated under the "seemingly irresistible appeal of memory stories of victimization, the more 'incredible' the better."[10]

One of the most recent expressions of this peculiar identification with Jewish victims is Binjamin Wilkomirski's "child survivor" memoir, *Fragment: Memories of a Wartime Childhood*. Wilkomirski's memoir transformed its author into a revered international hero and tragic figure, but turned out to be the story not of Binjamin Wilkomirski, but of Bruno Dössekker, a young Swiss boy abandoned ambivalently by his mother and adopted by parents he did not love and who showed him little affection. Dössekker rewrote his own childhood as the story of a young Jewish child who survived the camps. Until his fraud was exposed beyond a doubt, Dössekker held fast to his story, and was supported by Jewish organizations as well as groups of Holocaust survivors as he toured European and American cities as an 'authentic' survivor. Critics spilled a lot of ink discussing the success of *Fragments* once it was revealed to be a fake (though suspicions, largely ignored, were raised immediately upon its publication because of the unlikely survival of a young infant in death camps). They attributed all of the attention Wilkomirski received to the public's uncritical embrace of suffering. When everyone wants to be a victim, and a Jewish victim of the Holocaust brings the highest price, talk of Nazi criminality is cheapened, and there is no telling the difference between what really happened and what is mere dramatization. And, according to Wilkomirski's critics, it is the dubious fascination with Holocaust victims that has contributed to this sorry state of affairs: the appeal of victims' stories, the fear of appearing insensitive to a victim of genocide, our illusion that we know "their" suffering better if we figure out how vicariously to "feel" it.[11]

Jews have long been a specific kind of victim-object whose sufferings have become problematically iconic of "evil in our time" (a position many scholars reject and others embrace). Perhaps most significantly, the murder of European Jewry turned Jews into a new icon of the "innocent" victim (hence the peculiarly "sacred" status Jewish survivors of the camps achieved in the secular world after the 1970s). Hannah Arendt had already, in 1946, anticipated the problem of a cult of victimization among

Jews. Since all Jews, from the "newborn child" to the "repulsive usurer," were innocent in proportion to Nazi crimes against them, "we Jews are burdened by millions of innocents, by reason of which every Jew alive today can see himself as innocence personified." "We are simply not equipped to deal," she wrote to Karl Jaspers, "with a guilt that is beyond crime and an innocence that is beyond goodness or virtue."[12] Arendt feared that the burden of Jewish innocence—the inconceivable discrepancy between the conduct of the victims and the death to which they were condemned—would eventually transform itself into a necessarily insatiable demand for compensation and recognition. Since innocence can never be avenged and the guilty never sufficiently punished, Jews will forever renew demands for the recognition of betrayed innocence: each will see himself as "innocence personified" because he has suffered or belongs to a group that once did.[13]

Indeed, the nexus of discussion about Jewish memory of the Holocaust and the critique of "victim's culture" allows us to explore more generally the rhetorical and political consequences Arendt feared: if Jews are attached pathologically to being victims, the Holocaust is no longer an icon only of human tragedy, but also of the potential for the distortion and exploitation of human tragedy and even for the victimization of others. If Jews now over-identify with Holocaust victims, the Holocaust no longer represents a culturally privileged image of man's inhumanity to man, but also the anesthetic effects generated by the proliferation of media representations and memorials. And if Jewish trauma, to go beyond Arendt to current extrapolations, has come to stand not only for Jewish history, but is a paradigm of history *tout court*, then trauma paradoxically becomes a privileged marker of identity rather than a set of symptoms from which one might ideally recover.[14] Thus, the French historian Esther Benbassa denounces what she conceives as the over-identification with victimization among French Jews and an offensive "competition between victims" mobilized by both Jews and Blacks, in which the contest to have suffered more leads to an obsession with death. She also bemoans to what degree the "memory of the past and of the Shoah have been imposed on us to the point, sometimes, of suffocating life—to the point of legitimating a surprising tendency to victimization."[15] Heirs to Holocaust memory insist that Jewish suffering is no longer discussable in the language reserved for garden-variety agony because victims' "innocence beyond goodness or virtue" has no worldly equivalent save for the hushed tones of the memorial service. Thus, the "tendency to victimization" expresses not only the worship of survivors and the obsession with death, but also manifests the narcissistic appropriation of and identification with the pain of those one imagines to have suffered most unbearably.

Not surprisingly, then, many critics blame "victim's culture" for the "surfeit of memory" about the Holocaust. Identity is not developed over time, shaped by long and short-term events, effects, and particularities that define a specific relation to past and present, but is a wound that does not heal. "Wounded identity" thus has an origin, but no chronological limits or spatial boundaries: time collapses into media-saturated space, and history folds into a memory-screen onto which we publicly project private desires. The desire to be a victim blots out the victim's real suffering, and the "surplus of memory" about the Holocaust is shorthand for the narcissistic appropriation of suffering. Ian Buruma describes "victim's culture" as a masochistic attraction to injury, which has no substance other than its own oddly comforting self-gratification and thus its dissolution into nothingness and forgetfulness.[16] The sociologist Zygmunt Bauman offers a primarily psycho-cultural explanation about Jewish latter-day "martyrs," arguing that "hereditary victimization" is a peg on which other forms of anxiety hang themselves.[17] He allegorizes the Holocaust as a "ghost" who inhabits the would-be victims' bodies, makes their own relative comfort indistinguishable from survivors' trauma, and gives them license to feel "unequivocally wronged."[18] The literary theorist Walter Benn Michaels also uses the figure of the ghost, taken from Toni Morrison's novel about slavery, *Beloved*, as an allegory for a process of remembering what we have never lived through—in this case, slavery and the Holocaust. He argues that using the rhetorical device of the "deconstructive performative," that is, by performatively enacting a gap in understanding that, like trauma, is an experience "transmitted" but not conceptualized or "worked through," the "prohibition against understanding the Holocaust is at the same time formulated as the requirement that it be experienced instead of understood, and this requirement ... makes it possible to define the Jew ... as someone who, having experienced the Holocaust, can, even if he or she was never there, acknowledge it as part of his or her own history."[19] And this transmission of conceptually inassimilable experience becomes the defining feature of Jewish identity—an identity now shorn of any references to real Jewish persons or religious practices, but only to Jewish culture. Cultural memory replaces history, phantom-Jews replace "real" ones, and the performative enactment of the Holocaust in certain texts allows us, who were not there, to survive it.

Thus, "we" find ourselves in the peculiar position of experiencing a Holocaust we have not lived, or feel that this memory that we have not had is more painful than the real suffering of the victims. Such arguments about this phenomenon are properly impatient with grandiloquent representations of Jewish suffering, because they render it too familiar and encourage a narcissistic or sublime identification with suffering that is not your own, and which does not impart any meaningful knowledge of genocide. Jews' putatively pathological attachment to victimization is thus a cultural manifestation of "too much Jewish memory" and of the inflated prestige therefore accorded to Jewish wounds. Such wounded attachment, moreover, has also been conceived as an attribute of victims whose wounds have barely been remembered and have different experiences of violence and oppression. Thus, Jewish pathology becomes the pathology not only of Jews, but of all minority groups striving for cultural recognition.

The historian Peter Novick, whose contentious and most in-depth response to this question from the Left, *The Holocaust in American Life*, garnered much attention, argues that the rise of "identity politics" and a "culture of victimization" made it possible for Jews to "embrace a victim identity based on the Holocaust."[20] Though his is a long and detailed historical study of the Holocaust's increasing preeminence in American Jewish culture, his general argument is that the sacrosanct status of the Holocaust in American life is a pretext for the assumption of victim status, a surrogate identity in a Jewish world shorn of more traditional forms of affirmation, and that this "surplus" memory is part of a new emphasis on "surplus" suffering in which Jews suffer most of all. Novick rightly notes that the dubiously privileged status of Jews as the most victimized group of all problematically transforms them into objects of identification and envy or even icons of mysterious and sacred suffering. But his argument that Jews' embrace of the iconic status accorded Jewish pain *explains* the pathological attachment to wounds simply asserts tautologically that "victim's culture" accounts for a culture in which Jews embrace enthusiastically some form of victimization. That is, for Novick, Jewish pathology is clearly bound up with a broader cultural pathology in which the desire to be a victim is merely best symbolized by Jewish narcissism: the gap between empirically verifiable anti-Semitism and Jews' perception of their own vulnerability is, according to Novick, enormous, rendering Jewish perceptions particularly distorted and troubling. Jewish pain stands in for everyone's, so that all claims for restitution and recognition turn into a "competition of victims," a battle of cultural one-upmanship in which terms such as "holocaust envy" are rhetorical cannon fodder.[21] As the Left-wing French essayist Pascal Bruckner wrote tellingly in 1995, "The whole world wants to be Jewish."[22] The dubiousness (not to mention silliness) of his assertion brings into relief the perception of Jewish trauma now as an exaggerated attachment to one's wounds that stands in for the desires of all victims, who do not merely want recognition, but implicitly want to be acknowledged to be the most victimized of all. Thus, Benn Michaels' decontextualizes and equates the memory of slavery and the memory of the Holocaust, as if they generated exactly the same symptoms in a culture in which having been a victim is the only way to achieve recognition, or to have experienced historical trauma is the only way to have historical experience—in which traumatic and historical experience have thus been entirely conflated.

Surely quests for clear lines between better and worse ways of remembering, between respectful, bounded memory and the self-indulgent appropriation of memory, and even between real and fraudulent victims that have been obscured by culturally sanctioned, narcissistic investments in suffering constitute important critical ventures. They take on kitsch renderings of Jewish experience putatively wrought by "identity politics," and they underline the problematic sacralization of survivors, which makes it difficult to ask hard questions about victims' veracity. But these criticisms of "victim's culture" do not merely assert that "real" victims are those who were in the most literal sense "there," but also seek to define the meaning of reliable memory and thus how we best remember events. For all the emphasis on the contrast between empirical facts and the so-called surfeit of memory, these critics do not conceive empirical facts alone as sufficient to establish the veracity of memory. They seek instead to recover the history of injury undistorted by wounded attachments by designating what rhetorical relation to suffering represents reliable—insightful, useful, historically accurate, and ethically valid—memory, and what relation to suffering represents unreliable memory. Reliable memory of the past can counter the distortions generated by wounded identity and its various affirmations, whether these are illusions that one has "survived" a Holocaust that one has never experienced or the appearance of somatic symptoms resembling survivors' own, and thus distinguishes clearly between real and would-be victims. At the same time, these critics conflate traumatic memory so entirely with the pathological inflation of pain that they not only beg the historical question of how and when memory becomes traumatic, but also render trauma itself inconceivable except as an overwrought and potentially unreliable experience of suffering.[23] This is to say simply that the construction of "victim's culture" offers a significant and yet problematic interpretation of how best to remember Jewish suffering, and thus how insights into and information about the past can be gleaned reliably, and from whom.

What then is the proper relationship to the past suffering of one's group and to suffering humanity more generally? When does the relation to suffering become a self-indulgent, narcissistic projection? Michael A. Bernstein argues that the idea that victimhood should "endow one with special claims and rights" is part of an ideology in which extreme suffering underlines previously invisible worthiness and thus accords victims with special standing.[24] Those who use the rhetoric of victimization uncritically fail to realize that "victim" is a historically mutable category that must be pinned down: after the Great War, many Germans saw themselves primarily as victims, and elected Hitler to restore their "lost" honor.[25] Some historians have argued similarly that the fluidity of victim identity accounts for the perpetuation of modern war more generally: the use of sophisticated media, propaganda, and technology combined with impersonally waged warfare (because soldiers since the Great War for the most part do not literally "see" their enemy) constructs national, ethnic, or religious enemies as perpetrators and one's group as victims, regardless of their actual status.[26] In this context, the rhetoric of victimization becomes a means of mastering social crises by projecting responsibility for them onto enemy others who violate the nation's "innocence." War or a mental state of siege accompanies the construction of victimhood as a form of identity, since wounded national or religious aspirations by definition must be avenged or healed.

This intimate relation between the fluidity of the victim's role and outwardly projected violence also constitutes one of the main arguments against "victim's culture," since our perception of ourselves as a group besieged leads inevitably to the prevalence of violent self-defense as the only way to sustain group identity. As Zygmunt Bauman argues, "The thesis of hostility to the Jews being the prime mover of the Holocaust is sacralisation's principal, and most effective, instrument. In a perverse fashion, that hostility itself is thereby sacralized, exempt from contention, transplanted from the realm of empirical scrutiny into that of creed and an integral part of *doxa* ... Sacralisation sets the Jews as the sole bearers of the Holocaust memory, apart from the rest of the world incurably saturated with Jew-hatred, the site of the past holocaust and the hotbed of holocausts to come."[27] In the discourses of would-be victims—in this case, Jews who over-identify with Holocaust memory—the "sacralized hostility" that is deeply felt but not examined threatens to define the memory of the Holocaust itself. Literary theorist David Carroll writes: "The Shoah is for many the sign that no people can trust any other people ... and that aggressive 'self-defense' at all costs must be the political principle of the post-Shoah era."[28]

The "excessive" attention to the Holocaust is thus no longer merely about the event's commercialization, but also about how Holocaust memory is increasingly framed by an unbearable collective injury whose would-be victims inflate their agony. French historian Henry Rousso notes that such distortion—in his case, too, most contemporary Jews believe in the perpetual resurgence of anti-Semitism in spite of evidence to the contrary—occurs because now "Everyone wants his own 'genocide,'"[29] including Jews who did not live through the first one. Rousso famously outlined the collective symptoms of a nation, France, that had not worked through its relation to its collaborationist past. He later denounced the stubborn persistence of one of those symptoms, too much memory, and noted that the surfeit of memory about the Vichy period had become increasingly "Judeocentric." He says that this "Judeocentrism"[30] is a problem, because it "seeks to reread the entire history of the [Nazi] Occupation [of France] throught [sic] the prism of anti-Semitism."[31] He stresses that too many people believe that after the war, Jews wanted to be victims even when they "had refused at all cost to appear as victims distinct from the other victims of the Nazis."[32] In other words, today's self-appointed Jewish "victims" as well as those who claim that Jews have always been victims have a distorted memory of the past.

Thus, when the construction of the victim is located historically, when moral judgment can be reliably linked to a clear conception of who has been violated and who has not, when the heirs of sufferers do not confuse history and memory, but rationally assess the level of hostility toward them rather than projecting their own anxieties onto others, victims' heirs might establish a healthy relationship to reality. Arguments from the political Left believe the embrace of victimization led paradoxically to Israel's occupation of the West Bank. But those on the political Right, like Gabriel Schoenfeld, denounce the way in which "victim's culture" leads Jews to an emotional identification with suffering so devoid of content that a victim is a victim, and it is not at all clear what makes Jewish victimization specific and meaningful. For both Left and Right, the fluidity of victim identity threatens Jewish identity and even Israel's survival.

In this context, the refusal to succumb to emotions, to vengeance,[33] and to paranoia characterizes a healthy relationship to past suffering and allows for a proper assessment of the boundary between memory and history. The mastery of disorientation is essential to preserving those boundaries, and the loss of such mastery is also crucial to defining when a particular relation to past suffering will generate "surplus" memory that entirely absorbs history in the guise of recalling it. Those who have criticized the "surfeit of memory" have thus in this way sought to expose "our" investment in Jewish victimization as charged and problematic: we have attributed "revelatory virtues"[34] to catastrophe; are obsessed by victim's traumas; and we confuse trauma and historical experience. They believe that victimization now trumps heroism in conferring identity and prestige, and that public discourse is dominated by the narcissism of minority groups' claims to public recognition, and the putative distortion of history and obsession with memory their claims entail. They wish to ensure a clear distinction between history and memory, and recoil from an emphasis on the "unspeakability" of victims' suffering and from arguments about the "uniqueness" of the event in favor of an emphasis on the virtues of the ordinary.

The problem with these arguments is not that they are wrong, but that they tend to situate truth and clear-sightedness on the side of history, and opacity and trauma on the side of memory, far too simplistically via a particular rhetorical formulation of victimization as a trajectory from trauma to recovery, accomplished by force of ordinary virtues and a strenuous coming-to-terms. By this, I mean that these critics militate against the "misconceived selfishness" that constitutes the "sacralization"[35] of Jewish victims by stressing the virtues of the ordinary, the known, and the human dimension of catastrophic events: they do not merely affirm empiricist concepts of historical causation and accountability, but also link the moral project intrinsic in the historian's efforts to preserve "what happened" with having persevered in the face of "too much" memory. Indeed, they articulate a tendency within post-Holocaust discourses to struggle against the grandiloquence associated with contested claims that the Holocaust is unique, unspeakable, and therefore that its victims have suffered uniquely and unspeakably.[36]

The premises of this discourse against "victim culture" are not reducible to any particular philosophical approach.[37] Many critics insist, along with Michael Bernstein, that "the reserve of writers like Dan Pagis or Primo Levi may be invoked and held up as exemplary in numerous discourses, but, in fact, their suspicion of the sonorous and grandiloquent has been conspicuously *un*influential. Their rhetorical austerity has been praised precisely in order to be replaced by later critics' self-regardingly ornate and often explicitly rivalrous formulations."[38] This homage to the ordinary also shares the late historian Sybil Milton's impatience with what she called the "universal willingness to commemorate suffering experienced rather than suffering caused"[39]—to identify with victims' suffering while not knowing or wanting to know much about it, and thus to put one's self indulgently in their place. It emphasizes quiet meditation, and in particular references Primo Levi rather than Charlotte Delbo, and a minimalist style over an ornate one.

Bulgarian-born French literary theorist Tzvetan Todorov argues that, in contrast to those *hommes publics* who loudly decry the treatment of various marginal groups, and in contrast to grand discourses of good and evil which lead to overwrought rhetoric about catastrophe and *tremendum*, Primo Levi's words incarnate "humility: he doesn't shout, he speaks quietly, he weighs different options for and against, remembers exceptions to the rules, and seeks to understand his own reactions. He doesn't propose shattering accounts of things past, nor does he adopt the intonations of a prophet with a direct connection to the sacred: before the extreme, he knows how to remain human, too human."[40] Levi, he says, was "beyond both hatred and resignation."[41]

Levi's being "beyond resignation" allows him to move "beyond hatred," because it implies that Levi's writing represents judicious contemplation that recoils from abysses and extremities to conquer overwhelming emotions. Levi is an exemplary victim because he refuses to play the grand roles either of hero or innocent victim and focuses instead on how to understand the circumstances he has lived through, and thus to understand his own strengths and weaknesses as well as those of other victims.[42] Thus, in literary theorist Harald Weinrich's work, Levi's acute observation of the horror around him is also exemplary not only of how insights can most profitably be gained from suffering, but also how memory might remain untainted by forgetfulness, or at least undiminished in its power: "Primo Levi writes without hatred. He wishes to be not a judge but rather a witness, and his testimony, which is based on precise observation and a trained memory, must be reliable. It *is* reliable."[43] Levi's writing assures that memory not only never overwhelms history, but guarantees its veracity. Weinrich argues that Levi's precise observation and judicious, unemotional mode of approaching horror "scientifically," guarantees that memory will be truthful. From Weinrich's point of view, Levi guarantees that you can never really have too much memory if you know how to remember well.

Again and again, Levi's modesty and his embrace of ordinary virtues stand in for the veracity of memory. Indeed, the identification with Levi perhaps not surprisingly forms the common referent of those who denounce our attachment to injury from a humanist perspective. Thus, Gary Weissman contrasts Levi's testimony with those of "secondary" and other witnesses in order to demonstrate that "real" witnesses rarely claim to have been victims, and "secondary" witnesses often wish they had been victims of the Holocaust. Weissman claims that several generations of mostly Jewish intellectuals now vie to be "witnesses" to the Holocaust's horror.[44] He believes that survivors were victims, but also, as he says, he finds "value in the distinction [Klüger] makes between survivor stories and victim stories."[45] In Weissman's view, "real" victims are either dead or refuse to be labeled as victims. Paradoxically, it is the victim who refuses to embrace victimization that Weissman represents as the most reliable witness. They are not only more reliable since they were "there," but because being there apparently dictates a sense of proportion and measured response to events absent among those who can only fantasize having been there: respect for the memory of the dead together with a dramatic refusal to put themselves in the place of the dead victims.

In his most recent book, the philosopher Berel Lang too argues that Primo Levi demonstrates that we should "learn how to be surprised without becoming its victim."⁴⁶ That is, we should not confound the genocide of European Jewry with a great rupture in history and thus with unspeakable soul shattering, but must quietly interpret it in order to expand the category of the recognizable and thinkable. Our surprise at the Nazis' violation of humanist precepts during the Holocaust derives not from the intrinsic incomprehensibility of Jewish suffering, but from their contravention of a resolutely human world of predictable and well-ordered expectations. According to Lang, Levi's ability to draw universal principles from particular incidents renders him a crucial figure in post-Holocaust literature because he moves away from a focus on horror, the uncanny, and the unthinkable to the "recognizable." By stringing together a series of improbable incidents in Auschwitz, Levi demonstrates how even the most shocking transgressions are embedded in day-to-day life in the camps: that people transform human beings into things ceases to be an ungraspable horror, but something about which we can think. Our aim should be to reflect on and learn from surprise rather than sacralize horror. Thus:

> I would wish to claim that the Holocaust is distinctive—so much, in fact, that one need not step outside history or the standard patterns of historical, reflective, and social analysis to show this to be the case. The argument seems to me much weightier that through *standard* patterns and categories, one sees more of the individual character of the Holocaust, the deliberate effort at genocide which distinguishes it, and, behind that, the underlying will to violate all moral norms, than one does by projecting the features of that event on an extra-historical space—the tendency encouraged by claims for it as unique or incomprehensible.⁴⁷

And, Lang goes on a bit further, "the distinctiveness of the Holocaust becomes most visible not through the lenses of extra-historical categories but in the material and moral history of everyday causality and judgment."⁴⁸

Lang thus puts aside the question of how the Holocaust is both historical (it is motivated by a set of discernable perceptions and causes) and extra-historical (it cannot be reduced to "standard" patterns of historical experience) in favor of a conviction that all behavior, however unfamiliar, is explicable. In short, that inconceivable disproportion between Jews' conduct and their extermination, which Arendt believed bequeathed to Jews a never-to-be-quenched thirst for recognition, poses no problem if we stop treating it as an extra-historical phenomenon that challenges the "standard patterns" of history. The extra-historical dimension of analysis that Arendt proposed, one in which experience derives from or coincides with, but cannot be entirely reduced to the historical event, now becomes not an object of inquiry, but a conceptual obstacle to productive inquiry (a "projection" that distracts from the materiality of history).

In this way, Lang writes off discussions that emphasize the traumatic and the testimonial because, he argues, they tend to replicate the problem of "excess" posed by the Holocaust: we may want to understand the Holocaust as a traumatic event, but we should be forced to account for the event as traumatic, rather than presuming tautologically that its enormity and sheer excess is proof of its authentically traumatic nature. Thus, from Lang's point of view, many intellectuals and others claimed that Binjamin Wilkomirski's fraudulent autobiography of a child Holocaust survivor, Fragments, was authentic simply because he had been able to imagine it.

When Dössekker (alias Wilkomirski) proved uncooperative once questions about the veracity of his story finally became a chorus of demands for proof, the Swiss historian Stefan Maechler was asked by Dössekker's literary agent to get to the bottom of things, and wrote the definitive exposé of Wilkomirski's lies. Maechler's exemplary detective work and evenhandedness notwithstanding, his account of Dössekker's deception depicts most of Dössekker's defenders as hoodwinked because they wanted to believe in or identify with his suffering. Though he blames Dössekker for manipulating his audience, the book is nonetheless a far broader indictment of a culture so hungry for victim's stories that it has produced "professional victims"—in this case a woman who masqueraded as a child survivor as well as a victim of Satanic ritual abuse and who shares the stage with Wilkomirski at one of his readings. Maechler records the refusal of those who are skeptical of Wilkomirski's story generally to raise their voices, including some survivors. He is also careful to attribute some survivors' desire to believe Dössekker to their fear of victimizing him all over again by questioning his veracity. But what prevails above all is the grotesque spectacle of would-be victims wooing audiences with dramatic tales of atrocity, and a noisy parade of psychoanalysts, psychiatrists, and survivors' organizations all making claims on the "victim's" behalf.

This is not to cast an uncritical eye on Dössekker's fraud, but rather to put Maechler's interpretation of them in the context of recent critical frameworks within which real victims have become increasingly indistinct from fraudulent or would-be ones and in which claims to having been victimized are ever more inseparable from the narcissistic appropriation of suffering. Of course, none of the scholars we have discussed would deny that Primo Levi might have been traumatized by his experience. My point is not that this discourse denies the extraordinary nature of the Holocaust, but rather, that in seeking to be most loyal to memory, it figures paradoxically not only symptoms of trauma, but also of resentment, anger, and the desire for vengeance as an inassimilable residue of that event—as feelings that should ideally be always already mastered. Indeed, in this rhetorical context it is impossible to imagine any means of claiming to have been or to be a victim that might be legitimate other than by having already resolved one's relationship to that experience. The traumatized Jewish victim thus figures the memory of a history that cannot be assimilated or reconciled to any "standard pattern," so that, oddly, the historical and psychological experience of some Jews is erased or diminished in the high stakes effort to distinguish between history and memory, true and false claims to having been victimized, and measured and hyberbolic renderings of what actually happened. To the extent that this homage to the ordinary uses "victim's culture" as a stand in for an implicitly or explicitly hyperbolic, pathological memory that no longer references real victims, a certain kind of unrestrained relationship to victimization stands in for the perils of memory against history. Trauma, if unresolved, may figure the "wrong" sort of victim, one overly attached to her victimization. In the worst cases, the traumatized victim may be cast as not a "real" one.

Victims, in a culture that now casts suspicion on all those who claim to be victims or to have been victimized, become the repository of unconstrained affect and thus of experience not sufficiently "worked through." For critics of "victim culture," would-be victims are symptoms of democratic rationality gone awry, having now lost its bearings in a sea of feeling and thus of false claims. Moreover, they believe that empowered victimhood has replaced the disinterested indignation that permits the proper evaluation of grievances in democracies, so that the judicious examination of claims is swept away by the rhetorical force of the putative victim's "fearless" voice.[49] The grievance structure of rational, democratic contestation is replaced by the unconstrained projection of phantasmatic wounds.[50] The would-be victim becomes an allegory less for the quest for identity than for a wounded narcissistic investment: the discourse of "victim's culture" then tells the story of how democracies fail if we are not vigilant about the dangers of imagining ourselves only as victims, and in the process, risk confusing "real" victims and imaginary ones by conceiving us all as imaginary victims unless proven otherwise. The specter of Nazism, and indeed of all political ideologies which play upon perceptions of having been unfairly victimized, looms.

In opposition to this specter, allegations of "victim's culture" mark the fluidity of the very category "victim" (by insisting on a distinction between a real and a "would-be" victim), and insist on a normative framework within which victimization might be clearly defined. But this discourse also manifests deep ambivalence attending to the potential meaninglessness of suffering, and the disorientation, helplessness, or fragmentation of the victim that may result in a judgment about his inability to forgive, forget, and move on. The problem posed by that suffering is rendered particularly vivid by the constant struggle, as evident in Eva Hoffman's generally self-reflexive text about being the child of Holocaust survivors, *After Such Knowledge*. The struggle between critical distance from, and over-identification with, survivors marks just how profoundly difficult it is even (or especially?) for those spokespersons of the "second generation" to avoid the pitfalls of "vicarious witnessing," which Hoffman claims "tough-minded critiques" of the "Holocaust cult" underestimate and diminish.[51] She herself writes of feeling that a young woman's explicitly manifest grief at a memorial in a death camp was somehow inappropriate to the setting. And yet, as Ruth Franklin notes, might not such grief be appropriate?[52] On the one hand, Hoffman notes that perhaps Aharon Appelfeld's antidote to trauma—using ordinary language in its accessibility and humility—may not always be adequate, and on the other, she embraces her parents' trauma protectively in the guise of what one almost hesitates to call bourgeois propriety—one does not grieve so unabashedly in public. From a historical point of view, Ido de Haan argues that the reduction of Jewish persecution to a "psychotrauma" set up Jewish survivors as "original victim[s] against which all other forms of victimization would be measured," so that perhaps the so-called Holocaust cult is using the terms that historically legitimated Jewish experience, now at the expense of historical understanding. De Haan claims that various categories of victims were "grouped under the common denominator of a psychotrauma, even if the events that caused these traumata differed dramatically"; in his view, the whole meaning attributed to Jewish victims of the Holocaust is itself not a pathological symptom, but a form of cultural expression fashioned by the discomfort with which Jewish victims were originally diagnosed and which has been endlessly repeated—rendering their experience both diagnosable and yet fundamentally inconceivable.[53] But critics of "victim's culture" tend problematically not to attend to posttraumatic symptoms of the sort articulated by de Haan and Hoffman, but conceive them instead as part of the presumably excessive affect attached to victims that voids historical understanding.

We might ask if efforts to define victims rhetorically and culturally as those who have already survived, who have refused to succumb to the traumatic or other effects of events is not rather a defense against the inability really to distinguish clearly between the history of events and the never quite reliable and yet uncanny memory of those who have lived through them. We might ask if, aside from the surely appropriate criticism of masochistic attraction to injury and the persuasive critiques of identity politics, allegations of "victim's culture" also manifest a distaste for, and discomfort with, the putatively unrestrained claims of certain kinds of victims and those who claim to speak on their behalf.

Notes

1. Berel Lang, *Post-Holocaust: Interpretation, Misinterpretation, and the Claims of History* (Bloomington, IN, 2005), ix.
2. Norman Finkelstein's *The Holocaust Industry: Reflections on the Exploitation of Jewish Suffering* (London, 2000), exemplifies this perspective.
3. Robert Alter, "Deformations of the Holocaust," *Commentary* 71 (1981): 49.
4. Victimology was coined originally in the US, in the 1930s, by the American Benjamin Mendelsohn to refer to a branch of psychology that sought to explain the contexts of victims of crime. The study of victimology took off in the 1980s as a new concern with crime victims emerged. The term "victim's culture" seems to be an offshoot of this later development, though both victimology and victim's culture are used promiscuously and without precise references. See Robert Elias, *The Politics of Victimization: Victims, Victimology, and Human Rights* (New York, 1986), 17–21.
5. Tzvetan Todorov, "In Search of Lost Crime," *The New Republic*, 29 January 2001, 25.
6. See Ana Douglass and Thomas A. Vogler, *Witnesss and Memory: The Discourse of Trauma* (New York, 2003), 5.
7. See Wendy Brown, *States of Injury: Power and Freedom in Late Modernity* (Princeton, NJ, 1995), and Lauren Berlant, "The Subject of True Feeling: Pain, Privacy, and Politics," in *Cultural Pluralism, Identity Politics, and the Law*, ed. A. Sarat and T. Kearns (Ann Arbor, MI, 1999), 54–57.
8. Alvin H. Rosenfeld, "The Americanization of the Holocaust," *Commentary*, June 1995, 36.
9. Gabriel Schoenfeld, "Death Camps as Kitsch," *New York Times*, 18 March 1999.
10. Dagmar Barnouw, "The Certainties of Evil: Memory Discourses of the Holocaust," *Monatshefte für deutschesprachige Literatur und Kultur* 93 (2001): 106.
11. Stefan Maechler, *The Wilkomirski Affair: A Study in Biographical Truth*, trans. John E. Woods (New York, 2001).
12. Letter to Karl Jaspers, 17 August 1946, in Hannah Arendt and Karl Jaspers, *Correspondence 1926–1969*, ed. Lotte Kohler and Hans Saner, trans. Robert and Rita Kimber (New York, 1992), 54.
13. French philosophers Michel Feher and Alain Finkielkraut both insist that Jewish non-conformists of yesteryear now derive their identity from the "suffering of their parents." Feher warns of the dangers of seeking a coherent identity based on victimization by associating the American Left's multiculturalism with the now "Jewish" refusal of the "cosmopolitanism" with which they are "inevitably associated." They thus betray a "cosmopolitan sensibility" wary of grand commemorations in favor of an empty solidarity "founded on the sharing of suffering." In other words, multiculturalism is monological, conceives identity in terms of injury, and worships "grand" memorials that in reality are surrogate social bonds. Michel Feher, "1967–1992: Sur quelques recompositions de la gauche américaine," *Esprit* 187 (December, 1992): 75. See also Alain Finkielkraut, *The Imaginary Jew*, trans. Kevin O'Neil and Dvaid Suchoff (Lincoln, NE, 1994).
14. Dominick LaCapra has warned against the conflation of "structural trauma" and "historical trauma"—the confusion, that is, of all history with the state of being traumatized. See *History and Memory After Auschwitz* (Ithaca, NY, 2004), 194–210.
15. Esther Benbassa, "La Shoah comme religion; Les bien-pensants, juifs ou non, expient en ranimant la flame du souvenir face aux descendants de l'Holocauste," *Libération*,

11 September 2001. "Blacks" refers to a specific incident involving a French satirist from the Antilles.
16. Ian Buruma, "The Joys and Perils of Victimhood," *The New York Review of Books* 46, no. 6 (8 April 1999): 6.
17. Zygmunt Bauman, "Hereditary Victimhood: The Holocaust's Life as a Ghost," *Tikkun* 13, no. 4 (July/August 1998): 35–36.
18. Bauman, "Hereditary Victimhood," 35.
19. Walter Benn Michaels, "'You Who Never Was There': Slavery and the New Historicism—Deconstruction and the Holocaust," in *The Americanization of the Holocaust*, ed. Hilene Flanzbaum (Baltimore, MD, 1999), 195.
20. Peter Novick, *The Holocaust in American Life* (New York, 2000), 189.
21. Antonio de Figueiredo, "'Holocaust envy' or a better deal for Africa?," *New African* 409 (2002): 8–9.
22. Pascal Bruckner, *La Tentation de l'innocence* (Paris, 1995), 131–132.
23. See Gary Weissman, *Fantasies of Witnessing: Postwar Efforts to Experience the Holocaust* (Ithaca, NY, 2004), 21.
24. Michael André Bernstein, *Foregone Conclusions: Against Apocalyptic History* (Berkeley and Los Angeles, 1994), 91.
25. Ibid., 87.
26. Omer Bartov, *Mirrors of Destruction: War, Genocide, and Modern Identity* (Oxford, 2000).
27. Zygmunt Bauman, "Categorial Murder, Or: How to Remember the Holocaust," in *Re-Presenting the Shoah for the Twenty-First Century*, ed. Ronit Lentin (New York, 2004), 31.
28. David Carroll quoted in Alan Milchman and Alan Rosenberg, "The Problematics of Memory: A Hermeutical Inquiry Into the Holocaust," in *The Uses and Abuses of Knowledge: Proceedings of the 23rd Annual Scholars' Conference on the Holocaust and the German Church Struggle, March 7–9, 1993, Tulsa, Oklahoma*, ed. H.F. Knight and Sachs Littell (Lanham, MD, 1997), 45.
29. Éric Conan and Henry Rousso, *Vichy: An Ever-Present Past*, trans. Nathan Bracher (Hanover and London, 1998), 202.
30. Ibid., 51, 198.
31. Ibid., 199.
32. Ibid., 51–52.
33. Carroll quoted in Milchman and Rosenberg, "The Problematics of Memory," 44–45.
34. Michael André Bernstein, "Homage to the Extreme: The Shoah and the Rhetoric of Catastrophe," *Times Literary Supplement* (6 March 1998).
35. Bauman, "Categorial Murder," 30.
36. Bernstein, *Foregone Conclusions*, 93.
37. Ibid., 7.
38. Bernstein, "Homage to the Extreme."
39. Sybil Milton, cited in Edward T. Linenthal, *Preserving Memory: The Struggle to Create America's Holocaust Museum* (New York, 1995), 199.
40. Tzvetan Todorov, "Dix ans sans Primo Levi," *Esprit* 1 (1998): 135.
41. Tzvetan Todorov, *Facing the Extreme: Moral Life in the Concentration Camps* (New York, 1996 [1991]), 261.
42. Todorov, "Dix ans sans Primo Levi," 130.
43. Harald Weinrich, *Lethe: The Art and Critique of Forgetting*, trans. Steven Rendall (Ithaca, NY, and London, 2004), 193.

44. Weissman, *Fantasies of Witnessing*, 118.
45. Ibid., 75.
46. Lang, *Post-Holocaust*, 113.
47. Ibid., 85.
48. Ibid.
49. Jonathan Simon, "Parrhesiastic Accountability: Investigatory Commissions and Executive Power in an Age of Terror," *The Yale Law Journal* 114 (2005): 1421, 1450–1451, 1454. This commentary appears to be the underside of a new focus on "victim's rights": a phenomenon that Simon has argued is pervasive in the United States and Western Europe and represents the victim as hero and thus as the repository of "fearless"—deeply felt, morally suasive, and not self-interested—"speech." Simon takes the term "fearless speech" from a translation of Michel Foucault's own invocation of an ancient Greek concept.
50. It is important to note that these critics are not explicitly fearful of the moral damage and thus vengeful intentions victims presumably harbor—the scenario imagined by what Robert Meister has termed the "counterrevolutionary," who knows what damage he has wrought and hopes to stave off the consequences. At the same time, there is still an unacknowledged ambivalence about victims who cannot, as it were, master the symptoms of their once having been victimized. As described by Robert Meister, "Human Rights and the Politics of Victimhood," *Ethics and International Affairs* 16, no. 2 (2002): 94.
51. Eva Hoffman, *After Such Knowledge: Memory, History, and the Legacy of the Holocaust* (New York, 2004), 177.
52. Ruth Franklin, "Identity Theft: True Memory, False Memory, and the Holocaust," *The New Republic*, 31 May 2004.
53. Ido de Haan, "The Postwar Jewish Community and the Memory of the Persecution in the Netherlands," in *Dutch Jews as Perceived by Themselves and by Others: Proceedings of the Eighth International Symposium on the History of the Jews in the Netherlands*, ed. Chaya Brasz and Yosef Kaplan (Leiden, 2001), 432. For psychologists who work with survivors, however, the tendency to reduce survivors to pure victims or heroes is primarily related to our own narcissism, voyeurism, sadism, and above all, the need to displace our own rage or shame when confronted with those who have been brutally victimized. See the essays in John P. Wilson, Zev Harel, and Boaz Khana, *Human Adaptation to Extreme Stress: From the Holocaust to Vietnam* (New York, 1988).

Bibliography

Alter, Robert. "Deformations of the Holocaust." *Commentary* (February 1981).
Arendt, Hannah, and Karl Jaspers, *Correspondence 1926–1969*. Edited by Lotte Kohler and Hans Saner and translated by Robert and Rita Kimber. New York, 1992.
Barnouw, Dagmar. "The Certainties of Evil: Memory Discourses of the Holocaust." *Monatshefte für deutschsprachige Literatur und Kultur* 93, no. 1 (2001).
Bartov, Omer. *Mirrors of Destruction: War, Genocide, and Modern Identity*. Oxford, 2000.
Bauman, Zygmunt. "Categorial Murder, Or: How to Remember the Holocaust." In *Re-Presenting the Shoah for the Twenty-First Century*, edited by Ronit Lentin. New York, 2004.

———. "Hereditary Victimhood: The Holocaust's Life as a Ghost." *Tikkun* 13, no. 4 (July/August 1998): 35–36.
Benbassa, Esther. "La Shoah comme religion; Les bien-pensants, juifs ou non, expient en ranimant la flame du souvenir face aux descendants de l'Holocauste." *Libération*, 11 September 2001.
Berlant, Lauren. "The Subject of True Feeling: Pain, Privacy, and Politics." In *Cultural Pluralism, Identity Politics, and the Law*, edited by A. Sarat and T. Kearns. Ann Arbor, 1999.
Bernstein, Michael André. *Foregone Conclusions: Against Apocalyptic History*. Berkeley, CA, 1994.
———. "Homage to the Extreme: The Shoah and the Rhetoric of Catastrophe." *Times Literary Supplement*. 6 March 1998.
Brown, Wendy. *States of Injury: Power and Freedom in Late Modernity*. Princeton, NJ, 1998.
Bruckner, Pascal. *La Tentation de l'innocence*. Paris, 1995.
Buruma, Ian. "The Joys and Perils of Victimhood." *The New York Review of Books*, 8 April 1999
Conan, Éric and Henry Rousso. *Vichy: An Ever-Present Past*. Translated by Nathan Bracher. Hanover and London, 1998.
Douglass, Ana and Thomas A. Vogler. *Witnesss and Memory: The Discourse of Trauma*. New York, 2003.
Elias, Robert. *The Politics of Victimization: Victims, Victimology, and Human Rights*. New York, 1986.
Feher, Michel. "1967–1992: Sur quelques recompositions de la gauche américaine." *Esprit* 187 (December, 1992).
Figueiredo, Antonio de. "'Holocaust envy' or a better deal for Africa?" *New African*, no. 409 (July 2002): 8–9.
Finkelstein, Norman. *The Holocaust Industry: Reflections on the Exploitation of Jewish Suffering*. London, 2000.
Finkielkraut, Alain. *The Imaginary Jew*. Translated by Kevin O'Neil and David Suchoff. Lincoln, NE, 1994.
Franklin, Ruth. "Identity Theft: True Memory, False Memory, and the Holocaust." *The New Republic*, 31 May 2004.
Haan, Ido de. "The Postwar Jewish Community and the Memory of the Persecution in the Netherlands." In *Dutch Jews as Perceived by Themselves and by Others: Proceedings of the Eighth International Symposium on the History of the Jews in the Netherlands*, edited by Chaya Brasz and Yosef Kaplan. Leiden, 2001.
Hoffman, Eva. *After Such Knowledge: Memory, History, and the Legacy of the Holocaust*. New York, 2004.
Knight, H.F. and Sachs Littell, eds. *The Uses and Abuses of Knowledge: Proceedings of the 23rd Annual Scholars' Conference on the Holocaust and the German Church Struggle, March 7–9, 1993, Tulsa, Oklahoma*. Lanham, MD, 1997.
LaCapra, Dominick. *History and Memory After Auschwitz*. Ithaca, NY, 2004.
Lang, Berel. *Post-Holocaust: Interpretation, Misinterpretation, and the Claims of History*. Bloomington, IN, 2005.
Linenthal. Edward T. *Preserving Memory: The Struggle to Create America's Holocaust Museum*. New York, 1995.
Maechler, Stefan. *The Wilkomirski Affair: A Study in Biographical Truth*. Translated by John E. Woods. New York, 2001.
Meister, Robert. "Human Rights and the Politics of Victimhood." *Ethics and International Affairs* 16, no. 2 (2002): 91–108.

Michaels, Walter Benn. "'You Who Never Was There': Slavery and the New Historicism—Deconstruction and the Holocaust." In *The Americanization of the Holocaust*, edited by Hilene Flanzbaum. Baltimore, MD, 1999.

Novick, Peter. *The Holocaust in American Life*. New York, 2000.

Rosenfeld, Alvin H. "The Americanization of the Holocaust." *Commentary* (June 1995): 35–40.

Schoenfeld, Gabriel. "Death Camps as Kitsch." *New York Times*, 18 March 1999.

Simon, Jonathan. "Parrhesiastic Accountability: Investigatory Commissions and Executive Power in an Age of Terror." *The Yale Law Journal*, 114, (2005): 1419–1458.

Todorov, Tzvetan. *Facing the Extreme: Moral Life in the Concentration Camps*. New York, 1996 [1991].

———. "In Search of Lost Crime." *The New Republic*, 29 January 2001.

Weinrich, Harald. *Lethe: The Art and Critique of Forgetting*. Translated by Steven Rendall. Ithaca, NY, and London, 2004.

Weissman, Gary. *Fantasies of Witnessing: Postwar Efforts to Experience the Holocaust*. Ithaca, NY, 2004.

Wilson, John P., Zev Harel, and Boaz Khana. *Human Adaptation to Extreme Stress: From the Holocaust to Vietnam*. New York, 1988.

Paris, Capital of Anti-Fascism

Anson Rabinbach

Since the fall of communism, the intensity of debates over the legacy of anti-fascism is to no small degree the result of the fact that there has never been a consensus about the historical role of anti-fascism. Unlike Italian Fascism and German National Socialism, which were defeated and discredited militarily and politically in 1945, anti-fascism emerged from the war with its reputation enhanced by the aura of resistance movements and the Soviet victory. Postwar European communist parties and regimes, especially in the German Democratic Republic (GDR), drew their legitimacy from the sacrifices of heroes and martyrs who became the touchstone of myths and rituals until 1989. With the collapse of state sanctioned anti-fascist parties and regimes, anti-fascism emerged as the subject of a number of acrimonious public controversies as sensational archival revelations undermined the reputations of such once iconic figures as Stephan Hermlin, Ernst Thälmann, Arthur London, Jean Moulin, Paul Merker; but none of the public controversies was more passionate than the eruption over the now fairly well established evidence proving that Ignazio Silone (who was a hero both to Italian anti-fascists and anti-communists alike) had apparently been a police informant during his communist years.[1]

In 1994/1995, two distinguished historians, both of them veterans of the anti-fascist movement, retrospectively approached the subject from entirely opposing perspectives. In *The Age of Extremes*, British historian Eric Hobsbawm reprised the moment during the 1930s when the left abandoned its sectarian illusions, recovered from its earlier defeats, challenged the half-hearted and insincere policies of appeasement, and welded together a broad coalition of conservatives, liberals, socialists, and communists in a variety of countries "against the common enemy." By contrast, the late French historian François Furet claimed in his widely read *Le passé d'une illusion* that anti-fascism was the new face of Stalinism: a cynical and effective doctrinal shift that allowed European communists to change overnight from dedicated Bolsheviks into champions of liberty, democracy, humanity, and hatred of Hitler.[2]

Both of these books are symptomatic of the passions of the moment, at once too polemical and highly selective in scope and content. Both are far more works of memory than history. Neither draws on the rich new archival sources available since 1991. They ignore the fact that the ideology and practice of anti-fascism often varied greatly from the Comintern's official declarations linking fascism and monopoly capitalism. But taken together, they reveal the paradox of anti-fascism, which both mobilized genuine popular support for democratic currents while at the same time caused a fatal blindness that allowed many Western intellectuals to sacrifice their judgment and lead "double lives" guided by an opaque Stalinist "*apparat*."[3]

Neither Furet nor Hobsbawm distinguishes the official anti-fascism of the Comintern from local initiatives as well as from exile intellectuals and noncommunist resistance groups, which exhibited a much more complicated fiber of beliefs, convictions, hopes, emotions, and attitudes. Anti-fascism was more than the marriage of convenience between anti-Nazism and philo-Sovietism. It was less an ideology than a *mentalité*, more of a habitus than a doctrine. Its influence went far beyond the milieu of the Communist parties, extending not only to the left intellectuals and the "fellow-travelers," but to ordinary men and women, whether sympathizers of the Soviet "experiment" or not. In the 1930s, one could be an anti-fascist and not exclusively pro-communist, and one could also be pro-Soviet, but somewhat wary of the communists, as were many socialists, including Léon Blum. What did not exist after 1934 was a middle ground. The historian Richard Cobb, who lived in Paris during the 1930s, summed up the mood when he recalled that "France was living through a moral and mental civil war ... one had to choose between fascism and fellow traveling."[4]

In 1934, Paris became the capital of European anti-fascism. The most recent historiography has focused on four areas that offer some of the reasons for the effervescence of anti-fascism in France. Diplomatic and cultural historians have underscored the reorientation of Soviet foreign policy and reclamation of the "national" project of 1789 by the French Left.[5] Social historians have investigated the popular upsurge of anti-fascism from below (small "a" anti-fascism), while researchers in the Moscow archives have illuminated the well-orchestrated anti-fascism of the Comintern (capital "A" anti-fascism). Finally, a great deal of new research in the Soviet literary archives has revealed a major shift in attitude toward the intellectuals in the Fall of 1934. Anti-fascism can perhaps be best described as a cultural synthesis that combined the popular and the intellectual, the geopolitical and the local. The stations that marked the creation of that synthesis in the years 1934 and 1935 were the counter-demonstrations of the Left on 12 February, the burial of the communist writer Henri Barbusse on 7 September 1935, the International Congress of Writers for the Defense of Culture in July 1935, and the electoral victory of the Popular Front one year later.[6] During 1934, the mobilization of intellectuals, political organizations of the center Left, and the emergence of a genuinely popular anti-fascist movement also coincided with the rapid growth of a Germanophone exile community, composed almost entirely of refugees from Nazi Germany.

This essay surveys the four key elements in the creation of anti-fascist culture in France during the 1930s: (1) Soviet Foreign Policy and French Philo-Sovietism; (2) The Anti-fascist Campaigns of the Comintern and the exiles; (3) Popular Anti-fascism; (4) Literary Anti-fascism.

Soviet Foreign Policy and French Philo-Sovietism

Beginning in the fall of 1933, the French government, represented by Joseph Paul-Boncour, conducted negotiations with Soviet Foreign Minister Maxim Litvinov leading in September and October to the visits of Eduard Herriot and Pierre Cot to Moscow. On 19 May 1935, France and the Soviet Union concluded negotiations for a five-year Treaty of Mutual Assistance in the case of unprovoked aggression. A joint communiqué issued in Moscow stated that "these [two] governments are obliged in no way to weaken their weapons of national defense," and Stalin, in a famous statement, expressed his "complete understanding and approval of national defense pursued by France with a view to maintaining her armed forces at a level corresponding to the requirements of her security."[7] In other words, as the *Nation* journalist Louis Fischer put it: the French Communists were now required to be patriots and "to lay off the French army and stop their pacifist propaganda."[8] A few days later, Paris was plastered with posters announcing: "Stalin is right." The anti-militarism of the French communists was a dead letter.

The rapprochement led to official visits, diplomatic exchanges, tourism, and the promotion by both governments of a culture of official French philo-Sovietism, which played a key role in promoting the affirmative myth of the "new Russia." Though official France never completely embraced the new Russia; by the early 1930s, the older picture of the Soviet Union that prevailed in the 1920s—revolutionary, clandestine, strange, aggressive, subversive, and hostile to the West—began to compete with the new image of Soviet industrial modernity promoted by Soviet propaganda. Sixty percent of the funds of the Soviet Commissariat of Foreign Affairs were directed toward France, much of it going to contacts in the press, promoting well-orchestrated tours, and cultivating influential journalists. The intensity of the new "light from the East" drew its energy from the much touted Soviet economic and technological achievements of the Five Year Plans, whose devastating social costs were of course largely unknown. Whatever the faults of the new society in the East, its supporters contended, enmity to Fascism remained one of its central precepts.[9]

The Anti-fascist Campaigns of the Comintern and the Exiles

In August 1933, a small group of exile communists who had recently arrived in Paris produced a book that claimed that the Reichstag fire, which occurred just days before the first election faced by the new government, was the well-planned culminating act of terror that the Nazis used to secure total control over Germany. *The Brown Book of the Hitler Terror* and the campaign that accompanied it was the creation of Willi Münzenberg, the renowned Comintern impresario and Reichstag deputy, who earned the title of the "Red Hugenberg" for his organizational empire, which included the International Red Aid (IAH), numerous dailies and weeklies, journals, and the highly successful illustrated weekly, the *Arbeiter-Illustrierte-Zeitung*. His premise was that the fire could only have been a political crime, and—since only the National Socialists could benefit—was perpetrated by a Nazi cabal. Münzenberg seized the opportunity with characteristic skill and dramaturgical flair. He knew that "there was no more effective propaganda than an event that propagandized itself."[10] In the 1920s and early 1930s, Münzenberg enjoyed a greater measure of independence and freedom of action in the international field than did the German party or any other national communist organization. Münzenberg's style, his confabulation of organizations, commissions, and prominent public figures were already in place during the 1920s (Sacco-Vanzetti, Scottsboro). What was new was that Münzenberg, with his genius for propaganda, now faced Goebbels "in a head-to-head match, and in so doing, invented the new face of Stalinism: anti-Fascist communism."[11] In the same month, he founded the "World Committee for the Relief of the

Victims of German Fascism," created an international tribunal of lawyers to produce a counter-trial in London, and encouraged at least a dozen organizations worldwide to orchestrate an international campaign. Much of the campaign around the *Brown Book* concentrated on how the official Leipzig trial, which began in mid September, was conducted. From the first day to the close of the trial, when, on 31 December, the President of the Supreme Court, Dr. Karl Werner delivered a summation to refute explicitly the *Brown Book*'s claim that only the Nazis could have benefited from the fire, it remained an "active presence" in the courtroom. Goebbels himself called the *Brown Book* "the sixth defendant."[12]

The *Brown Book* simultaneously filled two urgent political and emotional needs, explaining how, without mentioning the utter impotence of the KPD or the unpreparedness of its leaders, that the Nazis were able to drive the party out of existence and its leaders into exile or prison. It surrounded that explanation with an image of the Nazis that in all respects ignored their popularity and electoral successes in favor of one in which conspiracy, blackmail, brutality, pathology, and sexual deviance took pride of place. The image of "Nazi fascism" that emerged from the *Brown Book* and the Reichstag Fire campaign no longer rested on the Marxist dogma of inevitable proletarian victory or on capitalist string-pulling, but rested instead on a newly fashioned image of heroic and innocent victims of degenerate homosexuals and morphine addicted fanatics. At the core of anti-fascism was a conspiracy narrative, or one might more accurately say, a counter-conspiracy narrative. The Nazis had accused the Communists of planning the fire as "das Fanal," the signal for an insurrection. Unexpectedly, the not yet Nazified German Supreme Court acquitted the four communist defendants on 23 December, giving not only Georgii Dimitrov, whose verbal dual with Goering electrified the court, but international communism an unexpected Christmas gift: the halo of innocence. As Koestler noted, "In the public mind, Dimitrov's acquittal became synonymous with the acquittal of communism in general from the charge of conspiracy and violence." Dimitrov became something that had eluded European communism since its inception: a genuinely popular "democratic" hero, the emblem of the new face of anti-fascist communism in the mid 1930s, no longer insular, illicit, clandestine, and proletarian, but virile, virtuous, and democratic. With Dimitrov's ascendancy to the symbolic leadership of the worldwide anti-fascist movement—soon followed by Stalin's decision in April 1934 to make him head of the Comintern—the style of international anti-fascism changed dramatically from the dour proletarian *"kumpel"* in his workers' *"Mütze"* (represented by the imprisoned German Communist Party head Ernst Thälmann) to the well-dressed, articulate, and cultivated European capable of quoting Goethe and Lenin in the same breath. The transformation of the image of communism during the Reichstag Fire campaign signaled an alteration in the self-representation of European and Soviet Communism at the same moment—from the rhetoric of the revolutionary vanguard to the rhetoric of the people and the nation.

After 1933, the main focus of all anti-fascist activity in Europe was France, where the majority of exiles had arrived. Among the émigrés, the major political casualty of Hitler's gaining power was the legitimacy of Social Democracy. Beginning in the second half of 1933, reports submitted to the German Social Democratic Party from its Prague exile revealed that the ideological and political authority of the party executive had all but disappeared, and that many of its former members in Germany—those engaged in underground activity—agreed with former party leader Rudolf Breitscheid's negative assessment of the intransigent leadership: "only a minority is willing to follow Prague."[13] The events of February 1934, and the echo of those events during the spring and summer of 1934, did not dissolve the enmities of the parties on the left, nor did they produce any new initiatives from either the leaders of the socialist or communist parties, but they did, as Gerd-Rainer Horn notes, force the "remaining of socialists of Europe, those who could still operate under conditions of legality, to take stock." As was the case in Spain and Austria, the French and Belgian Social Democratic politics definitely shifted to the left.[14] But the first Comintern sponsored anti-fascist Congress held in Paris in June 1933—so-called Amsterdam-Pleyel—was hardly the "most important demonstration of the will to fight of the anti-fascist forces of the majority of European countries," as its closing resolution proclaimed.[15] Its outcome was meager, resulting only in the merger of the anti-war Amsterdam Congress of 1932 and the anti-fascist Congress of 1933, under Henri Barbusse, André Gide, and André Malraux, as co-chairs.

Barbusse, who was considered by contemporaries to be a writer with strong communist sympathies, was in fact, as is now evident from his massive Moscow file, a major figure in the Comintern apparatus, working simultaneously as the head of half a dozen "supraparty" organizations. The Barbusse empire was actually managed by two German communists, his secretary, Alfred Kurella, and Albert Norden, who oversaw the day-to-day activity of the Committee against War and Fascism, the French "Thälmann Committee," and a "Women's Committee."[16] The two organizations, Barbusse's "World Committee for the Fight Against War and Fascism" and Münzenberg's "International Committee to Aid the Victims of Hitler Fascism," were distinct only insofar as the former was more influential among "certain proletarian masses and left oriented elements," while the latter tended towards more "left oriented bourgeois elements."[17]

Yet, there was a great deal of bad blood between the two leaders of the Comintern's "supraparty" organizations, resulting eventually in the compulsory adjudication of their dispute by a Moscow appointed delegation. Münzenberg was not terribly subtle in his high-handedness and disdain for Barbusse's French Committee, remarking that the French had not "produced any public events or actions of a legal nature," while his "World Committee to Aid the Victims of Fascism" had had "the greatest success." In his report of 19 November 1934, another Comintern plenipotentiary, Palmiro Ercoli-Togliatti, deplored the "lamentable *spirit of competition* [Togliatti's emphasis]" between the different mass organizations: the Amsterdam-Pleyel Committee against War and Fascism, the Münzenberg trust, the Red Aid (*Secours Rouge*), the women's youth, and intellectual groupings. The main cause of this state of affairs, according to Ercoli-Togliatti, was that "there were not enough 'masses' to go around," and all of these organizations were in fact "chasing the same few dozen intellectuals."[18]

At a deeper level, the question concerned not merely which Paris apparatus would take precedence in the lackluster campaign on behalf of Thälmann, but the future role of these supraparty organizations once national Communist Parties were required rather than prevented from participating in alliances with non-Communist organizations. At the end of July 1934, when the PCF-Socialist pact was struck, Barbusse appealed to the Comintern not to dissolve "Amsterdam-Pleyel," arguing that it was short-sighted to regard the pact between the two left parties (PCF and SFIO) as rendering supraparty organizations superfluous: "As you know, the Amsterdam-Pleyel movement has but one specific aim," he wrote, "the organization of a common front between the masses of both parties.... It safeguards the movement against setbacks and obstacles which might occur because of this or that momentary political conception that arises from the Socialist side."[19] In fact, with the shift to the Popular Front policy of the Comintern after the VIIth Comintern Congress in 1935, Münzenberg's *raison d'etre* was in jeopardy: his purpose of creating alliances with forces outside the sphere of the insular communist world was becoming superfluous, a reality that would become an even greater threat to his very existence in the coming years.

After the repatriation of Reichstag Fire defendants Dimitrov, Tanev, and Popov to Moscow on 28 February 1934, the fate of Thälmann became the sole aim of the campaign's efforts. Thälmann's legal situation remained precarious; after a brief torture session by the Gestapo, he landed in a kind of legal limbo between his Gestapo captors and the German judiciary. The denouement of the international campaign was Thälmann's fiftieth birthday on 16 April 1935, the obvious "occasion for a powerful intensification of the international movement for the release of Thälmann."[20] Telephone calls flooded the switchboards of German embassies throughout the world. Countless donations, bouquets, and resolutions were organized. Thalmann also received encomiums from famous writers such as Thomas and Heinrich Mann, Lion Feuchtwanger, Romain Rolland, Stefan Zweig, and Maxim Gorky.[21] His image adorned banners, posters, and thousands of postcards addressed to "Reichskanzler Adolf Hitler" with the words "We make you responsible for the life and safety of Ernst Thälmann."[22] Thälmann became the emblem of the anti-fascist "choice": "For Hitler or Thälmann—for war or peace" "Blood-tribunal or People's tribunal."[23] From the US alone, 50,000 birthday greetings arrived. Thälmann was portrayed as the tribune of the working class, but by the end of 1935, the highly sectarian Thälmann campaign had to be adjusted to conform to the results of the VIIth Congress. Efforts to involve German Social Democrats and Catholics in the movement produced little or no resonance. The Prague leadership of the SPD in exile (*Sopade*), did not express solidarity with Thälmann (who had of course been their arch-enemy) until January 1937.[24] In contrast to the Reichstag Fire campaign, the Thälmann effort was restricted to communists or the pro-communist milieu, and even in that community, they had little success in making the struggle for Thälmann "a matter of public opinion." The name Ernst Thälmann is "still completely inadequately popularized," an internal Comintern memorandum admitted in June 1935.[25]

The Aftermath of 6 February

The third vital element in the creation of a culture of anti-fascism was the crisis of February 1934. Though most historians today agree that Colonel François de la Rocque's *Croix de Feu* veterans' movement was far closer to the radical right than to Fascism, for contemporaries, especially the militants of the workers' parties, the paramilitary right seemed parallel to the movements that had destroyed the worker's parties in Italy and Germany.[26] For the French communists, 6 February was a political debacle. As opposed to the communist-led demonstrations on the 9th, which remained isolated, the SFIO/CGT's general strike on the 12th radiated far beyond Paris and its worker's suburbs to 346 localities, with the most spectacular successes occurring in municipalities with a strong trade-union presence.[27] In October 1933, Maurice Thorez, the French Communist Party's ever-subservient leader, could still explain Nazism as just one form of anti-communist monopoly capitalism among others, confidently predicting the rapid "bankruptcy of Hitler fascism which cannot realize its imaginary social program."²⁸ After 6 February, Thorez still refused to consider any alliance with the Socialists, who remained the primary "enemy," and despite the widely popular demand by the defiant Communist mayor of St. Denis, Jacques Doriot, and a number of other party leaders to end the "absurdity" of the old intransigence and enter into immediate negotiations to form a union with the Socialists, the Communists declared the government and Socialists "truly responsible" for the dead and injured of 6 February.²⁹

Internally, the PCF was rent by the gap between Comintern directives and the widespread sentiment for anti-fascist unity that emerged after the night of the Leagues and the unprecedented popularity of the dissident Doriot. In April, the Comintern declared a "cease-fire" between the two rival French leaders, demanding that both attend a conclave in Moscow to iron out the conflict. Instrumental in this French "turn" was a shadowy figure only recently illuminated by historical research, the Slovakian-born Comintern functionary Clément or Eugen Fried, a central European intellectual who had cut his political teeth in the Hungarian Soviet Republic of 1919, and who served as a kind of alter-ego or privy councilor to Thorez (who consulted him daily) and the PCF until 1939. The intransigent Doriot demurred, preferring to present his views to his own constituency during his campaign for reelection as mayor rather than to Stalin—a move that resulted in his denunciation and expulsion by the Comintern on 16 May for following the same road as Trotsky.³⁰

Four weeks later, the Comintern took a decisive step and on 11 June, the ECCI addressed a secret communiqué to the PCF to instruct the leadership in taking a decision at the National Party conference on the 23ʳᵈ in Ivry, recommending the party's willingness "at all costs" to strike an alliance with the Socialists and to attract the middle classes to the fight against fascism (while expelling Doriot for a lack of discipline). The Communists accepted the conditions set out by the Socialists at the beginning of June, to engage in the mutual campaign on behalf of Thälmann, and promised to refrain from accusations and slander. The Comintern message, conveyed by Ossip Piatnitsky, indicated for the first time that the Comintern was willing to abandon the immediate goal of the dictatorship of the proletariat and to adopt a political program more in conformity with the sentiments of the masses in a number of West European countries. The previous day, 10 May, Jacques Sadoul, the *Isvestia* correspondent in Paris, personally appealed to Dimitrov, who noted in his diary: "Threatening Fascism in France—United Front with Social Democracy—the incapacity of our leadership."³¹

This remarkable sea change in the Soviet—and the Comintern's—attitude remains perplexing. At the Seventeenth Party Congress in February, Stalin still considered the Nazi party an instrument of the big industrialists and the Reichswehr, which he believed could still be enticed to an entente with the Soviet Union, à la Rapallo. Karl Radek, the Comintern's German expert, said: "Only fools could imagine that we shall ever break with Germany."[32] "Fascism," Stalin told the Congress, "is not the issue here, if only for the reason that fascism in Italy has not prevented the USSR from establishing the best relations with that country." The Piatnitsky telegram of 11 June was the first sign of any change in the attitude of the Comintern. The upheaval taking place behind the scenes is evident in the recently published Dimitrov diaries. On 15 June, he registered his incredulity at the inability of the Comintern hierarchy to acknowledge the new situation: "With Piatnitsky—as if *nothing new* has happened!—And nothing new to say! ... Some want to change the revolutionaries! ... Terrible."[33] Two weeks later, on 2 July, Dimitrov posed the question to Stalin whether "it is correct to consider social democrats everywhere and under all circumstances the main social bulwark of the bourgeoisie." Stalin replied: "Not of course, in Persia. In the main capitalist countries yes, indeed."[34] It is hard to know what to make of this exchange; on the one hand, it shows Dimitrov pressing for a change and Stalin, as always, resistant to any abatement in the historic enmity to Social Democracy. The likelihood, though obviously a speculation, is that Stalin, who preferred to keep the question of German Communism separate from German-Soviet relations, was testing the waters of the Franco-Soviet alliance by permitting the change in the question of a working class union to be decided provisionally in the French case. On 27 July, the PCF and the SFIO signed the famous united action pact against fascism, war, and the decrees of the Domergue Government. The decision for a more general shift toward a Popular Front policy was not taken until October.

After February 1934, anti-fascist Committees sprang up more or less spontaneously throughout the country, made up in large part of those who took to the streets on the 12th of February. Throughout France, shops, offices, and ticket booths were closed. In more than nineteen mid sized towns, demonstrations of more than 5,000 persons were recorded. In the smaller villages, many with no significant trade-union presence, Socialists unfurled the red flag for the first time. France had not seen demonstrations of that magnitude since the protests demanding Dreyfus' exoneration in July 1906.[35] In the Loiret department, for example, where there were only 200 active communists in 1930, by 1935 more than 5,000 members had joined 77 local anti-fascist committees, not only in the workers districts of the city of Orléans where four to five thousand people demonstrated, but in rural villages where the left parties had little influence.[36] It is an exaggeration to conclude, as some historians have maintained, that these demonstrations in effect marked the "birth" of the Popular Front, but they did produce what was called in the jargon of the day, "one-time united fronts at the base." (*Front unique à la base*). Their combined impact brought down the government of Eduard Daladier, and its protean force could not be lost to the communist leaders, whose isolation from the broader currents of the left was now indelible, despite their continued assaults on the Socialists in the party press. In fact, a sort of Popular Front *avant la lettre* had occurred without orders from above, without direction, and in spite of the decades of rancor and polemic stances.

What this popular anti-fascism meant by "fascism" remained wholly ambiguous. For the communists, the term extended from the Action Française to the Radical Parti's Domergue government, which, according to them, appeased rather than suppressed the leagues and was "a movement of misery and fascism." Though far more circumspect, Léon Blum also spoke of the "French Hitlerites," who were abetting the danger of Nazi blackmail in Europe. Popular or "small a" anti-fascism was far more the expression of a symbolic politics of the street: a quantitative study of the "fashion" of demonstrations from 13 February to May 1936 counted more than a thousand marches, protests, and public gatherings, some 83 percent of the left, and 17 of the right, in all but five of France's departments.[37]

After 6 February, the French left underwent its own nationalization of the masses. The mass demonstrations, processions, and protests drew on a repertoire of rituals and symbols resting on the national memory of the revolutions of 1789, 1848, and 1871, while importing other elements to solidify the new politics of anti-fascist unity. Two months after the signing of the unity pact, a massive gathering of Socialists and Communists at the Panthéon commemorated the death of Jean Jaurès. It was on this occasion that the term "*Front Populaire*" appeared for the first time (as opposed to vague terms like "*Front Commun*"). The demonstrations at the wall of the communards a year later, under the inscription "1871–1936," was the first coordinated public expression of the Popular Front, with an estimated 600,000 participants.[38] In Danielle Tartakowsky's words, it was no longer a question of the living paying homage at the foot of the tombs of the martyrs, but of "summoning the breath of the history of the dead into the site of action, of history's forward march."[39]

One of the most symbolically weighted events of the newly elected Popular Front government was the death of Barbusse. Immediately after the celebrations of 14 July 1935, the sixty-two-year-old Barbusse traveled to Moscow to participate in the VIIth Comintern Congress where he contracted a lung infection and died on 30 August 1935. His death was an opportunity to celebrate a true and loyal "friend of the Soviet Union" (which was also the name of one of the many Comintern sponsored organizations that Barbusse headed). On 2 September, at 7:45 PM, as the orchestra played the *Internationale*, an honor guard headed by no less an august figure than Nikolai Bulganin, member of the Politburo and President of the Moscow Soviet, followed by the Comintern's Dimitri Z. Manuilsky, his protégé Nikita Khrushchev, and Lenin's former secretary, Elena Stasova, accompanied the writer's flower draped casket illuminated by four bright torches as it passed before rows of smartly saluting soldiers, grieving teachers, and official delegations of factory workers who lowered their flags as the procession passed. Overhead, an escadrille of airplanes flew in a spear formation as writers Alexei Tolstoi, Aleksei Koltsov, the French Communist leaders, Thorez, André Marty, Gaston Monmousseau, and Earl Browder of the CPUSA led the cortege with the body of Stalin's biographer through the streets of Moscow from the state hospital to the Grand Salle of the State Conservatory on the rue Herzen. "What sadness, but what joy," raptured *Humanité*, "for the victory of the idea for which the great departed man devoted himself."[40] Stalin sent a message that he "shared with you your pain on the occasion of the death of our friend, the friend of the French working class, the loyal son of the people of France, the friend of the workers of all countries, the tribune of the united front of workers against imperialist war and fascism, comrade Henri Barbusse."[41]

Barbusse lay in state for three days, whereupon he was carried by a carriage covered in flowers and drawn by six black horses to the Byelorussia Station. After two hours of eulogies, his body was placed on a train which, 23 hours later, arrived at the Gare de l'Est where it was met by a delegation including Jean-Richard Bloch, Francis Jourdain, Jacques Duclos, and Louis Aragon.[42] Barbusse's funeral, on 7 September was, unlike 14 July, a somber but impressive convocation of all of the forces that comprised the Popular Front. At the head of the funeral cortege was a large portrait of Barbusse surrounded by five hundred red flags with black borders.[43] At the last minute, at the insistence of the Soviets, his burial was shifted from the family tomb in d'Aumont (*Somme*) to *Père Lachaise*, where his internment became a massive display of anti-fascist solidarity and admiration for the anti-war writer and PCF militant. A distinguished committee headed by honorary presidents Maxim Gorky and Romain Rolland and dozens of famous intellectuals and politicians celebrated the author of the famous anti-war novel *Le Feu* (Fire), as he was buried in a plot exactly equidistant from the fresh tomb of the victims of 6 February 1934 and Le Mur des Fédérés, the holy burial shrine of French Communism. The contiguity of the two burial places was frequently invoked by the French leftist press, though ironically, the Communists avoided mention of it, preferring instead to emphasize the historical triumphs and heroes of the Republic at the expense of the defeat and victims of the

Commune. After 1934, the murder of the communards, which had been commemorated religiously for a decade, ceded its place to all the "victims of revolution"and 14 July and 1 May supplanted 29 May, the traditional memorial date of the Commune.[44] The site of Barbusse's tomb (which was likely the result of direct Soviet intervention with the Quay d'Orsay) was the perfect emblem of the new trajectory—a few meters of ground in the cemetery, but worlds apart in public memory—between the romanticism of the barricades symbolized by the wall of the executed communards and the new image of the heroic nation on the march.[45] It completed the martyrological syncretism of the Commune and February, solidifying, as *L'Humanité* elaborated a year later, "the resistance against fascism" and the tradition of the Commune, between the "hatred and corruption of Versailles in 1871" and the arousal of the people by the menace of the "seditious chiefs" on 6 February.[46] Not everyone present at the outpouring of public grief was acquainted with Barbusse's extensive *oeuvre*, however. One participant overheard a man asking his wife if she knew what famous book Barbusse had written, to which she answered, "you know, Pot-au-Feu!" (it was "*Le Feu*" [Fire], whereas Pot-au-Feu is a stew).[47]

During 1934, the "*lieux de mémoire*" of the left physically moved from the sacred wall of the Commune at the Mur de Fédéres at Pére Lachaise into the more prominent and nationally consecrated memorial spaces in the city of Paris—the place de la République, the place de la Concorde—which in turn diminished the symbolic power of the cemetery as a political site. By 1936, a "forest of placards and banners" displayed images of heroic precursors rather than fallen martyrs—Condorcet, Rousseau, Voltaire, and Diderot.[48]

A crucial factor in the success of French anti-fascism, as Thorez himself emphasized, was the rhetoric of democracy coupled with the "utilization of the revolutionary traditions of the French people."[49] The new language of anti-fascism, as historian Denis Peschanski observed, can be read in the changed political lexicon of *L'Humanité* in the late spring of 1935. Virtually overnight, the language of class, combat, struggle, and proletarian revolution gave way to a new language of "the people" and the "nation." Illustrative of this transformation was the new usage of the word liberty (*liberté*) from a modifier (liberty of the press, speech, etc.) to an abstract noun.[50] The communist calendar was integrated into the calendar of the Republic. The communist press—and beyond the press, the culture of the left–was awash in what Walter Benjamin called the "rhetorical furniture" of 1789.

Beyond words, new symbols were imported into the French lexicon of protest. On 1 June, the demonstration at the Mur de Fédéres was marked, as one observer noticed, by "something new." As the crowd passed in front of the tombs of the martyrs of February 1934, they silently raised their clenched fists.[51] The clenched or "raised fist," for example, initially adopted by the French left in the course of 1933, was a direct borrowing from the rituals of the German communists and was initially combined with the cry (in German) of *"Rotfront"* as a gesture of solidarity with the defeated German party. After the signing of the unity pact, the raised fist was adopted by all anti-fascists (including the left wing of the Radical Party).[52] Also new was the adoption of colored shirts (blue and red) by the youth movements of the left, and the creation of self-defense organizations among both communists and the socialists (though to a far more limited degree).

The Seduction of the European Intellectuals

In part, the receptivity of the intellectuals to anti-fascism was a response to the popular surge from below on 12 February. Intellectuals as diverse (and hostile to each other) as the Surrealists André Breton, René Crevel, and Paul Eluard, André Malraux, and the Radical philosopher Emile Chartier (Alain) signed the famous manifesto C.V.I.A. (*Comité de la vigilance des intellectuels anti-fascistes*). But during 1934 and 1935, Stalin also cautiously adopted a more positive attitude toward Sovietophile French intelligentsia—Rolland and Gide—whose vanity and pecuniary needs were nurtured by a trio: Alexander Arosev, head during the years of the Popular Front of the All-Union Society for Cultural Ties Abroad VOKS); Mikhail Koltsov, *Pravda* editor; and Ilya Ehrenburg for the Writer's Union. These organizations facilitated the smooth cultural associations between the Soviet Apparat and writers close to the party. The drive to recruit western intellectuals was evident in a note Barbusse wrote to the Comintern's propaganda chief Béla Kun in June,

> It appears to me that it is extremely important to win over the bulk of the intellectual masses to our cause. I don't just mean the eminent personalities, the masters of the pen and the sciences; we must also win over the institutions, the doctors, the engineers, the white collar employees, in short, the masses of intellectual workers. They are hit hard economically by the crisis which deprives them of their means of existence; they are fully aware—with more or less confusion—of the ideological crisis of the bourgeoisie; they want to find a new perspective, they are turning to us, in certain cases.[53]

It was not enough, Barbusse added, for them to join a committee, affix their signature to a petition, or for the Comintern just to use the intellectuals for the struggle; rather, it was necessary to "assist" the intellectuals in their search for a new ideology and to make them aware of their place in the new Socialist society. Barbusse's letter also referred to the upcoming Moscow writer's Congress to be held in August, which he anticipated would launch the initiative among the intellectuals.

The 1934 First All-Union Congress of Soviet Writers was aimed at gathering an elite of European writers, all by no means positively disposed to European Communism, but at the very least prepared to admire the achievements of Soviet society. As Klaus Mann, who attended the event, recalled,

> Never was I more intensely pained and puzzled by the inadequacies and errors inherent in the Marxism creed, than during my stay in Moscow. I went there in July 1934, to attend the first Congress of Soviet Writers. It was a large-scale affair remarkably staged and highly interesting. Many of the things I observed were indeed apt to impress on me not only the splendid efficacy of Soviet organization, but also the dynamic faith impelling this apparatus. It was fascinating—indeed elating—to witness the joyful élan with which the plain people participated in the collective effort of building the Socialistic society.[54]

The 1934 Congress was a major extravaganza dedicated to the veneration of the leading figures of classical European literature. Almost seven hundred Soviet and European writers, scores of party officials, Red Army soldiers, delegations from near and remote, Kolkhoz, and troops of young pioneers listened to some two hundred speeches for two entire weeks, from 17 August until 1 September.[55] Moscow's showplace of culture, the Hall of Columns, was decorated with the visages of Shakespeare, Tolstoy, Gogol, Cervantes, Heine, Pushkin, and Balzac, flanked by even more massive images of Stalin and Gorki, with a gigantic bust of Lenin adorning the red curtain festooned podium.[56]

The Congress combined the harsh Stalinist rhetoric of Zhdanov, who personally outlined the strictures of socialist realism, with a lighter salting of slightly more "liberal" and "tolerant" speeches such as Bukharin's, which mentioned the still largely taboo figure of Boris Pasternak and stressed the need for greater literary quality and "diversity." Hedging his bets, Malraux drew his famous distinction between the writers and intellectuals in the USSR who "can already work for the proletariat" and "us, the revolutionary writers of the West [who] are working against the bourgeoisie." But Malraux also used his unmatched "oratorical art" to challenge Stalin's dictum that writers are engineers of the soul: "If writers are engineers of the soul do not forget that the highest function of an engineer is to invent. Art is not a submission but a conquest."[57] If a Soviet writer had publicly taken issue with Stalin, dire consequences would no doubt have swiftly followed. Of the Soviets present, only Ehrenburg, Stalin's "cultural ambassador," supported the western writers in his pleas for tolerance and variety, individual taste and artistic excellence.[58] As the Paris correspondent of the *Isvestia* and the best known cultural mediator between Communist and non-communist writers and intellectuals inside and outside of Russia, the talented Ehrenburg shared with his close friend Malraux the conviction that the Soviet Union could be a bulwark against Nazi Germany and it was Ehrenburg who persuaded Malraux and his wife, Clara, to attend the Congress.[59] There is no reason to question the veracity of the novelist Isaac Babel's "confession" to his interrogator just before he was murdered in Butyrka prison on 27 January 1940: "Ehrenburg acquainted me with Malraux, of whom he thought very highly and whom he introduced to me as one of the brilliant representatives of young radical France. During our frequent meetings, Ehrenburg would tell me that the leaders of the most varied ruling groups in France listened to what Malraux had to say, and that his influence would grow as the years passed. Indeed, this would prove to be true."[60]

Even more important is the little known part played by Ehrenburg in persuading Stalin that European writers could be enlisted in the cause of anti-fascism. During his return to France from the conference in September 1934, Ehrenburg met privately with his childhood friend Nikolai Bukharin in Odessa where the two composed a detailed letter (his first ever) to Stalin. It is evident that Bukharin thought the letter important enough to travel to Odessa solely in order to advise Ehrenburg on how to present his case and what arguments would prove persuasive to the Soviet leader. The letter begins: "I hesitated for a long time, on whether or not I should write you this letter. Your time is precious not only to You but to all of us. If I have finally decided to write to You, it is only because without Your participation the question of organizing the writers of the West and America who are close to us can not be solved." Ehrenburg then noted that:

> the makeup of foreign delegations present at the writer's congress did not correspond to the weight and significance of their participation. With the exception of the two famous French delegates (Malraux and Bloch), the Czech poet [Vitslav] Nezval, two (not of the first rank, but nonetheless talented) German writers [Theodor] Plivier and Oskar Maria Graf, and finally the Dane [Martin Andersen] Nexö, there were no serious representatives of western European and American literature at our congress. This can be partly explained by the fact that the invitation to the congress was for some reason distributed not by Orgkomitet but by MORP [International Organization of Revolutionary Writers] and was for the most part poorly

conceived. They didn't invite the people who should have been invited. However, the main reason for the low quality of the international delegations at our congress is the entire literary politics of MORP (the International Writers Organization) and its national sections, which cannot be called anything else but Rappovian.[61]

The "RAPP," an acronym for Rossijskaja Associacija Proletarskisch Pisaletj or the Russian Association of Proletarian Writers that had dissolved two years earlier (23 April 1932), had served since 1929 as the umbrella Soviet writers organization that effectively oversaw the Bolshevization of all literature, by absorbing a wide variety of smaller organizations, initiating denunciatory campaigns, and promoting ideological conformity through draconian methods of exclusion, denunciation, and campaigns of defamation. By 1932, when it was officially dissolved, the RAPP dominated Soviet literature, and had ensured that all writers took an active part in socialist construction and class struggle by delivering literature that glorified the heroic role of workers and peasants in socialist construction.

Ehrenburg bemoaned the fact that the dissolution of the RAPP had still not changed the Comintern's literary politics: "Who runs MORP? A few third-rate Hungarian, Polish, and German writers. They've lived among us for some time, but this settled life has found no expression in their mentality or in their creative work. They are completely cut off from the life of the West and do not see those deep changes which have occurred in the western intelligentsia after the arrival of Fascism." Ehrenburg emphasized that, "the Western European and American intelligentsia pays attention to 'big names'." He emphasized the importance of the All-Union Writer's Congress for appealing to the European intelligentsia by demonstrating the extent that "our writers, both party and non-party, are rallied around the country in its constructive work and in its preparations for defense." The RAPP was a leftist club that diminished the legitimacy of the Soviet cause in the eyes of the really important writers.

> In America, the Rappovites push us away from such famous writers as Dreiser, Sherwood Anderson, and Dos Passos. They criticize them for not holding to the Party line in one or another of their literary characters. In France the journal *Commune* serves as the mouthpiece for the French section of MORP. In a recent survey of writers, most of them responded that often the journal published twenty lines of any writer and then forty lines of editorial explanation, usually in an incredibly rude tone and full of personal attacks. Such behavior pushes us away from the writers who are closest to us: Gide, Malraux, Du Gard, Fernandez etc. Suffice to say, even Barbusse finds himself in a situation that is barely tolerable. As for the Germans, Radek, in his concluding remarks [in Moscow], clearly displayed the nar-

rowness and, what is worse, the arrogance of the literary circles that have captured the leadership of revolutionary German literature.

Ehrenburg concluded with a plea to end this state of affairs and court the crème of western writers:

> The condition in the West right now is extremely advantageous: the majority of the most talented and famous writers sincerely want to join us in the fight against fascism. If instead of MORP there were to be a broad anti-fascist organization of writers almost all of the following writers would immediately join: Rolland, Gide, Malraux, Bloch, Barbusse ... Thomas Mann, Heinrich Mann, Sherwood Anderson, Dos Passos, ... Dreiser.... In short, such an organization with few exceptions, would unite all the great and loyal [uncorrupted]? writers. The political program of such an organization should be broad yet precise:
>
> 1. The struggle against Fascism
>
> 2. The active defense of the USSR.[62]

Clearly impressed with the proposal, Stalin immediately sent a note to Lazar Kaganovich endorsing its main points: "Read Comrade Ehrenberg's letter. He's right," Stalin wrote enthusiastically on 23 September. "The traditions of RAPP in the MORP must be liquidated. This is of the utmost necessity. Take up the matter along with Zhdanov. It would be good to broaden the framework of MORP ((1) The struggle against fascism. (2) The active defense of the USSR)[63] and place at the head of MORP Comrade Ehrenburg. This is an important matter. Please direct your attention to it."[64] In the end, however, Ehrenburg was not chosen to be head of MORP. Stalin hesitated to create a new organization, preferring instead to "liquidate the traditions" of the Russian Association of Proletarian Writers (RAPP) in the existing International Organization of Revolutionary Writers (MORP). Instead of installing Ehrenburg, Stalin preferred to appoint Barbusse as chairman of the International Organization of Writers and urged him to move its headquarters to Paris—which occurred in December 1934. Unlike Ehrenburg, Barbusse was opposed to replacing the MORP with a brand new organization of writers and proposed merely "issuing a manifesto, with the eventual goal of creating, on an international level, such an organization."[65] No doubt, Barbusse could not help but recall the events of November 1930, when he was vituperatively humiliated and denounced by Nizan for "rightist tendencies" at the Kharkov Congress of the RAPP and had to do penance (even before the Congress hurled its thunderbolts) by declaring that the literary heritage of the bourgeoisie could never be reconciled with the masses of the dispossessed, the proletariat.[66] In 1934, however, his considerable cultural capital was restored and Barbusse's "line" was once again in the ascendancy. With the German literary apparatchiks Kurella and Johannes R. Becher at his side, the venerable author and central figure in the Comintern's western literary apparatus would, until his death one year later, play a decisive role in recruiting Western writers to the new philo-Soviet anti-fascism.[67] In his diary, Dimitrov noted at the time, "Is there to be a new *Don Quixote* (the degenerate Bourgeoisie)? We need our Cervantes against Fascism."[68]

In the fall of 1934, writers were courted, seduced, invited, feted, and eulogized, especially if they were famous. The turn toward "socialist" humanism meant quite different things, however, to the influential western writers whose greatest works were published before World War I, and who, in their later years, were the object of sycophantic reviews, well-organized celebrations, and extremely expensive trips to the Soviet Union. Those who were truly famous—Rolland, Gide, Feuchtwanger, and Emil Ludwig—were granted an interview with Stalin himself. Yet, to understand the confluence of Soviet literary politics and the anti-fascist humanism of the senior writers of the West, two levels—the prosaic "seduction" of the intellectuals and their willingness to be "seduced," on the one hand, and the aesthetic transformation of Soviet literature into something called "humanism," on the other, has to be briefly addressed. Vladimir Paperny, in his sublime analysis of the culture of the Stalin era published in 1979 as *Architecture in the Age of Stalin: Culture 2*, distinguished between the aesthetic principles that governed the Lenin era (Culture I) and their transformation in Stalin's (Culture II).[69] Paperny argues that the culture of Stalinism cannot simply be reduced to ideology, because the ideology of Leninism and Stalinism, though distinct, does not sufficiently address the depth of the transformation that soviet culture underwent after 1932, far beyond the aesthetic and architectural dimension. As opposed to "Culture I," which emphasized the technological, the mechanical, the functional, and the biological (all of which became negative terms), Culture 2 "constantly declares its concern for the living person."[70] From a literary standpoint, the new "anthropomorphism" fit perfectly with the concepts of nineteenth-century realism, and in fact was itself in large part derived from literature. In the direct aftermath of the dissolution of the RAPP, which in turn destroyed the avant-garde both inside and outside the organization, the new "humanism" appeared as a direct analogue of the verticality symbolized in the architectural—aesthetic principles of the new and hierarchical (as opposed to egalitarian) society.

Under Arosev's capable direction, the All-Union Society for Cultural Ties Abroad (VOKS) coordinated the new cultural diplomacy paying special attention to the writers. The Soviets rolled out the red carpet for these well-attended travelers and Soviet ideologists, and functionaries displayed an unprecedented flexibility to outsiders that was unimaginable inside the Soviet Union and unthinkable within the Communist Parties in the West. The category "friend of the Soviet Union" conveyed a special status in the language of Soviet cultural diplomacy and, though they were hardly trusted, the goal was to turn these distinguished celebrities "into our defenders in the capitalist world."[71]

The undisputed literary icon in the era of high Stalinism (he died in 1936) was Maxim Gorky, who promoted the "heroic" and "monumental" virtues of Soviet Communism and drew into the philo-Soviet camp some of the venerable figures of European "high culture" in the early 1930s. Gorky courted Romain Rolland and played a major part, along with Arosev, in bringing about the famous meeting of Rolland and Stalin in July 1935, as well as enabling the interview with Andre Gide in December the following year. Rolland was especially instrumental in translating Stalin's platitudes about the "New Soviet Man" into his own language and lineage—from Beethoven to Tolstoy—of Humanism.

The seduction of the Europeans was not, however, a one-way street. The French literary elite endowed Soviet Europhile cultural apparatchiks such as Arosev and Ehrenburg (both of whom were Jews) with the patina of success; they profiled themselves as capable functionaries with access to influential figures outside of Russia, and they skillfully used their contacts with the "friends" among Western intellectuals and writers not only to promote Stalinist policies abroad, but to ingratiate themselves with the leader. Ambition, cynicism, self-preservation, and special access to literary celebrities helped Arosev enhance the luster of the VOKS by arranging high-profile visits culminating, when most successful, in an audience with Stalin. These Europhile intellectuals genuinely sensed the political advantages of bringing lesser known and more experimental writers over to the side of the revolution during the European crisis and participating in a common front against fascism.

The Congress for the Defense of Culture, attended by a sold out crowd of 3,000, opened on 21 June at the Salle Mutualité on the rue Saint-Victor and was the intellectual and political event of the decade, gathering the literary and cultural elite of Europe, including some 250 writers and intellectuals from thirty-eight countries.[72] "All of literary life was there; but there were also some representatives of the parties and the workers unions," wrote André Chamson, one of the Congress organizers. Significantly, the Congress was not primarily a Comintern affair. The relative absence of Münzenberg and even Barbusse in the story of its genesis and staging was no accident; once anti-fascism moved from the periphery of

Soviet policy to the center in 1934–1935, Münzenberg's role was eclipsed by the collaboration of Europhile Soviet functionaries and philo-soviet European writers and intellectuals. The Congress was run on the Soviet side by Koltsov and Ehrenburg, and on the French side by Louis Guilloux, Jean-Richard Bloch, René Lelu, Louis Aragon, and especially Andre Malraux. The Soviet delegation was headed by a prominent party figure, Shscherbakov and *Pravda* editor, Koltsov. Its members were chosen less for their literary skill than for of their fidelity to the Soviet system and proven subordination to Stalin, especially in their utterances on the subject of literature. Stalin personally selected the makeup of the Soviet delegation, but Malraux, Regler, and Ehrenburg persuaded Gide to convey a personal request to Stalin that Boris Pasternak and Isaac Babel be invited, in part to maintain the façade of broad participation—since Pasternak and Babel were known to be outside the strict parameters of the MORP, but also as a means to enhance their reputations in the West, which could help protect them in Moscow. Even the *Figaro*, no friend of the Soviet Union, praised the Writer's Congress' press organization and the fact that it was "superbly supplied with material." The care with which the Writer's Congress was managed emerges from Babel's KGB interrogation. Soviet writers allowed to travel to Paris relied on Ehrenburg and were not permitted to "converse with anyone or trust anyone other than Malraux."[73]

The bolshevization of the European left liberal intelligentsia went hand in hand with the transformation of European Bolshevism into anti-fascism. The international writer's conclave was in part the result of the Faustian pact between Europe's anti-fascist elite and Soviet Communism, at a particularly auspicious moment when both were seeking allies and a cultural bridge from Paris to Moscow. As Michael David-Fox has shown, this bridge was built out of the shared cultural and ideological stuff of humanist universalism, according to which the Soviet Union represented a supposedly universal path of development, the fulfillment of the revolutionary dreams of 1789, 1848, and 1872. In fact, in the 1930s, newly constructed Soviet socialism corresponded to the moment of its greatest particularism. These European intellectuals "intuitively felt they grasped and understood Soviet socialism so well at the very moment they misunderstood it so deeply."[74]

No doubt Stalin regarded European literary anti-fascism as window-dressing, but for Ehrenburg, Mann, Malraux, Gide, Bloch, and the hundreds of writers invited to attend the events in Paris it was an existential necessity. Ehrenburg aimed high but accurately: his ideal supporters were not the leading lights of the pro-Soviet avant-garde of the 1920s, but the major figures of French and German literature, the venerable generation of the 1860s (Rolland, 1866; Gide, 1869) and 1870s (Heinrich Mann,

1871; Thomas Mann, 1875). Of the younger authors he courted, Malraux was born in 1901, Gustav Regler in 1898, and Klaus Mann in 1906. None had joined the Communist Party; all were resolute in their hatred of Hitler. Referring specifically to Malraux, Regler made the decisive point: "the Party should be thankful for sympathizers of his stature who are worth a dozen Aragons."[75]

After the noisy success of the Paris Congress, the western writer's initiative threatened to quietly disintegrate. The reason for this, Koltsov wrote, "lies in the passivity of its leadership and in a total lack of funds."[76] Stalin ultimately supported Koltsov's request for more funds, but rejected his idea of "carrying out active, constant work, directed at consolidation of the broad circle of writers of all countries, aimed at fighting against fascism and war, the protection of cultural values, and active defense of the Soviet Union." As a concession, Stalin approved a Politburo decision to invite between ten and twelve prominent foreign writers to visit Russia each year. But by the end of 1934, after the murder of Kirov, roundups, repression, and executions of scores of party members were beginning to take their toll in Leningrad and Moscow. In May 1934, the first signs of the artistic and literary purges were abroad; the poet Osip Mandelstam had been arrested, although Stalin gave orders that he be "preserved" and was "merely" sent as an "outpatient" into internal exile at Voronezh near Moscow, probably because Stalin did not want to jeopardize the upcoming Soviet writer's Congress.[77] By the time Ehrenburg returned to Paris, Regler was repeating the joke the Soviet journalist had told him: "two men were walking across Red Square. One of them suddenly says, 'Watch out! Be careful!' The other says, 'But why? There's no one anywhere near us.' The other murmurs, 'One of us is bound to be a member of the GPU!'."[78]

Anti-fascism was a complex mix of ideas, images, and symbols, but also a mirage that ultimately divided the world into two hostile camps and subordinated all political judgment to a Manichean logic. In the struggle between "fascism" and its enemies, there could be no middle ground, no neutral space, and no non-combatants in a world divided between the forces of progress and decline, the friends and enemies of culture and civilization. Not unconnected to its friend-enemy logic was the anti-fascist myth of "virile innocence," especially of masculine heroes. "Better the widow of a hero than the wife of a coward" was an oft-repeated slogan. Many of the international volunteers who arrived in Spain in the heyday of anti-fascism during the Spanish Civil War (1936–1939) truly felt that they belonged not to a nation or class, nor to a party or a movement, nor a doctrine or a metaphysics, but to a common humanity whose adherents all spoke the same Spartan language, shared the same sacrifices, and were engaged in the same redemption of the world. The writer Milton Wolff, who joined the Abraham Lincoln Brigade, composed of three thousand American volunteers, wrote of his "Spanish Lesson": "He went to Spain in 1936 because he was an anti-fascist. He felt, although he did not know for sure, that if fascism were not stopped in Spain, it would sweep the world. He did not know beforehand what he was going to do when he got to Spain. Certainly he did not know anything about fighting or killing or dying; but he was a volunteer. In Spain he met a people who lived, slept and ate anti-fascism, who never tired of doing something about it." This rhetoric of innocence and the innocence of anti-fascist rhetoric may explain why anti-fascism remained so pure in the memory of its veterans. As George Orwell wrote in his classic *Homage to Catalonia* (1938), those illusions were in truth the correct "anti-fascist" attitude that had been carefully disseminated largely in order to prevent people from grasping the real political nature of the civil war within the civil war.

For opponents of Hitler, the news of the non-aggression pact signed between Foreign Ministers Vyacheslav Molotov and Joachim von Ribbentrop on 23 August 1939 was a devastating blow. Though Stalin had already begun to withdraw from the Spanish conflict, though explorations of a possible rapprochement with Hitler continued throughout 1937, and though the British and French alliance never materialized, no one anticipated what simply seemed inconceivable. While the majority of Communists quickly knuckled under and abandoned anti-fascism to pro-Sovietism, a minority of dissident intellectuals, such as Münzenberg, Manés Sperber, Arthur Koestler, Gustav Regler, Ignazio Silone, and Hans Sahl, broke ranks in order to remain anti-fascists. Forced to choose between loyalty to Communism and opposition to Hitler, these writers understood that the "Machiavellian powers," as Sperber called them, had struck up a totalitarian alliance. Even the word "fascist" disappeared from the communist lexicon.

Notes

1. On Silone, see Elizabeth Leake, *The Reinvention of Ignazio Silone* (Toronto, 2003).
2. Eric J. Hobsbawm, *Age of Extremes: The Short Twentieth Century, 1914–1991* (London, 1994); François Furet, *The Passing of an Illusion: The Idea of Communism in the Twentieth Century*, trans. Deborah Furet (Chicago, IL, 1999).
3. Stephan Koch, *Double Lives: Spies and Writers in the Secret Soviet War of Ideas against the West* (New York, 1994).
4. Cited in David Caute, *The Fellow-Travelers: Intellectual Friends of Communism*, rev. ed. (New York, 1988), 165.

5. A pioneering work in the diplomatic history of the 1930s is Sabine Dullin, *Des hommes d'influence: les ambassadeurs de Staline en Europe, 1930–1939* (Paris, 2001).
6. Sophie Coeuré, *La grande lueur à l'Est: les Français et l'Union soviétique, 1917–1939* (Paris, 1999), 200.
7. On the pact of 1935 see Dullin, *Des hommes d'influence*, 143.
8. Louis Fischer, "The Franco-Soviet Alliance," *The Nation* (19 June 1935): 705.
9. Coeuré, *La grande lueur*, 260.
10. Bruno Frei, *Der Papiersäbel: Autobiographie* (Frankfurt, 1972), 25.
11. Furet, *The Passing of an Illusion*, 216.
12. *Der Kampf um ein Buch: Wie im Dritten Reich gegen das Braunbuch gekämpft und gelogen wurde* (Paris, 1934), 5.
13. Rudolf Breitscheid to Paul Herz, 25 April 1935, cited in Gerd-Rainer Horn, *European Socialists Respond to Fascism: Ideology, Activism, and Contingency in the 1930s* (New York, 1996), 24.
14. Horn, *European Socialists Respond to Fascism*, 18, 20–25.
15. State Archive for Social and Political History, Moscow (RGASPI) (Comintern Archives), cited hereafter as RGASPI, "Resolutionsentwurf über den Europäischen Antifaschistenkongress und über die Aufgaben der Antifaschistischen Arbeitervereinigung Europas," 28 March 1933.
16. Stiftung Archiv der Parteien und Massenorganisationen der DDR im Bundesarchiv (SAPMO-DDR), cited hereafter as BA, TBS328/19562, "Abschrift aus Erinnerungen der Genossin Maria Rentmeister über Weltkomitee gegen Krieg und Faschismus und 'Weltfront'," n.d.
17. BA, TBS328/19562, "Abschrift aus Erinnerungen der Genossin Maria Rentmeister über Weltkomitee gegen Krieg und Faschismus und 'Weltfront'," n.d.
18. Annie Kriegel and Stéphane Courtois, *Eugen Fried: Le grand secret du PCF* (Paris, 1997), 275.
19. RGASPI, F.495, op. 60, d. 246, "22 July 1934," 4.
20. BA, NY4003/56, Letter from Wilhelm Pieck to Largo Caballaro, ca. March 1936.
21. BA, NY 4003/56, "Die Thälmann-Kampagne von Juli 1936 bis Juni 1937," 3.
22. BA, NY 4003/56, "Die Befreiungskampagne für Thälmann von New York bis Kapstadt," October 1934, 17.
23. BA, NY4003/57, "Für Ernst Thälmann," 1937.
24. BA NY 4003/56, "Letter to Paul Hertz 'Sopade' Prag," 3 November 1936.
25. BA, NY4003/56, "Bemerkungen zu Thälmannkampagne," n.d.
26. Zeev Sternhell, Mario Sznajder, and Maia Ashéri, *The Birth of Fascist Ideology: From Cultural Rebellion to Political Revolution* (Princeton, NJ, 1994).
27. Antoine Prost, "Les manifestations du 12 fevrier 1934 en province," *Le mouvement social* (January–March 1966).
28. Philippe Robrieux, *Maurice Thorez: Vie secrète et vie publique* (Paris, 1975), 174.
29. Phillippe Burrin, *La dérive fasciste: Doriot, Deat, Bergery, 1933–1945* (Paris, 1986), 169.
30. Ibid., 174–175; Kriegel and Courtois, *Eugen Fried*, 214.
31. Georgi Dimitroff, *Tagebücher 1933–1943*, ed. Bernhard H. Bayerlein, trans. Wladislaw Hedeler and Brigit Schliewenz, 2 vols. (Berlin, 2000), 1: 113.
32. Cited in A.M. Nekrich and Gregory L. Freeze, *Pariahs, Partners, Predators: German-Soviet Relations, 1922–1941* (New York, 1997), 85.
33. Dimitroff, *Tagebücher 1933–1943*, 1: 114.
34. Cited in Nekrich and Freeze, *Pariahs, Partners, Predators*, 261, n37.
35. Antoine Prost. "Les manifestations du 12 fevrier 1934 en province," *La France en*

36. *mouvement, 1934–1938*, ed. Jean Charles Asselain and Jean Bouvier (Paris, 1986), 20, 21.
36. François Marlin, "Le Réflexe anti-fasciste: Les comités de lutte contre le fascisme et la guerre dans le Loiret (1934–1936)," *Vingtieme Siecle* 8 (April–June 1983): 55–69.
37. Danielle Tartakowsky, "Strategies de la rue 1934–1936," in *La France en mouvement, 1934–1938*, ed. Jean Charles Asselain and Jean Bouvier (Paris, 1986), 32.
38. Danielle Tartakowsky, *Nous irons chanter sur vos tombes: le Père-Lachaise, XIXe–XXe siècle* (Paris, 1999), 131.
39. Tartakowsky, "Strategies de la rue 1934–1936," 32.
40. *L'Humanité*, 3 September 1935, 1.
41. Ibid.
42. Philippe Baudorre, *Barbusse* (Paris, 1995), 392–394.
43. Ibid., 394.
44. Tartakowsky, *Nous irons chanter*, 145–146.
45. Ibid., 147. In May 1936, at the request of Mme Barbusse, and perhaps through the good offices of "Moscow," Barbusse was exhumed and reinterred directly facing the wall of the communards. Cf. ibid., 149.
46. Danielle Tartakowsky, *Le pouvoir est dans la rue: crises politiques et manifestations en France* (Paris, 1997), 152.
47. BA, TBS328/19562, "Abschrift aus Erinnerungen der Genossin Maria Rentmeister über Weltkomitee gegen Krieg und Faschismus und 'Weltfront'," n.d., 12.
48. Tartakowsky, *Le pouvoir est dans la rue*, 132.
49. Robrieux, *Thorez*, 197.
50. Denis Peschanski, *Et pourtant ils tournent: vocabulaire et stratégie du P.C.F., 1934–1936* (Paris, 1988).
51. Tartakowsky, *Nous irons chanter*, 129.
52. Philippe Burrin, "Poings levés et bras tendus: La contagion des symboles au temps du front populaire," *Vingtième siècle* 11 (July–September 1986): 5–20.
53. RGASPI. 495.60.246, "Cher Comrade," 25 June 1934.
54. Klaus Mann, *The Turning Point: Thirty-Five Years of this Century* (New York, 1984), 285.
55. Joshua Rubenstein, *Tangled Loyalties: The Life and Times of Ilya Ehrenburg* (New York, 1996), 130.
56. Olivier Todd, *Malraux: A Life* (New York, 2005), 143.
57. Ibid., 145, 146.
58. Rubenstein, *Tangled Loyalties*, 133.
59. Ibid., 125.
60. Vitalii Shentalinskii, *The KGB's Literary Archive*, trans. John Crowfoot (London, 1995), 38.
61. Letter of 13 September 1934, cited in B.B.I Frezinskii, "Velikaia illuziia—Parizh 1935," *Minuvshee: Istoricheskii al'mankh Marerialy k istorii Nezhdunarodnogo kongressa pistalei v. zashitu kul'tury* 24 (1998): 171–185.
62. Ibid.
63. Similar to the incident with L. Brik's letter (on the legacy of Mayakovsky), Stalin uses the words of the author of the letter as his own.
64. Cited in Frezinskii, 171–185.
65. Ibid.
66. See the excellent study of Nizan's role in the Communist Party, Annie Cohen-Solal, with the collaboration of Henriette Nizan, *Paul Nizan, communiste impossible* (Paris, 1980), 97.

67. Rubenstein asserts that, "Kirov's murder prevented Ehrenburg from seeing Stalin though Frezinskii disputes this version of events, pointing to discrepancies in the chronology of Ehrenburg's memoirs."
68. Dimitroff, *Tagebücher*, 1: 119.
69. Vladimir Paperny, *Architecture in the Age of Stalin: Culture Two* (Cambridge and New York, 2002), 118–119.
70. Ibid.
71. Michael David-Fox, "The 'Heroic Life' of a Friend of Stalinism: Romain Rolland and Soviet Culture," *Slavonica* 11, no. 1 (2005): 3–29.
72. No complete collection of the speeches and materials relating to the congress was published until 2005. Its predecessor was Wolfgang Klein's *Paris 1935: Erster Internationaler Schriftstellerkongress zur Verteidigung der Kultur: Reden und Dokumente mit Materialien der Londoner Schriftstellerkonferenz 1936* (Berlin, 1982). This edition, put out by Akademie der Wissenschaften der DDR, Zentralinstitut für Literaturgeschichte, contained numerous unpublished documents and German versions of many contributions. A new and heavily expanded French edition was published in 2005 by Sandra Teroni and Wolfgang Klein, eds., *Pour la défense de la culture: les textes du Congrès international des écrivains, Paris, juin 1935* (Dijon, 2005).
73. Shentalinski, *The KGB's Literary Archive*, 40, 41.
74. David-Fox, "The 'Heroic Life,'" 3–29.
75. Gustav Regler, *The Owl of Minerva: the Autobiography of Gustav Regler* (New York, 1960), 182.
76. Cited in Leonid Maximenkov and Christopher Barns, "Boris Pasternak in August 1936—An NKVD Memorandum," *Toronto Slavic Quarterly*, no. 17 (Summer 2006), <http://www.utoronto.ca/tsq/06/pasternak06.shtml> (accessed 2 July 2008).
77. Shentalinski, *The KGB's Literary Archive*, 168, 169.
78. Gustav Regler, *The Owl of Minerva* (New York, 1960), 182.

Bibliography

Baudorre, Philippe. *Barbusse*. Paris, 1995.
Burrin, Phillippe. *La dérive fasciste: Doriot, Déat, Bergery: 1933–1945*. Paris, 1986.
———. "Poings levés et bras tendus: La contagion des symboles au temps du front populaire," *Vingtième siècle* 11 (July-September 1986): 5-20.
Coeuré, Sophie. *La grande lueur a l'Est: les Français et l'Union soviétique, 1917–1939*. Paris, 1999.
Caute, David. *The Fellow-Travelers: Intellectual Friends of Communism*. Rev. ed. New York, 1988.
Cohen-Solal, Annie. *Paul Nizan, communiste impossible*. Paris, 1980.
Der Kampf um ein Buch. Wie im Dritten Reich gegen das Braunbuch gekämpft und gelogen wurde. Paris, 1934.
Dimitroff, Georgi. *Tagebücher 1933–1943*. Edited by Bernhard H. Bayerlein. Translated by Wladislaw Hedeler and Brigit Schliewenz. 2 vols. Berlin, 2000.
Dullin, Sabine. *Des hommes d'influence: les ambassadeurs de Staline en Europe, 1930–1939*. Paris, 2001.

Furet, François. *The Passing of an Illusion: The Idea of Communism in the Twentieth Century.* Translated by Deborah Furet. Chicago, 1999.
Frei, Bruno. *Der Papiersäbel: Autobiographie.* Frankfurt, 1972.
Horn, Gerd-Rainer. *European Socialists Respond to Fascism: Ideology, Activism, and Contingency in the 1930s.* New York, 1996.
Hobsbawm, Eric J. *Age of Extremes: The Short Twentieth Century, 1914–1991.* London, 1994.
Koch, Stephan. *Double Lives: Spies and Writers in the Secret Soviet War of Ideas against the West.* New York, 1994.
Leake, Elizabeth. *The Reinvention of Ignazio Silone.* Toronto, 2003.
Kriegel, Annie and Stéphane Courtois. *Eugen Fried: Le grand secret du PCF.* Paris, 1997.
Marlin, François. "Le Réflexe antifasciste: Les comités de lutte contre le fascisme et la guerre dans le loiret (1934–1936)." *Vingtieme Siecle: revue d'histoire,* no. 8 (April–June 1983): 55–69.
Mann, Klaus. *The Turning Point: Thirty-Five Years of this Century.* New York, 1984.
Nekrich, A. M., and Gregory L. Freeze. *Pariahs, Partners, Predators: German-Soviet Relations, 1922–1941.* New York, 1997.
Peschanski, Denis. *Et pourtant ils tournent: vocabulaire et stratégie du P.C.F., 1934–1936.* Paris, 1988.
Prost, Antoine, "Les manifestations du 12 fevrier 1934 en province." *Le mouvement social* (January–March 1966).
Robrieux, Philippe. *Maurice Thorez: Vie secrète et vie publique.* Paris, 1975.
Rubenstein, Joshua. *Tangled loyalties: The Life and Times of Ilya Ehrenburg.* New York, 1996.
Shentalinskii, Vitalii. *The KGB's Literary Archive.* Translated by John Crowfoot. London, 1995.
Sterhell, Zeev, Mario Sznajder, and Maia Ashéri. *The Birth of Fascist Ideology: From Cultural Rebellion to Political Revolution.* Princeton, NJ, 1994.
Tartakowsky, Danielle. *Nous irons chanter sur vos tombes: le Père-Lachaise, XIXe–XXe siècle.* Paris, 1999.
———. *Le pouvoir est dans la rue: crises politiques et manifestations en France.* Collection historique. Paris, 1997.
———. "Strategies de la rue 1934–1936." In *La France en mouvement, 1934–1938,* edited by Jean Charles Asselain and Jean Bouvier. Paris, 1986.
Todd, Olivier. *Malraux: A Life.* New York, 2005.

Toward a Critique of Violence

Dominick LaCapra

> One can understand why Surrealism was not afraid to make for itself a tenet of total revolt, complete insubordination, of sabotage according to rule, and why it still expects nothing save from violence. The simplest Surrealist act consists of dashing down into the street, pistol in hand, and firing blindly, as fast as you can pull the trigger, into the crowd. Anyone who, at least once in his life, has not dreamed of thus putting an end to the petty system of debasement and cretinization in effect has a well-defined place in that crowd, with his belly at barrel level. The justification of such an act is, to my mind, in no way incompatible with the belief in that gleam of light that Surrealism seeks to detect deep within us.—André Breton, *Manifestoes of Surrealism*

Among the many farfetched aspects of my famous or infamous epigraph is the inchoate idea (could it be called instrumental?) that it is somehow a mark of distinction, if not elevating or even redemptive, to "dream" that random acts of violence may cause the downfall of a debased sociopolitical and cultural system. Evident as well is the conjunction of traumatizing violence and a sublimely abyssal "gleam of light ... deep within us." Breton expresses the fascination of figurations of violence that have played a prominent but differential role in the more or less symptomatic thought of noteworthy modern Western thinkers. I would like to inquire critically into these figurations and, in so doing, signal the questionable manner in which violence has been valorized and presented in foundational, sacralized, sublime, or redemptive terms.

A crucial problem is that such figurations of violence tend to free it from normative limits and associate it with excess. It is important, both analytically and critically, to understand the ideological and practical appeal of violence rendered sacred or sublime. It is equally important to appreciate the countervailing, normative role of orientations that seek alternatives to—or at least attempt to place limits on—violence, even when it is directed toward seemingly "emancipatory" ends. Indeed, an end, whose ostensible role is to limit violence, may itself become so abstract and ill-defined that it does not limit, but in fact legitimates the excessive use of violence, especially in the context of more or less covert interests (such as a quest for geopolitical dominance) and advanced technology that facilitate massive if not unlimited destruction and death. The violent pursuit of invasively expansive, utterly utopian ends (limitless conquest, total victory, uncompromisingly "radical" yet unrepresentable transformation, even fighting terror, and supposedly spreading freedom or equality) may fail systematically to work in strategic or tactical ways and be tantamount to, or at least have the same excessive effects as, a sacralization or rendering sublime of violence. The valorization of violence may serve to provide such extreme, phantasmatic ends with an aura of legitimation and may possibly be one of their disavowed motivations.[1]

Transfigurations of Violence and Trauma

Violence both poses problems that cut across disciplines and is closely related to other significant cross-disciplinary problems. It is, for example, difficult to see how one could discuss trauma, which has become an increasingly widespread concern, without relating it to violent processes of various kinds from the experience of physical assault to the symptom-inducing, imaginary identification with the victim of violence.[2] Indeed, violence is the typical manner of breaking the psyche's protective shield or forcefully transgressing normative limits and thereby causing traumatization. Terrorism may be seen at least in part as the systematic traumatization of a subject population, whether by a government or by nongovernmental groups. And traumatizing violence, including sacrificial violence, may be theorized and turned to in a deceptive effort to break through what is experienced as a deadly, compulsive cycle of repetition in the pursuit of hoped for purification, regeneration, or redemption—but with effects that instead intensify that cycle's vicious force. Moreover, the enumeration of formal analogies between trauma and the sublime may not extend analysis far enough.³ Certain theorists (at times themselves taking a formalistic or aestheticizing turn) may even conjoin trauma and violence conceptually and evaluatively in a manner that construes them as ecstatic experiences of the sublime or as sacralizing, redemptive, or foundational forces.⁴

A tendency to transfigure trauma into the sublime is especially prevalent in apocalyptic and postapocalyptic thinking, where violent, traumatizing action is understood as marking a radical, even total, rupture with the past—a kind of creation *ex nihilo*, conversion experience, or primal leap (origin as *Ursprung*) that is taken to be the necessary condition for a breakthrough into a typically blank or unknowable utopian future. This is one significant way in which violence may be glorified and made into an object of desire. The figuration of violence has been replete with sacrificial or sublime motifs and presented as a redemptive or regenerative force for the individual and the group.⁵ The foundation of a polity as well as of a personality is often traced to some violent, traumatic, transgressive, often sacralized or "sublimated" event, which is presumed to mark a turning point or rupture in history and the instauration of a new era. Among such events, often merging religious and political history, one may list the killing of Laius by Oedipus, the killing of Remus by Romulus, the killing of Abel by Cain, the intended sacrifice of Isaac by Abraham, the crucifixion of Christ (readable either as the self-immolation of the deity or the killing of the son abandoned by the father), the beheading of Louis XVI during the French Revolution (a regicide that was also a deicide), and the more abstract idea of the death of God who, as Nietzsche contends, was killed by us as the inaugural moment of modernity. Perhaps one might add the Nazi genocide against the Jews as well as other genocides or excessive, violent events, at least when they are construed in certain ways or function as foundational traumas and reference points or templates for later events and actions, often becoming constraining frames of reference. For example, the phantasm of the Nazis returns time and again—in Baader-Meinhof for the German government, in the German government for Baader-Meinhof, in the Arabs for certain Israelis, in the Israelis for certain Arabs, and so forth.⁶ It is also interesting to note that, about the time Nietzsche was announcing the death of God,⁷ the Catholic Church declared the infallibility of the Pope⁸—something it is tempting to see as a contested, anxious, anthropocentric gesture denying the possibly traumatizing recognition that the place of the Big Other might indeed be vacant or a void.

I would signal the importance of the founding or foundational trauma that paradoxically transfigures into an origin or source of identity what would seem to shatter identity or at least place it in question.⁹ Foundational traumas may of course become sacralized centerpieces of a civil religion (for example, the role of the atomic bombing of Hiroshima and Nagasaki for the *hibakusha* or the centrality of Holocaust commemoration, albeit differentially, for Jewish and German identity). A significant problem in comparative history and anthropology is whether there are myths of origin that resist or refuse to see the originary and ritualized, or at times compulsively repeated, inaugural event (or foundation) in terms of a traumatizing act of valorized or even sacrificial violence. For example, one may ask whether there are significant turns away from valorized and sacrificial violence in the peace and ecology movements (where *hibakusha* have played a role) or, in a different register, in the Abraham and Isaac story and in the crucifixion of Christ, turns suggested but not pursued in Derrida's *Gift of Death*, which may remain too much within a sacrificial frame of reference.[10] For example, the crucifixion might be read as a sacrifice to end further sacrifice, or even (more contestably) as a non-sacrifice, and not as a founding act to be emulated mimetically in the *imitatio Christi*. In this sense, it might be compared to the stoppage of sacrifice by God (or the Big Other) in the Abraham and Isaac story, although that tale still displaces sacrifice onto the nonhuman animal that is typically forgotten in analyses of the story, as is even the human victim, Isaac. (Accounts tend to focus on the relation between God and Abraham and perhaps oneself, often with a pronounced tendency to identify with Abraham, as in Kierkegaard.)[11]

In terms of recent events, it is noteworthy how rapidly 9/11 was converted into a foundational trauma, especially by the Bush administration with the active complicity of mainstream media. The very idea that the world changed totally after 9/11 gave the event an apocalyptic status. And its role as a foundational trauma or even a conversion experience could be seen in the idea that to be an American, or even a good person, you had to have been traumatized by 9/11—an idea that came close to normalizing trauma and ruling out, as unpatriotic or immoral, any critical analysis of the causes or political uses of 9/11, including its farfetched use as a pretext for war in Iraq. 9/11 starkly brings out the way trauma may be both given a politicized and foundational, if not an apocalyptic, status and subjected to manipulation and self-interested use.

I would also point to a broad intellectual and cultural current in modernity that is not restricted to the idea of the foundational trauma and encompasses some extremely problematic components. With varying degrees of critical distance on the intricate nexus linking violence, trauma, victimization, sacrifice, the sacred, and the sublime, this current includes many different figures and movements that in a more extended treatment would require greater differential analysis.[12] What I would underline is the dimension, coming into prominence in the twentieth century, wherein critical distance drops to a minimum or disappears, and violence is understood as definitive of agonistic human relations (as in social Darwinism) and valorized, justified, or even glorified as a transformative, regenerative, or originary/foundational force. In this sense, violence is not seen as significantly varied in its forms, as always problematic, and as at best only partially justifiable in terms of the context and the ends toward which it is directed (which is close to my own view as well as, I think, to an aspect of Marx's). In other words, violence, from the perspective I am analyzing critically, is not seen as never securely legitimate, whether by an appeal to God, the sovereign state, natural law, the terroristic threat of an elusive enemy, or the maintenance of an imperial order. Nor does it have only a contestable claim to legitimacy that is subject to argument in given circumstances. And an attempt is not made to disengage the sacred and the sublime (as well as the gift) from sacrificialism involving victimization and to subject the latter to sustained critique. Instead, the sacred or the sublime is indiscriminately or tendentiously validated (say, as foundational, radically transcendent, or beyond ethical judgment), and violence, including traumatization, is figured or experienced as something that runs counter to or even transcends instrumental reason, perhaps all reason, and constitutes an excessive, apocalyptic, redemptive power. Hence violence, from the latter perspective, is indeed sacred or sacralizing, or, in more secular terms, a glorious bearer and giver of an exhilarating, unrepresentable, ineffable, even "born-again" experience presumably beyond experience and transcendently out of this world.[13]

This process of sacralization even occurs in unlikely places, for example, toward the end of Temple Grandin's interesting book, *Thinking in Pictures and other Reports from my Life with Autism*, where the slaughterhouse and the killing of animals in it are sacralized, and there is not the full realization of what is at times intimated in the book, to wit, that the legitimate role of the sacred and ritual is not to sanctify or glorify violence and killing, but rather it is to limit and counteract their uncontrolled, invidious effects, including effects of victimization (such as extreme disempowerment).[14] Grandin states that one-third of the cattle and hogs in the United States are handled in equipment she has designed.[15] And she tries to build such equipment on humane principles. Her technique is to empathize or even identify with the animal on the apparatus that takes it to slaughter. She attempts to experience, from the perspective of the animal, the path, or rather the forced and often abusive preliminaries, to being slaughtered. Yet she also sacralizes the slaughterhouse, which I doubt is the animal's perspective. But she apparently does so because she believes, in however untimely a fashion, that it is only through the sacralizing role of ritual that some limits can be placed on the often-objectionable way animals are handled or mishandled on their way to death.

It would also be worth exploring the extent to which there are links between violence and the sublime or even the sacred in Burke, Kant, and the aesthetic of the sublime in general, including a dubious tendency for the sublime to function as a criterion of the transcendence, superiority, and sovereignty of humans over—and largely unlimited use of—other animals and the rest of nature, and at times, groups of abjected humans as well. In other words, there is a need to rethink the aesthetic of the sublime in a differential and other than dismissive or indiscriminately participatory way—to rethink it carefully neither as a categorical debunker nor as an unqualified enthusiast, especially when the sublime is linked not only to excess, but also to trauma and violence and becomes a force for foundation, transfiguration, or putative redemption.

Four Horsemen of Hyperbole? Sorel, Benjamin, Derrida, Bataille

To specify further the concerns I am evoking, I shall mention some significant texts that warrant further analysis.[16] I shall discuss them in a selective fashion to bring out aspects that are problematic and warrant critical reflection, even if these problematic aspects may not typify the entire thought or even a specific text of a given figure, for the latter issues could be addressed only in a much more extended treatment.

One finds an insufficiently guarded apology for violence in Georges Sorel's *Reflections on Violence* (first published in book form in 1915, but in periodicals as early as 1906 and 1908), a work that Zeev Sternhell has seen as significant for fascists despite its affirmed "leftist" anarcho-syndicalism and proletarian leanings.[17] Even if one disagrees with Sternhell in important ways, one may at the very least see Sorel's perspective as symptomatic of broader currents in the early twentieth century, and modernity more generally—currents exacerbated but not caused by World War I and the Great Depression as well as linked to forms of colonial and imperial violence. The crucial point for my account is that Sorel's apology focuses on violence as a regenerative or redemptive force that will transfigure civilization, mark the return of heroic values, and end the reign of despised bourgeois complacency and instrumental or calculative rationality. Its vehicle, the proletarian general strike, is termed a "complete catastrophe" and left utterly void of content.[18] The general strike signals the possible coming of what might be termed a blank utopia—a utopia about which one can say nothing and which marks a radical break or disjunction with the past, an end to the "burden" of history, and the inauguration of a brave new era. Proletarian violence is the good object in contrast to bourgeois violence, typified in the Terror during the French Revolution, which represents the bad object. With special reference to proletarian violence, the book's final words are: "It is to violence that Socialism owes those high ethical values by means of which it brings *salvation* to the modern world."[19] Here, one has the link between violence, seemingly sublime ethical values, and salvation—with violence itself invoked as a largely abstract concept bringing in its train a host of uncontrolled and unqualified connotations.

Sorel was quite important for the early Walter Benjamin essay of the "Critique of Violence," first published in the early twenties, which is a critique only in the most problematic of senses and conveys a rather uncritical, quasi-religious apology for a certain sort of violence or force. (*Gewalt* in German, meaning both violence and force, remains equivocal in Benjamin's text, yet often seems to mean violence.)[20] Active in Benjamin's essay is the binary opposition between mythical, state, representational violence, which is bad, and divine, absolute, pure, redemptive violence (linked at least implicitly to the revolutionary proletarian general strike), which is good. Good, or more precisely, pure, immediate, sovereign, divine violence (in a sense, inaugural, originary, or foundational violence situated beyond good and evil—analogous, I think, to the intended, divinely commanded violence of Abraham's sacrifice) is, for Benjamin, unrepresentable and performatively undermines the entire system of representation. Divine violence, with its invisible expiatory power, is even equated with what Benjamin terms bloodless but lethal annihilation.[21]

This is not the place for a more extended analysis of Benjamin's tangled discussion, but it may be noted that Derrida in "The Force of Law" provides a treatment of it that manifests a kind of *fort/da* attraction and repulsion with respect to Benjamin's line of thought, sympathetic if not emulative at points (notably with respect to an originary, revolutionary *coup de force*, a concept that Derrida seems to accept on his own behalf), and then drawing back, especially when extrapolations are made (at least in addenda) to Nazism and the "final solution."[22] Derrida's own text provides a complex, partially participatory reading of Benjamin's essay that is as intricate and open to diverse readings as the "Critique of Violence" itself, both inviting the mention of these texts in the series of discourses on violence I am exploring and making any clear-cut determinations of their status or import contestable.

Without claiming that it dominates the entire argument, I would single out as especially problematic a passage in the principal text of Derrida's "Force of Law" in which violence and force seem to assume an originary, performative role with interpretation, and, presumably, discourse (including normative discourse), having a derivative or at least secondary status.

> [Justice's] very moment of foundation or institution (which in any case is never a moment inscribed in the homogeneous tissue of a history, since it is ripped apart with one decision [*il le déchire d'une décision*]), the operation that consists of founding, inaugurating, justifying law (*droit*), making law, would consist of a *coup de force*, of a performative and therefore interpretive violence that in itself is neither just nor unjust and that no justice and no previous law with its founding anterior moment could guarantee or contradict or invalidate. No justificatory discourse could or should insure the role of metalanguage in relation to the performativity of institutive language or to its dominant interpretation.[23]

Continuing to write in a kind of discursive middle voice or participatory, free indirect style, Derrida goes on to call this foundational, performative, violent power the "mystical." He asserts that "silence is walled up in the violent structure of the founding act," and his stress moves to the *coup de force* and the performative, at least creating the impression that they transcend any "always-already" situatedness or supplementarity and alone institute or found justice and law.[24] Revolution as *coup de force* would seem to be cut off from its construction, in terms of a rethinking of historical temporality, as a radical modality of *différance* on the model of trauma, which would combine repetition with a decisive break or disjunction. Indeed, "performative and therefore interpretive violence" is dissociated from history (itself construed in reductively homogeneous, non-Derridean terms) and seemingly given a transcendental status as an *actus purus*, creation *ex nihilo*, perhaps an opening to the *tout autre* (totally other), or, at the very least, a foundational trauma.[25] (As in many other contestable contemporary discourses, the radically constructivist formula seems to be: All power to the performative!)

Here, one might object that in any historical situation, for example, the French Revolution, the *coup de force* is intimately bound up with legitimating or justificatory discourse that should not be understood as a metalanguage, but that is not simply derivative either—discourse that appeals to past discourses (Rousseau's, for example, or, on another level, both classical texts and Christian sacrificial and redemptive discourse) and informs the violent or forceful act or imbricates it with "immanent," sociopolitical, and ethical considerations, however misguided.[26] Yet one might counter this objection with an exegesis of Derrida's own discourse whereby it is interpreted not as isolating the *coup de force*, but as analytically distinguishing it and postulating at best a quasi-transcendental status for it that, in its performativity, situates it not as totally other than, but as irreducible to, prior situations or contexts. Such an exegesis would accord with Derrida's thought in other texts concerning *différance*, supplementarity, and a rethought historicity, but one might nonetheless be left with the impression that, in this text, Derrida's discourse is not as clear as it might be on the status of the *coup de force*, and, notably in its occasional appeal to violence (whereby history is "ripped apart by one decision"), might seem to be lending greater force to the performative *coup de force* than would be desirable (or than my suggested exegesis would allow). And the notion of violence is used in different registers, from interpretation to revolution, in a possibly bewildering and insufficiently regulated way (something that may be a constitutive problem in a discursive middle voice or participatory style that may perhaps be seen as enacting a transferential relation to the other—in this case, Benjamin's text and elsewhere, about the same time, Paul de Man and his World War II journalism).[27]

It is nonetheless significant that Derrida's treatment of divine violence, while it may be open to question as an exegesis of Benjamin, tries insistently to resist taking that violence as authorizing what is permissible in human action, thus countering the sacralization of human violence.[28] I would also recall that in the "Post-scriptum" added (to the best of my knowledge) after the initial presentation of his text at a conference at the Cardozo Law School (and in what I am tempted to see as a belated recognition that resonates with the concerns I am putting forward), Derrida saw, as dubiously symptomatic, crucial aspects of, and took critical distance from, Benjamin's "Critique of Violence" in a manner that, despite certain hesitations (*vide* the enigmatic parenthetical insertions of "perhaps, almost" and "perhaps, perhaps"), is more pronounced than anything to be found in the principal text of "The Force of Law":

> What I find, in conclusion, the most redoubtable, indeed (perhaps, almost) intolerable in this text, even beyond the affinities it maintains with the worst (the critique of *Aufklärung*, the theory of the fall and of originary authenticity, the polarity between originary language and fallen language, the critique of representation and of parliamentary democracy, etc.), is a temptation that it would leave open, and leave open notably to the survivors or the victims of the final solution, to its past, present or potential victims. Which temptation? The temptation to think the holocaust as an uninterpretable manifestation of divine violence insofar as this divine violence would be at the same time nihilating, expiatory and bloodless, says Benjamin, a divine violence that would destroy current law through a bloodless process that strikes and causes to expiate.... When one thinks of the gas chambers and the cremation ovens, this allusion to an extermination that would be expiatory because bloodless must cause one to shudder. One is terrified at the idea of an interpretation that would make of the holocaust

an expiation and an indecipherable signature of the just and violent anger of God.

It is at that point that this text, despite all its polysemic mobility and all its resources for reversal, seems to me finally to resemble too closely, to the point of specular fascination and vertigo, the very thing against which one must act and think, do and speak, that with which one must break (perhaps, perhaps). This text, like many others by Benjamin, is still too Heideggerian, too messianico-marxist or archeo-eschatological for me.[29]

In these passages, Derrida seems to oscillate between extremely decisive judgment and the kind of undecidability that is difficult to distinguish from more ordinary indecision and equivocation, perhaps attesting to his intense, impossibly mournful, not quite worked through relation to Benjamin and his text. Less self-questioning and hesitant are the sacralization and rendering sublime of violence that are at times quite forceful in the work of Georges Bataille. Still, Bataille explicitly yet tortuously engaged the problem of the relation between fascism and his own apology for violence in the traumatic context of sacrifice, unproductive or useless expenditure (*dépense*), and the uncompromising critique of instrumental rationality (including for a time a seeming defense of *surfascisme* or the escalating appeal to fascist procedures, including violence, in presumably opposing fascism). Within the larger notion of the heterogeneous, Bataille associated *dépense* not only with ambivalent affect involving attraction and repulsion, but also with "violence, excess, delirium, madness" and "extreme emotions" more generally.[30] For a linkage of trauma, the sublime, and *jouissance*, one might also refer to Bataille's ecstatic essay on the aftermath of the atomic bombing of Hiroshima discussed with reference to sovereign *dépense* beyond agency and politics (here there is no difference between natural disasters and bombings for Bataille—between the dropping of an atomic bomb and, say, a tsunami), "a core of darkness [that] remains untouchable," and "a boundless suffering that is joy, or a joy that is infinite suffering."[31] In effect, Hiroshima and its victims are seen in terms of a masochistic sublime that might be related to the transhistorical, traumatic "real" (somewhat like Agamben's dubious figuration of the *Muselmann*, the most abject victim in the camps, in *Remnants of Auschwitz*).[32] This correlation between the most abject or low, including the victim, even the victim of torture, and the ecstatic, sublime, or sacred is both commonplace in certain forms of thought and extremely dubious. (It is, for example, taken to an extreme in Mel Gibson's film *The Passion of the Christ*.) Bataille himself was fascinated, even obsessed, by 1905 photographs of a Chinese torture victim.[33] He described his response in terms that suggest mystical, if not pure and idealized masochistic identification:

The young and seductive Chinese man of whom I have spoken, left to the work of the executioner—I loved him with a love in which the sadistic instinct played no part: he communicated his pain to me or perhaps the excessive nature of his pain, and it was precisely that which I was seeking, not so as to take pleasure in it, but in order to ruin in me that which is opposed to ruin.[34]

Whatever one makes of the exoticized and eroticized aestheticization of the torture victim as *beau désastre*, or of the extreme gesture of ruining what is opposed to ruin, as well as of the figurations of sublimity or ecstasy such reversed ruination may induce (I fear they may contribute to a prevalent sense of abject but more or less enlightened or theorized disempowerment), one may acknowledge the importance of Bataille in bringing out both the limitations of instrumental rationality or economism and the persistent role of sacralizing and sacrificial forces, including their often covert or encrypted appeal in modernity. He also emphatically insisted on the value of spending the self without expecting a return on one's "investment." And his approach to the sacred and sacrifice stressed the role of voluntary victims, not scapegoated outsiders (except perhaps in the case of the bourgeoisie—not a subordinate or oppressed group, but one bearing the brunt of Bataille's polemical animus as boring, unheroic, and productive).[35] Moreover, Bataille's elated or effervescent rereading of Durkheim and Mauss, influenced in part by both surrealism and his reading of Nietzsche, tended to reverse Durkheim's and Mauss's emphasis on the role of legitimate limits as resistances to transgression and excess in order to formulate an influential view of social existence that stressed the value of excess, including violent and sacrificial excess, in which limits threatened to become little more than pretexts or inducements to transgression. A primary bearer of this excess and the vehicle of base materialism, stressing the dirty, ugly, repressed sides of being, was an anarchistic proletariat, or rather lumpenproletariat, that would not create a new order, as desired by Sorel, but would rather be an acephalic, self-dispossessing, disempowered, but nonetheless virile and ecstatic force for heterogeneity in which the role of recurrent violent sacrifice either seemed to be a necessary revitalizing force or at best remained equivocal. The goal of action was vague and addressed by Bataille only in resoundingly rhetorical, often violent phrases, such as the idea of life as a "virile unity" that has "the simplicity of an ax blow."[36] And a significant absence in Bataille's extensive reflection on sacrifice was any sustained concern with the problem of victimization and the perspective of the victimized themselves. Indeed, one might argue that a difficulty in Bataille is that he so internalized both conceptions of social constraint and modern atomistic individualism that he was unable to see any way around them other than through violent, sacrificial self-shattering.

Bataille had a pronounced, performative, participatory sense of the often encrypted role of the sacred and the sacrificial in modernity (for example, in self-mutilation) and was important in bringing a set of considerations into postwar French thought and modern thought more generally, not only for René Girard, but for many others (including Foucault, particularly in the abstract paean to both Bataille and transgression offered in his "Preface to Transgression").[37] How to arrive at an overall appreciation of Bataille, including the role of violence in his thought, is a complex task that has too often been met with rather uncritical apologetics (as in the recent studies of Michèle Richman or Michel Surya), an occlusion of political questions (as in the early essays of Foucault and Derrida), or an overly summary, even dismissive conception of Bataille's "left fascism."[38]

Passages to the Limit

The dubious sides of excess, transgression, and the apology for "sublime" violence were manifest in their role in fascism and Nazism, which one should take seriously as dimensions of modern thought and practice. If one makes selective use of it, Klaus Theweleit's *Male Fantasies* provides valuable analyses of the cult of violence, including misogynistic and antisemitic fantasies, of the Freikorps, notably in the writings of such important figures as Ernst Jünger and Ernst von Salomon.[39] For Jünger and Salomon, the *Fronterlebnis* (or experience of fighting on the front in the First World War) was itself an ecstatic existential peak that had sacrificial and regenerative force. It would be desirable to carry analyses such as Theweleit's forward into the discussion of fascists and Nazis, as well as to situate the latter with respect to earlier phenomena, including the cult of violence, World War I, colonialism, and imperialism. Such an approach is needed, especially in light of the overly restricted, even tendentious inclination to see the Holocaust predominantly if not exclusively in terms of instrumental (or means-ends) rationality, technology and modernization, the machinery of destruction, and industrialized mass murder or, more recently, biopolitics and mere, naked life or *homo sacer* (in Giorgio Agamben—but the general tendency in which Agamben may be situated is found in very different figures, including Raul Hilberg, Omer Bartov, Zygmunt Bauman, and Philippe Lacoue-Labarthe as well as in a crucial dimension of Horkheimer and Adorno's *Dialectic of Enlightenment*). This entire perspective on the Holocaust, stressing its modernizing, bureaucratizing, industrial, technological, biopolitical, analytically reductive aspects is indeed important, but it is also one-sided and insufficient.⁴⁰ One effect of a focus on bureaucratic structures as well as the everyday life and "ordinary" motivations of Germans in the Third Reich (one sense of the "banality of evil," at least for historians) is that, despite its partial validity, it may turn attention too much away from the group of committed Nazi militants and their ideological, at times quasi-sacrificial and "sublime," incentive that was bound up with the "everyday" yet extreme violence inflicted on victims. This shift of focus is one problem in Claudia Koonz's otherwise excellent *Nazi Conscience* as well as in the important work of Christopher Browning.⁴¹

In a different and at times dubious register, the American-born Jonathan Littell's prize-winning, massive historical novel, *Les Bienveillantes*, is also worth mentioning.⁴² Its often normalizing, first person, at times retrospective narrative offers an "it-could-happen-to-anyone" rendition of an SS-officer's experience during the Holocaust and the campaign on the eastern front, and familiar and copious, if at times disconcertingly gruesome, documentary material is downloaded and reprocessed with occasionally salacious twists (including the stereotyped figuration of the narrator-protagonist as having a phantasmatic and, in early life, actual incestuous relation to a sister with whom anal sex and identification induce in him a "passive" homosexual orientation). The title itself, which is gendered feminine, ostensibly refers to the (pacified) Furies and perhaps as well to the narrator-protagonist himself as well as his well-meaning, homoerotic, fellow SS officers who at one point are confusingly construed as being in basic human solidarity with the victims they torture and kill.⁴³ The often-leveling "machinery of destruction" seems to sweep up, mangle, and render choiceless even the lives of SS officers. Yet the narrator-protagonist, who starts his *Bildungsreise* with literary and philosophical ambitions and ends it by escaping punishment through a ruse and then directing a lace-making factory, occasionally has reflections of an other than normalizing sort:

> Since childhood I was haunted by the passion of the absolute and the transcendence of limits; now this passion had led me to the edge of common graves in the Ukraine [where Jews were shot and dumped during "killing" actions]. I always wanted my thinking to be radical; well the State, the Nation also chose the radical and the absolute; how could I, at this very moment, turn my back and say no, ultimately preferring the comfort of bourgeois laws and the mediocre assurance of the social contract? That was obviously impossible. And if radicality was the radicality of the abyss, and if the absolute revealed itself as the bad absolute, it was nonetheless necessary—I was intimately persuaded—to follow them to the very end, with my eyes wide open...

> The killing of the Jews at bottom serves no purpose ... It has no economic or political utility, no practical goal. On the contrary it is a rupture with the world of economics and politics. It is waste, pure loss. That's all. And thus what is happening can have only one meaning: that of a definitive sacrifice, which definitively binds us together and prevents us, once and for all, from turning back.[44]

The comments of Littell's narrator-protagonist serve to bring up the ways even a Himmler was neither a monstrous anomaly nor a banal "everyman," but an extreme and singular instance of more prevalent tendencies. Himmler took these tendencies in directions that were both entirely unacceptable and nonetheless construed or even experienced in ways that had resonances elsewhere, notably with respect to a variant of the aesthetic of the sublime oriented to violence, and lived in an extremely disconcerting kind of aporetic sensibility. The true Nazi, for Himmler, held together or was able to bear (*durchstehen*), in authentic hardness and self-possession, an aporia that joined the antinomies of existence: decency and the seemingly sublime ability to behold or witness mass slaughter (with the occlusion of the fact that the aesthetic spectators or bystanders in this case were also among the perpetrators).

I am, of course, alluding to a section of Himmler's now famous or infamous Posen speech of October 1943 (which Littell's narrator attends). It is worth quoting from, for it gives some sense of the meaning of genocidal violence (as well as its relation to achieving psychic hardness) for the *Reichsführer* and the Nazi upper-level SS officers to whom the speech was addressed—making the speech a kind of touchstone in this respect. Himmler's Posen speech was not propaganda for the public, but a communication by an insider to insiders, which of course does not mean that everything in it was true or even believed to be true by Himmler or his audience, for example, confidence about winning the war, especially after Stalingrad and losses in North Africa. But one may suggest that in important respects what Himmler asserted in the speech was performatively to be held as true, if not self-evident, by the committed Nazi elite, and anxiety about a possible or even likely loss of the war against the allies might heighten the significance, as well as the sacrificial and self-sacrificial quality, of a "victory" in the "war" against the Jews. In any case, evident in the speech is at least one way Nazi violence was not simply, and perhaps not primarily, a question of instrumental rationality, however self-defeating or unbalanced.

> I want to make reference before you here, in complete frankness, to a really grave matter. Among ourselves, this once, it shall be uttered quite frankly; but in public we will never speak of it. Just as we did not hesitate on June

30, 1934 [the so-called night of the long knives bringing about the purge of Ernst Röhm and the SA leadership], to do our duty as ordered, to stand up against the wall comrades who had transgressed, and shoot them, also we have never talked about this and never will. It was the tact which I am glad to say is a matter of course with us that made us never discuss it among ourselves, never talk about it. Each of us shuddered [*es hat jeden geschaudert*], and yet each one knew that he would do it again if it were ordered and if it were necessary. I am referring to the evacuation of the Jews, the annihilation of the Jewish people. This is one of those things that are easily said. "The Jewish people is going to be annihilated," says every party member. "Sure, it's in our program, elimination of the Jews, annihilation—we'll take care of it." And then they all come trudging, 80 million worthy Germans, and each of them has his one decent Jew [*seinen anständigen Juden*]. Sure, the others are swine, but this one is an A-1 Jew [*ein prima Jude*]. Of all those who talk this way, not one has seen it happen, not one has been through it [or been able to bear it or bear up under it—*keiner hat es durchgestanden*]. Most of you must know what it means to see a hundred corpses lie side by side, or five hundred, or a thousand. To have stuck this out and—excepting cases of human weakness—to have kept our integrity [or remained decent—*anständig geblieben zu sein*], that is what has made us hard. In our history this is an unwritten and never-to-be-written page of glory [*Ruhmesblatt*], for we know how difficult we would have made it for ourselves if today—amid the bombing raids, the hardships and the deprivations of war—we still had the Jews in every city as secret saboteurs, agitators, and demagogues. If the Jews were still ensconced in the body of the German nation, we probably would have reached the 1916-17 stage by now.[45]

At the end of this passage there is an appeal, however homophobic, to instrumental rationality, but it almost seems anti-climactic if not a non sequitur with respect to what precedes it. For Himmler and others in the Nazi elite, the annihilation of the Jews was among other things a quasi-sacrificial, redemptive act that eliminated a perceived source of pollution from the *Volksgemeinschaft* and obeyed the sacred command of the sovereign, supreme *Führer*.[46]

It would also be desirable to carry forward lines of inquiry already under way which examine the hypothesis that the Nazi genocide may have displaced or at least paralleled practices that were prevalent and, for many, acceptable in the colonies when applied to people of color.[47] There are indications of this view in the work of Frantz Fanon, although there is also the questionable tendency to dichotomize between good and bad violence and to justify anti-colonial violence undertaken by people of color not simply strategically, but as therapeutic and transfigurative in terms at times uncomfortably close to the views of Sorel or the early Benjamin. To quote but three statements that follow closely upon one another near the beginning of *The Wretched of the Earth*: "Decolonization is truly the creation of new men ... Its definition can, if we want to describe it accurately, be summed up in the well-known words: 'The last shall be first' ... The last can be first only after a murderous and decisive confrontation between the two protagonists."[48] In brief, at times for Fanon, the cathartic decolonization of the psyche, the overcoming of posttraumatic symptoms, and the achievement of virility and dignity required anticolonial violence on the part of the oppressed. But it is important both historically and critically to understand the way colonial violence of the sort Fanon counterattacked was at times of genocidal proportions and may well have been analogous to, or even one basis for, later initiatives that have been seen, at times in too unqualified a form and too much within an exclusively Eurocentric context, as unique, totally unexpected, and unprecedented. I would note as well that Hannah Arendt in *On Violence* argues that Sartre, notably in his preface to Fanon's *Wretched of the Earth*, is much less qualified than Fanon himself in his apology for, if not glorification and rendering sublime of, violence.[49] Indeed Sartre, in bringing his flamboyant preface to a close, states that, "violence, like Achilles' spear, can heal the wounds it has inflicted."[50] But the prevalence of such sentiments, especially on the far left and the far right, may be more significant than their appearance in this or that figure. Even Maurice Blanchot, in one of his less edifying, right-wing, at times anti-semitic and fire-breathing journalistic pieces of the 1930s (this one appeared in the 7 July 1936 issue of *Combat*), could write the following:

> It is necessary that there be a revolution because one does not modify a regime that controls everything, that has its roots everywhere. One removes it, one strikes it down. It is necessary that that revolution be violent because one does not tap a people as enervated as our own for the strength and passions appropriate to a regeneration of decency, but through a series of bloody shocks, a storm that will overwhelm—and thus awaken—it.... That is why terrorism at present appears to us as a method of public salvation.[51]

In this quotation, the phantasm of the totally pervasive and omnipotent system appears in a stark form, and it functions as a force for degeneration or enervation. Violence and terrorism are advocated as a kind of traumatizing shock therapy to regenerate and redeem a decadent, enervated (for André Breton, debased and cretinized) people—a perspective that seems light years away from the postwar Blanchot.

Two Historical Approaches and Beyond

It may be apt to discuss briefly the treatment of violence in its relation to ideology and practice in the work of two prominent historians, to whom

I have already referred. Zeev Sternhell and Isabel V. Hull may be seen as both converging and radically diverging in their insistent, and at times, one-sided emphases.[52] Both dichotomize between ideology and practice, with Sternhell emphasizing the former and Hull the latter. At present, Hull's orientation may be more prevalent in the historical profession, and that orientation has received much less sustained critical scrutiny than Sternhell's.[53]

Indeed, Sternhell has been criticized on numerous grounds: his exaggeration not only of the role of ideology in general, but of France in particular in the genesis and functioning of fascism; his idea that France had a special status with respect to the "essence" of fascism because it presumably existed in that country in its ideological purity and was not compromised in practice through embodiment in a regime; the insufficiently defined and qualified role he attributes to Sorel; his overemphasis on the slippage from the left to the right in the interwar period; and his underemphasis of the phenomenon of rightists staying on the right, supporting or not resisting fascism, believing they could manipulate it, and at times becoming radicalized in a fascist or *fascisant* direction. Despite the validity of these criticisms, one may nonetheless argue that Sternhell (like his teacher George Mosse, who also was a reference point for Hull) recognized and extensively analyzed the role of ideology even though he tended to see it in decontextualized if not Platonic terms and attributed to it an excessively causal role. Here the point would be that one should supplement and contest his account with an analysis of the complex relations of ideology to practice (movement, regime, and so forth)—ideology not simply as systematic philosophy, but as often vaguely articulated assumption or even prejudice that may be especially forceful in the formation of subjects, including fascist or *fascisant* subjects.

Instead of providing an account of the sustained interaction of ideology and practice, Hull, in *Absolute Destruction*, defines ideology narrowly and dismisses its relevance. She focuses exclusively on practice, which she even identifies with "culture"—at least with respect to German military culture. Yet, like Sternhell, she may also be seen as stressing particularity, indeed as developing another version of the German *Sonderweg* thesis that provides a new twist in construing the "special path" in terms of German military practice at home and in the colonies. But she reverses the more common "postcolonial" conception of the direction of influence in that she stresses the way the colonies provided a field of deployment for "beastly" practices first developed on the continent: "The point, at least for this study, is not that Europeans learned beastliness from their imperial encounters but that they could try out abroad the techniques, assumptions, doctrines, and scripts they carried with them, in an atmosphere relatively unlimited by law and conducive to the application of more force when the first allotment failed to achieve the goal."[54] Hull notes that what distinguishes the Third Reich from the earlier period, in which she believes excessive violence may be explained through "bureaucratic functioning," standard operating procedures, and means-ends rationality, all gone awry, was the importance of "Nazi ideology as interpreted by Hitler."[55] But, despite her expansive reference to "techniques, assumptions, doctrines, and scripts," she elaborates a restrictive notion of practice and contends that "the 'cult of violence' that epitomized National Socialism was simply the reification of practices and behavior (that is, action templates) that had become severed from the old Imperial military culture ... [and] easily harnessed for the ideological ends of even greater mass destruction and death."[56] Thus, with respect to the pre-Nazi period, the key for Hull is the role of a historically specific German military culture existing almost exclusively on the level of practice. It would be unfair to see Hull as isolating and exaggerating the role of Hitler in an ideologically tendentious manner. But, even with respect to the Nazi period, she does present a "cult of violence" as the reification of "action templates" that are somehow "harnessed" to "ideological ends" in what seems to remain an exclusive framework of means-end rationality. This framework may be analytically insufficient to account for the valorization and excessive enactment of violence, especially in the quasi-sacrificial context of a "cult."

One may argue that the broader problem is to analyze the interaction between ideology and practice in a wide-angled, yet differentiated, understanding of violence in particular and "culture" in general. One may also note that there is no need, as Hull at one point seems to assume, to confine explanatory or interpretive options to two extremes: the unmediated attempt to account for historical phenomena (à la Zizek) by appealing to a transhistorical "death drive" or traumatic real, on the one hand, and "ordinary organizational dynamics" or "practice" whereby violence has an inertial force unless countered by institutional limits, on the other.[57] One may certainly recognize the genuine significance of what Hull amply demonstrates: the importance of military culture and institutional dynamics, including limits they may create. But one need not exclude the more general role of ideology, which is at times related to practice. Ideology in this sense is not restricted to "a highly structured belief system"—the concept of ideology Hull invokes in order to downplay its role in pre-Nazi Germany.[58] As I have intimated, ideology may be understood in terms of more encompassing processes of subject formation, involving assumptions, prejudices, and (at times phobic or quasi-ritual) affect and fantasy, directed, for example, at other "races," in ways that may serve to enable or valorize violence, destruction, and death, or even render them "sublime." And attempts to interpret experience and practice can be divorced from ideology only insofar as behavior is robotic or compulsive (behavior that may nonetheless be legitimated ideologically, for example, in terms of hardness and imaginary body armor). (In reading *Absolute Destruction*, one may wonder what experiential and subject-forming processes, involving thought and feeling—or possibly the resistance to them—are touched on in the letters and other documentation left by Lt. Gen. Lothar von Trotha [the German commanding officer during the genocidal massacre of the Herero] to which Hull had access.) The question is whether ideology in a more comprehensive and historically pertinent sense played a significant role even in the historical phenomena Hull so usefully describes and analyzes.[59] Indeed, a prominent realization one derives from her extensively researched and documented book is how she joins others in recognizing the overall importance of analyzing closely the interactions between domestic, foreign, and colonial policy, notably in terms of mutually reinforcing processes. And, even if one stresses the need to understand complex processes involving the variable interaction of forces, one may construe in ideal-typical terms and recognize the value of both Sternhell's and Hull's approaches if they are seen in dialogic terms as thought provoking interventions that prompt further thought, argument, and conceptual refinement in the historical profession, notably with respect to the broad-gauged analysis of the nature and functioning of violence.

One could, of course, discuss still other, at times significantly different figures and processes in the terms I have offered, for example, Marinetti and Carl Schmitt or, in another register, Artaud and Heidegger. (I think Heidegger's attraction to the Nazis was in part related to his initial understanding of them as the possible bearers of a regenerative force that would end inauthentic modern civilization and, in an originary act or *Ursprung*, creatively repeat the so-called Greek miracle.)[60] And one detects an echo of Sorel's penchant for abstract, sensationalist assertion when one reads Zizek, in his "Plea for Ethical Violence," concluding that "authentic revolutionary liberation is much more directly identified with violence [than with a use of violence to establish a non-violent harmony]. It is violence as such (the violent gesture of discarding, of establishing a difference, or drawing a line of separation) that liberates."[61] These resounding words, with their "heads-must-roll" connotations, are immediately preceded by a reference to Che Guevara's putative conception of "revolutionary violence as a 'work of love.'"[62] (There is an element of projection at work here, since the quotation from Che that Zizek provides does not itself mention violence but refers to "the true revolutionary" as guided by strong feelings of love.) In any case, one cannot infer from Zizek's heady peroration that his article seems to be primarily a defense of a strong, censuring, Bartleby-the-scrivener-type superego that goes against the permissive grain of avoiding harsh, confrontational judgment, not so much by prohibiting enjoyment as by permitting non-enjoyment. Still, Zizek, in his typical gesture of taking it to the limit every time and seeing others as insufficiently radical (the assertion of a need for a "more radical" level, claim, or position appears three times on one page alone), asserts that what is missing in Judith Butler as well as in Adorno and Levinas (but presumably not in Lacan or himself) is a recognition of the "radical, 'inhuman' otherness" of "a terrifying excess ... inherent to being human."[63] Rather predictably, Zizek, like Agamben, locates this excess in the *Muselmann* ("the 'living dead' of the concentration camps"—but is this allusion to the vampire preceded by a reference to Stephen King really apt?). One might just as readily see a fascination with "inhuman," "terrifying excess" in Himmler and those in attunement with his Posen speech, and some discrimination between modalities and contexts of "terrifying excess" might well seem desirable. Moreover, one may acknowledge this "terrifying excess," and the threat it harbors for oneself as well as others, but still question certain approaches that compulsively return to it time and again or fixate on its sublimity or its relation to an iridescent if abstract and insufficiently specified figuration of violence. Or, to vary the formulation, one may affirm that there is a "totally other" or enigmatic, excessive dimension in every other, but not therefore conclude that every other is totally other or reducible to a terrifying excess.[64]

Critical Responses

I would conclude by observing that there have been powerful, substantive critiques of violence, at times in the same figures in whom there is a tendency to become fascinated with it, if not render it sacred or sublime. These critiques deserve sustained attention, for example, in dimensions of Arendt, Camus, Durkheim, Fanon, Heidegger, and Derrida. Without being able to provide that sustained attention in the present context, I would simply stress the point that in Arendt, while violence is recognized as at times necessary, political action is contrasted with violence or the imposition of will and bound up with deliberative judgment or *phronesis* arrived at through dialogic relations between and within selves—relations requiring open discussion, debate, institutionalized limits, and attempts at establishing validity through persuasion.[65] With respect to Camus, *L'homme révolté* could be reread beyond the Cold War polemics to which it gave rise in order to elicit the basic conception of the need for an ethic of violence in politics itself, an ethic setting limits to the use of violence that are not simply tactical or strategic. In a similar vein, the thought of Durkheim could be interpreted in the light of his insistence on an institutionally and normatively grounded sense of legitimate limits, which could serve as a basis of desirable social transformation and interact forcefully with transgressive and even anomic initiatives. Heidegger's *Gelassenheit* (or letting being be) and his critique of the conversion of the world, including all others, into a stock of raw material for narrowly human exploitation (or even endowment with meaning), might lead to a broadly ecological vision of existence that would counteract the violence of certain forms of human assertion, including interpretive ones (although there are certainly difficulties with Heidegger's views about nonhuman animals).[66] With respect to Derrida, I would stress the point that one of the principal implications of deconstruction is the undoing or unsettlement of sharp, decisive binary oppositions, which are essential for the *coup de force* that expels threatening alterity (including animality) from the self and projectively constitutes a violent scapegoat mechanism. This dimension of deconstruction is one of its principal ethical and political contributions.[67] From a Lacanian perspective, Zizek too provides a forceful critique of the projective nature of scapegoating, which forecloses an encounter with the traumatic "real" in those who resort to scapegoating. And in Fanon, one might emphasize the fruitful tension or internal self-contestation between the notion of violence as a therapeutic if not an apocalyptic, redemptive force for the oppressed person of color and the discussion, in *Wretched of the Earth* itself, of what Fanon terms "*troubles mentaux*," which colonialism engendered in the oppressed—mental dislocations that often seemed exacerbated rather than cured or redeemed by acts of violence.[68] In other words, the violent catharsis, if there was one, did not invariably regenerate; it might just as well undermine if not drastically disempower the self, making the "new men" prone to prolonged depression, nightmares, and other posttraumatic symptoms (including much-feared sexual impotence). (Here, a pertinent question would be the traumatization of one committing acts of violence, traumatization at times forceful enough to break through the protective shield provided by redemptive, self-justifying ideologies as well as militaristic discipline.)

The foregoing observations indicate the necessity of keeping in mind the limits and the limitations of my analyses, both of the series of figures or ideological currents I have referenced and of the treatment of the problem of violence and trauma. While I think it is credible to discuss them together, and raise the problem of the relationship among figures or movements I have discussed, it would be worse than a performative contradiction to conflate or amalgamate them. Each of the figures I mentioned (as well as others who might be mentioned) would of course require extensive, differential, and specific historical analysis with respect to their contexts and possibly to the intricacy of their thought in responding to those contexts, including in particular the role of violence in the political, economic, and social systems to which they were responding. As Homi Bhabha has noted: "Fanon forged his thinking on violence and counterviolence in ... conditions of dire extremity, when everyday interactions were turned into exigent events of life and death—incendiary relations between colonizer and colonized [Bhabha has just referred to particularly brutal aspects of the French policy of *regroupement* involving the killing and camp-like internment of Algerian peasants], internecine feuds between revolutionary brotherhoods [Bhabha refers to the 1957 bloodbath at Medouza in which the FLN slaughtered males over fifteen of the opposing Algerian political group, the MNA (Mouvement Nationaliste Algérienne), even ordering FLN operatives to "exterminate this vermin"], [and] terrorist attacks in Paris and Algiers by the ultra right-wing OAS (*Organisation [de l']Armée Secrète*) and their *pieds noirs* supporters (European settlers in Algeria). As a locus classicus of political resistance and the rhetoric of retributive violence, *The Wretched of the Earth* captures the tone of those apocalyptic times."[69]

As Martin Jay has reminded us in his *Refractions of Violence*, the entire question of the position, role, and response to violence offers a way of both rereading intellectual traditions and shaping one important approach to sociopolitical, economic, and cultural criticism.[70] One obvious implication of my discussion is that there is no inherently Nazi or fascist form of violence, but rather, in their nonetheless distinct cases (one should not simply conflate Nazism and all forms of fascism), an assimilation and usage of prevalent motifs in a particular political context and in an accentuatedly virulent manner. And it should be more than obvious that violence, including terrorism, with sacralizing, sacrificial, or sublime significations is not something that can be projected outside the West and localized in some "Oriental," Arab, or Muslim other. It is very much an "other" within, functioning as a constitutive outside, at times going beyond what is projected outside and deceptively localized in the other. It is important to distinguish, insofar as possible, limited or qualified, strategic and contextual justifications of violence, notably by the oppressed, from figurations of violence as sacred, sublime, or redemptive. Seen in the broadest sense, these considerations indicate that a key problem for contemporary critical thinking is to attend to various forms, modalities, and constructions of violence as well as to the forces in history that may help to limit if not avert the occurrence and to counteract the effects of at least certain forms of violence, notably those involving sacralizing or redemptive valorization, the establishment of oppressive power differentials, and attendant forms of victimization.

A revised version of this chapter is forthcoming in *History and Its Limits: Human, Animal, Violence* by Dominick LaCapra, from Cornell University Press. Copyright 2009 Cornell University Press. Used by permission of the publisher.

Notes

1. See the fruitful, cross-disciplinary engagement with the problem of violence and visual culture in Martin Jay, *Refractions of Violence* (New York, 2003).
2. Debarati Sanyal, in *The Violence of Modernity: Baudelaire, Irony, and the Politics of Form* (Baltimore, MD, 2006), tries to dichotomize between violence and trauma in the interest of stressing political agency, which she associates with a focus on violence. But in the course of her interesting study, the dichotomy breaks down, and it becomes evident that concerns with violence and with trauma need not be mutually exclusive. The literature on trauma is itself enormous and goes in various directions, not all of which are narrowly psychological. Still, much remains to be done in historiography in relating an informed, nonreductive approach to trauma and political, social, and more generally contextual analyses of violence. See the fruitful initiatives in Nancy Wood, *Vectors of Memory: Legacies of Trauma in Postwar Europe* (Oxford, 1999), Lawrence Douglas, *The Memory of Judgment: Making Law and History in the Trials of the Holocaust* (New Haven, CT, 2001), and *Traumatic Pasts: History, Psychiatry and Trauma in the Modern Age, 1870–1930*, ed. Mark S. Micale and Paul Lerner (Cambridge, 2001). My own contributions include *Representing the Holocaust: History, Theory, Trauma* (Ithaca, NY, 1994), *History and Memory after Auschwitz* (Ithaca, NY, 1998), *Writing History, Writing Trauma* (Baltimore, MD, 2001), *History in Transit: Experience, Identity, Critical Theory* (Ithaca, NY, 2004), and "Tropisms of Intellectual History" *Rethinking History* 8 (2004): 499–529. In the present essay, I return to, as well as attempt to further clarify and elaborate, some of the points made in these previous works.
3. See Frank Ankersmit, "The Sublime Dissociation of the Past: or How to Be(come) What One Is No Longer," *History and Theory* 40, no. 3 (October 2001): 295–323.
4. Aestheticizing sublimation was evident in Karl-Heinz Stockhausen's immediate response to the 11 September 2001 suicide bombing of the World Trade Center as "the greatest work of art imaginable for the whole cosmos." His entire comment, which he subsequently retracted, may be found at <http://www.osborne-conant.org/documentationstockhausen.htm> (Accessed on 3 July 2008). A sacralizing or sublime valorization of violence goes beyond aesthetic shock effects when it motivates or legitimates action.
5. For the American colonial context and the frontier experience, involving warfare against Indians, see Richard Slotkin's controversial, classical study, *Regeneration Through Violence: The Mythology of the American Frontier 1600–1800* (New York, [1973] 1996).

Toward a Critique of Violence • 233

6. On these problems see Jeremy Varon, *Bringing the War Home: The Weather Underground, the Red Army Faction, and Revolutionary Violence in the Sixties and Seventies* (Berkeley and Los Angeles, 2004) and Tom Segev, *The Seventh Million: The Israelis and the Holocaust*, trans. Haim Watzman (New York, 1991, 1993).
7. Section 108 of *The Gay Science* first published in 1882.
8. The First Vatican Council of 1870.
9. For a more extended treatment of the foundational trauma, see my "Trauma, Absence, Loss," in *Writing History, Writing Trauma*, chap. 2.
10. Jacques Derrida, *The Gift of Death*, trans. David Wills (1992; Chicago, 1995). For Saint Paul, the crucifixion and resurrection of Christ may not have been read in sacrificial terms, but they did mark a radical, foundational break in history (as did, in Paul's own life, his "conversion" on the road to Damascus). Alain Badiou argues that the "Christ-event" for Paul made Christianity an absolutely new phenomenon or "thought" that was radically incommensurable with Jewish and Greek thought. This event marked a caesura or break in history related to excess and grace, resistant to institutions and rituals, yet also bringing a nonliteral "law" of love for neighbor as well as self. In Badiou's formalizing and secularizing yet affirmative and participatory reading, Paul becomes an analogue of both Lacan, as abject-saintly analyst of the split subject, and the militant revolutionary of the act or event. Indeed, Badiou glosses faith, hope, and charity as conviction (requiring not only inward assurance, but public address), certainty (along with enduring fidelity and perseverance), and love (involving universalizing militancy). He is critical of—or at most (like Paul) indifferent to—all intermediary groups (or forms of "communitarism") and asserts the primacy of an unmediated, nondialectical link between the universal "truth" and the singular event (for the born-again Paul, Christ's Resurrection, which in Badiou becomes a dispensable myth). Badiou's "anti-philosophical" universalism is in one sense restricted (and remains within the philosophical tradition) in that it still assumes a sharp divide between the human (or man) and the animal, but it is unclear whether this divide replicates the Pauline/Lacanian subject's split between death and life or "flesh" and "spirit." And, in defending Paul and his thought against charges of sectarianism, Badiou does not address the obvious question of the "militant" use of violence or force against those who fail or refuse to see the universal "truth." In any event, in light of his approach, there is apparently much to be said for the contested understanding of Marxism as a secularized Christian heresy. See *Saint Paul: The Foundation of Universalism*, trans. Ray Brassier (Stanford, CA, 1997, 2003).
11. *Fear and Trembling*, ed., trans., intro. and notes Howard V. Hong and Edna H. Hong (Princeton, NJ, [1843] 1983).
12. The relations between the sacred and the sublime may also be approached in terms of the religious and the secular, especially the aesthetic. These often ill-defined and labile relations are not restricted to Romanticism. Still, see the analysis in M.H. Abrams, *Naturalism Supernaturalism: Tradition and Revolution in Romantic Literature* (New York, 1971). He quotes T.E. Hulme's provocative comment: "Romanticism, then, and this is the best definition I can give of it, is spilt religion" (68). For a more recent discussion of figures such as Benjamin, Durkheim, Matthew Arnold, and Virginia Woolf, see Vincent P. Pecora, *Secularization and Cultural Criticism: Religion, Nation, & Modernity* (Chicago, 2006).
13. While recognizing the importance of René Girard's work, I do not agree with the categorical ideas that the sacred may be reduced to the sacralization of violence or that violent sacrificial ritual is the root or foundation of all culture, at least until the coming of Christ that creates a putative Christian exceptionalism. The figures

and phenomena I discuss do, however, raise the problem of specific articulations of violence and the sacred and render more credible Girard's view that, in the absence of formal rituals that establish institutional limits (an absence or deficit common in modernity), sacrificial (or quasi-sacrificial) violence tends to become excessive and goes to the extreme of generalized crisis, mimetic rivalry, cycles of destruction, and, at times, "states of exception."

14. *Thinking in Pictures and Other Reports from my Life with Autism*, foreword Oliver Sacks (New York, 1995).
15. Ibid., 20.
16. See also the discussion in *History in Transit*, 263–270.
17. Sorel, *Reflections on Violence*, trans. T.E. Hulme (New York, [1915] 1941); Sternhell, *Neither Right nor Left: Fascist Ideology in France*, trans. David Meisel (Berkeley, [1983] 1986). It is noteworthy that Hulme was motivated to translate Sorel's book.
18. Sorel, *Reflections on Violence*, 147.
19. Ibid., 295.
20. Walter Benjamin, "Critique of Violence," in *Reflections: Essays, Aphorisms, Autobiographical Writings*, trans. Edmund Jephcott, ed. and intro. Peter Demetz (New York, [1920/21] 1978), 277–300.
21. Ibid., 297.
22. Jacques Derrida, "The Force of Law: The 'Mystical' Foundation of Authority," *Cardozo Law Review* 11 (1990): 920–1045, rpt. in *Deconstruction and the Possibility of Justice*, ed. Drucilla Cornell et al. (New York, 1992). See also my commentary on Derrida's essay as it was presented at a conference at Cardozo Law School, "Violence, Justice, and the Force of Law," *Cardozo Law Review* 11 (1990): 1065–1078. The translation that served as the basis of my commentary was somewhat faulty (the original French version was not made available to me), and Derrida's essay did not as yet include the footnotes and "Post-scriptum" on Nazism and the "final solution" (973–974 and 1040–1045). (I saw these addenda for the first time only in the published and corrected version of Derrida's essay in the *Cardozo Law Review*)
23. Derrida, "The Force of Law," 941–943.
24. Ibid., 943.
25. Derrida's analysis may be compared with Badiou's in *Saint Paul* and with comparable gestures in the work of Slavoj Zizek.
26. For a study of sacrificialism with respect to the French Revolution and such figures as Maistre, Sorel, and Bataille, see Jesse Goldhammer, *The Headless Republic: Sacrificial Violence in Modern French Thought* (Ithaca, NY, 2005). Despite differences in emphasis and interpretation, Goldhammer's analysis partially converges with my own. (I think he downplays the role of excess or, at times, indifference in apologies for violence, however abstractly conceived or formulated, notably in the mythologizing Sorel for whom the actual number of victims of violence in the proletarian general strike might—or possibly might not—be small.) Although problems concerning sacrificial and sacralized violence extend well beyond the figures and the French contexts he treats, Goldhammer has the virtue of emphasizing the often tangled and complex interactions of valorizations of sacrificial violence across the political spectrum.
27. On Derrida's treatment of de Man's World War II journalism, see my *Representing the Holocaust: History, Theory, Trauma*, chap. 4.
28. Derrida, "The Force of Law," 1033–1035. In contrast to Derrida's reading which develops an aporia with respect to Benjamin's concluding passage on divine violence, I would argue that the passage more plausibly is read as inducing advocacy of violent,

putatively revolutionary action in uncertainty about whether or not it is divinely sanctioned. See my "Violence, Justice, and the Force of Law," 1074–1076.
29. Derrida, "The Force of Law," 1044–1045)
30. Georges Bataille, "The Psychological Structure of Fascism," in the appropriately entitled *Visions of Excess: Selected Writings, 1927–1939*, ed. and intro. Alan Stoekl, trans. Allan Stoekl with Carl R. Lovitt and Donald M. Leslie, Jr. (Minneapolis, MN, 1985), 142.
31. Bataille, "Concerning the Accounts Given by the Residents of Hiroshima," in *Trauma: Explorations in Memory*, ed. and intro. Cathy Caruth (Baltimore, MD 1995), 221–235, at 221, 232. Bataille's essay, first published in 1947, takes the form of an extremely participatory reading of John Hersey's *Hiroshima* (1946; New York, 1985).
32. I discuss Agamben in *History in Transit: Experience, Identity, Critical Theory*, chap. 4.
33. Bataille, *The Tears of Eros*, trans. Peter Connor (San Francisco, 1989), 206.
34. Bataille, *Inner Experience*, trans. Leslie Anne Boldt (Albany, NY, 1988), 120.
35. Bataille also underscored the significance of laughter as a disorienting response to the Hegelian dialectic—one of Derrida's focal points in his early essay on Bataille. (One may nonetheless ask whether in Bataille, in contrast with Derrida, laughter remains humorless, and whether Bataille, even at his most disconcertingly ludicrous, has any sense of self-directed irony or parody.)
36. Bataille, "The Sorcerer's Apprentice," in *Visions of Excess*, 227.
37. Michèle Richman simply reads Durkheim through Bataille's pineal eye and makes him a theorist of the excess of "collective effervescence." A more critical procedure would bring out the significant tensions between Durkheim as well as Mauss, on the one hand, and Bataille, on the other, notably with respect to the issues of violence, sacrifice, potlatch, excess, limits, and desirable social change. See Michèle Richman, *Sacred Revolutions: Durkheim and the Collège de Sociologie* (Minneapolis, MN, 2002). See also Ivan Strenski, *Contesting Sacrifice: Religion, Nationalism, and Social Thought in France* (Chicago, 2002). Strenski stresses the extreme, darker side of sacrifice and focuses on the willing victim of self-sacrifice, having little to say about those who sacrifice others and seek regeneration through sacrificial violence. He traces what he sees as "the classic definition of sacrifice as a cosmic drama involving self-annihilation and expiation" (4) to seventeenth-century French Catholic thought and emphasizes the role of the sacrificial in both religious and secular thought and practice in France, including the French Revolution, the Dreyfus Affair, and the writing of such figures as Maistre, Durkheim, Hubert, Mauss, Girard, and Bataille. Although he ends his book by praising the valiant if inadequate effort of Durkheimians to validate social life and self-sacrifice while contesting more extreme versions of sacrifice, he nonetheless terms their approach "moderate," "prudent," or even "bourgeois." At points he seems to favor "extreme thinkers like Georges Bataille." In rather unqualified terms, he asserts of Bataille: "Far from shunning the perversity of sacrifice as unbridled self-destruction and violence, Bataille revels in it. Taking cues from Sade, 'cruelty,' essential at least to the ritual act of animal sacrifice, is for Bataille a virtue. All this trafficking in the extremism of total giving serves the goal of transcending our bourgeois humanist natures and ascending to the sacred" (176). Unable to develop certain lines of thought evident in Durkheim and Mauss themselves, Strenski apparently cannot envision a non-sacrificial critique of "bourgeois" humanism in which a sense of legitimate limits is both validated and related to desirable institutions, while justice is supplemented by gift-giving, but not indentured to the excesses of violence, victimization, and self-immolation.

38. Michel Surya, *Georges Bataille: An Intellectual Biography*, trans. Krzysztof Fijalkowski and Michael Richardson (London, 2002); Michel Foucault, "A Preface to Transgression," in *Language, Counter-Memory, Practice*, trans. Donald F. Bouchard and Sherry Simon (Ithaca, NY, 1977), 29–52; Jacques Derrida, "From a Restricted to a General Economy: A Hegelianism Without Reserve," in *Writing and Difference*, trans. Alan Bass (Chicago, 1978), 251–277. For the analysis in terms of "left fascism," see Richard Wolin, *The Seduction of Unreason: The Intellectual Romance with Fascism from Nietzsche to Postmodernism* (Princeton, NJ, 2004), 153–186. For a comparison of Bataille and Carl Schmitt, see Martin Jay, *Force Fields: Between Intellectual History and Cultural Critique* (New York and London: Routledge, 1993), 49–60. While one may debate its weight in the context of his thought, including postwar essays such as that on John Hersey's *Hiroshima*, one should nonetheless note Bataille's attempts at self-qualification once he saw the nature of fascism in power. And the designation of "left fascist," which might apply to Pierre Drieu la Rochelle, does not seem suitable for Bataille, whose labile thought is not readily adapted to left/right political oppositions. Sartre may not have been altogether wrong in his early appreciation of Bataille as a "new mystic," however ironically this designation was intended (1943; *Situations I* [Paris, 1947], 133–174).
39. *Male Fantasies*, 2 vols., trans. Erica Carter and Chris Turner in collaboration with Stephen Conway, foreword Anson Rabinbach and Jessica Benjamin (Minneapolis, MN, 1987, 1989).
40. Note, however, that the term "biopolitical" is subject to multiple, at times indeterminate meanings. In Michael Hardt and Antonio Negri's *Multitude: War and Democracy in the Age of Empire* (New York, 2004), it has a broadly encompassing meaning with respect to existential concerns and sociocultural forms of life.
41. Claudia Koonz, *The Nazi Conscience* (Cambridge, MA, 2003); Christopher Browning, *Ordinary Men: Reserve Police Battalion 101 and the Final Solution in Poland* (New York, 1992). I would note that Theodor Adorno's and Max Horkheimer's influential *Dialectic of Enlightenment* (New York, [1947] 1972) is marked by a possibly fruitful but unthematized tension between seeing Western history, culminating in the Nazi regime, as marked both by instrumental rationality gone awry and by sacrificialism and scapegoating, whose violence is not reducible to an instrumental, means-ends schema and whose role is especially emphasized by them in the chapter on "Elements of Anti-Semitism."
42. Jonathan Littell, *Les Bienveillantes* (Paris, 2006).
43. Ibid., 142.
44. Ibid., 95, 137, translations mine.
45. *A Holocaust Reader*, ed. and trans. Lucy Dawidowicz (West Orange, NJ, 1976), 132–133.
46. For an empirically based, archival study that provides evidence for the role of what he terms Nazi "redemptive anti-Semitism," see Saul Friedlander, *Nazi Germany and the Jews*, vol. I: *The Years of Persecution 1933–1939* (New York, 1997).
47. See Sven Lindqvist's suggestive *"Exterminate All the Brutes,"* trans. Joan Tate (New York, 1996). In her important book *Absolute Destruction: Military Culture and the Practices of War in Imperial Germany* (Ithaca, NY, 2005), Isabel V. Hull states, at least with respect to German colonial violence, which attained extreme or even genocidal proportions: "The continuities between colonial and European warfare are not due, as I thought at the beginning of this project, to Europeans learning evil lessons in the colonies and then applying them at home (though many an evil lesson was doubtless learned). Rather, Germans approached colonial wars from inside frames of

their military culture as it had developed in Europe. The colonial situation merely provided the opportunity to practice on Africans [the Herero in 1904–1907 and the Maji-Maji in 1905–1907] or Chinese [the German intervention in 1901] what the military experts took to be the immutable precepts of warfare" (2005: 3). (These comments run counter to the view of Aimé Césaire and Frantz Fanon, as formulated by Robert Young, that "Fascism was simply colonialism brought home to Europe" [*White Mythologies: Writing History and the West* (London, 1990), 125].) I shall return to more general features of Hull's analysis.

48. Frantz Fanon, *The Wretched of the Earth*, trans. Richard Philcox, foreword Homi Bhabha, pref. Jean-Paul Sartre (New York, [1961] 2004), 2–3.
49. Hannah Arendt, *On Violence* (New York, 1969).
50. Preface to *The Wretched of the Earth*, lxii.
51. "Terrorisme comme méthode de salut publique," *Combat* 1, no. 7 (7 July 1936).
52. I thank Samuel Moyn for bringing this point to my attention.
53. Gabrielle Spiegel, in her introduction to the book she edits, *Practicing History: New Directions in Historical Writing after the Linguistic Turn* (New York, 2005), may be seen as trying to provide the loosely formulated theory related to Hull's practice—what Spiegel oxymoronically terms "Practice Theory" and obviously sees as the wave of the future in historiography. Spiegel writes: "Although 'Practice Theory' as such has scarcely attained the status of a viable 'theory' in any real sense of the word, the accent it places on the historically generated and always contingent nature of structures of culture returns historiography to its age-old concern with processes, agents, change, and transformation, while demanding the kind of empirically grounded research into the particularities of social and cultural conditions with which historians are by training and tradition most comfortable" (25). Without implying a denigration of the unobjectionable defense of "empirically grounded research," I would observe that Spiegel's specific formulation might be read as a rationale for the resistance to theory, for the type of historian she invokes is apparently uncomfortable with forms of critical theory (for which intellectual history has been a primary conduit) that interrogate the assumptions and practices of historiorgraphy itself. Indeed, however unwillingly, Hull has been commended by V.R. Berghahn, for "an introduction [to *Absolute Destruction*] that is striking for its concise statement of her purposes and unencumbered by lengthy methodological and historiographical discussions" (*American Historical Review* 110 [2005]: 1269).
54. Hull, *Absolute Destruction*, 333.
55. Ibid., 326.
56. Ibid., 333.
57. Ibid., 331.
58. Ibid., 329.
59. In a relatively uncontested dimension of his influential *Orientalism* (New York, 1978, 2003), for example, Edward Said believed ideology did play a significant enabling and not only *ex post facto* rationalizing role with respect to English and French colonialism, which (as Hull observes), while at times was quite violent, did not go to the same genocidal extreme as the Germans. (For criticisms of Said, see the discussions in Young, *White Mythologies*, and in Robert J.C. Young, *Postcolonialism: An Historical Introduction* [Oxford, 2001].) This perhaps indicates both the significance of a broader concept of ideology and a differential causal status for "military culture," in its larger institutional context, as analyzed by Hull, since on one level ideologies with respect to the role of violence (such as racism and social Darwinism as well as *"pro patria mori"* sacrificialism and an aesthetic of the sublime) were probably not signifi-

cantly different in late nineteenth- and early twentieth-century Germany, England, and France, although there may have been differences in how they were experienced affectively or "lived" over time and place.
60. See my discussion in *Representing the Holocaust: History, Theory, Trauma*, chap. 5.
61. Slavoj Zizek, "A Plea for Ethical Violence," *Umbr(a): A Journal of the Unconscious* (2004): 89.
62. Ibid., 88.
63. Ibid., 86-7.
64. One should, however, be wary of the dubious cooptation of a prevalent animus against violence and, especially, terrorism to refer indiscriminately to activists who generally employ legal procedures and turn to civil disobedience or breaking the law in extreme circumstances not involving violence against persons. The branding as terroristic of animal-rights activists, who infringe existing property rights by spilling paint on high-priced fur coats or by setting free animals used for experimentation or confined in unacceptable factory-farm conditions, is a reminder of the way a critique of violence can be invoked for contestable purposes. According to a report in *The Chronicle of Higher Education*, Steven Best, a professor of philosophy at the University of Texas at El Paso who supports the Animal Liberation Front, was banned from traveling to Great Britain on the grounds that he was considered (in the words of an official with the Home Office) as "fomenting and justifying terrorist violence and seeking to provoke others to terrorist acts and fomenting other serious criminal activity." The grounds for this judgment were apparently comments Best had made at a conference and quoted in a British newspaper: "We are not terrorists, but we are a threat. We are a threat both economically and philosophically. Our power is not in the right to vote but the power to stop production. We will break the law and destroy property until we win." Responding to the decision of the Home Office, Best argued that his comments at the conference were taken out of context: "I argued that I didn't mean anything violent, that we'll wipe these guys off the face of the earth through legal means, through boycotts." (*Chronicle of Higher Education* [9 August 2005]: A10).
65. See the helpful discussions of Arendt in *The Cambridge Companion to Hannah Arendt*, ed. Dana Villa (Cambridge, 2000). As Dana Villa notes in his Introduction: "*The Human Condition* mines ancient Greek poetry, drama, and philosophy in order to show how, in its original understanding, political action was viewed as the very opposite of violence, coercion or rule. It was, in Arendt's rendering, the 'sharing of words and deeds' by diverse equals, whose 'acting together' generated a power quite different from the forceful ability to 'impose one's will' which we normally identify with political power" (12). In commenting on Arendt's understanding of phronesis and practical judgment in politics, in the same volume, Maurizio Passerin D'Entrèves states:
> In matters of opinion, but not in matters of truth, 'our thinking is truly discursive, running, as it were, from place to place, from one part of the world to another, through all kinds of conflicting views, until it finally ascends from these particularities to some impartial generality'... Arendt always stressed that the formation of valid opinions requires a pubic space where individuals can test and purify their views through a process of mutual debate and enlightenment. She was, however, quite opposed to the idea that opinions should be measured by the standard of truth, or that debate should be conducted according to strict scientific standards of validity. In her view, truth belongs to the realm of cognition, the realm of logic, mathematics and the strict sciences, and carries always an element of coercion,

since it precludes debate and must be accepted by every individual in possession of her rational faculties ... In this respect, truth is anti-political, since by eliminating debate and diversity it eliminates the very principles of political life. (254–255)

From an Arendtian perspective, a basic question would be the relation of politics and ethics, including its bearing on the limited use of violence.

66. On Durkheim, see my *Emile Durkheim: Sociologist and Philosopher*, rev. ed. (Aurora, CO, [1972] 2001). In a chapter of *History and Its Limits*, I treat the question of the human and the animal, focusing on the dubious quest for a decisive criterion dividing the two.
67. For an ambitious yet problematic combination of Benjamin and Derrida that affirms Derrida's later texts as "revolving around two central questions: politics and technology" and defends his "aporetic work of mourning that, so to speak, succeeds most when it fails, which is to say when it cannot be resolved," see Alessia Ricciardi, *The Ends of Mourning: Psychoanalysis, Literature, Film* (Stanford, CA, 2003), 12.
68. A graduate student at Cornell, Emma Kuby, has written an excellent paper on this topic.
69. Foreword to Fanon, *The Wretched of the Earth*, xxxiv–xxxv.
70. While it has obvious relations to the problem of trauma, this approach should not be limited to genocide and other extreme events, however important they may be in history and however much other forms of violence may at times induce or even lead to them. But one cannot equate trauma and history. On the contrary, one should devote sustained attention to less spectacular forms of "structural violence" discussed, for example, by Paul Farmer in his book of 2003, *Pathologies of Power: Health, Human Rights, and the New War on the Poor* (Berkeley and Los Angles, 2003). Farmer relies heavily on the crucial concept of "structural violence" wherein certain groups, notably the poor, are, because of their social position, subject to greater risks of violence and of largely untreated but treatable diseases such as AIDS. Indeed, their very conditions of life are in a non-trivial sense violent even if they are not subject to direct assault or massive injury, as they nonetheless too often are.

Bibliography

Abrams, M.H. *Naturalism Supernaturalism: Tradition and Revolution in Romantic Literature*. New York, 1971.

Adorno, Theodor and Max Horkheimer. *Dialectic of Enlightenment*. New York, [1947] 1972.

Ankersmit, Frank. "The Sublime Dissociation of the Past: or How to Be(come) What One Is No Longer." *History and Theory* 40, no. 3 (October 2001): 295–323.

Badiou, Alain. *Saint Paul: The Foundation of Universalism*. Translated by Ray Brassier. Stanford, 2003.

Bataille, Georges. "Concerning the Accounts Given by the Residents of Hiroshima." In *Trauma: Explorations in Memory*, edited by Cathy Caruth. Baltimore, MD, 1995.

———. "The Psychological Structure of Fascism." In *Visions of Excess: Selected Writings, 1927–1939*, edited and translated by Alan Stoekl, Carl R. Lovitt and Donald M. Leslie. Minneapolis, MN, 1985.

Benjamin, Walter. "Critique of Violence." In *Reflections: Essays, Aphorisms, Autobiographical Writings*, edited by Peter Demetz, translated by Edmund Jephcott. New York, [1920/21] 1978.
Blanchot, Maurice. "Terrorisme comme méthode de salut publique." *Combat* 1, no. 7 (7 July 1936).
Breton, André. *Manifestoes of Surrealism*. Translated by Richard Seaver and Helen R. Lane. Ann Arbor, MI, 1969.
Browning, Christopher. *Ordinary Men: Reserve Police Battalion 101 and the Final Solution in Poland*. New York, 1992.
Cornell, Drucilla, et al., ed. *Deconstruction and the Possibility of Justice*. New York, 1992.
Dawidowicz, Lucy, ed. and trans. *A Holocaust Reader*. West Orange, NJ, 1976.
Derrida, Jacques. "From a Restricted to a General Economy: A Hegelianism Without Reserve." In *Writing and Difference*, translated by Alan Bass. Chicago, 1978.
Douglas, Lawrence. *The Memory of Judgment: Making Law and History in the Trials of the Holocaust*. New Haven, CT, 2001.
Fanon, Frantz. *The Wretched of the Earth*. Translated by Richard Philcox. New York, [1961] 2004.
Farmer, Paul. *Pathologies of Power: Health, Human Rights, and the New War on the Poor*. Berkeley, CA, 2003.
Foucault, Michel. "A Preface to Transgression." In *Language, Counter-Memory, Practice*, translated by Donald F. Bouchard and Sherry Simon. Ithaca, NY, 1977.
Friedlander, Saul. *Nazi Germany and the Jews*, vol. I: *The Years of Persecution 1933–1939*. New York, 1997.
Goldhammer, Jesse. *The Headless Republic: Sacrificial Violence in Modern French Thought*. Ithaca, NY, 2005.
Grandin, Temple. *Thinking in Pictures and Other Reports from my Life with Autism*, New York, 1995.
Hardt, Michael and Antonio Negri. *Multitude: War and Democracy in the Age of Empire*. New York, 2004.
Hull, Isabel V. *Absolute Destruction: Military Culture and Practices of War in Imperial Germany*. Ithaca, NY, 2005.
Jay, Martin. *Force Fields: Between Intellectual History and Cultural Critique*. New York and London, 1993.
———. *Refractions of Violence*. New York, 2003.
Kierkegaard, Søren. *Fear and Trembling*. Edited and translated by Howard V. and Edna H. Hong. Princeton, NJ [1843] 1983.
Koonz, Claudia. *The Nazi Conscience*. Cambridge, MA, 2003.
LaCapra, Dominick. *Emile Durkheim: Sociologist and Philosopher*. Aurora, CO, [1972] 2001.
———. *History and Memory after Auschwitz*. Ithaca, NY, 1998.
———. *History in Transit: Experience, Identity, Critical Theory*. Ithaca, NY, 2004.
———. *Representing the Holocaust: History, Theory, Trauma*. Ithaca, NY, 1994.
———. "Tropisms of Intellectual History." In *Rethinking History* 8 (2004): 499–529.
———. "Violence, Justice, and the Force of Law." *Cardozo Law Review* 11 (1990): 1065–1078.
———. *Writing History, Writing Trauma*. Baltimore, MD, 2001.
Lindqvist, Sven. "*Exterminate All the Brutes*." Translated by Joan Tate. New York, 1996.
Littell, Jonathan. *Les Bienveillantes*. Paris, 2006.
Micale, Mark S. and Paul Lerner, eds. *Traumatic Pasts: History, Psychiatry and Trauma in the Modern Age, 1870–1930*. Cambridge, 2001.

Pecora, Vincent P. *Secularization and Cultural Criticism: Religion, Nation, & Modernity*. Chicago, 2006.
Ricciardi, Alessia. *The Ends of Mourning: Psychoanalysis, Literature, Film*. Stanford, CA, 2003.
Richman, Michèle. *Sacred Revolutions: Durkheim and the Collège de Sociologie*. Minneapolis, MN, 2002.
Said, Edward. *Orientalism*. New York, 1978, 2003.
Sanyal, Debarati. *The Violence of Modernity: Baudelaire, Irony, and the Politics of Form*. Baltimore, MD, 2006.
Segev, Tom. *The Seventh Million: The Israelis and the Holocaust*. Translated by Haim Watzman. New York, 1991, 1993.
Slotkin, Richard. *Regeneration Through Violence: The Mythology of the American Frontier 1600–1800*. New York, [1973] 1996.
Sorel, Georges. *Reflections on Violence*. Translated by T.E. Hulme. New York, [1915] 1941.
Spiegel, Gabrielle, ed. *Practicing History: New Directions in Historical Writing after the Linguistic Turn*. New York, 2005.
Sternhell, Zeev. *Neither Right nor Left: Fascist Ideology in France*. Translated by David Meisel. Berkeley, [1983] 1986.
Strenski, Ivan. *Contesting Sacrifice: Religion, Nationalism, and Social Thought in France*. Chicago, 2002.
Surya, Michel. *Georges Bataille: An Intellectual Biography*. Translated by Krzysztof Fijalkowski and Michael Richardson. London, 2002.
Theweleit, Klaus. *Male Fantasies*. 2 vols. Translated by Erica Carter and Chris Turner. Minneapolis, MN, 1987, 1989.
Varon, Jeremy. *Bringing the War Home: The Weather Underground, the Red Army Faction, and Revolutionary Violence in the Sixties and Seventies*. Berkeley and Los Angeles, 2004.
Wolin, Richard. *The Seduction of Unreason: The Intellectual Romance with Fascism from Nietzsche to Postmodernism*. Princeton, NJ, 2004.
Wood, Nancy. *Vectors of Memory: Legacies of Trauma in Postwar Europe*. Oxford, 1999.
Young, Robert. *Postcolonialism: An Historical Introduction*. Oxford, 2001.
———. *White Mythologies: Writing History and the West*. London, 1990.

Democratization, Turks, and the Burden of German History

Rita Chin

After the collapse of the Third Reich, democratization represented perhaps the most urgent political and ideological task facing West Germans. Both the ideal of democracy (liberty, equality, popular representation) and its concrete institutions (a constitution and popularly elected representative bodies) promised to act as bulwarks against repeating the barbarity of the Nazi dictatorship. By the mid 1980s, when the Federal Republic began to mark the fortieth anniversaries surrounding the war's end, many Germans—first and foremost, Chancellor Helmut Kohl—believed that the process of democratization was largely complete. West Germany, they argued, had demonstrated its unwavering commitment to the fraternity of Western capitalist democracies.

Yet, creating a stable democracy and measuring its success proved somewhat more complicated than both the fathers of the Federal Republic and their heirs anticipated. In the immediate postwar period, the issue of democratization became linked to a robust economy—in no small measure because the enemies of the Weimar Republic (Germany's first democratic experiment) had exploited a volatile economic crisis to undermine the regime. A quick economic stabilization program and the subsequent boon of the *Wirtschaftswunder,* in this respect, helped ensure that the new Bonn Republic was on the right path. But the postwar economic explosion required more manpower than the West German population could provide, and the government quickly turned to foreign guest workers to fill the shortage. Starting in 1955, the Federal Republic embarked on an eighteen-year period of labor recruitment, which included guest workers from southern Mediterranean countries as well as Muslim Turkey. Ultimately, the effort to democratize inadvertently produced postwar Europe's most extensive labor migration, bringing two million foreigners onto German soil.

In the late 1960s, democratization acquired a different set of meanings, as a younger generation of Germans, born during or immediately after the war, came of age. What had seemed to their parents like a grueling, yet courageous effort to rebuild the country and embrace Western-style democracy often appeared to these young people as an attempt to avoid coming to terms with the Nazi past. Critics on the left went so far as to condemn the Federal Republic's efforts to secure democracy through capitalism as a structural, political, and moral continuity from the Third Reich. It was precisely the obsession with the ever-expanding economic production and the self-congratulatory attitude toward prosperity, according to 1968ers, that obscured West German society's failure to deal with its troubling historical legacy.

For guest workers and their descendants, though, neither of these frameworks seemed adequate. As temporary labor recruitment evolved into *de facto* immigration during the mid 1970s, minority intellectuals began to address both the obvious and more subtle barriers to incorporation into German society. With the reunification of East and West Germany a decade and a half later, the second-generation Turkish-German author and cultural critic, Zafer Şenocak, formulated a key question with major implications for assessing democratization: "Is Germany a home for Turks?" This rather innocent query suggested a radically new definition of democracy. In Şenocak's view, it was no longer enough to evaluate Germany's democratic credentials according to the criteria of economic stability, or even a critical attitude toward the Nazi past. Somewhat paradoxically, he seemed to suggest, postwar labor recruitment had produced the demographic and cultural conditions for multiethnic democracy. Yet the ideological and political framework for democratization imagined by most Germans included little sense that guest workers might eventually become part of the nation's social and cultural fabric.

This essay explores the contested concept of democracy in the Federal Republic, a concept intimately bound up with the burden of the nation's past and the struggle over collective memory.[1] I deliberately focus on public discourse in order to highlight the ways that official national memory culture has often obscured the narratives and experiences of guest workers in German society. By revisiting some of the milestone moments in the Federal Republic's history, I aim to rethink the meanings of postwar democratization.

Paths to Democratization and the Guest Worker Program

As the US, British, and Russian armies converged on Berlin in May 1945, a top priority for the Allied forces was to prevent history from repeating itself. Less than thirty years before, the victorious powers laid the blame for the First World War at Germany's feet. The result was a punitive peace treaty that heaped humiliation and reparations on the conquered nation, sowing the seeds of a corrosive debate among many Germans about their country's shameful defeat culminating in significant popular support for National Socialism. When World War II came to an end, by contrast, the Allies vowed to practice restraint in implementing the peace. Not only did the victors wish to avoid creating new German resentments, they also sought to forestall the possibility of another dictatorship that might threaten world peace for a third time.[2] For the American, British, and eventually French occupying powers, this meant helping democratic institutions take firm root and preempting political upheaval by bolstering the economy.[3]

In order to lay a firm ideological foundation for democracy, the Western Allies proposed two key policies. The first, reeducation, sought to wean Germans from their undue respect for authority. The second, denazification, attempted to weed out Nazis from public life and civil service and included assessing individual guilt in war crimes trials such as Nuremberg.[4] During the occupation period, the Allies interned 200,000 former Nazi officials. In the first half of 1946 alone, 150,000 Germans lost their jobs in government and civil service, and 73,000 were removed from their positions in industry and commerce.[5] In practice, however, neither initiative proved as far-reaching or as thorough as originally envisioned. The nature of Allied occupation meant that each zone pursued these policies in different ways. The end result was an uneven and inconsistent reeducation program, prosecution of Nazi criminals, and treatment of former Nazi party members.

It is also important to acknowledge that the Allies defined these initiatives somewhat narrowly. Reeducation, for instance, targeted Germans' perceptions of authority rather than their feelings about racial difference, while denazification focused on party membership rather than social attitudes. Significantly, the Nuremberg Trials—the prime showcase for meting out justice for Nazi crimes—discussed the victims in terms of nationality and not in terms of ethnicity, race, or even religion.[6] Thus, it is not particularly surprising that just a few months into the Allied occupation, the actual practice of reeducation turned out to be more of a readjustment to ground-level social relations in which anti-Jewish biases largely persisted.[7] As one US government official complained, "denazification, which began with a bang, has since died with a whimper ... it opened the way toward renewed control of German public, social, economic and cultural life by forces which only partially and temporarily had been deprived of the influence they had exerted under the Nazi regime."[8] According to a 1947 survey conducted by the US Office of Military Government (known as OMGUS), even though most Germans were democratically inclined, a significant minority was undemocratic and continued to hold anti-Semitic and authoritarian views.[9]

Despite the limitations of US reeducation and denazification programs, John McCloy, head of the American administration in Germany, stated in 1949 that the behavior of Germans toward the few Jews in their midst would "be one of the real touchstones and the test of Germany's progress" in building a new state.[10] At least for some US officials, then, German attitudes toward their Jewish victims would serve as a barometer of democratization. Yet the shifting relations among the occupation powers pushed aside any concerns about the need for more justice or confrontation with the crimes of the Nazi past. As divisions hardened between the Western Allies and the Soviet Union along Cold War lines, the US and Britain prioritized efforts to rebuild the economy in their zones over the reeducation and denazification initiatives. The need to secure West Germany for capitalism and NATO took precedence over the initial desire to purge the remnants of Nazi influence. One consequence of this new concern was that economic recovery and entry into the Western security alliance eclipsed justice and memory as the primary measures of democratization.

This shift emerged especially clearly in the weeks after West Germany became a formal, separate state. In his inaugural address to the new Bundestag, Chancellor Konrad Adenauer expressed his concern at the lingering tendency toward anti-Semitism. In the face of hostile public opinion and even resistance from members of his own party, Adenauer spearheaded a compensation package for Jewish victims of the Holocaust.[11] But these acts, in a sense, completed the phase of democratization begun under American tutelage. As Diethelm Prowe has observed, "since Germans associated denazification with the occupation, they considered punishment of the guilty completed with the founding of their new democratic state."[12] The new task of democratization lay with building a strong and stable economy, shoring up the political democracy, and forging close economic and military relations with the Western powers.[13]

Meanwhile, the unexpectedly quick economic recovery from the war was extremely effective. For a large majority of Germans, rising prosperity helped establish the new republic's political legitimacy and quelled doubts about liberal democracy as the basic foundation for the West German state. Economic success began, at least, as a kind of insurance policy against a return to barbarism or a resort to Communism. Yet this path to democratization inadvertently introduced a new wrinkle into West German society. The *Wirtschaftswunder* created an urgent demand for manpower, which the native population was ill-equipped to provide. As a result of the high casualty rate among German men during the war and official efforts to encourage women in the wartime workforce to return to the home, authorities faced a massive labor shortage. The Federal Republic's solution to this problem was to implement a guest worker program, signing a labor recruitment treaty with Italy on 22 December 1955, and concluding subsequent agreements with Spain, Portugal, Turkey, Greece, and Yugoslavia. By the fall of 1964, the number of foreign workers in Germany surpassed one million, and five years later, it reached nearly two million.[14]

On one level, then, the large-scale importation of foreigners played a major role in pushing West Germany beyond its history of state-sponsored racial purification. But this connection between the guest workers and democratization went largely unacknowledged. One reason can be found in the basic parameters of the labor recruitment program. Initially, at least, government officials issued two-year employment permits to limit the length of residence in the Federal Republic. Workers consisted almost entirely of men between the ages of twenty and forty who were either single or left their families at home. Most lived in make-shift housing provided by their employers, often barracks situated on or near the factory site. These conditions framed the labor recruitment as a short-term expedient for the lack of native manpower. A 1959 *Frankfurter Allgemeine Zeitung* article, for instance, noted that "in the event of unemployment" or an economic downturn, "foreign workers could be sent back home again."[15] As a result, most West Germans took the euphemistic label "guest worker" literally; they assumed that the foreigners were temporary sojourners, present in the Federal Republic only until demand for their labor dried up. As transient beings, labor recruits were not associated with such longer-term processes as social reconstruction or democratization.

There were a few exceptions to this pattern. In 1964, Labor Minister Theodor Blank offered a more expansive significance for guest worker recruitment, casting the program as a sign of good will toward the international community. This arrangement, he explained, facilitated "the merging together of Europe and the rapprochement between persons of highly diverse backgrounds and cultures in the spirit of friendship."[16] Blank further argued that the labor migration would help promote "international understanding" and "European integration."[17] But even here, in Blank's broader understanding of the guest worker program, there was a basic failure to recognize the larger implications of this policy decision: by relying on foreign laborers to fuel the economic miracle, the very process of postwar democratization now required a renewed engagement with the question of difference.

In practice, the Federal Republic adopted precisely the opposite approach. The postwar guest worker program perpetuated many of Germany's older tendencies of social exclusion. Consider, for example, the legal status of those who came to the Federal Republic within the framework of labor recruitment. The original treaties and 1965 *Ausländergesetz* (Foreigner Regulation Law) categorized guest workers as foreigners. This distinction not only determined rights of work, social security, and residence, but also precluded (until 2000) the right to become naturalized citizens. The Federal Republic continued to reserve citizenship status for those with German blood, retaining the legal definition set out in 1913. The postwar guest worker program, in other words, presumed that West Germany was not an immigration country. Foreign laborers were not recruited to become permanent additions to German society, but rather to provide labor for a limited period and then return to their own homes. In this respect, the category of guest worker itself served to exclude labor migrants from the nation, making the distinction between foreigner and citizen appear natural and absolute. It was thus possible for guest workers to be physically present on German soil and, at the same time, remain entirely separate from the social body.

The New Left, the Nazi Past, and Democratization

What is perhaps more surprising than the initial failure to grasp the crucial place of labor recruitment in forging democracy is the fact that this blindness largely continued into the late 1960s and early 1970s. The 1960s, after all, marked the moment when the war baby generation reached adulthood, and the mostly middle class, mostly university educated New Left minority within this cohort began to level serious critiques at the democratizing process led by Adenauer.[18] In 1964, the Auschwitz trials in Frankfurt, along with a controversial parliamentary debate over extending the statute of limitations for Nazi war crimes, drew public attention once again to the presence of the National Socialist past.[19] That same year, the far right National Democratic Party was founded. These events "helped remind left-wing intellectuals that the Federal Republic had not yet fully shed its anti-democratic culture" and Nazi legacy.[20] In response, 1968ers demanded painstaking "*Vergangenheitsbewältigung*" (coming to terms with the past) and an end to their parents' silence concerning the Third Reich. To this younger generation,

> Adenauer Germany's coming to terms with its past seemed shallow and false. Instead of really getting to the roots of ... the origins of fascism, West Germany was busily constructing a self-serving ideology of rabid anti-communism. This credo ... had blocked the process of democratic reform in West Germany. Just as anti-communism had replaced democracy in this "feel good" Germany, so too did general prosperity mask the immense social costs of capitalism. It was necessary, the Left argued, to confront the brutal facts of the past head on.[21]

For members of the New Left, then, the hollowness of West German democracy was bound up with the nation's unselfconscious embrace of capitalism and endless pursuit of prosperity, which served as cover for the failure to deal with its shameful past.

Following earlier leftist critique, the New Left understood fascism as a product of the highest stage of capitalism. Yet the fixation on the intersection of capitalism and fascism unwittingly elided both systems' social and material impacts. At the most basic level, this focus "subsumed the singularity of the Nazis' systematic annihilation of the Jews under the generic term and structural concept of fascism."[22] The effect was to obscure the uniqueness of National Socialist crimes and to ignore its Jewish victims. At the same time, condemning international capitalism as a root cause of fascism did lead some New Left artists and intellectuals to extend their criticism to the Federal Republic's guest worker program. Rainer Werner Fassbinder's 1969 feature film, *Katzelmacher*, for example, depicted a vicious group of working class friends and their dealings with an imported laborer. That same year, the social activist Günter Walraff published a book of reportage on the living conditions of guest workers, *Bilder aus Deutschland—"Gastarbeiter" oder der gewöhnliche Kapitalismus (Images from Germany—"Guest Workers" or Capitalism as Usual)*.[23] In each case, however, self-congratulatory economic prosperity, social conformity, and ideological complacency emerged as the primary targets of critique. Foreign labor recruitment, in this view, simply represented the most extreme example of the Federal Republic's indifference to the human costs of the unbridled pursuit of capitalism. In *Katzelmacher*, for instance, the foreign laborer Jorgos functions as an abstract figure with no individual identity. He is virtually silent because of his inability to understand or speak much German, and his background remains obscure except for the fact that he has come from Greece.[24] Similarly, Walraff's book sought to challenge the idea of a surplus army of laborers, whose flexibility helped facilitate "capitalism as usual." Both guest workers and Jews remained remote as subjects, ancillary aspects of what were perceived as the more systemic problems of capitalism and fascism.

Ironically, then, this highly critical younger generation also had trouble seeing just how central the question of difference was to postwar democratization in the Federal Republic. To the extent that members of the New Left identified ethnic oppression as a product of capitalism or adopted anti-racism as part of their cause, they did so by criticizing the social conditions in other countries, and especially the United States.[25] The weekly *Welt am Sonntag* recognized the paradox as early as 1966: "Germans who work through their past by being outraged about apartheid in South Africa or race riots in America obviously do not have anything against the apartheid of alien workers [*Fremdarbeiter*] in the Federal Republic, against their social boycott and their displacement into ghettos."[26] Anti-racist and anti-imperialist struggles remained squarely outside West Germany. For 1968ers, just as for their parents, postwar recovery and democracy were strictly German projects, no more connected to the nation's Jewish (as opposed to National Socialist) past than to its multiethnic present.

The Bitburg Affair and the Renewal of German National Identity

The question of democratization resurfaced as a topic of heated public debate around 1982, when Helmut Kohl and other conservatives began to declare that the Federal Republic had proven itself a mature liberal democracy. This claim heralded the completion of the nation's democratizing process and was integral to Kohl's larger push to restore German patriotism and promote a more positive sense of national identity. Along the same lines, Kohl helped establish the *Deutsche Historische Museum* in Berlin and the *Haus der Geschichte* in Bonn in order to provide Germans with historical narratives that would instill pride (rather than shame or guilt). This return to nationalism also inspired revisionist histories of the Third Reich, precipitating the highly charged *Historikerstreit* (historians' debate) in 1986.[27]

The broader ideological stakes of Kohl's efforts became especially clear in the 1985 Bitburg affair, when the chancellor invited US President Ronald Reagan to lay a wreath at the Bitburg military cemetery to commemorate the fortieth anniversary of Germany's unconditional surrender at the end of World War II.[28] Although the request provoked an international uproar once it became known that SS soldiers had been buried there, Reagan completed the visit as planned and justified the decision by explaining that the ceremony was intended not to reawaken bad memories, but to commemorate the day peace began.[29] In many ways, the Bitburg ceremony was an audacious feat. As Geoff Eley has argued, Kohl orchestrated the event as "an act of symbolic resolution ... the consummation of Germany's long-earned return to normalcy."[30] Central to this process was an interweaving of democratic self-congratulation and the production of new historical narratives. Precisely because the Federal Republic had achieved four decades of democratic stability, Kohl's actions suggested, it had now earned the right to honor its war dead (many of whom had no specific ties to the Nazi Party) like other democratic nations. In the surrounding furor, leftist intellectuals such as Jürgen Habermas criticized what they considered a neoconservative attempt to "defuse the past."[31]

For critics on the left, Bitburg was especially problematic because it suggested that democratization and *Vergangenheitsbewältigung* were finite processes. With that work now complete, West Germans could leave the unpleasant and shameful Nazi legacy in the past and construct a useable national identity for the future. Yet one striking feature of this controversy was the common belief that democratic values should be gauged in terms of German attitudes toward Nazi crimes against the nation's largest minority group prior to 1945. This shared assumption between conservatives and progressives meant that the entire debate elided the question of multiethnic democracy in the present. Indeed, by driving home the importance of Germany's thorny past for any attempt to resuscitate national identity, Bitburg obscured the other major aspect of such a project: namely, that the effort to reclaim a patriotic nationalism also involved defining the parameters of Germanness, a process which necessarily took place in relation to the millions of guest workers now residing on West German soil.

By 1985, after all, the Federal Republic was home to the largest population of foreign residents in Western Europe. And as both Kohl and his critics knew quite well, the issue of the labor recruitment's domestic social (as opposed to economic) impacts had recently emerged as a topic of intense national debate. In 1979, Helmut Schmidt's socialist-liberal coalition had called for a major reformulation of the guest worker question. Leading Social-Democratic officials proposed abandoning the older notion of guest workers as temporary "labor forces" in favor of open acknowledgment that nearly two million foreign workers and their families were de facto immigrants in need of social, cultural, and economic "integration." To this end, the federal government took several dramatic steps: it funded numerous studies to assess the ground-level situation of migrants; it created the *Ausländerbeauftragte*, a new office to advocate on behalf of foreigners; and it promoted specific integration measures, such as curricular reform in the nation's schools. In response, Christian Democrats dedicated much of their 1983 campaign to the "problem of foreigners," making this an issue of partisan politics for the very first time. Insisting that SPD-sponsored integration had failed, the CDU called for a sweeping revision of foreigner policy, including measures to encourage guest workers to go home.

The basic connection between national identity and the guest worker question is readily apparent in a February 1982 parliamentary debate over *Ausländerpolitik*. Here, Alfred Dregger, a longtime Bundestag representative and the outspoken leader of the Christian Democratic-Christian Socialist (CSU) caucus, addressed the issue of integration. In contrast to the SPD, which defined this process as a reciprocal one that would transform both natives and migrants, Dregger placed the burden entirely on foreigners to adopt German values and lifestyles. Yet, he also insisted that some foreigners were more compatible with Germans than others.[32] Foreign citizens from Austria or Switzerland who spoke German, for example, presented little problem. Other Europeans, who shared common Christian roots, made integration and eventual assimilation likely. But Turks along with Asians and Africans possessed such unfamiliar cultures, religions, and values that integration seemed virtually impossible.

Focusing on Turks as the key group of unassimilable foreigners, Dregger stressed differences of culture and mentality. "The Turkish people," he argued:

> were not shaped by Christianity, rather by Islam—another high culture, and I stress, high culture. The fact that the state founded by Ataturk in 1918 is secular and understands itself as European changes nothing, anymore than the fact that our state is also secular rather than the earlier Holy Roman Empire. Even in its more secular form, Christian and Islamic high cultures have a lasting effect on our peoples. This contributes ... to the fact that they are not assimilable. They want to remain what they are, namely Turks. And we should respect this.[33]

As evidence of this incommensurable difference, Dregger pointed to the largely insular Turkish "ghettos" in Germany's major cities. While he praised the instinct of Turks to preserve their unique culture, he argued that they should do so in Turkey rather than in Germany.

What Dregger offered was a particular theory of culture. German culture, in his view, was neither superior nor inferior to its Turkish counterpart; each was simply different. Dregger did not question the value of multiple cultural traditions. Indeed, he celebrated the fact that historically rich cultures, by definition, operated according to distinct and specific logics. Yet the very strength and persistence of Turkish culture presented a new dilemma for postwar Germany. Turkish "ghettos" created pockets of an enduring minority culture within an equally strong majority culture.

Dregger likened this form of mixing to the unstable combination of oil and water, in which both cultures—discrete, impenetrable, and with fundamentally incompatible interests—coexisted uneasily in isolated enclaves. The CDU deemed this scenario unacceptable and proposed relocating Turks to their natural, original homeland. Ultimately, this theory posited a fixed and largely immutable ethnic core or essence. Whereas previous SPD integration policy had assumed that some kind of cultural adaptation or fluidity was possible, even desirable, the CDU view of culture foreclosed the potential for (much less the value of) reciprocal influence.[34]

This conservative theory of self-contained national cultures helps us to see that the CDU's energetic nationalism of the early 1980s was never simply an issue of moving beyond war guilt or *Wiedergutmachung*. The renewal of national identity also required a reassertion of borders and clear definitions of cultural membership. The new push for patriotism, moreover, seems to have undergirded the zero-sum logic central to CDU foreigner policy: migrants had to choose full assimilation or return to their countries of origin. Thus, as the party sought to restore national self-esteem based on the Federal Republic's position as a now mature liberal democracy, it increasingly maintained that strong national cultures could not cross pollinate and belonged to wholly separate natural habitats.

What becomes clear in the Bitburg controversy is that neither Kohl nor his leftist opponents recognized (or were willing to admit) that the effort to resuscitate German national identity involved both rewriting the Nazi past as a twelve-year lapse redressed through democratization *and* advocating a culturally homogeneous conception of belonging. Indeed, conservatives as well as progressives assumed that these interrelated tasks were entirely separate processes. For precisely this reason, leftist critics of Bitburg attacked Kohl for attempting to replace collective remembrance and atonement with unapologetic nationalism, but failed to note that the particular vision of national identity being advanced offered little room for the very guest workers whose labor did so much to secure postwar democratization.

Reverberations of a Reunified German Nation

Almost a decade later, guest workers and their descendants were again largely peripheral to the public discussions of German national identity precipitated by the sudden fall of the Berlin wall and the crumbling of the East German state. It was during the Monday demonstrations in Leipzig in October and November 1989 that the issue first surfaced. Protesting Leipzigers quickly moved from an initial universalist claim of "*Wir sind*

DAS *Volk*" (We are THE people) to the more particularist declaration, "*Wir sind EIN Volk*" (We are ONE people). Whereas the former slogan seemed directed at the German Democratic Republic's (GDR) repressive policies and called for representative democracy, the latter proclaimed a desire to reconstitute a single German people. Part of this shift had to do with a growing belief on the part of East Germans that unification offered the quickest path to a better life. Kohl's cabinet, in fact, made economic help for the East contingent upon the restoration of a national state.[35] Yet the question of what precisely "one people" signified was largely taken for granted as the push toward reunification gained momentum.

During the period from November 1989 to October 1990, public debate generally treated reunification as a foregone conclusion; most discussion focused on the practical aspects of the merger such as a single currency, the permanent resolution of Eastern borders, the privatization of GDR state property, and NATO membership. To the extent that that doubts about a restored German nation emerged, they tended to come from voices abroad raising questions about the effects of this imminent change on European integration. The *New York Times*, for example, issued an editorial on the rush to German unity that highlighted the misgivings expressed by the major powers in Europe. France, according to the editorial, viewed reunification as an obstacle in its attempt to move forward with Western European economic integration, while Britain perceived this development as a potential disruption of the current balance of power.[36] One of the few Germans to voice concern was the prominent intellectual Günter Grass, who specifically linked unification with the problem of a reinvigorated nationalism. "Once again," he observed, "it looks as if a reasonable sense of nationhood is being inundated by diffuse nationalist emotion. Our neighbors watch with anxiety, even with alarm, as Germans recklessly talk themselves into the will to unity."[37] For all of these skeptics, though, anxiety around reunification had to do with the age-old German question: could this major power in the center of Europe sustain itself peacefully, without encroaching on its neighbors either in terms of territorial expansion or nationalistic fervor?

It was not until the political process of reunification was complete that public debate explicitly turned to the question of what becoming "one people" again might mean. This conversation had two key focal points: the spate of brutal attacks on foreigners between 1991 and 1993; and the renewed effort to deal with the burden of the German past, which crystallized in the building of a Holocaust memorial in Berlin. One clear vision of how the German people should be defined was offered by young hooligans, skinheads, and right-wing extremists who carried out a series of vicious assaults against foreigners in both eastern and western parts of the new Federal Republic, often to the chorus of "Foreigners out" and "Germany for the Germans." In September 1991, the hostility reached a new level in the depressed eastern town of Hoyerswerda.[38] For nearly a week, gangs of young men, cheered on by hundreds of residents, besieged two apartment complexes that housed contract laborers from Mozambique and Vietnam who had been hired by the now defunct GDR. Armed with knives, rocks, bottles, and Molotov cocktails, the youths surrounded and blockaded the buildings. One man told newspaper reporters, "We are going to stay here until the blacks are gone."[39] Despite dozens of arrests, local police could not contain the violence and eventually used the cover of night to evacuate all 230 foreigners to the safety of a nearby army base. Significantly, this escalated aggression broke out in the weeks leading up to the first anniversary of German reunification. In the aftermath of the violence, Hoyerswerda residents appeared on national television and jubilantly proclaimed their town "foreigner-free."[40]

A similar assault took place on a refugee hostel in the eastern German city of Rostock in August 1992. Then, on 23 November 1992, two skinheads set fire to the home of a Turkish family in Mölln, killing two girls and their grandmother. Six months later, four German youths firebombed the house of another Turkish family in Solingen, killing five women and girls.[41] These xenophobic attacks functioned as a kind of grassroots referendum on who counted as the members of "ein Volk." On one level, at least, the violence itself was a visceral attempt to excise alien elements from the newly reconstituted nation. But there were clearly socioeconomic issues in play here, too. As numerous commentators have noted, skyrocketing unemployment plagued much of the East immediately following unification, fueling deep disappointment about the material rewards of a reunited German state. Meanwhile, resentment grew in the West as the federal government allocated large sums of money and resources to aid the new eastern states. Yet these economic factors cannot fully explain the ideological significance of the cheering onlookers in Hoyerswerda and Rostock. One source of the applause seems to have been a collective desire to remove any foreign body from the national imaginary—to create a "foreigner-free" Germany. Or perhaps the goal was actually more modest: to insist that the very presence of non-Germans on German soil represented an affront to the bystanders' dreams of reunification.

The views driving these anti-foreigner attacks, it is important to note, represented an extreme position rejected by most Germans. After the riots in Hoyerswerda and Rostock, several thousand demonstrators from western Germany descended on both cities to condemn the brutality, provoking clashes with the police and local residents. According to a *US News & World Report* journalist on the scene, even casual conversations had the potential to "erupt in rage." When Rostock resident Klaus Goetze criticized Georg Classen for coming from the West to demonstrate, for example, a furious Classen "shouted back: 'I'm here because I'm German, and it's the duty of all Germans to stand up at this moment and protest!'"[42] This sentiment was reaffirmed by tens of thousands who took to the streets all over the country to denounce the attacks in Mölln and Solingen. Between December 1992 and January 1993, nearly two million people (or one in every forty) participated in candlelight vigils, publicly repudiating the extreme Right's exclusionary vision of the nation.[43] An organizer of the 400,000-person-strong march in Munich pointed to the large turnout as a sign that "the majority of Germans are not secretly hostile to foreigners or sympathetic to fascism."[44] Even before most of the peace demonstrations took place, editors of the *Süddeutsche Zeitung* sought emphatically to counter any suggestion that migrants did not belong in the new Germany: "We demand protection of the constitution, police, and justice. We demand a politics which opposes extremism ... The integration of the foreigners residing here must no longer be the sole task of the groups we call the 'foreigner lobby.' The legal state must begin an offensive against the hatred of foreigners."[45]

In striking contrast, government leaders responded to the right-wing violence by skirting the issue of national belonging and pushing in a very different policy direction. Local officials such as the Interior Minister of Saxony, Rudolf Krause, explained the Hoyerswerda attacks by pointing to the abuse of Germany's asylum law.[46] His colleague, Saxon Minister President Kurt Biedenkopf, in turn, demanded a drastic reduction in the number of asylum seekers sent to the new (eastern) states.[47] At the federal level, Interior Minister Wolfgang Schäuble repeatedly attributed the anti-foreigner violence to the massive influx of refugees, adding that "large portions of the population" were alarmed at the "increase in asylum seekers."[48] He urged Kohl to take immediate steps to stem the "uncontrollable flow" of foreigners.[49] Leading policymakers, that is, emphasized a causal relationship between the nation's liberal asylum provision and xenophobic attacks, effectively avoiding the question at the heart of the violence: which vision of Germany ought to guide the newly unified nation's future?

This strategy of combating anti-foreigner sentiment by blaming refugees dominated the country's domestic agenda for well over a year, as the Kohl administration worked to pass a more restrictive asylum law. While opponents of the effort initially balked at the prospect of amending Article 16 of the Basic Law because of its historic anti-Nazi significance, the CDU managed to push through a constitutional change that went into effect in early 1993. In one sense, the widespread public handwringing about asylum seekers can be read as a response to the immediate problem of post-unification violence against migrants of varying types and backgrounds. What the asylum debates fostered was a kind of ideological quick fix. By stanching the flow of refugees, government officials positioned themselves as attentive to public discontent about foreigners more generally. Yet the decision to focus on asylum seekers ultimately meant that Germany's leaders elided the vast majority of foreigners, most of whom were long-time residents and came to the Federal Republic through some connection to the postwar labor recruitment. Reducing the numbers of refugees, that is, said nothing about the more fundamental question of whether guest workers and their descendants ought to count as part of the new German nation. In this way, the debate about national belonging continued to be framed in terms that excluded multiple generations of resident migrants.

The other focal point for postreunification discussions of "ein Volk" was the building of a Memorial for the Murdered Jews of Europe in the new capital city of Berlin. The project actually began in 1988, but only gained serious momentum in 1993 after political reunification was complete. Indeed, the memorial took on particular urgency in the wake of East-West consolidation, because it served as a vehicle to incorporate former East Germans into the work of commemoration, a process central to the West German path to democratization. Such work seemed especially necessary in light of the GDR's key founding myth, which maintained that "East Germany was the successor state to the anti-fascist resistance fighters, while West Germany was the successor to the fascists and Nazis."[50] One effect of this ideology, as Jeffrey Herf has argued, was that GDR *Vergangenheitsbewältigung* focused on celebrating anti-fascist resistance and fighting the Cold War, rather than acknowledging East German implication in the Third Reich or responsibility toward Jewish victims of the Holocaust.[51] The Berlin monument thus represented the first act of commemoration on behalf of Germans as an entire people.

But the construction of the Holocaust memorial was also crucial to the production of a collective national identity. As one of the first major public undertakings of the reunified Germany, the project placed the nation's relationship to its genocidal past at the center of the process. Even the plot of land set aside for the monument underscored this vital function. Located in the heart of Berlin, the site stands adjacent to other major symbols of the reunited nation and its historical antecedents: the Brandenburg Gate, the Reichstag, and Hitler's bunker. After nearly two decades of wrangling—over such questions as whether Germany needed a memorial, what form it should take, and whether it should commemorate all Nazi victims or only Jews—the monument was finally completed in May 2005. It was based on a design by American architect Peter Eisenman and comprised a vast field of undulating concrete slabs varying in height from three to ten feet. At the inauguration ceremony, President of the Bundestag Wolfgang Thierse emphasized the uniqueness of the event, explaining that no other country had erected a monument to "its biggest crime in history" in the middle of its capital. Here, we can see more clearly the conception of national identity that drove this German-German project. As Germany's "biggest crime in history," the Holocaust represented the national fate; it was what all Germans shared.

This idea, in fact, dominated discussions of national identity after reunification. In a 1993 op-ed piece for *Die Zeit*, the East Berlin theologian Richard Schröder suggested that Germans were linked by "a common responsibility": "We are responsible for our entire history with its highs and lows."[52] Five years later, in a public debate with Ignatz Bubis (head of the Central Council of Jews in Germany until his death in 1999), the novelist Martin Walser declared, "What we did in Auschwitz, we did as a nation and, by virtue of that alone, we must continue as a nation."[53] A subsequent commentary for the *Frankfurter Allgemeine Zeitung* by Klaus von Dohnanyi made the stakes of Walser's view explicit: "German identity, about which so many imprecise words have been spoken, this German identity cannot be defined today any more precisely than through our common descent from those who did it, who welcomed it or at least permitted it."[54]

By foregrounding a shared fate, these statements simultaneously advanced a highly particularist understanding of national belonging. Such a notion, Hanno Loewy has recently argued, "pushes off the German stage … all those who do not belong to the German community of fate because they can't be confronted with German 'disgrace': Jews, immigrant workers, refugees."[55] The insoluble link between German history and German identity, in other words, produced a homogeneous conception of the nation. And as the first official effort to advance a collective identity for a reunited Germany, the Berlin Holocaust memorial ultimately suggested that national belonging would remain exclusive to ethnic Germans.

Zafer Şenocak and Multiethnic Democracy

Not surprisingly, one of the first groups to grasp the fundamental limits of the discourse around German democracy and national identity was minority intellectuals. For our purposes, the ideas of the Turkish-German Zafer Şenocak are especially relevant. Born in Ankara in 1961, Şenocak moved to Munich in 1970 with his parents. There he attended elementary school and *Gymnasium* (academic high school), and after completing the *Abitur* (equivalent to a high school diploma), he studied German language and literature, politics, and philosophy at Ludwig-Maximilians-University. Shortly thereafter, Şenocak became an independent author, working first as a poet and then branching into prose fiction. During the mid 1980s, he translated Turkish folk poetry. He also received the Literary Prize of the City of Munich in 1984 and won the Chamisso Patronage Prize for foreign-born authors of German literature in 1988. Since 1990, Şenocak has written nonfiction essays for a number of prominent periodicals—most notably *Die Zeit, Die Welt,* and *Die Tageszeitung*—and has given countless readings around the world. He has become one of contemporary Germany's most important and critically acclaimed young intellectuals.

For Şenocak, the fall of the Berlin Wall and events in the GDR pushed previously unspoken questions of national belonging into the open and seemed to offer an opportunity for radically new answers. As thousands of ethnic Germans from the East arrived in the Federal Republic, Şenocak asked whether Germany was also a "homeland for Turks," criticizing the restrictive citizens' rights available to guest workers and their descendents.[56] The genealogical basis for German citizenship, he pointed out, meant that an ethnic German from Eastern Europe with only distant family ties to Germany and little ability to speak the language was considered a German, while a second- or third-generation Turk born, raised, and educated in Germany remained a foreigner. This moment of upheaval threw into stark relief one of the fundamental contradictions of West German democracy: namely, that its foundations had been laid with the labor of Turks and other foreign workers who continued to exist outside the legal parameters of the nation. In order to fulfill the promise of democratization, he argued, the Federal Republic needed to liberalize the definition of German citizenship.

But beyond the legal framework, Şenocak called for "a profound change of consciousness" on the part of both Germans and Turks to ensure that "native and future German citizens really live together successfully."[57] As an antidote to the tempting "phantasm of the lost homeland," he urged second-generation Turks to reject the one-sided orientation to Turkey of their parents and immerse themselves in questions of Germany's past and future. For Germans, on the other hand, "an important corrective in the process of rediscovering a new German national feeling," Şenocak reasoned, could be the "presence of a historical, cultural, and religious minority."[58] Writing just two months after the breaching of the wall, he declared somewhat optimistically: "We have the good fortune, which unfortunately goes unrecognized, of living in a time when concepts like fatherland, home, and nation can be seen from different perspectives and when they no longer function as key words that fit only one certain lock."[59]

Yet this sense of hopefulness and possibility dissipated quickly. Two years later, in January 1992, Şenocak again wondered whether Germany could be a homeland for Turks. This time his answer was quite different: "We have been asking ourselves this question for a year and a half. German unification was in process and stopped past us like a train that we ourselves were sitting on. We were inside this country that we grew up in, bound to its streets, plazas, cities, and people, but we were also outside it because the symbols which were suddenly resuscitated from the dusty files of history said nothing to us."[60] Part of the problem, he suggested, was that "rapid reunification ... created the illusion that current events and contemporary phenomena [could] be described with nineteenth-century language, with concepts such as *nation* and *Volk*. We have no concepts for the emotions and psychic structures to which recent historical ruptures have given rise, no concepts for the disarray of the new arrangements. The ones that are used are ripped out of context."[61] Şenocak, then, began his critique by calling for a new set of terms as well as a new way of thinking about the problem of difference in German history. But what exactly would this entail?

Part of an answer came in response to the spate of events in 1995 marking the fiftieth anniversary of the war's end. In an interview published by the Berlin daily, *Der Tagesspiegel*, Şenocak drew attention to the relationship between the boundaries of national identity and the injunction to Holocaust remembrance. When asked what the commemorative events meant to him as a Turkish author in Germany, he responded, "can immigrants participate in shaping the German future without having access to a shared history with the native population?"[62] At first glance, the inclination to involve Turks in coming to terms with German war crimes might seem counterintuitive. The millions of guest workers who came to the Federal Republic, after all, had no personal connection to or responsibility for the Third Reich. Şenocak's point, however, was that the process of Holocaust commemoration within its conventional framework inadvertently reproduced an ethnically homogeneous understanding of German identity. In the Federal Republic, he explained, "history is read as a diary of the 'community of fate,' the nation's personal experience, to which Others have no access. This conception of history as ethnic, collective memory was tied to the question of guilt after the crimes of the Nazis."[63] Only those who inherited the burden of responsibility for the Holocaust could lay claim to or share in German identity.

The very practices of *Vergangenheitsbewältigung*, Şenocak asserted further, tended to package "history, as one packs up things or buildings: in commemorative speeches, in commemorative plaques, in rituals."[64] This compartmentalized perspective was problematic because it obscured the ways the past reverberates in the present—in particular, the connections between German attitudes toward Jews in the Wilhelmine era and Weimar Republic and German attitudes toward Turks in the postwar period. Dividing the nation's history into discrete periods and discontinuous episodes made it much harder to see that the question of difference represented an ongoing problem, one of the recurring issues for German democratization.

But Şenocak's goal was not to reject Holocaust commemoration per se. Instead, he wanted to reformulate the nation's approach to its troubled history by disrupting the binary logic of categories such as self/other, inside/outside, German/foreigner. Unpacking German history and recognizing continuities between past and present, Şenocak insisted, required bringing immigrants into the historical imaginary, into the shared burdens and responsibilities that were an inevitable part of living in postwar German society. In short, he proposed introducing a third term into the compulsive, but stagnant commemorations of Jewish victims by German perpetrators. In his 1998 novel *Gefährliche Verwandschaft* (*Perilous Kinship*), Şenocak fleshed out this triangular relationship. Describing "today's Germany," narrator Sascha Muteschem, son of a German-Jewish mother and Turkish father, observes:

> Jews and Germans no longer face one another alone. Instead, a situation has emerged which corresponds to my personal origin and situation. In Germany now, a trialogue is developing among Germans, Jews, and Turks, among Christians, Jews, and Moslems. The undoing of the German-Jewish dichotomy might release both parties from the burden of their traumatic experiences. But for this to succeed they would have to admit Turks into their domain. And for their part, the Turks in Germany would have to discover the Jews, not just as part of the German past in which they cannot share, but as part of the present in which they live. Without the Jews the Turks stand in a dichotomous relation to the Germans. They tread in the footprints of the Jews of the past.[65]

The literary critic Leslie Adelson has usefully cautioned against a linear interweaving of Turkish and German national memory cultures, suggesting that Şenocak "write[s] a new subject of remembrance into being" rather than presenting a transparent window into Germany's struggle with diversity on a sociological level.[66] Yet it is worth emphasizing that Şenocak's primary preoccupation was with history, a topic that resonates in aesthetic, as well as political, registers. And it is precisely the perspective enabled by triangulation that made it possible for Şenocak to ask new kinds of questions about the relationship between history and contemporary German society. In "Thoughts on May 8, 1995," for instance, he recounted how his father listened to the war on the radio in his Turkish village. When the conflict ended, Şenocak explained, his father "experienced neither a liberation nor a collapse. He was neither victim nor perpetrator," adding: "this vantage point allows me to raise a few questions."[67] For Şenocak, this anniversary was an important occasion on which to connect past and present, especially in light of reunified Germany's newly attained sovereignty. "Germany lost World War II in 1945," he stated. "The Nazi regime was defeated. On the other hand, the subtle consequences of National Socialism continue to affect Germany even today. Does the Nazis' brutal effort to render Germany ethnically homogeneous have nothing to do with the present resistance to acknowledging, in Germany in 1995, the ethnic diversity that has arisen through migration?"[68] Here, in plain language, was the crux of the matter: fifty years of democratization and Holocaust commemoration had not brought West Germans any closer to recognizing the ongoing pattern of social exclusion bound up with public national memory discourse and accepted notions of collective identity. But a triangulated debate among Germans, Turks, and Jews, Şenocak suggested, might help Germans begin to grasp ethnic diversity not simply as a temporary problem or a singular tragic episode from the past, but as a central narrative of the nation's historical development. In this respect, Şenocak's larger goal was not so much to use Jews or Turks as analytic tools for unsettling the binary of German and foreigner, but rather to cultivate a *shared* sense of history and nationality, to redefine the very boundaries of national belonging.

What Şenocak shows us with striking clarity is that the discussion about German democratization and national identity after 1945—both at key historical moments and in the historiography—has recapitulated older ideological patterns, which presumed and projected ethnic homogeneity. Ultimately, one of Şenocak's greatest contributions (and what makes his work so crucial today) is his ability to see that diversity and difference have always been integral to the postwar project of German democracy. The work of democratization, in this view, is never simply finished, and is never measured according to a fixed historical standard. Indeed, it is precisely the shifting social relations—and the new kinds of epistemological vantage points—fostered by the migration process that continually revitalize German democracy.

Notes

1. In this respect, I am working within historiographical debates about collective memory. This field has been explored in detail by Alon Confino, "Collective Memory and Cultural History: Problems of Method," *American Historical Review* 102, no. 5 (1997): 1386–1403; Susan A. Crane, "Writing the Individual Back into Collective Memory," ibid., 1372–1385; and more recently, Peter Fritzsche, "The Case of Modern Memory," *Journal of Modern History* 73 (2001): 87–117. Studies specifically on national memory in Germany include: Saul Friedländer, *Memory, History, and the Extermination of the Jews of Europe* (Bloomington, IN, 1993); Andreas Huyssen, *Twilight Memories: Marking Time in a Culture of Amnesia* (New York and London, 1995); Wolfgang Wippermann, *Umstrittene Vergangenheit: Fakten und Kontroversen zum Nationalsozialismus* (Berlin, 1998); and Wulf Kansteiner, *In Pursuit of German Memory: History, Television, and Politics after Auschwitz* (Athens, OH, 2006).
2. Josef Foschepoth, "German Reaction to Defeat and Occupation," in *West Germany under Construction: Politics, Society, and Culture in the Adenauer Era*, ed. Robert G. Moeller (Ann Arbor, MI, 1997), 76, 87.
3. The Soviets were less sanguine about democracy for recent Nazi supporters. See Jeffrey Herf, *Divided Memory: The Nazi Past in the Two Germanys* (Cambridge, MA, 1997), 33–37.
4. The Soviets also advocated denazification, but generally implemented it on the basis of class lines. See Herf, *Divided Memory*, 74. The Soviet approach also maintained that the rise of fascism in Germany resulted from structural causes and the elimination of fascism required structural changes. See Foschepoth, "German Reaction," 75–79.
5. Herf, *Divided Memory*, 204.
6. Michael R. Marrus, *The Nuremberg War Crimes Trial 1945–1946: A Documentary History* (New York, 1997) and Donald Bloxham, *Genocide on Trial: War Crimes Trials and the Formation of Holocaust History and Memory* (New York, 2001).
7. Frank Stern, "The Historic Triangle: Occupiers, Germans and Jews in Postwar Germany," in Moeller, *West Germany under Construction*, 202.
8. Quoted in Stern, "The Historic Triangle," 223.
9. Anna J. Merritt and Richard L. Merritt, *Public Opinion in Occupied Germany: The OMGUS Surveys, 1945–1949* (Urbana, IL, 1970), cited in Herf, *Divided Memory*, 205. See also Werner Bergmann and Rainer Erb, *Anti-Semitism in Germany: The Post-Nazi Epoch since 1945*, trans. Belinda Cooper and Allison Brown (New Brunswick, NJ, 1997), esp. 1–17.
10. John McCloy, Remarks at the Heidelberg Conference, 1949, Truman Library, Papers of H.N. Rosenfeld, Box 16. Quoted in Stern, "The Historic Triangle," 225.
11. Robert G. Moeller, "Remembering the War in a Nation of Victims: West German Pasts in the 1950s," in *The Miracle Years: A Cultural History of West Germany, 1949–1968*, ed. Hanna Schissler (Princeton, NJ, 2001), 86.
12. Diethelm Prowe, "The 'Miracle' of the Political-Culture Shift: Democratization between Americanization and Conservative Reintegration," in Schissler, *The Miracle Years*, 456.
13. For a useful discussion of the efforts to deal with the Nazi past during the early Federal Republic, see Norbert Frei, *Adenauer's Germany and the Nazi Past* (New York, 2002).
14. The arrival of the one-millionth guest worker, Armando Rodrigues of Portugal, was officially celebrated on 10 September 1964. See Rita Chin, *The Guest Worker Ques-*

tion in *Postwar Germany* (Cambridge, 2007), 1–6. According to the Statistisches Bundesamt, there were 1.8 million labor migrants from Italy, Spain, Greece, Turkey, and Yugoslavia at the end of 1971. See *Statistisches Jahrbuch für die Bundesrepublik Deutschland* (Stuttgart, 1973), 52.

15. "Italiener in der deutschen Industrie—Ergebnis eines Experiments," *Frankfurter Allgemeine Zeitung*, 21 October 1959, quoted in Ulrich Herbert, *Geschichte der Ausländerbeschäftigung in Deutschland 1880 bis 1980* (Bonn, 1986), trans. by William Templer as *A History of Foreign Labor in Germany, 1880–1980: Seasonal Workers/Forced Laborers/Guest Workers* (Ann Arbor, MI, 1990), 211.
16. Quoted in Herbert, *A History of Foreign Labor*, 213.
17. Theodor Blank, "Ein Schritt zur Völkerverständigung," *Der Arbeitgeber* 17 (1965): 280.
18. For a more detailed discussion of this mounting generational critique, see Harold Marcuse, "Revival of Holocaust Awareness in West Germany, Israel, and the United States," in *1968: The World Transformed*, ed. Carole Fink, Philipp Gassert, and Detlef Junker (Cambridge, 1998), 421–438.
19. Andrei S. Markovits and Philip S. Gorski, *The German Left: Red, Green, and Beyond* (Oxford, 1993), 51–53; and Herf, *Divided Memory*, 340–344.
20. Markovits and Gorski, *The German Left*, 52.
21. Ibid.
22. Ibid.
23. It is worth noting that recent scholarship has claimed that Walraff was a paid informant for the Stasi, the East German secret police. According to Hubertus Knabe, for example, Walraff received information for his books from the Stasi. See Knabe, *Die unterwanderte Republik: Stasi im Westen* (Berlin, 1999).
24. See Linda Alcoff, "The Problem of Speaking for Others," *Cultural Critique* 20 (1991–92): 5–32.
25. In her discussion of West German feminism's blindness to the question of race, Sara Lennox briefly notes that members of the student movement and New Left supported anti-imperialist and anti-racist struggles outside of the Federal Republic during the 1960s and 1970s. She suggests that it was not until the 1980s that West German feminists began to consider racism within the ranks of German feminism itself. See her "Divided Feminism: Women, Racism and German National Identity" in *Engendering Identities*, ed. Susan Castillo (Porto, 1996), 30.
26. H. von Studnitz, "Sind wir unfair zu den Gastarbeitern?" *Welt am Sonntag*, 20 March 1966. Quoted in Julia Woesthoff, "Ambiguities of Antiracism: Representations of Foreign Laborers and the West German Media, 1955–1990" (Ph.D. diss., Michigan State University, 2004), 61.
27. Discussions of the *Historikerstreit* and the relationship between the Nazi past and German national identity include: Richard J. Evans, "The New Nationalism and the Old History: Perspectives on the West German Historikerstreit," *Journal of Modern History* 59 (1987): 761–797; Hans-Ulrich Wehler, *Entsorgung der deutschen Vergangenheit? Ein polemischer Essay zum "Historikerstreit"* (Munich, 1988); Charles Maier, *The Unmasterable Past: History, Holocaust, and German National Identity* (Cambridge, MA, 1988); Geoff Eley, "Nazism, Politics and the Image of the Past: Thoughts on the West German Historikerstreit 1986–1987," *Past and Present*, no. 121 (1988): 171–208.
28. For more on the Bitburg affair, see Geoffrey Hartman, ed., *Bitburg in Moral and Political Perspective* (Bloomington, IN, 1986).
29. Evans, "The New Nationalism," 789.

30. Eley, "Nazism, Politics and the Image," 176.
31. Jürgen Habermas, "Defusing the Past: A Politico-Cultural Tract" in Hartman, *Bitburg*, 43–44.
32. Deutscher Bundestag, *Verhandlung des Deutschen Bundestages: Stenographische Berichte*, 9. *Wahlperiode* (Bonn, 1982), 4892.
33. Deutscher Bundestag, *Verhandlung*, 4893.
34. This pattern of cultural racism links the German debates to similar ideological and political struggles taking place in Britain during the same time period. See, for example, Martin Barker, *The New Racism: Conservatives and the Ideology of the Tribe* (London, 1980), 1–53; Paul Gilroy, *Against Race: Imagining Political Culture beyond the Color Line* (Cambridge, MA, 2000), 32–39.
35. Konrad Jarausch and Volker Gransow, "The New Germany: Myths and Realities" in *Uniting Germany: Documents and Debates, 1944–1993*, ed. Jarausch and Gransow (Providence, RI, 1994), xxvi.
36. *New York Times* editorial, 19 November 1989, cited in Jarausch and Gransow, *Uniting Germany*, 83–84.
37. Günter Grass, n.t., *New York Times*, 7 January 1990.
38. This was not the first violent attack in unified Germany, but was one of the largest and most protracted. For a chronology of hate crimes in western and eastern Germany between 1989 and 1994, see Hermann Kurthen, Werner Bergmann, and Rainer Erb, eds., *Antisemitism and Xenophobia in Germany after Unification* (Oxford, 1997), 263–285.
39. Leon Mangasarian, "Police Evacuate Mozambicans after Racist Attacks in Eastern Germany," *United Press International*, 21 September 1991.
40. Stephen Kinzer, "A Wave of Attacks on Foreigners Stirs Shock in Germany," *The New York Times*, 1 October 1991, A1.
41. For analysis of the violence against foreigners in the Federal Republic during the early 1990s, see Gabriele Nandlinger, "Chronik der Gewalt," in *Die zweite Vertreibung: Fremde in Deutschland*, ed. Klaus Henning Rosen (Bonn, 1992), 119–158; Armin Pfahl-Traughber, *Rechtsextremismus: Eine kritische Bestandaufnahme nach der Wiedervereinigung* (Bonn, 1993); and Claus Leggewie, *Druck von rechts: Wohin treibt die Bundesrepublik?* (Munich, 1993).
42. John Marks, "The Fight for a New Germany's Soul," *US News & World Report* 113, no. 10 (14 September 1992): 21. I include this American news source because it provides a perspective on the riots quite unlike any of those captured in the German media.
43. Stephen Kinzer, "Germany Ablaze: It's Candlelight, Not Firebombs," *New York Times*, 13 January 1993, A4, cited in Jarausch and Gransow, *Uniting Germany*, 268.
44. Ibid.
45. Heribert Prantl, "Eine deutsche Pubertät," *Süddeutsche Zeitung*, 10 October 1991.
46. Knut Pries, "Die Krawalle in Hoyerswerda," *Süddeutsche Zeitung*, 24 September 1991, 3.
47. Giovanni di Lorenzo, "Der Mob siegt in Hoyerswerda," *Süddeutsche Zeitung*, 25 September 1991.
48. David Gow, "Bonn Condemns Neo-Nazi Clashes," *The Guardian*, 24 September 1991.
49. Kinzer, "Germany Ablaze," A1.
50. Herf, *Divided Memory*, 177.
51. For a useful analysis of how this political discourse developed, see ibid., 13–200.
52. Richard Schröder, *Die Zeit*, 29 January 1993, cited in Jarausch and Ganserow, *Uniting Germany*, 273–274.

53. Martin Walser, "Erfahrungen beim Verfassen einer Sonntagsrede," *Frankfurter Rundschau*, 12 October 1998, 10, cited in Hanno Loewy, "A History of Ambivalence: Post-Reunification German Identity and the Holocaust," *Patterns of Prejudice* 36, no. 2 (2002): 10. The Walser-Bubis debate was sparked by remarks—most famously that Auschwitz should not be a "moral cudgel"—which Walser made during his acceptance speech for the Peace Prize of the German Book Trade in October 1998.
54. Klaus von Dohnanyi, "Eine Friedensrede. Martin Walsers notwendige Klage," *Frankfurter Allgemeine Zeitung*, 14 November 1998, cited in Loewy, "A History of Ambivalence," 11.
55. Loewy, "A History of Ambivalence," 11.
56. Zafer Şenocak and Bülent Tulay, "Germany—Home for Turks? A Plea for Overcoming the Crisis between Orient and Occident" in Şenocak, *Atlas of a Tropical Germany: Essays on Politics and Culture, 1990–1998*, ed. and trans. Leslie Adelson (Lincoln, NE, 2000).
57. Ibid., 2.
58. Ibid., 7.
59. Ibid., 3.
60. Zafer Şenocak, "Ein Türke geht nicht in die Oper," *Die Tageszeitung*, 21 January 1992, 11.
61. Zafer Şenocak, "What Does the Forest Dying Have to Do with Multiculturalism?" in Şenocak, *Atlas*, 26.
62. Zafer Şenocak, "May One Compare Turks and Jews, Mr. Şenocak?" in Şenocak, *Atlas*, 53.
63. Ibid.
64. Ibid.
65. Zafer Şenocak, *Gefährliche Verwandschaft* (Munich, 1998), 40. Literary scholar Andreas Huyssen has argued that the perilous kinships confronted by the novel's protagonist emerge in the shrouded family history of his Turkish grandfather, a history that Germany and Turkey share around "genocides that have left a burden of guilt to successive generations." But the real stakes of this legacy, according to Huyssen, involve the question of "how such histories are remembered and how they can be imagined and written at a time when the changing memory culture of Germany poses new problems of memory for the Turkish immigrants and their descendants." See Andreas Huyssen, "Diaspora and Nation: Migration into Other Pasts," *New German Critique*, no. 88 (2003): 160.
66. Leslie A. Adelson, "The Turkish Turn in Contemporary German Literature and Memory Work," *Germanic Review* 77, no. 4 (2002): 333.
67. Zafer Şenocak, "Thoughts on May 8, 1995," in Şenocak, *Atlas*, 58–59.
68. Ibid., 59–60.

Bibliography

Adelson, Leslie A. "The Turkish Turn in Contemporary German Literature and Memory Work." *Germanic Review* 77, no. 4 (2002): 326–338.

Alcoff, Linda. "The Problem of Speaking for Others." *Cultural Critique* 20 (1991–92): 5–32.

Barker, Martin. *The New Racism: Conservatives and the Ideology of the Tribe*. London, 1980.
Bergmann, Werner, Rainer Erb, and Hermann Kurthen, eds. *Antisemitism and Xenophobia in Germany after Unification*. Oxford, 1997.
Bergmann, Werner and Rainer Erb. *Anti-Semitism in Germany: The Post-Nazi Epoch since 1945*. Translated by Belinda Cooper and Allison Brown. New Brunswick, NJ, 1997.
Blank, Theodor. "Ein Schritt zur Völkerverständigung." *Der Arbeitgeber* 17 (1965).
Bloxham, Donald. *Genocide on Trial: War Crimes Trials and the Formation of Holocaust History and Memory*. New York, 2001.
Chin, Rita. *The Guest Worker Question in Postwar Germany*. Cambridge, MA, 2007.
Confino, Alon. "Collective Memory and Cultural History: Problems of Method." *American Historical Review* 102, no. 5 (1997): 1386–1403.
Di Lorenzo, Giovanni. "Der Mob siegt in Hoyerswerda." *Süddeutsche Zeitung*, 25 September 1991.
Eley, Geoff. "Nazism, Politics and the Image of the Past: Thoughts on the West German Historikerstreit 1986–1987." *Past and Present*, no. 121 (1988): 171–208.
Evans, Richard J. "The New Nationalism and the Old History: Perspectives on the West German Historikerstreit." *Journal of Modern History* 59 (1987): 761–797.
Frei, Norbert. *Adenauer's Germany and the Nazi Past*. New York, 2002.
Fritzsche, Peter. "The Case of Modern Memory." *Journal of Modern History* 73 (2001): 87–117.
Friedländer, Saul. *Memory, History, and the Extermination of the Jews of Europe*. Bloomington, IN, 1993.
Foschepoth, Josef. "German Reaction to Defeat and Occupation." In *West Germany under Construction: Politics, Society, and Culture in the Adenauer Era*, edited by Robert G. Moeller. Ann Arbor, MI, 1997.
Gilroy, Paul. *Against Race: Imagining Political Culture beyond the Color Line*. Cambridge, MA, 2000.
Gorski, Philip S. and Andrei S. Markovits. *The German Left: Red, Green, and Beyond*. Oxford, 1993.
Gow, David. "Bonn Condemns Neo-Nazi Clashes." *The Guardian*, 24 September 1991.
Gransow, Volker, and Konrad Jarausch. "The New Germany: Myths and Realities." In *Uniting Germany: Documents and Debates, 1944–1993*, edited by Jarausch and Gransow. Providence, RI, 1994.
Habermas, Jürgen. "Defusing the Past: A Politico-Cultural Tract." In *Bitburg in Moral and Political Perspective*, edited by Geoffrey Hartman, 43–51. Bloomington, IN, 1986.
Herbert, Ulrich. *Geschichte der Ausländerbeschäftigung in Deutschland 1880 bis 1980*. Bonn, 1986.
Herf, Jeffrey. *Divided Memory: The Nazi Past in the Two Germanys*. Cambridge, MA, 1997.
Huyssen, Andreas. "Diaspora and Nation: Migration into Other Pasts." *New German Critique*, no. 88 (2003): 147–164.
———. *Twilight Memories: Marking Time in a Culture of Amnesia*. New York and London, 1995.
"Italiener in der deutschen Industrie—Ergebnis eines Experiments." *Frankfurter Allgemeine Zeitung*, 21 October 1959.
Kansteiner, Wulf. *In Pursuit of German Memory: History, Television, and Politics after Auschwitz*. Athens, OH, 2006.
Kinzer, Stephen. "A Wave of Attacks on Foreigners Stirs Shock in Germany." *The New York Times*, 1 October 1991.

Knabe, Hubertus. *Die unterwanderte Republik: Stasi im Westen*. Berlin, 1999.
Leggewie, Claus. *Druck von rechts: Wohin treibt die Bundesrepublik?* Munich, 1993.
Lennox, Sara. "Divided Feminism: Women, Racism and German National Identity." In *Engendering Identities*, edited by Susan Castillo. Porto, 1996.
Loewy, Hanno. "A History of Ambivalence: Post-Reunification German Identity and the Holocaust." *Patterns of Prejudice* 36, no. 2 (2002): 3–13.
Maier, Charles. *The Unmasterable Past: History, Holocaust, and German National Identity*. Cambridge, MA, 1988.
Mangasarian, Leon. "Police Evacuate Mozambicans after Racist Attacks in Eastern Germany." *United Press International*, 21 September 1991.
Marcuse, Harold. "Revival of Holocaust Awareness in West Germany, Israel, and the United States." In *1968: The World Transformed*, edited by Carole Fink, Philipp Gassert, and Detlef Junker, 421–438. Cambridge, 1998.
Marks, John. "The Fight for a New Germany's Soul." *U.S. News & World Report* 113, no. 10 (14 September 1992).
Marrus, Michael R. *The Nuremberg War Crimes Trial 1945–1946: A Documentary History*. New York, 1997.
Merritt, Anna J. and Richard L. Merritt. *Public Opinion in Occupied Germany: The OMGUS Surveys, 1945–1949*. Urbana, IL, 1970.
Moeller, Robert G. "Remembering the War in a Nation of Victims: West German Pasts in the 1950s." In *The Miracle Years: A Cultural History of West Germany, 1949–1968*, edited by Hannah Schissler. Princeton, NJ, 2001.
Nandlinger, Gabriele. "Chronik der Gewalt." In *Die zweite Vertreibung: Fremde in Deutschland*, edited by Klaus Henning Rosen. Bonn, 1992.
Pfahl-Traughber, Armin. *Rechtsextremismus: Eine kritische Bestandaufnahme nach der Wiedervereinigung*. Bonn, 1993.
Prantl, Heribert. "Eine deutsche Pubertät." *Süddeutsche Zeitung*, 10 October 1991.
Pries, Knut. "Die Krawalle in Hoyerswerda." *Süddeutsche Zeitung*, 24 September 1991.
Prowe, Diethelm. "The 'Miracle' of the Political-Culture Shift: Democratization between Americanization and Conservative Reintegration." In *The Miracle Years: A Cultural History of West Germany, 1949–1968*, edited by Hanna Schissler. Princeton, NJ, 2001.
Şenocak, Zafer. *Atlas of a Tropical Germany: Essays on Politics and Culture, 1990–1998*. Translated by Leslie Adelson. Lincoln, NE, 2000.
———. *Gefährliche Verwandschaft*. Munich, 1998.
Stern, Frank. "The Historic Triangle: Occupiers, Germans and Jews in Postwar Germany." In *West Germany under Construction: Politics, Society and Culture in the Adenauer Era*, edited by Robert G. Moeller. Ann Arbor, MI, 1997.
Studnitz, H. von. "Sind wir unfair zu den Gastarbeitern?" *Welt am Sonntag*, 20 March 1966.
Walser, Martin. "Erfahrungen beim Verfassen einer Sonntagsrede." *Frankfurter Rundschau*, 12 October 1998.
Wehler, Hans-Ulrich. *Entsorgung der deutschen Vergangenheit? Ein polemischer Essay zum "Historikerstreit."* Munich, 1988.
Wippermann, Wolfgang. *Umstrittene Vergangenheit: Fakten und Kontroversen zum Nationalsozialismus*. Berlin, 1998.
Woesthoff, Julia. "Ambiguities of Antiracism: Representations of Foreign Laborers and the West German Media, 1955–1990." Ph.D. diss., Michigan State University, 2004.

WEST GERMAN GENERATIONS AND THE GEWALTFRAGE
The Conflict of the Sixty-Eighters and the Forty-Fivers

A. Dirk Moses and Elliot Neaman

Introduction

Die Gewaltfrage—the question of violence—haunted West Germans in the 1960s despite the fact that the country was at peace. As might be expected, the memories and consequences of the Second World War remained palpable. Over five million German soldiers had fallen between 1939 and 1945, more than half of them in the final year of hostilities, while tens of thousands of women suffered horrific sexual abuse at the hands of Soviet occupation forces. Over 500,000 civilians were killed in allied bombing and, of the 14 million Germans expelled from central and eastern Europe, 1.71 million perished.[1] Hundreds of thousands of other Germans, namely Jews and those classified as Jews by the Nazis, had fled the country in the 1930s or been murdered soon thereafter. Millions of Jews in other parts of Europe had less chance of refuge; they were exploited, starved, shot, or gassed in the millions by a wide variety of German organizations, ranging from the SS, the *Wehrmacht*, the railways, and civilian occupation authorities.[2]

What is more, violence had been a continuous presence in the lives of older Germans who had endured the first global conflagration of 1914–1918 and subsequent street fighting of the Weimar Republic. Even members of the celebrated "sixty-eighter" generation, born roughly between 1938 and 1948, possessed childhood memories of cowering in bomb shelters or marching in refugee columns; those without such direct experiences grew up in ruined towns and cities, with devastated families, amid the national shame for the Holocaust. Not surprisingly, pacifism was a popular political current after the war.[3]

Yet, if peace had finally come to continental Europe after two world wars, the tension between the west and communist countries, decolonization, and the subsequent Vietnam War meant that violence was always more than a memory. The mortal struggle of national liberation movements with European counterinsurgency, as well as the prospect of nuclear Armageddon, appeared each evening on television screens. For West German intellectuals of all generations, these pictures were not only interpreted through the lens of the Cold War, as they were elsewhere. Images of the Nazi/fascist past were linked with contemporary events such as the Vietnam War (Would communism triumph as it almost had in Germany in the early 1930s, conservatives feared? Or would capitalist elites unleash global war yet again, leftists worried?), because these intellectuals suffered from the "Weimar Syndrome," the acute anxiety that the Bonn Republic might suffer the fate of the first, ill-fated German experiment in democracy.[4] "Bonn is not Weimar," the Swiss journalist F.R. Alleman assured Germans in 1956, confirming what was uppermost in people's minds. Twelve years later, in the wake of right-wing electoral success and student mobilization, the political scientist Karl Dietrich Bracher (born 1922) was also moved to ask whether Bonn was in fact Weimar after all.[5]

Who was to blame for 1933, asked intellectuals, and are they carrying out their evil work today? In a discourse of crisis structured in this manner, different factions of the intelligentsia defined one another as standing in the tradition responsible for the destruction of German democracy in the past. The syndrome thus tended to escalate debates because opponents always fulfilled the threatening clichés of the other.[6] By framing contemporary public dramas in terms of Weimar politics, the syndrome contributed to the hysteria and paranoia of postwar West German politics. Ironically, then, the passionate effort of Bonn intellectuals to ensure that the turmoil of the 1920s would not ruin the Federal Republic meant that some of the spirit of those years—including the question of the legitimacy of political violence to defend democracy against the perceived enemies of democracy—was imported into the political discourse of the 1960s and 1970s of and about the student movement.

Thanks to the terrorism of the Red Army Faction (RAF), political violence in the Federal Republic is often associated, however obliquely, with the student movement and New Left, that is, with "'68." Instead of participating in the Weimar Syndrome by asserting that '68 was either the enemy or savior of West German democracy, we propose to historicize this contentious period by observing how the events of the day were interpreted by intellectuals as acts in a drama whose script was provided by German history itself. This essay, an exercise in the political history of ideas, examines the question of political violence in the "red decade" after 1967 among the sixty-eighters and their older counterparts, the forty-five generation of intellectuals, born roughly between 1922–1932.[7] The ideological and political conflicts around '68, we will see, reflected many of the themes of generational tension elsewhere in the world, but were overlaid with a specifically German concern: the legitimacy of violence to defend democracy. Political action in Germany, then, was characterized by "melancholic repetition" (Martin Jay), never solely future-oriented, but framed by traumatic memories that defined the temporal horizon in terms of historically embedded moral imperatives.[8]

The New Left, the Student Movement, and the *Gewaltfrage*

If the German student movement took its cues, tactics, and rhetoric from the youth culture of the United States, its members also saw themselves as inheritors of European social radicalism. This dual influence meant they struggled with the question of the extent to which social change could be accomplished by peaceful, legal protest, or by subversive, revolutionary tactics. But the "question of violence" (*die Gewaltfrage*) was not solely self-generated or driven by a dynamic internal to the student movement. It developed in relation to considerable state and right-wing violence, as well as to anxieties about the course of West German politics. The students interpreted the Grand Coalition of 1966–1969 as a reenactment of Weimar and themselves as anti-fascists who would not make the same mistakes as when the Weimar Left underestimated the threat of Hitler's movement. Two texts were very important in situating the years 1966–1969 within the Weimar context of 1930–1933, by delivering a concept of *authoritarianism* against which to agitate: Max Horkheimer's *Autoritärer Staat* and Adorno (and others') *The Authoritarian Personality*. The Grand Coalition appeared as a reincarnation of the last years of the Weimar democracy, as broad coalitions operated on the basis of emergency decrees that eventually gave Hitler the opening he needed to transform the system into an explicit dictatorship. It also appeared to confirm Carl Schmitt's analysis of parliamentary democracy as the triumph of interest groups masquerading as representatives of the peoples' interests. The fact that Karl Schiller, the finance minister from the SPD, also succeeded in forging bodies of co-determination between the employers associations and the unions, was seen as another sign of the ultimate integrative power of the capitalist state to close down opposition and exclude possibilities of other social and economic models. The students also saw confirmation of Adorno's "authoritarian personality" in the hostile attitude of the West German population to their politics. In particular, they viewed the Springer media empire as an incubator for the fascist personality—a resentful middle class with ego-weak characteristics, such as the love of order, hierarchies, and the subordination to power. The rising popularity of the far-right NPD only added to the students' fears, as did the looming passage of the emergency laws (*Notstandsgesetze*).

Student opposition to the emergency laws was linked with opposition to US foreign policy, and its war in Vietnam in particular: both were attacking democracy and socialism. This opposition reached a boiling point in Germany in 1967 to 1968 with street demonstrations, strikes, sit-ins, the fatal shooting of a student on 2 June 1967, and the attempted assassination of the leader of the Berlin chapter of the SDS (Students for a Democratic Society), Rudi Dutschke, on 11 April 1968, which set off a convulsion of violent protests against the German state and other institutions. This included the police, the university, and mass media, all viewed by the students as conspiring to destroy German democracy.

The radicalization of the student movement was presaged by a growing split, beginning in the mid 1950s, between the venerable Social Democratic party and its youth organization, the SDS. Herbert Wehner and other party leaders led the SPD away from orthodox Marxism toward reform socialism and away from nationalism towards liberal internationalism, looking to the United States as the protector and guarantor of West German sovereignty. Many of the leaders of the SDS disliked the growing anti-communism of the SPD and were suspicious of NATO and the United States. When the US became involved in the conflict in Indochina after 1954, the suspicion that United States foreign policy was neither leading the free world, nor embodying the principles of the United Nations, but rather reflected neocolonial aspirations, only seemed to confirm their darkest fears. The SPD also became increasingly irritated with the attitude of the young cadres in the late 1950s over the question of how to deal with the East German State (GDR). In May 1960, the left-wing of the SDS split from the SPD, while moderates and the right-wing of the organization formed the Social-Democratic University Association (SHB). The SDS announced the split on 8 May 1960, the fifteenth anniversary of the capitulation of Germany in World War II.[9]

Two strains developed in the burgeoning student radical movement after the SDS broke with the SPD in 1960/61, one "anti-authoritarian," the other "classical" Marxist.[10] The former was inspired by situationism and was centered in Munich around a group called "Subversive Aktion," while in other major centers, Frankfurt, Bochum, Hamburg, and Berlin, classical Marxism, or more precisely Marxist-Leninism and later Reform (Frankfurt School) Marxism constituted the ideological core of the movement. Rudi Dutschke began as a proponent of the anarchic version of radical politics associated with the Munich subversives, but he later moved in the direction of a non-sectarian, heterodox Marxism, based on Luxemburgian revisionism. Dutschke's genius was to be able to combine many elements together, as the German media elevated him to celebrity status from mid 1967 onward.[11]

Like the situationist movement in general, the German group, founded in 1957, saw itself as the inheritors of the Dadaist innovation that equated the artist with an avant-garde revolutionary. The German chapter of the Situationist International, called SPUR, was based on the name of the journal founded in 1960 by the German organ of the Situationist International (SI).[12] The artist Dieter Kunzelmann, who joined in 1960, became the most prolific theoretician of the movement. In his view, the working class was no longer a revolutionary subject, but rather had become the passive object of manipulation in an age of Cold War and restorative tendencies in Western Europe. The remaining revolutionary subject was the artist him or herself, who, through experiments in living and public provocation (hence the title "provos" for its members), could hope to build the basis for future revolutionary movements. In the place of organized mass movements, led by the Marxist vanguard, the situationists embraced the notion that small groups could use targeted violence to attack the bourgeois order.[13] Kunzelmann passed onto the SDS an eclectic mix of surrealism, Dadaism, psychoanalysis, and German philosophy, in the main derived from the Frankfurt School.

Kunzelmann imported the peace-love-drugs culture of San Francisco, which was encapsulated in his famous reply to what he would do about the war in Southeast Asia: "What do I care about Vietnam, when I have orgasm difficulties."[14] By contrast, by 1967 Dutschke was married and considered Kunzelmann's emphasis on sexual freedom a distraction for the movement ("pseudo-sexualization").[15] But German situationism was not just playful Bohemianism, since it also anticipated both the theory and praxis of the extreme radical wing of the student movement. Kunzelmann himself organized a terrorist group, after training with Al-Fatah in Jordan, in the mid 1960s called the "Tupamaros West-Berlin," whose most spectacular and troubling act of violence was planting a bomb in a Jewish community center in Berlin on the carefully chosen date of 9 November 1969. Fortunately, the bomb failed to explode.[16] The Tupamaros called for attacks on judges, lawyers, and the destruction of American, Jewish, and

Israeli property in Germany, and were thus the direct predecessors to and inspiration for the later *Red Army Fraction* (RAF).[17]

Around early 1965, Dutschke and his friend, another former citizen of East Germany, Bernd Rabehl, decided to join the SDS, partly because of their distrust of the links developing between the SDS and the East German Freie Deutsche Jugend (FDJ). For them, both East and West Germany were occupied by an imperialist superpower and therefore "coexistence" would simply stabilize a status quo that perpetuated Germany's subjugation. They favored instead a *Deutschlandpolitik* that would ratchet up, not decrease, confrontation between East and West. The logic of this position can only be understood against the background of how the Cold War conflicts over decolonization were interpreted in the mid 1960s.

Dutschke captured the essence of the student movement's fascination with Third World revolutionary movements by pointing to the parallels he saw between neocolonialism and a divided Germany. Just as Georg Lukács had tried to explain the problem of a gradually deradicalized proletariat in Western Europe after World War I as the result of the reification of consciousness (in *History and Class Consciousness*), Dutschke interpreted the lack of opposition to modern imperialism in the 1960s along the same lines and relegated to the extra-parliamentary opposition the task of opposing neocolonialism as a new revolutionary subject. In the Cold War, Germany was just as much the object of imperialism as Vietnam.[18] A contemporary poem nicely captured this widespread perception:

Vietnam is Germany
Her fate is our fate
The bombs for her freedom
Are bombs for our freedom.[19]

These lines, written by Erich Fried, a German-Jewish exile and Holocaust survivor, introduce a curious inversion. The American bombs being dropped on the North Vietnamese, to make them "free," could not help but bring forth in postwar Germans' imagination the trauma of allied bombs that destroyed German cities to make them free. In a world turned upside down by US imperialism, the Germans and Vietnamese alike are akin to Jews facing extermination. That a leftist thinker like Fried could not see the nationalist-revolutionary implications of that analogy was only possible because the self-identification with the victims of the Holocaust was actually part of the international student movement, often led by Jews, outsiders, and minorities. In France particularly, for many leaders of 1968 (Cohn-Bendit, Glucksmann, Finkielkraut), the French state had not only failed to own up to its fascist-Vichy past, but had perpetrated another holocaust in Algeria. When Cohn-Bendit, a son of Berlin Jews, was expelled from France in 1968, thousands of Parisian students took to the street shouting, "*Nous somme tous des juifs allemands.*"[20] By equating the anti-imperial struggle with the Holocaust, Bonn was not so much Weimar, but rather a subordinate player in a neofascist axis that circled the globe.

The Students' Confrontation with the German State

In following the tactics of the Berkeley Free Speech movement and the SNCC (student Non-Violent Coordinating Committee), the German radicals adopted their methods as well: sit-ins, strikes, peaceful demonstrations, poster actions, etc. The Berlin students developed a method of sending small groups of students (provos) through crowded shopping streets to attract attention through political clownery, such as holding out tins to collect money for "warm underwear for the police."[21] The police responded by invoking Article 3 of Germany's Basic Law and sent undercover policemen into the crowds to arrest the students.[22] There was also persistent tension between the provos and the "classical" Marxists. The latter frowned upon what they viewed as undisciplined spontaneous actions, such as throwing eggs at the *Amerika Haus* and attacking the American flag—as happened after an anti-Vietnam demonstration on 5 February 1966—or a happening in front of the popular Berlin café Kranzler on 10 December 1967, where two papier mâché puppets of Lyndon Johnson and Walter Ulbricht were fed to the flames. Actions of this type were designed to incite and provoke the authorities, not much more, but they edged ever further into the gray areas of illegality.

Inside the SDS, the question of violence was debated repeatedly before the death of Benno Ohnesorg. Not unlike the splits that occurred inside the SNCC, after the election of Stokely Carmichael as chairman in 1966, some SDS activists questioned the effectiveness of relying solely on nonviolent tactics. Acts of provocation that only destroyed objects, or simulated violence, were the first actions in a more confrontational direction that led to a loss of support among moderates and "bourgeois" liberals, but also led to recriminations from other SDSers.

In early 1966, German student demonstrations against the Vietnam War began in earnest. The students called the winter of 1965/1966 the "Vietnam Semester."[23] Bernd Rabehl and Rudi Dutschke had formed a small group called "*Anschlag*" (attack) that used the SDS name in placards during demonstrations. During the night of 3 and 4 February, they and a small group of SDSers carried out an illegal "*Plakataktion*" blanketing Berlin with posters calling Chancellor Ernard and the Bonn coalition a band of murderers for supporting the war in Vietnam and the repression of colonial peoples.[24] The old guard at the SDS was extremely unhappy with the provos and tried to have them thrown out of the SDS, but ultimately they could not gain enough votes to carry out such a disciplinary action. After a sit-down strike on 9 February, modeled on Berkeley, students marched to the *Amerika Haus*, pelted it with eggs and ripped down the American flag. Berlin's mayor, Willy Brandt, and other dignitaries, rushed to apologize to the American authorities. Inside the SDS, a fiery internal discussion ensued, in which Fritz Haug, an orthodox Marxist professor of philosophy and editor of the influential journal *Das Argument*, inveighed against Dutschke for trying to push the working class prematurely into a revolutionary situation. The discussion was a key moment that showed fissures within the SDS on the issue of violence. Haug invoked Marx's thesis against Putschism, and Dutschke responded with Lukács' theories from the early 1920s on the failure of the Russian Revolution to abolish the state. According to Dutschke's interpretation of Lukács, the working class, while objectively the subject of history, was objectively stuck in encrusted class relations and so the revolutionary agent, the student movement, had to lead the workers into a new mode of consciousness. Rabehl, who had written a doctoral dissertation on the Paris Commune as reflected in Soviet historiography, also argued against Dutschke that the situation in 1966 was neither pre- nor postrevolutionary, as had been the case in 1920.[25]

Global politics and the German past merged on 2 June 1967 when the Shah of Persia, Mohammad Reza Pahlavi, and his wife Farah Diba arrived at the Schöneberger City Hall to present an exquisite carpet to the Mayor, Heinrich Albertz. The Shah was of particular significance to the students because of the perceived centrality of his role in the Cold War as a puppet of the United States and as an example of a Third World tyrant "of the Free World" who lived in splendor while his people starved.[26] Outside the City Hall, pro-Iranian students (probably organized by the Persian secret police) faced off against the anti-Shah demonstrators.[27] The *Jubelperser* (cheering Persians) suddenly brandished long, wooden clubs and flailed wildly at the students while the police watched passively for ten minutes before intervening. The students vowed to return that evening, when the Shah and his wife were to attend a performance of Mozart's *Magic Flute* at the Opera House. On the Bismarckstrasse, the demonstrations became even more bloody as eight hundred police started clubbing the students without any warning. At around 8:20 PM, Karl-Heinz Kurras, a criminal inspector, shot Benno Ohnesorg as he was trying to flee the demonstration.

Had one of the ringleaders been shot, perhaps in the act of throwing a brick, the Springer Press would have poured out indignant rage and the students would have been put on the defensive. As it was, the *Bildzei-*

tung was hardly reticent. The headlines the next day read, "Who produces terror must be prepared for a harsh response." But Ohnesorg was an entirely different case. He came from Hannover, was twenty-six years old, recently married and was then studying modern languages and philology at Braunschweig. He was a pacifist, described by friends as an independent type who would not join any student groups, though he did attend some events put on by the Evangelical Students Association. In hindsight, Ohnesorg's death provided a perfect grounding mythology for the student movement. Thousands watched as his casket was transported from West Berlin to Hannover, through East Germany, where the SED had made a special exception to the transit rules in order to embarrass the West German government.[28] Like Americans who remember where they were when they heard the news of the death of John or Robert Kennedy, the shooting of Ohnesorg remained etched upon the collective memory of the generation of 1968.

The events of 2 June 1967 reverberated throughout the nation, but the center of gravity was located in Berlin. As political scientist Richard Löwenthal and others noted at the time, the fact that the Wall had been built in Berlin drew politically interested students—the FU had the most politics majors in the nation, nine hundred and seventeen to be precise. Second, the special Berlin Model of co-determination actually increased, not decreased, potential tensions. Third, the island character of the city and Cold War pressures made the Berlin citizenry particularly sensitive, sometimes even panicky, about the rebellious and seeming anarchic behavior of students, so many of whom came from outside the city.[29]

Die Gewaltfrage and the Split Inside the SDS

From the point of view of the students, the German state and the police were acting in concert to suppress their legitimate desire for social change. And like in the Weimar years, the state did in fact put pressure on left-wing political dissent, by responding to street demonstrations with phony invocations of the Basic Law, clubs, dogs, and high-pressure water hoses. Unlike in Weimar, however, there was no organized right-wing street violence to offer some kind of comparison. Violence was thus both a political reality, driven by escalating confrontations between the authorities and the students, and a theoretical discourse to justify the necessity of violence as a means to effect social change.

Both aspects were on clear display when Herbert Marcuse visited the FU in July to give four talks before a packed audience of student radicals. The leadership of the SDS heralded Marcuse as the preeminent theoretician of the student movement, because he offered not only a post-Marxist analysis of late capitalism and consumer society, but seemed to accept, with some reservations, the guru role offered to him by the students.[30] The students were particularly attracted to Marcuse's contention that late industrial capitalism opened up the possibilities for an entirely new kind of human being who could transcend aggressive animal instincts in the building of a new society. Marcuse's main topic was the "End of Utopia," which he interpreted as the opposite of realism. Realists believe that social problems are inevitable, while modernist utopians could point to the advances of material productive forces as proof that concerted social action could lead to a free society. If one succumbed to the realists, one might as well concede the "end of history."[31] His second talk, "The Problem of Violence in the Opposition," was crucial. Here, he pointed to the civil disobedience movement in the United States as an example for the German students, even though he never explained who were the equivalent agents of socially oppressed African Americans in Germany. Marcuse saw violence as legitimate when it countered what he considered to be the illegitimate use of violence by the state (as in, for example, Martin Luther King's opposition to the war in Vietnam). Marcuse's final lecture on this topic, "The Problem of Violence and the Radical Opposition," was a decisive influence on Dutschke's thinking on this issue.[32]

Dutschke's development in fact highlighted the acute tensions that soon arose inside the SDS and the student movement in general over the question of political violence. Dutschke was directly blamed for the violent turn of the protests that occurred in front of the Moabit courthouse in the fall of 1967, as a student agitator, Fritz Teufel, sat in custody awaiting trial on charges of inciting a riot.[33] Dutschke suggested storming the courthouse and invoked the burning of the Supreme Court in Vienna by workers on 15 July 1927, implying that the students might wish to follow their example. Everyone, he said, "should think about what it means for him or herself."[34] Bernd Rabehl began to break with Dutschke at this point and made contact with the Berlin police, because he did not want to see the student opposition spiral out of control.[35]

Worry about Democracy

Beginning in May 1966, the SDS had established a Study Group on Vietnam and held a series of popular conferences on the war. The national leaders at the time, Helmut Schauer and Hartmut Dabrowski, were able to follow up on the success of these events by getting the largest of the German unions, the IG Metall, to finance another conference at the end of October 1966 in Frankfurt. The topic, "Democracy at Risk" (*Notstand der Demokratie*), was aimed at the emergency laws that were being discussed at the time between the potential partners of the Grand Coalition, the SPD, CDU, CSU, and FDP. The laws would curtail some civil liberties and give the police wider powers to infiltrate subversive political groups and clamp down on violent acts by protesters. More importantly, the laws would give a special commission, made up of representatives from the *Bundestag* and the states, the right to declare war by a simple majority in the case of a threat of external danger (*Zustand der äusseren Gefahr*). Critics warned that this undemocratic procedure was analogous to the almost unanimous granting of war credits to the Kaiser in 1914 and the Reichstag's support for Hitler in May of 1933.[36] The ideas behind the emergency laws had been discussed since 1958, but through the early 1960s, the conservatives had not been able to pass them. Both the unions and the students feared that the price of power for the SPD would be agreeing to the emergency laws. In fact, after much tumult and controversy, they were finally enacted on 30 May 1968, with a two-thirds majority to amend the German constitution. The fears that the laws would be used to undermine Germany's parliamentary system proved, of course, to be unfounded.

The German "1968"

Youth social protest was a global phenomenon in 1968. Historically, the German "1968" as a movement can be dated from 1966 to 1969, though the "hot period" lasted only from the acquittal of Kurras in December 1967 to the "Battle on Teglerweg," an extremely violent demonstration in front of a courthouse on 4 November 1969, in which 500 demonstrators threw molotov cocktails at police, injuring 130 of them, some seriously.[37] After those kinds of protests died down, the *Bewegung* was without a leader who could orchestrate public protests that commanded media attention. Throughout the fall of 1968 and all of 1969, the student opposition splintered into cells and diverse grouplets, and organized student groups at the universities quarreled about tactics and strategies. There were still many large demonstrations throughout 1969, but they seemed more and more like repeat performances and historical reenactments. One can date the end of APO with fair precision with the beginning of the SPD/FDP coalition in 1969. In general terms, one could argue that "1968" was coexistent with APO (*Ausserparlamentanische Opposition*) and therefore with the Grand Coalition from December 1966 to October 1969. But at the start, from 1966 to mid 1967, the active members of the radical student groups were small in number. Even in Berlin, the SDS only held two seats in the nine-seat executive council of the General Students Association (AstA). By the beginning of 1968, however, Dutschke's call alone could bring six or seven thousand students onto the streets of Berlin. That was a potent weapon in a city whose leaders were jittery about the moral authority of the youth and in fact were imbued with general guilt, carried over from the Weimar period, about the use of military and police force against the left, and specifically felt guilt in relation to the events of 2 June 1967.

Dutschke realized the power of the student movement and exploited it with deftness. But in hindsight, including his own, his plans were megalomaniacal. He believed that the student movement alone had the power to confront NATO and change what he perceived to be the German government's acquiescence in the US's global imperial strategy. His geopolitical vision included the reunification of Germany, followed by a Council Republic (*Räterepublik*) along the lines of the early Soviets, before Lenin crushed them in 1918. Dutschke's other model was the Paris commune of 1871. He foresaw a breaking down of the barriers between the worker and the intellectual, the disappearance of crime, and a reduction of the workweek. When asked (by H.M. Enzensberger) whether or not the allies would not impose a blockade in the event that Berlin became a Council Republic, Dutschke replied that just as with the Paris Commune, the workers and students would organize to break it.[38]

Dutschke was so convinced of the possibility of revolution at this time that he even became involved in a bizarre plot to blow up ships in the Hamburg harbor that were carrying weapons for the US war effort in Vietnam. The explosives were actually delivered to Dutschke's apartment in Berlin, thanks to an eccentric Milanese millionaire and radical publisher, Giangiacomo Feltrinelli. Dutschke hid the explosives for several days, even transporting them in his infant son, Che's, baby carriage, before finally abandoning the plot as too risky.[39]

Violence Against the Students

During the winter months of 1968, Dutschke's role as supra-leader of the movement became increasingly evident. He traveled the country incessantly, giving speeches and organizing student demonstrations. He also made the cover of Germany's major magazines, even receiving money for his efforts, all of which led to a countermovement against him inside the SDS, but even more ominously, created an image in the public's eye of a

Lenin-like figure emerging to lead the students. There was an air of hysteria surrounding Dutschke, which became evident on 21 February at a pro-American demonstration held in front of the Schöneberger City Hall, during which a young man who resembled Dutschke was kicked to the ground and almost trampled to death. Harking back to the "people's justice" atmosphere of Weimar, posters called Dutschke the "public enemy," a "Jewish pig," and other obscenities.[40]

The assassination attempt on Dutschke confirmed the worst fears of the students, that the combined power of the anti-student Springer press and proto-fascist sympathies of middle class Germans would eventually result in the murder of one of their own. The martyrdom of Dutschke seemed apocalyptic: he was born on Easter Day, he was shot during Easter week (*Gründonnerstag*), and he often invoked Jesus as an inspiration.[41] The political violence also had a world-historical parallel. On 4 April 1968, Martin Luther King was gunned down in Memphis by James Earl Ray, a loner and petty criminal. Joseph Bachman, Dutschke's assailant, likewise a loner and down on his luck, had read about King and wondered to himself why the American civil rights leader, a pacifist, was killed, while the German student leader who promulgated violence, was free to draw thousands of young people onto German streets.[42]

Up until Dutschke's shooting, the student movement did not possess a coherent organization or worldview. The small student groups were good at setting into motion waves of political action, but they were not well equipped to harness the energy and create lasting institutions. Since the Federal Republic could boast, by any measure, a very wealthy economy, the students were much less interested than traditional socialists in issues such as economic inequality. They did not want a better standard of living; they wanted a different kind of living, one beyond industrial society. The political spectrum was correspondingly wide, reaching from libertarian anarchists to hippies to Trotskyites to Stalinist die-hards.

The events of Easter 1968 finally gave the students a sense of unity of purpose and provided them with a single object for their anger and frustration, thus solidifying the movement. But Dutschke would soon go into exile, and his parting also signaled the beginning of the end of the movement. The *Gewaltfrage* as theory was put, as it were, into suspended animation. The possibility to use it remained, and was of course used in the 1970s by small underground groups, but the question for most—when and to what extent it was legitimate to employ violence—was never resolved: could German democracy and society be saved with the application of calibrated doses of provocation and violence, or did one have to smash the system and start all over again?

The Forty-Fivers and the Sixty-Eighters

These events and the question of violence after 1966 revived traumatic memories for all Germans because they interpreted it in terms of the "Weimar Syndrome." As might be expected, this syndrome affected older Germans who had experienced the Weimar years as adults more than it did younger Germans. The leftist and liberal members of the generation between them, the forty-fivers, who were children during the Weimar years, maintained remarkable sympathy for the student movement, even after the *Gewaltfrage* was posed, but there were limits to their tolerance, as we shall see. At some point, even they could not escape the Weimar Syndrome.

Ludwig von Friedeburg (born 1923) made clear where he and Habermas, who were in close communication with the SDS leadership in Frankfurt and West Berlin, stood. He called them the "democratically engaged minority," and at the SPD congress in 1968, Horst Ehmke hailed the students as "the generation for which we have been waiting."[43] Leftist and some liberal forty-fivers saw in the sixty-eighters images of themselves and the opportunity to realize those ambitions that had been thwarted since 1945.

By the winter of 1967/68, this support became more difficult when the humanities and social science departments in many German universities were taken over by students who proclaimed the inauguration of the "critical university," as in Berlin, or the "political university" as in Frankfurt.[44] Some of the occupiers were simply enthusiastic reformers who sought to integrate the learning process more closely with their most pressing political concerns, as Habermas, Hofmann, and others had recommended. Others were more radical and, according to one historian, adopted a "guerrilla strategy," wanting to "set up bases at the universities that would offer a collective opportunity to discover and develop long-term social-revolutionary strategies for the cities."[45]

At the SDS conference in Hannover on 9 June 1967—one week after Ohnesorg's death— Habermas used the infelicitous term "leftist fascism" to characterize the mentality and strategy of actionism.[46] His reaction underscored the common posture of all forty-fivers to revolutionary rhetoric, whether of the left or the right. Their commitment was to the Federal Republic as a project of reform, either radical or conservative; having witnessed it in their youth, blind actionism was an anathema. Thus, novelist Günter Grass condemned the violence and confrontational posture of the SDS, saying that, "The slogans 'ban the SDS' and 'Expropriate Springer' are written in the same authoritarian ink."[47] Marxist political scientist Peter von Oertzen, in taking issue with Habermas' controversial term and distancing the students from fascism, had to admit that one had to regret "the actionism of the radical wing of the rebelling students, and one needed to criticize most harshly their partly irrational character, lack of tactical wisdom, their strategic aimlessness, and often bitter intolerance."[48] And in his criticism of the conservative reaction to the students' call for the democratization of society, the pedagogue Hartmut von Hentig referred disparagingly to the left's program as "either breathtakingly naïve or ideologically strained."[49] Ralf Dahrendorf famously crossed swords with Rudi Dutschke on the roof of a van before thousands of students in Freiburg in 1967, putting his case against the New Left, utopianism of any sort, or criticism of representative democracy.[50]

Nonetheless, despite the violence and revolutionary rhetoric of key student leaders, leftist intellectuals continued to support their aims insofar as they coincided with their own. West Berlin professors and writers were more worried about the escalation of the street clashes, and especially by what they called the "pogrom atmosphere" among the population and the police described above. "The disturbance of the youth is justified," they wrote in an open declaration in Die Zeit that was probably penned by Habermas, because the parliaments were not discussing the pressing issues like Vietnam.[51]

Such support was not surprising. What was significant was that many liberals also affirmed the movement after 1968 despite the radicalization. Figures like political scientist Kurt Sontheimer, Bracher, and political theorist Alexander Schwan, who are today thought of as anti-student neoconservatives, were among those liberals affirming the movement. Typical was Horst Krüger's reaction. While highly critical of the radical wing of the student movement, he argued that one should not reduce the protest movement to this dimension. On the whole, the protest movement was effecting a liberalization of society, and the sooner some of its members abandoned revolutionary activity and devoted themselves to concrete matters, like anti-authoritarian kindergartens, reformed doctors, and legal practices and so on, the better. "The fork in the road [Kreuzweg] between romanticism and reality, between anarchy and social engagement, is still open."[52] Writing in 1969, Bracher had no doubt that the danger to the Republic still came from the right. He remained disturbed by the passive character of the population regarding the state, and the "frighteningly little" identification with its democratic institutions. "Here also lie the constructive aspects of the current 'disturbances' insofar as they are directed towards inner reform and the recognition of the GDR."[53]

Even the chief editor at the Norddeutscher Rundfunk and later anti-leftist editor of the conservative Frankfurter Allgemeine Zeitung Joachim

Fest (1926–2006) ran this argument. "Their [the students'] legitimate need for suggestive future options have been neither recognized nor addressed for twenty years."⁵⁴ Unbridled utopianism, revolutionary rhetoric, and violence were the fruit of such neglect. The student movement's inability to articulate coherently its demands and utopian vision merely reflected the muteness of the establishment. The one-sidedness of both parties, Fest suggested, put the Republic in danger, but the real problem was the German prejudice against the left. "Not in student annoyance, in their lack of respect and call to action, but in the authoritarian reaction against it, lies also well-founded what will be essentially the real test for the Federal Republic in the near future."⁵⁵ Sociologist M. Rainer Lepsius made precisely the same point.⁵⁶

Kurt Sontheimer was even harder on the establishment. The threat continued to come from the right, he argued in 1968, because the conservative establishment could not distance itself satisfactorily from the far right, sharing as it did an ensemble of dubious concepts and categories. To be sure, the APO had some anti-parliamentary streams, but it presented no danger and was in fact a salutary challenge to the regime.⁵⁷ Like Fest, Sontheimer insisted that the real danger to the Republic did not come from a revolutionary but essentially isolated and impotent group of students, but rather from the latent authoritarian, indeed, fascist sentiments they might evoke in the population. The electoral success of the right-wing National Party of Germany (NPD) should be a lesson to politicians that only through the true grounding of democracy in public institutions would the country be rendered immune from such threats in the future.⁵⁸ The alarmist "Cassandra calls" of conservative professors that students were paralyzing the universities were understandable, he agreed, for it was true that some of them had resolved to use the campuses as launching pads for revolution. But the professors had to realize that the student push for a direct, plebiscitary input into university decisionmaking represented a frustrated reaction to stalled university reform.⁵⁹

There were, of course, forty-fivers who opposed the students from the outset. Two of the most significant interventions were Erwin Scheuch's *Die Wiedertäufer der Wohlstandsgesellschaft* (The Anabaptists of the Affluent Society) and Wilhelm Hennis' *Die deutsche Unruhe* (The German Disturbance). Their main argument expressed the Weimar Syndrome: the students and New Left had imported the intellectual currents of the 1920s, namely that truth was beyond academic proof and scrutiny, into the 1960s. This was the ideology in which the crimes of the twentieth century had been committed, and it was typical of youth movements possessing a pre-critical desire for total explanation in the manner of theology or philosophies of history. Scheuch went so far as to lend academic credibility to the popular canard that linked the left-wing students to right-wing Nazi students from the 1930s by employing the term *"linke Leute von Rechts"* (left people from the right). Not for nothing did he think that the students reincarnated the Anabaptist religious chiliasm of the radical Reformation.[60]

With the sixty-eighters, he contrasted members of his forty-fiver generation, who were replacing the older reconstruction generation whose work they viewed "mostly with critical distance." The main conflict between the generations, however, was not between the sixty-eighters and the reconstruction generation, but between the sixty-eighters and what Scheuch called his own "middle generation." The latter were appalled by the ideological protest of the New Left, unlike some members of the older generation such as the Marxists Ernst Bloch and Wolfgang Abendroth, who were sympathetic to the students. Why did the forty-fivers find the emphasis on political spirit and orientation (*Gesinnung*) so disturbing?

> This generation remembers its elementary experiences that in modernity all the great crimes were committed by people and groups who asserted that the content of their politics was an ideology and that their spirit and orientation could not be questioned. The *Gesinnungskriminelle* of politics is the typical arsonist and murderer of great magnitude of this century.[61]

The social democratic philosopher Hermann Lübbe agreed. He thought that the student generation of the 1920s and the culture of the First World War experience had been replicated in the 1960s and 1970s by a "world wide student-intellectual partisan cult." It represented a "flight from reality," indicative of those who had been unable to stabilize their identities due to the pace of the modernization process. As a result, they exhibited a sectarian worldview well known since the nineteenth century as "partisan romanticism." In short, the students were the apostles of the counter-enlightenment because they "rediscovered the old political 'truths' that not only decisive arguments but violence also cuts the Gordian Knot, clarifies situations, and simplifies everything."[62] This was the argument about the "second student movement" (the first being that of the turn of the century feeding into right-wing student radicalism in the Weimar Republic) made popular by Rudolf Krämer-Badoni.[63] The radical wing of the student movement represented precisely the totalitarian agent that many of the liberals and conservatives who had studied with the neo-Hegelian philosopher Joachim Ritter in Münster feared: a social group that identified its own interests as universal and which justified itself by an appeal to a philosophy of history. The antidote was to protect the state from a totalitarian seizure of power.

The SDS-Nazi analogy was popular in these circles. Moderate students were entreated to resist the attempts of the SDS to democratize and politicize scholarship that one commentator argued were akin to Goebbels' attempts to control university life in the Third Reich.[64] The journalist Giselher Schmidt published a book in 1969, *Hitler's and Mao's Sons*, in which he equated the anti-parliamentary stance of Germany's neo-Nazis and the New Left, although admitting that the latter was at least honest about its program.[65] The philosopher Ernst Topitsch, who had spent the 1950s and 1960s campaigning against conservative clericalism, argued that the students' claim to a privileged insight into truth was just the latest in a long line of threats to academic freedom that went back through the Nazis to the Church.[66] These provocative analogies drew a sharp response from leftists and some liberals. Peter Glotz thought the comparison "unbearably tasteless,"[67] while the historian Helga Grebing (born 1930) wrote a book that aimed to invalidate the equation of left- and right-wing radicalism.[68]

Conservatives failed to criticize the violence of the state, of which they implicitly approved. A typical response was from the conservative Roman Catholic historian, Konrad Repgen (born 1923), who, in condemning student violence, did not mention the attempted assassination of Dutschke in April 1968, or the press campaign against the student leader to which the shooting on a Berlin street was obviously related, as the subsequent statements of the perpetrator indicated.[69] Liberal critics pointed out that conservatives had nothing to say about the pressing problems that outraged the consciousness of younger Germans, above all the eight-month silence of the Berlin city government about the shooting of Ohnesorg, and the establishment's exaggerated outrage about a few thrown rocks and protests.[70]

Terrorism and Critical Theory

If the forty-fivers were divided about the meaning of the student movement, they did not fight among themselves in the 1960s. The Weimar Syndrome did not have them in its thrall. During the 1970s, however, when what even liberals as well as conservatives called the campus-based "nihilistic counterculture" developed, along with its perceived poison fruit—leftist terrorism—the familiar crisis mentality began to spread to forty-fiver intellectuals as well.

Their debates were accordingly acrimonious. Liberals who had first expressed sympathy for the students now joined conservatives in denouncing Critical Theory and the supposed violent effects of the Frankfurt School.

Bracher complained that the "Habermas-wave" had been "eagerly adopted and vulgarized" by young radicals, who had collapsed knowledge into interest, and society into the state.[71] Hans Maier thought that the youth movement's "vulgar brand of actionistic Marxism" was becoming increasingly embarrassing for Adorno and Habermas.[72] Writing in 1976, the philosopher Nicholas Lobkowicz agreed that Habermas's influential *Knowledge and Human Interests*,[73] whose central thesis he recognized the critical theorist himself had by then largely abandoned, had nevertheless "become, in varying degrees of vulgarization, an article of faith for many self-styled critical academic politicians and theoreticians."[74] The socialist critique, Bracher continued, "culminated in a sociologically and psychologically founded emancipation protest against society *as such*, against its values and taboos, and ultimately as political criticism of the system generally."[75] The problem of left-wing extremism, the philosopher Robert Spaemann declared, did not issue from *any* political theory, but one that was unable to justify authority short of the ideal speech situation.[76]

Hermann Lübbe, too, argued against the conflation of the theoretical and social grounding of norms, maintaining that it contained the basic structure of totalitarian domination and terrorism. Grounding norms on the basis "of the most compelling argument" did not lead necessarily to extremism, he implied. Its "political meaning," however, when combined with what he called the "terroristic imperative"—the identity of the empirical subject (an individual or a party) with the transcendental—was that a group with the "terrorist imperative" considered itself in possession of norms that were more "real" (i.e., true and just) than the norms that were actually obtained. The inevitable consequence was the transition of the terrorist imperative into terrorist action. Lübbe did not go so far as to name which individuals or groups were possessed by the "terrorist imperative" (other than the terrorists themselves, of course), but his use of the Habermasian vocabulary in the context of the public attack on the Frankfurt School in the Fall of 1977 would have left his readers with a clear picture of who he had in mind.[77] Prominent conservative politicians such as Franz Joseph Strauss and Hans Filbinger (the latter being disgraced by revelations of his activities as a Nazi judge, partly on the basis of misinformation fed to the German media by the STASI[78]) publicly laid the blame for terrorism at the feet of the Frankfurt School, who, they claimed, were the terrorists' "spiritual fathers."

Sontheimer, who had defended the students, now came to the same conclusion as Lübbe. Characterizing the Bonn Republic in terms of "structural" or "objective violence" logically implied a utopian state of equality, the unrealizability of which could lead to terrorism.[79] The analogy had unnecessarily accentuated nagging doubts about the system and had thereby destabilized its institutions. Left-wing theory that had its origins in the systemic social crisis only served to worsen it.[80]

For these liberals and conservatives, living proof of the fruit of the "cultural revolution" was the leftist milieu on the campuses.[81] During the notorious fall of 1977, when numerous terrorist attacks provoked a mood of hysteria among middle class Germans and the state took extraordinary security measures that were interpreted by many as a resurrection of authoritarianism, the campuses were targeted as the breeding ground of the so-called terrorist "sympathizers." The social democratic politician Peter Glotz estimated that about fifteen to twenty percent of students (about 140,000 to 170,000) agreed with the student author of a notorious article who admitted he had experienced "clandestine joy" at the recent assassination of Federal prosecutor Siegfried Buback.[82] This shared joy was evidence enough for Sontheimer and others that the left as a whole was responsible for the terrorist disaster.[83]

Habermas naturally rejected Sontheimer's implicit Weimar analogy only to substitute it with one of his own. The official ban on employing radicals was akin to Bismarck's anti-socialist laws a century later. Once again, the only progressive element in the Republic, its intellectuals, was being demonized. Old authoritarian traditions were rearing their ugly heads. The real threat was not the left, but an establishment that was able to use terrorism to identify an internal enemy (i.e., the left) and thereby stifle any critique. "Only a state that makes the fascist self-understanding of Carl Schmitt its own, needs internal enemies that it can fight, as is the case with foreign enemies during war."[84]

He reminded everyone that he and other leftist intellectuals had been among the first to criticize what Adorno called "student activism." He himself had referred to "leftist fascism" because the ideology of radical voluntarism and violence reminded him of the German conservative revolutionary professors of his youth, Carl Schmitt and Martin Heidegger. This was his generational experience speaking. The conservative argument that the Frankfurt School was somehow "objectively responsible" for the terrorism was the kind of argument Stalinists used in another context. Invoking the specter of Weimar, he suggested that Strauss wanted to impose "Franco's legacy in the Federal Republic."[85]

The reflex to identify one's own tradition with the victims of Nazism appeared unavoidable. Hans Buchheim (born 1922), the political scientist and contemporary historian at the *Institut für Zeitgeschichte* in Munich who had written early books on the Nazi regime, reversed the meaning of the Weimar Syndrome. He went so far as to argue that the older generation (the forty-fivers and older Germans) were being condemned by the sixty-eighters in terms of the same group-think as the Jews were in the 1930s and 1940s.[86]

Conclusion

The notorious "German Autumn" of 1977, with its terrorist killings and police reaction, marked the highpoint of intellectual and political polarization in the Federal Republic. Hereafter, the question of political violence subsided as much of the sixty-eighter milieu found a political vehicle in the new Green party, although anarchist and squatter scenes lived on in many German towns and cities. Massive demonstrations against the stationing of US missiles were a feature of the peace movement in the early 1980s, but public protest was the legitimate exercise of a democratic right, not a paranoid expression of political violence. The Weimar Syndrome seemed to lessen as the different fractions of the intelligentsia realized that changes in government did not spell the end of democracy, however defined. The political alignments of the "Historians' Dispute" of the mid 1980s, in which liberal intellectuals such as Bracher supported Habermas, showed they had other concerns. Now, many intellectuals worried that Helmut Kohl's stated intention to renationalize German politics entailed a reversion to the cultural politics of the 1950s rather than of the 1920 and 1930s.[87] Memory of the Holocaust and "overcoming the Nazi past" became a central question rather than *die Gewaltfrage* and West German democracy.[88] From 1982 to 1998, the student radicals accomplished the "long march through the institutions" that would create a new elite in the media, the universities, and with the Greens, at the highest branches of the German government.[89] If in the 1960s the students had seen themselves as "Hitler's children," that is, brought into the world by Nazified mothers and fathers, by the 1980s their opposition to the institutions of West Germany lessened as their own influence grew.[90] The anti-authoritarians had in their own way become a new kind of authority—and in that dialectical process had finally overcome the Weimar Syndrome.

Notes

1. Hans Ulrich Wehler, *Deutsche Gesellschaftsgeschichte*, 5 vols. (Munich, 1987–2008), 4: 942–44; Michael Geyer, "The Place of the Second World War in German Memory and History," *New German Critique*, no. 71 (Spring–Summer, 1997): 5–40; Atina

1. Grossmann, "A Question of Silence: The Rape of German Women by Soviet Occupation Soldiers," in *Women and War in the Twentieth Century*, ed. Nicole Ann Dombrowski (New York, 1999), 122–185.
2. Ulrich Herbert, ed., *National Socialist Extermination Policies* (New York, 2000).
3. Andrew Oppenheimer, "West German Pacifism and the Ambivalence of Human Solidarity, 1945–1968," *Peace and Change* 29, nos. 3–4 (2004): 353–389.
4. A. Dirk Moses, "The Weimar Syndrome in the Federal Republic of Germany: Carl Schmitt and the Forty-Fiver Generation of Intellectuals," in *Leben, Tod und Entscheidung: Studien zur Geistesgeschichte der Weimarer Republik*, ed. Holger Zaborowski and Stephan Loos (Berlin, 2003), 187–207.
5. Karl Dietrich Bracher, "Wird Bonn doch Weimar?" *Der Spiegel*, 13 March 1967, 60.
6. J.G.A. Pocock, "Verbalizing a Political Act: Toward a Politics of Speech," in *Language and Politics*, ed. Michael Shapiro (Oxford, 1984), 38–39.
7. A. Dirk Moses, "The Forty-Fivers: A Generation Between Fascism and Democracy," *German Politics and Society* 17 (1999): 95–127.
8. Martin Jay, "When Did the Holocaust End? Reflections on Historical Objectivity", in his *Refractions of Violence* (New York, 2003).
9. Ibid., 374.
10. See Jens Hager, ed., *Die Rebellen von Berlin: Studentenpolitik an der freien Universität* (Cologne and Berlin, 1967), 50–51.
11. See Ulrich Chaussey, *Die Drei Leben des Rudi Dutschke* (Frankfurt, 1989), on Subversive Aktion, 37–39. On Dutschke's brand of Marxism, see Bernd Rabehl, *Rudi Dutschke, Revolutionär im geteilten Deutschland* (Dresden, 2002).
12. Lothar Fischer et al., *Gruppe SPUR, 1958–1965* (Regensburg, 1986).
13. See Dieter Kunzelmann, *Leisten Sie Keinen Widerstand* (Berlin, 1998).
14. Ibid., 51–73.
15. Rudi Dutschke, *Die Revolte* (Hamburg, 1983), 169.
16. Wolfgang Kraushaar, *Die Bombe im Jüdischen Gemeindehaus* (Hamburg, 2005), 29–30.
17. Ibid. See also Kraushaar's *Die RAF und der linke Terrorismus* (Hamburg, 2006).
18. See Rudi Dutschke, "Die Widerspruche des Spätkapitalismus, die anti-autoritären Studenten und ihr Verhältnis zur Dritten Welt," in Uwe Bergman et al., *Rebellion der Studenten* (Frankfurt, 1968), 33–57. See also his interview with Günther Gaus from 1970, in Rudi Dutschke, *Mein langer Marsch* (Hamburg, 1980), esp. 51.
19. Cited by Ingo Juchler, *Rebellische Subjektivität und Internationalismus* (Marburg, 1989), 8.
20. Wolfgang Kraushaar, *1968 als Mythos, Chiffre und Zäsur* (Hamburg, 2000), 329.
21. See Bernard Larrson, *Berlin—Hauptstadt der Republik—Fotographien aus einer geteilten Stadt 1961–1968* (Göttingen, 1968).
22. See Hager, *Die Rebellen von Berlin*, 50–52. The Basic Law, Article 3, paragraph 1 states that, "all persons shall be equal before the law." The police asserted (with dubious legal reasoning) that the students were placing themselves above the law.
23. Bergmann et al., *Rebellion der Studenen*, 18.
24. See Jürgen Miermeister and Joachem Staadt, *Provokationen: Die Studenten und Jugendrevolte in ihren Flugblättern* (Darmstadt, 1980), 82.
25. Interview with Bernd Rabehl, Berlin, 27 August 2006. On the three different strands inside the New Left in relation to the seizure of power (Neo-Marxists, Anti-Authoritarians, and Radical Socialists), see Wighard Härdtl, "Strategie der neuen Linken zur Machtergreifung," in *Die Studentische Protestbewegung*, ed. Heinrich Barth (Mainz, 1971), 95–123.

26. A bestseller at the time popularized these ideas: Bahman Nirumand, *Persien, Modell eines Entwicklungslandes oder Die Diktatur der Freien Welt* (Hamburg, 1967).
27. The presence of the Iranian secret police was widely reported, see "Berlin—Knüppel frei," *Der Spiegel*, 12 June 1967, 41. See also "Die Jubelperser," *Die Zeit*, 30 June 1967.
28. "Die FDJ senkte die Fahnen," *Der Abend*, 9 June 1967.
29. "Die aufsässigen Studenten von Berlin," *Der Spiegel*, 5 June 1967, 48–50.
30. See Bernd Rabehl, *Am Ende der Utopie* (Berlin, 1988), 238–242.
31. Herbert Marcuse, *Five Lectures: Psychoanalysis, Politics and Utopia*, trans. Jeremy J. Shapiro and Shierry M. Weber (Boston, 1970), 62.
32. See "Diskussion zu 'Das Problem der Gewalt in der Opposition' vom 10–13 Juli 1967 in Berlin," in Rudi Dutschke, *Die Revolte* (Hamburg, 1977), 183–205.
33. Chaussey, *Die Drei Leben des Rudi Dutschke*, 168.
34. "Studenten—der lange Marsch," *Der Spiegel*, 11 December 1967, 52.
35. Gretchen Dutschke-Klotz, *Wir hatten ein schönes barbarisches Leben* (Cologne, 1996), 183.
36. See Dietrich Thränhardt, *Geschichte der Bundesrepublik* (Frankfurt, 1986), 175. See also Rudolf Augstein, "Notstand durch Gesetz?" *Der Spiegel*, 6 November 1967.
37. "Gewaltsamer Aufruhr vor dem Landesgericht," *Berliner Morgenpost*, 5 November 1968.
38. All of these ideas can be found in a discussion between Dutschke, Rabehl, Enzensberger, and Semmler in "Ein Gespräch über die Zukunft," *Kursbuch* 14 (October 1967): 146–174.
39. See Chaussey, *Die Drei Leben des Rudi Dutschke*, 179–180.
40. Jürgen Miermeister, *Rudi Dutschke* (Hamburg, 1986), 92–94.
41. Jürgen Miermeister has noted the many parallels between Jesus and Dutschke's messianism, see his ibid., 38–39.
42. "Durch den Mord an King angeregt," *Tagesspiegel*, 14 April 1968.
43. Horst Ehmke, "Die Generation, auf die wir gewartet haben [1968]," in his *Politik der praktischen Vernunft* (Frankfurt, 1969), 187–207.
44. See the documentation in Wolfgang Kraushaar, ed., *Frankfurter Schule und Studentenbewegung. Von der Flaschenpost zum Molotowkocktail, 1945 bis 1995*, 3 vols. (Hamburg, 1998); Detlev Claussen and Regine Dermitzel, eds., *Universität und Widerstand. Versuch einer Politischen Universität in Frankfurt* (Frankfurt, 1968).
45. Rolf Wiggershaus, *The Frankfurt School: Its History, Theories, and Political Significance*, trans. Michael Robertson (Cambridge, MA, 1994), 632–633.
46. Jürgen Habermas, "Diskussionsbeiträge," in his *Protestbewegung und Hochschulreform* (Frankfurt, 1969), 148. He later regretted and withdrew the term.
47. Günter Grass, "Gewalt ist wieder Gesellschaftsfähig," *Der Spiegel*, 6 May 1968, 57.
48. Peter von Oertzen, "Was ist eigentlich Linksfaschismus?" *Süddeutsche Zeitung*, 13/14 January 1968.
49. Hartmut von Hentig, "Die Sache und die Demokratie," *Die Neue Sammlung* 9 (1969): 121; von Hentig, "Die grosse Beschwichtigung," *Merkur* 22 (1968): 385–400.
50. Ralf Dahrendorf, "Aktive und passive Öffentlichkeit," *Merkur* 21 (December 1967): 1109–1122; von Hentig, "Sozialismus oder Liberalismus," *Die Zeit*, 21 November 1969, 59–60.
51. "Appel an den Berliner Senat," *Die Zeit*, 8 March 1962, 6. The signatories included Wolfgang Abendroth, Theodor W. Adorno, Richard F. Behrendt, Dieter Claessens, Wolfram Fischer, Otto Flechtheim, Ludwig von Friedeburg, Günter Grass, Jürgen Habermas, Werner Hofmann, Walter Jens, Walter Killy, Alexander Kluge, Christian

Graf von Krockow, Werner Maihofer, Fritz Raddatz, Hans Werner Richter, Wolfgang Schnurre, Jakob Taubes, Harald Weinrich.
52. Horst Krüger, "Wohin treibt die Protestbewegung?" *Merkur* 23 (September 1969): 883–886.
53. Karl Dietrich Bracher, "Die zweite Demokratie," *Die Zeit*, 12 December 1969, 54–55.
54. Joachim Fest, "Das Dilemma des studentischen Romantizismus," in *Revolution gegen den Staat? Die ausserparlamentarische Opposition-neue Linke*, ed. Hans Dollinger (Bern, 1968), 225.
55. Ibid., 239, 232.
56. M. Rainer Lepsius, "Unruhe als Studentenpflicht?" *Stimmen der Zeit*, no. 180 (1967): 299–310.
57. Kurt Sontheimer, "Antidemokratisches Denken in der Bundesrepublik," in his *Antidemokratisches Denken in der Weimarer Republik. Die politischen Ideen des deutschen Nationalismus zwischen 1918 und 1933* (Munich, 1968), 317–347.
58. Kurt Sontheimer, "Gefahr von rechts—Gefahr von links," in *Der Überdruss an der Demokratie: Neue Linke und alte Rechte—Unterschiede und Gemeinsamkeiten*, ed. Kurt Sontheimer et al. (Cologne, 1970), 1–43.
59. Kurt Sontheimer, "Die Demokratisierung der Universität," in *Reform als Alternative. Hochschullehrer antworten auf die Herausforderung der Studenten*, ed. Alexander Schwan (Cologne, 1969), 63–73.
60. Erwin Scheuch, "Zur Einleitung," in *Die Wiedertäufer der Wohlstandsgesellschaft. Eine kritische Untersuchung der "Neuen Linken" und ihrer Dogmen*, ed. Erwin Scheuch (Cologne, 1967), 7–13.
61. Ibid., 11.
62. Hermann Lübbe, "Das Elend der Universitäten [1970]," in his *Hochschulreform und Gegenaufklärung* (Freiburg, 1972), 62–64.
63. Rudolf Krämer-Badoni, "Die zweite Jugendbewegung," *Aus Politik und Zeitgeschichte* 44 (1967): 3–16.
64. Karl Willy Beer, "Die Demokratie in Gefahr," *Die Politische Meinung* 13 (1968): 3–6.
65. Giselher Schmidt, *Hitlers und Maos Söhne* (Frankfurt am Main, 1969), 17.
66. Ernst Topitsch, *Die Freiheit der Wissenschaft und politischer Auftrag der Universität*, 2nd ed. (Neuwied, 1969).
67. Peter Glotz, "Die bündischen Professoren," *Süddeutsche Zeitung*, 18 November 1970, 8.
68. Helga Grebing, *Linksradikalismus gleich Rechtsradikalismus: Eine falsche Gleichung* (Stuttgart, 1971).
69. Konrad Repgen, "Staatskrise?" *Hochland* 60 (1967/8): 474–477. See the letter from Josef Bachman to Dutschke, 15 January 1969, in Rudi Dutschke, *Mein langer Marsch*, 134.
70. Hans Schwab-Felish, "Versuch einer Replik," *Merkur* 23 (February 1969): 121–124.
71. Karl Dietrich Bracher, *Schlüsselwörter in der Geschichte* (Düsseldorf, 1978), 28.
72. Hans Maier, "Reform in der Demokratie," in Schwan, *Reform as Alternative*, 26.
73. *Der Spiegel* described his influence in the following manner: "No work by a German philosopher over the past decade has found as much international resonance." In "Immer Diskutieren," *Der Spiegel*, 28 March 1973, 141.
74. Nicholas Lobkowicz, "Erkenntnisleitende Interessen," in *Die politische Herausforderung der Wissenschaft. Gegen eine ideologisch verplante Forschung*, ed. Kurt Hubner et al. (Hamburg, 1976), 55.
75. Karl Dietrich Bracher, *The Age of Ideologies. A History of Political Thought in the Twentieth Century* (New York, 1984), 213.

76. Robert Spaemann, "Die Utopie des guten Herrschers," *Zur Kritik der politischen Utopie* (Stuttgart, 1977), 135.
77. Hermann Lübbe, "Freiheit und Terror," *Merkur* 31 (September 1977): 819–829.
78. See Günter Bohnsack and Herbert Brehmer, *Auftrag Irreführung* (Hamburg, 1992), 59.
79. Kurt Sontheimer, "Gewalt und Terror in der Politik," *Neue Rundschau* 1 (1977): 1–12.
80. Kurt Sontheimer, *Das Elend unserer Intellektuellen. Linke Theorie in der Bundesrepublik* (Hamburg, 1976), 278, 289.
81. Jeremy Varon, *Bringing the War Home: The Weather Underground, the Red Army Faction, and Revolutionary Violence in the Sixties and Seventies* (Berkeley and Los Angeles, 2004).
82. Peter Glotz, "Jeder fünfte denkt etwa so wie Mescalero," *Der Spiegel*, 3 October 1977, 54.
83. Kurt Sontheimer, "Um eine Basis der Gemeinsamkeit," *Süddeutsche Zeitung*, 26/27 November 1977.
84. Jürgen Habermas, "Verteuflung kritischen Denkens," *Süddeutsche Zeitung*, 26/7 November 1977.
85. Jürgen Habermas, "Probe für Volksjustiz," *Der Spiegel*, 10 October 1977, 32.
86. Hans Buchheim, "Der Protest aus falsch bewältigter Vergangenheit," *Frankfurter Allgemeine Zeitung*, 6 March 1968, 2.
87. See Elliot Neaman, *A Dubious Past: Ernst Jünger and the Politics of Literature after Nazism* (Berkeley and Los Angeles, 1999), chap. 7.
88. A. Dirk Moses, *German Intellectuals and the Nazi Past* (Cambridge, 2007).
89. Rudi Dutschke would not have recognized this process as his "long march," by which he meant subverting, not joining, the elite. Tony Judt is correct in his assessment that Dutschke managed to combine in this phrase both Mao and Trotsky, since the contemporary Trotskyite strategy was "enterism," that is, the infiltration of institutions such as trade unions and universities and subverting them from the inside. See his *Postwar: A History of Europe Since 1945* (New York, 2005), 407.
90. In 1998, the fourteenth *Bundestag* under Gerhard Schroeder had 332 members from the 1968 generation (out of a total of 669). They were far more likely to be working at the universities, or in the sphere of art, literature or media, than in business, administration or the military. Niklas Luhmann, *Zum Begriff der sozialen Klasse*, cited by Heinz Bude, *Das Altern einer Generation* (Frankfurt am Main, 1995), 95n1.

Bibliography

"Appel an den Berliner Senat." *Die Zeit*, 8 March 1962.
Augstein, Rudolf. "Notstand durch Gesetz?" *Der Spiegel*, 6 November 1967.
Barth, Heinrich, ed. *Die Studentische Protestbewegung*. Mainz, 1971.
Bergmann, Uwe et al. *Rebellion der Studenen*. Frankfurt, 1968.
"Berlin—Knüppel frei." *Der Spiegel*, 12 June 1967.
Bohnsack, Günter and Herbert Brehmer. *Auftrag Irreführung*. Hamburg, 1992.
Bracher, Karl Dietrich. *The Age of Ideologies. A History of Political Thought in the Twentieth-Century*. New York, 1984.

———. *Schlüsselwörter in der Geschichte*. Düsseldorf, 1978.
———. "Wird Bonn doch Weimar?" *Der Spiegel*, 13 March 1967.
———. "Die zweite Demokratie." *Die Zeit*, 12 December 1969.
Buchheim, Hans. "Der Protest aus falsch bewältigter Vergangenheit." *Frankfurter Allgemeine Zeitung*, 6 March 1968.
Bude, Heinz. *Das Altern einer Generation*. Frankfurt, 1995.
Chaussey, Ulrich. *Die Drei Leben des Rudi Dutschke*. Frankfurt am Main, 1989.
Claussen, Detlev and Regine Dermitzel, eds. *Universität und Widerstand: Versuch einer Politischen Universität in Frankfurt*. Frankfurt, 1968.
Dahrendorf, Ralf. "Aktive und passive Öffentlichkeit." *Merkur* 21 (December 1967): 1109–1122.
———. "Sozialismus oder Liberalismus." *Die Zeit*, 21 November 1969.
"Die aufsässigen Studenten von Berlin." *Der Spiegel*, 5 June 1967, 48–50.
"Die FDJ senkte die Fahnen." *Der Abend*, 9 June 1967.
"Durch den Mord an King angeregt." *Tagesspiegel*, 14 April 1968.
Dutschke-Klotz, Gretchen. *Wir hatten ein schönes barbarisches Leben*. Cologne, 1996.
Dutschke, Rudi. *Mein langer Marsch*. Hamburg, 1980.
———. *Die Revolte*. Hamburg, 1977.
———. "Die Widerspruche des Spätkapitalismus, die anti-autoritären Studenten und ihr Verhältnis zur Dritten Welt." In Bergman et al., *Rebellion der Studenten*. Frankfurt, 1968.
Ehmke, Horst. "Die Generation, auf die wir gewartet haben [1968]." In *Politik der praktischen Vernunft*. Frankfurt, 1969.
"Ein Gespräch über die Zukunft." *Kursbuch*. 14 October, 1967.
Fest, Joachim. "Das Dilemma des studentischen Romantizismus." In *Revolution gegen den Staat? Die ausserparlamentarische Opposition-neue Linke*, edited by Hans Dollinger. Bern, 1968.
Fischer, Lothar et al. *Gruppe SPUR, 1958–1965*. Regensburg, 1986.
"Gewaltsamer Aufruhr vor dem Landesgericht." *Berliner Morgenpost*, 5 November 1968.
Geyer, Michael, "The Place of the Second World War in German Memory and History," *New German Critique*, no. 71 (Spring–Summer, 1997): 5–40.
Glotz, Peter. "Die bündischen Professoren." *Süddeutsche Zeitung*, 18 November 1970.
———. "Jeder fünfte denkt etwa so wie Mescalero." *Der Spiegel*, 3 October 1977, 54.
Grass, Günter. "Gewalt ist wieder Gesellschaftsfähig." *Der Spiegel*, 6 May 1968.
Grossmann, Atina. "A Question of Silence: The Rape of German Women by Soviet Occupation Soldiers." In *Women and War in the Twentieth Century*, edited by Nicole Ann Dombrowski. New York, 1999.
Habermas, Jürgen. "Diskussionsbeiträge." *Protestbewegung und Hochschulreform*. Frankfurt, 1969.
———. "Probe für Volksjustiz." *Der Spiegel*, 10 October 1977.
———. "Verteuflung kritischen Denkens." *Süddeutsche Zeitung*, 26/7 November 1977.
Hager, Jens, ed. *Die Rebellen von Berlin. Studenenpolitik an der freien Universität*. Cologne and Berlin, 1967.
Herbert, Ulrich, ed. *National Socialist Extermination Policies*. New York, 2000.
Jay, Martin, "When Did the Holocaust End? Reflections on Historical Objectivity." In *Refractions of Violence*. New York, 2003.
"Die Jubelperser." *Die Zeit*, 30 June 1967.
Juchler, Ingo. *Rebellische Subjektivität und Internationalismus*. Marburg, 1989.
Judt, Tony. *Postwar: A History of Europe Since 1945*. New York, 2005.
Kraushaar, Wolfgang. *1968 als Mythos, Chiffre und Zäsur*. Hamburg, 2000.

———. *Die Bombe im Jüdischen Gemeindehaus*. Hamburg, 2005.
———. *Die RAF und der linke Terrorismus*. Hamburg, 2006.
———, ed. *Frankfurter Schule und Studentenbewegung. Von der Flaschenpost zum Molotowkocktail, 1945 bis 1995*. 3 vols. Hamburg, 1998.
Krüger, Horst. "Wohin treibt die Protestbewegung?" *Merkur* 23 (September 1969): 883–886.
Kunzelmann, Dieter. *Leisten Sie Keinen Widerstand*. Berlin, 1998.
Larrson, Bernard. *Berlin—Hauptstadt der Republik—Fotographien aus einer geteilten Stadt 1961–1968*. Göttingen, 1968.
Lepsius, M. Rainer. "Unruhe als Studentenpflicht?" *Stimmen der Zeit*, no. 180 (1967): 299–310.
Lübbe, Hermann. "Freiheit und Terror." *Merkur*, no. 31 (September 1977): 819–829.
Marcuse, Herbert. *Five Lectures: Psychoanalysis, Politics and Utopia*. Translated by Jeremy J. Shapiro and Shierry M. Weber. Boston, 1970.
Miermeister, Jürgen. *Rudi Dutschke*. Hamburg, 1986.
———, and Joachen Staadt. *Provokationen: die Studenten und Jugendrevolte in ihren Flugblättern*. Darmstadt, 1980.
Moses, A. Dirk. "The Forty-Fivers: A Generation Between Fascism and Democracy." *German Politics and Society* 17 (1999): 95–127.
———. *German Intellectuals and the Nazi Past*. Cambridge, 2007.
———. "The Weimar Syndrome in the Federal Republic of Germany: Carl Schmitt and the Forty-Fiver Generation of Intellectuals." In *Leben, Tod und Entscheidung: Studien zur Geistesgeschichte der Weimarer Republik*, edited by Holger Zaborowski and Stephan Loos. Berlin, 2003.
Neaman, Elliot. *A Dubious Past; Ernst Jünger and the Politics of Literature after Nazism*. Berkeley, CA, 1999.
Nirumand, Bahman. *Persien, Modell eines Entwicklungslandes oder Die Diktatur der Freien Welt*. Hamburg, 1967.
Oppenheimer, Andrew. "West German Pacifism and the Ambivalence of Human Solidarity, 1945–1968." *Peace and Change* 29, nos. 3–4 (2004): 353–389.
Pocock, J.G.A. "Verbalizing a Political Act: Toward a Politics of Speech." In *Language and Politics*, edited by Michael Shapiro. Oxford, 1984.
Rabehl, Bernd. *Am Ende der Utopie*. Berlin, 1988.
———. *Rudi Dutschke, Revolutionär im geteilten Deutschland*. Dresden, 2002.
Scheuch, Erwin. "Zur Einleitung." In *Die Wiedertäufer der Wohlstandsgesellschaft. Eine kritische Untersuchung der 'Neuen Linken' und ihrer Dogmen*. Cologne, 1967.
Sontheimer, Kurt. "Antidemokratisches Denken in der Bundesrepublik." In Sontheimer, *Antidemokratisches Denken in der Weimarer Republik. Die politischen Ideen des deutschen Nationalismus zwischen 1918 und 1933*, 317–347. Munich, 1968.
———. "Die Demokratisierung der Universität." In *Reform als Alternative. Hochschullehrer antworten auf die Herausforderung der Studenten*, edited by Alexander Schwan, 63–73. Cologne, 1969.
———. *Das Elend unserer Intellektuellen. Linke Theorie in der Bundesrepublik*. Hamburg, 1976.
———. "Gewalt und Terror in der Politik." *Neue Rundschau* 1 (1977): 1–12.
———. "Um eine Basis der Gemeinsamkeit." *Süddeutsche Zeitung*, 26/27 November 1977.
———, ed. "Studenten; der lange Marsch." *Der Spiegel*, 11 December 1967.
——— et al., ed. "Gefahr von rechts—Gehahr von links." In *Der Überdruss an der Demokratie: Neue Linke und alte Rechte—Unterschiede und Gemeinsamkeiten*, 1–43. Cologne, 1970.

Spaemann, Robert. "Die Utopie des guten Herrschers." In *Zur Kritik der politischen Utopie*. Stuttgart, 1977.
Thränhardt, Dietrich. *Geschichte der Bundesrepublik*. Frankfurt am Main, 1986.
Varon, Jeremy. *Bringing the War Home: The Weather Underground, the Red Army Faction, and Revolutionary Violence in the Sixties and Seventies*. Berkeley and Los Angeles, 2004.
von Hentig, Hartmut. "Die grosse Beschwichtigung." *Merkur* 22 (1968): 385–400.
———. "Das Sache und die Demokratie." *Die Neue Sammlung* 9 (1969).
von Oertzen, Peter. "Was ist eigentlich Linksfaschismus?" *Süddeutsche Zeitung*, 13/14, January 1968.
Wehler, Hans Ulrich. *Deutsche Gesellschaftsgeschichte, 1914–1949*. 4 vols. Munich, 2003.
Wiggershaus, Rolf. *The Frankfurt School: Its History, Theories, and Political Significance*. Translated by Michael Robertson. Cambridge, MA, 1994.

Part III

Critical Theory and Global Politics

From "The Dialectic of Enlightenment" to "The Origins of Totalitarianism" and the Genocide Convention
Adorno and Horkheimer in the Company of Arendt and Lemkin

Seyla Benhabib

Martin Jay has devoted his distinguished career to articulating that unique blend of philosophical analysis and social-scientific research that we have since come to characterize as "The Critical Theory of the Frankfurt School."[1] Jay's early book, *The Dialectical Imagination*, conveyed the originality and depth of this project to a generation of graduate students and young scholars.[2] And it contributed in no small measure to the decision of many of us to go to Germany to study this tradition. This was certainly the case for me in going to the Max Planck Institute in Starnberg to study with Jürgen Habermas from 1979 to 1981. For that inspiration, and guidance throughout the years, I am grateful to Marty.

* * * * *

At the center of the Critical Theory of the Frankfurt School is the reckoning with the European catastrophe of the past century—the rise of National Socialism, Soviet Communism, and the Holocaust.[3] One of the earliest undertakings of the Institut für Sozialforschung was the study on "Authority and the Family," investigating why the German working and salaried classes shifted their support away from left parties generally and toward more authoritarian political solutions.[4] The study found that the undermining of the authority of the father through the loss of his economic independence in the marketplace and his increasing subjection to the "impersonal" forces of the growing economic and state conglomerates drained the sources of revolt against patriarchy, which led to the emergence of weakened personality types, incapable of resisting the established status quo.

Already in this study a strong presupposition emerged that would guide the work of the Frankfurt School: the assumption that the rise of European anti-Semitism, and eventually the Holocaust, needed to be explained within a *universalistic* framework, within which anti-Semitism was *one* among many other kinds of prejudice that still existed in European society in the wake of the Enlightenment. This universalist orientation continued in the major study in which Adorno collaborated during his stay in New York in the 1940s, and for which Max Horkheimer acted as Director of the Department of Scientific Research of the American Jewish Committee. It was named *The Authoritarian Personality* and appeared in the series *Studies in Prejudice*, edited by Horkheimer and Samuel H. Flowerman.[5] As Jay notes, when questioned about the absence of a study of anti-Semitism in relation to authoritarianism, in the earlier studies on authority and the family, Friedrich Pollock replied, "'one didn't want to advertise that.' It perhaps also corresponded to the Institut's unwillingness to draw unnecessary [sic!] attention to the overwhelmingly Jewish origins of its members."[6] Even the more psychoanalytically oriented passages on "Elements of Anti-Semitism" in the *Dialectic of Enlightenment* do not abandon this universalistic perspective.

By contrast, for many Jewish thinkers and historians of this period, such as Gershom Scholem, Leo Strauss, Jacob Taubes, Martin Buber, Leo Baeck, and Kurt Blumenfeld, among others,[7] the European catastrophe was first and foremost a Jewish catastrophe that only manifested the transmutation of traditional Christian-Jewish hatred or "Jew hatred" (Leo Strauss) into the modern project of mass extermination, supported now by all of the means at the disposal of a technologically advanced state. According to this view, only the technology and mechanism of Jewish extermination were different, not the logic or structure of century-old hatred toward the Jews. Still, what remained unintelligible to many thinkers, as well as to many functionaries and officials of Jewish organizations inside and outside the Reich—what in fact was almost beyond comprehension for them—was the *totalizing* logic of the Nazi program of Jewish genocide.[8] Settling itself beyond instrumental logic, Nazi anti-Semitism aimed at the elimination of the Jewish race as such. This defied categories of Christian "Jew hatred" or even modern German anti-Semitism, both of which still permitted salvation to individual Jews through conversion, intermarriage, societal passing, and other kinds of compromise and subterfuge, while denying a distinct Jewish collective existence. Nazi anti-Semitism, which was based on pseudo-scientific race thinking, defied particularistic Jewish logics of explanation. In the more than half century since the end of World War II, these differences in theoretical orientation between the *universalistic* and *particularistic* modes of considering anti-Semitism and the events of the Holocaust have continued, and even intensified, as the scope and magnitude of the destruction of European Jewry have become manifest.[9]

In this essay, I wish to examine Adorno and Horkheimer's views on anti-Semitism in relation to Hannah Arendt's theses in *The Origins of Totalitarianism* and elsewhere.[10] Adorno and Horkheimer, as well as Arendt, are universalists in their methodological and normative orientations to the "Jewish question," and their explanations of anti-Semitism. What divides them in their approach to these matters is the theoretical utilization of political economy and psychoanalysis in the case of Adorno and Horkheimer, versus idiographic[11] historical narrative and culturally more holistic sociology in the case of Arendt. By exploring this topic, I hope to contribute to the beginnings of a long-overdue conversation and confrontation among these thinkers, who have marked many of us very deeply on both sides of the Atlantic. With the collapse of "really existing socialism" and the eclipse of Marxism, Hannah Arendt's star has risen in recent decades, while that of the Frankfurt School has dimmed. Nevertheless, there is still much to be gained from a careful comparative analysis of their work, because however deep their differences, their reaction to the catastrophe of the twentieth century was a *political* as opposed to a *theological* or a merely *philosophical* one. They never lost faith in human beings' capacity to "start anew" and change their collective conditions of existence (Arendt), or to anticipate the "wholly other" and imagine a better future (Horkheimer). Arendt tried to retrieve the project of political freedom, in the sense of building republics in which freedom could be housed, from the mystificatory clutches of Heideggerian philosophy. Members of the Frankfurt School evoked repeatedly the hope that human emancipation was not an empty, but a concrete, utopia. Hannah Arendt and members of the Frankfurt School are fundamentally united in their insistence upon the power of human beings to change their world even in the face of developments where despair seemed more plausible. Yet these subterranean bonds have not always been visible, and competition among these "émigré intellectuals" and their personal dislikes and old accounts, have dominated our understanding of their legacy.

To initiate this dialogue between Arendt and the Frankfurt School, I will focus on their approaches to anti-Semitism. The question of anti-

Semitism is a particularly sharp lens through which to observe Arendt's and Adorno and Horkheimer's theoretical commitments. Arendt's universalistic approach to explaining the origins of European anti-Semitism, and the solutions she offers to go beyond it, are strongly inflected by her more particularistic commitments to an autonomous Jewish politics in the interwar period of the nineteen-twenties and early nineteen-thirties that is neither simply Zionist nor anti-Zionist. She urges the Jews to defend themselves *politically as* Jews against the assault on them. In highlighting this aspect of Arendt's thought, I also wish to argue that Martin Jay's 1978 description of Arendt as a "political existentialist," who believes in the "primacy of the political," is not indebted to Carl Schmitt and Alfred Bauemler, as he asserts,[12] but is grounded in her own historical attempt to explain the rise of European anti-Semitism in the light of the political paradoxes and eventual failures of the modern nation-state in Europe in the interwar period and beyond. Arendt discovered politics, as a young student at the Universities of Marburg and Freiburg, not in the lectures or arms of Martin Heidegger, but through her interest in the Jewish question and through her friend and guide, Kurt Blumenfeld, the Zionist leader, whom she met in Heidelberg in 1926.

In the concluding sections of this essay, I briefly contrast Adorno and Horkheimer's, as well as Arendt's, considerable skepticism toward the "force of law" (Derrida), with Raphael Lemkin's response to the destruction of European Jewry by developing, from within the law of nations, a conception of genocide which is comparative and historical in scope. Lemkin's "legal universalism," much like Arendt's and that of Adorno and Horkheimer's, also attempts to mediate the universal and the particular. The Holocaust, for him, becomes *an example* rather than the *unique paradigm* of that chief crime against humanity, the crime of genocide.

The "Jews and Europe" (1939) and "Elements of Anti-Semitism" (1941)

Max Horkheimer's 1939 essay, "The "Jews and Europe," is a terse piece, written in apodictic style, with many memorable phrases, such as "He who does not wish to speak of capitalism should also be silent about fascism."[13] The essay is dominated by the contention that fascism and/or National Socialism, which are not distinguished from one another, "is the truth of modern society."[14] Horkheimer argues that in the general transition from liberal society to the authoritarian state (an ambiguous formula which refers to National Socialism as well as to Stalinist communism), the decline in relevance of the sphere of circulation has rendered the Jews also "superfluous," i.e., dispensable from the standpoint of state power. The Jews represented individualism and the principle of exchange and thus embodied the ideals and illusions of liberal capitalism in the nineteenth century. With the rise of "state capitalism,"[15] which imposed direct political controls on the economy and suspended, without wholly eliminating, the laws of the market, the function and usefulness of the Jews were coming to an end.

Not only in its reductionist explication of the complexity of Jewish experience in modern society since the Enlightenment in terms of political economy, but also in its insistence on the primacy of the economic, this early essay displays a "functionalist" account of anti-Semitism which was extremely short-sighted. Would any other group besides the Jews, occupying a similar position in the economy and society, have been subject to the same kinds of prejudice? Was anti-Semitism merely a function of economic positionality? Was not the presence of the Jews in the sphere of circulation as bankers and moneylenders, itself only explicable in the light of the anti-Semitic measures which in much of Europe prohibited the Jews from owning land, joining the military, and holding public office until and even after the French Revolution? How could the position of the Jews in modern European society be abstracted from the long history of reprisals and exclusions and eliminations to which they had been subject? Horkheimer's formulae fall very short here.

The only place in which Horkheimer shows some cultural sensitivity to the particular fate of European Jews, rather than viewing them only as placeholders within a general theory of class society, is in his comments on their condition as refugees and asylum seekers. He finds it understandable that the Jews as "emigrants" are unlikely to hold a mirror to capitalism, in which it may see its own fascist core, precisely in those countries where they are granted asylum.[16] Yet Horkheimer's empathy has its limits: the Jewish lamentations about the lost past, about the failure of liberalism, etc., he argues, are short-sighted as well as hypocritical, since "Even the French Revolution, which helped bourgeois economics gain a political victory and which gave Jews equality, was more ambivalent than many Jews today can even imagine. Not their ideas but usefulness defines the bourgeoisie ... The order which started as progressive in 1789 carried from its inception the tendency towards National Socialism within it."[17]

As Jay has documented, Horkheimer and Adorno's position on anti-Semitism was shifting throughout the 1940s.[18] In a letter to Herbert Marcuse of 1943, Horkheimer argued that "the problem of anti-Semitism is much more complicated than I thought in the beginning. On the one hand we have to differentiate radically between the economic-political factors which cause and use it, and the anthropological elements in the present type of man which respond to anti-Semitic propaganda as they would to other oppressive incentives; on the other hand we must show these factors in their consistent interconnection and describe how they permeate each other."[19]

Anson Rabinbach has noted that in this period, while the economic dimension continues to be very significant in Adorno and Horkheimer's explication of anti-Semitism, "the emphasis here is no longer on the *presence* of the Jews in the sphere of circulation, but on the Jews in the mental 'imagery' of Nazism, which metaphorically substitutes the Jews as the 'hated mirror image of capitalism.'"[20] This new analysis of anti-Semitism is announced in the "Elements of Anti-Semitism" in the *Dialectic of Enlightenment*.

In the *Dialectic of Enlightenment*, Adorno and Horkheimer maintain that the two moments which constitute the legacy of western modernity and the Enlightenment—namely the value of the autonomous personality and the emergence of a "value-free" and technologically based science of nature—are mutually incompatible. The promise of the Enlightenment to free humans from their self-incurred tutelage cannot be attained via a reason that functions as a mere instrument of self-preservation. "The worldwide domination of nature turns against the thinking subject himself; nothing remains of him but this eternally self-identical 'I think' that should accompany all my representations."[21]

The critique of the domination of nature, which is one of the central themes of this work, means that the Marxist view of history as enabling human emancipation through the increasing control of nature via the technological organization of social labor is wrong. Man's emancipation from nature is not progress; rather, it carries within itself the seeds of regression, and ultimately, of the oppression of inner as well as outer nature. The Marxian philosophy of history is now replaced by a Nietzschean vision of "progress" as sublimation of life instincts, self-repression, and the increase of resentment. Laboring activity, the act through which man uses nature for his own ends by acting as a force of nature himself, is indeed an instance of human cunning. As the interpretation of Odysseus reveals, however, the effort to master nature by becoming like it (*mimesis*) is paid for by the internalization of sacrifice. Labor is indeed the sublimation of desire; but the act of objectification in which desire is transformed into a product is not an act of self-actualization, but an act of fear which leads to the control of the nature within oneself. The Marxian view of the humanization of the species through social labor must be rejected.

One of the Notes appended to the text, "The Interest in the Body," announces this new orientation: "Beneath the familiar history of Europe runs another, subterranean one. It consists of the fate of those human instincts and passions repressed and displaced by civilization. From the perspective of the fascist present, in which what was hidden emerged to light, manifest history appears along with its darker side, omitted by the legends of the national state no less than by their progressive criticisms."[22] The stories of Odysseus and the Holocaust act almost as bookends of this self-destructive dynamic of Western Enlightenment: the myth which is Enlightenment and the Enlightenment which becomes myth through Nazi propaganda. We witness the birth of western civilization and its transformation into barbarism. The Jews are caught in the wild currents of this civilizational dynamic and become its privileged objects of sacrifice.

Myth, which relates how the hero constitutes his identity by repressing the forces of nature which threaten to engulf him, also expresses its obverse. Humanity pays for overcoming the fear of the other by internalizing the victim in an act of *mimesis*.[23] Yet, as the regression from culture to barbarism brought about by National Socialism shows, Odysseus's cunning (*List*), the origin of western *ratio*, has not been able to overcome humanity's original fear of the "other." The Jew remains the other, the stranger: the one who is human and subhuman at once. Whereas Odysseus's cunning consists in the attempt to appease otherness by becoming like it—Odysseus offers the Cyclops human blood to drink, sleeps with Circe, and listens to the Sirens—fascism, through false projection, makes the other like itself. "If mimesis makes itself like the surrounding world, so false projection makes the surrounding world like itself. If for the former the exterior is the model which the interior has to approximate, if for it the stranger becomes familiar, the latter transforms the tense inside ready to snap into exteriority and stamps even the familiar as the enemy."[24]

Fascism is a special case of organized paranoid delusion. Under the pressure of the super-ego, claim Adorno and Horkheimer, the ego projects its aggressive wishes as "evil intentions onto the outside world ... either in fantasy by identification with the supposed evil, or in reality by supposed self-defense."[25] What makes the Jews especially suitable to be the object of such paranoid fantasies, however, is not clearly identified. This choice, if one may call it that, is related less to the condition of the Jews in modern society than more to the history of Christian anti-Judaism. The God of Judaism is distant, forbidding, and "entangles his creatures in the net of guilt and merit";[26] Christianity, by contrast, tries to "lessen the horror of the absolute" by imagining God in the image of man. The Jewish God, who forbids representation in "graven images," is the originator of Enlightenment: further, also, of the distinction between religion and magic; of word and object; concept and referent. Monotheistic Judaism heralds the beginning of the *Entzauberung* (the loss of magic) in the world. God is not in nature, but the Lord of Nature and its Creator. Furthermore, through the covenant with their God, the Jewish race oblige themselves not to be tempted by natural instincts alone. The Ten Commandments are moral instruments of repression, contributing no less than the "wily" Odysseus himself, to the emergence of the subject of western civilization, as the subject of rational self-mastery and repression.

Adorno and Horkheimer draw upon the treasure throve of anti-Jewish imagery, amply present in German Philosophy from Hegel to Nietzsche.[27] What is noteworthy is that the metaphoric significations associated with the Jews are multiple, unstable, and equivocal: the Jews are viewed not only as the *originators* of the Enlightenment, but also as a nomadic people *resisting* Enlightenment; they are not only *enemies* of magic, but also suspected, throughout the Middle Ages, of *engaging* in magic; they are not only the source of *repressive morality*, but also the source of *immorality and of licentiousness*. The Jews are the floating signifiers of the National Social imagination. But if the sources of anti-Semitism lie in the deep entanglements of mimesis and false projection; of self-identity and through the domination of the other in the phylogenetic development of the human species, then as Anson Rabinbach points out, "It is ultimately not clear whether this version of primal anti-Semitism can usefully distinguish modern racism, Christian Jew-hatred (ancient or primordial), anti-Judaism, or whether—in the end—it has anything to do with the Jews at all."[28] By locating the sources of anti-Semitism in what has been called "the primordial history of subjectivity,"[29] Adorno and Horkheimer go so deep that they come dangerously close to dehistoricizing anti-Semitism and making it an eternal aspect of western and Christian thought. As Jay also notes, "For Horkheimer and Adorno, then, perhaps the ultimate source of anti-Semitism and its functional equivalent is the rage against the nonidentical that characterizes the totalistic dominating impulse of western civilization."[30] But at this level of generality, concrete Jewish historical experiences throughout different centuries and across countries of the Western world become mere "ciphers" of forces that lie much deeper. This is a conclusion with which Adorno and Horkheimer could have been satisfied, but which, bereft of specification, seems to repeat the thesis of "eternal anti-Semitism."

In Adorno and Horkheimer's various attempts to explain anti-Semitism, we witness a dilemma which is conceptual in nature: not only in the case of the explanation of anti-Semitism, but with prejudice and racism generally, if one's explanatory scheme is too general it will miss the specific constellation of experiences, images, and metaphors, which define others as "the Other"; if, on the other hand, one attempts to account for the "othering" of human groups in terms of the specific qualities of these groups themselves, one can be accused of blaming the victim. Attaining the right balance between the standpoint of the victim and that of the victimizer, between the agent of racism and the object of it, is a difficult task. Not only Adorno and Horkheimer, but Arendt as well has been accused of blaming the victim.[31]

Hannah Arendt and the "Jewish Question"

Arendt met the Zionist leader Kurt Blumenfeld in 1926 at a student event in Heidelberg. The two formed a life-long friendship, only to be interrupted by the publication of Arendt's book, *Eichmann in Jerusalem* (1963).[32] When Arendt was arrested by the Gestapo in the Spring of 1933, and was forced to flee to Paris from Prague with her mother, she had been carrying out research in the Prussian State Library at the request of Blumenfeld on the extent of anti-semitic measures undertaken by non-governmental organizations, business associations, and professional clubs, etc. Blumenfeld, in turn, was preparing to present this material at the eighteenth Zionist Congress.

Arendt's interest in Jewish matters has been amply documented, but what remains perhaps unexplained is why this interest was so acute on the part of the daughter of a middle class assimilated Jewish family. Undoubtedly, as Elisabeth Young-Bruehl has argued, part of the answer lies in the familial background.[33] Arendt's paternal grandfather, Max Arendt, was a staunch leader of the Jewish Community in Königsberg, and although an anti-Zionist, clearly a man who explicitly identified himself as a Jew. Her mother, an early sympathizer of Rosa Luxembourg, was a fiercely proud woman, who instructed her daughter to report to her immediately every word or gesture of anti-Semitism in school. Also not incidental is Arendt's deep awareness of the contrast between the experience of German Jewry, to whom she belonged, and East European Jewish refugees and permanent and temporary workers, who flocked to the city of Königsberg (now Kalinigrad), where Arendt grew up. This contrast between the affluent and emancipated German Jewry, who enjoyed civil and political rights, and their Eastern brethren, affected Arendt deeply and gave her a sense for the contrast among the experiences of various Jewish communities, which was unusual for its time.[34]

After completing her dissertation on St. Augustine's concept of love, Arendt turned to the biography of Rahel Levin Varnhagen, a Jewish *salonnière* born in Berlin in 1771, whose salon enjoyed considerable prestige until Napoleon's invasion of Germany in 1806. Intended as her *Habilitationsschrift*, this study was completed in 1933 except for the last two chapters, which were finished during her exile in 1938 in France. It appeared in English first in 1957 and in German second in 1959.[35]

There are manifold layers of reading that must be disentangled in approaching Arendt's attempt to tell Rahel Levin Varnhagen's story as she herself "might have told it."[36] In the early 1930s, Arendt's own understanding of Judaism in general and her relationship to her own Jewish identity were undergoing profound transformations, which were taking her away increasingly from the egalitarian, humanistic ideals of Kant, Lessing, and Goethe toward a recognition of the ineliminable fact of Jewish difference within German culture. The Rahel book documents the paradoxes of Jewish emancipation between the breakdown of the ghetto and the emergence of the nineteenth-century bourgeois Christian modern nation-state. It is in this small intermezzo between 1790 and 1806, at which point Napoleon enters Berlin, that Rahel Levin's salon in her "Berliner Dachstube" flourishes.

From the standpoint of Arendt's political philosophy as a whole and her subsequent analysis of anti-Semitism, the book on Varnhagen puts forth a category toward which Arendt remains deeply ambivalent—namely "society" and "the social." Varnhagen presided over an ephemeral social phenomenon, namely the *salons*, which were often held in the drawing rooms of well-to-do bourgeois houses, in which the public and the private, and the personal and the collective mixed and mingled, in unpredictable and flowing ways. Intimacy was encouraged, although one pretended not to notice; one had to take care not to violate the unwritten rules of good manners—"salonfähiges Verhalten."

Almost in every respect, the salons, as models of public space, contradict the *agonal* model of the public sphere that predominates Arendt's *The Human Condition*. Whereas the Greek polis and the public sphere characteristic of it exclude women (and children and servants generally), the salons are spaces dominated by female presence. Whereas in the public spaces of the polis speech is "serious," guided by the concern for "the good of all," the speech in salons is playful, amorphous, and freely mixes the good of all with the advantage of each. Whereas the public sphere of the polis suppresses eros, the salons cultivate it.

Yet Arendt does not use the salons as an alternative model of the public sphere in her later work, rather seeing in them the shortcomings of the "social" in general. The social tends toward conformity and the ennobling of private pursuits at the expense of collective goals. I believe Arendt thought this not because she was under the spell of Martin Heidegger, with whom she had already concluded her affair when she began writing the Varnhagen book, but because she became an increasingly political person, and critical of the illusions of the German-Jewish assimilated bourgeoisie. As the years proceeded and Arendt experienced the collapse of the political order upon her own flesh, in order to understand anti-Semitism, her schemata shifted from "the social" to the "political."[37] Much later, in *The Origins of Totalitarianism*, and with respect to Jewish acceptance into society, she was to remark: "This perversion of equality from a political into a social concept is all the more dangerous when a society leaves but little space for special groups and individuals, for then their differences become all the more conspicuous."[38]

In her reflections on anti-Semitism in the aftermath of the Holocaust and after the fate of German-Jewry had become sealed, Arendt put forth a radical contention: modern anti-Semitism, she argued, far from being an "eternal" dimension of the relationship between Jews and gentiles, represented, rather, a thoroughly modern phenomenon.[39] As such, it reflected the disintegration of traditional political structures in Europe and, in particular, the decline of the nation-state in the aftermath of European imperialism. According to Arendt, anti-Semitism had to be understood not in isolation, but in the context of a crisis of Western civilization that far exceeded the importance of the "Jewish Question."

In thus framing the "Jewish Question" against a much broader political background, Arendt challenged a number of traditional views on anti-Semitism. Foremost among them was the idea that modern anti-Semitism simply represented a new form of religiously motivated "Jew hatred." Against this view, Arendt argued that, in effect, "even the extent to which the former derives its arguments and emotional appeal from the latter is open to question." As she wrote in a crucial and characteristically controversial passage from the *Origins of Totalitarianism*:

> The notion of an unbroken continuity of persecutions, expulsions and massacres from the end of the Roman Empire to the Middle Ages, the modern era, and down to our own time, frequently embellished by the idea that modern anti-Semitism is no more than a secularized version of popular medieval superstitions, is no less fallacious (though of course less mischievous) than the corresponding antisemitic notion of a Jewish secret society that has ruled, or aspired to rule, the world since antiquity.[40]

Arendt's strong language in this passage is meant to drive home her point unambiguously: to understand the new in light of the old was, she suggests, to fundamentally misunderstand it. No amount of historical detail about the persecution of Jews could explain what she considered an unprecedented phenomenon. An adequate understanding of modern anti-Semitism therefore required new categories of thought. And to forge these categories, Arendt believed, it was necessary to reassess not only Jewish history, but European history as a whole.[41]

Arendt's understanding of anti-Semitism challenged established views on the "eternal" aspect of anti-Semitism in several important ways. First, it suggested that it was possible, and, indeed, necessary to construct a *theory* of anti-Semitism. Second, Arendt insisted that, in contrast to the religiously motivated anti-Semitism of the Middle Ages, modern anti-Semitism was a *political* phenomenon. And, third, she argued that, as a political phenomenon, it was situated at the nexus of three fundamental developments: European imperialism, the decline of the nation-state, and the failure of liberal emancipation. Underpinning all of these contentions, and thus Arendt's theory of anti-Semitism as a whole, was a fundamental paradox: modern anti-Semitism rose as the modern nation-state declined; therefore, the suggestion that anti-Semitism was a by-product of extreme nationalism was simply mistaken. As she explained, "unfortunately, the fact is that modern anti-Semitism grew in proportion as traditional nationalism declined, and reached its climax at the exact moment when the European system of nation-states and its precarious balance of power crashed."[42] It was only in light of these events, unfolding on a European and indeed a global scale, that it was possible to understand what would have been an otherwise deeply perplexing development: the enormous significance that the "Jewish problem" acquired for the Nazis.

Why is it that the "infernal machine" of Nazi totalitarianism was set in motion by the seemingly unimportant "Jewish problem"? The first two parts of *The Origins of Totalitarianism*, first published in 1951, represent Arendt's most comprehensive attempt to offer an answer. Arendt's answer breaks down the question into two parts: part I represents her attempt to explain "why the Jews"; part II, building on part I, grapples with the question of "why Nazism?" This answer is, however, inseparable from explaining "why the Jews." Both approaches treat anti-Semitism as a fundamentally political phenomenon that emerges as a consequence of radical transformations in the European balance of power.

Arendt's view, which is reflected in her careful historical reconstruction of the "Jewish Question" in part I, is that at least part of the explanation is to be found in the convergence of political, economic, and psychological factors that both tied the Jews to the nation-state and undermined their ability to adapt to its transformations. In effect, the story of part I is fundamentally an analysis of the self-destructive alliance between Jews and state power. The point of this analysis is to identify the circumstances that led to the emergence of modern anti-Semitism, as well as to challenge the idea that Jews were simply the hapless victims of eternal prejudice. The doctrine of "eternal anti-Semitism," Arendt argues, offered a convenient cover for "professional anti-Semites," for, "if it is true that mankind has insisted on murdering Jews for more than two thousand years, then Jew-killing is a normal, and even human, occupation and Jew-hatred is justified beyond the need of argument."[43] More disturbingly, however, it had also led Jews to abdicate responsibility for their own fate and thus to fatally underestimate the novelty and danger of modern anti-Semitism. As Arendt explains,

> Ignorance or misunderstanding of their own past were partly responsible for their fatal underestimation of the actual and unprecedented dangers which lay ahead. But one should also bear in mind that lack of political ability and judgment have been caused by the very nature of Jewish history, the history of a people without a government, without a country, and without a language.[44]

It was this apolitical condition of the Jews that had historically made the Jews indispensable allies of the nation-state.

The nation-state needed the Jews, since, from its very emergence, it relied both on their financial resources and on their political loyalty for its consolidation. In return, it rewarded wealthy Jews with a host of social privileges that made them dependent upon state power and prevented their integration into society. The Jews did not much object, as this privileged status coincided with their own aspiration to maintain a separate identity. The interests of the state and the interests of the Jews therefore seemed perfectly well matched.[45]

It is precisely because the nation-state, unlike its absolutist predecessor, was not allied with any specific class in society that it allied itself with the Jews.[46] The class of Jews that had inherited their wealth from the Court Jews of absolutist times seemed ideally suited for this purpose, as they formed the only group in society that "did not form a class of [its] own and ... did not belong to any of the classes in their countries."[47] As a result, they could offer the emergent state both the financial backing and the political loyalty it so desperately needed. The distance from Court Jew to European banker seemed but a short step away. And indeed, the European banker continued to be of use to the state even as it subsequently achieved a higher degree of consolidation. Even as their political role diminished as the result of subsequent political developments, Jewish bankers nevertheless remained useful as international mediators *among* nation-states.

As the fortunes of the nation-state waned, so did those of the Jews. The extraordinary capitalist development of the nineteenth century pushed the expansion of national economies eventually beyond the borders of the nation-state and came to rely increasingly on the exploitation of external resources. Unluckily for the Jews, in the ensuing imperial scramble, the bourgeoisie, which constituted the driving force behind economic expansion, came to rely on a very different kind of ally, "the mob" (*les declassés*), in its quest for power.

What, exactly, the "mob" is and who falls into that category is an issue of some difficulty in Arendt's thought. As Margaret Canovan explains, Arendt "speaks of the Mob as the 'residue' or even 'the refuse of all classes' accumulated from those left behind after each of capitalism's economic cycles. These individuals have lost their place in the class structure. They are burning with resentment against ordered society, and easily mobilized for violence by demagogues."[48] Nevertheless, one thing is clear: the mob has no interest in, or regard for, any of the institutions that had sustained the nation-state and disdained especially the institution at its very heart—the rule of law.

For their greed, then, Arendt argues, the bourgeoisie paid a high price indeed. Even though they had been initial allies, bourgeoisie and the mob soon found themselves at mortal odds, as the imperial scramble for Africa[49] turned out to be less a display of imperial power and more of a dress rehearsal for the bourgeoisie's own destruction at home.[50] Indeed, there was little reason why the violence, greed, and lawlessness unleashed by imperialism should stop at the boundaries of Europe. "The bourgeoisie succeeded in destroying the nation-state but won a Pyrrhic victory; the mob proved quite capable of taking care of politics by itself and liquidated the bourgeoisie along with all other classes and institutions."[51]

First and foremost among the mob's victims were the Jews, who had failed to make the transition from nation-state to imperialism, and thus became the most vulnerable group in European society and an easy target for the murderous impulses of the mob. What made the Jews particularly vulnerable to the mob, according to Arendt, was their status as both political and social outsiders. On this latter point, Arendt points to the fact that Jewish political emancipation coincided with the rise of imperialism in the late nineteenth century (in Germany, Jews achieved full political emancipation in 1871). As a result, Jews were cast into society *en masse*, that is, wealthy bankers and impoverished Jewish masses alike. Society, however, was no more inclined to accept the newly emancipated Jewish masses as equals than the new imperialist regimes were to maintain the formerly privileged status of wealthy Jews under the nation-state. In contrast to the nation-state, imperialism had little use for either. Politically obsolete and socially vulnerable, they were rendered "superfluous" in the context of the general disintegration of traditional political and social structures in the aftermath of the imperial collapse in World War I. "Anti-semitism reached its climax when the Jews had … lost their public functions and their influence, and were left with nothing but their wealth"[52]—a turning point in European history that coincided with "the exact moment when the European system of nation-states and its precarious balance of power crashed."[53]

It is instructive to compare Arendt's and Horkheimer's views here: they agree that the peculiar economic position occupied by the Jews as lenders and bankers, bailing out and supporting first the absolutist regimes of Europe and subsequently national governments, gave them a unique and problematical profile. They were "within the nation," but never really "of the nation." Both touch upon the resentment that the economic condition of the Jews gave rise to: for Horkheimer, given their prominence in the circulation sphere, the Jews became like a lightning rod toward which all sorts of anti-capitalist resentment would be channeled on the part of the masses. For Arendt, the economic position of the Jews gave them a "supra-national" and "proto-cosmopolitan" existence, which at one and the same time called forth and belied the universal belief in "the rights of man." The Jews seemed to represent "human rights as such." Yet at the same time, their problematic position within the nation also evidenced the vulnerability to which they were subject in virtue of not clearly belonging to a collectivity that would stand up for them. This is why for Arendt, as well as for Theodor Herzl, the Dreyfus case was so significant. Even after the legacy of the French Revolution, and within the "civic nation" of France, the Jews remained outsiders. After the Franco-Prussian War (1870–1871), Dreyfus, an Alsatian Jew and an officer in the French army, was accused of being a spy for the Germans. Jewish existence thus revealed the fragile balance between the universalistic aspirations of the modern nation-state and the principle of "national sovereignty." Such sovereignty would repeatedly be defined not in terms of a community of citizens and equals, but in terms of an ethnos of blood and belonging.[54]

Arendt's attempt to locate the sources of anti-Semitism not in the economic sphere alone, which she certainly did not ignore, but in the unresolved paradoxes of the modern state after the French Revolution would have seemed to the members of the Frankfurt School as a case of naïve idealism or even worse, liberalism. They never accepted the autonomy of the state from the economy and never really developed a theory of the modern liberal state, even when they speculated, as in Marcuse's case, on its demise.[55] Arendt, who saw the fate of the Jews as bound up with the frailty of the ideals of human rights, the rule of law for all, and popular sovereignty, was on firmer ground here. Her analysis of anti-Semitism led her to unearth much deeper tensions in the modern state system as such.

Undoubtedly, however, Arendt's antagonism toward psychological and psychoanalytical explanations in general within the realm of the political are exaggerated. Every citizen was also a child, and a woman or a man, or may be both or neither, and of ambiguous sexuality. By focusing on the "dignity of the public sphere," Arendt accomplished a much-needed correction against the reduction of political phenomena to the economic by the Marxists. But in decidedly pushing away the socio-psychological and cultural context that also shaped the sphere of the political and the psyche of the individual citizen, she may have undercut some of the prescience of her own vision of the political.

What has increasingly gained prominence in our times, during which the nation-state system of the post–WW II period is caught in the throes of deep and unpredictable transformations at times referred to as "postnationalism" or "postsovereignty," are Arendt's reflections on minorities, statelessness, and the plight of refugees. It is also at this point that we can see the threads connecting the experiences of the failed liberal emancipation of the German Jews to the collective experiences of the majority of Eastern European Jews, as articulated for us most poignantly through Raphael Lemkin's category of "genocide."

Arendt on Statelessness and "The 'Right to Have Rights'"

Arendt was one of the few political theorists of the past century who focused on the significance of the nationalities and minorities question that emerged in the wake of World War I as a harbinger of totalitarianism. The dissolution of the multinational and multiethnic empires such as the Russian, the Ottoman, and the Austro-Hungarian, and the defeat of the Kaiserreich led to the emergence of nation-states, particularly in eastern-central Europe, which enjoyed little religious, linguistic, or cultural homogeneity. These successor states—Poland, Austria, Hungary, Czechoslovakia, Yugoslavia, Bulgaria, Lithuania, Latvia, Estonia, the Greek and the Turkish republics—controlled territories in which large numbers of so-called "national minorities" resided. On 28 June 1919, the Polish Minority Treaty was concluded between President Woodrow Wilson and the Allied and Associated Powers, to protect the rights of minorities who made up nearly 40 percent of the total population of Poland at that time and consisted of Jews, Russians, Germans, Lithuanians, and others. Thirteen similar agreements were then drawn up with various successor governments "in which they pledged to their minorities civil and political equality, cultural and economic freedom, and religious toleration."[56] Not only were there fatal unclarities in how a "national minority" was to be defined; but the fact that the protection of minority rights applied only to the successor states of the defeated powers, and not to Great Britain, France, and Italy, which refused to consider the extension of the minority treaties to their own territories, created cynicism about the motivations of the Allied Powers in supporting minority rights in the first place. This situation led to anomalies whereby, for example, the German minority in Czechoslovakia could petition the League of Nations for the protection of its rights but the large German minority in Italy could not. The position of Jews in all successor states was also unsettled: if they were a "national minority," was it in virtue of their race, their religion, or their language that they were to be considered as such, and exactly which rights would this minority status entail?

For Arendt, the growing discord and political ineptitude of the League of Nations, and the emerging conflicts among so-called national minorities themselves, as well as the hypocrisy in the application of the Minority Treaties, all were harbingers of the developments in the 1930s. The modern nation-state was being transformed from an organ that would execute the rule of all for all of its citizens and residents into an instrument of the nation as a narrow "imagined" ethno-national community. "The nation has conquered the state, national interest had priority over law long before Hitler could pronounce 'right is what is good for the German people.'"[57]

The perversion of the modern state from an instrument of law into one of lawless discretion in the service of the nation was evident when states began to practice massive denaturalizations against unwanted minorities, creating millions of refugees, deported aliens, and stateless peoples across borders—special categories of humans created through the actions of nation-states. For in a territorially bounded nation-state system or in a "state-centric" international order, one's legal status is dependent upon protection by the highest authority controlling the territory upon which one resides and issuing the papers to which one is entitled. One becomes a *refugee* if one is persecuted, expelled, and driven away from one's homeland; one becomes a *minority* if the political majority in the polity declares that certain groups do not belong to the supposedly "homogeneous" people; one is a *stateless* person if the state whose protection one has hitherto enjoyed withdraws such protection, nullifying the papers it has granted; one is a *displaced* person if, having been rendered a refugee, a minority, or a stateless person, one cannot find another polity to recognize one as its member and remains in a state of limbo, caught between territories, none of which desire one to be its resident. It is here that Arendt concludes:

> We become aware of the existence of a right to have rights (and that means to live in a framework where one is judged by one's actions and opinions) and a right to belong to some kind of organized community, only when millions of people emerge who had lost and could not regain these rights because of the new global political situation.... The right that corresponds to this loss and that was never even mentioned among the human rights cannot be expressed in the categories of the eighteenth-century because

they presume that rights spring immediately from the "nature" of man ... the right to have rights, or the right of every individual to belong to humanity, should be guaranteed by humanity itself. *It is by no means certain whether this is possible.*[58]

Published in 1951, seven years before *The Human Condition*, this analysis of anti-Semitism both in terms of the crisis of the nation-state and the demise of the interwar state system, establishes that what Martin Jay calls "the primacy of the political,"[59] was central to Arendt's attempt to understand modern Jewish experience in Europe.[60] Her "political existentialism" owed, as far as I can tell, nothing to Carl Schmitt but everything to her own existential and political confrontation with the fate of the German Jews.

Conclusion: From *The Origins of Totalitarianism* to the Genocide Convention

Whether it be through the language of political economy, of psychoanalysis, or of German philosophy and sociology, Arendt and Adorno and Horkheimer remained German—more accurately, Western European—Jews in their reflections on anti-Semitism. For them, the Jewish faith was a private matter, guaranteed by the freedom of religious belief of the modern liberal state. The collective aspects of Jewish existence had become for their generation a matter of familial or social choice alone: one could go to synagogue or not; one could marry a Jew or not; one could raise one's children in the Jewish community or not. Of course, there were other thinkers and traditions more attuned to the collective dimension of Jewish existence in Germany as well and its transmission through the Hebrew language, liturgy, and tradition. "Das Jüdische Lehrhaus" and the Institut für Sozialforschung were housed in the same building.[61] Yet it was rare for the more traditional Jewish orientation to share universalist and universalizing impulses. This is precisely the legacy of Raphael Lemkin (1901–1959), whose efforts to have the United Nations adopt a Genocide Convention transformed the memory of the Holocaust into a universal experience of humankind as such. Lemkin attempted to have the law mediate the universal and the particular; he tried to reconcile the law of all nations with the irreducibly specific memories of nations and peoples facing extermination. It may be instructive in conclusion to briefly compare the dialectic of the universal and the particular for Lemkin, as well as for Arendt and Adorno and Horkheimer.

Arendt's, Adorno's, and Horkheimer's decided attempts to explain the phenomenon of Nazi anti-Semitism through categories situating this phenomenon within the broader history of western civilization and Enlightenment cannot be separated from their moral and political commitments to envisage a world in which human equality and human difference, tolerance and the acceptance of otherness prevail. For all of their dyspeptic, and often careless, dismissals of political liberalism, Adorno and Horkheimer are political liberals in the sense clarified for us by John Rawls.[62] The memory of the Holocaust and the destruction of European Jewry are transformed in their works into the utopian hope that an emancipated society can be housed within a republican framework. Put succinctly: their methodological universalism in explaining anti-Semitism cannot be separated from their belief that Jews can live a life of dignity, freedom, and tolerance only in a society that aspires to human emancipation or that guarantees public freedoms to all of its citizens.[63] In her emphasis on the good of politics and the dignity of the political, Arendt takes issue with the more privatistic conceptions of liberal freedoms as "negative liberties" and seeks ultimately a republican correction of liberal individualism.

Transforming the persecution not only of the Jews, but also of other peoples such as the Roma, the Poles, the Slovenes, and the Russians, into a universal legacy for mankind, actionable under the law of nations, was Raphael Lemkin's desideratum. In the Preface to *Axis Rule in Occupied Europe*, he writes: "The practice of extermination of nations and ethnic groups as carried out by the invaders is called by the author 'genocide,' a term deriving from the Greek word *genos* (tribe, race) and the Latin *cide* (by way of analogy, see homicide, fratricide)."[64] These few famous lines offered a term for what Churchill had called "a crime without a name." Lemkin himself, it has been pointed out, did not insist on the uniqueness of the Holocaust, but he attempted to formulate "a broad theory and definition of genocide, in which the Holocaust served as prime example, not as an exception."[65] Lemkin's broad conception of genocide, which in his unpublished notes was extended back to the history to the colonization of the Aztecs and the Incas, as well as the destruction of early Christians by the Romans, and less controversially to the genocide of Ottoman Armenians by the young Turks, has spawned a new field of "comparative genocide studies."[66]

Not only in terms of historical research, however, but in terms of more technical legal considerations as well, Lemkin's various definitions of genocide are elastic, and exhibit an "'instability' between the historical and the legal, between the cultural and the 'ethnical,' between intent and consequence."⁶⁷ According to The Genocide Convention, adopted on December 9 1948,

> genocide means any of the following acts with intent to destroy, in whole or in part, a national, ethnical, racial or religious group, as such: (a) Killing members of the group; (b) Causing serious bodily or mental harm to members of the group; (c) Deliberately inflicting on the group conditions of life calculated to bring about its physical destruction in whole or in part; (d) Imposing measures to prevent births within the group; (e) Forcibly transferring children of the group to another group.⁶⁸

Debates as to the degree of "intent" which must accompany these acts; the definition of "the group," and whether social classes should or should not be considered groups; and what degree of destruction of the cultural legacy of the group constitutes genocidal intent as opposed to forced assimilation, ethnic cleansing, or displacement have accompanied these words from their inception and will continue to do so. But Lemkin, who worked as an attorney in the Polish State Prosecutor's Office and fled to the United States in 1939 via Sweden, not only brought a legal imagination and perspective to the understanding of anti-Semitism and the extermination of the Jews; he also introduced the category of "the group" and emphasized that "The objectives of such a plan would be the disintegration of the political and social institutions, of culture, language, national feelings, religion, the economic existence of national groups, and the destruction of the personal security, liberty, health, dignity, and even the lives of individuals belonging to such groups."⁶⁹ I will conjecture that neither Arendt nor Adorno and Horkheimer, emerging as they did out of the more liberal and individualistic traditions of German-Jewish emancipation, would be as accepting as Lemkin of the concept of the group or of the moral and political imperative to preserve groups. Groups, for them, would be worth defending only insofar as they served the prospects of the emancipation or freedom of their members. Nevertheless, in Arendt's prescient reflections on the minorities question in interwar Europe and on "the right to have rights," we sense anticipations of the problem of cultural groups and the protection of the cultural legacy of minorities that dominated Lemkin's work.

What we gain by evaluating Adorno and Horkheimer's and Arendt's explanations of Nazi anti-Semitism in comparative perspective, and in extending this evaluation briefly to touch upon the legacy of Raphael Lemkin, is insight into the dialectic of the universal and the particular that inevitably and necessarily accompanies all reflections on the fate of European Jewry. And all such reflection remains a testimony to that unprecedented spiritual and intellectual legacy of the twentieth century's émigré intellectuals, whom Martin Jay has brilliantly named "permanent exiles."

Notes

1. See Max Horkheimer's classical statement. "The critical theory of society ... has for its object men as producers of their own historical way of life in its totality. The existing relations which are the starting point of science are not regarded simply as givens to be verified and to be predicted according to the laws of probability. Every given depends not on nature alone but also on the power man has over it.... [Critical theory] is not just a research hypothesis which shows its values in the ongoing business of men; it is an essential element in the historical effect and powers of men ... Its goal is man's emancipation from relationships that enslave him." Max Horkheimer, "Traditionelle und Kritische Theorie," (Nachschrift), Zeitschrift für Sozialforschung, ed. by Alfred Schmidt, 9 vols. (Munich, photomechanical reprint of original 1980), 6, no. 3 (1937): 625; English translation consulted in Max Horkheimer, Critical Theory. Selected Essays, trans. Matthew J. O'Connell et al. (New York, 1972), 244.
2. Martin Jay, The Dialectical Imagination. A History of the Frankfurt School and the Institute of Social Research, 1923–1950, foreword Max Horkheimer (Boston, 1973).
3. Jay's pioneering work was followed by several other monographs in the 1970's and 1980's. See Susan Buck-Morss, The Origin of Negative Dialectics (New York, 1977); Andrew Arato and Eike Gebhardt, eds., The Essential Frankfurt School Reader (New York, 1978); Thomas McCarthy, The Critical Theory of Jürgen Habermas (Cambridge, MA, 1978); David Held, Introduction to Critical Theory (Berkeley and Los Angeles, 1980); Helmut Dubiel, Wissenschaftsorganization und politische Erfahrung: Studien zur frühen kritischen Theorie (Frankfurt am Main, 1978), English trans. Benjamin Gregg (Cambridge, MA, 1985); Wolfgang Bonss and Axel Honneth, eds., Sozialforschung als Kritik (Frankfurt am Main, 1982); Axel Honneth, Kritik der Macht: Reflexionsstufen einer kritischen Gesellschaftstheorie (Frankfurt, 1985); Seyla Benhabib, Critique, Norm and Utopia: A Study of the Foundations of Critical Theory (New York, 1986); cf. for others who identified less with the project than the previously listed authors, Raymond Geuss, The Idea of a Critical Theory: Habermas and the Frankfurt School (Cambridge, 1981); Zoltan Tar, The Frankfurt School: The Critical Theories of Max Horkheimer and Theodor Adorno (New York, 1977). In this period, Albrecht Wellmer's Critical Theory of Society, trans. John Cumming (New York, 1974) was also enormously influential in educating many of us (Andrew Arato; Jean Cohen; Susan Buck-Morss; Joel Whitebook; Dick Howard, and myself) who were affiliated with the journal, Telos, edited by Paul Piccone, about critical theory. See Axel Honneth's excellent laudatio to Albrecht Wellmer upon his receiving the Adorno prize of the city of Frankfurt, "Artist of Dissonance: Albrecht Wellmer and Critical Theory," Constellations 14, no. 3 (2007): 305–315. More than a decade later, and relying upon recently available archival material, Rolf Wiggershaus published, Die Frankfurter Schule: Geschichte, theoretische Entwicklung, Politische Bedeutung (Munich and Vienna, 1986). Wiggershaus was less ceremonial and less protective of Max Horkheimer's intellectual and personal failing as the Institute's director than was Jay.
4. As Jay explains in The Dialectical Imagination (with Erich Fromm as the project's director, and the cooperation of Paul Lazarsfeld, Ernst Schachtel, and others), three

thousand questionnaires were distributed to workers, "asking their views on such issues as the education of children, the rationalization of industry, the possibility of avoiding a new war, and the locus of real power in the state" (116). The individually conducted interviews, which were written down verbatim, were then analyzed for the latent personality traits they disclosed. Of the 586 respondents, 10 percent exhibited an "authoritarian" character; 15 percent were deemed anti-authoritarian, even revolutionary: "The vast majority, however, were highly ambivalent. As a result, the Institut concluded that the German working class would be far less resistant to a right-wing seizure of power than its militant ideology would suggest." Jay, *The Dialectical Imagination*, 117; cf. *Studien über Autorität und Familie* (Paris, 1936). The empirical sections, penned by Erich Fromm, were not included in the original study and were published much later as *Arbeiter und Angestellte im Vorabend des dritten Reichs: Eine sozialpsychologische Untersuchung* (*Workers and Civil Servants on the Eve of the Third Reich: A Sociopsychological Study*), ed. Wolfgang Bonss (Stuttgart, 1980).

5. See T.W. Adorno, Else Frenkel-Brunswik, Daniel J. Levinson, and R. Nevitt Sanford, "The Authoritarian Personality," abridged ed., in *Studies in Prejudice*, ed. Max Horkheimer and Samuel H. Flowerman (New York and London, 1950; reissued as Norton paperback in 1969 and 1982). There were actually two studies conducted by members of the Institute, one was the study of anti-Semitism within American labor sponsored by the Jewish Labor Committee, and the other was on the authoritarian personality and was sponsored by the American Jewish Committee.

6. Jay, *The Dialectical Imagination*, 133 (my emphasis). Right after the publication of Jay's book, there were some caustic criticisms of the Frankfurt School's neglect of anti-Semitism, drawing attention precisely to these passages. See Erhard Bahr, "The Anti-Semitism Studies of the Frankfurt School: The Failure of Critical Theory," *German Studies Review* 1, no. 2 (1978): 125–138.

7. Cf. Gershom Scholem on the failure of the "German-Jewish" symbiosis, "Jews and Germans," in *On Jews and Judaism in Crisis: Selected Essays*, ed. Werner J. Dannhauser (New York, 1976); Leo Strauss, *Jewish Philosophy and the Crisis of Modernity. Essays and Lectures in Modern Jewish Thought*, ed. and intro. Kenneth Hart Green (Albany, NY, 1997); Leo Strauss, "German Nihilism (lecture delivered on February 26, 1941)," *Interpretation* 26 (1999): 353–378. I thank my colleague Steven Smith for helpful references to Strauss's work. Jacob Taubes, *The Political Theology of Paul*, trans. Dana Hollander (1987; Stanford, CA, 2004); Martin Buber, *Zwei Glaubensweisen*, in *Werke*, 22 vols. (1950; Munich, 1962), 1: 651–782; Leo Baeck, *Das Wesen des Judentums*, 3rd ed. (1923; Darmstadt, 1985); Kurt Blumenfeld, *Erlebte Judenfrage. Ein Vierteljahrhundert Deutscher Zionismus* (Stuttgart, 1962).

8. On the defiance of instrumental logic by the Nazis and hence the uselessness of the category of "instrumental reason" generally to understand Nazi anti-Semitism, see Dan Diner, "Historical Understanding and Counterrationality: The Judenrat as Epistemological Vantage," in *Probing the Limits of Representation. Nazism and the "Final Solution,"* ed. Saul Friedländer (Cambridge, MA, 1992), 128–142, and most recently Dan Diner, *Gegenläufige Gedächtnisse. Über Geltung und Wirkung des Holocaust, Essays zur jüdischen Geschichte und Kultur* (Göttingen, 2007).

9. I am thinking, of course, of Daniel Goldhagen's, *Hitler's Willing Executioners. Ordinary Germans and the Holocaust* (New York, 1996) versus Christopher Browning, *Ordinary Men: Reserve Police Batallion 101 and the Final Solution in Poland* (New York, 1992); Christopher Browning, *The Origins of the Final Solution: The Evolution of Nazi Jewish Policy, September 1939–March 1942* (Jerusalem, 1992); and Dan Stone, ed., *The Historiography of the Holocaust* (Houndsmills, 2004). George Steiner has continued to

emphasize the unique position of the Jews within Western and Christian culture as outsiders, as "guests," who through their irredeemable otherness also remind western culture of their failed aspirations and cosmopolitan ideals. See George Steiner, "The Wandering Jew," *Petahim* 1, no. 6 (1988); George Steiner, *Errata: An Examined Life* (London, 1997). I am relying here on the critical but very insightful essay by Assaf Sagiv, "George Steiner's Jewish Problem," *Azure*, Summer 5763 (2003): 130–154. Sagiv approaches Steiner's work from a Zionist perspective, skeptical of cosmopolitan aspirations.

10. There are many other themes and concepts which may serve as entry points for a useful, and long overdue, conversation between Arendt and the Frankfurt School: the critique of liberalism, mass society, and bureaucracy; the skepticism toward orthodox Marxism and its philosophy of history; the critique of Hegel and the move back to Kant; and of course, the shared admiration, on the part of Adorno and Arendt in particular, toward Walter Benjamin. I choose the topic of "anti-Semitism" because I have always believed that the origins of Hannah Arendt's political philosophy owed more to her reflections on "the Jewish question," and the rise of European anti-Semitism than to Heidegger's influence upon her. It is around this point as well that some of the most striking differences between Arendt and Horkheimer and Adorno come to the fore. See note 12 below.

11. I use this term with reference to Weber's distinction between "generalizing" and "idiographic" social science. On the difficulties of characterizing Arendt's methodology, see the early review essay by Eric Voegelin of *The Origins of Totalitarianism* in *Review of Politics* 15 (January 1953), and my discussion in Seyla Benhabib, "Hannah Arendt and the Redemptive Power of Narrative," *Social Research* 57, no. 1 (1990): 167–196.

12. See Martin Jay and Leon Botstein, "Hannah Arendt: Opposing Views," *Partisan Review* 45, no. 3 (1978): 348–381. [This text has been reprinted with no revisions in Martin Jay, *Permanent Exiles: Essays on the Intellectual Migration From Germany to America* (New York, 1986), as "Hannah Arendt's Political Existentialism," pp. 237–256. I am using the original *Partisan Review* here]. In the "Introduction" to *Permanent Exiles*, Jay discusses the controversy his essay has generated but sees no need to revise its claims (xix–xx).

On the supposed influence of Carl Schmitt and Alfred Baeumler on Arendt, see Jay, "Hannah Arendt," 353. Jay writes, "As its own end, politics should not be conceived as a means to anything else whether it be domination, wealth, public welfare, or social justice; in short, *politique pour la politique*" ("Hannah Arendt," 363). There is very little textual evidence in any of Arendt's oeuvre that she was influenced either by Schmitt (to whom there are barely two references in *The Origins of Totalitarianism*) or by Alfred Bauemler. These assertions, as Jay himself acknowledges, are a matter of conjectural contextualization ("Hannah Arendt," 351). What is certainly not open to dispute is the influence of Heidegger's thought on Arendt, however one is to interpret it. Jay also focuses on Arendt's early essay in *Partisan Review* to support his claims about her "political existentialism," but he does not clearly distinguish this from "political decisionism." (See Hannah Arendt, "What is Existenz Philosophy?" *Partisan Review* 18, no. 1 (1946): 35–46, rpt. as "What is Existential Philosophy?" in Arendt, *Essays in Understanding: 1930–1954*, ed. Jerome Kohn (New York, 1994), 163–187). I note the differences between the original title and this later version and comment on it in Seyla Benhabib, *The Reluctant Modernism of Hannah Arendt*, new ed. (New York, 2003), 59–60, n. 35. The two are not the same: one can be a political existentialist, believing that there are no ultimate guarantees and foundations in the political

sphere which can be provided either by reason or history, without at the same time accepting the characteristic theses of political decisionism about the significance of the single, individual act upon which sovereignty is grounded, such as in Schmitt's claim that "Sovereign is he who decides on the exception" (Carl Schmitt, *Political Theology. Four Chapters on the Concept of Sovereignty*, trans. and intro. by George Schwab [1922; Chicago, 1985], 5). Jay does not cite the all too crucial passage in Arendt's critique of Heidegger in this essay, which applies equally to all politically decisionist illusions. Arendt writes about Heideggerian *Dasein*: "The essential character of the Self is its absolute Self-ness, its radical separation from all its fellows ... Later, and after the fact, Heidegger has drawn on mythologizing and muddled concepts like 'folk' and 'earth' in an effort to supply his isolated Selves with a shared, common ground to stand on ... All that can result from that is the organization of these Selves intent only on themselves into an Over-self in order somehow to effect a transition from resolutely accepted guilt to action" (Arendt, "What is Existential Philosophy?" in *Arendt: Essays in Understanding*, 181–182). This passage hardly displays political decisionism; in fact, it is ironic and almost contemptuous of the amateurish way in which Heidegger seeks to proceed from the isolated self—Dasein—to politics, which is always engaged in with others. Whatever Arendt's later predilections to minimize Heidegger's involvement with National Socialism, she never abandoned her thesis that to think politically one needs to proceed from the premise of irreducible human plurality and not from an isolated Dasein. On Arendt and Heidegger, see my *The Reluctant Modernism of Hannah Arendt*, chap. 4, "The Dialogue with Martin Heidegger: Arendt's Ontology of *The Human Condition*," 102–123; on this relationship and its misinterpretation in the hands of Elzbietta Ettinger, *Hannah Arendt-Martin Heidegger* (New Haven, CT, 1995) and Richard Wolin, *Heidegger's Children: Hannah Arendt, Karl Löwith, Hans Jonas and Herbert Marcuse* (Princeton, NJ, 2003), see Seyla Benhabib, "The Personal is not the Political," *Boston Review* (October–November 1999): 45–48, reprinted in revised and enlarged form as "Appendix" to *The Reluctant Modernism of Hannah Arendt*, 2nd ed., 221–233. See also my review of Richard Wolin's *Heidegger's Children*, "Taking Ideas Seriously," *Boston Review* (December 2002/January 2003).
13. Max Horkheimer, "Die Juden und Europa," *Zeitschrift für Sozialforschung*, ed. Marx Horkheimer, dtv. Repr. of vol. viii (1939); ed. used (Munich, 1980): 115.
14. The whole sentence, with its obscure syntax reads, "Der Faschismus ist die Wahrheit der modernen Gesellschaft, die von der Theorie von Anfang an getroffen war. Er fixiert die extremen Unterschiede, die das Wertgesetz am Ende produzierte." (Fascism is the truth of modern society, which was identified by Theory since its inception. Fascism fixates the extreme differences which are ultimately produced by the law of value.) Ibid., 116.
15. See Friedrich Pollock's subsequent article, "State Capitalism: Its Possibilities and Limitations," *Studies in Philosophy and Social Sciences* 9, no. 2 (1941): 200–255. On Pollock's discussions as early as 1932 of achieving a stabilized capitalist economy despite the Depression, and his rejection of orthodox Marxist crisis theory, see also Jay, *The Dialectical Imagination*, 153–55.
16. Jay, *The Dialectical Imagination*, 115.
17. Ibid., 129. Allegedly concluded in September 1939, this article expresses extreme skepticism toward British and French intentions and capacities to fight National Socialism. Horkheimer sees the coming war as an imperial, and indeed a global, one for world domination among "the superpowers" (see Jay, *The Dialectical Imagination*, 128 and 135). Much of the poisonous quality of his comments about liberalism can be

accounted for in the light of his deep skepticism that Great Britain and France would or could really resist National Socialism alone, without the aid of the United States.
18. Martin Jay, "The Jews and the Frankfurt School: Critical Theory's Analysis of Anti-Semitism," in *Permanent Exiles: Essays on the Intellectual Migration from Germany to America* (New York: Columbia University Press, 1985), 90–100.
19. Max Horkheimer to Herbert Marcuse, 17 July 1943, in *Gesammelte Schriften* 17, ed. Alfred Schmidt and Gunzelin Schmid Noerr (Frankfurt, 1985), 463. Cited in Anson Rabinbach, "Why Were the Jews Sacrificed?: The Place of Anti-Semitism in *Dialectic of Enlightenment*," *New German Critique*, no. 81, special issue on *Dialectic of Enlightenment* (Autumn 2000): 51–52.
20. Rabinbach, "Why Were the Jews Sacrificed?" 52.
21. Theodor Adorno and Max Horkheimer, *Dialektik der Aufklärung*, 7th ed. (1944; Frankfurt, 1980), here 27; *Dialectic of Enlightenment*, English trans. John Cumming (New York, 1972). I have mostly used my own translations. I have discussed this text as well as Horkheimer's concept of "self-preservation" more extensively in Seyla Benhabib, *Critique, Norm and Utopia*, 163–171 and 190–205.
22. Adorno and Horkheimer, *Dialectic of Enlightenment*, 207; see also Benhabib, *Critique, Norm and Utopia*, 166–167.
23. On the origins and significance of this concept, see Jay, *The Dialectical Imagination*, 269–273; Rabinbach, "Why Were the Jews Sacrificed?" 56–59.
24. Horkheimer and Adorno, *Dialectic of Enlightenment*, 167.
25. Ibid., 192.
26. Ibid., 177.
27. Yirmiyahu Yovel, *Dark Riddle. Hegel, Nietszche and the Jews* (University Park, PA, 1998).
28. Rabinbach, "Why Were the Jews Sacrificed?" 61.
29. Thomas Baumeister and Jens Kulenkampff, "Geschichtsphilosophie und philosophische Aesthetik," *Neue Hefte für Philosophie* 5 (1973): 74–105.
30. Jay, "The Jews and the Frankfurt School," 99.
31. See Bahr, "The Anti-Semitism Studies of the Frankfurt School," 133–38; on Arendt, see Leon Wieseltier, "Understanding Anti-Semitism: Hannah Arendt on the Origins of Prejudice," *The New Republic*, 7 October 1981, 20–32.
32. Hannah Arendt, *Eichmann in Jerusalem: A Report on the Banality of Evil*, rev. and enlarged ed. (New York, 1965); originally published in 1963; this reprint 1992. On Arendt's meeting Blumenfeld, see Elisabeth Young-Bruehl, *Hannah Arendt: For Love of the World* (New Haven, CT, 1982), 70–74. On the correspondence of Hannah Arendt and Kurt Blumenfeld, see: "...*in keinem Besitz verwurzelt": Die Korrespondenz*, eds. Ingeborg Nordmann and Iris Philling (Hamburg, 1995), 257–265, and Ingeborg Nordmann, "Nachwort. Eine Freundschaft auf des Messers Schneide," in "...*in keinem Besitz verwurzelt": Die Korrespondenz*, 349–55.
33. For more details on the family background, see Young-Bruehl, *For Love of the World*, 8–12.
34. In a letter to Heinrich Bluecher, her husband, who is here playfully referred to as "the Golem," Arendt writes: "The Golem is wrong when he argues that the Jews are a people, or a people which, like others, is in the process of realizing itself. In the East they are already a people without a territory. And in the West, God knows what they are (including myself)." *Hannah Arendt-Heinrich Bluecher, Briefe. 1936–1968.* ed. Lotte Koehler (Munich, 1996), 58 (my translation). For further discussions of the Eichmann book, see also Seyla Benhabib, "Arendt's *Eichmann in Jerusalem*," in *The Cambridge Companion to Hannah Arendt*, ed. Dana Villa (Cambridge, 2000), 65–86.

35. Hannah Arendt, *Rahel Varnhagen: The Life of a Jewish Woman*, rev. ed., trans. Richard and Clara Winston (New York, 1974).
36. The phrase is from Arendt's "Preface" to *Rahel Varnhagen*, xv–xvi. I have discussed this work at great length in Benhabib, *The Reluctant Modernism of Hannah Arendt*, chap. 1, "The Pariah and Her Shadow: Hannah Arendt's Biography of Rahel Varnhagen," 1–34.
37. Dana Villa is certainly correct in noting that Arendt's characterization of "the social" owes a great deal to Heidegger's characterization of "das Man" in *Being and Time* (Dana Villa, *Arendt and Heidegger. The Fate of the Political* (Princeton, NJ, 1995)). But equally interesting is the way in which Arendt commingles the three dimensions of the social: mass society; society based on commodity exchange; and, new sphere of social relations in modern society or "civil society." This categorical conflation of the various dimensions of the social is the major weakness of Arendt's social theory and at the root of her neglect of economics in political life. See Benhabib, *The Reluctant Modernism of Hannah Arendt*, "The Social and the Political: An Untenable Divide," 138–172.
38. Hannah Arendt, *The Origins of Totalitarianism* (1951; New York, 1979), 54; abbreviated in the text as OT and all references in parenthesis are to the 1979 edition. Originally published in Britain as *The Burden of Our Time* (London, 1951).
39. Parts of this section have previously appeared in Seyla Benhabib and Raluca Eddon, "From Anti-semitism to the 'Right to Have Rights.' The Jewish Roots of Hannah Arendt's Cosmopolitanism," *Babylon: Beiträge zur jüdischen Gegenwart*, no. 22 (Frankfurt, 2007), 44–62. For general discussions on the significance of Jewish politics for Arendt's conception of politics and philosophy, see Richard Bernstein, *Hannah Arendt and the Jewish Question* (Cambridge, MA, 1996); Seyla Benhabib, *The Reluctant Modernism of Hannah Arendt*. Cf. also, Jerome Kohn, "Preface: A Jewish Life: 1906–1975," in *Hannah Arendt. The Jewish Writings*, eds. Jerome Kohn and Ron H. Feldman (New York, 2007), ix–xxxiii.
40. Arendt, *Origins of Totalitarianism*, xi.
41. Arendt's insistence on the centrality of Jews to the larger story of the moral and political collapse of Europe reveals a complex and ambivalent philo-Semitism that underpins her theory of anti-Semitism. While she famously declared that "I have never in my life 'loved' any people or collective," and, indeed, that the "'love of the Jews' would appear to me, since I am myself Jewish, as something rather suspect," she nevertheless attributed to Jews a privileged cultural as well as political role in European history, see, Hannah Arendt, *The Jew as Pariah*, ed. and intro. Ron H. Feldman (New York, 1978), 247. See also, the expanded and revised edition of the essays from *The Jew as Pariah*, supplemented by other materials in: Arendt, *The Jewish Writings*. In one sense, for example, in the figure of the *schlemihl* as embodied by Heine and in Bernard Lazare's *pariah*, Arendt discerned a unique model of humanity, which, "excluded from the world of political realities," could at one time "preserve the illusion of liberty." While Nazi totalitarianism erased this illusion, Arendt regarded the pariah's humanity and independence of mind as eminently political qualities in her own time—indeed, as the conditions sine qua non of human freedom.
42. Arendt, *Origins of Totalitarianism*, 3.
43. Ibid., 7.
44. Ibid., 8.
45. Ibid., 13.
46. Ibid., 17.

47. Ibid., 13.
48. Margaret Canovan, "The People, the Masses, and the Mobilization of Power: The Paradox of Arendt's Populism," *Social Research* 69 no. 2 (2002): 405.
49. In the opening sections of part II of OT, entitled "Imperialism," Arendt's thesis is that the encounter with Africa allowed the colonizing white nations such as the Belgians, the Dutch, the British, the Germans, and the French, to transgress those moral and civil limits abroad that would normally control the exercise of power at home. In the encounter with Africa, civilized white men, regressed to levels of inhumanity by plundering, looting, burning, and raping the "savages" whom they encountered. Arendt uses Joseph Conrad's famous story, "The Heart of Darkness," as a parable of this encounter. The "heart of darkness" is not in Africa alone; twentieth-century totalitarianism brings this center of darkness to the European continent itself. The lessons learned in Africa seem to be practiced in the heart of Europe. Her discussion of imperialism, which begins with the European "scramble for Africa," concludes with "The Decline of the Nation-State and the End of the Rights of Man." Arendt was ahead of her time here. On recent explorations of the relationship between the Holocaust and Imperialism, see Richard King and Dan Stone, eds., *Hannah Arendt and the Uses of History. Imperialism, Nation, Race and Genocide* (Oxford and New York, 2007).
50. As Arendt explains: "Only when the nation-state proved unfit to be the framework for the further growth of the capitalist economy did the latent fight between state and society became openly a struggle for power. During the imperialist period neither the state nor the bourgeoisie won a decisive victory.... This changed when the German bourgeoisie staked everything on the Hitler movement and aspired to rule with the help of the mob, but it then turned out to be too late." Arendt, *Origins of Totalitarianism*, 124.
51. Ibid., 124.
52. Ibid., 4.
53. Ibid., 3.
54. These philosophical theses about the contradictions between "human rights" and "national sovereignty" are more clearly analyzed in Hannah Arendt's *On Revolution* (New York, 1963). Arendt's antagonism toward the concept of sovereignty in political thought shows again that she does not share "decisionist" premises. For a more detailed discussion of these themes, see Seyla Benhabib, *The Rights of Others: Aliens, Citizens and Residents*, The John Seeley Memorial Lectures (Cambridge, 2004), chap. 2.
55. Cf. Herbert Marcuse, "Dear Kampf gegen den Liberalismus in der totalitären Staatsauffassung," *Zeitschrift für Sozialforschung* 3 , no. 1 (1934): 161–95.
56. Carole Fink, "Defender of Minorities: Germany in the League of Nations, 1926–1933." *Central European History* 5, no. 4 (1972): 331. See also Fink, *Defending the Rights of Others. The Great Powers, the Jews and International Minority Protection* (Cambridge, 2004).
57. Arendt, *Origins of Totalitarianism*, 275.
58. Ibid., 296–297 (my emphasis).
59. We should not forget that this phrase also has a history within the Critical Theory of the Frankfurt School and is used to describe the transformation of critical theory in the wake of Friedrich Pollock's very important essay on "State Capitalism," and "Is National Socialism a New Order?" *Studies in Philosophy and Social Science* 9 (1941): 440–455. For a critical discussion of Pollock's position, see Moishe Postone, *Time,*

Labor and Social Domination. A Reinterpretation of Marx's Critical Theory (Cambridge, 1993), section on "Friedrich Pollock and the Primacy of the Political," 90–96.

60. There is yet another source of "the primacy of the political" in Arendt's work. This is the critique of orthodox Marxism-Leninism that her husband Heinrich Bluecher shared with other members of the *Spartacist* party. Arendt was much more aware of these discussions among various communist and ex-communist militants, many of whom, like her, were in exile in Paris in the mid to late nineteen-thirties, than we are wont to believe. On the significance of the Paris exile for Arendt, see my "Hannah Arendt's Political Engagements," *Hannah Arendt Centenary* (forthcoming). As Jay perceptively notes, Rosa Luxemburg's polemic against Lenin was quite significant for Arendt's own understanding of the significance of democratic participation of the masses in self-governance. (Jay, "Hannah Arendt: Opposing Views," 358). But this observation is dismissed with the further claim that Arendt misunderstood "that the spontaneity Rosa Luxemburg championed meant the *unforced combination of objective and subjective factors produced by the logic of capitalism and raising the consciousness of the working class.*" (Jay, ibid., 358 [my emphasis]) "The primacy of the political" has returned in the writings of East European dissidents such as Vaclav Havel, Adam Michnik, Jacek Kuron, Janos Kis, and others, after 1989, precisely because this faith in "the unforced combination of objective and subjective factors" has revealed itself to be exactly what Arendt said the Marxian conception of history had been all along, namely, the unproven faith that one had the key whereby to unlock the meaning of history. For Arendt's oft-misunderstood critique of Marx, see the important and neglected section on "The Labor Movement," in Hannah Arendt, *The Human Condition* (Chicago and London, 1958), 212–220.
61. Jay, *Dialectical Imagination*, chap. 1.
62. John Rawls, *Political Liberalism* (New York, 1993; repr. 1996). The core of political liberalism is the freestanding justification of the principles, which legitimize political rule in terms of nonsectarian and nondivisive understandings of what constitutes "the right" for us all, as opposed to what we may conceive of individually as "the good." There would be many other respects in which a Frankfurt School perspective would be critical of political liberalism, but the conflation of political liberalism as a theory of government with the free market is a red herring. Political liberalism is not dependent upon economic liberalism; and, in fact, it requires a social democratic restructuring of the economy.
63. There is an important distinction in Arendt's work between "liberation" and "freedom." See, *On Revolution* (New York, 1963), 22–27, 54–61, and also, Benhabib, *The Reluctant Modernism of Hannah Arendt*, 157–65. In this essay, I cannot provide the more detailed analyses of "liberation" vs. "freedom" in the works of Arendt and the Frankfurt School that would be required.
64. Raphael Lemkin, *Axis Rule in Occupied Europe. Laws of Occupation, Analysis of Government, Proposals for Redress* (Washington, DC, 1944), xi.
65. Dan Stone, "Raphael Lemkin on the Holocaust," *Journal of Genocide Research* 7, no. 4 (2005): 546.
66. See the special issue of *Journal of Genocide Research* 7, no. 4 (2005) devoted to the work of Raphael Lemkin; Michael A. McDonnell and A. Dirk Moses, "Raphael Lemkin as Historian of Genocide in the Americas," in the same issue, 501–529, and A. Dirk Moses, "The Holocaust and Genocide," in Stone, *The Historiography of the Holocaust*, 533–555.
67. Anson Rabinbach, "The Challenge of the Unprecedented—Raphael Lemkin and the Concept of Genocide," *Simon Dubnow Institute Yearbook* 4 (2005), 401.

68. United Nations Convention on the Prevention and Punishment of the Crime of Genocide. Adopted by Resolution 260 (III) A of the UN General Assembly on 9 December 1948 (Chapter II).
69. Lemkin, *Axis Rule*, 79.

Bibliography

Adorno, Theodore, Else Frenkel-Brunswik, Daniel J. Levinson, and R. Nevitt-Sanford. "The Authoritarian Personality." In *Studies in Prejudice*, edited by Max Horkheimer and Samuel H. Flowerman. New York and London, 1950; reissued as Norton paperback in 1969 and 1982.

Adorno, Theodore and Max Horkheimer. *Dialektik der Auflärung*. 7th ed. 1994; Frankfurt, 1980.

Arato, Andrew and Eike Gebhardt, eds. *The Essential Frankfurt School Reader*. New York, 1978.

Arendt, Hannah, and Heinrich Blücher. *Hannah Arendt-Heinrich Bluecher, Briefe. 1936–1968*. Edited by Lotte Koehler. Munich, 1996.

Arendt, Hannah. *Eichmann in Jerusalem: A Report on the Banality of Evil*. Revised and enlarged ed. New York, 1965; Reprint in 1992.

———. *Essays in Understanding: 1930–1954*. Edited by Jerome Kohn. New York, 1994.

———. *The Human Condition*. Chicago and London, 1958.

———. *The Jew as Pariah*. Edited and introduction by Ron H. Feldman. New York, 1978.

———. *The Jewish Writings*. Edited by Jerome Kohn and Ron H. Feldman. New York, 2007.

———. *On Revolution*. New York, 1963.

———. *The Origins of Totalitarianism*. 1951; New York, 1979.

———. *Rahel Varnhagen: The Life of a Jewish Woman*. Edited and translated by Richard and Clara Winston. New York, 1974.

———. "What is Existential Philosophy?" *Partisan Review* 18, no. 1 (1946): 35–46.

Baeck, Leo. *Das Wesen des Judentums*. 3rd ed. 1923; Darmstadt, 1985.

Bahr, Erhard. "The Anti-Semitism Studies of the Frankfurt School: The Failure of Critical Theory." *German Studies Review* 1, no. 2 (1978): 125–138.

Baumeister, Thomas and Jens Kulenkampff. "Geschichtsphilosophie und philosophische Aesthetik." *Neue Hefte für Philosophie*, no. 6 (1974): 74–104.

Benhabib, Seyla. *Critique, Norm and Utopia: A Study of the Foundations of Critical Theory*. New York, 1986.

———. "Arendt's Eichmann in Jerusalem." In *The Cambridge Companion to Hannah Arendt*, edited by Dana Villa, 65-86. Cambridge, 2000.

——— and Raluca Eddon. "From Antisemitism to the 'Right to Have Rights': The Jewish Roots of Hannah Arendt's Cosmopolitanism." In *Babylon: Beiträge zur jüdischen Gegenwart*, no. 22 (Frankfurt, 2007): 44–62.

———. "Hannah Arendt and the Redemptive Power of Narrative." *Social Research* 57, no. 1 (1990): 167–196.

———. "The Personal is Not the Political." *Boston Review* 23 (October–November 1999): 45–48.

———. *The Reluctant Modernism of Hannah Arendt*. New York: Rowman and Littlefield Publishers, 2003.
———. *The Rights of Others: Aliens, Citizens and Residents*. The John Seeley Memorial Lectures. Cambridge, MA, 2004.
———. "Taking Ideas Seriously." *Boston Review* 27, no. 6 (December 2002/January 2003).
Bernstein, Richard. *Hannah Arendt and the Jewish Question*. Cambridge, MA, 1996.
Blumenfeld, Kurt. *Erlebte Judenfrage. Ein Vierteljahrhundert Deutscher Zionismus*. Publication of the Leo Baeck Institute. Stuttgart, 1962.
Bonss, Wolfgang and Axel Honneth, eds. *Sozialforschung als Kritik*. Frankfurt, 1982.
Browning, Christopher. *Ordinary Men: Reserve Police Batallion 101 and the Final Solution in Poland*. New York: Harper and Collins, 1992.
———. *The Origins of the Final Solution: The Evolution of Nazi Jewish Policy, September 1939–March 1942*. Jerusalem: Yad Vashem and University of Nebraska Press, 1992.
Buber, Martin. *Zwei Glaubensweisen*. In *Werke*, 22 vols. 1950; Munich, 1962.
Buck-Morss, Susan. *The Origin of Negative Dialectics*. New York, 1977.
Canovan, Margaret. "The People, the Masses, and the Mobilization of Power: The Paradox of Arendt's Populism." *Social Research* 69, no. 2 (2002): 403–442.
Diner, Dan. *Gegenläufige Gedächtnisse. Über Geltung und Wirkung des Holocaust, Essays zur jüdischen Geschichte und Kultur*. Göttingen, 2007.
———. "Historical Understanding and Counterrationality: The Judenrat as Epistemological Vantage." In *Probing the Limits of Representation. Nazism and the "Final Solution,"* edited by Saul Friedländer, 128–142. Cambridge, MA, 1992.
Dubiel, Helmut. *Wissenschaftsorganization und politische Erfahrung: Studien zur frühen kritischen Theorie*. Frankfurt, 1978.
Ettinger, Elzbietta. *Hannah Arendt-Martin Heidegger*. New Haven, CT, 1995.
Fink, Carole. "Defender of Minorities: Germany in the League of Nations, 1926–1933." *Central European History* 5, no. 4 (1972): 330–357.
———. *Defending the Rights of Others. The Great Powers, the Jews and International Minority Protection*. Cambridge, 2004.
Fromm, Erich. *Arbeiter und Angestellte im Vorabend des dritten Reichs: Eine sozialpsychologische Untersuchung*. Edited by Wolfgang Bonss. Stuttgart, 1980.
Geuss, Raymond. *The Idea of a Critical Theory: Habermas and the Frankfurt School*. Cambridge, 1981.
Goldhagen, Daniel J. *Hitler's Willing Executioners: Ordinary Germans and the Holocaust*. New York: Alfred Knopf, 1996.
Held, David. *Introduction to Critical Theory*. Berkeley and Los Angeles CA, 1980.
Honneth, Axel. "Artist of Dissonance: Albrecht Wellmer and Critical Theory." *Constellations* 14, no. 3 (2007): 305–315.
———. *Kritik der Macht: Reflexionsstufen einer kritischen Gesellschaftstheorie*. Frankfurt, 1985.
Horkheimer, Max. *Critical Theory. Selected Essays*. Translated by Matthew J. O'Connell et al. New York, 1972.
———. *Gesammelte Schriften*. Edited by Alfred Schmidt and Gunzelin Schmid Noerr. 19 vols. Frankfurt, 1985.
———. "Die Juden und Europa." In *Zeitschrift für Sozialforschung* 8 (1939): 115–137.
———. "Traditionelle und Kritische Theorie." In *Zeitschrift für Sozialforschung* 6 (1937): 245–294.
Jay, Martin. *The Dialectical Imagination. A History of the Frankfurt School and the Institute of Social Research, 1923–1950*. Boston, 1973; Berkeley and Los Angeles, 1996.

――― and Leon Botstein. "Hannah Arendt: Opposing Views." *Partisan Review* 45, 3 (1978): 348–381.
―――. "The Jews and the Frankfurt School: Critical Theory's Analysis of Antisemitism." In *Permanent Exiles: Essays on the Intellectual Migration from Germany to America*. New York, 1985.
King, Richard and Dan Stone, eds. *Hannah Arendt and the Uses of History: Imperialism, Nation, Race and Genocide*. Oxford and New York, 2007.
Kohn, Jerome. "Preface: A Jewish Life: 1906–1975." In *Hannah Arendt. The Jewish Writings*. Edited by Jerome Kohn and Ron H. Feldman, ix–xxxiii. New York, 2007.
Lemkin, Raphael. *Axis Rule in Occupied Europe. Laws of Occupation, Analysis of Government, Proposals for Redress*. Washington, DC, 1944.
McCarthy, Thomas. *The Critical Theory of Jürgen Habermas*. Cambridge, MA, 1978.
McDonnell, Michael A. and A. Dirk Moses. "Raphael Lemkin as Historian of Genocide in the Americas." *Journal of Genocide Research* 7, no. 4 (2005): 501–529.
Moses, A. Dirk. "The Holocaust and Genocide." In *The Historiography of the Holocaust*, edited by Dan Stone, 533–555. Houndmills, 2004.
Marcuse, Herbert. "Der Kampf gegen den Liberalismus in der totalitären Staatsauffassung." In *Zeitschrift für Sozialforschung* 3, no. 1 (1934): 7–44.
Nordmann, Ingeborg and Iris Philling. "... in keinem Besitz verwurzelt": Die Korrespondenz. Hamburg, 1995.
Rabinbach, Anson. "The Challenge of the Unprecedented—Raphael Lemkin and the Concept of Genocide." *Simon Dubnow Institute Yearbook* 4 (2005).
―――. "Why Were the Jews Sacrificed?: The Place of Anti-Semitism in Dialectic of Enlightenment." *New German Critique*, no. 81 (Autumn 2000): 49–64.
Pollock, Friedrich. "Is National Socialism a New Order?" *Studies in Philosophy and Social Science* 9 (1941): 440–455.
―――. "State Capitalism: Its Possibilities and Limitations." *Studies in Philosophy and Social Sciences* 9, no. 2 (1941): 200–255.
Postone, Moishe. *Time, Labor and Social Domination. A Reinterpretation of Marx's Critical Theory*. Cambridge, MA, 1993.
Rawls, John. *Political Liberalism*. New York, 1993; Reprint 1996.
Sagiv, Assaf. "George Steiner's Jewish Problem." *Azure*, Summer 5763 (2003): 130–154.
Schmitt, Carl. *Political Theology. Four Chapters on the Concept of Sovereignty*. Translated and introduction by George Schwab. 1922; Chicago, 1985.
Scholem, Gershom. *On Jews and Judaism in Crisis: Selected Essays*. Edited by Werner J. Dannhauser. New York, 1976.
Steiner, George. *Errata: An Examined Life*. London, 1997.
―――. "The Wandering Jew." *Petahim* 1, no. 6 (1968).
Stone, Dan, ed. *The Historiography of the Holocaust*. Houndmills, 2004.
―――. "Raphael Lemkin on the Holocaust." *Journal of Genocide Research* 7, no. 4 (2005): 539–550.
Strauss, Leo. "German Nihilism (lecture delivered on February 26, 1941)." *Interpretation* 26 (1999): 353–378.
―――. *Jewish Philosophy and the Crisis of Modernity. Essays and Lectures in Modern Jewish Thought*. Edited and introduction by Kenneth Hart Green. Albany, NY, 1997.
Tar, Zoltan. *The Frankfurt School: The Critical Theories of Max Horkheimer and Theodor Adorno*. New York, 1977.
Taubes, Jacob. *The Political Theology of Paul*. Translated by Dana Hollander. Stanford, CA, 2004.

Voegelin, Eric. Review of *The Origins of Totalitarianism*, *Review of Politics* 15, no. 1 (1953): 68–76.
Wellmer, Albrecht. *Critical Theory of Society*. Translated by John Cumming. New York, 1974.
Wieseltier, Leon. "Understanding Anti-Semitism: Hannah Arendt on the Origins of Prejudice." *The New Republic*, 7 October 1981, 20–32.
Wiggershaus, Rolf. *Die Frankfurter Schule: Geschichte, Theoretische Entwicklung, Politische Bedeutung*. Munich and Vienna, 1986.
Wolin, Richard. *Heidegger's Children: Hannah Arendt, Karl Löwith, Hans Jonas and Herbert Marcuse*. Princeton, NJ, 2003.
Young-Bruehl, Elisabeth. *For Love of the World*. New Haven, CT, 1982.
Yovel, Yirmiyahu. *Dark Riddle: Hegel, Nietzsche and the Jews*. University Park, PA, 1998.
Villa, Dana. *Arendt and Heidegger: The Fate of the Political*. Princeton, NJ, 1995.

THE ANTI-TOTALITARIAN LEFT
BETWEEN MORALITY AND POLITICS

Dick Howard

Martin Jay introduces his study of *Marxism and Totality* with a "topography of Western Marxism" that concludes with some remarks about what he calls the "generation of 1968."[1] They were a "distinct generation of non-dogmatically leftist intellectuals," in whose number he counts himself. Similarly, in the Introduction to a collection of his essays published two years later,[2] he explains that although he wanted to move beyond Critical Theory to other projects, "I was drawn back into its orbit." The reason for this continued appeal was first of all intellectual curiosity, because he was "never certain that Marxism, Western or otherwise, offered all the answers." But there was a political appeal as well, since he thereby avoided the deadening experience of a "deradicalization" when the excitement of the initial discoveries gave way to a "theoretical and practical" loss of confidence. That changed mood, he goes on to say, is "evident" in my 1977 study of *The Marxian Legacy*, and "apparent" also in articles in the journal *Telos*. In contrast, Martin Jay cites the volume that Karl Klare and I had published only five years earlier as part of "a burgeoning awareness of the richness as well as the inadequacies of a tradition of thought."[3] Could it have been simply what he calls the "disheartening events of the 1970s" that explains the changed intellectual landscape?

As always with Martin Jay's historical reconstructions, the picture is not black and white. He points out that the loss of confidence had not produced a kind of "dogmatic anti-New Leftism comparable to the 'God that failed' anti-Communism ... of an earlier disillusionment." He does not believe that "the story is over," or that the historian's task is simply to trace a "bleak tale of dashed expectations." After all, he had described the search for what Karl Klare and I called an "unknown dimension" as seeking both its "richness as well as [its] inadequacies." But just that duality was what I had sought to portray in The Marxian Legacy. That is why I insisted that the publisher replace the proposed cover photo of a May 1968 demonstration in Paris with Breughel's painting "The Blind Leading the Blind."[4] True, I left the editorial committee of Telos around that time because it seemed to me that the journal was increasingly publishing what I called "meta-commentaries" that veered ever more toward "traditional" rather than critical theory. But when Telos rediscovered the political-intellectual project that had inspired its first phase—as it became increasingly involved in understanding the new social movements that emerged first within the Communist bloc and then also in the West—I had no problem rejoining the editorial group, and published a second, updated edition of The Marxian Legacy in 1988.

Rereading Marxism and Totality recently, I could not help but wonder why Martin Jay stressed the signs of defeat—even when he also insisted that "the story" would also continue. I then looked back at my own two books to which he referred. The major difference between them (aside from the fact that one is the product of many hands) is that The Marxian Legacy concludes with two long chapters on the work of Claude Lefort and Cornelius Castoriadis.[5] I had managed, with great difficulty and over many objections, to have essays by each of them published in Telos, but their critique of Marxist pieties grated on many an ear. It has to be recalled that while the New Left was "new" in that it challenged the bureaucratic politics of communism, it also was "left" in its refusal of reflexive anti-communism as well as in its unreflective identification of democracy with capitalism. The fact that Lefort and Castoriadis had taken the critique of totalitarianism as the fundamental thread that could lead to the invention of a radical politics was hard to digest. That is why I was not surprised when I read in Marxism and Totality that while they had "a period of influence" in 1968, it was "short-lived."[6] Not surprising, if frustrating, was the fact that this brief allusion opened the path to a new chapter, on Louis Althusser's structuralism. While the intellectual historian is not a prophet, Martin Jay does consider his goal to be the "rescue [of] the legacy of the past in order to allow us to realize the potential of the future."[7] Needless to say, in the two decades since he wrote, the structuralist vogue has come and gone. What frustrated me, however, is that the anti-subjectivism preached by Althusser and his disciples was in its essence *anti-political*. Its claim to justify its radical politics by an appeal to a new "science" denies its own role and political responsibility. In so doing, it turns out to be another variant of the basic structure that Lefort and Castoriadis's critique showed as the foundation of what can best be called the totalitarian temptation. In its broadest sense, their critique did not denounce a specific political regime for this-or-that concrete action, but it more broadly criticized the denial of the very autonomy of the political domain as such. By contrast, radical politics—as it shot forth in the 1968 movements—could be understood as a reclaiming of the political.[8]

Marxism and Totality is only incidentally the history of a generation, but the idea that the "adventures" of a *concept* can tell us something about a concrete political experience is worth exploring. The difficulty is that the sixty-eighters were also—and perhaps primarily—concerned to develop a new politics. That is why the first chapter of *The Unknown Dimension* is Karl Klare's essay, "The Critique of Everyday Life, the New Left and the Unrecognizable Marxism." At a time, not so long ago, when very little of Marx's work was available in the United States,[9] there was a new politics in gestation, emerging from the civil rights and then the anti-war movement, but branching quickly from feminism outward toward what Klare described as the "critique of everyday life." Concepts were needed if the experience was to take hold, and give itself a coherence by which to avoid the fate of being "short-lived." Thus, after 1968, US New Leftists (such as the readers of *Telos*, *New German Critique* or *Radical America*) tended to seek a renewal of critical Marxism, whereas the Europeans, feeling the need to draw conclusions from the failed General Strike of May–June in Paris, and the crushing of the Prague Spring by the Warsaw Pact, turned (slowly but steadily) away from Marx and toward the idea of an autonomous civil society and the renewal of democratic politics.[10]

These different orientations within the New Left are explained in part by the history and the institutional structures of the European and US state. Without going back to the old topos of the "two revolutions,"[11] it suffices to recall that the civil rights movement, despite its moral power and civic mobilization, demanded the interventions of the central state (the courts, and eventually presidential leadership) to impose change on a recalcitrant society. And many of those who mobilized for that cause remembered their grandparents telling them how the New Deal made possible the trade unions that helped them escape dependence and to create a (limited but real) social safety net. The US Americans' goal, which they could not express in so many words, was the creation of what may well be a contradiction in terms: a radical social democracy.[12] The radicalism remained, but as a moral imperative and criticism rather than as a positive political project.

The experience of leftists in Eastern as well as Western Europe was practically the inverse of their US comrades. On the one hand, French Jacobinism and Soviet-style command economies made clear the constraints of statist centralism on civic autonomy. But on the other hand, it was clear that the creation of a political machine capable of transforming or taking over the state in order to eliminate the hindrances to free and full development demanded the constitution of a hierarchical organization that was the antithesis of the liberation that was sought. The result was a sort of dual alienation—fearing the very state that seemed needed in order to liberate the individual—which helps to understand the origin of their concern with totalitarianism as a kind of anti-politics threatening the quest for political renewal. By the same token, they were forced to reevaluate the project of democracy, which could no longer be treated as merely the formal legitimation of capitalist material exploitation.

If the Marxist option has today been finally played out, the question remains whether the European critique of totalitarianism and the consequent recognition of the radical role of democracy could be transplanted to the New World. In the wake of 9/11, such an experiment can be seen in the activities of a group of sixty-eighters who have been labeled as "liberal hawks." They represent a putatively "European" political sensibility, although the path that led them to that style of thinking differs in specific cases. The similarity is suggested, for example, by their adoption of the rhetorical denunciation of Saddam Hussein as a "fascist totalitarian" who would surely make, and make use of, weapons of mass destruction (as he had done already in the Anfal attacks on Iraqi Kurds). The problem is that this is the rhetoric of the Bush administration and its neoconservative supporters, who claim to support the furtherance of democracy and to combat the protean threat of a totalitarianism that did not disappear with the demise of the Cold War. These new-style "European" New Leftists had somehow to convince themselves that the victory over communism (and fascism before it) had been achieved by an alliance with the devil—such as in the 1986–1988 decision to install cruise and Pershing missiles in Germany, which seemed to have convinced Gorbachev of the need for radical reform, and later with NATO interventions in Bosnia (and, conversely, by the failure to intervene in Rwanda).

But there is a slippage in this claim, which is in the last resort the same as the one that is made by supporters of "realism" in international relations (who in fact opposed the war in Iraq). What these neo-European Americans have forgotten is that anti-totalitarianism supported a politics of human rights, which began to take shape in the late 1970s with Poland's *Solidarnosc* and Czechoslovakia's *Charter 77*. It was *only then*, when an *immanent* foundation existed, that there could be hope for a *domestic, self-*

generated democratization of society. In a word, the liberal hawks' attempt to unite politics and morality ignores Aristotle's warning that the good man is not necessarily a good citizen. At the same time, they forget Kant's distinction between the political moralist (or moralizing politician) and the moral politician (who recognizes the place of political prudence).[13] Although they would never admit it, rather than bringing morality to politics, they may be the last heirs of political Leninism!

Generational Stories

Although the liberal hawks have—with the aid of a Bush administration that, in spite of the dubious election of 2000, has shown itself more unscrupulous than even the most paranoid imagined—painted themselves into a corner, the political logic that led them there is not therefore simply wrong. Their voluntaristic moralism did not come from nowhere, and its abuse does not mean that it is or will be always and everywhere without use. Two decades after Martin Jay questioned the effect of the "disheartening events of the 1970s" on the "distinct generation of non-dogmatically leftist intellectuals" who were the heirs of Western Marxism, Paul Berman, an active member of that generation, published *Power and the Idealists*.[14] His title captures a bit of the *frisson* no doubt felt by many of the newly minted hawks that remembered their New Leftist past, but still dared play with fire. Indeed, this element of risk is what makes Berman's text a *Bildungsroman* rather than simply a political tract. He reconstructs the evolution of an international, and internationalist, generation that learned how to translate its moral ideals into a practical politics understanding the need to use power to defend human rights.

The generational story is recounted in a lengthy first chapter that just happened to have been published one week before the terrorist attacks of 9/11. It weaves together the biographies of emblematic figures of the international new left of the 1960s—many of whom we had met in Berman's 1996 reconstruction of the paradoxical birth, and fate, of that generation, *A Tale of Two Utopias*[15]—by means of a reflection on the odyssey of Joschka Fischer, a high school dropout and street fighter who became Germany's foreign minister and its most popular politician. The terror attacks that occurred the following week, leading *Le Monde* to headline famously "*Nous sommes tous américains*," had the paradoxical effect of first affirming but then quickly destroying the ascendance of the power of morality that Berman described in the Fischer case. For a moment, left and right joined in what seemed a common cause in which justice was allied with the state. But for the right, morality is the homage that vice pays to virtue;

and many on the left were too self-satisfied by their new legitimacy (and the power it brought) to recognize that they were being played for a sucker. In the eyes of his critics, Berman belongs to the latter category—and on one level, his book gives comfort to the enemies of that new twenty-first century renegade: the "liberal hawk," a contemporary avatar of the postwar anti-fascist transformed into an unconditional Cold Warrior.

But to reduce a book to its "thesis" is to do violence to an exercise in political thought that is also an autobiography and the biography of a generation. True, Berman does express clear political choices, particularly with regard to the invasion of Iraq. But even if one disagrees with him, it must be conceded that he presents nothing so crude as the unabashed boosterism found, for example, in the work of the former French ultra-leftist, Yves Roucaute, who with no sense of self-parody, titles his recent book *Le néo-conservatisme est un humanisme*.[16] Berman is less pretentious and not so self-assured. But the *Bildung* of the idealists he portrays does have its Hegelian touch insofar as their journey is a sort of *Aufhebung*, preserving while raising to a higher level their immediate intuition of the need to "resist" what they first experienced as "fascism" and finally came to recognize as "totalitarianism."[17] He mourns the end of what Daniel Cohn-Bendit described as the "imaginary sixty-eighters International" in *We Loved the Revolution So Much* (1992). But melancholy is not Berman's response; generations pass, life goes on, and a new generation will find its own language to speak of "the tragedies that descend all too fatefully upon the people who struggle against tragedies." The New Left he has described are "the risk-takers. The resisters." And the author of these lapidary final words, like the generation he has portrayed, is clearly on their side, whatever political "position" he may adopt yesterday or tomorrow.

The Totalitarian Temptation

"Resistance" is an ethical maxim whose political translation is problematic. As with the generals, politicians often fight the last war. So too with the sixty-eighters, who were brought up on the legend of anti-fascism. They first translated this heritage into a paradoxical pacifism, combining an ethics of militant resistance with an ideal of revolution that would eliminate the immorality of liberal, bourgeois capitalism. Why call them "idealists"? Theirs was a faith that drew a straight line from resistance to revolution, leaving no time for reflection, no space for compromise, and no place for inconvenient realities. It is not surprising that some adopted an imperious logic identifying politics with war, passing effortlessly from word to deed, that is, in this case: to terrorism.[18] And many of their comrades found it difficult not to sympathize silently or actively, or to explain away what they refused to denounce as unjustified excesses, calling them simple accidents that did not invalidate the revolutionary essence of the left. Their anti-fascist parents had apologized for Stalin's abuses as bumps on the rocky road to real communism, or (after 1956) distortions due to the cult of personality; now the *résistants* of the new generation were prisoner to their own ideals (even more than to their ideology).

The identification of anti-fascism with anti-capitalism (or of fascism with capitalism) was never intellectually satisfying; it was political positioning, which is always problematic. If you did not equate economic domination with political domination, it was hard not to wonder about the repressive regimes in the Soviet Union and its *glacis*. But even if you made that critical judgment, your faith still could be firmed up by the allure of Mao's "cultural" revolution, or the Latin American Davids taking on the North American Goliath. The French, no doubt because they had been the most dogmatic (and least theoretical), were the first to fall victim to reality; after a moment of renewed dogmatism that blamed the "defeat" of May 1968 on its bourgeois anarchism, they suffered the "Solzhenitsyn Shock," given popular appeal by the so-called New Philosophers (among whom the best known today are André Glucksmann and Bernard-Henri Lévy) who pillaged shamelessly—without the slightest acknowledgment—the work of Lefort and Castoriadis.[19] But for the young French leftists, the negation of their old faith did not lead to despair; that negation was soon negated (and thus *aufgehoben*) as they learned to appreciate the resistance of the East European sixty-eighters, who were turning civil society against the state. They failed to see that, at least at first, this option was a revival of their old reflex: they had found in the East European dissident movements the idea that civil society can bring to its knees the power of the political state, which was another way of creating an *ersatz*-proletariat that could move History.

But these young leftists soon came to a more important realization: that their "resistance" had a more serious transnational enemy, a "totalitarianism" that was, moreover, flesh-of-their-flesh. Historical materialism's certainties, they began to understand, could justify a smothering paternalist dogmatism unwilling to tolerate difference. But the lesson was not easily accepted for a reason that in retrospect sounds childish: since the bourgeoisie defined its enemies as "totalitarian," the self-defined radical left could hardly accept as its enemy the enemy-of-their-bourgeois-enemy. And this new left could not compete with the academic political scientists in formulating checklists of criteria to distinguish true enemies from merely apparent ones. Instead, as Berman puts it, with just enough vagueness to capture the uncertainty of the participants, they ultimately came "to judge by smell and feel" in order to awaken their spirit of *resistance*. This is philosophically naïve, and it fecklessly ignores historical conditions. "Resistance" acquires a political force only when confronted by a totalitarian power; otherwise, it is just plain garden-variety liberalism—a good thing, to be sure, but not the political terrain on which a critical left can grow and redefine itself by building on immanent contradictions within existing conditions.

Berman's *éloge* to resistance praises sometimes opposition to dictatorship, sometimes refusal of totalitarianism—and the difference makes a difference.[20] Rights are violated in both cases (they may also be violated in democracies). But totalitarianism's denial of individual rights is essential to its main—but of course unadmitted—goal, which is to put an end to *all* of the effects of democracy, especially the assertion of the idea of rights, which is the precondition for moral action. This goal was shared by Stalinism and Nazism, both of which were born in reaction to the breakdown of old, hierarchical social and political order. But the totalitarian project can never be completely successful; if it were, it would choke off the energy of society and destroy its own capacity for renewal. More important is the recognition that the totalitarian *temptation* remains present also in existing democracies, which often find it hard to live with the demons unleashed by their own freedoms. It is the existence of *this immanent threat*—whose presence or absence is the concern of a modern critical theory, just as the presence or absence of an immanent force making possible the transcendence of capitalism was the concern of classical critical theory—that distinguishes totalitarianism from dictatorship. This is what ultimately distinguishes political resistance from moral righteousness.

Once this logic of New Left politics is distilled, it becomes possible *both* to understand, *and* to criticize the politics of the "liberal hawk" that Paul Berman presents skillfully. *If* Saddam's regime was indeed totalitarian—and Berman names many facts that point to such a genealogy, from the history of the foundation of the Baath party to the Fedayeen Saddam continuing to harass the invaders as they dashed toward Baghdad—then (critical!) support for the US project is *as* justified as was, for example, the leftist and liberal support of the Soviet Union against Hitler. But analogies compare things that are similar in some ways but different in others, and the difference is important. The interrogation has to continue. Does the analogy justify the claim that "Islamo-fascism" is the new Enemy? Does it justify a further analogy between the elimination of this Islamic totalitarianism and the fall of the Soviet empire? If totalitarianism were only a violent reaction crushing the emerging democratic energies, its defeat should permit those young flowers to bloom again, like young trees after the forest fire has passed over them. Berman rightly recalls that Iraq had a cosmopolitan middle class in the years before Saddam (although its survival might be questioned, especially as the occupation has gone on, and on). But the US wagered on the import of exiles who, it was clear even then, were not the kind of *résistants* whose story Berman wanted to tell in *Power and the Idealists*. In the language of critical theory, the attempt to import democracy by force did could not count on the existence of an internal resistance whose negation of the old order could provide a positive foundation for the creation of something new.

The Right to Be Wrong

The right to be wrong is basic to any political democracy. But that right does not extend to morality—there are limits that cannot be violated. The "liberal hawks" are not morally wrong, but they take their moral wishes for political reality, becoming idealists in the pejorative sense of the term. My disagreement with this political choice is based on the fact that resistance is a moral stance (a "thou shalt not") that cannot be translated directly into political practice. To think politically about the new choices facing the twenty-first century demands, first of all, that we understand those of the twentieth century. Berman's *Bildungsroman* is a vital contribution to that understanding. My criticism points to the need to rethink the *political* implication of the critique of totalitarianism whose one-sided (moral) character explains how the liberal hawks' support of the Iraq invasion did not recognize that it could be abused by political opportunists in the Bush government. They forget that democratic politics depends on political *judgment*, which is fallible, not on a moral will that is always identical to itself, and therefore incapable of anything other than resistance. The moral will that turns to politics is a kind of totality folded in upon itself, jealously guarding its own purity even when it is forced to reckon with the reality of "power." There is a basic difference between what I have called elsewhere a politics of will and the open-ended quest that marks a politics of judgment.[21]

The political problem posed by the refusal to distinguish morality and politics can be expressed differently if we recall an episode in intellectual history that preceded the idealist search for a philosophical system in which subject and object, thought and being, politics and society would be reconciled.[22] Writing in 1784, a few years after the publication of the first edition of the *Critique of Pure Reason*, Kant sought to integrate the causal determination of events in the phenomenal world with the existence of a noumenal (and thus unknowable) realm of freedom in a short essay called "The Idea of History from a Cosmopolitan Point of View."

He pointed to what he called the "unsocial sociability" of humans, which leads them to create political and cultural institutions incarnating a progress that none of the actors consciously intended. Only the philosopher, as *spectator*, recognizes the sense or meaning created by the participating actors. This specification is important. Kant is not Marx; he does not claim to know the direction of historical progress, or to give instructions on its realization. As if to underline this limitation, Kant published in the same year his essay "What is Enlightenment?" His answer to the question was simple: it is liberation from one's "self-incurred tutelage" by the participants who, while not living in an "Enlightened Age," live in an "age of Enlightenment," defined also as an "age of criticism." In other words, although the philosopher-as-spectator may know the deeper meaning of human action, that action has to retain its autonomy, even while it is caught up in the causal networks of the phenomenal world.

When he turned to morality proper, Kant of course formulated his "categorial imperative" that binds the will while insuring its purity. But he worried about what a later essay called "The Old Proverb: That may be True in Theory but It is of no Practical Use." Writing in 1793, as the Terror was on the agenda, he reaffirmed his enthusiastic reception of the French revolution. In spite of the unexpected political violence that was occurring, he argued on moral grounds that, although the deposition of a tyrant does no injustice to that ruler (whose unjust rule disqualifies him from office), "it is in the highest degree illegitimate for the subjects to seek their rights in this way. If they fail ... and are then subjected to severe punishment they cannot complain about injustice."[23] There seems to be a conflict here between Kant's morality of the pure will and his political judgement—the one anti-revolutionary, the other enthusiastic about the particular French experience. But the difficulty is only apparent: in the one case, Kant is speaking from the standpoint of the actor; in the second, from that of the spectator. In other words, the politics of will must be distinguished from the politics of judgment. The former is based on an a priori purity that allows no exceptions; the latter starts from particular conditions and asks whether and how they manifest an "exemplary" universality analogous to the way a singular work of art incarnates a norm of beauty to which all must give their assent.

The political implications of Kant's arguments were drawn together in the 1795 essay "On Perpetual Peace," from which the just cited passage rejecting a politics of revolutionary will was taken. In this masterful and yet often enigmatic late essay, Kant proposes what he calls a "transcendental principle" according to which "All actions relating to the right of other men are unjust if their maxim is not consistent with publicity." This means that the actor must take into account the rights and choices of a plurality of other actors, recognizing the existence of a plurality of wills. But, typically, Kant adds first of all to the transcendental principle a critique. It points out that there are some actions that may become public without therefore being just, as in the case of the aforementioned tyrant who is sufficiently strong that he need not conceal his plans. The critique leads in turn to the proposal of an "affirmative and transcendental principle," which asserts that "All maxims which *stand in need* of publicity in order not to fail in their end agree with politics and right combined." There is little that needs to be added to this lapidary synthesis, whose implications ring as true today as they did when moral voluntarism culminated in Robespierre's equally concise but more frightening phrase: "virtue, without which terror is fatal; terror without which virtue is impotent. Terror is nothing but prompt, severe, inflexible justice; it is therefore an emanation of virtue." Robespierre too was an idealist who was trying to face up to the paradoxes of power by adopting a moral stance. Kant was a critical theorist, who reminds his reader of the difference between real power and political ideals.

Kant's critical distinction between the domains of will and judgment suggests the need to distinguish morality from politics. Their identification creates a false totality. Martin Jay's *Marxism and Totality* alludes to this difficulty when he recognizes the deadend that goes with a "God-that-failed" resentment against Marxism's avatars, insisting that "the story is not over" and the "adventures" of the concept of totality are not played out. In the Introduction to *Permanent Exiles*, Jay insists that the quest for "a variety of non-transcendent grounds for critique" remains on the agenda, referring particularly to Jürgen Habermas, who would later formulate a "discourse theory of law and democracy" that, without abandoning the goals of Western Marxism and Critical Theory, takes important steps toward realizing the imperatives laid down by Kant. But Jay does not comment on the curious fact that, in the course of his development, Habermas never addressed himself to the problem of totalitarianism, which was so fundamental to the development of new left politics. Why Habermas did not do so, and at what cost to his own thinking, is a question that deserves an essay of its own.[24] As for the author of *Marxism and Totality*, it is perhaps because the intellectual historian was, in spite of himself, a part of the story he undertook to narrate that his account at one and the same time points toward political developments to come, and yet is blind to others that do not appear to fit the intellectual paradigm that he had made his own. Blindness and insight, as Paul de Man's poststructuralist theory proposes, are identical twins in a way that politics and morality are not. That curious right to be wrong that is essential to politics is perhaps also the foundation of the history that attracts the intellectual historian.

Notes

1. Martin Jay, *Marxism and Totality: The Adventures of a Concept from Lukács to Habermas* (Berkeley and Los Angeles, 1984). Unless otherwise indicated, citations in the next paragraphs are from pages 19 and 20.
2. Martin Jay, *Permanent Exiles: Essays on the Intellectual Migration from Germany to America* (New York, 1986), xiv.
3. Dick Howard and Karl E. Klare, eds., *The Unknown Dimension: European Marxism since Lenin* (New York, 1972). The book contained a chapter on the Frankfurt School, excerpted from *The Dialectical Imagination: A History of the Frankfurt School and the Institute for Social Research, 1923–50* (Boston, 1973; Berkeley and Los Angeles, 1996), by Martin Jay.
4. Although that cover may explain why Martin Jay found here an "evident" disillusionment, a more telling illustration is found in the difference between the presentation of Rosa Luxemburg in the first chapter—which insists *equally* on her "richness" and her "inadequacies"—and the less nuanced 1971 Introduction to my edition of *Selected Political Writings of Rosa Luxemburg* (New York, 1971).
5. I had wanted a chapter on the political group the two had created, *Socialisme ou Barbarie*, and had met with both of them in Paris to try to arrange a contribution. They were encouraging and the meetings became the basis of long friendship. They had overcome the divergences that led to earlier splits, and had co-authored (with Edgar Morin) the first major interpretation of May 1968, *La brèche* (Paris, 1968). But neither had the time to write the chapter, and the person they tried to convince to write it never turned in the promised essay.
6. Jay, *Marxism and Totality*, 383–384.
7. This is the last sentence of the Introduction to ibid., 20. In the Introduction to *Permanent Exiles*, Martin Jay recalls that a critique of his work published in *Telos* cited an "uncharacteristically bold" remark of Horkheimer to the effect that Critical Theory "confronts history with that possibility which is always concretely visible within it" (xv). Would one, he asks skeptically, still say the same thing in the 1980s?
8. My claim is not that Lefort and Castoriadis were read by all (or any!) of the participants; rather, their critique managed to capture a shared spirit that animated them even when, as in the case of the West Germans, the issues posed by totalitarianism were far distorted by their concern with the Nazi past and the "really existing socialism" in East Germany. In the US case, it was the politics called "anti-anti-communism" that turned attention away from the implications of their own actions.
9. Recall that the translations of Marx's early works began to be available only in the mid to late 1960s. As a student at the University of Texas, I bought my copies of the *Capital* (and Lenin) from the truck of a still loyal communist who drove to Austin every few weeks to peddle the products of Progress Publishers in Moscow.
10. This claim refers, of course, not to the movements as a whole but to their intellectual and political leaders. Each of the European cases has its historical specificity, the French long enchained to the mythologized communist *résistance*, the Germans haunted by the Nazi past.
11. The theme goes back to Gentz, whose pamphlet denouncing the French revolution was translated into English by John Quincy Adams to aid his father's campaign against Jefferson. I have tried to present a more systematic and modern formulation by distinguishing between the creation of a "democratic republic" (the French goal) and a "republican democracy" (that the US created almost in spite of themselves). Cf., *The Specter of Democracy* (New York, 2002).

12. Of course, not everyone was drawn toward statist solutions. There were constant battles within SDS between the "Social Democratic" New York faction and the "Anarchist" Texas and Californian groups. The problem of state or civil society was not unique to the US. In spite of the massive support for the *Solidarnosc* trade union movement, the Polish government was able to impose a State of Siege in December 1981. While the social movement did, over time, reconstitute itself, that bitter experience taught an important lesson, which led its leaders to agree to negotiate with the old regime at the Round Table making possible a successful (and peaceful) transition out of communism.
13. Cf., Immanuel Kant, *Perpetual Peace*, ed. and trans. Lewis White Beck (New York, 1957), Appendix I, "On the Disagreement between Morals and Politics in Relation to Perpetual Peace." I will return to Kant in my concluding remarks. Note, for the moment, that "the moralizing politician, by glossing over principles of politics which are opposed to the right with the pretext that human nature is not capable of the good as reason prescribes it, only makes reform impossible and perpetuates the violation of law" (Kant, *Perpetual Peace*, 121).
14. Paul Berman, *Power and the Idealists or, The Passion of Joschka Fischer and its Aftermath* (Brooklyn, 2005). A paperback edition was published by Norton in 2007. Cf., my review essay in *Constellations* 14, no. 3 (September 2007): 445–453. It should be noted that Berman's argument here is far more subtle than his over-simplified *Terror and Liberalism*, written in the immediate aftermath of September 11 (New York, 2003).
15. Paul Berman, *A Tale of Two Utopias: The Political Journal of the Generation of 1968* (New York, 2005).
16. Yves Roucaute, *Le néo-conservatisme est un humanisme* (Paris, 2005). A former student of Louis Althusser and Nicos Poulantzas, Roucaut teaches at the Nanterre branch of the University of Paris. His book was published by the Presses Universitaires de France in 2005. I mention him in this context simply because his book's title—with its allusion to Sartre's famous *Existentialism is a Humanism*—expresses more clearly than many of today's French anti-totalitarians a specific *political* orientation. Others who come from a similar lineage are more nuanced or, in cases such as André Glucksmann, underline the *moral* foundation of their interventions.
17. The scare quotation marks are mine. I use them to make clear that the recent rhetorical coinage of "islamo-fascism" differs from the twentieth-century totalitarianisms in an essential point: there are no homegrown militants who claim to be actualizing from within (i.e., "critically") values that have been betrayed by democratic societies. The lesson of the critique of totalitarianism is that democracies are haunted by an *anti-political* temptation, which can take many forms. While religious fundamentalism is a form of anti-politics, so too is the belief in the self-curative virtues of the free market, as is what Kant calls a "moral despotism," whose purity stands above and outside of the messy world of politics. I will return to this point in the concluding section.
18. Hannah Arendt warned against this danger already in *On Revolution* (New York, 1962). She returned to it in "Thoughts on Politics and Revolution," an interview from 1970, dealing specifically with the New Left, and reprinted in *Crises of the Republic* (New York, 1972). Arendt's arguments in this context put into question aspects of Martin Jay's critique of "The Political Existentialism of Hannah Arendt," in *Permanent Exiles: Essays on the Intellectual Migration from Europe to America* (New York, 1986).
19. In fact, the most serious study of the implications of Solzhenitsyn was Lefort's *Un homme en trop* (Paris, 1976). It should be noted that the journal *Esprit*, which played

an important role in disseminating the ideas of Lefort and Castoriadis, was a significant force in bringing together the East European dissidents with their Western counterparts. I discussed the background of *Esprit* and its contribution to these debates in *Telos*, no. 36 (1978), reprinted in *Defining the Political* (Minneapolis, MN, 1989), 135–149.
20. Berman fails to see the implications of what he describes as his "idealists" recognition of the need to revise their vision of politics when the ultra-leftists of the Red Brigades or the Red Army Fraction tried to use violence in order to provoke the establishment to reveal its "totalitarian" or "fascist" essence.
21. Cf., for example, "Intersecting Trajectories of Republicanism in France and the United States," in *The Specter of Democracy*, 173–196.
22. I am condensing here the line of argument that I suggested in *From Marx to Kant* (New York, 1985, 1993), whose first edition published in 1985 followed out implications of *The Marxian Legacy*. A second edition in 1993 elaborated the theoretical paradigm, while a recent essay "Von der Politik des Willens zur Politik der Urteilskraft: Eine Deutung des Marxschen Systems," in the *Marx-Engels-Jahrbuch* (2005): 9-62 reconsiders the issues in the new political context.
23. This passage, as well as the following arguments, are found in the Second Appendix to *Perpetual Peace*, titled "On the Agreement between Politics and Morality under the Transcendental Concept of Public Right," which is available in different translations.
24. While some Americans might claim that Habermas never analyzed the nature and theoretical/political implications of communism for the same reason that they neglected it—anti-anti-communism—he himself has explained (in an interview with Adam Michnik, in *Die Zeit*, no. 53, 1993) that he simply never found them to be important. When I tried to interpret Habermas's democratic theory of law at a symposium in honor of the English translation of *Between Facts and Norms*, the argument fell on deaf ears, and the essay was not reprinted in the book version of the symposium. It is available as "Law and Political Culture," *Cardozo Law Review* 17, nos. 4–5 (March 1996). A condensed version of the arguments is found in *The Specter of Democracy*.

Bibliography

Arendt, Hannah. *Crises of the Republic*. New York, 1972.
———. *On Revolution*. New York, 1962.
Berman, Paul. *Power and the Idealists or, The Passion of Joschka Fischer and its Aftermath*. Brooklyn: Soft Skull Press, 2005.
———. *A Tale of Two Utopias: The Political Journal of the Generation of 1968*. New York, 2005.
———. *Terror and Liberalism*. New York, 2003.
Howard, Dick. *From Marx to Kant*. New York, 1985, 1993.
———. *The Specter of Democracy*. New York, 2002.
———. "Von der Politik des Willens zur Politik der Urteilskraft: Eine Deutung des Marxschen Systems." *Marx-Engels-Jahrbuch* (2005): 9–62.
———, ed. *Selected Political Writings of Rosa Luxemburg*. New York, 1971.

——— and Karl E. Klare, eds. *The Unknown Dimension: European Marxism since Lenin*. New York, 1972.

Jay, Martin. *The Dialectical Imagination: A History of the Frankfurt School and the Institute for Social Research, 1923–50*. Boston, 1973; Berkeley and Los Angeles, 1996.

———. *Marxism and Totality: The Adventures of a Concept from Lukács to Habermas*. Berkeley and Los Angeles, 1984.

———. *Permanent Exiles: Essays on the Intellectual Migration from Germany to America*. New York, 1986.

Kant, Immanuel. *Perpetual Peace*. Edited and translated by Lewis White Beck. New York, 1957.

Lefort, Claude. *Un homme en trop*. Paris, 1976.

Roucaute, Yves. *Le néo-conservatisme est un humanisme*. Paris, 2005.

Sovereign Equality vs. Imperial Right
The Battle over the "New World Order"

Jean L. Cohen

The nature and direction of the international system is hotly contested today. Developments since the last decade of the twentieth century suggest to some that the organizing principle of international society—the principle of sovereign equality entrenched in the UN Charter system—has become anachronistic.[1] Reform proposals are proliferating and, given the high stakes, the theoretical and political assumptions informing them are well worth the attention of critical theorists.[2]

There are certainly important changes that indicate the need for legal and institutional reform in the international domain. The proliferation of new threats to international peace and security coming from civil wars, failing states, transnational terrorism, grave human rights violations, and the risk that private individuals or "rogue" states will acquire weapons of mass destruction seem to indicate the necessity to transcend the sovereignty-oriented, "state-centric" approach to international law. Indeed, today the problem requiring regulation seems to be anarchy and tyranny within states rather than anarchy between them. Moreover, the expansion of human rights law and the expectation that it should be backed up by strong sanctions, including military intervention to protect citizens against their own state (humanitarian intervention and/or democratic imposition), suggest that the juridical sovereignty of the state has become contingent on outside judgments based on cosmopolitan principles. Rules protecting the sovereignty of failed or "outlaw" states, such as the principles of nonintervention and domestic jurisdiction appear out of date, and the international order based on them is becoming increasingly illegitimate.

In short, it appears as if the battle over the international order is one between *sovereigntists* who are still enchanted by the state, and *cosmopolitans* who are entranced, rather, by human rights and who seek a fundamental revision of the principles of international law and politics. The latter construe the expansion and individualization of international criminal law and the proliferation of human rights discourse as the call for humanitarian and democratic interventions and as indicative of an emergent consensus on the basic values of the "international community" challenging atavistic rules about sovereignty, state consent, state majoritarianism, and the "legalism" pervasive in the UN Charter system. This development is hailed by adherents of an increasingly influential version of moral cosmopolitanism—*cosmopolitan liberalism*—for it indicates that justice is becoming a primary goal of the international community.[3]

According to cosmopolitan liberals, it is time to systematize the emergent conception of the moral basis of the global condition theoretically, and to take the next steps, pragmatically to complete the moralization and "individualization" of the global political system. Despite disagreements over what these steps should be, all concur that "state-centrism" and the principle of the sovereign equality of states in international law has to be abandoned and replaced by a *direct focus* on the individual (one's security, one's basic human rights) as the *subject* of cosmopolitan law and justice.[4] From this perspective, the problem today is how to order and regulate the world community so as to *protect the rights of world citizens*, i.e., justice to *persons*, not how to preserve the sovereign equality of states.[5]

I will argue that this approach to constructing a "new world order" is normatively flawed and politically dangerous. My thesis is that this version of cosmopolitanism rests on a form of moral (and political) monism that wrongly reduces the basis of political legitimacy and legal validity to a single external, substantive criterion—justice to persons—equated with respect for basic human rights; hence the instrumentalist approach to the concept of sovereignty, the denigration of the principle of sovereign equality that has been the foundation of international law, and the quixotic search for a new "basic norm" for a cosmopolitan legal system. Constructed as antithetical to the view that asserts the value of political autonomy of states (labeled statist), it translates into an interventionist version of liberal anti-pluralism.[6] Indeed, it reintroduces hierarchy and exclusion back into the international system on the level of basic norms. Undesirable political and institutional consequences follow directly from it is premises. The relentless attack on the principle of sovereign equality makes it complicit with imperial projects of powerful states interested in weakening the principles that constrain the use of force, and that deny them legal cover or political legitimacy when they violate international law. Worse, it plays a negative role of blocking reflection on reform projects that are desirable and feasible, while playing into the hands of those seeking to undermine international law and transform it an imperial direction.

Against this moral reductionism, I will offer an alternative approach that acknowledges the need for institutional and legal reform, but which gives both the political values that sovereignty articulates and human rights their due without being "state-centric." What I call the "dualist model" of international political theory avoids the reductionism of the cosmopolitan liberal approach.[7] It seeks to preserve the principled, inclusive, egalitarian features of the international legal and political order and to strengthen the restraints on the illegitimate use of force while providing for the protection of human rights. Yet it challenges the unhelpful dichotomy erected between "state centrism" and cosmopolitan principles of human rights. While I will argue in favor of the notion of a responsibility to protect against grave human rights violations, I shall also insist on maintaining the universalistic principle of sovereign equality as the foundational meta-norm of the "new" world order alongside human rights principles. Indeed, I contend that the dualist model, based upon the values of autonomous political community and human rights, offers the only acceptable basis on which to reform legal and political institutions so that they become more just, more legitimate, and more effective.

After briefly discussing the tenets of cosmopolitan liberalism (I), I will analyze the principle of sovereign equality that is at the core of contemporary international law (II), present an ideal-typical description of the structure and logic of imperial law (III), and offer an alternative approach to institutional and legal reform (IV).

Cosmopolitan Liberalism

The basic assumption informing cosmopolitan liberalism is that one can assert a framework of moral rights and obligations applicable to all human beings on the basis of their "common humanity"—their equal dignity and equal worth as moral agents, i.e., their personhood. As Thomas Pogge put it in an early article, three elements are shared by all cosmopolitan liberal theories: *individualism*—the ultimate units of concern are human beings; *universality*—the status of the ultimate unit of concern attaches to every human being equally, and *generality*—this status has global force such that personhood must be respected in everyone, not only fellow nationals, co-religionists, etc.[8] The abstract moral principle of equal dignity is cast in the language of *human rights* and formulated as a theory of justice to persons. Violation of basic human rights is an injustice and, from the cosmopolitan point of view, it is a matter of universal concern that such injustice be rectified.

This idea is important and would be unobjectionable were it not wed to two further claims that have rather disturbing institutional and political implications, disclaimers notwithstanding. The first is the insistence not only that *all* individuals have intrinsic worth, but that *only* individuals have such worth. In order to establish that people have moral obligations beyond state borders, cosmopolitan liberals seem to think it necessary to deny that there is independent value to autonomous political community, or that it can be a source of *sui generis* obligations and loyalties owed exclusively to compatriots.[9] They reason from the perspective of the individual construed as a rights-bearing moral person, not as a member of a political community who is involved in a special political relationship or engaged in a common political project—*self-government under law*—*with compatriots*. Political communities, solidarities, and loyalties are deemed mere (and mutable) historically contingent facts.[10] Accordingly, there is no normative significance to state sovereignty: *there is nothing inviolable or even morally special about political and legal relationships among citizens and their polity, and about domestic principles of legitimacy that internal sovereignty articulates and external sovereignty (independence from the jurisdiction of other states although not from international law) protects.*

Indeed, *state boundaries have a merely derivative significance*.[11] Those who accord moral significance to the political autonomy of states (polities) are accused of "statism," and of falling for the "domestic analogy," which misleadingly compares communal to individual autonomy and the equality of states to the equality of individuals.[12] But states are not persons, and only the latter can be respected as autonomous sources of ends with a moral claim to autonomy. Accordingly, state autonomy (sovereignty) is neither fundamental, nor adequate as a justification of the derivative principles of nonintervention and self-determination. Claims to political autonomy, sovereignty, nonintervention and self-determination are contingent.

The question remains, contingent on what? The second fateful move of cosmopolitan liberalism is to turn respect for the "fundamental" human rights of persons into the *sole* criterion for assessing the legitimacy for states and supranational institutions.[13] In short, recognition of a state's "sovereignty" should turn on the degree to which it respects persons in its care rather than on its efficacy in maintaining control. Moreover, cosmopolitan liberals *purport to infer a determinant and allegedly non-controversial list of basic human interests from the moral principle of equal respect for the dignity of persons and insist that contemporary human rights law demonstrates that there is a global consensus on these interests and on the obligation to protect them.* The philosopher's interpretation of what specific basic rights the moral principle of justice to persons entails thus *trumps the constitutional specification of the content of rights through the public law and domestic political processes within states.* As Allan Buchanan puts it, "We believe persons as such have certain basic rights because of the exceptional moral importance of certain fundamental interests all persons have. We have been able to identify these fundamental interests because we have a clear enough idea of what the requirements for a decent life are."[14] He comes up with his own far from minimal list by cherry picking from human rights documents.[15] Thus, in a rather un-Kantian move, these self-dubbed "neo-Kantian" cosmopolitans seem to think that moral reflection can yield not only an abstract principle such as equal liberty, but also the specification of the content of a list of basic rights, which can serve as the criterion of legitimacy for legal and political systems. *It is this move that is objectionable, for it loses sight of the indispensable role of the domestic politics and legal systems, in the constitution of freedom and the concretization of rights, and it makes the mistake of reducing the legal and the political to the moral, a fateful error* that Kant did his utmost to avoid.[16] Respect for persons thus seems to deny respect for their political agency in the primary context where it is possible: domestic society!

Justice to persons thus becomes *the external moral standard of legitimacy* for every polity and every legal system. Accordingly, states must satisfy an overarching, "universal" monistic substantive standard of political morality—respect for some set of human rights—in order to be deemed legitimate, to be recognized as a full member of the "international community," and to qualify for the always conditional rights of autonomy, domestic jurisdiction, and nonintervention. Since national borders are the "serendipitous result of past violence and other kinds of morally objectionable or irrelevant historical facts" and since the nation is a myth, states have no basic right to nonintervention.[17] Thus, the deeper logic of the argument undermines the "conventional view" that "the right against intervention applies symmetrically to all sovereign states—indeed as an attribute of the status of sovereignty itself."[18] On the "asymmetrical view," state autonomy is respected only if it is instrumental to social justice: "benevolent intervention," including the use of military force by outsiders, is warranted if it would foster just domestic institutions and protect human rights. In other words, the nonintervention principle protects only one class of states.

The same holds for the general right of self-determination, the other key principle of international law expressing the ideal of political autonomy in a plural political universe. If claims to self-determination cannot invoke injustice as the reason for the demand for political autonomy, they must fail. From this perspective, *it makes no difference whether one's rights are violated by one's own or by a foreign government.*[19] Accordingly, claims to decolonization, independence from "benevolent" occupations and trusteeships, and secession are contingent on demonstrating that "self-determination" will be foster "social justice."

Cosmopolitan liberalism purports to offer a coherent, systematic foundation for international political theory as well as a theoretically sound basis for legal reform. Accordingly, a focus on "human security" and basic human rights should replace the particularistic, power-oriented statist approach "unfortunately" embodied in the UN Charter, and it should become *the* criteria for the recognition and ascription of "conditional" autonomy to states. Appropriate reforms would thus entail a leap from the classical international law of states, to a global legal system that would turn international policy and law into "world domestic policy" and "cosmopolitan right." This argument implies that the ultimate members of the international community are individuals, not states.[20]

The shift to a monistic, rights-based theory of international law and legitimacy would therefore entail a certain *Gleichschaltung*. States would be construed as the instruments of the international community—still perhaps the most important functional units in implementing principles of global right, but with no fundamental role in creating it. They would be reduced to the status of administrative units in a decentralized "multi-leveled" global governance structure that accords "autonomy" provisionally, conditioned on how well they comport with the norms of global justice. Indeed, in the cosmopolitan imaginary, what is envisioned is a global order in which the rights-based value consensus of the international community would replace state consent as the main source of international law. *Thus, moral monism translates into institutional monism*, disclaimers notwithstanding. The just world order imagined by the cosmopolitan liberal is not an international system populated by supranational institutions, transnational organizations, and sovereign states, whose coexistence and cooperation is regulated by rules based on the *dual* principles of sovereign equality and human rights.[21] Rather, it would be a monistic global international community (of individuals) based on a universal substantive value consensus in which there is no meaningful distinction between the internal and the external, in which the principle of sovereign equality is no longer constitutive of international relations or law, and in which only some states deemed morally legitimate have, conditionally, some of the prerogatives once associated with sovereignty. The political implications of such a shift with respect to rules regulating the use of force are articulated quite openly, particularly with regard to humanitarian intervention and preventive war.[22]

There has been a much talk in cosmopolitan circles of shifting the discussion of humanitarian intervention toward a focus on "the responsibility to protect" rather than the permissibility to intervene; on human rather than state security; and on the right of individuals to be rescued and the duty to rescue, instead of who has the right to do the rescuing.[23] The claim is that while the state has the primary responsibility to protect its citizens, if it is unwilling or unable to do so, the default responsibility lies with the "international community." Thus, we should abandon the "sovereignty/intervention" frame (too dependent on the presumption of sovereign equality) in favor of the "right to be rescued/responsibility to protect" frame for addressing instances of grave rights violations and the apparently interrelated issues of humanitarian intervention, preventive war, and regime change.

This discourse has come into vogue due to the influential report of the International Commission on Intervention and State Sovereignty (ICISS) set up by the Canadian government for the UN in 2001, and it reappears in the recent reform proposal drafted in 2005 by the UN High-Level Panel on Threats, Challenges and Change, both of which are clearly influenced by the tenets of cosmopolitan liberalism.[24] Cosmopolitan liberals use the discourse of the "responsibility to protect" articulated in these reports as a way to redefine sovereignty and to demote it from its place in international law, thereby dethroning the nonintervention principle, and the corollary of sovereign equality. Sovereignty is *disaggregated into a bundle of prerogatives* and reduced to a *function*—protection—of the welfare, dignity, and basic subsistence rights of citizens—that can be performed by others if the state reneges. As such, state "sovereignty" has only instrumental value. From the perspective of human rights and justice to persons, *it makes no difference* which entity performs this function. Allan Buchanan and Robert Keohane maintain that the sovereignty bundle can be disaggregated; other states or coalitions of states can assume by default the function of protection and role of *instantiation of the "international community."*[25] Thus, states that fail to measure up to the external moral standard of a justice-based theory of international law lose their legitimacy and right to political autonomy. They can be placed in a trustee relationship, to the "international community," and accorded, piecemeal, elements of "quasi-sovereignty" as they reform and develop in the "proper" direction. Accordingly, human rights will trump atavistic concerns with sovereign autonomy and state security, and intervention into (and occupation of) unjust states will protect what really matters, human security and human rights. However, since the United Nations is allegedly a "statist organization" of questionable legitimacy, cosmopolitan liberals extract the discourse of the responsibility to protect from the UN reform project in which it was originally embedded, and invoke it in order either to justify unilateral humanitarian interventions or as the basis for "reform" proposals that would establish "multilateral" alternatives to UNSC authorization mechanisms.

Despite its growing influence and superficial attractiveness, I argue that in the current context, this conception is abstract and utopian in the worst sense. Indeed, there is another way of interpreting recent changes in the international system. From a different perspective, the sovereignty-based model of international law appears to be ceding not to cosmopolitan justice, but to an imperial project of dominance and indirect control of key "peripheries." The world's sole superpower makes good use of cosmopolitan discourse in its efforts to marginalize international institutions and undermine international law, especially law restraining the use of force and the legal principles of nonintervention and self-determination. What we face is not a simple effort to evade international law by a powerful actor, but rather a serious bid to *reorient it* in an imperial direction—under the heading of "global right."

The target of this project is the foundational principle on which contemporary international law and the multilateral (pluralistic) UN Charter system is based: the *legal principle of sovereign equality*;[26] for it is this principle that asserts the equal status of all polities and this system of collective security that places the burden of proof on would-be interveners supposedly acting to "enforce" human rights law or to impose democracy. I support the further constitutionalization of international law if this means reinforcing rules regulating the use of force, updating the UN Charter and Security Council membership to reflect current realities, rendering the latter more accountable through institutional and procedural reform, and formalizing the legal rules regulating humanitarian interventions in case of grave violations. Reforms are needed to avoid morally arbitrary selective and/or unjustified "humanitarian" interventions, be they unilateral or UN sponsored. But I insist that the logical consequence of abandoning the discourse of sovereign equality in favor of cosmopolitan human rights discourse is to play into the imperialists' hands. Why?

There is in fact no cosmopolitan order in place today nor is there one on the immediate horizon. There are instead two contending legal orders each of which is in transition: international law and imperial right. Undermining the former gives free reign to the latter. Let me present an ideal type of each.

Sovereign Equality

International law can be recognized by its twin principles of the sovereign equality of states and a relatively balanced relation of the rule of law and political will. International law has an egalitarian structure and cannot be made by one actor. It presupposes, as does the idea of *collective* security, a *plurality* of autonomous political actors with equal status in the international system, whose practice and input into international law making (consent) is crucial. For it to function at all, international law does require a certain balance of power, but not the techniques associated with that term from the nineteenth century. Ideal typically, it constrains power, yet powerful states can also benefit from international legal regulation. The complex relation of law and power in the international domain suggests that international law can be both an instrument of power and an obstacle to its exercise.[27]

Indeed, the second half of the twentieth century witnessed an unprecedented effort to legally regulate the use of force and install a collective security regime. But it also witnessed a great wave of "declarations of independence," i.e., of assertions of political autonomy and sovereignty by states emerging out of the debris of European empires. The legal principle of sovereign equality and its corollary, the principle of nonintervention, are key elements of this effort. In the aftermath of decolonization, when it became interpreted in light of the concept of self-determination, sovereign equality was invoked to generalize the principle of political autonomy, and nonintervention to *all* member states in the UN (191 as of 2006)—i.e., to all states. The international order thereby became more inclusive, more egalitarian, and more "legalized" than ever before, seriously restricting the space for the legitimate exercise of power outside the law. Sovereign equality became the counter-concept to empire.

Accordingly, all states have an equal entitlement to participate in the formation of international law (consent) and to take on international obligations because they are equalholders of full international legal personality. A *principle of reciprocity* with legal effect follows from this assumption: all states are formally entitled to the same general rights and subject to the same general obligations. Any state claiming a right under international law has to accord all other states the same right. *Sovereign equality is thus a relational concept.* The legal principle of sovereign equality also entails *jurisdiction:* the authority to make and enforce rules within a certain geographic area, limiting the application of external power. From the juridical perspective, *domestic jurisdiction* and *immunity* from foreign laws (autonomy) is the *sine qua non* for international law as it delimits legal systems from one another and thus articulates plurality. It means that states are not subject to other states' jurisdiction, although the scope of acts for which state officials have immunity can be restricted by international law (today restrictions concern acts of aggression, forced annexation, genocide, and other international crimes). In other words, a state is sovereign because it is normatively and legally deemed independent from any other state: it is bound only by international law.[28]

External sovereignty—independence—is matched by internal sovereignty—the domestic supremacy of the state's legal system and political institutions. From the domestic point of view, sovereignty is also a relational concept: it involves a distinctive political and legal relationship between a citizenry and a state. The citizen is the referent of public power and of the constitutional principles (public law) regulating the exercise of sovereign power. From this perspective, the citizen is construed as a member of a political and legal community involved in a collective project of governing itself under law, as the discourse of popular sovereignty implies. Accordingly, citizens are subjects and potentially construed as authors of the laws and political institutions under which they are governed. *Shaping these political relationships, assessing their legitimacy, involves political participation in processes and relationships that are and ought to be uniquely theirs.* By implication, internal and external sovereignty entail each other. Together they comprise the unity and indivisibility of sovereignty: domestically, the indivisibility of sovereignty signifies the unity of the polity and its legal system; internationally, it means the legal personality of the state, its autonomy, its ability to enter into treaties, and assume obligations, etc.

This sovereignty does not mean, however, that the *prerogatives* associated with sovereign power must be exercised by one instance domestically, that a sovereign state is impermeable to international law, or that its officials can hide behind the legal personality of the state when they violate it. Nor does it mean that the prerogatives ascribed to sovereign states cannot be "unbundled," i.e., ascribed to various actors or restricted by international law. But it does mean that the unity of sovereignty in the above sense of legal supremacy domestically and political autonomy/equal legal standing internationally cannot be "disaggregated," nor can it be reduced to one of the functions of a state (protection).

It is nonetheless important to keep the internal and external perspectives analytically distinct: supremacy domestically of a legal system (necessarily linked to de facto control even though we are defining sovereignty as a norm) cannot mean, from an international law perspective, that a state's legal system is deemed globally supreme. That would be to equate sovereignty with an imperial perspective. Rather, one has to recall that the autonomy ascribed via the principle of sovereign equality to all states is normative and relational; accordingly, no state is legally supreme. The external sovereignty ascribed to all states by the principle of sovereign equality arises within a *plural* normatively egalitarian political universe based on institutionalized multilateralism: one in which neither a world empire nor imperialist polities ruling over colonies or "peripheries" can be tolerated. Sovereignty is a form of legal empowerment to act with legal effect that is ascribed by international law to every state; it is thus a legal institution, not a mere fact. Consequently, the principle of sovereign equality indicates that "the rules according to which international law is interpreted, developed and changed are not the billiard balls of classical realism, but rather the table upon which the game is played."[29] Indeed, vis à vis the old Westphalian conception, *a key change* occurred with the principle of sovereign equality: instead of seeing sovereignty as existing apart from and prior to international law—as a pre-existing political "fact" of absolute and impermeable state power—"sovereign equality" is now seen as the core rule set up by the international system itself. Moreover, this principle has always been linked with a utopian ideal of greater substantive equality in lawmaking—the trend toward a more inclusive international community has been accompanied by a push in that direction.[30] It is important to note that de facto inequalities of power and privilege in the international system do not violate the legal principle of sovereignty; it remains the organizing principle so long as equal legal standing, domestic jurisdiction, sovereign immunity, and reciprocity apply to all states. Sovereign equality means equality before the rule, not within the rule.[31] It is a "constitutive legal fiction," an institution that structures the entire edifice of international law. But it is also the basis on which claims to actual equalization of conditions can be and are raised. The same holds true for domestic legal systems, as is well known.

Understanding the principle of sovereign equality as a legal norm allows one to see that the prerogatives ascribed to sovereign states can change—that there can be *different sovereignty regimes*. This is the way to understand the key transformations in international law since the Second World War: sovereign states gave up their "sovereign" right to go to war, and aggression and annexation became illegal; colonialism was dismantled and "empire" was deemed a violation of the principle of self-determination. Sovereign states cooperate in a multiplicity of international institutions, and they accept being limited by human rights principles, renouncing impermeability to international law in this domain. Since the 1990s, human rights principles codified earlier have been taken very seriously and extreme violations such as genocide, ethnic cleansing, and enslavement are not considered today to be within the domestic jurisdiction of any state. These are the new rules of sovereignty in the society of states, not indications of its abolition. The equal status of all polities—within an international community based on collective security—is meant to bolster international comity, to help avoid conflicts, and to protect weak states against strong ones.

Imperial Law

This order is just what the imperial project and its alternative understanding of global right aims to undermine. Since its emergence as the sole superpower, the US has claimed *major revisions regarding constraints on the use of force*; it actively seeks to undermine the UN and to block reforms that would reinforce it and the international rule of law. It has sought to undermine the principle of sovereign equality by making use of moral humanitarian discourse to unilaterally designate polities as "rogue states," and thereby denying them the protection of international law. The US claims the right to unilaterally "enforce" UN resolutions (against Iraq) without Security Council authorization, it has invoked a new doctrine of preventive self-defense in the absence of immanent threat, and it pretends that the principle of unilateral intervention on humanitarian grounds has the status of customary law.[32] It has arrogated to itself the "responsibility to protect" individuals around the world against tyranny and grave human rights violations by invoking the concept of human security and blurring the distinctions between humanitarian aid, intervention, preventive war, and regime change (aided and abetted by cosmopolitan rhetoric in this project). Indeed, it is creating a militarized "preventive" paradigm based on the themes of security and emergency that is undermining the rule of law in foreign and domestic affairs. In the name of a vague and general global right and an absolutist conception of its own sovereignty, the US positions itself as the provider of "human security" against internal and external threats, while insisting on the privilege to be above the law because it is the only entity capable of assuming that "burden." The US has also sought to evade, undermine, and unilaterally alter international humanitarian law on the detention and treatment of prisoners in its "war on terror," arbitrarily designating people "unlawful enemy combatants" without status tribunals, "rendering" alleged terrorists to countries that are known to torture, and issuing rules allowing torture of its own detainees despite the fact that the US Senate ratified the torture convention and that prohibitions against it have *jus cogens* status.[33] These violations of international law framed and justified within a juridical discourse ("faux law") allow the US to position itself as lawmaker and law enforcer, but not equally subject to the law.

In short, this is a project to create a contemporary version of imperial right abandoning the principle of sovereign equality and the egalitarian structure of international law. The predominance of powerful countries in shaping international law to their advantage is not new. But the imperial posturing of the US in a context in which it is unchallenged by any other great power with sufficient military might or will to "balance" it since 1989 is new and dangerous. I do not believe that the American imperial project will succeed. But cosmopolitan rhetoric, an old imperial companion, gives it cover and aid in undermining existing international law and blocking constructive and progressive reform.

What is the distinctive structure of imperial law? *Imperial legality* can be recognized by its hierarchical structure and its solipsistic conception of "sovereignty"—only one state is truly sovereign and its will trumps any existing rules of law. An empire knows no equals or clear boundaries, it regards its domestic law as global right, it sees the independence of other polities as contingent on its will, and it exists in a hierarchical relation with a shifting "periphery." The imperial power posits equivalence between its interests and those of the "international community," and in the name of the latter, it construes *human security* and justice as its responsibility.[34]

Several interrelated strategies are involved here. One, as already indicated, is to claim *systematic* exception or exemption from international law. This is only possible for an unchecked superpower with imperial pretensions. No state is obligated to ratify a treaty, but nor is a third party state legally justified in trying to change the content of a treaty during negotiations that it has no intention of signing. This was US practice in relation to the Convention on the Law of the Sea, the Land Mines Treaty, and most notably, the Rome Statute of the ICC. The recent attempt to exempt itself from the torture convention and the "new thinking" claiming that treaties are political commitments, not legal obligations for the United States, along with the denial that that international law is law at all, are further examples.[35]

Another strategy is to reintroduce hierarchy and exclusion into the international system through various labels, such as "rogue," "terrorist," and "axis of evil," that serve to strip a state of its sovereignty and equal standing in the international community and place it beyond the protection of the nonintervention principle. The idea is to deny the legal personality of some states, to strip them of immunity and suspend application of the principle of jurisdiction and reciprocity to them by subjecting them to external control. These states become the new periphery of imperial right and potential targets of "preventive self-defense" and humanitarian intervention. Reminiscent of the bad old days of colonialism, this strategy seeks to create gradations of sovereignty based on external assessment of regime type or degrees of rights violations, replacing the old criteria of degree of civilization and/or development, and recreating semi-sovereign statuses and a revived form of trusteeship for "outlaws."[36] The functional and bundle theories of sovereignty are useful to this gambit and to justify transformative occupations with necessary tutelage in democracy and in the rule of law![37] So are the justification of unilateralism and/or coalitions of the willing (democracies) who engage in military intervention without UN authorization for "humanitarian" purposes. The discourse of "rogue state," "axis of evil," and even "failed state" (Iraq has been labeled a failed state even though it was a strong state) is thus used to reverse the trend toward ascribing sovereign equality and the principle of nonintervention to all states. The definition of a rogue state is intentionally vague and arbitrary: apparently a state is a rogue state because the United States so decides.[38] Even if this political decision is acquiesced by others, the effect would be the denial of equal membership and hence a severe challenge to sovereign equality.

A third strategy is to alter the way international law is made. At stake in the contentious debate over the "sources" of international law—consensus vs. consent—is the principle of reciprocity and the protections it provides weak states. The US effort to erode consent as the basis for new norms, to shorten the time in which customary law and even *jus cogens* principles are made, the substitution of acts for statements, and the attack on state majoritarianism in favor of a vague "consensus" of the international community are all tactics aimed at enabling the superpower to regain control over international lawmaking in a context in which numbers and the principle of reciprocity strengthen the weak.[39] The claim that there is an emerging right of unilateral humanitarian intervention, that preventive war is included in the right of self-defense under article 51 of the UN Charter, and the invocation of categories like "unlawful combatant" or "terrorist" in order to place individuals in the category of *hostis humani generis*, like the pirate and slave trader of the past, thereby depriving them of the protections of international law, are part and parcel of this project.[40]

Attempting to bring other polities under the domestic law or jurisdiction of a hegemon is another imperial strategy. The US has claimed that states it designates as "sponsors of terrorism" lose their immunity before American courts, and are subject to their jurisdiction.[41] The recent American pretension to extraterritorial application of national law, especially when associated with coercive sanctions, is another example.[42] It goes without saying that these measures are deeply incompatible with the principles of sovereign equality and domestic jurisdiction.

A fifth strategy of imperial law is to deformalize international lawmaking so that it becomes flexible and indeterminate. The idea is to block the development of formal legal criteria and procedures for determining and applying the law and to replace these with substantive moral-ethical standards that reflect the "universalistic" principles of the hegemon's foreign policy. Vague and open-ended ethical standards such as the "interest of the international community," or "humanitarian exigencies," or the "responsibility to protect" create flexibility that suits the imperial project. Invocation of consensus of the "international community" legitimates military interventions that violate formal international law in the name of a global right. Such interventions are presented as supreme emergencies so as to block legal formalization of the rules that could carefully circumscribe exceptions to the nonintervention principle by articulating the proper authority to make the decision, determining the thresholds or criteria and procedures that should guide it, as well as developing accountability mechanisms for such decisions. It should be noted that a powerful hegemon with imperial intentions need not act unilaterally. It may prefer to instrumentalize the key multilateral political body, the Security Council, by acting in ways to block formalization of the rules that could regulate the latter's new legislative and interventionist posture. In short, if the US can get UNSC policy serving its purposes and if the latter is informal and not fully reciprocal, the imperial power can bask in UN legitimacy while subtly transforming the international system in its favor. The vague and open-ended rules on the listing of "terrorists" (sorely lacking due process protections) and the notoriously ambiguous and enabling Resolution 1483 that gave the occupying "Authority" in Iraq virtual carte blanche to transform the Iraqi political and legal regime with no independent mechanism to ensure that it meets its obligations are two disturbing examples.[43] In other words, while unilateral action is obviously an imperial strategy, acting through the UNSC without clear legal rules and accountability mechanisms, and without reciprocity, can also serve the imperial project.

Reform Proposals

This project may not succeed—it is doing rather badly as the debacle in Iraq indicates, and there are important challenges to some of its worst excesses in US courts. But it has already played a destructive role in the domain of international law with the help of the rhetoric of cosmopolitan liberalism. Recall that the latter also attacks the principle of sovereign equality, denies the intrinsic value of autonomous, self-determining and self-governing political community, challenges the legitimacy of the UN because it is "statist" and inegalitarian, while insisting on the futility of

UN reform, and proposes alternatives that would be even more inegalitarian and hierarchical.

Let me be clear—I take human rights and justice to persons seriously, and I believe that legal and institutional reform is needed. I do not believe, however, that the step from an international to a cosmopolitan world order *without* the sovereign state or the principle of sovereign equality has or should be taken. *In short, we must not fall into the conceptual trap that construes sovereignty and human rights as components of two antithetical, mutually exclusive legal regimes.* Rather, we should realize that since 1945, we have been confronted with a new and contradictory institutionalization of both principles and that their interrelation has to be periodically readjusted. The task before us is to strengthen universalistic supranational institutions, foster formal legal reform to norm the exception, and help create a global rule of law that protects *both* the sovereign equality of states and human rights. If we abandon the principle of sovereign equality and the present rules of international law on aggression and collective security, we lose an important barrier to the proliferation of imperial projects and regional attempts at *Großraum* ordering by emerging twenty-first century great powers.

This project entails acknowledging the existence and value of what I call a *dualistic* world order whose core remains the international society of states embedded within (suitably reformed) international institutions and international law, that also has important cosmopolitan elements.[44] The latter, especially *jus cogens* human rights principles and individual liability of officials, should be seen as part of a *new sovereignty regime*: signaling changes in the prerogatives of sovereignty, setting new limits to its legitimate exercise, and as indicative of shifts in the cultural understanding of what falls within the "domestic jurisdiction" of a state and what are legitimate acts of a state for which an agent can no longer evade responsibility by ascribing authorship to a fictional legal person. The *tension* in this dualist model between the principles of sovereignty and "cosmopolitan" human rights does exist and as already indicated, *periodic adjustments between its components elements will have to be made*. The point is that both sovereign equality—and the values of political plurality, political autonomy (the precondition for democracy) for the weak as well as the strong, that it protects—and human rights, and the justice and personal autonomy they secure, are both worth preserving.

Conclusion

As we have seen, the monist approach to international justice typical of cosmopolitan liberalism screens out the political values on which the principle of sovereign equality is based. The bundle theory of sovereignty and its functionalist reduction to the responsibility to protect undermines the key principle that constitutes political plurality, safeguards political autonomy and the space within which political freedom can emerge, secures the main context of justice, and helps protect the weak against the strong states. The a-political and even anti-political stance of cosmopolitan liberalism sees sovereignty as anachronistic, because it reduces citizens to moral persons whose abstract rights can be articulated and given content by the moral philosopher standing outside and above the domestic polity, by purporting to articulate and systematize the basic values of the international community. The fiction of a global legal system in the process of being constitutionalized based exclusively on the individualistic principle of justice to persons fosters this hubris. Despite the claim that theirs is an agency-based view, reasoning only from the perspective of the victim who needs to be saved places political agency on the back burner. Instead of political judgment, we get moral absolutism.

My defense of sovereign equality does not mean I believe a legal principle alone can block great power predations or imperial projects. Only the emergence of effective counter-powers willing to balance the superpower of the US and the infra-power of private transnational organizations can ensure that the international rule of law can block imperial right. Viable counter-powers included within the Security Council that are committed to the rule of law and to the principles of the Charter are absolutely crucial for preventing the degeneration of international law into a mere medium for a hegemon's imperial will to power. Plurality in the political sense of a counter-power must operate today on a larger scale than the old European nation-state: very large states like the US, China, India, Russia, and regional quasi-polities like the EU or others in the making will be the key players. It would be disastrous if the emerging great powers of the twenty-first century emulated the disdain for international law and the imperial gesturing of the present US, or embraced its replacement of sovereign equality with hierarchical principles. Far better are regional federations along the lines of the EU, that are committed to shouldering the responsibilities of their combined power of enforcing international law and fostering a global rule of law. Membership in regional associations could protect the sovereign equality of small polities and make their voice matter more on the world scene. It would also help enormously if the regional association stood for democratic principles, self-determination, and human rights, and encouraged its members to foster and maintain them. Perhaps such future regional associations would some day attain standing within a reformed UN system of collective security.

The dualistic model I have in mind thus involves the articulation of public power and public law on multiple levels of the world political system. But it would seek to harmonize the core principles of international law—sovereign equality and human rights—not abandon one in favor of the other.

Notes

1. On the concept of sovereign equality, see Hans Kelsen, "The Principle of Sovereign Equality of States as a Basis for International Organization," *Yale Law Journal* 53, no. 2 (1944): 207–220.
2. In the spirit of Martin Jay, I approach these questions from the perspective of critical theory. This means that one must be aware of ideological uses of the moral discourses of human rights, globalization, interdependency, and cosmopolitanism, and resist the relations of force and domination that these can be invoked to serve or institute. Others who approach cosmopolitanism within the tradition of critical theory include Jürgen Habermas, "Does the Constitutionalization of International Law Still Have a Chance?", in Habermas, *The Divided West*, ed. and trans. Ciaran Cronin (Cambridge, MA, 2006), 113–194; Hauke Brunkhorst, *Solidarity: From Civic Friendship to a Global Legal Community* (Cambridge, MA, 2005); and Rainer Forst, "Towards a Critical Theory of Transnational Justice," *Metaphilosophy* 32 (January 2001): 160–179.
3. The term comes from Charles Beitz, "Social and Cosmopolitan Liberalism," *International Affairs* 75, no. 3 (1999): 515–529. It includes "radical Rawlsians," such as Brian Barry, Charles Beitz, Allan Buchanan, Thomas Pogge, Fernando Tesón, among others, who link the liberal conception of the person as a free and equal being to the older cosmopolitan idea that every human being has a global stature as an ultimate unit of moral concern.
4. Allan Buchanan, *Justice, Legitimacy and Self-Determination* (New York and Oxford, 2004). For a critique, see Michael Byers, *War Law* (New York, 2006), 107–108.
5. Charles Beitz, *Political Theory and International Relations* (Princeton, NJ, 1979). See also Thomas Pogge, "The Problem of Global Justice," *Philosophy and Public Affairs* 33, no. 2 (2005): 113–147.
6. See Gerry Simpson, *Great Powers and Outlaw States* (Cambridge, MA, 2004), 76–86, on liberal anti-pluralism.
7. Jean L. Cohen, "Whose Sovereignty? Empire versus International Law," *Ethics & International Affairs* 18, no. 3 (2004): 1–24.
8. Thomas Pogge, "Cosmopolitanism and Sovereignty," *Ethics* 103, no. 1 (1992): 48–49.
9. Moderate cosmopolitans acknowledge these duties, but see them as derivative of the obligation of equal treatment that applies to all persons. See Samuel Scheffler, *Boundaries and Allegiances: Problems of Justice and Responsibility in Liberal Thought* (Oxford, 2001), 115.
10. Beitz, *Political Theory of International Relations*, 138.
11. Ibid., 181–182.
12. Ibid., 40.

13. Allan Buchanan, *Justice, Legitimacy and Self-Determination* (New York and Oxford, 2004).
14. Ibid., 439. See also Fernando Tesón, "Ending Tyranny in Iraq," *Ethics & International Affairs* 19, no. 2 (2005): 20.
15. Buchanan, *Justice*, 129-30.
16. Kant insisted that equal liberty or "external freedom" can only be constituted via the political authority of the state exercised through formal legal procedures with direct effect on individuals.
17. Tesón, "The Liberal Case for Humanitarian Intervention," in *Humanitarian Intervention: Ethical, Legal, and Political Dilemmas*, ed. J.L. Holzgrefe and Robert O. Keohane (Cambridge, 2003), 102.
18. Beitz, *Political Theory of International Relations*, 192.
19. Ibid., 119.
20. The "radical Rawlsians" insist against Rawls' own views that rational deliberators in the "global original position" assessing global principles of justice represent individuals, not peoples or states. By implication, the global order consists fundamentally not of sovereign states but of individuals. See John Rawls, *The Law of Peoples* (Cambridge, MA, 1999), and Beitz, *Political Theory of International Relations*; Buchanan, *Justice, Legitimacy and Self-Determination*. But see Pogge, "The Incoherence between Rawls' Theories of Justice," *Fordham Law Review* 72 (2004): 17–56, for a dualist position that comes close to mine.
21. Cohen, "Whose Sovereignty?"
22. See Allan Buchanan and Robert O. Keohane, "The Preventive Use of Force: A Cosmopolitan Institutional Proposal," in *Ethics and International Affairs* 18, no. 1 (2004): 1–22; Charles Beitz, "Nonintervention and Community Integrity," *Philosophy and Public Affairs* 9 (1980): 211–238; Fernando Tesón, *Humanitarian Intervention: An Inquiry into Law and Morality* (Irvington-on-Hudson, 1997).
23. See Terry Nardin and Melissa S. Williams, eds., *Humanitarian Intervention*, NOMOS XLVII (New York, 2006).
24. *The Responsibility to Protect: Report of the International Commission on Intervention and State Sovereignty* (Ottawa, 2001). Report of the High-level Panel on Threats, Challenges and Change," submitted in 2004. "Report of the Secretary General's High Level Panel on Threats, Challenges and Chance. A more secure world: Our shared responsibility" (New York, 2004), <http://www.un.org/secureworld> (Accessed on 8 July 2008).
25. Buchanan, *Justice, Legitimacy and Self-Determination*, 280–288, and Robert O. Keohane, "Political Authority after Intervention: Gradations in Sovereignty," in Holzgrefe and Keohane, *Humanitarian Intervention*, 275–282.
26. UN Charter, Article 2:1 <http://www.un.org>.
27. See Michael Cosnard, "Sovereign Equality—'the Wimbledon sails on'," in *United States Hegemony and the Foundations of International Law*, ed. Michael Byers and Georg Nolte (New York, 2003), 117–134. See also Gerry Simpson, *Great Powers and Outlaw States: Unequal Sovereigns in the International Legal Order* (Cambridge, 2004), 25–61.
28. Michael Byers, *Custom, Power and the Power of Rules* (Cambridge, 1999), 53–124.
29. Byers and Chesterman, "Changing the Rules about Rules," in Holzgrefe and Keohane, *Humanitarian Intervention*, 296.
30. See Nico Krisch, "More Equal Than the Rest? Hierarchy, Equality and U.S. Predominance in International Law," in Byers and Nolte, *United States Hegemony and the Foundation of International Law*, 135–175.

31. Cosnard, "Sovereign Equality," 122. But see Simpson, *Great Powers and Outlaw States* for an argument that the UN Charter system combines "legalized hegemony with sovereign equality."
32. See Michael Byers, *War Law*, for an overview. For the Bush doctrine of preventive military action, see *The National Security Strategy of the United States*, September 2002 (<http://www.whitehouse.gov/nsc/nss.pdf>).
33. White House counsel Alberto Gonzales advised Bush to rescind the Geneva Conventions and declared that the President is not bound by the Convention against Torture. For a discussion, see Byers, *War Law*, 132–135.
34. What follows on imperial law is heavily indebted to Nico Krisch, "More Equal than the Rest? Hierarchy, Equality and US Predominance in International Law," in Byers and Nolte, *United States Hegemony*, 135–175.
35. Dupuy, "Comments," in Byers and Nolte, *United States Hegemony*, 182. John R. Bolton, "Is there Really Law in International Affairs?," *Transnational Law and Contemporary Problems* 10 (2000): 1–47.
36. On the imperialist concept of quasi-sovereignty see Lauren Benton, "Landlocked: Colonial Enclaves and the Legal Puzzles of Quasi-Sovereignty" (unpublished).
37. Keohane, "Political Authority after Intervention," 275–282.
38. R.S. Litwak, *Rogue States and US Foreign Policy* (Washington, DC, 2000).
39. Michael Byers and Simon Chesterman, "Changing the Rules about Rules," in Holzgrefe and Keohane, *Humanitarian Intervention*, 187–194. See also Nico Krisch, "More Equal than the Rest?,"142–144.
40. Krisch, "More Equal than the Rest?," 143.
41. As per the extension of the scope of application of the Alien Tort Claims Act to violations of international law committed abroad, affirmed in *Filartiga v. Pena-Irala*, 630 F2d 876, 890 (2d Cir., 1980), cited in ibid., 143.
42. See the discussion in Cosnard, "Sovereign Equality," 127–129, of the Helms-Burton Act and the D'Amato-Kennedy Act adopted by Congress to prevent companies engaged in international trade from dealing with Cuba and Iran. Even though these efforts failed, they are indicative of imperial thinking.
43. For an excellent discussion see Jose E. Alvarez, "Hegemonic International Law Revisited," *American Journal of International Law* 97, no. 4 (2003): 873–888.
44. See Cohen, "Whose Sovereignty," 19–24.

Bibliography

Alvarez, Jose E. "Hegemonic International Law Revisited." *American Journal of International Law* 97, no. 4 (2003): 873–888.

Beitz, Charles. "Non-Intervention and Community Integrity." *Philosophy and Public Affairs* 9 (1980): 211–238.

———. *Political Theory and International Relations*. Princeton, NJ, 1979.

———. "Social and Cosmopolitan Liberalism." *International Affairs* 75, no. 3 (1999): 515–529.

Benton, Lauren. "Landlocked: Colonial Enclaves and the Legal Puzzles of Quasi-Sovereignty." Unpublished.

Bolton, John R. "Is there Really Law in International Affairs?" *Transnational Law and Contemporary Problems* 10 (2000): 1–47.

Brunkhorst, Hauke. *Solidarity: From Civic Friendship to a Global Legal Community*. Cambridge, MA, 2005.
Buchanan, Allan. *Justice, Legitimacy and Self-Determination*. New York and Oxford, 2004.
——— and Robert O. Keohane. "The Preventive Use of Force: A Cosmopolitan Institutional Proposal." *Ethics and International Affairs* 18, no. 1 (2004): 1–22.
Byers, Michael. *Custom, Power and the Power of Rules*. Cambridge, 1999.
———. *War Law*. New York, 2006.
——— and Simon Chesterman. "Changing the Rules about Rules: Unilateral Humanitarian Intervention and the Future of International Law." In *Humanitarian Intervention: Ethical, Legal, and Political Dilemmas*, edited by J.R. Holzgrefe and Robert O. Keohane, 177-204. New York and Cambridge, 2003.
——— and Georg Nolte, eds. *United States Hegemony and the Foundations of International Law*. New York, 2003.
Cohen, Jean L. "Whose Sovereignty? Empire versus International Law." *Ethics & International Affairs* 18, no. 3 (2004): 1–24.
Cosnard, Michael. "Sovereign Equality—'the Wimbledon sails on'." In *United States Hegemony and the Foundations of International Law*, edited by Michael Byers and George Nolte. New York, 2003.
Forst, Rainer. "Towards a Critical Theory of Transnational Justice." *Metaphilosophy* 32 (January 2001): 160–179.
Habermas, Jürgen. "Does the Constitutionalization of International Law Still Have a Chance?" In Habermas, *The Divided West*, edited and translated by Ciaran Cronin. Cambridge, MA, 2006.
Holzgrefe, J.R. and Robert O. Keohane, eds. *Humanitarian Intervention: Ethical, Legal and Political Dilemmas*. Cambridge, 2003.
Kelsen, Hans. "The Principle of Sovereign Equality of States as a Basis for International Organization." *Yale Law Journal* 53, no. 2 (1944): 207–220.
Krisch, Nico. "More Equal Than the Rest? Hierarchy, Equality and U.S. Predominance in international law." In *United States Hegemony and the Foundations of International Law*, edited by Michael Byers and George Nolte, 135–175. Cambridge, MA, 2003.
Litwak, R.S. *Rogue States and US Foreign Policy*. Washington, DC, 2000.
Nardin, Terry and Melissa S. Williams, eds. *Humanitarian Intervention, NOMOS XLVII*. New York, 2006.
The National Security Strategy of the United States, September 2002 (<http://www.whitehouse.gov/nsc/nss.pdf> Accessed on ???)
Keohane, Robert O. "Political Authority after Intervention: Gradations in Sovereignty." In *Humanitarian Intervention: Ethical, Legal and Political Dilemmas*, edited by J.R. Holzgrefe and Robert O. Keohane, 275-94. Cambridge, 2003.
Pogge, Thomas. "Cosmopolitanism and Sovereignty." *Ethics* 103, no. 1 (1992): 48–75.
———. "The Incoherence between Rawls' Theories of Justice." *Fordham Law Review* 72 (2004): 17–56.
———. "The Problem of Global Justice." *Philosophy and Public Affairs* 33, no. 2 (2005): 113–147.
Rawls, John. *The Law of Peoples*. Cambridge, MA, 1999.
"Report of the Secretary General's High Level Panel on Threats, Challenges and Chance. A more secure world: Our shared responsibility." New York, 2004, <http://www.un.org/secureworld>
The Responsibility to Protect: Report of the International Commission on Intervention and State Sovereignty. Ottawa: IDRC, 2001.

Scheffler, Samuel. *Boundaries and Allegiances: Problems of Justice and Responsibility in Liberal Thought*. Oxford, 2001.

Simpson, Gerry. *Great Powers and Outlaw States: Unequal Sovereigns in the International Legal Order*. Cambridge, 2004.

Tesón, Fernando R. "Ending Tyranny in Iraq." *Ethics & International Affairs* 19, no. 2 (2005): 1–20.

———. "The Liberal Case for Humanitarian Intervention." In *Humanitarian Intervention: Ethical, Legal, and Political Dilemmas*, edited by J.L. Holzgrefe and Robert O. Keohane, 93-129. Cambridge, 2003.

———. *Humanitarian Intervention: An Inquiry into Law and Morality*. Irvington-on-Hudson, 1997.

The Myths of Modern Identity as Ersatz Ideologies

Detlev Claussen and Michael Werz

Whether directly experienced or not, we all have in our mind's eye the images of a surprisingly changed world—the fall of the Berlin Wall and the collapse of the Twin Towers. These two events mark unmistakably the beginning of a new era, one with enormous uncertainties. The social changes of the last twenty years have altered the globe so fundamentally that one would almost think the old world views have come crashing down. But the images that humans create in response to conditions change more slowly than the conditions themselves—and yet they are also a component of them. The combination of global simultaneity and the time lag of world images make the latter attractive, because they appear to guide the new into the familiar trajectories of the past. Looked at more closely, however, it becomes clear that the seemingly old worldviews already carried traces of modernity. It is precisely the apostles of the contemporary, above all in the media and the sciences, that often deny the new that appears dressed up in old clothes, and that prefer to present the new in the guise of the old and familiar.

It soon became clear that the images from 11/9/1989 and 9/11/2001 could be read as hieroglyphics of an epoch-making social transformation. Although the events of 11/9 and 9/11 had universal significance, they were understood within national contexts. Indeed, one could get the impression that the nineteenth-century age—the birth of nation-states—was returning. But the differences are key. The task of theory depends on understanding and formulating them; the *differentia specifica hides the memory of possible transformation*—exactly at the moment when the contemporary social conditions seem to offer no alternatives. US American society has kept this experience of resistance to alternatives much longer than European societies. As an American experience, it became one of the constitutional conditions of Critical Theory in the middle of the twentieth century. Theodor W. Adorno's *Minima Moralia* can be read in this sense as a seismograph pointing to the transformation of the whole in the self-reflective intellectual subject. The critical theorists in exile experienced the changed role of intellectuals in the flesh; they were forced to anticipate their own integration into a general culture industry. This progressive basis of their experience made Critical Theory enormously productive, and it was taken up and expanded by later generations, not only in the US and Germany.

If after 9/11 anti-americanism became a global phenomenon, one has to ask what people meant by "Americanization," since anti-americanism can be understood as a distorted reaction to real occurrences. Anti-americanism allows differences to be asserted in spite of increasing similarities of lifestyle. This is particularly true at a time when one does not have to worry about the name one gives to the reigning economic order, which one can correctly characterize as a capitalist production system without being accused of promoting Marxism. But even this characterization is more effulgent than enlightening. It seems as if every day the world is made anew on the model of progressive America. Out of this mix of perceptions and fantasies, the United States emerges as the winner in the globalization process, about which many people outside of the US are highly ambivalent. Even inside the US, many feel threatened by a process that at its hard economic core represents a worsening of the position of labor in relation to capital. But after the rueful end of socialist experiments, no dispossession of property can offer the promise of redemption. The current situation seems to be literally without an alternative. But because so many societies are in the midst of radical change, a paradoxical situation emerges: the connected whole is so thick and nontransparent, and at the same time so brittle, that no one ideology is in a position to offer a justification for it.

This factual constellation, which became ever more evident after 9/11, in fact did replace the ideology whose demise Daniel Bell had recognized with great sociological acumen in the 1950s. The concept of ideology he employed related to various bodies of political ideas. It was a concept of ideology that became a Western way of speaking in the 1950s. This social scientific concept moved in a complimentary way to the Marxist-Leninist variations, which already had been forgotten and which were related to the critical concept of ideology developed by Marx, referring to the core of verity in the false and thus referenced truth. In the work of the Frankfurt School since the 1950s, the Sisyphean attempt was made time and time again to connect to this critical category. But Helmuth Plessner had already indicated how pointless would be the attempt to restore the actual meaning of a concept against the way it functioned in general use. Not only had economic values, but also concepts experienced a secular inflation during the twentieth century.

The inflation of language today is a good way to read the loss of substance. It is an impossible task to try and restore the actual meaning of words against their everyday use. From Francis Bacon to Karl Kraus, this dilemma of a critical thought was a fundamental aspect of the Enlightenment. The words "culture," "nation," and "society" have all undergone an alteration of meaning that forces every author to rethink their use. The philosophy of language, by ignoring extra-linguistic reality, irrevocably has cut through the umbilical cord that connected concept and thing. The survival of theory depends, however, on precisely that relationship, since every conceptual transformation leaves trace elements, beyond concepts, in the context of life. The point is to follow their tracks.

Looking back at the intellectual cycles since the 1970s, it is striking that the prophets of the new fancied up their inventions with the prefix "post." The competing social scientists reacted with a change of attribution; the new became subordinate, such as the "second modernity," which took the place of the first. In this way, the past remained dominant in many social scientific interpretations. Lacking any kind of concept, one seized on what was already known in order to make a determination. In reality, under these conditions, the old Hegelian insight returns: "what is merely familiar is not as such properly known."

As if by appointment, the twenty-first century supposedly started on 9/11. Out of a need to find a clear marker for the new, a feeling about substantial social change was validated. The lack of conception that went along with dating the new must have had a reason, for there is no scarcity of nominalist creativity across the world. The social sciences are experiencing quick changes to their language, out of which slogans are passed on to the media to describe reality. One should take seriously these nominal changes as moments of changes to reality, without fetishizing them as causes of a changed reality. The separation of material objects from their concepts was one of the most important alterations in the scientific landscape of the twentieth century. Anyone in the scientific community today who dares to speak of materialism outside of the context of intellectual history risks being viewed as an outsider. During the entire nineteenth century—which one can in the strictest sense call the bourgeois age—materialism, as an anti-traditional tradition, challenged science to prove its power of reality.

The basis for modern society was laid in that "long century," which began with the almost simultaneous American declaration of independence and the industrial revolution in England, and lasted until World War I. This must be remembered, because nominalist creations such as "globalization" again define the new as derivative. The long nineteenth century also witnessed the discovery of history and the concept of the end of history, both of which were used again at the end of the short twentieth century as ways to interpret the world. At the end of the nineteenth century, one observes an unprecedented invention of traditions, which strengthened the ontological semblance of modern society. The structural contradiction between historical understanding and historical interpretation of reality accompanied all of the great theories of society in the bourgeois era. The political theories of Francis Fukuyama and Samuel Huntington at the end of the short twentieth century seemed to bring this contradiction back into view. The disintegration of the Cold War alliances provoked a desire to dig up buried national traditions; it was not only in Germany that a "politics of the past" became an unavoidable motif of national self-perception. Both as a catchword and as a social scientific discipline, "history" took on a decisive, legitimizing function. "Society," by contrast, the key category of the period when the blocks confronted each other, suffered a massive loss of meaning. And the apparent lack of alternatives to a market economy reduced all emphatic visions of society to a skeleton. One searched in the past to establish differences, which became apparent in the present as cultural distinctions.

Within this context, the speechless violence of 9/11 called up a wave of interpretations that, through the media, were able to access the entire reservoir of the social sciences and humanities. An entire repertoire of experts appeared among the individual disciplines; from terrorist specialists to Islamic scholars, the academy had something to offer everyone. The specialist's knowledge was enhanced by emotive personal perspectives and intellectual debates, in which experts spoke about the larger picture. The speechlessness of the perpetrators challenged the global communication machine, which reacted to the affront by pouring forth an entire world of opinions. Right down to the controversies about the bin Laden videos on Al-Jazeera and CNN, the media presented the world as a global market of opinion that, like individual economies, was structured in specifically national ways. There is something arbitrary and vague, however, about differentiating the world according to national cultures, because it comes out of an enduring nineteenth-century tradition of a natural connection between culture and nation that has been long in decline.

In order to overcome this dilemma, a new form of cultural conservatism has arisen that proclaims itself the defender of a problematic tradition, and tries to maintain a culture whose social underpinnings have already dissolved. The fictive nature of lumping together bourgeois class, nature, and culture was criticized previously in the nineteenth century, but positivism, with its hostility to theory, led many to forget about that critique during the twentieth century. Against this background of social amnesia, postmodernism was able, during the last half of the twentieth century, to enjoy a triumphant march through the humanities and the media, reaching its zenith in an omnipresent pattern of identity. If is true that almost no one speaks anymore of "postmodernity," everyone does speak still about "identity." The word is not only pervasive in universities and talk shows, but also shows up in everyday speech whenever one has an opinion one feels no need to justify.

The attractiveness of this category, already three decades old, throws light on the death of theoretical thought, a process that pervades the entire short century. This destruction of intellectual potential had catastrophic consequences, particularly in the wake of the changes in 1968, and their effect on the global academic marketplace. The self-incrimination of the sixty-eighters—of participating in the destruction of this tradition—contributed little to this complicated situation because their analysis had nothing to do with self-reflection. The surviving rhetoricians of 1968 created the space for a discourse on identity, as an abstract negation of their own practices, and carried out in a broad way throughout society. "Identity" as it is discussed today, is nothing more than a slogan into which needs, such as the demand for purity, unity, and meaning, are interjected. It is entirely separated from the original concept in German Idealism. "Identity" today simulates the identity of the singular and the universal, into which the particular vanishes.

In the last thirty years, the social sciences have done much to establish the category of "identity" in the public sphere without criticizing the dubious nature of its use or function. In contrast to Kant's time, the critical method is no longer an option, unless one is prepared to fall down at the door of empirical reality. Today "critique" most often establishes itself in the realm of criticism of science, and in doing so comes dangerously close to anti-rational currents. In addition, more so than ever before, the sciences are being asked to prove their usefulness. In proportion, as a science has less economic value, the more the scientists try to prove its legitimacy to the powers that be. The traditional ideas of honor, such as scientific or artistic notions of autonomy, are more and more becoming antiquated. The changing conditions of the international marketplace have not only devalued the worth of physical work, but have also put pressure on intellectual labor. Politics and the economy increasingly tend to demonstrate to the intellectuals that they are becoming redundant. In the realm of technology and science, this is limited to showing them that they are globally exchangeable; those in the human sciences, though, can only demonstrate their usefulness by serving some higher material interest.

The legitimizing potential of a category like "identity" proved itself already in the fights among various groups in the 1970s. The pressure did not come in any way from a reactionary corner; one only has to think of the establishment of Holocaust and Gender Studies, and special academic programs for African Americans in US universities. Their rise was accompanied by an erasure of the political distinction, still a product of the nineteenth century, between left and right, which at its hard core was based on the substance of class society with a bourgeois and a proletariat. These categories became problematic because of the dynamism of a progressive industrial society in its golden age between 1950 and 1973. An added dimension was that, with the exception of Japan, all of these societies, as they transitioned to affluence, also became more homogeneous though immigration, professional mobility, and ethnic and religious invention of traditions. As a result, it became even easier to transfer categories of identity into the world beyond the university, where in the 1980s they came to be taken for granted, consciously as "national identities," out of which groups could articulate various demands on society. The ethnic-national dissolution of Soviet-style societies could be legitimized in this way, just as for variably sized groups of Muslims, the diversification of progressive postindustrial societies could be described with those categories just as well as the transnational claims of Islamic groups. The discussions about "multiculturalism," which became more intense everywhere in the West after 9/11, except in the United States, took on, once more, quite exemplary dimensions in Germany. That perhaps had to do with the remnants of the German concept of *Kultur*, which is echoed in the demands for a *Leitkultur* (dominant culture), whether it be aggressively German or embarrassingly European.

This German concept of culture became formulated pointedly not in the classical or idealist age—that is, at a time when no German national state actually existed—but rather in the last third of the nineteenth century, as the citizens stopped believing in human progress and pitted an aggressive German culture against Western civilization. Just as citizenship rights became established in the Second Empire as *ius sanguinis*, that is, by ancestry, so the German concept of culture dragged with it an ethnic connotation that a reader, who could not identify with it, would never have been able to find in Schiller or Goethe, Hegel or Kant. This ethnic poisoning began at the same time as the history of German nationalism, as a genuine product of the long nineteenth century. Since then, the demand for a German *Leitkultur* manages to hide the reactionary impulse for ethnic homogeneity, in its everyday, practical, taken-for-granted articulation, by which one demands that in common social intercourse, all members of society have to make a greater effort. The slogan of multiculturalism negated precisely these "efforts," by treating all of the different cultures as tightly fitted entities existing in one space. Dig down deep enough and one will find at the core of multiculturalism again the category of identity, which in a reversal of tolerant pluralism contributed to a taken-for-granted national dominant culture by establishing the idea that one's self-understanding and one's cultural ascriptions are in harmony.

That is why Christianity, understood as part of the secular state and secular society, slips back into current discussions through the back door. This contemporary form of identification and self-identification allows new groups to develop. Paradigmatic examples of this are the transformations of earlier "guest workers" and later asylum seekers from so-called Islamic countries: they and their families are considered Muslims no matter what their religious affinities might be. Their past citizenship and the religion of their places of origin determine how the groups are classified in their new places of residence. In this way, the actual secularization process is revoked and becomes a non-reality, both in the lands of origin and in their new homes.

What is denied is secularization as a two hundred year old process that, in a contradictory fashion, has changed not just western societies. The simplified idea of progressive secularization was modeled on the belief in progress from the nineteenth century, although in its last third period, there occurred massive counter-reactions to the increasing worldliness of bourgeois society. In that period, the reaction delivered up the slogan of "culture wars" used a hundred years later, ironically, to refer to the controversies taking place at US universities over competing politics of identity. This kind of acculturation of politics can be understood as a reaction to the failures of the new social movements at the end of the 1960s. As usual, this process played out faster in the United States than in other places. Just waiting to be picked up during the world historical conflicts of the 1980s were all of the categories in which collective self-understanding and analytic claims could be articulated. The catchword "multiculturalism" tied together social interpretation and collective self-consciousness; an imprecise mixture that corrupts all theory. A reactionary politics of national identity established itself everywhere in Europe after the fall of real socialism, and mercilessly exploited this weakness of multiculturalism. "Multicultural" was portrayed as a malevolent ideological program of the intellectual élites, against which a poisonous but popular common sense could be easily mobilized. And, in fact, multiculturalism is not only a reflexive reaction to changed ethnic structures of western society, but also a political claim to bestow a voice on variously constituted groups of intellectuals, marginalized persons, and discriminated segments of the population. An ongoing struggle over the legitimacy of those voices takes place between these groups and their representatives. By contrast, it is easy to speak for the apparently silent majority that is in league with so often called upon social traditions.

Whereas in the United States the struggle over new interpretations of society and its traditions is carried out within an academic establishment to which someone like Samuel Huntington belongs, the front lines in Germany are staffed by the academically trained print (and now web) journalists. They know all of the academic debates over definitions, and use their extra-academic power of the press in order to put into play a new self-understanding of society in the style of an anti-authoritarian revolt against a purported dominant political culture of the so-called sixty-eighters that occasionally is pilloried as a dictatorship of political correctness. The syncretistic power of society is at work here, in so far as that power connects the vaunted "values" of the educational elite with the anti-intellectual resentments of a silent majority. The sociological miracle of being part of the elite and the majority is made possible by the postulated *Leitkultur*, since the autochthonous participants of the *dominant culture* consider themselves to have acquired the distinction at birth. No subjective effort is needed anymore to inherit what the fathers apparently passed on to the children in the manner conceptualized by Goethe for the German bourgeoisie. The bourgeois "invention of tradition," which since the late nineteenth century let a national self-consciousness take form, does not work anymore. Only a conscious reestablishment of tradition would, one hundred years later, be an alternative to a politics of history and identity. In that way, substantive democratic rules of interaction for a heterogeneous society politically could have been secured; a project that failed in 1968 and which, after 1989, no one thought of starting up again.

The aversion to the new is not a German invention, but after 1989 the barrier against the new in its German form saw the light of day again in world history. Germany lay at the vertex of two alternative systems, and a unique situation in history came to pass as the two very different social forms were united politically and, apart from a few nostalgic dreamers, this event was not supposed to be viewed by either side as anything new. From the far right to the far left, everyone came to agree with the phrase "reunification." The events of the late fall of 1989 allow us to study the reality of collective subjectivity in an exemplary manner. The social discontent with the undemocratic SED regime, encapsulated in the phrase "We are *the* people," transformed itself into the phrase "We are *one* people," which pointed to a national exit from social misery. In Germany, the name "reunification" had already been coined by the German constitution (Basic Law). But in the other "real-socialist" nations of Eastern Europe, the dissolution of the Eastern Bloc occurred under the promise of a "return to Europe." The nation proved itself to be a transmitted form of collective subjectivity, whose past could be more easily idealized than in Germany. The formula of national identity treats an imagined community as identical with an idealized past of the nation. Nobody wished to take away this fantasy from the new nations of the middle Eastern European states, which were reclaiming old histories—especially in light of the reality of the still existing Soviet Union—and where the national form of dissolution seemed to speed up democratic progress. But in Germany this process of idealizing national identity through a socially unconceptualized past became difficult, since it would have meant incorporating National Socialist history as well. Thus, the formula of identity evoked even more strongly than usual the acculturation of social differences. A renewed substantialization of German culture was bound to clash with the transformed composition of the West German population, a phenomenon that from the point of view of identity was labeled "multiculturalism." The xenophobic attacks of the early 1990s can be traced to these tensions of "Reunification": Rostock-Lichtenhagen, Hoyerswerda, Solingen.

In its abstractness, the slogan "identity" fits together logically with the same claim to breadth as the word "globalization." Against this background, abstract identity appears fetishistically as something concrete onto which everything can be projected that is supposed to save society from leveling down. The imagined collective subjectivity can become more than fiction, it can become a *real fiction* that creates a new situation. The way this fiction took on a kind of reality became manifest in Germany in the late fall of 1989. It does not make any sense from a critical perspective to point to the fictitious moment of that time, because what was important was its *real* character. The identity politicians made a lot of interest off this currency and rendered their critics speechless. The critics, who wanted to be heard, used the same means as those they criticized. They presupposed a collective subjectivity and proposed identity in the same way, it was just supposed to be something other than national. The discourse of national identity and the voices of multiculturalism ended up meeting in a conceptual prison house. The enlightened multiculturalists have long ago left behind the naïve ideas about pure origins and have come up with hybrid forms. But the discovery of hybrids did not lead to an abandonment of the category of identity; quite the opposite, it became an attempt to save the concept in the face of a society that seemed to be incessantly producing the non-identical. The paradox of the new society consists precisely in destroying traditional forms of belonging, while at the same time producing new needs for identity. In the culture industry's system of needs, "collective identity" operates like a psychic inlay, as the psychoanalyst Paul Parin has called it. It promises to repair the damaged confidence of the subject.

The way that collective identity functioned psychologically in Germany became very obvious after 1990. The damaged self-confidence reached an almost cult-like status in post–Nazi Germany. Since after 1945 it was not possible to separate cleanly the nation from the Nazi past, the complaints about an abandoned national feeling were part of the arsenal of reactionary cultural criticism. The GDR invented a separate form of nationalism, which did have the effect of keeping alive injured national pride: seldom was Johannes R. Becher's GDR hymn "Risen From the Ashes (*Auferstanden aus Ruinen*)," with its line "Germany One Fatherland," sung so loud as it was in 1989. While jeremiads about a missing national feeling were aired in West Germany until 1990 only with a little embarrassment, in the Soviet-occupied zone they had the effect of sounding like the legitimate striving for freedom against the oppression of a police state. Because the Nazis had been fought against under the banner of national liberation, once "real existing socialism" was toppled, one could fall back on the same formula. But in contrast to the collapse of National Socialism, this time the Germans could mimic the form of national liberation. In light of the wave of black, red, and gold colors during political demonstrations, the progressive ideas of the actual GDR dissidents melted away like snow in the sun. The illusion of national identity merged with "reunification" and never before had the category of identity enjoyed more reality than during that period.

National identity commands a high price, for who can expect a newly emigrated citizen to avow all of German history, including the making of a confession of guilt? Anyone who avoids doing so will be confronted with a feeling of being an outsider, one of the more unusual ethnicizing exclusions in the world. Is there an alternative to national identity politics? A critical social theory could show its usefulness with a critique of collective perceptions of subjectivity. Social self-understanding becomes transparent through remembering how the category of identity came to penetrate everyday life, and the genesis of national collective consciousness documents that it is subjectively produced. The category of identity becomes successful when feelings are played off against consciousness; and as long as a difference still exists between feeling and consciousness, the possibility of transformation still exists. The dominance of the social whole becomes true when overwhelmed by feeling. "Collective identity," far from empowering the subject as an individual, unmasks itself as a category of subjugation. Nowhere did this become so shockingly evident in the recent past as in the dissolution of Yugoslavia.

The best example of this form of collective subjugation occurred in Bosnia in the early 1990s: after ethno-nationalist aggressors divided up Sarajevo with barricades, armed bands marauded through the country, confronting people under penalty of death to identify their origins and, depending on the answer, one could either walk away with one's skin intact or be raped, exiled, tortured, or murdered. Especially in a heterogeneous society like the Bosnian one, the borders had to be created violently to constitute the new collective. In light of these events, it would be a denial of reality to stress the fictional quality of the category of identity. Authority and violence are the mediators between fiction and material reality. In no way was it the old animosity between nationalities, religions, and different cultures that brought forth the conflict. It was rather the aspirations for power by old and new elites that corresponded to a general insecurity about the future of a society whose particular nexus, the real-socialist mediating relationship between centralized power and economic distribution, was threatened. The pacification of the conflict could only come from the outside. The Dayton Peace Accords of 1995 led to an institutionalization of ethnicity that has paralyzed the country to this day.

One could claim this was a special, regional case, but the conflict occupied the entire world that would neither countenance a repeat of the massacre at Srebrenica, nor deny the newly created social realities. The conflict in the Balkans palpably puts the categories of how societies are interpreted to the test. The arbitrary side of the collective categories, hidden in public discourse, here becomes visible and throws a shadow back onto the scholarly and journalistic discussions from which they emanated.

The new world can be so easily interpreted with collective categories because its economic conjunctions have lost all alternatives. In this manner, US society delivers, with its ontological pretense, the paradigmatic model of interpretation that is applied to other, very distant societies. They are allegedly constituted by groups of varying origins that, competing over institutions, must learn to regulate their conflicts. What disappears from this social conception are the things that are mediated by activities of human beings among themselves. But the differences between the groups can be described more easily and, above all, more equivocally when they are traced back to supposed cultural differences. Culture becomes transformed, as if by magic, into a dematerialized category that raises the economically determined value of the category into a heavenly virtue, stripping it of its thing-like character. This process of displacement was already evident at the end of the long nineteenth century. It came in the form of the time-transcendent appearance of nations that had "always" differed culturally. This illusion was finally undermined in the last half of the twentieth century. It is true that in this period more nations than ever before were constituted and new and old empires dissolved. But what emerged was a unifying economic global system threatening to destroy all of the individually state-secured distributive economies. The world is still going through this process of dissolution, and the concept "globalization" describes it, while the slogan "Americanization" interprets it in a reactionary manner.

These are worldwide changes, but the reactions to them were differentiated. A theory of social differences could prove its usefulness if it were in a position to explain the variations historically. An essential aspect of global modernization consists in a progressive experience of secularization. Fundamentalist counter-movements therefore can be best understood as a reaction to this process, since it is not the old that returns in them, or even the power of the old; rather, the new takes on an atavistic appearance. But this atavism has a Janus face that opens itself up to a sociological explanation. Secularization pushes up against the border of the Enlightenment, since the individual itself is a real fiction. The idea of radical individualism denies the real existence of the active subject inside of the given social conditions of production.

The bourgeois subject at least needed property and family to develop self-consciousness. The individualized human being has only subjective qualities that can be devalued, however, on any given day. More than ever, today it is the secondary virtues in a knowledge economy, like flexibility, which are supposed to guarantee survival in a dynamic society. But this promise of security stands in opposition to the social experience of the twentieth century in which everyone could become an object of economic or political caprice. The artifact "holocaust," which has become disassociated from the actual events at Auschwitz, mediates this message on a global scale. The latent as well as manifest universalizing of fear increases the appetite for trans-individual security, and only those who deny social reality cannot notice the hunger for it. 9/11 reproduced this feeling of powerlessness among all of those who could not identify with those who committed the crime.

The inability to see the victims of the attacks on the Twin Towers as part of a cosmopolitan globally connected life points to the power of collective categories that divide the world into "us" and "the others." It requires human solidarity and social awareness to reach a grounded perception of the individual as weak and in need of reciprocal assistance. The disavowal of weakness appears to coincide perfectly through the identification with the aggressor. The hidden and open jubilation expressed in some parts of the world can be explained by resentment-filled impotence, which transforms the victims into wards of the strongest power in the world. The deceptive religious aura around this deed, which in a moment of indiscretion the composer Stockhausen called "sublime," feeds from the triumph of the failure of secularization, from which all fundamentalists draw. The terror, which is set loose from any kind of real political calculation—the kind which showed itself again on 11 March 2004 in Madrid—is not a question of definition; rather, it interprets itself in the language of violence that the whole world is supposed to understand as follows: nobody and nothing is safe from us. The figure of the suicide bomber embodies through the deed a complete ruthlessness in which the individual cancels out itself. The perpetrator and the sympathizers are not bound together by any common convictions or common goals, and a mediation is not possible or even necessary.

The groundwork for a collective whose constitution needs no individuals was already laid in the antiquated form of nineteenth century nationalism, which separated itself from the very society which created it. For this reason, the national dissolution of empires were often accompanied by a hint, sometimes even more than that, of xenophobia, ethnic cleansing, and pogroms. In regard to National Socialism, the emptiness of horror will be remembered in a distorted form. Exactly this vacuum is filled by the new collective categories and their symbols, like the national flags at concentration camp museums, the national and international days of remembrance, which cannot make do anymore without differentiating between the other and one's own "identity." The quotidian repetition of memory as praxis strengthens the consciousness not only of the reality of collective categories, but also the feeling of partaking in something primordial.

Although the social sciences today criticize the notion of the "primordial" as a false illusion, this criticism does little to reduce the discrete charm of the category. In fact, it seems to guarantee knowledge about origins, which secures its media successes. The forms of collective subjectivity are still connected to the mediation between nation and society, even in their ethnic or multicultural variety. Still, neologisms such as "transnational" reflect the manner in which particular national perceptions are constituted. The media organizations also have not shaken off the national form of communication. An individual who wishes to mark oneself off from the collective is still constitutively dependent on the nation. A critique thus must begin by dismantling the illusion of the unchanging dominance of the social collective. The relationship between the nation and society is always changeable, and by deduction so are the categories in which one understands both oneself and the world. The ever-increasing social pressure to attach oneself to one kind of collective identity evokes the growing pressure not only to attach, but also to subordinate to the collective. Collective becomes identical with the illusion of self-realization. It is not a humanity without memory one needs to fear—the nightmare that stood out in Adorno's eye—but rather an endless number of people who cannot identify with humanity as a whole because their social fantasy is buried under the myths of particular ideologies of identity. The universal ideology of identity that pushes aside the image of an emancipated humanity amounts to a reverse transformation of enlightenment into a mythology that only can be countered with a new enlightenment, albeit this time aware of its very real limitations.

Translated by Elliot Neaman

Part IV

Coda

Ten Questions for Martin Jay

1. Your book, *The Dialectical Imagination*, was first published in 1973 and it launched your scholarly career; that's about thirty-five years ago now. That book and subsequent work in the following decade, e.g., *Marxism and Totality*, and the Adorno book for the "Modern Masters" series, expressed a certain fidelity to the Western Marxist tradition, and implied that you harbored a certain faith in the longevity and even the validity of a perspective we might broadly describe as "critical theory." Do you think that your turn toward other themes in more recent work—the French critique of ocularcentrism, the discourses of experience, the new work on mendacity in politics—suggests that your faith in critical theory has diminished? Does your turn to new themes mean you've lost some of your earlier enthusiasm for the intellectual resources of critical theory?

MJ: My initial interest in Western Marxism in general and the Frankfurt School in particular was more that of an intellectual historian than a committed advocate, which led certain early critics of my work—for example, Gillian Rose, Russell Jacoby, and James Schmidt—to worry that I had come to bury rather than praise. One of my first publications, in fact, was a critique of what I feared were the metapolitical implications of Marcuse's utopianism. I was, however, sufficiently drawn to certain of the assumptions and goals of the tradition to be a sympathetic chronicler, who has never lost a certain respect for its legacy. Although in subsequent years I've been concerned with other figures and other themes, I have never repudiated Critical Theory and often return to the remarkably rich corpus of writings it produced (and its second and third generation descendants continue to produce). In my book on experience, for example, I have a chapter on Adorno and Benjamin, and in my current work on lying in politics, I have learned from Adorno's critique of authenticity, which I explored in a recent piece in *New German Critique*. This year, Judith Butler and I, along with a very extensive group of Berkeley colleagues, launched a graduate "designated emphasis" in Critical Theory, under whose auspices I will be giving a seminar on the Frankfurt School in the spring of 2008. So although I have certainly broadened my interests, I continue to drink at the well from which I first sipped back in the 1960s.

2. In his famous essay on the German-Jewish Intellectuals, Habermas made the interesting statement that German-Jewish thought has always remained "critique." What's your perspective on that claim? More importantly, do you think of yourself as in any sense working out of an intellectual tradition inflected in any way by the Jewish experience? This is a theme you've rarely touched upon in your writings. And it's clear to most readers that you share a certain reluctance to identify yourself with any ethno-religious perspective, since any such identification risks blunting or even openly conflicting with one's universalist aspirations as a cosmopolitan intellectual. Still, even granting that point, in what sense do you think you've been shaped by your own (admittedly complicated) historical-biographical and sociological trajectory as an American Jew?

MJ: To give more than a superficial answer to this question would take at least a lengthy essay. I have for a very long time been a non-observant Jew unable to share in the religious practices and rituals of the community with any serious commitment, at least since my bar mitzvah in 1957. Because my parents had themselves more or less abandoned the piety of their first-generation forebears, my own drifting away from observance was not a wrenching decision, nor have I ever been tempted to recover what had been lost. Marrying out of the tribe, as I did, was thus not a problematic choice, and my family never hesitated to support it.

That said, I have always considered myself deeply and proudly Jewish in the way that so many secular Jews of my generation do, and I have often written about Jewish issues and for journals like *Midstream*, *Commentary* (before their lurch to the right), and *Tikkun*. This has led to a certain public recognition that I am, however one might define it, a Jewish intellectual (or at least an intellectual who is definitely Jewish). Thus, to cite two examples, the Union College Encyclopedia identifies me as one of its prominent Jewish alumni, and the comedian Alan King asked me to contribute to a book about growing up Jewish, which he edited under the awful title *Matzoh Balls for Breakfast*—and where I found myself in the unlikely company of figures like Sid Caesar, Billy Crystal, and Don Rickles!

More seriously, I have been fascinated by the writings of European Jewish thinkers, and not only the secular ones like the majority of the Frankfurt School, but also more religiously inclined ones like Buber, Rosenzweig, Scholem, and Levinas. My attitude, to be sure, has never been reverential or celebratory, largely because I have taken seriously that imperative to practice critique Habermas identifies as one of the legacies of the German-Jewish interaction. This inclination extends as well to Israel, whose existence I have always unequivocally defended, but whose current regime I do not. In fact, one of the most controversial pieces I've ever written, a 2003 column for *Salmagundi*, dealt with the relationship between the new anti-Semitism and the policies of Ariel Sharon. It resulted in a violently aggressive, ad hominem attack by a right-wing Zionist named Edward Alexander, reprinted many times and then included in a book he coedited on allegedly self-hating Jewish foes of Israel. Here I was placed not in the company of borscht belt comedians, but of figures like Noam Chomsky, George Steiner, Tony Judt, Seymour Hersh, Thomas Friedman, Judith Butler, and Michael Lerner. While I don't share all of their arguments, I have no trouble feeling honored by the inclusion.

3. Freud and Freudian concepts have long been central to critical writing, broadly defined. To what extent has Freud been influential for you?

MJ: For my generation, Freud was a major influence, especially in the wake of his reassessment as a potentially radical figure by Norman O. Brown, Herbert Marcuse, Juliet Mitchell, and others. I was never convinced, however, that intellectual history might be enriched by the straightforward application of psycho-historical interpretations to figures or their ideas. The brief moment of its efflorescence following the pioneering work of Erik Erikson ended fairly rapidly, and the results were mixed at best. If I had to look back and see how Freud has left a mark on my own work, it would have been through the impact of some of his less central ideas, such as on the uncanny, the abject, mourning, and melancholy. And, of course, I have been interested in trying to make sense of the ways in which psychoanalytic explorations of visuality and the unconscious, most notably those of Lacan and Lyotard, have enriched our understanding of visual experience. The recent assault on Freud has done a lot to discredit his work, but I still find much of it very stimulating.

4. In your more recent writings you have tended to side with Habermas's critique of poststructuralism. Do you consider it a theoretical cul-de-sac?

MJ: My sympathies for Habermas, which were perhaps most extensively elaborated in work I did in the 1980s, has never meant a simplistic rejection of the various positions that were lumped together under the awkward rubric of "post-structuralism." I have always taken the provocations of Foucault, Lacan, and Derrida very seriously, as well as those of earlier figures like Bataille who anticipated some of their arguments. In essays such as my comparison of modernist and postmodernist paganism, represented respectively by Peter Gay and Jean-Francois Lyotard, I have tried to draw out the virtues in each position. Now that the so-called "theory wars" of the 1980s have waned, it is even easier to avoid a "for or against" stance towards traditions that are too rich and productive to warrant wholesale judgments.

5. What do you see as the primary mission of intellectual history to the humanities?

MJ: Intellectual history has many valuable missions to perform. It serves, for example, as a holding pen for theories and figures that are not at the moment at the cutting edge of their disciplines, but might one day enjoy an unexpected renaissance of interest. It reminds present-minded scholars that the terms they use have complicated, sedimented histories, that defy reduction to legislated definitions. It opens up horizons across disciplinary lines, allowing us to see parallels or interactions that might be missed by concentrating on only one narrow historical trajectory. It makes us attend to the institutions of intellectual life and the fields of force in which ideas emerge, are disseminated and transmitted, and compete for hegemony. It gives us permission to take ideas unreductively and on their own merits, but also to situate them in the contexts which enabled them to flourish or languish. And as history, it helps us to appreciate the narrative and dramatic ways in which ideas and culture develop over time, often with unintended consequences and creative misreadings that defy the control of those who first elaborate them.

It also can illuminate the hitherto unexplored histories of disciplines in ways that may have an impact on the present practices of those within them. By far the most influential essay I have ever written is "Scopic Regimes of Modernity," which has been anthologized, translated, and taught widely. To my great surprise, it has not only become a touchstone for scholarly histories of visual culture, but also an inspiration for artists working in different media, or at least a way for them to make sense of the work they are doing.

6. How do you think intellectual history will fit into the current constellation of the humanities in the next decade or so? Is there a "crisis" of identity in the field now?

MJ: I have always resisted the easy invocation of "crisis" talk, which melodramatically suggests we have reached a point of heightened significance in which something decisive will occur. Intellectual history has survived the surge of interest in social and then cultural history, learning from both without succumbing to the charge that it is inherently elitist or Eurocentric or patriarchal in nature. Although we are less quick now to assume a hierarchy of "high" and "low" or "avant-garde" and "traditional" ideas or cultural practices, intellectual historians are normally drawn to the more demanding, complex, and difficult end of the spectrum. I have always encouraged my students to work on figures or themes they can take seriously in their own terms and not see simply as symptoms of something else, if only to get the stimulation from encountering challenging, even counterintuitive ideas rather than reinforcing familiar and conventional ones.

Insofar as there is a creative dialogue between historicist and antihistoricist impulses in the humanities, between contextualizing and anticontextualizing approaches, and between narrative and synchronic methods, intellectual history will continue to be an important participant in the larger conversation of the humanities. It has, to be sure, a great deal to learn from other approaches, especially those that have gone under the rubric "the linguistic turn," and has also been much enriched by absorbing lessons from social scientists like Bourdieu. The robust vitality of the field is apparent in the new energy evident in older journals such as *The Journal of the History of Ideas* and new ones like *Modern Intellectual History*. Lots of smart people doing first-rate, creative work!

7. You went to Union College and received your PhD from Harvard University, where you studied intellectual history with H. Stuart Hughes. Are there elements of Hughes's method or are there substantive interests in his oeuvre that you feel shaped your own practice as an intellectual historian? Are there other teachers and scholars, at Union College and at Harvard, whose influence might be detected in your work, and if so, how? What might this tell us about successive schools and institutional forces that have contributed to the character of European intellectual history in the United States today?

MJ: I was first introduced to Stuart Hughes in 1962, when he came to Union to give a talk. He was running at the time for Senate in Massachusetts as a peace candidate, opposing Teddy Kennedy, Edward McCormick (nephew of the Speaker of the House), and George Cabot Lodge. Hughes, of course, came in a distant fourth, losing much of his already modest support after the Cuban Missile Crisis undermined the pacifist cause. I mention this background because Hughes, himself the scion of a distinguished political family, was always more than a scholarly figure for me. He embodied the ideal of an activist intellectual, willing to combine his work as an historian with political commitment. I had no trouble deciding which graduate mentor I wanted when I applied for graduate school in 1965.

As an intellectual historian, Hughes was also a model in his willingness to yoke together a disparate cast of characters from several countries and fields, and find larger patterns in their ideas. His most successful and influential book, *Consciousness and Society*, is one I still ask my students to read fifty years after its publication. I think it is fair to say that I've been more comfortable engaging with the intricacies of the thought of the figures I treat than he was, as he painted with fairly broad-brush strokes. But he was certainly a model in terms of his combining scholarly and non-scholarly commitments and looking for figures in carpets that could be discerned only from above. I should add that his interest in the intellectual migration from Germany and personal friendship with figures like Marcuse helped to orient and validate my first project.

As for even earlier mentors at Union, I'm very pleased to have a chance to acknowledge the impact and inspiration of historians Joseph Finkelstein, Neal Allen, and Manfred Jonas, literary critics Carl Niemeyer and John Mason Bradbury, and philosopher Sven Peterson. It may be of some interest that my senior honors thesis was on the reception of Nietzsche's thought in prewar Europe; I later discovered that Eugene Lunn and Mark Poster, who also became European intellectual historians, likewise wrote as undergrads on Nietzsche, a reflection of the impact of Walter Kaufmann's influential reevaluation of his impact a few years earlier.

8. Some scholars have tried to ascribe a "Jay method" to intellectual history (for example, Dominick LaCapra). Is there a "Jay method?"

MJ: No, happily, no. I have always been opposed to developing a replicable method that can be applied like a recipe to any question in intellectual history. Although Dominick once perceptively described my work as "synoptic content analysis," I don't think all of it can be so neatly defined. What I've tried to convey to students is the conviction that they have to fix on a theme or figure or problem that really excites them and will be worth absorbing their talents and energies for a very long time. I've tried to get them to conceptualize their work as an answer to an exigent question and to spend time framing that question as precisely as they can in order to know what is relevant and what is not in their research and the presentation of the results. And I've tried to relieve them of the burden of writing a definitive answer to that question, encouraging them instead to see their work as part of an ongoing discussion that will inevitably surpass their efforts. Important work, it seems to me, wants to open up further debate and welcomes being surpassed in time, rather than closing down a discussion and serving as a tombstone for a question no one wants to open again. One of the greatest satisfactions of my earliest work on Critical Theory is the way in which it helped generate an international interest in the Frankfurt School, which shows no signs of abating well into the twenty-first century.

9. How would you describe Adorno's influence on the way you write intellectual history? For example, in both your scholarly writing and social commentary, you often describe two (or more positions), set them off against each other in order to sublate them, add several layers that combine elements of each, but finally distance yourself from the original arguments in order to leave the reader with a hard-to-reverse tapestry of ideas, but no definitive resolution. Is there any of *Negative Dialectics* in this strategy?

MJ: At times I have found Adorno's notion of a force field or constellation of countervailing and unreconciled elements a suggestive metaphor for the presentation of intellectual positions. Rather than forcing a smooth sublation, mediating contradictions in a higher synthesis, I have been drawn to tense contests of ideas without easy resolution, creating a kind of negative dialectic in Adorno's sense of that term. In fact, in the little book I did on Adorno himself for the "Modern Masters" series, I used the concept to define his own complicated formation at the intersection of—or perhaps better put, within the gravitational field—of several, very different impulses, both generative and receptive. That is, in addition to those that provided a context for the formation of his ideas, I tried to include others that were operative in the ways in which the ideas have been understood since their inception, thus incorporating Gadamer's insight that meaning is not fixed by those whose signatures are on ideas, but also generated by the unexpected ways in which they are later interpreted. The bi-annual column I've done for *Salmagundi* since 1987 is called *Force Fields*, as is one of my essay collections, which points to the power of this model in my work. In addition to its substantive implications, I've also sought to mobilize it to highlight the different voices in which I write, scholarly and colloquial, best illustrated by the mixture of texts in my volumes of essays, which undercut the impression of a smoothly coherent subject behind all of my writing.

10. The hallmarks of your work are its catholicity and generosity. While you may have inclined in books like *Marxism and Totality* and *Downcast Eyes* to a rationalist Enlightenment tradition in your conclusions, you always showed keen interest in the insights of alternative traditions, in-

cluding most recently the English conservative tradition. You tend to interpret charitably what other rationalist intellectual historians sometimes put on trial or treat as threats. But it is striking—especially as a defender of Enlightenment rationalism—that you have never written about the liberal theoretical traditions of any country. There is no chapter in your books on Constant, Mill, or Tocqueville in the nineteenth century or Berlin or Rawls in the twentieth (though Habermas in the end approached the latter), and some of your most incisive criticism has been reserved for contemporary attempts to revive liberalism. Is this an asymmetry in your work? Is it intentional? What does it tell us about your approach to intellectual history?

MJ: You are right to highlight my desire to be as charitable as I can to positions I instinctively find implausible or even unappealing. It has always seemed to me a wise rule of thumb to engage with opponents at their strongest, rather than seek to destroy them in advance by focusing only on their vulnerabilities. Constructive intellectual discussion is not like a battle in a court of law in which the goal is to win by any means possible. In fact, I always get more satisfaction out of losing an argument to someone I've learned from than out of winning an easy victory over an opponent whose positions are too weak to take seriously. In the case you have mentioned, that of British conservatism, I would agree that a thinker like Burke or more recently Oakeshott—whose lectures I attended during my junior year abroad at the London School of Economics—are worthy interlocutors from whom much can be learned. One of the great disappointments of contemporary American politics is that the revival of conservatism has been so lacking in serious intellectual substance. What you call my charitable openness to other positions has, of course, also been the source of criticism by those who feel more partisan in their commitments, the most amusing recent example being the generally positive review Terry Eagleton wrote of *Songs of Experience* in *The London Review of Books*, where he complained that the book would do little to drive Donald Rumsfeld from power (and although Rumsfeld did, in fact, fall soon after, I can't claim that Eagleton was wrong).

As for my relative neglect of liberalism, I think the reason is simply that my own default prejudices are so hopelessly liberal that I don't find it interesting to explore the origins of what seems so self-evident to me. If, as I claimed in my last book, experience is often an encounter with otherness, a perilous journey that takes us some distance from where we began, I like to venture into foreign intellectual waters in order to come home changed, hopefully for the better, by the adventure.

PUBLICATIONS OF MARTIN JAY

Books

The Dialectical Imagination: A History of the Frankfurt School and the Institute of Social Research, 1923–50 (Boston: Little, Brown and Co., 1973); English, Japanese, Spanish, French, German, Italian, Dutch, Chinese, Indonesian, and Serbo-Croatian editions; pirated Korean and Turkish editions; Portuguese and official Turkish editions forthcoming; second American edition with new preface (Berkeley: University of California Press, 1996).

Marxism and Totality: The Adventures of a Concept from Lukács to Habermas (Berkeley: University of California Press; Cambridge, England: Polity Press, 1984); Japanese edition, Chinese and Serbo-Croatian editions forthcoming.

Adorno (London: Fontana [Modern Masters]; Cambridge, MA: Harvard University Press, 1984); Italian, Portuguese, Slovenian, Spanish, Japanese, Korean, Turkish, and two Chinese editions (PRC and Taiwanese).

Permanent Exiles: Essays on the Intellectual Migration from Germany to America (New York: Columbia University Press, 1985); Japanese edition.

Fin-de-Siècle Socialism and Other Essays (New York and London: Routledge, 1988); Spanish and Japanese editions.

Force Fields: Between Intellectual History and Cultural Critique (New York and London: Routledge, 1993); Japanese and Spanish editions.

Downcast Eyes: The Denigration of Vision in Twentieth-Century French Thought (Berkeley: University of California Press, 1993); Korean and Spanish editions forthcoming.

Cultural Semantics: Keywords of Our Time (Amherst, MA: University of Massachusetts Press, 1998).

Refractions of Violence (New York: Routledge, 2003); Japanese edition.

La Crisis de la experiencia en la era postsubjetiva, edited by Eduardo Sabrovsky (Santiago de Chile: Universidad Diego Portales Press, 2003).

Songs of Experience: Modern European and American Variations on a Universal Theme (Berkeley: University of California Press, 2004); Polish edition forthcoming.

Edited Volumes with Introductions

Festschrift for Leo Lowenthal, *Telos*, no. 45 (Fall 1980).
An Unmastered Past: The Autobiographical Reflections of Leo Lowenthal (Berkeley: University of California Press, 1987).
The Weimar Republic: Sourcebook (with Anton Kaes and Edward Dimendberg) (Berkeley: University of California Press, 1994).
Vision in Context: Historical and Contemporary Perspectives on Sight (with Teresa Brennan) (New York and London: Routledge, 1996).
America Hihvo-Riron No Shin Dankai (The New State of American Critical Theory), vol. I (Tokyo: Aoki Shoto, 1997); vol. II (Tokyo: Kouchi Syobah, 2000).
"The Current State of Visual Culture Studies," *Journal of Visual Culture* 4, no. 2 (August, 2005).
Axel Honneth, *Reification: A New Look at an Old Idea*, with commentaries by Judith Butler, Raymond Geuss and Jonathan Lear (Oxford: Oxford University Press, 2008).

Book Introductions

Helmut Dubiel, *Theory and Politics* (Cambridge, MA: MIT Press, 1985).
Franz L. Neumann, *The Rule of Law* (Leamington Spa, England: Berg Publishers, 1986).
Alain Boureau, *Kantorowicz: Stories of a Historian* (Baltimore: The Johns Hopkins University Press, 2001).
Leo Lowenthal and Siegfried Kracauer, *In steter Freundschaft: Briefwechsel*, edited by Peter-Erwin Jansen and Christian Schmidt (Hamburg: Zu Klampen, 2003).
Ales Erjavec, ed., *Postmodernism and the Postsocialist Condition: Politicized Art under Late Socialism* (Berkeley: University of California Press, 2003).

Articles

"The Permanent Exile of Theodor W. Adorno," *Midstream* (December, 1969).
"Metapolitics of Utopianism," *Dissent* (July–August, 1970); reprinted as "How Utopian is Marcuse?" in *The Revival of American Socialism*, edited by George Fischer (New York: Oxford University Press, 1971).
"The Politics of Terror," *Partisan Review* 38, no. 1 (1971).
"The Frankfurt School in Exile," *Perspectives in American History* 6 (1972).
"The Frankfurt School," in *The Unknown Dimension: European Marxism Since Lenin*, edited by Karl Klare and Dick Howard (Basic Books: New York, 1972).
"The Frankfurt School's Critique of Marxist Humanism," *Social Research* 39, no. 2 (Summer, 1972); Hebrew translation in *Basha'ar* 18, no. 1 (January–February, 1975); Swedish translation in *Tekla*, nos. 12/13 (August, 1982).
"Recent Developments in Critical Theory," *The Berkeley Journal of Sociology* 18 (1973–1974).
"The Loss of George Lichtheim," *Midstream* 19, no. 8 (October, 1973).
"Anti-Semitism and the Weimar Left," *Midstream* (January, 1974).
"The Frankfurt School's Critique of Karl Mannheim and the Sociology of Knowledge," *Telos*, no. 20 (Summer, 1974).

"Crutches vs. Stilts: An Answer to James Schmidt on the Frankfurt School," *Telos*, no. 22 (Winter, 1974–1975).

"Marxism and Critical Theory: Martin Jay and Russell Jacoby," *Theory and Society* 2 (1975).

"The Extraterritorial Life of Siegfried Kracauer," *Salmagundi*, nos. 31–32 (Fall 1975– Winter 1976).

"The Politics of Translation: Kracauer and Benjamin on the Buber-Rosenzweig Bible," *The Leo Baeck Institute Year Book* 21 (1976).

"The Concept of Totality in Lukács and Adorno," in *Varieties of Marxism*, edited by Shlomo Avineri (The Hague: Kluwer Academic Publishers, 1977), and *Telos*, no. 32 (Summer, 1977).

"Further Considerations on Anderson's *Considerations on Western Marxism*," *Telos*, no. 32 (Summer, 1977).

Biography of Franz Neumann in the *Dictionary of American Biography*, Supplement 5 (1951–1955) (New York, 1977).

"Adorno and Kracauer: Notes on a Troubled Friendship," *Salmagundi*, no. 40 (Winter, 1978); German translation in *Hannoversche Schriften* 6, edited by Detlev Claussen, Oskar Negt, and Michael Werz (Frankfurt: Verlag Neue Kritik, 2005).

"Hannah Arendt: Opposing Views," with a rejoinder by Leon Botstein, *Partisan Review* 45, no. 3 (1978).

Biographies of Herbert Marcuse and Max Horkheimer in *International Encyclopedia of the Social Sciences* 18 (New York: The Free Press, 1979).

"Kurt Mandelbaum: His Decade at the Institute of Social Research," *Development and Change* 10, no. 4 (October, 1979).

"Frankfurter Schule und Judentum, Die Antisemitismusanalyse der Kritischen Theorie," *Geschichte und Gesellschaft* 5, no. 4 (1979); English version as "The Jews and the Frankfurt School," *New German Critique*, no. 19 (Winter, 1980), and *Germans and Jews Since the Holocaust: The Changing Situation in West Germany*, edited by Anson Rabinbach and Jack Zipes (New York: Holmes and Meier, 1986); Portuguese translation in *Construindo a Imogem do Juden*, edited by Nelson H. Vierra (Rio de Janeiro, 1994).

"Introduction," Festschrift for Leo Lowenthal, *Telos*, no. 45 (Fall, 1980).

"Remembering Henry Pachter," *Salmagundi*, nos. 52–53 (Spring-Summer, 1981).

"Vico and Western Marxism," in *Vico: Past and Present*, edited by Giorgio Tagliacozzo (Atlantic Highlands, NJ: Humanities Press, 1981).

"Back to the Starting Line After the Theories Misfire," *The Times Higher Education Supplement*, 18 December 1981.

"Anamnestic Totalization: The Function of Memory in Herbert Marcuse's Thought," *Theory and Society* 11, no. 1 (1982): reprinted in *Marcuse: Critical Theory and the Promise of Utopia*, edited by Robert Pippin, Andrew Feenberg, and Charles Webel (South Hadley, MA, 1988); German translation in *Befreiung denken—Ein politischer Imperative: Ein Materialienband zu Herbert Marcuse*, edited by Peter-Erwin Jansen (Offenbach, Verlag 2000, 1989).

"Should Intellectual History Take a Linguistic Turn? Reflections on the Habermas-Gadamer Debate," in *European Intellectual History: Reappraisals and New Perspectives*, edited by Dominick La Capra and Steven L. Kaplan (Ithaca, NY: Cornell University Press, 1982); German translation in 1988.

"Positive and Negative Totalities: Implicit Tensions in Critical Theory's Vision of Interdisciplinary Research," *Thesis Eleven*, no. 3 (1982). German translation in *Sozialforschung als Kritik*, edited by Wolfgang Bonß and Axel Honneth (Frankfurt: Suhrkamp Verlag, 1982).

"Misrepresentations of the Frankfurt School," *Survey* 26, no. 1 (Summer 1982).

"For Gouldner; Reflections on an Outlaw Marxist," *Theory and Society* 11, no. 6 (November 1982).
Introduction to Max Horkheimer, "Egoism and the Freedom Movement," *Telos*, no. 54 (Winter 1982–1983).
"Habermas and Modernism," *Praxis International* 4, no. 1 (April, 1984), and Richard Bernstein, ed., *Habermas and Modernity* (Cambridge, MA: MIT Press, 1985); Greek translation in *Leviathan* 3 (Athens, 1989).
"Adorno in Amerika," in *Adorno-Konferenz 1983*, edited by Ludwig von Friedeburg and Jürgen Habermas (Frankfurt: Suhrkamp Verlag, 1983); English translation in *New German Critique*, no. 31 (Winter, 1984); reprinted in *Hannoversche Schriften* 1 (Frankfurt: Verlag Neue Kritik, 1999).
"Culture—A World Exclusive," *The Times Higher Educational Supplement*, 16 September 1983.
"I Never Wanted to Play Along: A Profile of Leo Lowenthal," *California Monthly* 95, no. 2 (December 1984).
"Hierarchy and the Humanities: The Radical Implications of a Conservative Idea," *Telos*, no. 62 (Winter, 1984–1985), and David Wallace, ed., *Tradition and Modernity: Contemporary Perspectives on the Humanities* (Burnaby, British Columbia: Simon Fraser University 1985).
"Lukács, Bloch in Boj za Marksisticni Koncept Totalnosti," *Filofski Vestnik* (Ljubljana, Yugoslavia), 1985/2; French version in *Editions Actes Sud* (1986)
"Two Cheers for Paraphrase: The Confessions of a Synoptic Intellectual Historian," *Stanford Literature Review* 3 (Spring, 1986).
"In the Empire of the Gaze: Foucault and the Denigration of Vision in Twentieth-Century French Thought," in *Foucault: A Critical Reader*, edited by David Hoy (London, Basil Blackwell, 1986) and *ICA Documents* 4/5 (London, 1986); reprinted in Lisa Appiginesi, ed., *Postmodernism: ICA Documents* (New York, 1989); French and Spanish translations, 1988 and 1989, German translation in *Leviathan*, 19, 1 (1991).
"Resettlement of German Jews: Comments on the Papers of Steven M. Lowenstein, Mordechai Eliav and Monika Richarz," *Leo Baeck Institute Year Book* 30 (1985).
"Mass Culture and the Intellectual Migration from Germany: the Cases of Max Horkheimer and Siegfried Kracauer," in *On Max Horkheimer*, edited by Seyla Benhabib, Wolfgang Bonss, and John McCole (Cambridge, MA: MIT Press, 1993) and in *Exil. Wissenschaft. Identität*, edited by Ilja Sruber (Frankfurt, 1988).
"Reconciling the Irreconcilable? Rejoinder to Kennedy," *Telos*, no. 71 (Spring, 1987) and *Geschichte und Gesellschaft* 13, no. 4 (1987).
"Sigmund Freud," *Encyclopedia Britannica*, Macropaedia (1988).
"Habermas and Postmodernism," *The Journal of Comparative Literature and Aesthetics* 11, nos. 1–2 (1988); Irit Rogoff, ed. *The Divided Heritage* (Cambridge, 1991); and Ingeborg Hoesterey, ed., *Zeitgeist in Babel: the Postmodernist Controversy* (Bloomington, IN, 1991).
"The Rise of Hermeneutics and the Crisis of Ocularcentrism," *Poetics Today* 9, no. 2 (November, 1988); *The Rhetoric of Interpretation and the Interpretation of Rhetoric* (Durham, 1989); *Journal of Contemporary Thought* (Varoda, India), 1991.
"Urban Flights: the Institute of Social Research Between Frankfurt and New York," *The University and the City*, edited by Thomas Bender (New York: Oxford University Press, 1988); and *Critical Theory Today: the Frankfurt School: How Relevant Is It Today?*, edited by Ph.V. Engeldorp Gastelaars, S.S. Magala, and O. Preuss (Rotterdam, 1990).
"Scopic Regimes of Modernity," in *Vision and Visuality; Discussions in Contemporary Culture* 2, edited by Hal Foster (1988); expanded version in *Modernity and Identity*, edited by Scott Lash and Jonathan Friedman (London: Wiley-Blackwell, 1992); German

translation in *Leviathan* 20, 2 (Berlin, 1992); Polish translation in *Prezestrzen, filosofia i architektura*, edited by Ewy Rewars (Poznan, 1999).

"The Debate over Performative Contradiction: Habermas vs. the Post-structuralists," *Zwischenbetrachtungen: Im Prozess der Aufklärung*, edited by Axel Honneth et al. (Frankfurt: Suhrkamp Verlag, 1989) and *Philosophical Interventions in the Unfinished Project of Enlightenment* (Cambridge, MA: MIT Press, 1992).

"The Descent of De Man," *Salmagundi*, nos. 78–79 (Spring-Summer, 1988); reprinted in *The Salmagundi Reader*, edited by Robert and Peggy Boyers (New York and Indianapolis: Indiana University Press, 1996).

"Fin-de-siècle Socialism," *Praxis International* 8, no. 1 (April, 1988); Dutch translation in L.W. Nauta and J. P. Koenis, eds., *Een toekomst voor het socialisme?* (Amsterdam, 1988); Danish translation in *Grus*, 26 (1988).

"Songs of Experience: The Debate over *Alltagsgeschichte*," *Salmagundi*, no. 81 (Winter, 1989).

"The Morals of Genealogy, or Is There a Post-Structuralist Ethics?" *Cambridge Review*, no. 110 (June 1989); and *The Subject in Postmodernism* I (Ljubljana, 1989); translated into Norwegian in *Tidens Verdier: Variasjoner over Moral og Samfunn*, edited by Torben Hviid Nielsen (Oslo: Universitetsforlaget, 1995).

"Photography and the Mirror of Art," *Salmagundi*, no. 84 (Fall, 1989).

"Klassenkampf im Seminar: Amerikanische Kontroversen um den Marxismus," *Frankfurter Allgemeine Zeitung*, 6 September 1989; "Class Struggle in the Classroom? The Myth of American 'Seminar Marxism'," *Salmagundi*, nos. 85–86 (Winter–Spring, 1990).

"Name-Dropping or Dropping Names? Modes of Legitimization in the Humanities," in *Theory Between the Disciplines*, Martin Kreiswirth and Mark Cheetham (Ann Arbor, MI: University of Michigan Press, 1990).

"Topografia Marksizmu Zachodniego," *Edukacia Filozoficzna* 8 (Warsaw, 1989) (translation of first chapter of *Marxism and Totality*).

"Habermas in Estetska Ideologija," *Filozofski Vestnik* 2 Ljubljana, 1989), and Serbo-Crotian in *Delo* 36, 11–12 (November–December, 1990).

"The Textual Approach to Intellectual History," in Karen J. McHardy, ed., *Fact and Fiction: German History and Literature, 1848–1924* (Tübingen: Francke Verlag, 1990); and *Strategies* 4, no. 5 (1991).

"Fieldwork and Theorizing in Intellectual History: A Response to Fritz Ringer," *Theory and Society* 19, no. 2 (1990); Spanish translation in *Prismas* 10 (Quilmes, Argentina, 2006).

"Women in Dark Times: Agnes Heller and Hannah Arendt," in *The Social Philosophy of Agnes Heller. Poznan Studies in the Philosophy of Sciences and the Humanities* 37 (1994); in German in *Leviathan* 2 (Berlin, 1994).

"Ideology and Ocularcentrism: Is There Anything Behind the Mirror's Tain?" in Charles Lemert, *Intellectuals and Politics: Social Theory Beyond the Academy* (Newbury Park, CA: Sage Publications, 1990); and *Indian Journal of American Studies* 18, no. 1 (Winter, 1988); German translation in *Leviathan* 23, no. 1 (1995).

"The Disenchantment of the Eye: Surrealism and the Crisis of Ocularcentrism," *Visual Anthropology Review* 7, no. 1 (Spring, 1991); *Visualizing Theory: Selections from V.A.R. 1990-1993*, edited by Lucien Taylor (New York: Routledge, 1994).

"Materialism and the Retreat from Form," in *Filozofski Vestnik* (Ljubljana, xii, 1, 1991).

"Who's Afraid of Christa Wolf? Thoughts on the Dynamics of Cultural Subversion," *Salmagundi*, no. 92 (Fall, 1991).

"The Aesthetic Alibi," *Salmagundi*, no. 93 (Winter, 1992); reprinted in *The New Salmagundi Reader*, edited by Robert and Peggy Boyers (New York: Syracuse University Press, 1996).

"Of Plots, Witnesses and Judgments," in *Probing the Limits of Representation: Nazism and the "Final Solution,"* edited by Saul Friedlander (Cambridge, MA: Harvard University Press, 1992).

"The Aesthetic Ideology: as Ideology: or, What Does It Mean to Aestheticize Politics?" *Cultural Critique* 21 (Spring, 1992). German translation in Peter Kemper, ed., *Die Zukunft des Politischen: Ausblicke auf Hannah Arendt* (Frankfurt: Fischer Taschenbuch Verlag, 1993).

"Erfahrungen und/oder Experimentieren: Löwenthal und die Herausforderung der Postmodernismus," in Frithjof Hager, *Geschichte Denken: Ein Notizbuch für Leo Löwenthal* (Leipzig: Reclam Verlag, 1992); Polish translation in *Pojednenie Tozsamocsi z Roznica?*, edited by Ewy Rewers (Poznan: Wydawnictwo Fundacji Humaniora, 1995).

"Lyotard and the Denigration of Vision in Twentieth-Century French Thought," *Thesis Eleven*, no. 31 (1992).

"European Intellectual History and the Specter of Multi-Culturalism," *Salmagundi*, no. 96 (Fall, 1992); French translation in *X-Alta*, 2/3 (November, 1999).

"Once More an Inability to Mourn? Reflections on the Left Melancholy of Our Time," *German Politics and Society* 27 (Fall, 1992).

"The Academic Woman as Performance Artist," *Salmagundi*, nos. 98–99 (Spring–Summer, 1993).

"Sartre, Merleau-Ponty, and the Search for a New Ontology of Sight," *Modernity and the Hegemony of Vision*, edited by David Michael Levin (Berkeley: University of California Press, 1993).

"Experience without a Subject: Walter Benjamin and the Novel," in Greek in *Leviathan*, 13 (Athens, 1993); *New Formations* 20 (Summer, 1993); *Rediscovering History: Culture, Politics and the Psyche*, edited by Michael S. Roth (Stanford, CA: Stanford University Press, 1994); and *The Actuality of Walter Benjamin*, edited by Laura Marcus and Lynda Nead (London: Lawrence & Wishart, 1998).

"Postmodern Fascism? Reflections on the Return of the Repressed," *Tikkun* 8, 6 (November/ December, 1993).

"The Apocalyptic Imagination and the Inability to Mourn," in *Rethinking Imagination: Culture and Creativity*, ed. Gillian Robinson and John Rundell (London: Routledge, 1994); German translation in *Wer Inszeniert das Leben?*, edited by Frithjof Hager and Hermann Schwengel (Frankfurt: Fischer, 1996).

"Educating the Educators," *Salmagundi*, nos. 101–102 (Winter–Spring, 1994).

"Abjection Overruled," *Salmagundi*, no. 103 (Summer, 1994).

"Mimesis und Mimetologie: Adorno und Lacoue-Labarthe," in *Auge and Affekt: Wahrnehmung und Interaktion*, edited by Gertrud Koch (Frankfurt, 1995); in English in *The Semblance of Subjectivity: Essays in Adorno's Aesthetic Theory*, edited by Tom Huhn and Lambert Zuidervaart (Cambridge, MA: MIT Press, 1997).

"Limites de l'éxperience-limite: Bataille et Foucault," in *Georges Bataille aprés tout*, edited by Denis Hollier (Paris, 1995); in English in *Constellations* 2, no. 2 (October 1995); Polish translation in Marek Kwiek, ed., *"Nie Pytajcie Mnie, Kim Jestem..."*: *Michel Foucault Dzisiaj* (Posnan, 1998).

"The Manacles of Gavrilo Princip," *Salmagundi*, nos. 106/107 (Spring–Summer, 1995), reprinted in Michael Lerner, ed., *Best Contemporary Jewish Writing* (New York: Jossey-Bass, 2001).

"Vracanje pogleda: ameriski odziv na francosko kritiko okularcentrizma," *Filosofski Vestnik* (Ljubljana), 1 (1995); in English as "Returning the Gaze: The American Response to the French Critique of Ocularcentrism," *Definitions of Visual Culture II, Modernist Utopias, Postformalism and Pure Visuality*, edited by Chantal Charbonneau (Montreal:

Museé d'art contemporaine, 1996); *Perspectives on Embodiment*, edited by Gail Weiss and Honi Fern Haber (New York: Routeldge, 1999); and in *Traveling Theory: France and the United States*, edited by Ieme van der Poel and Sophie Bertho (Madison, NJ: Fairleigh Dickinson University Press, 1999); German translation in *Privileg Blick: Kritik der visuellen Kultur*, edited by Christian Kravagna (Berlin: Id Verlag, 1997); Spanish translation in Estudios Visuales 1 (Madrid, November, 2003).

"Photo-unrealism: The Contribution of the Camera to the Crisis of Ocularcentrism," *Visuality and Textuality*, edited by Stephen Melville and Bill Readings (London: Macmillan, 1995).

"From Modernism to Post-Modernism," *The Oxford Illustrated History of Modern Europe*, edited by T.C.W. Blanning (Oxford: Oxford University Press, 1995).

"The Uncanny Nineties," *Salmagundi*, no. 108 (Fall, 1995); in German as "Das unheimliche Manöver oder: Über ein unbehagen in der Moderne," *Frankfurter Rundschau*, 31 December 1996.

"Response to George Mosse and David Myers," *Judaism* 45, no. 2 (Spring, 1996).

"For Theory," *Theory and Society* 25, no. 2 (April, 1996).

"Modernism and the Specter of Psychologism," *Modernism/Modernity* 3, no. 2 (May, 1996); reprinted in *The Mind of Modernism*, edited by Mark S. Micale (Stanford, CA: Stanford University Press, 2004).

"Peace in Our Time," *Salmagundi*, III (Summer, 1996).

"Disciplinary Prisms: Responding to My Critics," *Comparative Studies in Society and History* 38, no. (April, 1996).

"Must Justice be Blind? The Challenges of Images to the Law," *Filozofski Vestnik* 2 (1996); reprinted in *Law and the Image: The Authority of Art and the Aesthetics of Law*, edited by Costa Douzinas and Lynda Nead (Chicago: University of Chicago Press, 1999); Korean translation in *Bol*, 4 (Winter, 2006).

"The Conversion of the Rose," *Salmagundi*, no. 113 (Winter, 1997).

"The German Migration: Is There a Figure in the Carpet?" *Exiles and Emigrés: The Flight of European Artists from Hitler*, edited by Stephanie Barron (Los Angeles: Los Angeles County Museum of Art, 1997); translations in the French and German editions of the catalogue.

"1920: The Free Jewish School is Founded in Frankfurt am Main under the Leadership of Franz Rosenzweig," in Sander L. Gilman and Jack Zipes, eds., *Yale Companion to Jewish Writing and Thought in German Culture, 1096–1996* (New Haven: Yale University Press, 1997).

"Un Monumento alla Libertà di Espressione," *Il Manifesto* (Rome, December 19, 1997).

"Kwangju: From Massacre to Biennale," *Salmagundi*, no. 120 (Fall, 1998).

"Against Consolation: Walter Benjamin and the Refusal to Mourn," in Jay Winter and Emmanuel Sivan, *War and Remembrance in the Twentieth Century* (Cambridge, 1999); reprinted in *Philosophical Designs for a Socio-Cultural Transformation: Beyond Violence and the Modern Era* (Tokyo: Ecole des Hautes Etudes en Sciences Culturelles, 1998) and *Review of Japanese Culture and Society*, special issue on "Violence in the Modern World," 11–12 (December, 1999–2000), and *Benjamin Studies* 1 (Amsterdam, 2002); Japanese translation in *Thought* 9, no. 1 (2001).

"The Ungrateful Dead," *Salmagundi*, no. 123 (Summer, 1999); German translation in *Frankfurter Rundschau*, 18 September 1999.

"Onko kokemus edeleen kriisissa? Ajatuksia Franfurtin koulun kainosta," *Kritikin Lupaus*, edited by Olli-Pekka Moisio (Helsinki, 1999); in English as "Is Experience Still in Crisis? Reflections on a Frankfurt School Lament," *Kriterion: Revista de Filosofia* (Belo Horizonte, Brazil), 100 (July/December, 1999); in *Critical Theory: Current State and*

Future Prospects, edited by Jaimey Fischer and Peter Uwe Hohendahl (New York: Berghahn Books, 2001); and in *The Cambridge Companion to Adorno*, edited by Tom Huhn (Cambridge: Cambridge University Press, 2004); in French in *X-Alta*, 5 (October, 2001.

"Drifting into Dangerous Waters: The Separation of Aesthetic Experience from the Work of Art," *Filozofski Vestnik*, 2 (1999); reprinted in *Aesthetic Subjects*, edited by Pamela Matthews and David McWhirter (Minneapolis: University of Minnesota Press, 2003).

"The Speed of Light and the Virtualization of Reality," in *The Robot in the Garden: Telerobotics and Telepistemology in the Age of the Internet*, edited by Ken Goldberg (Cambridge, MA: MIT Press, 2000); Slovenian translation in *Levitate, What's Next/Lebdim, Kaj Potem*, edited by Aleksandra Kostic (Maribor, Slovenia: zalonik: Association for Culture and Education KIBLA, 2000).

"Pen Pals with the Unicorn Killer," *Salmagundi*, nos. 126–127 (Summer, 2000).

"Diving into the Wreck: Aesthetic Spectatorship at the Fin-de-Siècle," *Critical Horizons* 1, no. 1 (February, 2000); Portuguese translation in *Caleidoscópio*, nos. 1–2 (2001).

"Modern and Postmodern Paganism: Peter Gay and Jean-François Lyotard," in *Enlightenment, Passion, Modernity: Historical Essays in European Thought and Culture*, edited by Mark S. Micale and Robert L. Dietle (Stanford, CA: Stanford University Press, 2000).

"Posthumer Pop: Im Intertextuellen Netz: Nietzsche am Ende des amerikanischen Jahrhunderts," *Frankfurter Rundschau*, 3 August 2000.

"The Paradoxes of Religious Violence," *Salmagundi*, nos. 130–131 (Spring–Summer, 2001); French translation in *X-Alta* 8 (November, 2004).

"Roland Barthes and the Tricks of Experience," *The Yale Journal of Criticism* 14, 2 (2001).

"Lafayette's Children: The American Reception of French Liberalism," *SubStance*, no. 97 (2002).

"Somaesthetics and Democracy: Dewey and Contemporary Body Art," *The Journal of Aesthetic Education* 36, 4 (Winter, 2002); German translation in *Kunst und Demokratie: Positionen zu Beginn des 21. Jahrhunderts*, edited by Ursula Franke and Josef Früchtl (Hamburg: Felix Meiner Verlag, 2003).

"Cultural Relativism and the Visual Turn," *Journal of Visual Culture* 1, 3 (2002); Portuguese translation in *Aletria*, nos. 10/11 (2003-2004); reprinted in *Images: A Reader*, edited by Sunil Manghani, Arthur Piper, and Jon Simons (London: Sage, 2006).

"La crisis de la experiencia en la era post-subjetiva," *Prismas* 6, no. 6 (2002).

"Ariel Sharon and the Rise of the New Anti-Semitism," *Salmagundi*, nos. 137–138 (Winter–Spring, 2003).

"Mourning a Metaphor: The Revolution is Over," *Parallax* 27 (April–June, 2003); reprinted in *Rethinking Modernity*, edited by Santosh Gupta, Prafulla C. Kar, and Parul Dave Mukerji (Delhi: Pencraft International, 2005).

"Det uaegetes Stigma: Adornos Kritik af Autenticiten," *Kritik*, no. 165 (Copenhagen, 2003).

"No State of Grace: Violence in the Garden," *Reflections on Literature, Criticism and Theory: Essays in Honour of Professor Prafulla C. Kar*, edited by Sura P. Rath, Kailish C. Baral, and D.Venkat Rao (Delhi, 2004); *Sites Unseen: Landscape and Vision*, edited by Dianne Harris and D. Fairchild Ruggles (Pittsburgh: University of Pittsburgh Press, 2007).

"Experience in America," *Keywords: Experience*, edited by Nadia Tazi (New York: Other Press, 2004).

"The Ambivalent Virtues of Mendacity," *Index on Censorship* 33, no. 2 (April, 2004).

"Intellectual Family Values," *Salmagundi*, no. 140 (Summer, 2004).
"Geschichte und Erfahrung: Dilthey, Collingwood, Scott und Ankersmit," *Vorträge aus dem Warburg-Haus* 8 (Berlin: Akademie-Verlag, 2004).
"Lo squadro di Foucault tra ciò che l'occhio vede e la verità della pittura," *Il Manifesto*, Rome, 25 May 2005.
"Epilogue: Visual Worlds, after 9/11," *Visual Worlds*, edited by John R. Hall, Blake Stimson, and Lisa Tamaris Becker (London: Routledge, 2005).
"The Kremlin of Modernism," *Salmagundi*, nos. 148–149 (Fall 2005–Winter 2006).
"Phenomenology and Lived Experience," *Blackwell's Companion to Phenomenology and Existentialism*, edited by Hubert Dreyfus and Mark Wrathall (New York: Blackwell, 2006).
"Still Waiting to Hear from Derrida," *Salmagundi*, nos. 150–151 (Spring–Summer, 2006).
"The Ambivalent Virtues of Mendacity: How Europeans Taught (Some of) Us to Love the Lies of Politics," in *The Humanities and the Dynamics of Inclusion Since World War II*, edited by David A. Hollinger (Baltimore: The Johns Hopkins University Press, 2006); and *Education and the Spirit of Time: Historical, Global and Critical Reflections*, edited by Olli-Pekka Moisio and Juha Suoranta (Rotterdam: Sense Publishers, 2006).
"Aesthetic Experience and Historical Experience: A Twenty-First Century Constellation," catalogue for *Ahistorical Occasions*, edited by Nato Thompson (North Adams, MA: MASS MoCA, 2006).
"Ocularity," *Sensorium: Embodied Experience, Technology, and Contemporary Art* (Cambridge, MA: MIT Press, 2006).
"Taking on the Stigma of Inauthenticity: Adorno's Critique of Genuineness," *New German Critique*, no. 97 (Winter, 2006); and *Theory as Variation*, edited by R. Radhakrishnan et al. (Delhi: Pencraft India, 2007).
"Still Sleeping Rough: Colin Wilson's *The Outsider* at Fifty," *Salmagundi*, nos. 155–156 (Summer–Fall, 2007).
"Czy Politykom Wolno Kłamać," *Gazeta Wyborcza* (Warsaw, Poland), 7–8 September 2007.

Reviews

Peter Gay, *Weimar Culture* and Walter Benjamin, *Illuminations*, *Midstream* 15, no. 2 (February, 1969).
Istvan Deak, *Weimar Germany's Left-wing Intellectuals*, *Commentary* 48, 4 (October, 1969).
Donald Fleming and Bernard Bailyn, ed., *The Intellectual Migration*, and Hans Wingler, *The Bauhaus*, *Commentary* 49, no. 3 (March, 1970).
Fritz Stern, *The Failure of Illiberalism*, *Midstream* 18, no. 8 (October, 1972).
Wilhelm Reich, *Sex-Pol*, *The Daily California Book Review* (Spring, 1973).
Joachim Radkau, *Die Deutsche Emigration in den USA: Ihr Einfluss auf die Amerikanische Aussenpolitik, 1933-1945*, *Journal of Modern History* 45, no. 2 (June, 1973).
Robert Boyers, ed., *The Legacy of the German Refugee Intellectuals*, *Journal of Modern History*, 45, 2 (June, 1973).
Reinhard Bendix and Guenther Roth, *Scholarship and Partisanship*, *Isis* 69, no. 2 (1973).
William Johnston, *The Austrian Mind*, *Journal of Modern History* 45, no. 4 (December, 1973).
Eugene Lunn, *Prophet of Community*, *Central European History* 8, no. 1 (March, 1975).

Max Horkheimer, *Aus der Pubertät and Notizen 1950 bis 1969 und Dämmerung*, The Times Literary Supplement, 4 July 1975.
Uriel Tal, *Christians and Jews in Germany*, American Political Science Review 77, no. 2 (June, 1978).
Melvin Lasky, *Utopia and Revolution*, Partisan Review 45, no. 2 (1978).
Ruth Link-Salinger, *Gustav Landauer, Philosopher of Utopia*, American Historical Review 83, no. 3 (June, 1978).
Zoltan Tar, *The Frankfurt School*, Central European History 12, no. 1 (March, 1979).
Leszek Kolakowski, *Main Currents in Marxism*, American Historical Review 85, no. 1 (February, 1980).
Thomas E. Willey, *Back to Kant*, Partisan Review 47, no. 1, 1981.
Ronald Aronson, *Jean-Paul Sartre—Philosophy in the World*, The New Republic, 21 February 1981.
James Miller, *From Marx to Merleau-Ponty*, Clio 11, no. 2 (1982).
Theodor Adorno, *Prisms*, Bennington Review (Summer, 1983).
Joseph Bendersky, *Carl Schmitt: Theorist for the Reich*, Journal of Modern History 56, no. 3 (September, 1984).
Lee Congdon, *The Young Lukács*, The Times Literary Supplement, 7 October 1983.
Jarrell C. Jackman and Carla M. Borden, eds., *The Muses Flee Hitler*, Society 22, no. 1 (November-December, 1984).
Perry Anderson, *In the Tracks of Historical Materialism*, The Times Literary Supplement, 5 October 1984.
Hans Blumenberg, *The Legitimacy of the Modern Age*, History and Theory 24, no. 2 (1985).
Lewis Coser, *Refugee Scholars in America*, Contemporary Sociology 14, no. 4 (July, 1985).
Jürgen Habermas, *Autonomy and Solidarity*, The New York Times Book Review, 9 November 1986.
Judith Marcus and Zoltan Tar, eds., *Foundations of the Frankfurt School of Social Research*, Journal of the History of the Behavioral Sciences 11, no. 1 (January, 1987).
Karl Dietrich Bracher, *The Age of Ideologies*, American Historical Review 91, no. 4 (October, 1986).
Alvin Gouldner, *Against Fragmentation*, Theory and Society 15, no. 4 (1986).
Mary Gluck, *Georg Lukács and His Generation*, Contemporary Sociology 15, no. 5 (1986).
Jurgen Habermas, *The Philosophical Discourse of Modernity*, History and Theory 28, no. 1 (1989).
Cornelius Castoriadis, *Political and Social Writings*, 2 vols., Dissent (Summer, 1990).
Seán Hand, *The Levinas Reader*, Tikkun 6 (November/December, 1990), reprinted in *The Tikkun Reader*, edited by Michael Lerner (Oakland, CA, 1992).
Fredric Jameson, *Postmodernism: Or, The Cultural Logic of Late Capitalism*, History and Theory 32, no. 3 (1992).
Theodor W. Adorno, *Notes on Literature*, 2 vols. London Review of Books, 10 June 1993.
Michael Taussig, *The Nervous System* and *Mimesis and Alterity*, Visual Anthropology Review 9, no. 2 (Fall, 1993).
Moishe Postone, *Time, Labor and Social Domination*, New German Critique 60 (Fall, 1993).
Mitchell Cohen, *The Wager of Lucien Goldmann* in The American Historical Review 101, no. 1 (February, 1996).
William Scheuerman, *Between the Norm and the Exception*, International Studies in Philosophy, 28, no. 4 (1996).
Stephan Oetterman, *The Panorama*, Bookforum (March, 1998).
George Stephanopolous, *All too Human* and Christopher Hitchens, *No One Left to Lie To*, London Review of Books, 29 July 1999.

Russell Jacoby, *The End of Utopia*, Catriona Kelly, ed., *Utopias*, John Carey, ed., *The Faber Book of Utopias*, Robert Proctor, *The Nazi War on Cancer*, London Review of Books, 1 June 2000.

Massimo Cacciari, *Architecture and Nihilism*, Design Book Review, nos. 41/42 (Winter/Spring, 2000).

Alexander Stephan, *"Communazis": FBI Surveillance of German Émigré Writers*, New York Times Book Review, 28 January 2001.

David Simpson, *Situatedness: Or, Why We Keep Saying Where We are Coming From*, London Review of Books, 28 November 2002.

Mark Lilla, *The Reckless Mind* and Eric Hobsbawm, *Interesting Times*, Modern Intellectual History 2, no. 2 (August, 2005).

Espen Hammer, *Adorno and the Political*, Notre Dame Philosophical Reviews, 12 May 2006.

Susanne Kirkbright, *Karl Jaspers: A Biography*, London Review of Books, 8 June 2006.

Erdmut Wizisla, *Benjamin und Brecht: Die Geschichte einer Freundschaft*, The Brecht Yearbook 31 (2006).

Doctoral Students Directed by Martin Jay

(through June 2008)

John Abromeit
Paige Arthur
Avner Ben-Amos
Theodore Bogacz
Julian Bourg
Warren Breckman
Alice Bullard
Rita Chin
Carolyn J. Dean
Lawrence Frohman
Martin Gammon
Elizabeth Goodstein
Peter E. Gordon
Lohren Green
Richard Gringeri

Michael Gubser
Andrew Jainchill
Richard Kim
Eiko Kuwano
James Kwak
Benjamin Lazier
A. Dirk Moses
Samuel Moyn
Gregory B. Moynahan
Elliot Neaman
Melissa Ptacek
Emanuel Rota
Abraham P. Socher
David Sorkin
Anna Wertz

Contributors

Seyla Benhabib is Eugene Meyer Professor of Political Science and Philosophy at Yale University and Director of its Program in Ethics, Politics, and Economics. Her many books include *Critique, Norm and Utopia: A Study of the Normative Foundations of Critical Theory* (New York, 1986); *The Reluctant Modernism of Hannah Arendt* (New York, 1996, 2002); *The Claims of Culture: Equality and Diversity in the Global Era* (Princeton, 2002); *The Rights of Others: Aliens, Citizens and Residents* (Cambridge, 2004); and *Another Cosmopolitanism: Hospitality, Sovereignty and Democratic Iterations* (New York, 2006).

Warren Breckman is associate professor of history at the University of Pennsylvania. He is the author of *Karl Marx, the Young Hegelians and the Origins of Radical Social Theory* (Cambridge, 1999) and the editor of *European Romanticism: A Brief History with Documents* (New York, 2007). An editor of the *Journal of the History of Ideas*, he is currently writing *Adventures of the Symbolic: French Post-Marxism and Democratic Theory* (New York, forthcoming), a study of political philosophy in France from 1968 to the present.

Rita Chin is associate professor of history at the University of Michigan. She published *The Guest Worker Question in Postwar Germany* (New York, 2007), which explores the postwar labor migration's social, cultural, and ideological impacts, both on guest workers and German society at large. She has begun research on a second book, which examines how leftist groups in Germany, Great Britain, and France have grappled with the questions of racial/ethnic difference raised by the arrival of millions of new immigrants after 1945.

Detlev Claussen is Professor for Theory of Society, Sociology of Culture, and Science at Leibniz-University in Hannover, Germany. He studied with Theodor Adorno and Max Horkheimer, was a member of the German SDS, and has been a political commentator. His publications include several studies of violence, anti-Semitism, and racism. His books include *List der Gewalt: soziale Revolution und ihre Theorien* (Frankfurt, 1982); *Grenzen der Aufklärung* (Frankfurt, 1987, 2005 and forthcoming in translation with University of California Press); *Was heisst Rassismus?* (Darmstadt, 1994); and *Aspekte der Alltagsreligion* (Frankfurt, 2000). His most recent book in German is *Béla Gutmann: Weltgeschichtes des Fussballs in einer Person* (Berlin, 2006); his biographical study, *Theodor W. Adorno: One Last Genius*, has been published in translation by Harvard University Press (2008).

Jean L. Cohen is professor of political science at Columbia University. She is the author of many articles and books including *Civil Society and Political Theory*, co-authored with Andrew Arato (Cambridge, MA, 1992) and *Regulating Intimacy: A New Legal Paradigm* (Princeton, 2002). She is currently working on a new book tentatively entitled *Rethinking Sovereignty, Rights and Democracy in the Epoch of Globalization*.

Carolyn J. Dean is John Hay Professor of International Studies at Brown University, where she is also associate dean of the faculty. She is the author of *The Self and Its Pleasures: Bataille, Lacan, and the History of the Decentered Subject* (Ithaca, NY, 1992); *Sexuality and Modern Western Culture* (New York, 1996); *The Frail Social Body: Pornography, Homosexuality, and Other Fantasies in Interwar France* (Berkeley, 2000); and, most recently, *The Fragility of Empathy after the Holocaust* (Ithaca, NY, 2004). She is working on a new project, *Too Much Jewish Memory: On Disbelief, Exaggeration, and the Making of Jewish Victims*.

Peter E. Gordon is professor of history at Harvard University. He was a member in the Society of Fellows in the Liberal Arts at Princeton University from 1998 to 2000. Since joining the Harvard faculty in 2000, he has taught courses primarily in modern European intellectual history. His publications include *Rosenzweig and Heidegger: Between Judaism and German Philosophy* (Berkeley, 2003) and, as co-editor, *The Cambridge Companion to Modern Jewish Philosophy* (Cambridge, 2007). His new study,

Continental Divide: Heidegger, Cassirer, Davos is forthcoming from Harvard University Press, and his edited collection, *Weimar Thought*, is forthcoming from Princeton University Press.

Dick Howard is Distinguished Professor of Philosophy at the State University of New York at Stony Brook. Thirty-five years ago, he edited (with Karl Klare) *The Unknown Dimension: European Marxism since Lenin* (New York, 1972), in which one of Martin Jay's first publications appeared. His many works include *The Marxian Legacy* (Houndsmills, 1977, 1988); *The Birth of American Political Thought, 1763–87* (Houndsmills, 1990); and *The Specter of Democracy* (New York, 2002). He recently completed a new study of the history of political thought in the West, and comments frequently in the French media.

Andreas Huyssen is Villard Professor of German and Comparative Literature at Columbia University where he founded and directed the Center for Comparative Literature and Society (1998–2003). One of the founding editors of *New German Critique* (since 1974), his books include *After the Great Divide: Modernism, Mass Culture, Postmodernism* (Bloomington, 1986); *Twilight Memories: Marking Time in a Culture of Amnesia* (New York, 1995); and *Present Pasts: Urban Palimpsests and the Politics of Memory* (Stanford, 2003). His new book is *Other Cities, Other Worlds: Urban Imaginaries in a Globalizing Age* (Durham, NC, 2008).

Lloyd Kramer is Dean Smith Distinguished Term Professor at the University of North Carolina-Chapel Hill, where he also chairs the department. His writings include *Threshold of a New World: Intellectuals and the Exile Experience in Paris, 1830–1848* (Ithaca, NY, 1988); *Lafayette in Two Worlds: Public Cultures and Personal Identities in an Age of Revolutions* (Chapel Hill, NC, 1996); and *Nationalism: Political Cultures in Europe and America, 1775–1865* (New York, 1998). He is also co-author, with R.R. Palmer and Joel Colton, of *A History of the Modern World*, 10th edition (New York, 2007) and, co-editor, with Sarah Maza, of *A Companion to Western Historical Thought* (New York, 2002).

Rosalind Krauss is University Professor in the Department of Art History at Columbia University, where she formerly held the Meyer Schapiro Chair in Modern Art and Theory. A specialist in twentieth-century art, her published works include *Passages in Modern Sculpture* (New York, 1977); *The Originality of the Avant-Garde and Other Modernist Myths* (Cambridge, MA, 1985); *Cindy Sherman* (New York, 1993); *The Optical Unconscious* (Cambridge, MA, 1993); *Formless: A User's Guide* (New York,

1997); and *The Picasso Papers* (New York, 1998). With Yve-Alain Bois, Benjamin Buchloh, and Hal Foster, she published *Art Since 1900* (New York, 2001).

Dominick LaCapra is professor of history and comparative literature, the Bryce and Edith M. Bowmar Professor of Humanistic Studies, and director of the School of Criticism and Theory at Cornell University. He is the author of twelve books, the most recent of which are *History and Reading: Tocqueville, Foucault, French Studies* (Toronto, 2000); *Writing History, Writing Trauma* (Baltimore, 2001); and *History in Transit: Experience, Identity, Critical Theory* (Ithaca, NY, 2004).

A. Dirk Moses has taught history at the University of Sydney since 2000 after studying in Australia, Scotland, the USA, and Germany. He is interested in twentieth-century Germany, colonialism, world history, and genocide studies. His publications include *German Intellectuals and the Nazi Past* (Cambridge and New York, 2007) and, as editor, *Empire, Colony, Genocide: Conquest, Occupation, and Subaltern Resistance in World History* (Oxford and New York, 2008), *Genocide and Settler Society: Frontier Violence and Stolen Indigenous History in Australian History* (Oxford and New York, 2004) and, as co-editor, *Colonialism and Genocide* (New York, 2007). He is currently coediting the *Oxford Handbook on Genocide Studies*.

Samuel Moyn is professor of history at Columbia University. He has published two books, *Origins of the Other: Emmanuel Levinas between Revelation and Ethics* (Ithaca, NY, 2005) and *A Holocaust Controversy: The Treblinka Affair in Postwar France* (Waltham, MA, 2005). His new books in progress are *The Last Utopia: On the Recent History of Human Rights* (Harvard University Press, forthcoming) and *A New Theory of Politics: Claude Lefort and Company in Contemporary France* (Columbia University Press, forthcoming).

Gregory B. Moynahan is associate professor of history at Bard College, where he co-directs the science, technology, and society program. The winner of many fellowships, he works in the area of German social and scientific thought, has published articles on Georg Simmel, and has a forthcoming monograph on Ernst Cassirer's philosophy in historical context.

Elliot Neaman is professor of history at the University of San Francisco, with a specialty in late modern European thought. He is the author of *A Dubious Past: Ernst Jünger and the Politics of Literature* (Berkeley, 1999) and is currently working on a book on the political and cultural legacy of 1968 in German history.

Anson Rabinbach is professor of history and director of the European cultural studies program at Princeton University, where he has taught since 1998. His books include *The Crisis of Austrian Socialism: From Red Vienna to Civil War, 1927–1934* (Chicago, 1981); *The Human Motor: Energy, Fatigue, and the Origins of Modernity* (New York, 1991); and *In the Shadow of Catastrophe: German Intellectuals Between Apocalypse and Enlightenment* (Berkeley, 1996). His current projects include a study of concepts transformed by the Cold War and a political and intellectual history of European anti-fascism.

Jerrold Seigel is William R. Kenan, Jr. Professor Emeritus of History at New York University. His books are *Rhetoric and Philosophy in Renaissance Humanism* (Princeton, NJ, 1968); *Marx's Fate: The Shape of a Life* (Princeton, NJ, 1978; University Park, PA, 1993); *Bohemian Paris: Culture, Politics, and the Boundaries of Bourgeois Life, 1830–1930* (New York, 1987; Baltimore, MD, 1999); *The Private Worlds of Marcel Duchamp: Desire, Liberation and the Self in Modern Culture* (Berkeley, 1995); and *The Idea of the Self: Thought and Experience in Western Europe since the Seventeenth Century* (Cambridge, 2005). He is currently working on bourgeois culture.

David Sorkin is professor of history and Frances and Laurence Weinstein Professor of Jewish Studies at the University of Wisconsin-Madison. He has written *The Transformation of German Jewry, 1780–1840* (New York, 1987); *Moses Mendelssohn and the Religious Enlightenment* (Berkeley, 1996); *The Berlin Haskalah and German Religious Thought* (London, 2000), and edited several collections.

Michael Werz is a transatlantic fellow at the German Marshall Fund in Washington, D.C. and visiting scholar at the Institute for the Study of International Migration at Georgetown University. His books include *Grenzen der Säkularisierung* (Frankfurt, 2000) and, as editor or co-editor, *Bosnien und Europa* (Frankfurt, 1999), *Antisemitismus und Gesellschaft* (Frankfurt, 1995), *Keine Kritische Theorie ohne Amerika* (Frankfurt, 1995), *Kritik des Ethnonationalismus* (Frankfurt, 2000), and *Veränderte Weltbilder* (Frankfurt, 2005). His recent research focuses on the socio-historical and academic factors involved in the invention of ethnicity and identity politics.

Index

A
Abendroth, Wolfgang, 284
Adams, John Quincy, 342n11
Adelson, Leslie, 260
Adenauer, Konrad, 245, 247–48
Adorno, Theodor, xvii, xx, xxi–xxii, xxiv, xxvi–xxvii, xxix–xxx, xxxiii, xxxv, xxxviin3, xxxixn49, 77–97, 221, 229, 236n41, 270–71, 286–87, 300–307, 316–19, 321n10, 369, 381, 386, 391
Agamben, Giorgio, 219, 221, 229
Albers, Joseph, 139
Alexander, Edward, 387
Allemann, F.R., 269
Allen, Neal, 390
Althusser, Louis, xxiv, 100, 139, 332, 343n16
Anderson, Sherwood, 199–200
Ankersmit, F.R., xxvi
Antifascism, 183–209, 336–37
Appelfeld, Aharon, 177
Arad, Michael, 156–59
Aragon, Louis, 194, 203–204
Arendt, Hannah, 165–66, 174, 225, 229, 238n65, 301–302, 307–19, 321n10, 321n12, 323n34, 324n37, 324n41, 325nn49–50, 325n54, 326n60, 343n18
Arendt, Max, 307
Arosev, Alexander, 196, 201–202
Arp, Hans, 140
Artaud, Antonin, 228
Assmann, Jan, 152
Augustine, 307

B
Babel, Isaac, 198, 203
Bachman, Joseph, 280
Bacon, Francis, xxv, 370
Badiou, Alain, 233n10, 234n25
Baeck, Leo, 300
Balibar, Étienne, 123
Balla, Giacomo, 139

Balzac, Honoré de, 197
Barbusse, Henri, 185, 188–89, 193–97, 199–200, 202
Barnouw, Dagmar, 165
Barry, Brian, 363n3
Barthes, Roland, xxvi, xxxv
Bartov, Omer, 221
Bataille, Georges, xix, xxvi, xxxv, 139–40, 219–21, 235n35, 235–36nn37–8
Bauemler, Alfred, 302, 321n12
Bauman, Zygmunt, 162, 167, 170, 221
Becher, Johannes, 201
Beckett, Samuel, 90
Beethoven, Ludwig van, 77–97, 202
Beitz, Charles, 363n3
Benbassa, Esther, 162, 166
Benhabib, Seyla, 96n52
Benjamin, Walter, xxiv, xxvi, xxx, xxxiii, xxxviin3, 29, 80, 85, 94, 144, 195, 216, 218–19, 234n28, 239n67, 321n10, 386
Berg, Alban, 77–78
Berghahn, Marion, xi
Berghahn, V.R., 237n53
Bergson, Henri, xviii, 52n19, 139, 141
Berkowitz, Roger, 62
Berlant, Lauren, 163
Berlin, Isaiah, 392
Berman, Paul, 335–39, 343n14, 344n20
Bernstein, J.M., 90, 97n55
Bernstein, Michael André, 162, 169–70, 172
Bertolio, Antoine, 19n48
Best, Steven, 238n64
Bhabha, Homi, 231
Biedenkopf, Kurt, 255
Blackstone, William, 69
Blanchot, Maurice, 225
Blank, Theodor, 246–47
Bloch, Ernst, 284
Bloch, Jean-Richard, 194, 192, 200, 203
Bluecher, Heinrich, 326n60
Blum, Léon, 184, 193

Blumenfeld, Kurt, 300, 302
Bonaparte, Napoleon, 82, 307–308
Bonnenville, Nicolas, 10
Bossuet, Jacques-Bénigne, 5
Bourdieu, Pierre, 389
Bourgeois, Bernard, 121, 124
Bracher, Karl Dietrich, 269, 282, 285–86, 288
Bradbury, John Mason, 390
Brandt, Willy, 275
Breitscheid, Rudolf, 188
Breton, André, 196, 210, 225
Breughel, Pieter, 332
Brezhnev, Leonid, 117
Browder, Earl, 194
Brown, Norman, 387
Brown, Wendy, 163–64
Browning, Christopher, 222
Bruckner, Pascal, 168
Buback, Siegfried, 287
Buber, Martin, 300, 387
Bubis, Ignatz, 257, 265n53
Buchanan, Allan, 350, 352, 363n3
Buchheim, Hans, 287–88
Bukharin, Nikolai, 197–98
Buñuel, Luis, 140
Burke, Edmund, 59, 215, 392
Buruma, Ian, 167
Bush, George W., 335
Butler, Joseph, 47–48
Butler, Judith, 229, 386–87

C

Cabane, Pierre, 26, 30
Caillois, Roger, 143
Calhoun, Craig, xxxi, xxxiv
Camus, Albert, 229
Canovan, Margaret, 312
Carmichael, Stokely, 274
Carroll, David, 170
Cassini, Giovanni, 6
Cassirer, Ernst, xxxii, 55–73
Castoriadis, Cornelius, 332–33, 337, 342n8, 343n19
Ceaucescu, Nicolai, 130
Celan, Paul, 90
Cervantes, Miguel de, 197, 201
Césaire, Aimé, 237n47
Chaix, Richard, 19n44
Chamson, André, 202
Chartier, Emile, 196
Christianity, xxv, 3–16, 48, 164, 217, 233n10, 233n13, 250–51, 300, 305–306, 317, 374
Chomsky, Noam, 387
Classen, Georg, 255

Cobb, Richard, 184
Cohen, Hermann, 55–58, 61–63, 67
Cohn-Bendit, Daniel, 273–74, 336
Coleman, James, 141–42
Communism, xxiii, 104, 108, 117, 122, 124, 129, 183–205, 246, 248, 269, 271, 279, 302, 326n60, 332, 337, 342nn9–10, 343n12, 244n24
Condorcet, Marquis de, 195
Confucius, 36
Conservatism, 120, 165, 249–50, 252, 269, 278, 281–87, 336, 392
Constant, Benjamin, 392
Copernicus, 6
Cornell, Drucilla, 56
Cot, Pierre, 185
Crary, Jonathan, 137–38
Crevel, René, 196
Croce, Benedetto, xviii

D

Dabrowski, Hartmut, 277
Dahrendorf, Ralf, 282
Daladier, Eduard, 193
Dali, Salvador, 140
Darnton, Robert, 3, 4
David-Fox, Michael, 203
De Man, Paul, 218, 341
Debord, Guy, 138
Delaunay, Robert, 139
Delbo, Charlotte, 172
Delehelle, Abbé, 19n44
Dempsey, Jack, 141
Derrida, Jacques, xix, xxiv, 119, 123, 127, 132, 139, 145, 213, 216–19, 221, 229–30, 233n10, 234n22, 234n25, 234n28, 235n35, 239n67, 302, 388
Descartes, Rene, xxiii, xxv, 103
Dewey, John, xxvi
Diderot, Denis, 195
Dilthey, Wilhelm, xxxviin6, 56, 73n6
Dimitrov, Georgii, 187, 189, 192, 201
Dohnanyi, Klaus von, 257
Doriot, Jacques, 191
Dos Passos, John, 199–200
Dregger, Alfred, 251–52
Dreiser, Theodore, 199–200
Dreyfus, Alfred, 192, 313
Drieu la Rochelle, Pierre, 236n38
Duchamp, Marcel, 24–53, 140–1
Duclos, Jacques, 194
Durkheim, Emile, xviii, 220, 229–30, 235n37
Dutschke, Rudi, 271–74, 277, 279–80, 285, 290n41, 292n89

E

Eagleton, Terry, xxxi–xxxiv, 392
Eckhart, Meister, 41
Ehmke, Horst, 281
Ehrenburg, Ilya, 196, 198–200, 202–4
Eisenman, Peter, 156–58, 256–57
Eley, Geoff, 250
Eluard, Paul, 196
Enlightenment, the, x, xiii–xix, xxii–xxiv, xxvii, xxxi, xxxiii, xxxv, 3–16, 61, 66, 79, 158–9, 221, 236n41, 299–319, 340, 379, 391–2
D'Entrèves, Maurizio Passerin, 238n65
Enzensberger, H.M., 279
Ercoli-Togliatti, Palmiro, 189
Erhard, Ludwig, 274
Erikson, Erik, 387
Experience, ix, xv, xvii–xix, xxiii–xxix, xxxi–xxxii, xxxv, 35–6, 44, 46–7, 49, 57, 60, 61, 65, 90–1, 97n55, 102, 106, 112, 130–31, 138–41, 144, 152, 163, 167–69, 171, 174–77, 211–14, 221–23, 228, 238n59, 243, 159–60, 284, 287, 303, 306, 316, 331, 333, 364, 374, 385–87, 392

F

Fanon, Frantz, 224–25, 229–31, 237n47
Farmer, Paul, 239n70
Fascism, 183–209, 219, 221, 226, 231, 236n38, 248, 255, 262n4, 281–82, 287, 302, 305, 322n14, 334, 336, 338, 343n17
Fassbinder, Rainer Werner, 248
Fauchet, Claude, 5, 10, 19n48, 20n54
Feher, Michel, 178n13
Feltrinelli, Giangiacomo, 279
Fénelon, François, 5
Fernandez, Ramon, 199
Fest, Joachim, 282–83
Feuchtwanger, Lion, 190, 201
Fichte, Johann Gottlieb, 56, 70
Filbinger, Hans, 286
Finkelstein, Joseph, 390
Finkielkraut, Alain, 162, 178n13, 273
Fischer, Joschka, 335
Fischer, Louis, 185
Fleck, Ludwig, 70
Flowerman, Samuel, 300
Flynn, Bernard, 112n4
Foster, Hal, 155
Foucault, Michel, xix, xxiv, xxvi, xxxv, 72, 139, 180n49, 221, 388
France, 3–23, 99–100, 109–12, 118–23, 138–39, 162–63, 170–71, 184–209, 226–27, 235n37, 253, 273–74, 313, 340, 385
Franco, Francisco, 287

French Revolution, xviii, 3–23, 91, 120, 212, 216–7, 234n26, 235n37, 303, 313, 340, 342n11
Freud, Sigmund, xviii, xxxi, 30, 387
Fried, Clément (or Eugen), 191
Fried, Erich, 273
Friedeburg, Ludwig von, 281
Friedman, Thomas, 387
Fukuyama, Francis, 371
Furet, François, 16, 100, 184

G

Gadamer, Hans-Georg, xix, 391
Galileo, 6
Gallagher, Catherine, xi
Gauchet, Marcel, 100, 110–11
Gay, Peter, 388
Geertz, Clifford, 43
Genlis, Madame de, 10
Gentz, Friedrich von, 342n11
Geoffrin, Marie-Thérèse, 19n45
Germany, 55–58, 60, 62–64, 93–94, 153–55, 158, 169–70, 183–209, 212–3, 222, 226–28, 236n47, 237–38n59, 242–95, 299, 306–18, 319–20n4, 334–35, 342n8, 342n10, 369–71, 373–77, 386–87, 390
Geuss, Raymond, 90
Gibson, Mel, 219
Gide, André, 188, 196, 199–203
Girard, René, 221, 233n13
Glotz, Peter, 285, 287
Gluck, Carol, 152
Glucksmann, André, 122, 273, 337, 343n16
Goebbels, Joseph, 186–87, 285
Goering, Hermann, 187
Goethe, Johann Wolfgang von, 187, 308, 373, 375
Goetze, Klaus, 255
Gogol, Nikolai, 197
Goldhammer, Jesse, 234n26
Gorky, Maxim, 190, 194, 197, 202
Gouldner, Alvin, xxviii
Graf, Oskar Maria, 198
Gramsci, Antonio, 79
Grandin, Temple, 214
Grass, Günther, 253
Grebing, Helga, 285
Greenberg, Clement, 140
Greenspan, Liz, 154
Grégoire, Henri, 4, 5, 19n48
Grotius, Hugo, 62, 64–66
Guevara, Che, 228
Guilbaut, Serge, 90
Guilloux, Louis, 203

H

Haan, Ido de, 177
Habermas, Jürgen, xv, xix, xxii, xxvii, xxix, xxxiii, xxxv, xxxviin9, 55, 57, 67, 72, 96n52, 250, 281–82, 286–88, 299, 341, 344n24, 386–88, 392
Hardt, Michael, 236n39
Haug, Fritz, 275
Havel, Václav, 326n60
Haydn, Joseph, 92
Hegel, G.W.F., xxviii, xxxixn44, 61, 82–85, 117–35, 306, 321n10, 373
Hegelianism, xxii, xxviii, 82–5, 103, 106, 117–33, 235n35, 284, 336, 370
Heidegger, Martin, 101, 109, 113n7, 119, 123, 125, 228–30, 287, 302, 308, 321n10, 321n12, 324n37
Heine, Heinrich, 197
Helvétius, Anne-Catherine, 10
Hennis, Wilhelm, 283
Hentig, Hartmut von, 282
Herf, Jeffrey, 256
Hermlin, Stephan, 183
Herriot, Eduard, 185
Hersey, John, 236n38
Hersh, Seymour, 387
Herzl, Theodor, 313
Hilberg, Raul, 221
Himmler, Heinrich, 223–24
Hitchcock, Alfred, 143
Hitler, Adolf, 170, 184, 188, 190, 205, 227, 256, 270, 278, 315, 325n50, 338
Hobbes, Thomas, 62
Hobsbawm, Eric, 183–84
Hoffman, Eva, 176–77
Hofmann, Werner, 281
d'Holbach, Baron Paul Thiry, 19n45
Holism. *See* totality
Holocaust, the, 152–58, 162–82, 213– 218, 221–22, 245, 253, 256–57, 259–61, 268–69, 273–74, 288, 299–329, 373, 379
Hontheim, Johann Nikolaus von, 5
Horkheimer, Max, xvii, xx, xxii, 221, 236n41, 270, 300–307, 313, 316–19, 319n1, 321n10, 322n17, 322n19, 323n21, 342n7
Horn, Gerd-Rainer, 188
Hughes, H. Stuart, xvii–xix, xxxviiin27, 389–90
Hull, Isabel, 226–28, 236n47, 237n53, 237n59
Hulme, T.E., 233n12, 234n17
Human rights, 67, 151, 153, 164, 313, 315–16, 325n54, 334–35, 346–67
Humboldt, Wilhelm von, 57–61, 68
Hume, David, 19n42, 44–7, 49–50
Huntington, Samuel, 371, 375

Hussein, Saddam, 334, 338
Husserl, Edmund, 101–102, 105
Huyssen, Andreas, 265n65

I

Ihmig, Norbert, 56, 70
Irigaray, Luce, 139
Itten, Jonannes, 139

J

Jacoby, Russell, 385
James, William, xxvi
Jameson, Frederic, 95n17, 96n53, 138
Jarry, Alfred, 34
Jaspers, Karl, 166
Jaurès, Jean, 193
Jay, Martin, ix–xl, 50, 79–80, 93, 99–100, 106, 113n21, 117–18, 126, 137–39, 144–46, 152, 231, 270, 299–300, 302–303, 316, 319n4, 320n6, 321n12, 326n60, 331–33, 335, 341, 342n4, 343n18, 363n2, 385–92.
Jay, Martin, works of: *Adorno*, ix, xxxviinl, 385, 391; "Changing Names," 386–87; *Cultural Semantics*, xxviii; *The Dialectical Imagination*, ix, xvii, xx–xxii, 299, 320n6, 385; *Downcast Eyes*, ix, xix, xxiii, xxxi, xxxiv, xxxviin2, xxxixn53, 137–47, 391; "For Theory," xxviii; "Hannah Arendt: Opposing Views," 302, 321n12, 343n18; *Marxism and Totality*, ix, xxi–xxiv, xxvii, 79–80, 93, 117–8, 126, 132, 331–33, 341, 385, 391; Introduction to *Permanent Exiles*, 342; *Refractions of Violence*, 231; "Scopic Regimes of Modernity," 137, 388; *Songs of Experience*, ix, xix, xxiii–xxv, xxvii, xxxi–xxxii, 386, 392; "The Ungrateful Dead", xxixn49; "Unsympathetic Magic," xxx–xxxi; "When Did the Holocaust End? Reflections on Historical Objectivity," 152
Jefferson, Thomas, 342n11
Jellinek, Georg, 69
Jesus, 7, 9, 11, 36, 280, 290n41
Johnson, Lyndon, 274
Jonas, Manfred, 390
Jourdain, Francis, 194
Judaism, 66, 85, 154, 156, 162–77, 178n13, 213, 224, 233n10, 244–5, 248–49, 256, 260, 272–73, 280, 300–13, 316, 318, 324n41, 386–87
Judt, Tony, 292n89, 387
Jumel, Abbé Jean-Charles, 19n44
Jünger, Ernst, 221

K

Kafka, Franz, 156

Kaganovich, Lazar, 200
Kandinsky, Wassily, 139
Kant, Immanuel, xxvi, xxvii, 61, 64–65, 68, 71–2, 143, 215, 308, 321n10, 335, 339–41, 343n13, 343n17, 350, 364n16, 372–73
Kaufmann, Walter, 390
Kelsen, Hans, 62–65, 68, 71–72
Kentridge, William, 145–46
Keohane, Robert, 352
Khrushchev, Nikita, 194
Kiefer, Anselm, 91
Kimmelmann, Michael, 158
King, Alan, 386
King, Martin Luther, 277, 280
Kirov, Sergey, 204
Kis, Janos, 326n60
Klare, Karl, 331–33
Klee, Paul, 139
Klein, Felix, 70
Klüger, Ruth, 173
Koestler, Arthur, 103, 187, 205
Kohl, Helmut, 242, 249–50, 252–53
Koltsov, Aleksei, 194
Koltsov, Mikhail, 196, 203–204
Koonz, Claudia, 222
Kracauer, Siegfried, ix
Krämer-Badoni, Rudolf, 284
Krause, Rudolf, 255
Kraus, Karl, 370
Krüger, Horst, 282
Kuhn, Thomas, 70
Kun, Bela, 196
Kunzelmann, Dieter, 272
Kurella, Alfred, 188, 201
Kuron, Jacek, 326n60

L

Lacan, Jacques, 111, 113n8, 118–19, 127, 130, 139, 143, 229, 233n10, 387–88
LaCapra, Dominick, xxxii, xxxviin13, 178n14, 390
Laclau, Ernesto, 131
Lacoue-Labarthe, Philippe, 123, 221
Lamourette, A.-A., 3–16
Lang, Berel, 162, 173–75
LaVerdiere, Julian, 159
Lefort, Claude, 99–115, 122–25, 131, 134n11, 332–33, 337, 342n8, 343n19
Leibniz, G.W.F., 56, 58, 60–62, 64–65, 67–72
Lelu, René, 203
Lemkin, Raphael, 302, 314, 316–19
Lenin, Vladimir, 133, 188, 194, 197, 201, 279, 326n60, 342n9
Lennox, Sara, 263n25
Lepsius, M. Rainer, 283
Lerner, Michael, 387
Lespinasse, Julie de, 19n48
Lessing, Gotthold, 308
Levi, Primo, 172–74
Levinas, Emmanuel, 229, 387
Lévy, Berhard-Henri, 337
Liberalism, 57–58, 60, 313, 317, 321n10, 322n17, 326n62, 338, 347–49, 351–52, 360–62, 392
Libeskind, Daniel, 156–57
Lin, Maya, 157, 159
Lipton, David, 57
Littell, Jonathan, 222–23
Litvinov, Maxim, 185
Lobkowicz, Nicholas, 286
Locke, John, xxv, 47–50, 57–58
London, Arthur, 183
Louis XV, 4
Louis XVI, 5, 14, 212
Lovejoy, Arthur O., xxi, xxxii, xxxviiin27
Löwenthal, Leo, ix
Löwenthal, Richard, 276
Lübbe, Hermann, 284, 286
Ludwig, Emil, 201
Lukács, Georg, 79, 103, 273, 275
Lunn, Eugene, 390
Luxemburg, Rosa, 307, 326n60, 342n4
Lyotard, Jean-François, xxiv, 132, 387–88

M

Mach, Ernst, 24, 56–57
Maechler, Stefan, 175–76
Mahler, Gustav, 78
Maier, Hans, 286
Maimon, Solomon, 56
Maimonides, Moses, 56
Malpighi, Marcello, 6
Malraux, André, 188, 196–200, 203–204
Malraux, Clara, 198
Mandelstam, Osip, 204
Mann, Heinrich, 190, 200, 203
Mann, Klaus, 197, 204
Mann, Thomas, 190, 200, 204
Mannheim, Karl, ix
Manuilsky, Dimitri, 194
Marbeuf, Yves-Alexandre de, 13
Marck, Siegfried, 63
Marclay, Christian, 146–47
Marcuse, Herbert, 276–77, 303, 385, 387
Marinetti, Filippo, 228
Martin du Gard, Roger, 199
Marty, André, 194
Marx, Karl, 103–104, 108, 120–21, 127, 130, 164, 214, 275, 326n60, 333, 340, 342n9, 370

Marxism, ix, xxi–xxiv, xxvii, 77, 79, 93, 94–112, 114n26, 117–33, 233n10, 271–72, 286, 301, 321n10, 326n60, 331–33, 335, 341, 369, 385, 391
Mauss, Marcel, 220, 235n37
McCloy, John, 245
Meister, Robert, 180n50
Memory, 48, 119, 139, 151–59, 160n4, 162–72, 184, 193, 195, 205, 243, 245, 259–61, 276, 288, 316–17, 369, 380–81
Mendelsohn, Benjamin, 178n3
Merker, Paul, 183
Merleau-Ponty, Maurice, 99–115
Michaels, Walter Benn, 167–68
Michaux, Henri, 112
Michnik, Adam, 326n60
Mill, John Stuart, 56, 58, 60–61, 392
Milton, Sybil, 172
Mirabeau, Victor de Riqueti, Marquis de, 10, 12
Miro, Joan, 140
Mitchell, Juliet, 387
Modernism, 24–50, 30, 89–90, 109, 138–39, 142, 145–47, 388
Molotov, Vyacheslav, 205
Monmousseau, Gaston, 194
Montaigne, xxiii, xxv
Montesquieu, Charles-Louis de Secondat, Baron de, 19n42, 57
Morin, Edgar, 342n5
Morrison, Toni, 167
Mosse, George, 226
Mouffe, Chantal, 131
Moulin, Jean, 183
Müller-Doohm, Stefan, 78
Mulot, François, 19n48
Münzenberg, Willi, 186–88, 202–203, 205
Musil, Robert, 24–53, 152
Muteschem, Sascha, 260
Myoda, Paul, 159
Myth, 183, 186, 204, 213, 233n10, 234n26, 256, 276, 305, 350, 380–81

N
Nancy, Jean-Luc, 117–35
Nauman, Bruce, 141
Necker, Suzanne, 19n45
Negri, Antonio, 236n39
Neufchâteau, François de, 21n71
Newton, Issac, 58
Nexö, Martin, 198
Nezval, Vitslav, 198
Nicholas of Cusa, 56, 58
Niemeyer, Carl, 390
Nietzsche, Friedrich, 36, 117, 152–3, 164, 212, 220, 306, 390

Nora, Pierre, 152
Nordon, Albert, 188
Novick, Peter, 162, 168

O
Oakeshott, Michael, 392
Oertzen, Peter von, 282
Ohnesorg, Benno, 274, 276, 285
Orwell, George, 117, 205

P
Paddison, Max, 77, 80
Pagis, Dan, 172
Pahlavi, Mohammad Reza, 275
Paperny, Vladimir, 201
Parin, Paul, 377
Pascal, Blaise, 6
Pasternak, Boris, 197, 203
Paul (Apostle), 233n10
Paulsen, Samuel, 63
Payne, Philip, 34
Pels, Peter, xxxi
Peschanski, Denis, 195
Peterson, Sven, 390
Phenomenology, 91–116
Piatnisky, Osip, 191–92
Plato, xxiii
Plessner, Helmut, 370
Plivier, Theodor, 198
Pogge, Thomas, 348, 363n3
Pollock, Friedrich, 300, 325n59
Popov, Blagoj, 189
Poster, Mark, 390
Postmodernism, 24, 127, 138, 372, 388
Poststructuralism, xxii–xxv, xxix–xxxiii, 47, 100, 117–18, 126, 131–32, 137–38, 145, 341, 387–88
Poulantzas, Nicos, 343n16
Prowe, Diethelm, 245
Pudovkhin, Vsevolod, 147
Pushkin, Alexander, 197

R
Rabehl, Bernd, 274
Rabinbach, Anson, 304
Radek, Karl, 192, 199
Rancière, Jacques, 123
Rawls, John, 392
Reagan, Ronald, 132
Regler, Gustav, 203–205
Repgen, Konrad, 285
Ribbentrop, Joachim von, 205
Ricci, Scipio de, 5
Richman, Michèle, 221, 235n37
Ritter, Joachim, 284

Robespierre, Maximilien, 341
Rocaute, Yves, 336, 343n16
Rodrigues, Armando, 262n14
Roland, Jean-Marie, 15
Rolland, Romain, 190, 194, 196, 200, 202–203
Rorty, Richard, xxvi
Rosanvallon, Pierre, 100–101
Rose, Gillian, 385
Rose, Jacqueline, 137
Rosenfeld, Alvin, 164
Rosenzweig, Franz, 387
Rossellini, Roberto, 143
Rousseau, Jean-Jacques, 5, 7, 10, 57, 195, 217
Rousso, Henry, 170
Ruge, Arnold, 120
Ryan, Michael, xxx, xxxii, xxxviin13

S
Sadoul, Jacques, 191
Sahl, Hans, 205
Said, Edward, 96n50, 237n59
Salcedo, Doris, 159
Salomon, Ernst von, 221
Sanyal, Debarati, 232n2
Sartre, Jean-Paul, xxiv, 106, 108, 113n8, 114n26, 139, 225, 236n48, 343n16
Schäuble, Wolfgang, 255
Schauer, Helmut, 277
Scheuch, Erwin, 283–84
Schiller, Friedrich von, 373
Schiller, Karl, 270
Schmidt, Giselher, 285
Schmidt, Helmut, 250
Schmidt, James, 385
Schmitt, Carl, 64, 129, 228, 236n38, 270, 287, 302, 316, 321n12
Schoenberg, Arnold, 79, 90
Schoenfeld, Gabriel, 162, 165, 171
Scholem, Gershom, xxxixn49, 300, 387
Schopenhauer, Arthur, 71
Schröder, Richard, 257
Schroeder, Gerhard, 292n90
Schwan, Alexander, 282
Schwarz, Arturo, 30
Scott, Joan Wallach, xxvi
Selfhood, xxvi–xxvii, 24–50, 58, 68, 70–71, 82, 109, 145, 220, 230, 321n12
Şenocak, Zafer, 243, 257–61
Serra, Richard, 141, 157–58
Shakespeare, William, 197
Sharon, Ariel, 387
Sherman, Cindy, 142–44
Shscherbakov, Aleksandr, 203
Silone, Ignazio, 183, 205
Simmel, Georg, 66

Simon, Jonathan, 180n49
Sirk, Douglas, 143
Smith, Adam, 46–7, 49–50
Solzhenitsyn, Aleksandr, 337, 343n19
Sontheimer, Kurt, 282–83, 286–87
Sorel, Georges, xviii, 215–6, 225–6, 228
Spaemann, Robert, 286
Sperber, Manès, 205
Spiegel, Gabrielle, 237n53
Ssélavy, Rrose, 30–32, 34, 140. See also Duchamp, Marcel
Stahl, Friedrich Julius, 120
Stalin, Joseph, 129, 185, 187, 191–92, 194, 196–98, 200–205, 207n63, 337
Stasova, Elena, 194
Steiner, George, 320n9, 387
Sternhell, Zeev, 215, 226, 228
Stockhausen, Karl-Heinz, 232n4
Stoller, Paul, xxxi
Strauss, Franz Joseph, 286
Strauss, Leo, 300
Strenski, Ivan, 235n37
Structuralism, 70, 119, 332
Subotnik, Rose Rosengard, 80
Surya, Michel, 221

T
Tanev, Vasi, 189
Tartakowsky, Danielle, 193
Taubes, Jacob, 300
Taussig, Michael, xxx, xxxi, xxxiii
Taylor, Charles, 24
Terrorism, 211, 225, 231, 238n64, 269, 285–88, 336–37, 346, 359
Téson, Fernando, 363n3
Teufel, Fritz, 277
Thälmann, Ernst, 184, 189–90
Theweleit, Klaus, 221
Thierse, Wolfgang, 257
Thorez, Maurice, 190, 194
Tiedemann, Rolf, 78, 80
Tocqueville, Alexis de, 392
Todorov, Tzvetan, 172–73
Tolstoi, Alexei, 195
Tolstoy, Leo, 197, 202
Topitsch, Ernst, 285
Torricelli, Evangelista, 6
Totalitarianism, 119, 122, 124, 299–319, 324n41, 325n49, 332, 334, 336, 338–39, 341, 342n8, 343n17
Totality, ix, xxi–xxiv, 71, 73, 79, 82–85, 87–89, 94, 95n17, 96n53, 94–112, 117–18, 121–28, 131–32, 138, 319n1, 339, 341
Trotha, Lothar von, 228
Tunney, Gene, 141

U

Ulbricht, Walter, 274
United States, 137, 178n4, 290, 244,-45, 249, 271, 273, 279, 288, 333–34, 338–39, 342n8, 342n11, 343n12, 357–62, 369, 373, 378

V

Varnhagen, Rahel Levin, 307–308
Victimhood, 143, 153–58, 162–77, 178n4, 178n13, 180n49, 180n50, 180n53, 187–89, 194–95, 211, 213–14, 218–20, 232, 234n26, 235n37, 244–45, 248, 256, 260–62, 273, 287, 305–307, 310, 312, 337, 362, 379–80
Villa, Dana, 238n65, 324n37
Violence, 129, 152, 168, 170, 187, 210–39, 254–56, 264n41, 268–70, 272, 274–77, 279–88, 312, 336, 340, 344n20, 350, 371, 378, 380
Vision, xxii–xxiv, xxxi, xxxv, 26, 137–47, 387–88
Visuality. *See* Vision
Voltaire, 14, 195

W

Wagner, Richard, 78
Wahrman, Dror, 43–50
Walker, Peter, 157–9
Walraff, Günther, 248, 263n23
Walser, Martin, 257, 265n53
Warhol, Andy, 145
Weber, Max, xviii
Wehner, Herbert, 271
Weil, Eric, 121
Weiner, Lawrence, 140
Weinrich, Harald, 173
Weissman, Gary, 173
Werner, Karl, 187
Wilkomorski, Binjamin, 165, 175
Wilson, Woodrow, 314
Woffington, Peg, 49–50
Wolff, Christian, 60, 69
Wolff, Milton, 205

Y

Young-Bruehl, Elisabeth, 307
Young, James, 157
Young, Robert, 237n47

Z

Zedong, Mao, 337
Zhdanov, Andrei, 197, 200
Zizek, Slavoj, 117–35, 227–30, 234n25
Zweig, Stefan, 190

www.ingramcontent.com/pod-product-compliance
Lightning Source LLC
Chambersburg PA
CBHW051415290426
44109CB00016B/1313